The 1994 SANDERS PRICE GUIDE to AUTOGRAPHS

NUMBER 3

George Sanders, Helen Sanders, and Ralph Roberts

Alexander Books
65 Macedonia Road
Alexander, North Carolina USA

Publisher: Ralph Roberts

Cover Design: WorldComm®

Executive Editor: Kathryn L. Hall

Editor: Pat Hutchison

Interior Design and Electronic Page Assembly: WorldComm®

Printed in the United States of America

10 9 8 7 6 5 4 3 2 1

ISBN 1-57090-003-5

Library of Congress Catalog Card Number: 94-070942

Alexander Books—a division of Creativity, Inc.—is a full-service publisher located at 65 Macedonia Road, Alexander NC 28701. Phone (704) 252-9515 or (704) 255-8719 fax.

Alexander Books is distributed to the trade by **Associated Publishers Group**, 1501 County Hospital Road, Nashville, Tennessee 37218. Telephone (800) 327-5113 or (615) 254-2450. Fax (615) 254-2405. Telex SAN: 630-818X

Contents

14 THE C.A.C.C. by Matt Mrowicki 119

15 THE PRESERVATION OF YOUR COLLECTION by Ralph Roberts 127

16 HOW TO USE THIS PRICE GUIDE by Helen Sanders 137

17 A FINAL WORD ON PRICING by Helen Sanders 143

Section II: PRICES

PRICES 149

Section III: FACSIMILES

Section IV: DEALERS

1968 Democratic Presidential nominee and former Vice President of the United States Hubert Humprey was only one of thousands of celebrities interviewed by George Sanders during decades as a broadcast and print journalist.

PREFACE

by Charles Hamilton

Throw out your other price guides on autographs! This one is the best. It is the most complete and the most accurate, nothing less than the philographic Baedeker. It is without equal. My own copy is almost worn out. *In* fact, if there is a prize for the most tatterdemalion copy, I herewith enter mine into the competition.

One of the most *intriguing* things about the Sanders price guide is that it casts light on the autographic values of people you never heard of and makes you *want* to look at their handwriting. But the best thing about it is that it's a great browsing book. A book to keep at your bedside. Better than Montaigne, and more illuminating. I never pick it up without adding to my fund of autographic knowledge.

If I had owned a book like this fifty years ago, it would have changed the course of my life. I would have wound up today not just older and wiser, but smarter and richer.

I am often asked by young collectors and dealers for my groat's worth of advice. Here it is: Read and study this book.

A collector for over 65 years, Charles Hamilton is acknowledged worldwide as the leading expert on autographs, their authenticity, and rarity. He is the author of over a dozen books, most of them concerning autographs. His impact on the autograph field has been immense and lasting.

About This Price Guide

This is our fourth autograph price guide. The first two were published by the Wallace-Homestead Book Company of Radnor, Pennsylvania—owned by Capital Cities/ABC. These are **The Price Guide to Autographs** 1st and 2nd editions, and were released in 1988 and 1991 respectively. Our third price guide, **The 1994 Sanders Price Guide to Sports Autographs**, was published recently by Scott Publishing, the famous stamp guide people. Our fourth price guide you now hold in your hands, **The 1994 Sanders Price Guide to Autographs**.

The autograph field has grown dramatically in the last few years; just as our efforts in compiling the best price guides in the hobby have also expanded severalfold. Our sports price guide, for example, contains more prices than our first general price guide in 1988! This price guide that now weights down your arms reaches new heights of completeness with the most names and prices of any autograph price guide ever published. That's the good news.

The bad news is this book—even though it has more names and more prices than you've ever had in one convenient place before—has no sports-related names or prices. All sports material is now found in**The 1994 Sanders Price Guide to Sports Autographs**. We simply have too many names and prices to put everything into one volume any more. So, yes, you'll need both books, but these two volumes together give you a thousand pages of the best information available in the world of autographs.

Acknowledgments

These are the splendid men and women (in alphabetical order) who have made the interesting hobby of autograph collecting one of the most rewarding experiences of our lives. They are, in varying degrees, responsible for the happiness and financial gains that make this never-ending pursuit such a truly exciting undertaking. In most cases this list includes personal friends, acquaintances, competitors, suppliers, members of the media, and, most importantly, learned advisors. Not one forger or spin doctor is included.

Jon Allan
Bob Allen (*Antique Week*)
Allan Abrams (Toledo *Blade*)
Tim Anderson
Charles Apfelbaum
Jack L. Bacon
Edward Baig (*Business Week*)
Catherine Barnes
Robert F. Batchelder
Mary A. Benjamin
Saimi Rote Bergmann (The Repository, Canton, OH)
Jim Berland
Roger W. Bertoia
Barbara Bigham (*Autograph Times*, Phoenix,AZ)
Norman Boas
Warren Boroson (Hackensack *Sunday Record*)
Harvey Brandwein
Brenda Burch (WLOS-TV, Asheville, NC)
Walter Burks
Carol Cain (Mobile Alabama *Register*)
Dr. Ronald R. Caldwell
Dwight Chapin (San Francisco *Examiner*)
Gary E. Combs
Danny Cox (Dallas, Texas)
John Crudele (New York *Post* Syndicate)
Duane Dancer (KLIF, Dallas)
Herman Darvick
Roy Deeley (England)
Suzanne Dolezal (Detroit *Free Press*)
Amy Dunkin (BusinessWeek)
Sophie Dupre (England)
Carla Eaton

Robert "Bob" Eaton
Tom Eisaman
Bob Erickson (Pres., UACC)
Joe Fawls
Clifford O. Feingold, D.D.S.
Phillip Fiorini (*USA Today*)
Cathy & Roger E. Gilchrist
Bud Glick
Anita Gold (Knight-Ridder)
Miegan & Chandler Gordon
Marilyn Greenwald (Boys Life magazine)
Diane & Charles Hamilton
Donn Harmon
Geoffrey *Buzz* Harte (New Zealand)
Celie & Jim Hayes
Gary Hendershott
Stephen Hisler
Jeanne Hoyt
A. Bruce Hunt III
Pat Hutchison
Christopher C. Jaeckel
Curry & John Jamison
Mia & Chris Jaquette
Betty, Susan & Greg Johnson
Eileen Keiter
Kristin & Michael Kern
Carol King (Asheville,NC)
Stephen Koschal
Pierce A. Koslosky, Jr. (Omaha,Neb.)
Ann Krafthofer
Maggie Lauterer (WLOS-TV,Asheville,N.C.)
John Laurence
Kenneth R. Laurence
Gary Lawrence (IL)
Robert A. LeGresley
Alan Levi
William Linehan
Jerry D. Litzel (Ames, Iowa)
James Lowe
David H. Lowenherz
George S. Lowry
Bill Luetge
Joe and Scott Lusk (TN)
Joseph Maddalena
Cathy Marshall (CNN News)
J.L. Mashburn
Dr. Michael J. & Patrice Masters
Frank & Ruth Ann Matthews
Ann McCutchan (Gannett News Service)
Peggy & George McGill
Nancy L. McGlashan
Pam & Chuck McKeen
Beth McLeod (South Palm Beach *County Living*)
Jack Menges
Harold P. Merry
C.J. Middendorf (San Diego, CA.)
Bill Miller (Autograph Collector magazine)
Bonni J. Miller (Goldmine magazine)
George Robert Minkoff
Michael Minor
Gil Moody
Stuart J. Morrissey (Scott Publishing)
Howard S. Mott
Matthew Mrowicki and the CACC
Alfred *Chip* Muchin
Shirley & Eugene Muchin
J.B. Muns
Dr. F. Donn & Barbara Nidiffer

Donn Noble
William J. Novick
Karen & James Oleson
Nancy Page
Jerry E. Patterson
Louise Pennisi
Cordelia & Tom Platt
Robert L. Polk
Angelica Giesser & Udo Prager (Germany)
ProComm Studio Services (Arden, N.C.)
Stephen S. Raab
Celeste & Ray Rast
Diana J. Rendell
Kenneth W. Rendell
Tracy & John Reznikoff
Brian Riba
Stanley J. Richmond
Hinda Rose (England)
Joyce & Earle Rowell (New Zealand)
Joseph Rubinfine
Sheila & Rhodes T. Rumsey
Joseph R. Sakmyster
Nate Sanders
Rebecca & Stephen G. Sanders
George M. "Sandy" Sanders
Richard Saunders
David Schulson
Charles Searle
Kevin Sherman (Autograph Collector magazine)
Gemma Sica
Ann & Louis Sica, Jr.
Kaye & Merv Slotnick
James Smalldon
Dr. Leslie Smart
Pat & Jim Smith (Acton, Maine)
Dr. Lewis C. Sommerville
William W. Stanhope
Christophe Stickel
Gerard A.J. Stodolski
Darrell Talbert (Autograph Collector magazine)
Georgia Terry
Bob Tollett
E.N. Treverton
Louis Trotter
Wallace Turner (New York *Times*)
Jim Twelmeyer
Larry Vrzalik
Mark Vardakis
Susan & Eliot Wadopian
Joan, Erin & Lael Wadopian
Joel Sanders Wadopian
John Waggoner (*USA Today*)
Dewey Webb (Phoenix, Arizona *New Times*)
Daniel Weinberg
Michelle and Tom Williams
John Wilson (England)
Al Wittnebert (Treasurer, UACC)
Chris Wloszczyna (*USA Today*)
Jaye Wright (*Florida Today*)
Dr. Ellis "Bill" Zussman

When the snows come to the nearby mountains creating our sudden isolation, or, whenever we need a helping hand in any way, a big erstwhile New Zealander comes to our rescue without hesitation. As many of our readers know, his name is Roger E. Gilchrist. He has been our best friend, ex-son-in-law, strongest supporter, loyal confidant, fellow autograph dealer and now owner of a new autograph auction house. It seems we are always expressing our sincere thanks to Roger and his lovely wife, Cathy, North Carolina's most eclectic hairdresser-stylist, for their gentle kindnesses to two senior citizens overladen with autographs and computers.

A special thanks to all the members of our *country* friendly Enka, North Carolina Post Office (28728) including neighborly Charles Poss, Vicki Morgan, sore-footed Ruth Treadway, Postmistress Betty Joan Rice, lovely Brenda Case, former Postmaster and fellow Lion Club member Paul Carlock, and the greatest tall storyteller who ever manned a small-town post office, LeRoy *Semper Fi* Moore. They haven't lost or misplaced a single treasured autograph (incoming or outgoing) or a copy of our various Price Guides in 17 years. Their courteous and efficient service to Autograph House encourages us to believe that the United States Postal Service is the finest of its kind in the world!

The 1994 SANDERS PRICE GUIDE to AUTOGRAPHS

Section I: INFORMATION

NUMBER 3

Chapter 1

THE WORLD OF AUTOGRAPHS

by George and Helen Sanders

From 1983 to 1993 the hobby of collecting pieces of paper bearing the handwriting and signatures of celebrated people has grown in an awesome fashion. Some of the statistics are worthy of your attention as a collector or as a seller of such precious pieces of our worldly history.

A few months ago, we watched an interesting television program dedicated to collectibles on which urbane autograph dealer Paul Hartunian was asked about the estimated population of our hobby and he quickly replied, "I believe there are approximately five million collectors in America today." As he said that, we were remembering that only ten years earlier, we had read an estimation in one of Charles Hamilton's many wonderful books on autographs in which he had said, "There are about 15,000 philographers (autograph collectors) in America and around three million autograph seekers." Think of it. A growth factor of over two million interested, dedicated human beings who are constantly searching for old and new autographic material.

The Growth of the Hobby

Here are some additional numerical facts for your consideration as an autograph hobbyist in the fastest growing collectible in the world. In 1983, gallery owner Todd Axelrod, complete with his lengthy cigar, pocketful of dreams and a bulging wallet, visited us here at **Autograph House**. Without hesitation, he purchased $200,000-worth of our precious signatures and returned to his only gallery located in frenetic Las Vegas, Nevada. At that time, there were only eight galleries open for business in the entire nation. Today, Axelrod, himself, owns and operates that many posh emporiums of framed memorabilia. More importantly, today there are over three hundred such galleries operating in just about every major and many minor cities in this great nation of ours.

Antiquities gallery owners Sheila and Rhodes Rumsey have watched their attractive stores expand from minor operations in Greensboro, North Carolina to a posh Phipps Plaza location in Atlanta as well as their colorful gallery in that city's famed Underground Atlanta; a great gallery at the Marriott Hotel in Washington, D.C.; and a special operation in Charleston, South Carolina's rich resort area. From the early '80s to 1994 the hard-working Rumseys have shown

Antiquities owners Rhodes and Sheila Rumsey with George Sanders (center) during a vacation in Warm Springs, Georgia in 1992.

In a broadcast career spanning several decades, George Sanders (right) has interviewed and collected the in-person autographs of literally thousands of celebrities. Here he is with actor Henry Fonda on location in 1957.

spectacular growth in their sales of framed autographic treasures.

Auctions

A decade ago, you would have been hard-pressed to locate more than a baker's dozen of auction houses that devoted entire auctions exclusively to autographs, manuscripts and other related items. Today, over fifty-six such auction establishments are acquiring mail and telephone bids or pounding gavels at sit-down sessions with in-person bidders. One autograph dealer, with whom we have dealt for over a decade, Bill Luetge (of Wauwatosa, Wisconsin) has recently foregone weekly sales catalogues and now peddles his autographs exclusively via auctions. He told us that he sold over 7,500 lots via 56 different auctions in 1992-1993. It is just one more example of the hobby's amazing growth in a very brief period of time.

A classic success story engendered in the past five years involves our very good friends Pat and Jim Smith, proprietors of **Remember When Auctions** in Maine, whose unstinting efforts have brought them and their clients some hefty profits. In their initial 1988 auction they sold a paltry $6,000-worth of autographs but just five years later (November 20, 1993) they held an auction that realized over $800,000 in autograph sales. By early 1994, they had sold over 1.1 million dollars in their most recent auction. Other major auction houses such as Sotheby's, Christie's, Riba, Darvick, and so forth have also enjoyed record sales in recent years. The hammering of gavels has brought smiles to the faces of collectors and sellers alike from coast-to-coast. Furthermore, we must also acknowledge the huge successes of major autograph auctions held in Europe as interest in philography grows internationally. Even the sales of our price guides have tripled worldwide since 1988!

Autograph Dealers

There's more to this success story. In 1988, when we joined forces with brilliant author Ralph Roberts creating the initial edition of **The Price Guide to Autographs**, we were able to list just 133 full or part-time autograph dealers in the back of that green-covered book. By 1991, in the 2nd edition, we were listing 182 such dealers, a growth factor of fifty. With this publication of **The 1994 Sanders Price Guide to Autographs**, we cannot dedicate the space required to list the 600 autograph dealerships now involved with daily sales in this obviously burgeoning collectible. In

George interviews famed comedienne Phyllis Diller (pre-facelift) in 1971. Ever the collector, George is getting her to sign her book.

other words, there are now approximately 467 more dealers than in 1988. In the words of the mysterious informer "Deep Throat" to the Watergate investigative reporters Woodward and Bernstein, "follow the money!" The autograph hobby has become one of the smartest depositories for greenbacks since grandpa stuffed such things in his horsehair mattress.

The Strength of the Autograph Business

Another heartwarming example of the strength this business seems to manifest is the saga of autograph dealer Charles Searle. In February of 1990, thanks to the financial ramifications of an unexpected divorce, his highly successful business dropped to near bankruptcy. His usually quick-selling, middle-priced stock of autograph material was decimated by the legal settlement and his cash-flow was practically nonexistent.

Charles Searle

With a little help from his friends and unlimited hours of tedious labor, Searle has had a sensational comeback and is once again enjoying wonderful sales and highly comfortable profits. His mailing list is bulging with the names of countless new collectors who seem to be joining all of us daily in this rapidly growing hobby and/or "industry."

Obviously, most of our collector colleagues are not big spenders as they stalk celebrities for in-person signings; address countless polite letters requesting treasured autographs; peruse varied and reasonably-priced dealer cata-

If you don't ask for an autograph, you'll never get it. Here Sir Leslie Munro, then president of the United Nations General Assembly, graciously signs for George Sanders.

logues searching for bargains that may or may not exist. These folks are the backbone of the hobby and the Sanders happily cheer them on as their respective collections grow in leaps and paraphs. (A *paraph* is those squiggles under signed names used long-ago to prevent forgeries—John Hancock's famous signature is a prime example.) However, in the past ten years, we've seen the invasion of so-called "heavy hitters" looking for expensively rare material to fuel their quick-buck cannons on a field of collectibility that has become an hysteric battleground littered with forged "Stonewall" Jackson Civil War-time letters; bogus Presidential signatures and stolen-from-archives collections.

Investing in Autographs

Because of the massive infusions of investment capital we now have large, and frequently well-informed, financial organizations who acquire and offer spectacular autographic treasures. Last year, we saw a very special letter of Abraham Lincoln sell at auction for well over one-million U.S. dollars. We had written several years ago that the day would come when rare pieces *would* sell at prices in the range of rare oil paintings. Frankly, we were thinking in terms of the year 2000. But now, six years before the turn of the century, we find the aforementioned Lincoln letter leading the way.

Long after we're gone, you will be reading about some amazing prices realized for classical composers' manuscripts; artists' sketches and letters; special historic content letters bearing enlightening secrets; Civil War collections featuring the scrawls of Robert E. Lee, U.S. Grant, Jeb Stuart, T.J. Jackson, William T. Sherman, James Longstreet, P.T. Beauregard, Hooker, Burnside, Early, Meade, Buckner, and so many others who proudly wore the blue or the grey.

Various categories in the collection of autographs are

going to hit the blue skies in value but we have always suggested that extreme caution is a required asset when investing hard-earned currency for richly-priced paper of another kind, such as autographs. Collecting for fun is not related to collecting for profit. One collector has nothing to lose and the other risks a great deal. The latter must seriously consider every aspect of their fiscal involvement with autographs. If their respective advisors are not sufficiently well-informed with years of scholarly experience in this field, some investors will learn some very hard lessons

Due to the popularity of special content letters, colorful

George with legendary entertainer Jimmy Durante. In-person autographs were the start of the vast Sanders autograph collection.

From collecting autographs to giving autographs, coauthor Helen Sanders happily signs copies of our previous autograph price guide.

documents and beautiful signed photographs, they have become rare and exceedingly expensive. As a result, in the last ten years we have seen the lowly SIG (autographese for *signature*) become more and more desirable. The SIG is versatile, available and now accepted as a legitimate member of the autograph field.

What's Hot and What's Not

Because the five books we've authored about this hobby are now available on the reference shelves of thousands of U.S. public and collegiate libraries, we are frequently asked about what's hot and what's not! Collecting the signatures or any material autographed by U.S. Presidents is, of course, very popular. But, for those without a budget for the Chief Executives, the acquisition of U.S. Vice Presidents has become most appealing. They are all available at reasonable prices with a few exceptions such as Aaron Burr, Elbridge Gerry, Richard M. Johnson and a few others.

Men and women of science, with special emphasis on Nobel laureates, are equally appealing at low cost. The heroes of The War of 1812, The Spanish-American War, World Wars I and II have become quite popular with today's collectors. Lest we forget, there is still much interest and investment in such categories as Cabinet members, prominent U.S. senators and congressmen, aviation pioneers, men and women whose names have become trade names *a la* Elizabeth Arden, Helena Rubinstein, John Deere, David Buick, Ransom Olds, Henry Ford, Louis B. Mayer, Jack Warner, Walt Disney, Clarence Birdseye, Joyce C. Hall

In 1991, German dealers Angelica and Udo Prager visited Autograph House and viewed the Sanders' prized Button Gwinnett authograph (in frame behind them). The signature was recently sold for six figures.

of Hallmark Cards and on and on and on. Air aces, sports stars, Academy Award winners, country music stars and the ever popular catchall category of "celebrities" which includes well-known people from every walk of life who just happen to turn you on and open your purse or wallet with their peculiar desirability.

During the past five years we've seen some "collector creativity" infused into this hobby. There are now many hobbyists acquiring collections of signatures of just those celebrated people appearing on U.S. postage stamps. Using the popular editions of Linn's *Who's Who on U.S. Stamps*, authored by Richard Louis Thomas (1991 and 1993), collectors are building interesting and valuable material.

Since the U.S. Postal Service was created in 1971, replacing the U.S. Post Office Department, the United States has issued an increasing number of stamps portraying individuals such as Joe Louis, Bob Wills, Dr. Paul Dudley White, the Carter Family, Bobby Jones, Francis Ouimet, Edgar Bergen, Fannie Brice, Laurel & Hardy, Abbott and Costello, Sojourner Truth, Dr. Martin Luther King, Nicola Tesla, Dr. Lee DeForest, Clark Gable and Vivien Leigh, Judy Garland, Gary Cooper, John Wayne, William Saroyan and countless others. These novel postage stamps open a wide vista of collectibles never before considered. We have a collection of our own that just includes those philatelic celebrities with whom we've met and been photographed.

In the final analysis you alone are the best authority on the kind of autograph collection you personally enjoy. If you spend a fortune on material that brings you no hobby happiness, why bother to invest? On the other hand, if you are creating a collection that excites, interests and entertains you, why worry about the cost?

If you are purely an investor with your sights solely on

Another legend, longtime country music and Grand Old Opry star Little Jimmy Dickens signs for George Sanders in 1970.

profits, we suggest you become tremendously cautious and understand that not everything offered to you is the buy of this or the next century. As collectors for nearly 60 wonderful years, who have bought and sold some grand collections, we have learned that not all famous people remain of permanent interest to a multitude of collectors. Stars rocket into the press agents' heavens and seem to shine for decades before plunging into the seas of oblivion. Other names have the staying power of fast-exploding rockets or sparklers and seldom retain any value at all. History is a cruel sustainer of fame with no will to substantiate or protect the values contained in your particular collection.

Pay Attention, It Pays!

Any hobby worth its salt requires almost constant attention and a considerable amount of investment. Autograph collecting is no exception. Pay attention! Receive true value for every dollar! Do not be hoodwinked by fast-buck artists! Read every word written about your particular specialty as this is a scholar's hobby and don't be afraid to return material that does not resemble the description you were originally presented. It's a great hobby and it's becoming more exciting with the passing of each day. Every day is Christmas and/or Hanukah. For autograph collectors "the postman rings *more* than twice."

Chapter 2

AUCTIONS ARE FOR EVERYONE

by John and Tracy Reznikoff

An overwhelming percentage of the material our company purchases originates from estates and individuals. We buy enough material for our stock so that if we never went to another auction, it really would not make a difference to our success. However, the electricity of the auction arena can easily attract all levels of buyers to its forefront.

There are few things in life that can equal the thrill of the gavel pounding down; the sounding bell of ones' success on a lot that is truly desired. The thrill is always directly proportional to the degree of bargain that has just occurred, and while exhilarating, this does not even take into account the education one receives when attending an auction.

There is Nothing to Fear

Surprisingly, many collectors and dealers shy away from auctions for a number of reasons. Statements such as "they are too highbrow," "I won't get anything," or "it's all dealer material with preset reserves" are a few comments that are heard all the time. While these claims may be true on some occasions, they are hardly reflective of auctions as a whole. Auctions are never constructed to discourage buyers. In fact, the various state consumer laws that govern all auction houses are implemented and enforced strictly to protect and favor all buyers. Logically, auction houses understand they would not be in business for very long if people were unable to actually buy material from them.

Learn How to Take Advantage

Auctioneers are constantly pressed by deadlines and restricted by printing costs as to the length of descriptions they can allow. Thus, time is a major advantage for the buyer. Buyers should learn when and how this time advantage can create opportunity. After 20 years of attending auctions we can "smell" a potential bargain. For those not as experienced, there are telltale signs of things that could easily "fall between the cracks."

Taking a contrary attitude can be beneficial. If you come upon a little country auction that has a Lincoln letter and you think that no one is going to know about the auction and you will be able to buy the letter for a song, unfortunately, you will be sorely mistaken.

The extensive network of "pickers" and agents provide many dealers with information beforehand on the whereabouts of autograph material that is available both privately and at auction. Likewise, the same letter in a fancy New York manuscript auction might get overlooked or perhaps outshined by other items in the sale. Using your time wisely to pre-select where and when you intend to bid will be one of your greatest assets.

Taking time to review the auction catalog is of equal importance. Learn to read between the lines. For instance, look for inordinately brief descriptions, as these may be lots you wish to inspect personally due to the possibility that there might be much more than meets the eye. If you see sub-lots, also referred to as "A" lots (for instance lot 310 followed by lot 310A) be aware that these are, in all likelihood, late arrivals to the auction that may not have received the same attention as other lots in the sale. Large lots of multiple items can be either treasure troves or mine fields, thus, inspection of these lots is always essential. When there are many examples of the same item, there will most likely be significant opportunity. For example, ten consecutive lots of JFK letters will almost always bring less on an individual basis than one or two. You are more apt to get a bargain in the middle than at the beginning or end of a run of repeating lots.

Keep It to Yourself

It is important to remember to keep those bargains to yourself. Appropriate auction etiquette is always appreciated. Not only is it in the best interest for all involved to remain humble about your personal gains, but ironically, the person to whom you may boast about your great fortune, could very likely end up being your underbidder or outbid you the next time around.

Psychology and common sense will play a great role in your auction strategy as it develops. Who is bidding or outbidding on what items along with why and how much will all be part of a developing picture of exactly what transpires behind the scenes. We recommend that you take notes in your auction catalog, as this will greatly aid you in the future. Writing down the amount a lot opens for, what it actually sold for and to whom the lot is sold are all important information to document.

While recording the underbidder and final buyer may seem extraneous or insignificant to you for many reasons it may, in fact, be of great importance to you at a later date.

This underbidder or final buyer may prove to be a potential client for you for a similar item in the future.

In addition, you may want to keep notes as to the general "spiritedness" of the bidding on a particular lot and likewise, those lots which receive no attention at all. These notes can specifically help you to evaluate future purchases and provide you with a more secure knowledge of the current market. Always keep an open mind but be influenced mostly by your own experience. Soon enough you too will be able to "smell a bargain" from around the corner. Happy bidding!

John and Tracy Reznikoff: John Reznikoff was studying pre-law at Fordham University when he founded his collectibles company in 1979. **University Archives**, located in Stamford, Connecticut, is one of the nation's premier autograph dealers. John recently married Tracy Levy from New York City. Tracy, a *magna cum laude* graduate from Barnard College, plans to continue on to graduate school this coming Spring.

Tracy and John Reznikoff with George Sanders at a recent UACC show.

Chapter 3

FIRST LADIES OF THE UNITED STATES

by Michael Minor and Larry Vrzalik

An exciting yet little known area of autograph collecting.

The autographic material of America's First Ladies remains one of the best kept secrets in the annals of autograph collecting and, generally speaking, it is one of the most under priced areas of collecting. In several notable instances, First Lady material is among the rarest of all Americana. However, it is also an area of collecting whose hour has come and which is beginning to be collected by both the wise collector and investor.

While it is an impossibility to assemble a complete collection of all our First Ladies, those First Ladies whose material is in abundant supply more than compensate for the rarities. And, happily, in most instances there are desirable and often relatively inexpensive substitutes for those First Ladies whose material is unobtainable, such as daughters or daughters-in-law who acted as White House hostesses in their behalf.

A collection of First Lady material is, by its very nature, both a history of the Presidency and of the Republic. It is also a history of feminism in this country and even of our social mores.

America's First Ladies are an interesting and varied

group and are truly representative of the great nation they represented. They came in all ages and sizes, ranging from the lovely young First Lady Frances Cleveland, who was only 21 when she married 49-year-old bachelor president Grover Cleveland, to 66-year-old Anna Harrison whose husband died before she could make the arduous trip to Washington. She was also the only living First Lady who never set foot in the White House.

The Youngest and the Oldest

The youngest First Lady at the time of her marriage to a president was Eliza McCardle Johnson who was only 16 when she married Andrew Johnson. The oldest First Lady at the time of her marriage to a president was Caroline Carmichael McIntosh Fillmore, second wife of Millard Fillmore, who was 44. The youngest wife of a president at the time of her death was Alice Hathaway Lee Roosevelt, first wife of Theodore Roosevelt and mother of the indomitable "Princess Alice" Roosevelt (Longworth), who was only 23 at the time of her death. She and Theodore Roosevelt's mother died on the same day, Valentine's Day, 1884. Shortly thereafter, Theodore Roosevelt went west to recover from his double tragedy. He wrote a glowing account of his life with Alice and never again mentioned her name as long as he lived. The oldest president's wife at the time of her death was Bess Truman who lived to be 97 years old.

The Short , the Tall, and the Smart

First Ladies have ranged in height from the diminutive Martha Washington, who was only 5' tall, to the stately Eleanor Roosevelt, who was 5'11" tall.

The educational backgrounds of our First Ladies range from the scholarly Lou Hoover, who had a geology degree—

the first in that field conferred by Stanford University on a woman, and who was fluent in several languages, including Chinese, to the semiliterate Rachel Jackson, who smoked a pipe!

And, the physical attributes of our First Ladies range from the lovely Julia Gardiner Tyler, second wife of John Tyler, a great beauty who was known as the "Rose of Long Island", and who was only 24 when she married the 54-year-old widower president to the cross eyed, portly Julia Dent Grant who was adored by her "Ulys." Some presidential marriages, such as the Polks, Grants, Hayeses, and Trumans were happy ones, while others have been hellish, such as the John Quincy Adamses, the Pierces, the Lincolns, the Hardings and the Franklin Roosevelts.

Death, Marriage, and Divorce

It is a little known footnote to history that six of our First Ladies were widows when they married their presidential husbands. They were: Martha Washington, Martha Jefferson, Dolley Madison, Caroline Fillmore, Edith Wilson and Mary Lord Harrison. Four of our First Ladies were divorcees when they married their presidential husbands. They were: Rachel Jackson, Florence Harding, Betty Ford and Sara Jane Fulks Futterman Reagan Karger, the actress Jane Wyman.

Interestingly, only two of our First Ladies remarried after the deaths of their presidential husbands. Our youngest First Lady, Frances Cleveland, remarried five years after Cleveland's death when she was 49. She married 33 year old Princeton Archaeology professor Thomas Preston, who was 16 years her junior. Strangely, after she remarried she signed herself as "Frances F. Cleveland Preston." The second First Lady to remarry, Jacqueline Kennedy, married Greek shipping magnate Aristotle Onassis.

Influence

The wives of the Presidents have come to be known as "First Ladies." The early presidential wives were known by various titles, e.g., "Lady Washington", "Mrs. President Tyler", and even as "Presidentess". While all presidential wives exerted varying degrees of influence over their husbands, all have been powerful and influential women on the institution of the presidency.

In several instances First Ladies, e.g., Martha Jefferson and Rachel Jackson, were influential by their absence. But almost all influenced their husbands and their presidential policies, either directly or indirectly. For example, it is well known that the talented and articulate Abigail Adams had great influence on her staid and dogmatic husband John Adams. Many of her colorful and brilliant letters to John Adams survive. It is evident that John Adams shared everything with Abigail and that he sought and valued her advice.

The lovely and ambitious Sarah Polk was her husband's only confidant and she also acted as her husband's presidential secretary. Deeply religious, she banned dancing, liquor and cards from the White House. And, it was to her that James Knox Polk directed his dying words: "I love you Sarah. For all eternity I'll love you." Her influence on her husband's administration cannot be underestimated, and the Polk administration may have been the most successful presidential administration on record. Polk fulfilled all his campaign promises, fought a successful war, greatly expanded the size of the United States, and served but a single term!

The saintly Rachel Jackson influenced her husband's administration from the grave. The presidential campaign of

1828, in which Jackson was elected president, was one of the dirtiest on record. In the campaign Jackson's deceased mother was branded as a whore for British soldiers and Rachel was slandered as a bigamous adulteress. Andrew Jackson always believed that the cruel attacks on his deeply religious wife precipitated her untimely death, probably from a heart attack, shortly after he was elected president. Rachel was buried in what would have been her inaugural gown.

The loss of Rachel's softening influence on her husband was keenly felt during his tumultuous presidency, and the attacks on Rachel's character during the presidential campaign indirectly caused the resignation of Jackson's entire cabinet. It seems that John H. Eaton, Jackson's Secretary of War, was married to a vivacious and lovely woman named Peggy, who was regarded as an adulteress by the wives of Jackson's other cabinet members, who refused to accept or receive Mrs. Eaton socially. Jackson, feeling that Mrs. Eaton's treatment was similar to that accorded his beloved Rachel, staunchly defended her and demanded that the cabinet wives receive her. When they refused, the choleric Jackson asked for and received the resignations of almost his entire cabinet! The widower Martin Van Buren, who was serving as Jackson's Secretary of State (1829-1831), sided with the President in the Eaton affair. As a result Jackson threw his considerable support behind Van Buren who was elected the next vice president and then the next president.

Thomas Jefferson's Lovely Black Mistress

Worn out from child bearing, Martha Jefferson died at an early age. On her death bed Jefferson reportedly promised never to remarry—a promise which he kept. However, not long thereafter, Jefferson took one of Martha's slaves as his mistress. The slave was a lovely octaroon creature named Sally Hemings, whom Martha Jefferson had inherited from her father.

Ironically, Sally was Martha Jefferson's half-sister, having been sired by Martha's father with one of his slaves. According to contemporary accounts Sally Hemings bore a striking resemblance to Martha Jefferson. Jefferson fathered seven children by Sally, some of whom looked like him. Jefferson's relationship with the lovely Sally was, perhaps, the greatest scandal of his administration and became a campaign issue. It is an historical irony that Jefferson's black descendants still have an annual family reunion.

Tragedy

Our most tragic First Lady was Jane Means Pierce, who hated politics and politicians. She fainted when she learned of Pierce's presidential nomination and fervently prayed for his defeat. Shortly after Pierce's election, but before his inauguration, he, his wife, and their only surviving son, Benny, were involved in a train accident. Benny was tragically killed and his decapitated head rolled down the aisle and came to rest at the feet of his horrified parents.

Neither Franklin nor Jane Pierce were ever the same thereafter, and from that time Jane Pierce never again functioned as a normal person. She refused to attend Pierce's inauguration, and didn't arrive at the White House for several weeks after his inauguration. After she arrived, she draped the White House in black and remained in mourning throughout Pierce's entire administration. She refused to perform her duties as First Lady, delegating that task to an aunt, Abigail Means. Jane Pierce spent much of her time as First Lady in a darkened room in the White

House writing letters to her dead son. Pierce blamed himself for Benny's death. As a result of his towering guilt, he was perhaps our weakest and most ineffective president at a crucial time in our history before the Civil War. Pierce's indecision allowed the country to drift toward conflict which might have been averted.

Another tragic First Lady, Mary Lincoln, suffered the death of a son in the White House and witnessed her husband's assassination. She has the dubious distinction of being the only First Lady accused of being a traitor, as well as of being committed to a mental institution. She was also our only expatriate First Lady, choosing to live abroad for many years after Lincoln's assassination.

The Rarest and Most Mysterious

Margaret Taylor is one of our most mysterious First Ladies of whom even no known likeness exists. She, like Jane Pierce, prayed for her husband's defeat, fearing the presidency would kill him. Her fears were, sadly, well founded. Until recently it was erroneously thought that only one example from her pen existed, which example, in fact, was not written by her. However, recently, through the brilliant research of Dr. Walter Ostromecki, a First Ladies scholar and historian, three examples of her incredibly rare signatures were found on attested legal documents dealing with the disposition of Taylor's estate, one of which is illustrated in this article. None of the known, unquestionably authentic signatures of Margaret Taylor will ever come on the market, as all are in archives.

The rarest of the First Ladies, autographically speaking, as well as the most mysterious, is Hannah Hoes Van Buren of whom not a single word from her pen is known to exist and virtually nothing is known about her. She was a cousin of

Martin Van Buren and bore him four sons and a daughter, dying at an early age. Strangely, Van Buren did not mention her in his autobiography.

Rare, too, is the autographic material of Martha Jefferson Elizabeth Monroe, Rachel Jackson, Letitia Tyler, Abigail Fillmore, Caroline Fillmore, Harriet Lane, Eliza Johnson, Ellen Arthur, Alice Lee Roosevelt, Ida McKinley, Ellen Wilson, and Jacqueline Kennedy Onassis.

The Expensive and Inexpensive

The most expensive First Lady, autographically speaking, is Martha Washington, followed as a close second by Mary Todd Lincoln. Pricey, too, is the autographic material of Abigail Adams, whose chatty and opinionated letters are avidly sought and prized by collectors.

Although scarce, the material of many First Ladies is not comparatively expensive. In this category are Louisa Adams, Anna Harrison, Julia Tyler, Sarah Polk, Jane Pierce, Julia Grant, Lucy Hayes, Caroline Harrison, Ida McKinley, Ellen Wilson, Helen Taft, Florence Harding, Lou Henry Hoover and somewhat surprisingly, Barbara Bush. Refreshingly abundant and moderately priced is the material of Dolley Madison, Lucretia Garfield, Frances Cleveland, Mary Lord Dimmick Harrison, Edith Roosevelt, Edith Bolling Wilson, Grace Coolidge, Eleanor Roosevelt, Bess Truman, Mamie Doud Eisenhower, Lady Bird Johnson, Patricia Nixon, Betty Ford, Rosalynn Carter and Nancy Reagan.

Books

Perhaps the first First Lady of whom signed books are obtainable is Harriet Lane, niece of her bachelor uncle, James Buchanan. She inherited Buchanan's library and signed the volumes below Buchanan's signature as "Harriet Lane Johnston." Interestingly, her signature is much scarcer and more expensive than that of her presidential uncle. The first First Lady to write her memoirs and of whom signed copies exist, was Helen Herron Taft, whose autobiography is entitled *Recollections of Full Years*, published in 1914 (Julia Grant's autobiography was published posthumously).

Edith Bolling Wilson published her memoirs, entitled *My Memoir*, in 1938. A lovely, boxed signed limited edition of 1000 was published in lavender covers and box. Although the book had a relatively large signed limited edition, few copies appear on the market.

The brilliant and scholarly Lou Henry Hoover collaborated with her engineer husband in translating an early mining treatise into English. The book is entitled *De Re Metallica* by Georgius Agricola (1556), and was republished by the Hoovers in 1912. Signed copies are avidly sought, as well as rare and expensive.

Eleanor Roosevelt authored several books, signed copies of which are usually modestly priced. The only book written by Jacqueline Kennedy Onassis is a whimsical self-illustrated tome coauthored by she and her sister Lee. It is entitled *One Special Summer* and was published in a boxed, signed limited edition of 500 in 1974, and was signed by Mrs. Onassis with a very rare form of her signature, "Jacqueline Bouvier," her maiden name.

Lady Bird Johnson wrote an interesting autobiography entitled *A White House Diary*, published in 1970, and signed copies are plentiful. A highly desirable, rare and little known book was also done by Mrs. Johnson entitled *The White House Library*. The book is beautifully done in red morocco in a boxed, signed limited edition of only 300 copies. It is a bibliography of the books in the White House Library and contains an actual book plate of the type used in books in the White House Library. Mrs. Johnson has also authored or collaborated on several wild flower books, all of which are beautifully and profusely illustrated. Available, too, are signed copies of the autobiographies of Betty Ford, entitled *The Times of My Life*, published in 1978, Rosalynn Carter, entitled *First Lady From Plains*, published in 1984, and Nancy Reagan, entitled *Nancy*, published in 1980, and her most recent book is *My Turn* published in 1993. Barbara Bush wrote a charming and witty book about her dog "Millie" and signed copies are avidly sought. She also has a just-released autobiography.

Cards

Signed First Lady Executive Mansion or White House cards are another interesting area of collecting. Although the Executive Mansion card was introduced by U. S. Grant, no signed Executive Mansion cards of Julia Dent Grant are known to the authors. The first First Lady available in this format is Lucy Webb Hayes, who is rare but obtainable in this format. Also rare but obtainable in this format are Lucretia Garfield, Caroline Harrison, Ida McKinley, Edith Roosevelt, Helen Taft, Ellen Wilson, Edith Bolling Wilson, Florence Harding, Jacqueline Kennedy (Onassis), Nancy Reagan and Barbara Bush. Relatively common in Executive Mansion or White House cards are Frances Cleveland, Grace Coolidge, Lou Henry Hoover, Eleanor Roosevelt, Bess Truman, Mamie Doud Eisenhower, Lady Bird Johnson, Patricia Nixon, Betty Ford, Rosalynn Carter, Nancy Reagan, Barbara Bush and, presumably, Hillary Clinton.

Signed Photographs

Another interesting but challenging area of collecting is First Lady signed photographs. The earliest First Lady of whom a signed photograph is known to exist is an old age example of Sarah Polk. Obtainable but extremely costly are signed photographs of Mary Todd Lincoln.

Obtainable but rare, although only moderately expensive in most instances, are signed photographs of Julia Grant, Lucy Hayes, Lucretia Garfield, Caroline Harrison, Mary Lord Dimmick Harrison, Ida McKinley, Edith Roosevelt, Helen Taft, Edith Bolling Wilson, Florence Harding, Grace Coolidge, Eleanor Roosevelt, and Jacqueline Kennedy Onassis. Common and moderately priced are the signed photographs of Frances Cleveland, Lou Henry Hoover, Bess Truman, Mamie Doud Eisenhower, Lady Bird Johnson, Patricia Nixon, Betty Ford, Rosalynn Carter, Nancy Reagan and Barbara Bush.

Frankly Speaking

Still another interesting area of collecting First Lady material is that of "franking signatures" or "widows' franks", which privilege twenty two presidential widows were granted upon the deaths of their presidential husbands. Although Margaret Taylor was granted the franking privilege no example of her frank is known.

The following list of First Lady franks is in order of rarity (but not necessarily of cost), of their hand written franking signatures: Margaret Taylor (unknown), Martha Washington, Louisa Adams, Sarah Polk, Jacqueline Kennedy Onassis, Julia Grant, Anna Harrison, Dolley Madison, Ida McKinley, Mary Lincoln, Edith Wilson, Florence Harding, Helen Taft, Eleanor Roosevelt, Mamie Doud Eisenhower, Bess Truman, Lady Bird Johnson, Lucretia Garfield, Edith Roosevelt, Grace Coolidge and Mary Lord Harrison. The franking signature of Frances Cleveland by that name is scarce; however, her franking signature as "Frances F. Cleveland Preston," which form she used after her remarriage, is the most common of all First Lady franks.

Exciting and Rewarding

The autographic material of America's First Ladies is among the most exciting and rewarding of all areas of collecting. Compared to their presidential husbands, their material is many times scarcer. There are literally hundreds of letters of Washington and Lincoln for every letter of Martha's and Mary's. The dignified George was even known to act as secretary for his beloved Martha as letters signed by her but in his holograph are known, and our martyred Civil War president took time from his heavy burdens of office to personally (and illegally!) frank private, nonofficial letters of his fiery wife Mary.

Today these rarities are worth far more than their weight in gold. Happily, many other First Lady rarities are still available at surprisingly modest prices, given their scarcity. Even more serendipitous is the fact that approximately half the First Lady series can be obtained at very modest prices; however, it is the opinion of the authors that this area of collecting is greatly under priced and it is not a matter of "if" but "when" the prices of First Lady material will sharply escalate.

We wish to acknowledge and give special thanks to Dr. Walter Ostromecki, First Lady historian, for the information he kindly provided in connection with this article.

Michael Minor and **Larry Vrzalik** have been partners in Lone Star Autographs for many years. Lone Star Autographs, P. O. Drawer 500, Kaufman Texas 75142, has a Gallery and Retail offices and issues free bimonthly catalogs. Historical research is the avocation of both Minor and Vrzalik, who are coauthors of a book on presidential autographs *From The President's Pen*, and numerous historical articles and articles about autographs. They are currently writing a book on First Lady autographs.

First Lady Facsimile Signatures

Martha Dandridge Custis Washington
1731-1802

Abigail Smith Adams
1744-1818

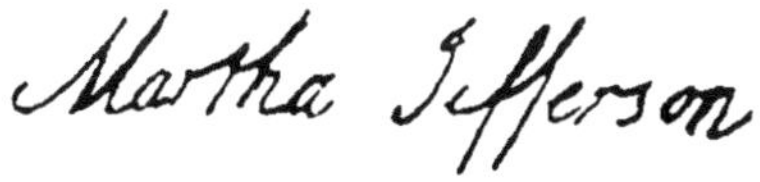

Martha Wayles Skelton Jefferson
1748-1782

Martha Jefferson Randolph
Proxy First Lady 1802-3, 1805-6

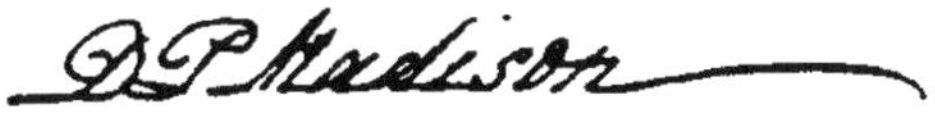

Dolley Payne Todd Madison
1768-1849

Elizabeth Kortwright Monroe
1768-1830

Eliza Monroe Hay
Proxy First Lady 1817-1825

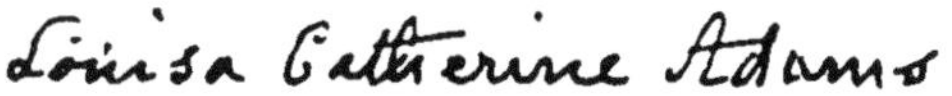

Louisa Catherine Johnson Adams
1775-1852

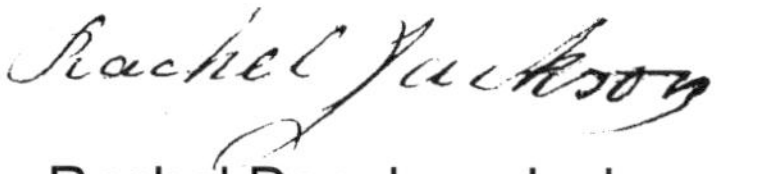

Rachel Donelson Jackson

Emily Jackson Donelson
Proxy First Lady 1829-1836

Angelica Singleton Van Buren
Proxy First Lady 1839-1841

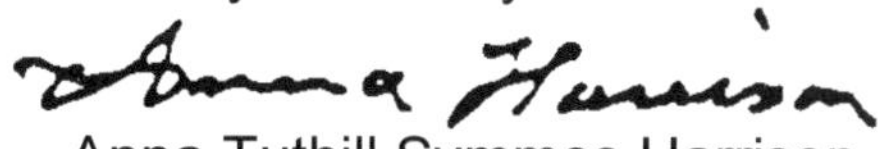

Anna Tuthill Symmes Harrison
1773-1861

E. Priscilla Cooper Tyler
1816-1889
Proxy First Lady 1842-1844

Julia Gardiner Tyler
1820-1889

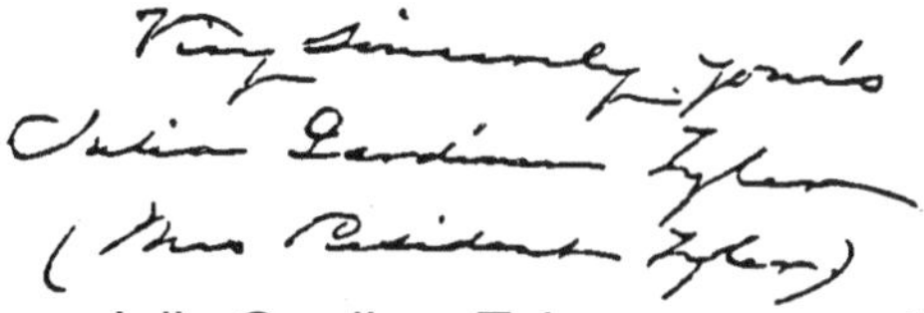

Julia Gardiner Tyler, an unusual form of her signature with notation, "Mrs. President Tyler"

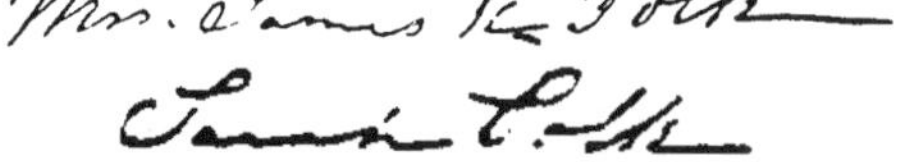

Sarah Childress Polk
1803-1891

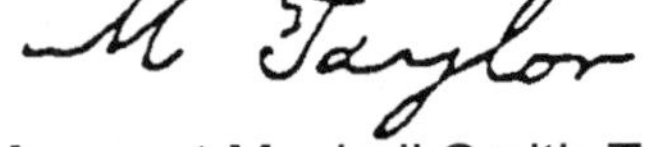

Margaret Mackall Smith Taylor
1788-1852

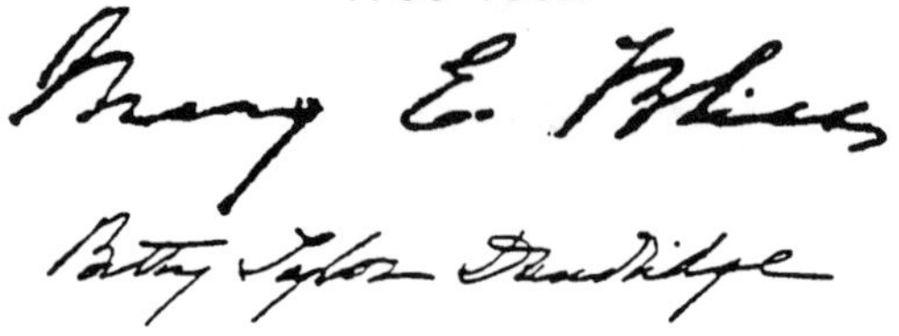

Mary Elizabeth (Betty) Taylor Bliss
(Dandridge)
Proxy First Lady 1849-1850

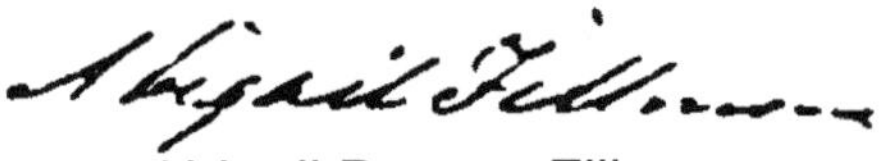

Abigail Powers Fillmore
1798-1853

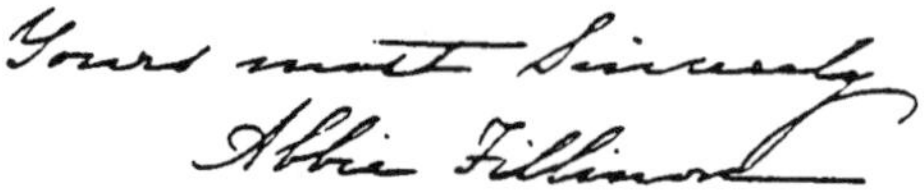

Mary Abigail Fillmore
Proxy First Lady 1832-1854

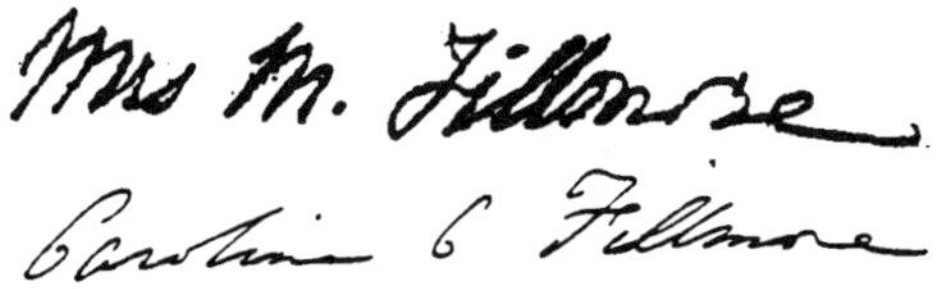

Caroline C. McIntosh Fillmore
1813-1881

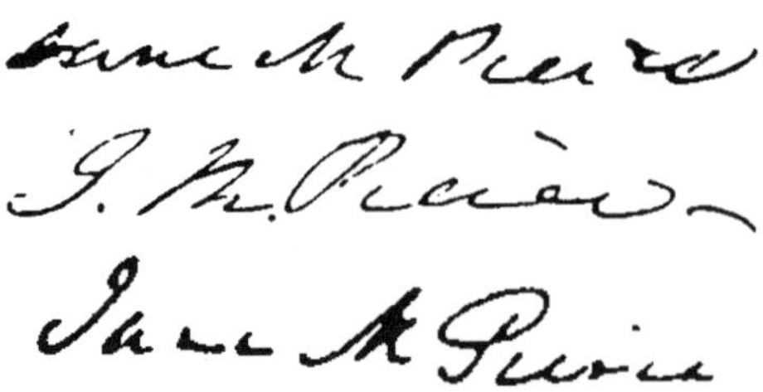

Jane Means Appleton Pierce
1806-1863

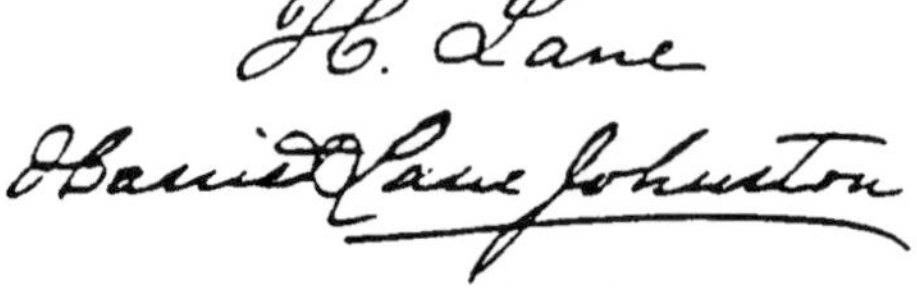

Harriet Lane
1830-1903

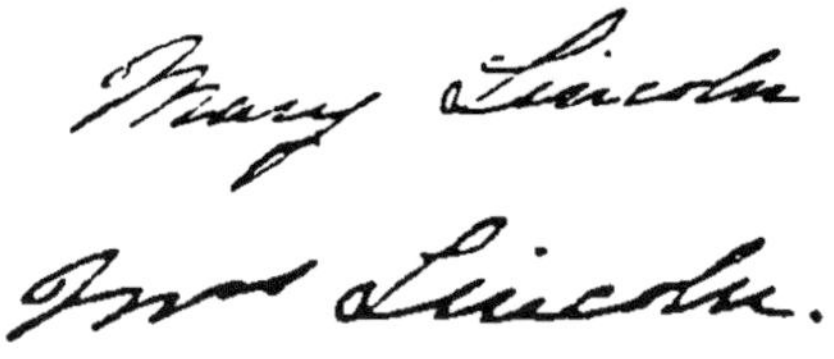

Mary Todd Lincoln
1818-1882

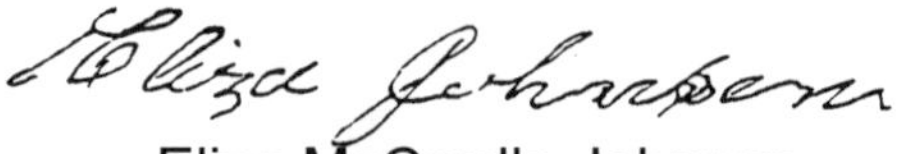

Eliza McCardle Johnson
1810-1876

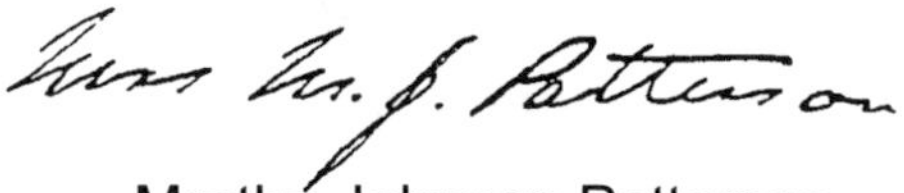

Martha Johnson Patterson
1828-1901
Proxy First Lady 1865-1869

Julia D. Grant
1826-1902

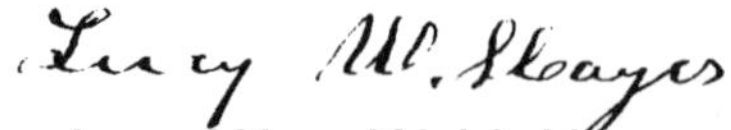

Lucy Ware Webb Hayes
1831-1889

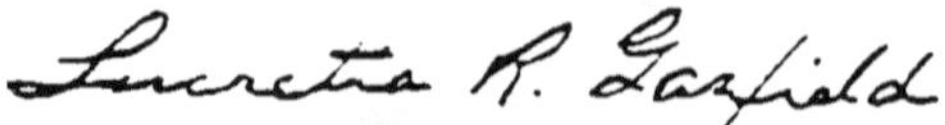

Lucretia Rudolph Garfield
1832-1918

Ellen Lewis Herndon Arthur
1837-1880

Mary Arthur McElroy
Proxy First Lady 1881-1885

Rose Elizabeth Cleveland
Proxy First Lady 1885-1886

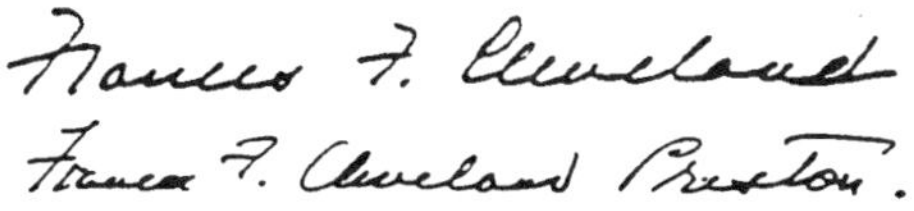

Frances Folsom Cleveland
1864-1947

Caroline Lavinia Scott Harrison
1832-1892

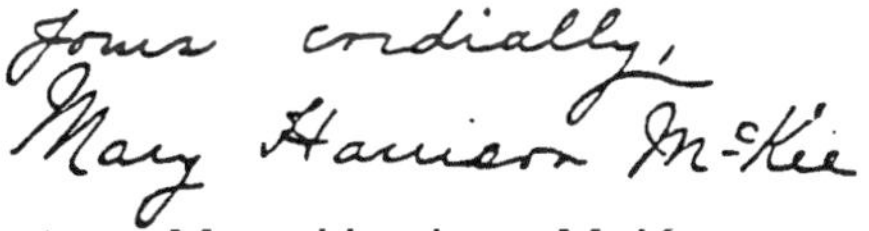

Mary Harrison McKee
Proxy First Lady 1892-1893

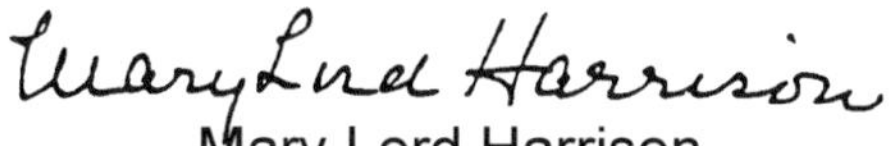

Mary Lord Harrison
1858-1948

Ida Saxton McKinley
1847-1907

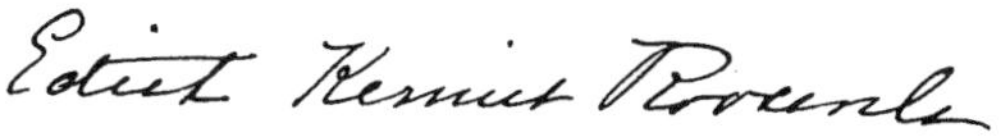

Edith Kermit Carow Roosevelt
1861-1948

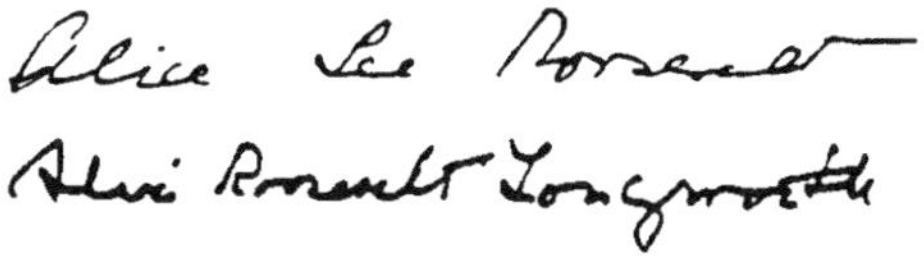

Alice Lee Roosevelt (Longworth)
1902-1990
Proxy First Lady

Helen Herron Taft
1861-1943

Helen Taft Manning
Proxy First Lady 1910-1911

Ellen Louise Axson Wilson
1860-1911

Margaret Woodrow Wilson
Proxy First Lady 1914-1915

Edith Bolling Galt Wilson
1872-1961

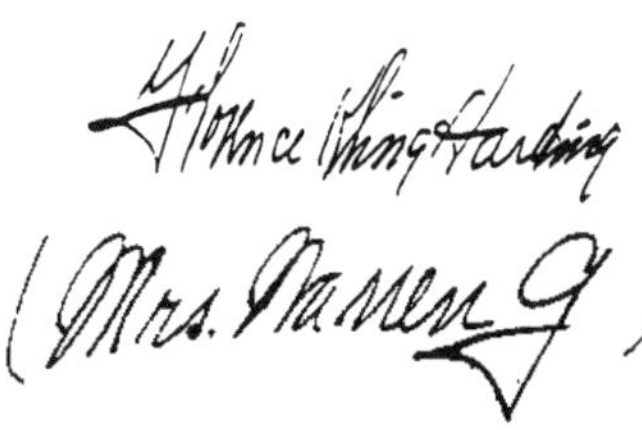

Florence Kling Harding
1860-1924

Grace Anna Goodhue Coolidge
1879-1957

Lou Henry Hoover
1874-1944

Anna Eleanor Roosevelt Roosevelt
1884-1962

Elizabeth Virginia Wallace Truman
1885-1982

Mamie Geneva Doud Eisenhower
1896-1979

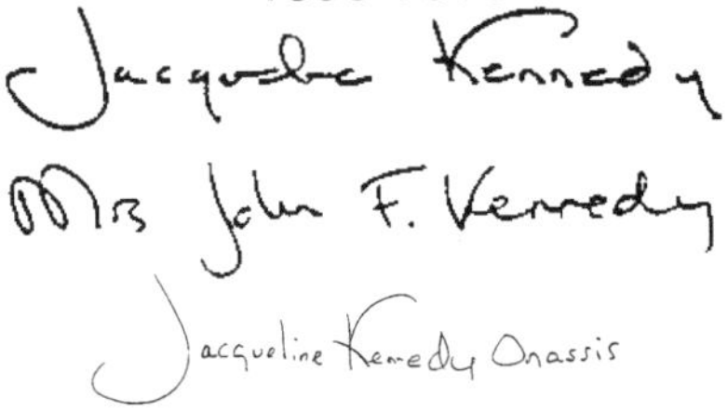

Jacqueline Lee Bouvier Kennedy Onassis
1929-1994

From her limited edition book *One Special Summer* (as Jacqueline Bouvier)

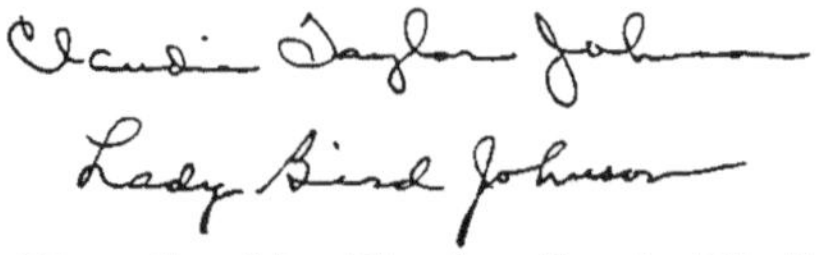

Claudia Alta Taylor (Lady Bird) Johnson
1912-

Patricia Ryan Nixon
1912-1993

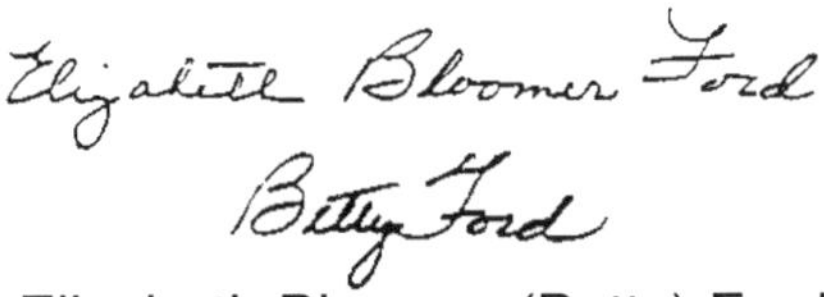

Elizabeth Bloomer (Betty) Ford
1918-

Rosalynn Smith Carter
1927-

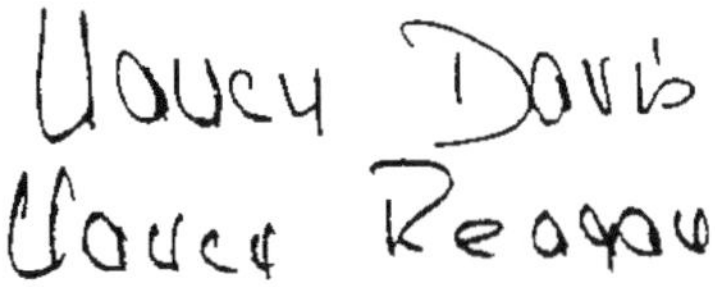

Nancy Davis Reagan
1923-

Barbara Pierce Bush
1925-

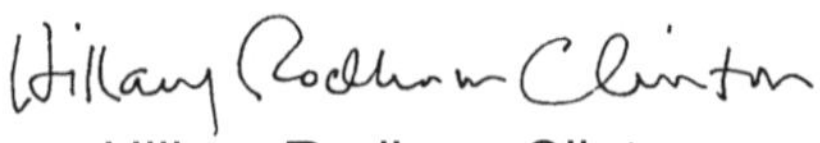

Hillary Rodham Clinton

Chapter 4

WORLD WAR II

by Don Nidiffer

It is now almost 53 years after the bombing of Pearl Harbor. As such, the next few years are likely to find the area of World War II autographs receiving more attention, and possibly, higher prices as a result.

My good friend, the late B.C. West, has said that Hitler signed 20,000 items in his lifetime and that 50,000 of them are in the United States. With the possible exception of recent 20th century U.S. presidents (JFK to present), no field of collecting is beset by more "land mines" than World War II autographs. Of outright forgeries worldwide, Hitler is the most fabricated (most people feel Abraham Lincoln holds this title domestically). If the reader gains nothing else from consuming this chapter, let him/her beware that the need for an experienced hand in purchasing WW II material may be almost as important today as the outcome of the war itself. *Caveat emptor.*

To those, however, who care to tread, World War II offers many avenues to collect with perhaps a few good investment opportunities and certainly some undervalued arenas. The most popular, and the most expensive, by far, come from Germany.

Autographs from most other major powers are often neglected with some offering significant potential for the future financially. Lest one become bored, topical collections can be based upon gatherings from a variety of areas. Aviators, top military commanders, submariners, military scientists and inventors, political figures, holocaust victims, Nuremberg trial defendants, soldier letters, top medal winners (U.S. Medal of Honor or Germany's Knight's Cross of the Iron Cross) are all areas which have avid followers.

As Germans go, collectors of the infamous have a considerable number of choices. Due to his well-deserved immortal reputation as "pure evil" incarnate, Hitler is the target of many collectors. Other frequently sought political figures include party leader Martin Bormann, Reichsmarshal Hermann Goering, Deputy Fuhrer Rudolf Hess, Propaganda Minister Dr. Joseph Goebbels, Reich Foreign Minister Joachim Von Ribbentrop, Head of German Labor Front Dr. Robert Ley, and most of the Nuremberg trial defendants.

Other German military commanders often requested include the most brilliant strategists of the Field Marshals and field commanders. Examples are Field Marshals Erwin Rommel (who never became a Nazi) and Erich von Manstein (even more popular than Rommel among German soldiers), tank commanders Heinz Guderian (some feel the most brilliant strategist in the German military) and Hasso von Manteuffel (Battle of the Bulge fame), and top naval commanders Erich Raeder (very successful U-Boat usage at beginning of the war) and Karl Doenitz (succeeded Hitler as Fuhrer).

Top U-Boat commanders include Otto Kretchmer, Erich Topp, and Gunther Prien (exceedingly rare due to death in 1941). Alfred Jodl is also collectable as the German commander who surrendered in person to Allied Supreme

Commander Dwight D. Eisenhower (who refused to shake his hand). And for irony, the only Field Marshal known to have been of Jewish descent was Erhard Milch, readily available on signed photos.

There are those who seek only officials/soldiers from Hitler's elite guard, the SS. Heinrich Himmler tops this list and is generally available. In contrast, a great rarity is Himmler's Deputy and first administrator of concentration camps, Reinhard Heydrich, nicknamed "The Hangman." Heydrich was assassinated in 1942 by two free Czechs who parachuted into Prague. Predictably, the Nazi's leveled the village of Lidice and killed many of its inhabitants in reprisal.

Among Germany's finest pilots are the "Blond Knight" Erich Hartmann, Gerd Barkhorn, and Gunther Rall, all of whom survived the war. Hartmann's record of 352 kills will undoubtedly preserve his position of the highest scoring ace of all time. At the time of this writing, Hartmann and Rall (275 kills) are still alive. Barkhorn (301 kills) was killed in a car accident in the mid 1980's.

Other Luftwaffe heroes include commander of the fighter pilots and ace Adolf Galland, the flamboyant "Star of Africa" Hans-Joachim Marseille and other early top award winners Werner Moelders, Walter Oesau, and Gunther Lutsow. All but Galland died during the war. So that aviator collectors may remain busy, there are over 5,000 Luftwaffe aces with 107 German aces who shot down at least 100 enemy planes. Major Emil Lang holds the record for the number shot down in a single day—18!

The twenty-two Nuremberg trial defendants of Germany and their little known corresponding Japanese counterparts who were also tried and selectively executed are particularly popular among survivors of the war who were persecuted by an Axis powers.

German soldier letters are not yet and may never become highly sought after, possibly due to language differences. Concentration camp identification papers or letters, especially from the most infamous, Dachau or Auschwitz, have a small but determined market. Finally, there are more than 8,000 winners of Germany's top award, the Knight's Cross of the Iron Cross. Hitler embellished this award further by adding the higher grades (in ascending order) of Oak Leaves, Oak Leaves with Swords, and Oak Leaves with Swords and Diamonds. A special order was singularly given to Hans-Ulrich Rudel who received the Knight's Cross with Golden Oak Leaves, Swords, and Diamonds for his 2,530 operations and 532 tank kills during the war, which he survived. Otto Skorzeny is also a standout KC winner for his numerous exploits, not the least of which was his daring rescue of Mussolini from captivity in 1943.

Collectors of Japanese material are not as limited as the availability of what they seek. Emperor Hirohito's autograph is difficult to find and relatively expensive. Minister of War General Hideki Tojo is perhaps the most desirable of the Japanese military, who along with several of his comrades, was executed following the Tokyo War Crimes Trials. Only seven of the twenty-eight defendants were executed following the trials (two others died during the trial of natural causes) with this group representing the significant political and military circle for collectors. Trial defendants do not include, however, Japanese pilot aces such as Sabruno Sakai or the pilot commander of the Pearl Harbor attack force Mitsuo Fuchida (later moved to the U.S. and joined the clergy). Nor does it include Admiral Isoroku Yamamoto, General Tomoyuki Yamashita, or the Japanese Ambassador to Germany Hiroshi Oshima who was felt to be as much a Nazi as most of his hosts.

For those who wish to round out their Axis collection, the demand for Italian figures mirrors the lack of strength their forces exhibited during the war. Mussolini is needed to supplement a dictator set (which may also include Spanish Generalissimo Francisco Franco). Perhaps Mussolini's "predecessor," King Victor Emmanuel, III, who appointed him Prime Minister or his son-in-law, Count Ciano, are of interest as well if one collects Italians.

Forgeries and superb facsimiles of Germans abound. Japanese and Italian material generally have not reached sufficient popularity to be heavily fabricated. German award documents, in particular, are collected for their decorative as well as their associative value.

At a major military show several years ago, a dealer quietly confided in me that a G.I. had told him that when he broke into Hitler's Chancellory, he discovered a "pile" of Knight's Cross documents. He also found "a little old man" who claimed that he signed these most prestigious awards for Hitler. While this story is unlikely, the determination of genuineness of any Hitler signature is the most difficult one that will be encountered by World War II enthusiasts. I have personally examined Hitler signatures with crossovers, ink shade variations, on original paper, depicting an authentic event, and which can be bled. And yet, they were not actually signatures of Hitler but a type of "lithograph" that is exceptionally deceptive. In fact, they would forever be declared genuine were it not for their perfect overlay over other examples, thus being the equivalent of a Nazi "autopen."

Other German signatures to approach with caution include a very deceptive facsimile of Hermann Goering *on photographs* (I have seen perhaps one or two from 1940-1945 I thought were genuine), printed signatures of von Manstein, von Richthofen, Himmler, Marseille, Goebbels,

Goring (on the Luftwaffe goblet document), the ink stamp of Erwin Rommel, and photographs "signed" by an important figure and inscribed to another important figure.

One final note on German forgeries I have learned from another good friend, Jack Hatter of Volume Control, that there are many aspects to verification of authenticity. While a forger may be familiar with how a signature looks, he/she may not be knowledgeable as to typical format, ink color, corresponding dates and events, what rank or what place relates to the person signing, the peculiarities of German language at that time, etc. As with many historical documents, there are at least five aspects to any item which should be verified.

Allied material currently seems to be undervalued and represents the greatest potential for the future. "Old Blood and Guts," George S. Patton, Jr., is by far the most expensive autograph of the U.S. military (As one veteran of his command once told me, his "guts," our "blood"). Few people are aware that Dwight D. Eisenhower has numerous "undiscovered" autopens as well as several known secretarial signatures. Besides Eisenhower, other five-star Generals are Omar Bradley, Hap Arnold, Douglas MacArthur, George Marshal, and Admirals Ernest King, William Leahy, Chester Nimitz, and William "Bull" Halsey. Other generals of interest are British Field Marshal Montgomery of Alamein and Russia's hero, Marshal Zhukov.

Winston Churchill heads the list of Allied political figures, although an authentic signed picture of Joseph Stalin would command a much higher price. U.S. presidents Harry Truman and Franklin D. Roosevelt are readily available and modestly priced, although war date letters with good related content are rarely encountered. Neville Chamberlain, the Prime Minister of England who signed a peace treaty with

One World War II general's autograph that millions of soldiers, sailors, and flyers saw was that of Lieutenant General Lewis B. Hershey, Director of the Selective Service System from 1940 to 1964. General Hershey's signature was at the bottom of that greetings from Uncle Sam letter so many received during and after the war. General Hershey is shown here being interviewed by author George Sanders in 1960.

Hitler a year before England entered the war, is a good conversational autograph.

The American ace list comprises about 1,200 or so pilots with only 29 scoring more than 20 kills (the American pilots faced a more formidable foe than Russian biplanes frequently shot down by the Germans in great numbers). Major Richard Bong (died 1945) heads the list with 40 kills from the Pacific Theater. Major Francis Gabreski was the top ace of the European Theater with 21 kills. Col. Paul Tibbets and the crews of Enola Gay and Bock's Car are widely known for the two atomic/hydrogen bomb missions. Col. James Doolittle's first raid on Japan is also familiar to many.

Albert Einstein, Robert Oppenheimer (developed atomic bomb), and Edward Teller (developed hydrogen bomb) head the list of most requested scientists of the World War II era. Niels Bohr, a Nobel prize winner and argumentative (at times) peer of Einstein's, is of interest as a contributing physicist of the period.

Please keep in mind that entire collections may be built upon even one of the many areas discussed above. As such, credit has not been done to any single area, but rather a sampling of each has been offered. World War II was devastating as are all wars. It is best we remember and study such events in our own ways so that we can do our best to avoid future tragedies.

Dr. Don Nidiffer is a doctor of psychology and also a longtime collector and widely-recognized expert in World War II autographs. He lives in Charlottesville, Virginia.

Chapter 5

THE REALLY BIG SIGS

by George and Helen Sanders

Ever since the publication of our first edition of "The Price Guide to Autographs" in 1988, we have been asked to list the TOP 60 signature values. Fellow collectors and dealers seem to enjoy reading about the BIG SIGS just for the fun of learning whose signature is earning the highest price on the current market.

Most of us will probably never own all of the top 60 heavy hitters but we all dream of owning at least a couple of them. After all, aren't the catalogs of dealers and auction houses our ultimate "wish books"?

The autograph market has expanded to approximately six million collectors competing, in one fashion or another, for the handwritten treasures of U.S Presidents, vice presidents, movie & TV stars, composers, artists, scientists, astronauts, sports stars, military leaders, clergy, world leaders and other categories too numerous to mention. Our hobby has become one of the most frequently mentioned collectibles throughout the world. Hence, the intense interest in what items cost and what actual value they might sustain in the 21st Century .

In the past decade, all of us have become acutely aware

that the once "lowly" signature that had heretofore played second fiddle to the obviously more important ALS, document, quotation or precious manuscript was fast becoming a valuable adjunct to our respective collections. In the good, old days, most dealers seldom listed such scrawls in the front of their catalogs but did offer, at very reasonable prices, signatures for the fledgling collector in the back of their respective price lists. Many still do but not with the former casual nonchalance they had mustered when there was so much good material readily available.

Good Items Are Disappearing From the Market

In today's frenetic marketplace, we are more likely to acquire a signature of Greta Garbo than one of her childlike handwritten or hand-printed letters. It's easier to purchase an Abraham Lincoln autograph than to locate one of his letters that hasn't been priced beyond the means of Mr. or Ms. Average Collector. Rare and outstanding signatures are now listed in the front of most top dealers' fine catalogs and are no longer considered a cheap or relatively unappealing item.

As we've warned so many times in our various books or articles, as this exciting hobby grows, good items are fast disappearing from the market. The modern collector has to be quick, educated, sure-footed and carry a respectable wallet. Yes, there are still wondrous "bargains" to be found but today we face much stiffer competition for those low-cost items than ever before.

In short, the SIG is in! When all else becomes too pricey or totally unavailable to average folk, the signature of your most favorite celebrity continues to be accessible for a valued spot in your binders or carefully framed with an attractive photo or engraving. Collectors and/or dealers no longer turn up their respective noses to a good signature when that SIG might be the only available piece awaiting your attention and your investment. By comparison, most signatures are relatively reasonable in cost. However, we are about to list for your edification the Top Signature Values selected from over 50,000 prices in this book. Hardly a list of something for everyone but surely a clear indication that the rarest of SIGS demand the highest prices.

All of these signatures, by the way, are ones that are available to collectors. Other much more valuable autographs exist, but only in museums.

Top Signature Values

	PERSON	PRICE
1.	Button Gwinnett (Signer)	$100,000.00
2.	Ivan the Terrible (Tsar)	$ 35,000.00
3.	Shoeless Joe Jackson (Baseball)	$ 23,000.00
4.	King Edward IV (England)	$ 22,500.00
5.	Sir Thomas More (Clergy)	$ 19,750.00
6.	Rain-In-The-Face (Native American)	$ 13,000.00
7.	Martin Luther (Clergy)	$ 10,000.00
8.	Barbara Fritchie (Revolutionary War)	$ 8,800.00
9.	Sitting Bull (Native American)	$ 7,500.00
10.	Geronimo (Native American)	$ 6,750.00
11.	John Paul Jones (Naval Hero)	$ 6,050.00
12.	Lewis Meriwether (Explorer)	$ 4,500.00
13.	Thomas Lynch, Jr. (Signer)	$ 4,200.00
14.	George Washington (President)	$ 4,070.00
15.	J.E.B. Stuart (Civil War)	$ 3,650.00
16.	Raphael (Artist)	$ 3,500.00
17.	T.J. "Stonewall" Jackson (Civil War)	$ 3,500.00
18.	Ludwig van Beethoven (Composer)	$ 3,300.00

19.	Benjamin Franklin (Statesman)	$ 3,275.00
20.	Robert E. Lee (Civil War)	$ 3,200.00
21.	Alfred Moore (U.S.Supreme Court)	$ 3,200.00
22.	Adam Smith (Economist)	$ 3,080.00
23.	Capt. James Cook (Naval Explorer)	$ 3,000.00
24.	Andrew "Rube" Foster (Baseball)	$ 3,000.00
25.	John Wesley Hardin (Western Outlaw)	$ 2,900.00
26.	Pat Garrett (Western Lawman)	$ 2,700.00
27.	Abraham Lincoln (President)	$ 2,700.00
28.	Rembrandt van Rijn (Artist)	$ 2,500.00
29.	Wolfgang A. Mozart (Composer)	$ 2,500.00
30.	George Pickett (Civil War)	$ 2,500.00
31.	Albrecht Duerer (Artist)	$ 2,500.00
32.	Johann S. Bach (Composer)	$ 2,500.00
33.	Michelangelo (Artist)	$ 2,250.00
34.	Queen Elizabeth I (England)	$ 2,250.00
35.	Marilyn Monroe (Actress)	$ 2,250.00
36.	Francisco Goya (Artist)	$ 2,200.00
37.	Joseph Haydn (Composer)	$ 2,200.00
38.	Captain John Smith (Colonial)	$ 2,200.00
39.	Lyman Hall (Signer)	$ 2,200.00
40.	King Henry VIII (England)	$ 2,150.00
41.	George A. Custer (Civil War)	$ 2,100.00
42.	Vincent van Gogh (Artist)	$ 2,050.00
43.	John Hancock (Signer)	$ 2,050.00
44.	John Adams (President)	$ 2,000.00
45.	Emperor Hirohito (Japan)	$ 2,000.00
46.	Peter Paul Rubens (Artist)	$ 2,000.00
47.	Daniel Boone (Frontiersman)	$ 1,700.00
48.	Paul Revere (Revolutionary War Hero)	$ 1,700.00
49.	Sojourner Truth (Abolitionist)	$ 1,650.00
50.	Walt Disney (Cartoonist)	$ 1,500.00
51.	Dr. Albert Einstein (Scientist)	$ 1,500.00

52. States Rights Gist (Civil War) .... $ 1,375.00
53. Adolf Hitler (German Dictator) .... $ 1,350.00
54. Gen. George S. Patton (Military) .... $ 1,200.00
55. John Andre (Revolutionary War) .... $ 1,200.00
56. Buddy Holly (Rocker) .... $ 1,200.00
57. Johann von Goethe (German Poet) .... $ 1,200.00
58. George Gershwin (Composer) .... $ 1,200.00
59. Ernest Hemingway (Author) .... $ 1,000.00
60. Jean Harlow (Actress) .... $ 1,000.00
61. Fyodor Dostoevsky (Author) .... $ 1,000.00
62. Stephen Foster (Composer) .... $ 1,000.00
63. Jimi Hendrix (Rocker) .... $ 1,000.00

Top Prices Will Continue to Rise

The aforementioned prices for signatures represent the average current selling prices of the celebrated people listed above. The values presented are the result of extensive research through thousands of recent dealer offerings and autograph auction catalogues. Since prices change frequently, please be aware of the flexibility in the autograph marketplace. Further, we take no responsibility for quoting others' published prices in the compilation of our data. In closing we feel bound to exclaim, the day of the once lowly signature has dawned, giving philography's child its proper place in the sun—hopefully protected by acid free plastic or matting and ultraviolet glass.

We feel relatively certain that in the few short months since we compiled this information, many of the above listed signatures have shifted into even higher prices. As many of you know, our TOP 25 lists have been published annually in nearly 900 newspapers, magazines, periodicals and mentioned by radio & TV talk show hosts and hostesses on countless occasions. Thus it was decided to offer even more information and the above TOP 60 is the result. Obviously, the multitude of collectible signatures are not to be found in such a "high-rent" district but average anywhere from $5.00 to $50.00 and truly offer something for everyone's budget. What is the very best deal? Acquiring autographs the old-fashioned way IN PERSON. The latter are always costless to the seeker, genuine beyond a doubt and a heluva lot more exciting to collect. Happy hunting to all.

James A. Farley—FDR's Postmaster General and later president of The Coca-Cola Company—chats with George, who is wisely drinking a Coke.

Chapter 6

AUTOGRAPHS OF THE WAR BETWEEN THE STATES

by Michael J. Masters, M.D.

Charles Marshall, an attorney after the war, was A.A.G. on Robert E. Lee's staff. He was the only other Confederate at the Appomattox surrender besides Lee, serving as General Lee's secretary, at the McLean house in front of General U.S. Grant and his high command. After the war he was besieged with requests for autographs of southern notables, especially Robert E. Lee.

Being a collector myself, I have enjoyed finding letters written by luminaries of the war in response to autograph collectors. I have one of Marshall's letters from 1891 to such an autograph collector from Texas in which Marshall sounds decidedly testy. He says: "I regret to say that I have no letters or other papers signed by any of the persons named by you, nor have I any photographs. I have letters and papers signed by Gen. R.E. Lee, but I believe I have parted with the last one that I could spare. I am now in the country and all my papers are at my house in town which I seldom visit. If I find a paper signed by General Lee which I can spare, I will send it to you."

I can certainly identify with that collector; I have received several similar exasperated responses with thinly veiled irritation from Civil War dealers when I have wanted autographs of Robert E. Lee or other "big names" from that conflict.

Even Northerners Admire Robert E. Lee

Because I live in the South, my interest in the Confederacy comes naturally. Today, however, it is very common for Northerners to admire Robert E. Lee, T. J. "Stonewall" Jackson, J. E. B. Stuart or A. P. Hill and to collect their autographs. There is a sense in which collecting Northerners or Southerners transcends geography; both are collected throughout the country. The name used to identify the conflict—Civil War, War Between the States, War for Southern Independence, War of the Rebellion, War of the Northern Aggression, War of Secession, and even The Late Unpleasantness—reflects the speaker's attitude toward the war. While I am more comfortable with other nomenclature, it is hard to avoid the term "Civil War" when writing because of its brevity and the general usage of the term.

I never cease to be amazed at how widespread the interest in the Civil War is. My medical office has a Civil War decor, which daily generates passionate and exciting discussions with my patients about the Civil War on many levels.

The Civil War still represents the crossroads of American history. Actually this should not be so surprising. The Civil War was above all an American fight—fought by Americans, on American soil, over American issues. The heroes on both sides were American. The Civil War was the biggest war ever fought on the American continent. The number of men killed was greater than the sum of all casualties in other wars from the Revolution through the Korean conflict. It was the last "old-fashioned" war in which men charged in mass formation with the generals out in front. It was the first

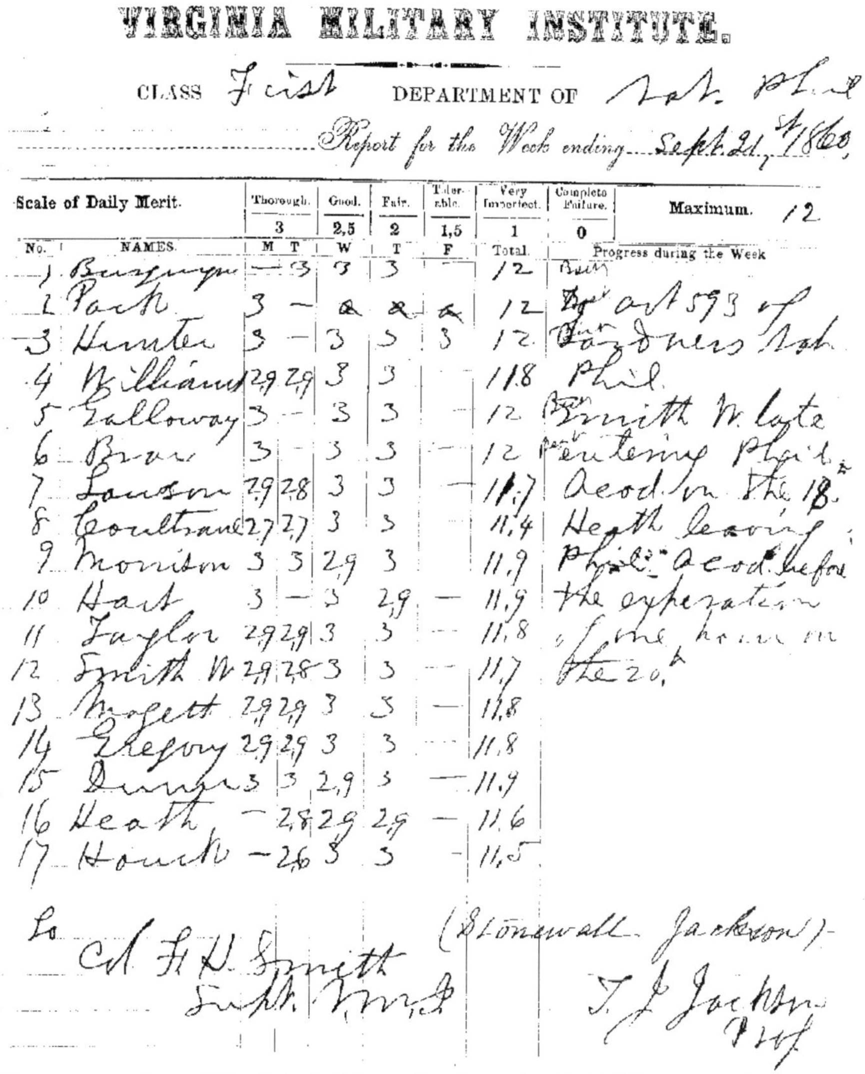

VIRGINIA MILITARY INSTITUTE.

CLASS First DEPARTMENT OF Nat. Phil.

Report for the Week ending Sept. 21st 1860.

Scale of Daily Merit.	Thorough.	Good.	Fair.	Tolerable.	Very Imperfect.	Complete Failure.	Maximum. 12
	3	2,5	2	1,5	1	0	

No.	NAMES.	M	T	W	T	F	Total.	Progress during the Week
1	Burgwyn	—	3	3	3		12	
2	Park	3	—	a	a	a	12	
3	Hunter	3	—	3	3	3	12	
4	Williams	2,9	2,9	3	3		11.8	
5	Galloway	3	—	3	3	—	12	
6	Brown	3	—	3	3	—	12	
7	Lawson	2,9	2,8	3	3	—	11,7	
8	Coultrane	2,7	2,7	3	3		11,4	
9	Morrison	3	3	2,9	3		11,9	
10	Hart	3	—	3	2,9	—	11,9	
11	Taylor	2,9	2,9	3	3	—	11,8	
12	Smith W	2,9	2,8	3	3	—	11,7	
13	Moffett	2,9	2,9	3	3	—	11,8	
14	Gregory	2,9	2,9	3	3		11,8	
15	Dungres	3	3	2,9	3	—	11,9	
16	Heath	—	2,8	2,9	2,9	—	11,6	
17	Houck	—	2,6	3	3	—	11,5	

Progress during the Week: Burg. ... art 593 of Gardners Nat. Phil. Smith W. late entering Phil. Recd on the 18th. Heath leaving Phil. recd before the expiration of one hour on the 20th.

To Col F. H. Smith Supt. V.M.I.

(Stonewall Jackson)

T. J. Jackson Prof.

Class report from Virginia Military Institute by T. J. "Stonewall" Jackson with cadets' names, grades, and progress in his hand. This class marched to Richmond on April 21, 1861, under Jackson's direction to act as drillmasters for the new Confederate army. Five of the top ten men in Jackson's class died in the war, including the top student, Henry King Burgwyn, the "Boy Colonel," who was killed on the first day of the Battle of Gettysburg. The words "Stonewall Jackson" were written by Francis H. Smith, Superintendent of VMI. Jackson never signed his name using "Stonewall."

modern war with new technology such as ironclad battleships, land mines, submarines, repeating shoulder arms, rifled artillery, aerial observation with balloons, strategic use of railroads and telegraph, trench warfare of an extensive nature and even primitive machine guns.

It was the first war to be comprehensively photographed. And, fortunately for autograph collectors, it generated a mountain of paperwork during four years of intense fighting and maneuvering by Union and Confederate armies. In addition, the level of literacy on both sides was surprisingly high. Consequently, countless soldiers' letters and diaries flowed from the war. The beginning Civil War collector has some decisions to make because of the many options available to him.

It has been almost 130 years since the end of the War Between the States. Many participants have been forgotten. But numerous soldiers' memories have been preserved through the diaries, letters, photographs and other official paper records that have survived insects, rodents, fires, damp basements and "official purging" of old documents. Official military documents included endorsements, orders, reports, passes, and letters between active participants. The Civil War was a conflict with constantly changing military conditions that required participants to sign a great deal of paperwork.

"Wardate" and Endorsements

Documents or photographs that were signed during the years of the war are considered "wardate." These are the most sought after of Civil War documents and, unfortunately, the most expensive. Often documents involving requests for relatively mundane matters such as pay, leave, passes or transfers went up and down the chain of command gathering comments and, more importantly, signatures with ranks at each step. These endorsements are a large source for war-dated materials. Because of this, when scouting groups of old Civil War documents, one's guard can never be let down lest a seemingly routine document contain an endorsement from an important general. I have a report from an assistant surgeon stating that a soldier from the 12th North Carolina is unfit for duty because he lost his right arm at the battle of Chancellorsville. (Somehow that seems obvious to me.) To my surprise it is endorsed by three generals including Robert Rodes as Major General and Richard S. "Baldy" Ewell as Lieutenant General.

Confederate Material Harder to Find

Confederate autograph material is as a rule rarer than Union for several reasons. First many buildings and records were burned, especially toward the end of the war when the Confederates evacuated a town. Because of the scarcity of paper, many Confederate military documents were written on cheap brown and even reddish paper which had a tendency to get brittle and crumble. The ink often contained gunpowder or soot and gave only a pale gray line at the time of writing that tended to fade.

Signatures of some generals such as George Pickett and A. P. Hill always seem to be light, possibly because of the thin writing pens they used. Blue and red inks are seen, the latter used primarily by clerks. Documents written with pencil were often hurriedly scrawled during the heat of battle when pen and ink were not available. These documents have a sense of urgency with interesting battle content. The devastation of the postwar South and inherent heat and humidity also contributed to the loss of many Confederate documents. It seems that the Confederate generals are more sought after. They have attained an almost mythical quality. They are the most romantic characters in American military history and the most studied in the history of the Civil War. Thus supply and demand for the few materials of these generals that are available play a role in their scarcity.

Most people in the autograph field believe that the Civil War is among the "hottest" areas of collecting interest at this time. Some of the interest has been fueled by major productions such as the movie "Glory" and Ken Burns' PBS series on the Civil War. Sure to keep the pot boiling is the more recent TNT production of Michael Shaara's Pulitzer prize-winning novel *The Killer Angels* (renamed "Gettysburg").

What to Collect?

In spite of the increased media visibility of the Civil War, some individuals predict an eventual correction of the very high prices being realized at some of the larger auctions. There has also been a lot of "big money" that has entered the Civil War area recently, cutting a large swath, driving up prices, and making quality material harder to find. All of these factors create a dilemma for the Civil War collector. What should one collect?

The first step should be to narrow collecting down to a particular focus. Comprehensive collections, such as collecting all the Confederate generals, are unrealistic at this point in time.

I have good friends who have collected generals for decades and still do not have them all, so starting at this point to collect all Union or Confederate generals is not realistic. But while comprehensive collections may not be feasible, the Civil War offers an extensive array of other collecting possibilities. I know people who collect all the generals associated with a particular battle such as Franklin.

(Gettysburg tends to be the most popular, and with all the new interest likely to be generated from the movie "Gettysburg," material from this battle seems to be at a premium.) Collecting all the generals, either Union or Confederate, from a particular state can be an interesting pursuit. I know someone who collects all the Confederate generals who were major generals. There are a number of people who collect a particular subject area such as medicine, photography, railroads, prisons, cavalry, Army of Northern Virginia, Army of the Potomac, Trans-Mississippi, naval, or routine documents concerning a particular battle.

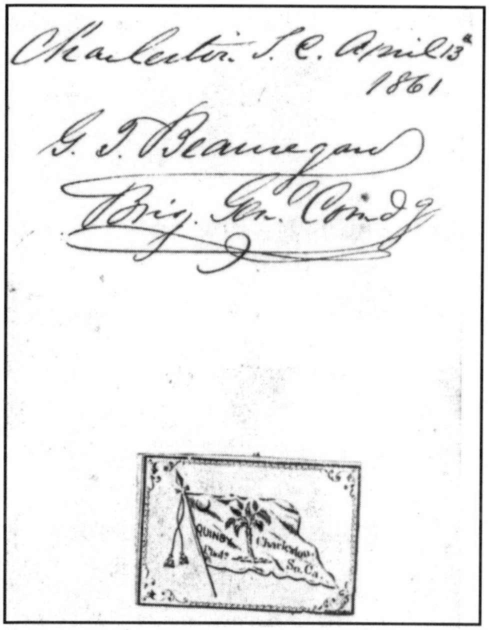

Reverse of *carte de visite* with Charleston, S.C. backmark signed by Confederate General G.T. Beauregard on April 13, 1861, the day that Fort Sumter surrendered.

Sometimes collectors focus on one or two generals only, such as Custer. I have another friend who is a direct descendant of John Bankhead Magruder and avidly collects anything to do with him. Another friend collects generals who were killed in action (KIA's). My wife, who has a background in music, collects (out of self defense, I think) photographs of soldiers holding musical instruments. Generally if there is an area of interest, there is an area of Civil War collecting that can be applied to that interest.

Cost

Regrettably, the other factor to consider is one's budget. The spiralling increase of prices for the well-known names on both sides has to be faced realistically before embarking on a collecting endeavor. This is especially true for the Confederate "superstars." Signatures of Robert E. Lee, Stonewall Jackson, J.E.B. Stuart, and A.P. Hill are virtually unobtainable on any kind of modest budget. Additionally, practically all of the Confederate generals are rare in wardate, and Union generals are rapidly gaining that status (at least for the well-known names). If the general was killed during the war, there is an even greater difficulty in obtaining his signature in any form, with expected higher costs. Stonewall Jackson, J.E.B. Stuart, Albert S. Johnson, Stephen D. Ramseur (I just had to add a North Carolinian) for the Confederates and Philip Kearny, Nathaniel Lyon, and James Birdseye McPherson for the Union represent some of the rare, highly sought after KIA's that have become rather pricey. Generals with less stable commands because of raiding or extensive cavalry activities, such as John S. Mosby or Nathan Bedford Forrest, may be available in postwar writings or railroad bond signatures respectively but impossible to obtain in wardate.

Not too many years ago when material was more plentiful, I thought all I wanted was war-dated signatures. I sometimes viewed with a measure of disdain pre- and postwar clipped signatures. I know now that I have missed obtaining generals that I have not seen since that time because I was waiting for wardate. My advice would be to obtain a desired signature, if the price seems reasonable, in any form and then upgrade as more desirable forms are found. Trading material with other collectors and dealers is

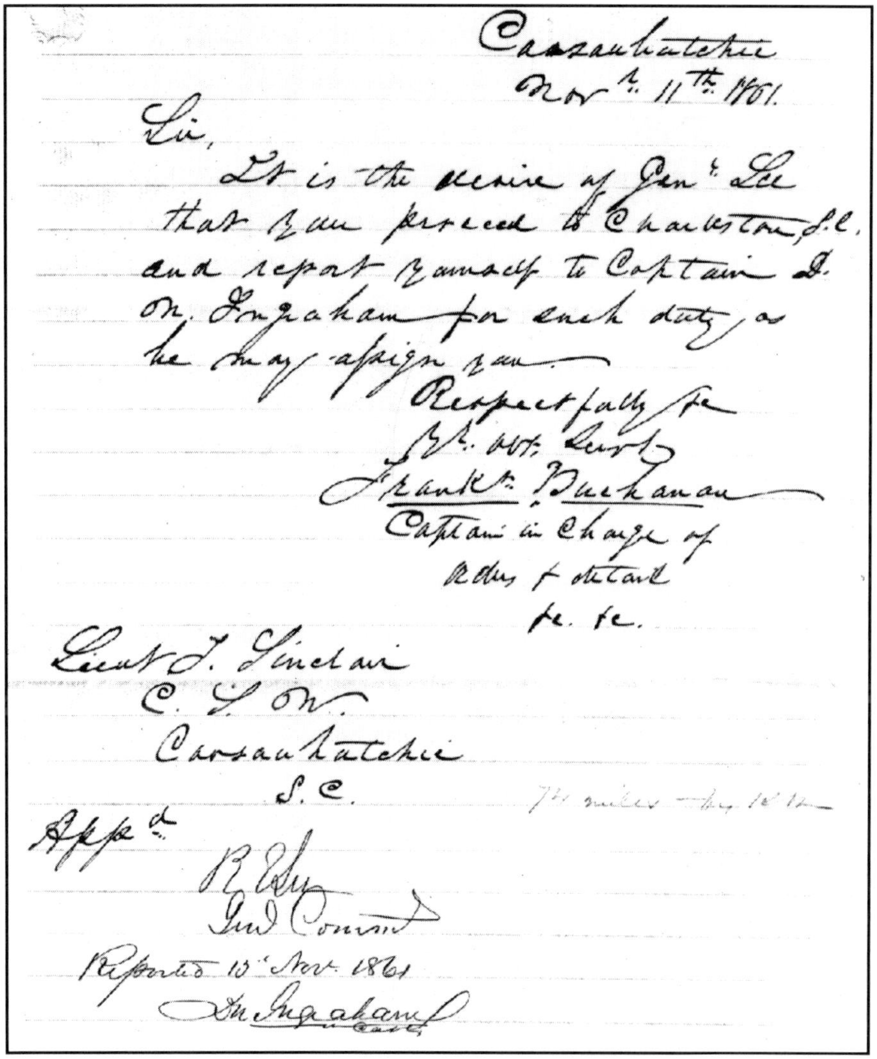

Coosawhatchie
Nov. 11th 1861.

Sir,

It is the desire of Gen. Lee that you proceed to Charleston, S.C. and report yourself to Captain D. N. Ingraham for such duty as he may assign you.

Respectfully &c
Yr. obt. Servt
Franklin Buchanan
Captain in Charge of Orders & detail
&c. &c.

Lieut. J. Sinclair
C. S. N.
Coosawhatchie
S. C.

Appd.
R E Lee
Genl Comdt

Reported 13th Nov. 1861
D. N. Ingraham

Wardate ALS by Franklin Buchanan, Commander of the *Virginia* (*Merrimac*), endorsed by Robert E. Lee and Duncan Ingraham, Navy Chief at Charleston, S.C.

common in Civil War circles and frequently can be more advantageous to both parties than straight cash purchases because of appreciated value.

If "investment" is one's sole concern, the parameters are

different. In that case, the war-dated documents, especially letters with historically important content, have realized larger jumps in prices over the years but at considerably larger outlays initially. Collectors are not bound by the same restraints as investors, and all the Civil War material has increased in value especially in the last two years.

When there is a heavy demand for a limited amount of autograph material, establishing a specific price for an item is usually very subjective and complicated by the uniqueness of each item. Because the Civil War market is so fluid, any estimates of price are really a snapshot of that point in time. Next month all bets are off, and new numbers apply. Additionally there is a distinct subculture of Civil War collecting.

There are numerous private sales of which the general public is unaware. The prices of these private sales cannot be reflected in price guides. Consequently, prices are considered in somewhat subjective ranges rather than specifics. This is not very satisfying but does underscore the fact that in active (frenzied?) areas of collecting continued involvement in the current market is the only way to keep up.

In addition to obvious factors such as condition and legibility, price is most affected by date, military or historical significance, and the importance of the individual who signed the document. I am convinced that in Civil War documents, there is the largest premium for individual signatures during the war versus non wardate signatures of the same individual than in any other war or collecting area including presidents. U. S. Grant tends to be more expensive as Civil War general than as president.

Date within the war can affect the price also. A document in which a general is writing close to the time of an important battle tends to be more desirable regardless of content. A

Original salt print of abolitionist John Brown with attached clipped signature.

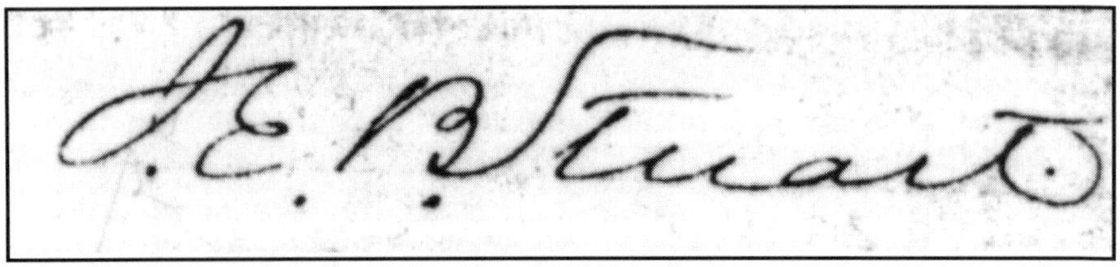

Clipped signature of Robert E. Lee's famous Chief of Cavalry, J.E.B. Stuart.

letter from George Meade written on July 4, 1863, the day after his victory at Gettysburg, would be a prize for any collector, even if it were only answering an autograph request. Likewise, militarily significant battle reports, historically important documents, or particularly revealing letters signed by the major players transcend all price guides and are worth whatever the buyer and seller agree upon.

Signatures on documents of routine content by some of the legendary generals are much more expensive than important content by much lesser generals. J.E.B. Stuart's signature on a forage report is much more valuable than a wardate ALS by Daniel Ruggles with good content about military maneuvers at Port Hudson in August 1862. At this writing, clipped signatures of the more pedestrian Confederate and Union generals can be obtained in the two figure amounts. (War-dated clips signed with rank are more costly.)

As the generals become more important or rarer, the prices rise into the hundreds and ultimately end with a simple clip of Robert E. Lee being valued in the low three thousands and Stonewall Jackson in at least the four thousands but may be more, considering the competition to obtain his signature. It is my experience that for every Jackson one sees 10 to 15 Robert E. Lees. A.P. Hill is probably rarer, and J.E.B. Stuart is rarer still. It is easy to see that war-dated ALS's of these individuals go into the five figures in wardate. I would hope that these expensive items would not discourage collectors from participating in Civil War collecting.

Soldiers' Letters

One area that is still reasonably priced is soldiers' letters. While it can be thrilling to own a signature of a famous Civil War participant, the truest picture of the war is grasped by reading the letters of the not so famous, the men in the ranks who really fought the war. Their perceptions of the fighting and their leaders can be illuminating. While military critics have not been kind to George McClellan, the letters of the soldiers who fought under him reveal that they loved him and held him in high esteem.

The daily routine, the constant rumors about the enemy, the drunken leaders, and often explicit eyewitness battle content have propelled soldiers' letters upward in price, but individual letters from both sides are still relatively available. Even more desirable would be a series of letters by one soldier describing his experiences over a period of time. As in autograph material, the Confederate soldier's letters are rarer and more expensive than his Union counterparts.

Where to Find Civil War Autographs

Where can Civil War material be acquired? The primary source is reputable autograph dealers or Civil War dealers who handle the type of material you desire. The dealers who have more extensive stock of Civil War items usually have more specialized knowledge of the war and can be teachers and confidants as well as purveyors. Their catalogues or monthly lists can be educational apart from any material you purchase.

Another source of material can be auctions. Many auction houses do not necessarily guarantee the authenticity of

Wardate clipped signature of Confederate General A.P. Hill

the material. Also, the collector has to take care not to get caught up in the excitement of the moment and pay more than he has budgeted. Fellow collectors can also be a source of material. I enjoy talking to other collectors and vicariously enjoy their acquisitions. Often they may be willing to sell a lesser piece if they have upgraded to a better document.

Civil War shows can be a source as well. I have learned a great deal going to these shows. I have met other collectors, learned which dealers handle the type of material I most want to acquire, and enjoyed perusing other Civil War material that I might not collect (guns, swords, dug relics, and so forth).

Over the last two years I have noticed there has been progressively less autograph material at the Civil War shows, reflecting the increasing scarcity of Civil War material in general. Dealers at these shows are very approachable and most have specific areas of expertise within the Civil War (photography, uniforms, medicine, documents, and so on). Civil War book dealers exhibit at these shows and their book displays of both current and out of print books can be perused to obtain reference books or more detailed information about a personality or collecting interest.

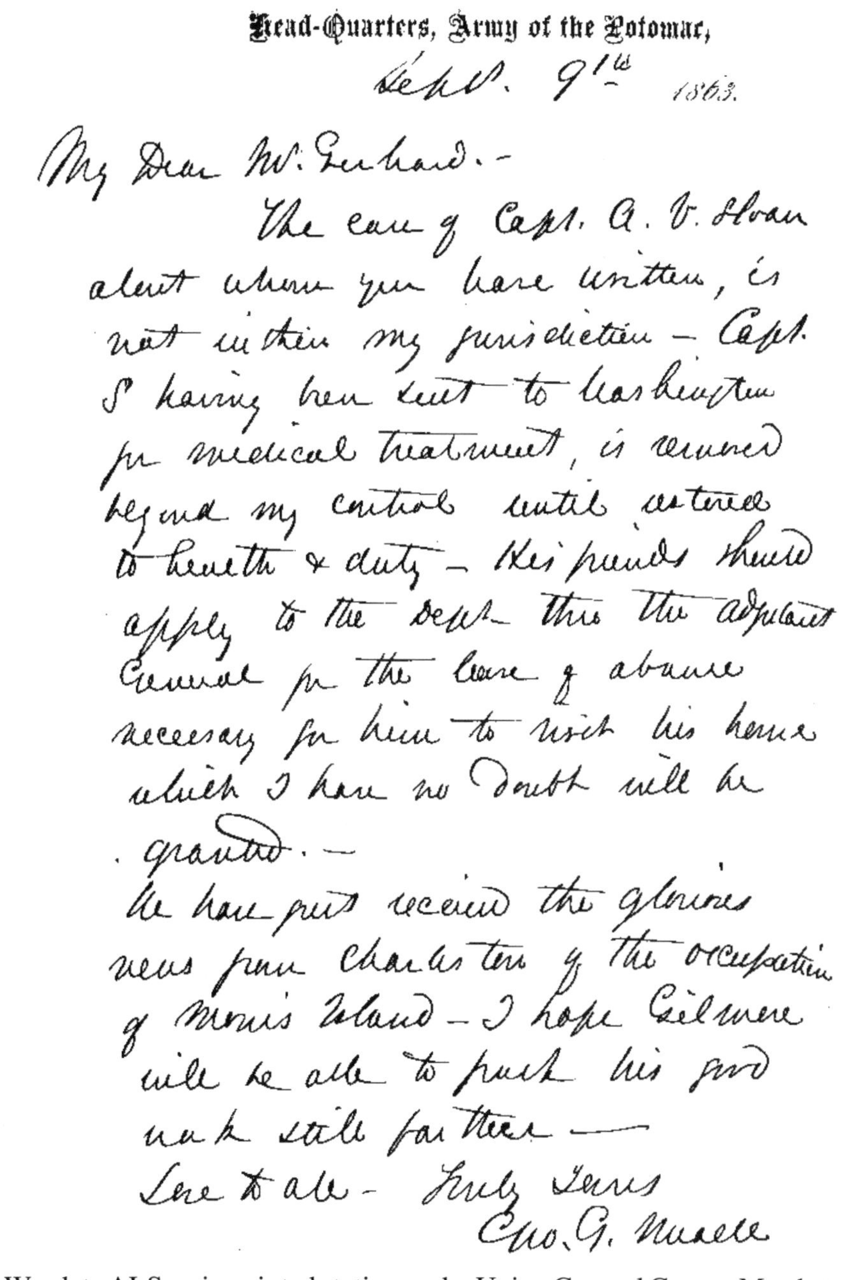
Head-Quarters, Army of the Potomac,
Sept. 9th 1863.

My Dear Mr. Gerhard.—
The case of Capt. A. V. Sloan about whom you have written, is not within my jurisdiction — Capt. S having been sent to Washington for medical treatment, is removed beyond my control until restored to health & duty — His friends should apply to the Dept. thro the Adjutant General for the leave of absence necessary for him to visit his home which I have no doubt will be granted.—
We have just received the glorious news from Charleston of the occupation of Morris Island — I hope Gillmore will be able to push his good work still farther —
Love to all — Truly Yours
Geo. G. Meade

Wardate ALS on imprinted stationery by Union General George Meade two months after his victory at Gettysburg.

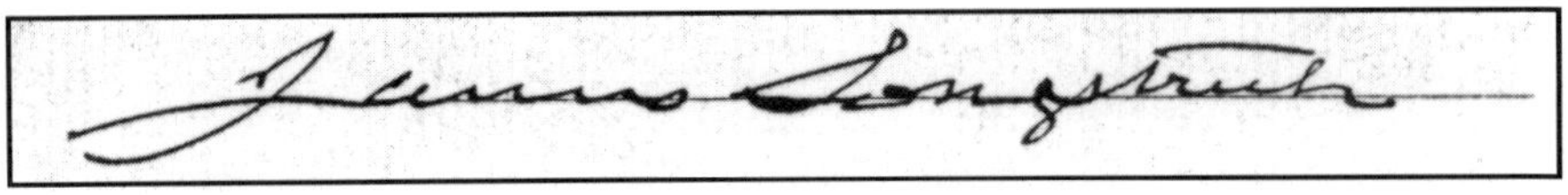

The signature of "Lee's Fighting General," James Longstreet.

Civil War shows are held in different locations throughout the year but are mostly held east of the Mississippi. Periodicals such as *The Civil War News*, a newspaper, and *Civil War Times Illustrated*, a magazine (there are many others) contain numerous advertisements and classifieds by Civil War dealers, book shops and collectors, enabling individuals in all geographic areas to have access to Civil War material.

Fascination

The enduring fascination with the War Between the States has created a Civil War autograph market that currently may be somewhat out of control. The collector faces the difficulty of scarcity of material and burgeoning prices. But those with a spark of interest (in my case it is more of a conflagration) and continued diligence can enjoy this field of collecting on whatever level they choose. My perceptions may not be shared by everyone. I am reminded of what William T. Sherman said when criticized for alleged errors in his memoirs: "I may be wrong, but that's the way I remembered it. These are my memoirs, not the memoirs of anybody else."

Chapter 7

EXECUTIVE MANSION & WHITE HOUSE CARDS

by Stephen Koschal

With prices for Presidential material at an all time high and much of it quickly becoming relatively scarce, Executive Mansion/White House Cards have become very popular once again. The ideal item to add to your Presidential collection is generally an item signed by the President while he was in office. Relatively speaking, due to the high costs of such material the least expensive yet respectable way of adding to your collection are examples of Executive Mansion/White House Cards.

These cards measure approximately 2.75 x 4.25 inches, are white in color and bear the imprint in the upper right hand corner "Executive Mansion" with the word "Washington" imprinted just below and somewhat to the right. On a few occasions I have seen these cards during the Arthur administration where the words "Executive Mansion, Washington" was much more centered on the card.

Developed Especially for Autographs

It is said these cards were created due to the increasing demand for the autograph of the President. During nearly two thirds of the 19th century autograph requests were generally answered with small slips or small plain cards that were signed to fulfill the requests. This accounts for the occasional sheet of paper that turns up with several examples of a Presidential signature on it which a secretary was able to tear off an example as the requests came in.

What's True and What's Not

In at least a half dozen books that have been written on the subject of autograph collecting since the 1940s that we have seen, it is stated that these Executive Mansion cards were first introduced by President Hayes. Only has it been in recent years that we have now seen in print that possibly President Grant may have introduced these cards and that only one or two examples may exist. We have also read, which is true, "For all practical purposes Hayes is the first President available in these cards."

We have also read that if a Grant card does exist, it was signed after his administration by a collector who was able to acquire a blank card from President Hayes and had Grant sign it at a later date. False. To set the records straight here for the first time we not only show a U.S. Grant Executive Mansion Card but also one that he has dated as well, proving without a doubt that Grant was the first President to introduce these popular collectibles. Please see the top of the facing page for an illustration of this card.

Several administrations later—on September 14, 1901 (due to the death of President McKinley by an assassin's bullet)—Theodore Roosevelt became president. Approximately one month later, he changed all Executive Mansion stationery and Executive Mansion cards to read "White House, Washington." This lasted until approximately 1905 when he once again changed his stationery to read "The White House."

Executive Mansion card signed and dated in 1872 by President U.S. Grant, proving he was the first to use these cards.

It is also important to mention here that during the Arthur administration, although the Executive Mansion Card was widely distributed, he improved on this card by issuing a much larger card measuring 6 x 8 which is usually referred to as a "White House Vignette Card." There are generally two types of this card, one, the front view of The White House which shows the driveway which leads up to the entrance and is filled with horses, carriages and pedestrians in the foreground. The other example of a White House Vignette Card portrays the back of the Executive Mansion with children playing on the lawn.

The cards were also generally distributed through the administration of Warren G. Harding. We have seen examples signed by every President since Harding, except for Clinton, including a few genuinely autographed by President Bush.

These particular cards became very popular in recent years for many collectors have turned to collecting multiple signatures on a single card. These cards are available today through the Bureau of Engraving and Printing in Washington at a nominal cost.

Facsimile Cards

The modern White House since the Eisenhower administration has sent out White House Cards bearing the President's printed signature, some even bear a printed sentiment along with the signature. Other recent Presidents have done the same. Kennedy, Johnson and Nixon all sent out White House cards with a printed sentiment and signature. In many cases these cards have the word "FACSIMILE" or "This is a facsimile reproduction" printed on the verso.

A word of caution, many of these cards were pasted in albums and later hastily removed, leaving mounting traces

Facsimile signature of Jimmy Carter on a White House card.

on the backs of these cards covering the printed information advising you the card is not genuinely signed. These cards are still somewhat collectible and have some value. We are also aware that some modern cards that have been sent out by The White House that do not bear the warning, are usually signed for the President by a secretary or the autopen. Genuine White House cards signed by any modern President since Eisenhower can be considered to be extremely scarce.

Be On Guard

There are two other reasons for collectors to be on their guard while collecting these gems. For one, a few examples have appeared on the market that were genuinely signed by a modern First Lady. Holding on to these cards for a few years collectors were able to acquire a President's signature on the same card after his term in office. Although both signatures are genuine, in most cases, the President did not sign the card while he was in office. These cards are still very desirable and actively sought after by collectors.

The second example, and much more serious, refers to the brazen individual who several years ago printed up at least two different White House Cards. These were sold in volume, unsigned for collectors to eagerly acquire a Presidential signature. The first type is a card somewhat identical to a genuine White House card except that the printing is in flat blue ink. The genuine White House card is printed with a more glossy blue ink and the words are *raised*.

The second card is similar to the one above, however this card does not have a smooth finish to the touch but rather has a more textured surface. On this same card at the top left corner, a Presidential seal has been printed.

We have seen many of these spurious examples signed

by Gerald Ford and President Bush has also been duped into signing a few. These bogus cards have little or no value over ordinary signature value whereas a genuine White House card is usually worth at minimum double the price of a mere signature.

Values

Starting with President Grant, his cards are virtually unobtainable. As mentioned above books state one or two may exist, I know of no other than my own. This unique card measures 3 x 4 which is slightly larger than the other Executive Mansion cards. This card also has a space for the date just after the word Washington. Should a Grant card appear on the market its value would be $3,000.

President Hayes Executive Mansion cards are available from time to time. He usually simply signed his cards "R.B. Hayes." Occasionally he used these cards for short notes to friends which also become available. Signed Executive Mansion cards of Hayes are valued at $375.00

President Garfield who held the office for such a short time signed very few Executive Mansion cards. Most bear his full signature and some are dated as well. Beware: a genuine Executive Mansion card was also sent out with a stamped signature. The cards bearing a stamped signature are still quite collectible and sell for $150. A genuine signature on an Executive Mansion card would be worth in excess of $4500.00.

President Arthur always affixed a beautiful bold full signature to these cards. His is one of the most attractive looking examples. Presently valued at $450.00

Grover Cleveland examples are usually available on the market with many of them dated as well. He is presently the least expensive of the 19th century Presidents. His cards sell for $250.00

Benjamin Harrison can be considered somewhat scarce. Not many examples have appeared on the market for it is believed that he preferred to send out the White House Vignette Card to autograph seekers. A few Executive Mansion cards have appeared on the market with short notes signed by President Harrison however a very few simply signed examples are known to exist. One of these would be worth in excess of $1500.00.

William McKinley cards are quite desirable as is most anything signed by him while in office. His cards are still available and sell for $375.00

Theodore Roosevelt cards are actively sought after by collectors. They are usually found signed with a bold, full signature. "White House" cards are valued at $500-$600. "The White House" cards are valued at $450.

William Howard Taft usually signed these cards as Wm. H Taft along with a three or four word sentiment that he usually dated. With his writing being so large, the short sentiment usually fills up the entire card, looking quite attractive. Value $225.00.

Woodrow Wilson cards are available and are always signed in full and in the top left corner of the card. By doing this it would avoid any one from writing anything additional above his name. Value $400.00.

Warren G. Harding are also very desirable as is most anything he signed while in office. These cards are signed in full and are available from time to time. Value $375.00.

Calvin Coolidge is the most common of all the Presidents in this format. His cards are readily available and can be obtained for $200.00.

Herbert Hoover's autographs considered by many to be uncommon as President are available in the form of White House cards. A nice clean example would be worth $325.00.

Franklin D. Roosevelt held the office of President for a record length of time. Items signed by Roosevelt as President are still plentiful however signed White House cards are seldom offered in recent years. Several collections I am presently aware of contain an Executive Mansion, Albany card till it can be replaced with a genuine White House card. A White House card signed by Roosevelt is worth $400.00.

Harry S. Truman cards are also sought after. He usually signed these cards with a fine bold signature. They become available from time to time and are valued at $400.00

Dwight D. Eisenhower can be considered uncommon in this form. Due to his extreme popularity as General and President he had difficulty coping with the many requests for his autograph. During his first Presidential term he did personally sign White House cards but later had cards printed with a facsimile sentiment and signature. The verso of the card states this is a facsimile. More commonly found is a card with the embossed Presidential seal surrounded by stars which are available signed. The traditional White House cards signed by Eisenhower are worth $450.00.

Recent Presidents

John F. Kennedy. Requests to the White House were answered with cards that contained a printed sentiment and signature. On the verso was a printed statement that these were facsimiles. These cards are still collectible and sought by collectors throughout the world. No genuinely signed White House cards have yet to appear on the market to my knowledge.

Lyndon B. Johnson. Many requests for Johnson signatures were answered with a White House card that bore a signature of Johnson written by his secretary Bruce Thomas. Many of these cards contain a three word sentiment

Example of a White House Vignette Card. This one has been signed by (at the time) five living presidents—Gerald R. Ford, George Bush, Ronald Reagan, Jimmy Carter, and Richard Nixon.

"with best wishes." I have also seen cards containing an autopen signature of Lady Bird with the secretarial signature of Lyndon B. Johnson just above the First Lady's. A few genuine White House cards signed by LBJ do exist.

Richard Nixon. The White House sent out printed examples of his signature. Some of these cards also have a printed sentiment. Some of the Nixon cards were sent out signed by secretaries and have no disclaimer on the verso. Most of the cards that are available were signed by Patricia Nixon and a few enterprising collectors managed to have Nixon sign these cards several years later after leaving the White House.

Gerald R. Ford. Genuine signed White House cards are to be considered very rare. Bogus White House cards mentioned earlier have found their way in the market signed by

Ford. Some he has signed as G. R. Ford and a few others with the more desirable Gerald R. Ford signature.

Jimmy Carter. Requests to the White House were answered with a slightly different card. The words "The White House, Washington" were shifted to the top left corner, a portrait of the rear of the White House is printed in the center of the card and a printed signature of Jimmy Carter is near the bottom of this portrait. All the printing was done in light green ink. On the verso of the card is the printed statement: "Facsimile Signature of Jimmy Carter, 39th President of the United States." As with any modern U.S. President a genuine signed White House card would be considered very scarce.

Ronald Reagan. The Reagan White House kept the same format as the Carter administration. The words "The White House Washington" remained at the top left corner. The only change was that the printing was changed to blue ink on the Reagan cards and his facsimile signature is more centered on the White House. A few genuine examples signed by Reagan have surfaced but are still considered rare.

George Bush. As of this writing I am not aware of any genuine examples of signed White House cards. I have personally seen three or four of the spurious White House cards mentioned above that appear to have been genuinely signed but these did not come out of the White House. These cards were signed by Bush when put in front of him for an autograph request at functions outside the White House.

Bill Clinton. At this time I am also not aware of any examples of signed White House cards by Bill Clinton.

Stephen Koschal is the author of *Collecting Books and Pamphlets Signed by The Presidents of the U.S.* He is also the author of dozens of articles on the subject of autograph collecting. A long time collector and dealer who issues catalogs on a regular basis and former Director of the Universal Autograph Collectors Club. 1980-1984.

Chapter 8

AUCTION TRENDS

by Jim Smith and Jim Berland

Specialized autograph auctions have been around for a long time. With the increased popularity of our hobby, they have quickly grown in numbers and in the quantity of items offered. Today they have become the primary source of fresh material on the market, offering pieces seldom matched in diversity and quantity by any but the very largest dealers.

If you have been in this hobby for even a short period of time, you have often asked yourself the question "What is this worth?" The answer is really very simple. It is worth what someone else is willing to pay for it.

Auctions have become the stage upon which this question is answered. It is here that dealers and collectors meet to compete for the desired autographs, and where new price levels are set.

You can be certain that auction results are thoroughly analyzed and studied by the professionals in our hobby. It is this raw data that allows them to find competitively priced pieces for their own collections and/or for resale.

Auction results can be used by virtually all of us, whether we are interested in U.S. Presidents, Colonial era, Civil War generals, aviators, royalty, scientists, sports heroes, composers, entertainers, artists, authors, or all of the above.

What we will attempt here is to give you a five year overview (1988-1993) of auction trends, with prices fetched on various items in specific categories.

We have limited ourselves to "fair-traded" items, signatures and letters/documents with little or no content. These are the type of pieces that allow an accurate tracking and hopefully realistic expectations for the future. You should be able to see specific growth patterns, with many excellent increases in value.

The examples are quoted with 1988 prices first, followed by prices into 1994. We have selectively chosen categories and names that we believe accurately reflect market conditions during this 5 year period.

American Colonial Era

Overall strong, steady growth in prices, with a moderate increase in the number of collectors. Examples: John Hancock, DS ($2,600-5,000), Sig ($800-2,100); Patrick Henry, DS ($550-1,450), Sig ($200-700); Thomas Mifflin, DS ($225-300); William Shirley, DS ($175-550); John Jay, ALS ($2,000-3,300); Benjamin Franklin, Sig ($1,100-2,500); Benedict Arnold, ALS ($3,500-6,000); Charles Carroll, Check ($200-350); Horatio Gates, LS ($300-550); Robert Morris, DS ($300-550); J.B.D. Rochambeau, LS ($400-650); Philip J. Schuyler, ALS ($400-660); Fredrick von Steuben, DS ($600-2,100); Marquis de Lafayette, ALS ($425-1,200); and Charles Cornwallis, ALS ($350-650).

Americana

Overall steady growth in prices, with particular interest in Western Americana. Examples: Daniel Boone, Sig ($900-

1,500); Samuel Francis Smith, AQS: one stanza from "My Country 'tis of Thee' ($300-850); Annie Oakley, Sig ($950-3,300); William F. Cody, double Sig ($250-650); Pat Garrett, ALS ($1,200-2,800); Emmett Dalton, Sig ($250-850); Sitting Bull, pencil Sig ($2,600-6,500); Geronimo, pencil Sig ($2,500-6,000); Sam Houston, Sig ($250-450), DS: Treasury Warrant ($350-660); Samuel F. Austin, DS ($950-1,700); and A.L. de Santa Anna, DS ($600-1,250).

Civil War

Frantic growth in popularity and geometric price increases. Examples: Robert E. Lee, Sig ($900-2,700), signed CDV ($2,800-6,600); James Longstreet, Sig ($50-275); T.J. "Stonewall" Jackson, Sig ($1,750-2,800), wardate ALS ($6,500-23,000); States Rights Gist, Sig ($140-1,375); Simon B. Buckner, Sig ($40-130); Fitzhugh Lee, Sig ($30-110); Nathan Bedford Forrest, DS: Railroad Bond ($400-1,400); Raphael Semmes, Sig ($80-330); Pierre G.T. Beauregard, Sig ($60-250), signed CDV ($220-1,850); Jefferson Davis, Sig ($225-500); Alexander Stephens, ALS ($50-220); Judah P. Benjamin, Sig ($80-270); William T. Sherman, Sig ($40-275), SP ($350-3,500); Philip H. Sheridan, Sig ($30-175); George A. Custer, Sig ($1,200-3,000); John C. Fremont, Sig ($70-250); George G. Meade, Sig ($30-150); Abner Doubleday, ALS ($550-1,800); Philip St. George Cooke, signed CDV ($125-1,000); Winfield S. Hancock, signed CDV ($150-925); Joshua L. Chamberlain, Sig ($25-450), DS ($50-1,050); Ambrose E. Burnside, ALS ($80-340), signed CDV ($125-880); and Hiram G. Berry, wardate AES ($125-1,150).

Military

A steady growth in prices, with particular increased

interest in American World War II personalities. Examples: George S. Patton, Sig ($650-1,100), SP ($1,600-6,000); Chester Nimitz, Sig ($40-70); Douglas MacArthur, SP ($300-550), Sig ($100-160); George C. Marshall, TLS ($70-165); Bernard Montgomery, DS ($120-600); Benito Mussolini, SP ($210-460); Adolf Hitler, 5 x 7 SP ($2,100-4,500), DS ($1,200-2,200); Heinrich Himmler, DS ($370-750); Martin Bormann, TLS ($400-770); Karl Doenitz, SP ($100-100); Joseph Goebbels, Sig ($125-220), TLS ($500-2,200); Hermann Goering, TLS ($500-750); Erwin Rommel, DS ($1,500-1,600); Horatio Nelson, LS ($1,400-2,400); William Bainbridge, LS ($100-220); George Dewey, SP ($140-330); Hyman Rickover, signed book ($110-165); John J Pershing, TLS ($80-130); and Robert Baden-Powell, TLS ($160-360).

Aviation and Explorers

Overall strong, steady growth in prices. Examples: Orville Wright, Sig ($150-310), Check ($325-450), TLS ($500-1,200); Wilbur Wright, ALS, (2,200-4,400); Charles Lindbergh, SP ($700-1,550), ALS ($600-1,450); Amelia Earhart, Sig ($210-480), 5"X4" SP ($525-1,800); Glenn Curtiss, Sig ($110-190); Igor Sikorsky, signed book ($70-150); Pappy Boyington, Check ($30-120); Eddie Rickenbacker, TLS ($40-140); William "Billy" Mitchell, Check ($220-600); Ferdinand von Zeppelin, TLS ($250-290); Louis Bleriot, 4"X5" SP ($210-440); Richard E. Byrd, Check ($90-100); Henry M. Stanley, Sig ($70-140); and David Livingstone, Sig ($90-170).

U.S. Presidents

Still the most popular category in terms of interest, substantial price increases to the "major" Presidents. Examples: George Washington, Sig ($2,500-4,100), DS: Society of Cincinnati document ($6,100-12,000), DS (with Jefferson): 4 Language Ship's Paper ($7,100-16,500); John Adams, Sig ($800-2,000), DS ($2,200-5,500); Thomas Jefferson, Free Franked envelope ($1,300-3,500); James Madison, Sig ($240-440); James Monroe, DS: Land Grant ($275-550); John Quincy Adams, Sig ($110-230), DS: Land Grant ($340-550); Andrew Jackson, DS: Land Grant ($600-1,250); Martin Van Buren, Sig ($110-165); William Henry Harrison, Check ($450-1,500); John Tyler, DS ($550-880); James K. Polk, DS ($850-1,400); Zachary Taylor, DS ($750-3,600); Millard Fillmore, DS ($500-450); Franklin Pierce, Free Franked envelope ($200-280); James Buchanan, Free Franked envelope ($200-330); Abraham Lincoln, full Sig ($1,200-3,500), DS: Military Commission ($4,250-6,600), Check ($6,500-9,900); Andrew Johnson, DS ($725-1,650); Ulysses S. Grant, Sig ($180-660), DS ($400-1,100); Rutherford B. Hayes, Sig ($110-165); James A. Garfield, ALS ($550-770); Chester A. Arthur, DS ($220-330); Grover Cleveland, DS ($220-220); Benjamin Harrison, Sig ($90-130); William McKinley, DS ($170-330); Theodore Roosevelt, signed White House card ($240-410); William H. Taft, TLS ($90-140); Woodrow Wilson, DS ($220-350); Warren G. Harding, TLS ($110-140); Calvin Coolidge, signed White House card ($110-160); Herbert Hoover, TLS ($60-110); Franklin D. Roosevelt, TLS as Governor ($150-220); Harry Truman, TLS ($110-165); Dwight D. Eisenhower, TLS ($110-190); John F. Kennedy, TLS ($600-1,100); Lyndon B. Johnson, TLS ($150-220); Richard Nixon, TLS ($80-160); Gerald R. Ford, TLS ($60-110); Jimmy Carter, Check ($130-115); Ronald Reagan, Check ($385-260); George Bush, TLS ($220-180) and the "4 Presidents" (Reagan, Ford, Carter & Nixon), SP ($3,300-1,500).

Heads of State

Slow, steady growth in prices, with a moderate increase in the number of collectors, probably an undervalued field. Examples: Napoleon Bonaparte, LS signed "Bonaparte" ($930-1,750); Maximilien Robespierre, DS ($2,200-3,400); Joseph-Ignace Guillotin, DS ($1,300-2,300); Francis I (France), DS ($550-700); Charles DeGaulle, TLS ($440-590); Winston Churchill, Sig ($450-550), TLS ($850-1,300), ALS ($1,100-1,800); Duke of Wellington, 3rd person ALS ($160-160); Oliver Cromwell, DS as "Oliver P" ($2,400-3,200); George II, DS ($270-370); George III, DS ($260-380); William IV, ALS ($160-280); Victoria, DS ($180-260); Duke & Duchess of Windsor, SP ($660-550); Frederick II (Germany), LS ($450-550); Bismarck, AQS ($175-330); Paul von Hindenburg, DS ($160-180); Catherine II (Russia), LS ($1,100-1,650); Alexander II, DS ($440-510); David Ben-Gurion, TLS ($225-490); Mohandas K. Gandhi, ALS signed "Bapu" ($700-1,100); Simon Bolivar, ALS ($3,300-3,800); and Francisco Franco, postcard SP ($110-190).

Scientists

Very strong, recent rapid growth in prices, one of the hottest fields in the hobby. Examples: Isaac Newton, Sig ($1,100-3,300), DS ($3,300-6,600); Albert Einstein, Sig ($600-950), TLS ($1,200-1,800), 4"X5" SP ($1,100-2,300); Nikola Tesla, Sig ($140-330); Wernher von Braun, SP ($125-330); J. Robert Oppenheimer, signed currency ($140-400); Max Born, TLS ($90-200); Otto Hahn, TLS ($70-275); Guglielmo Marconi, Sig ($70-180); Michael Faraday, ALS ($275-470); Samuel F.B. Morse, ALS ($370-950); Lee DeForest, TLS ($75-290); Robert Brown, ALS ($330-930); Charles Babbage, ALS ($275-1,000); Alexander Graham

Bell, TLS ($550-1,000); Thomas A. Edison, Check ($275-450), DS: Minutes of a Meeting ($400-600), SP (850-1,200); Charles Darwin, ALS ($1,400-2,500); Louis Pasteur, ALS ($1,000-1,600); George Washington Carver, ALS ($500-880); Sigmund Freud, ALS ($2,200-4,900); and Carl Jung, TLS ($650-1,000).

Sports

Continued steady growth in prices, always a popular category. Examples: Babe Ruth, Sig ($440-950), SP ($1,100-2,200), signed ball ($1,400-3,800); Ty Cobb, Check ($285-440), ALS ($880-1,700); Tris Speaker, SP ($280-675); Kenesaw Mountain Landis, Sig ($110-150); Miller J. Huggins, Sig ($440-710); Cy Young, TNS ($300-510); Roberto Clemente, SP ($220-340); Knute Rockne, Sig ($140-280), signed book ($350-1,400); Vince Lombardi, SP ($340-480); Robert T. "Bobby" Jones, Sig ($180-700), SP ($450-2,200); Walter Hagen, Sig ($120-290); Ben Hogan, TLS ($50-180); Joe Louis, signed book ($240-600); Muhammad Ali, Sig as "Cassius Clay" ($80-230); and Jesse Owens, SP ($80-290).

Entertainers

Steady growth in prices for "major" performers, stagnant results for the more obscure, consistent group of collectors. Examples: Clark Gable, Check ($200-385); Stan Laurel and Oliver Hardy, SP ($600-925); Jayne Mansfield, signed program ($60-140); Bert Lahr, DS ($180-250); Marilyn Monroe, SP ($3,300-3,700); Bette Davis, DS ($110-170); Greta Garbo, DS ($1,600-1,200); Katharine Hepburn, SP ($160-250); George Reeves, Sig ($550-600); John Wayne, SP ($330-360); Audrey Hepburn, DS ($80-260); Bela Lugosi, SP ($490-725); Basil Rathbone, DS ($330-450); Humphrey Bogart, DS ($1,100-1,500); Boris Karloff, DS ($310-390);

Montgomery Clift, DS ($660-1,000); W.C. Fields, Sig ($210-350); Lucille Ball, DS ($220-340); Elvis Presley, SP ($660-825); and Beatles, SP ($1,100-2,600).

Composers

Consistent and steady growth in prices, with a recent surge in collector's interest. Examples: Sergei Rachmaninov, Sig ($100-140); Irving Berlin, Sig ($75-165); Johannes Brahms, ALS ($1,300-2,000); Giuseppe Verdi, ALS ($1,200-1,900); Duke Ellington, AMuQS ($660-1,200); Thomas "Fats" Waller, AMuQS ($660-880); George M. Cohan, postcard SP ($260-550); Richard Rodgers, AMuQS ($210-460); Franz Liszt, Sig ($140-340); Richard Strauss, postcard SP ($380-460); Gustav Mahler, ALS ($1,350-1,550); George Gershwin, Check ($770-1,200), AMuQS ($3,300-4,400); Igor Stravinsky, Sig ($140-310); Claude Debussy, ALS ($770-990); Camille Saint-Saens, AMuQS ($260-550); Edvard Grieg, Sig ($160-385); Bela Bartok, Sig ($140-340); Nicolo Paganini, ALS ($660-1,200); and John Philip Sousa, Check ($160-240).

Artists

Consistent and steady growth in prices, another category with increased collector's interest. Examples: Raoul Dufy, ALS ($280-600); Pierre Auguste Renoir, ALS ($1,100-1,600); Edgar Degas, ALS ($1,200-1,750); Claude Monet, ALS ($1,200-1,800); Camille Pissarro, ALS ($660-1,300); Edouard Manet, ALS ($880-1,400); Henri Toulouse-Lautrec, ALS ($1,900-3,300); Pablo Picasso, SP ($770-2,300); Diego Rivera, Sig ($120-240); Maxfield Parrish, ALS ($330-600); Georgia O'Keefe, ALS ($440-800); Grandma Moses, Sig ($55-140); Norman Rockwell, signed FDC ($25-110); Walt Disney, signed book ($1,100-1,700); Charles Schulz,

SP ($45-140); Thomas Nast, Sig ($20-110); Auguste Rodin, ALS ($220-400); and Frederic Auguste Bartholdi, ALS ($220-880).

Literary

Substantial growth in prices for "major" names, with moderate increases for others. Examples: Francois Voltaire, ANS ($1,400-3,000); Jules Verne, ALS ($330-990); Marcel Proust, ALS ($440-900); Robert Browning, ALS ($325-550); Elizabeth Barrett Browning, ALS ($990-1,300); Charles Dickens, Check ($420-660); Rudyard Kipling, Sig ($100-140); Alfred Lord Tennyson, Check ($130-240); George Byron, Free Franked panel ($550-1,150); Robert Louis Stevenson, DS ($180-480); J.R.R. Tolkien, TLS ($360-850); Jack London, Check ($200-385); Nathaniel Hawthorne, DS ($450-880); J. Fenimore Cooper, Check ($55-180); Ernest Hemingway, pencil Sig ($250-490); Mark Twain, single Sig ($375-550), double Sig ($490-925); H.G. Wells, ALS ($120-360); Robert Frost, signed book ($65-220); Erle Stanley Gardner, TLS ($40-170); Henry W. Longfellow, Sig ($55-120); Harriet Beecher Stowe, Sig ($55-130); and John Steinbeck, Sig ($140-290).

Miscellaneous Autographs

Examples: Andrew Carnegie, Sig ($50-110); Henry Ford, SP ($1,250-1,600); J. Pierpont Morgan, DS ($440-660); Andre Citroen, TLS ($110-475); Harvey S. Firestone, Sig ($90-130); Jay Cooke, LS ($100-180); James Rothchild, LS ($260-440); John D. Rockefeller Sr., TLS ($375-660); Isaac M. Singer, TLS ($550-1,650); George Westinghouse, TLS ($330-575); Albert Schweitzer, SP ($250-440), ALS ($210-420); Joseph Smith, signed currency ($770-1,200); Brigham Young, Sig ($210-500), Check ($550-1,050); Pope Pius XII, signed benediction ($440-770); Pope Innocent XI, DS ($440-710); Mother Teresa, SP ($60-140); Louis Brandeis, ALS ($325-600); Benjamin Cardozo, ALS ($425-460); Salmon P. Chase, ALS ($110-310); Clarence Darrow, Sig ($110-335); Frederick Douglass, DS ($110-280); Booker T. Washington, TLS ($70-180); Clara Barton, ALS ($275-600); Florence Nightingale, ALS ($440-700); Mata Hari, ALS ($1,450-2,500); Belva Lockwood, Sig ($120-220); Helen Keller, Sig ($55-110), TLS ($240-260); Ayn Rand, Sig ($135-390); Maria Montessori, ALS ($330-750); and Elizabeth Cady Stanton, Sig ($35-100).

The Hobby is Healthy!

We hope that you have found this brief analysis of auction price trends as interesting as we have. The names and prices that we used in this comparision were specifically selected because in our opinion they represent accurate examples of market conditions. If we had wished to be more dramatic, we would have certainly included some of the outstanding prices fetched on letters or documents with content. Many of these wonderful items have sold for over $100,000.00, with a couple actually breaking the $1,000,000.00 barrier.

Our hobby certainly appears to be in a vibrant state. Prices are up substantially in every category, with many having made truly dramatic increases. Most of the major auction houses are reporting increases in the number of bidders at each event. It is an exciting field, and growing in size annually. Much more quality material is coming on the market, items that heretofore were kept in attics.

While the press reports mostly revolve around content letters by Abraham Lincoln, George Washington, Robert E. Lee, "Stonewall" Jackson, and others important in American history, there has been a new awareness in categories like artists, composers and scientists. There is a treasure trove of material available in these underutilized fields. Imagine reading the words written by such notables as Renoir, Degas, Monet, Brahms, Verdi, Gershwin, Edison, Darwin, Pasteur and many others. It is an exciting time in this hobby, and we look forward to many more grand years.

Jim Smith is the owner of **Remember When Auctions, Inc.**, P.O. Box 629, Acton, Maine, 04001, phone 207-477-8111. Jim, and his wife Pat, have been conducting specialized autograph auctions for 6 years. They issue 4 catalogs per year, 600 to 2,000 lots each, with quality autographs in all fields. Catalogs are issued at no charge, simply call or write and your name will automatically be added to their mailing list. Quality consignments are always being sought, again simply call or write for details.

Jim Berland is a Lawyer/Commodity Trader in Chicago and an ardent autograph collector. He served as the Auction Editor for the U.A.C.C.'s publication "Pen and Quill" from 1991-1993. He follows the auction market worldwide, and has an unrivaled knowledge of auction results.

Auctioneers Jim and Pat Smith of **Remember When Auctions** hosted George Sanders on the Maine coast in 1991 and again in 1993.

BONUS 1950s HOLLYWOOD HISTORICAL PHOTOGRAPH

Well (heh, heh) George may kill us but this picture we found while going through some old photographs from his Hollywood days is too good not to publish. That's actress Rhonda Fleming laying a big kiss on George!

Chapter 9

PERFORMING ARTS

by Bill Safka and Arbe Bareis

In recent years there has been tremendous interest in autographed material relating to the performing arts. Film stars, composers, opera stars, classical instrumentalists, and popular performers are highly sought after by both collectors and dealers. The great performers of the past and present will be remembered long after ordinary mortals are gone.

The Stars of Yesteryear Can Now Be Seen Again

Video and audio recordings are available to the general public as never before. Complete recordings of such luminaries as Enrico Caruso, Sergei Rachmaninov, and Edith Piaf can be heard on compact disc. Arturo Toscanini conducting the NBC Symphony and a recently discovered performance of Verdi's *La forza del destino* featuring Renata Tebaldi, Franco Corelli, and Boris Christoff in addition to "Voice of Firestone" programs starring the likes of Jussi Björling, Lauritz Melchior, Helen Traubel, and Leonard Warren can all be seen on video for the first time since their initial respective telecasts in the 1950s.

A whole new generation can view the films of Bette

Davis, Joan Crawford, Spencer Tracy, and James Dean by renting them at their nearest video stores. Listening and watching inspire many people to collect autographs of the artists they have seen in performance.

Composers and Other Musicians

Composer autographs are more highly prized today than ever before. Among the rarest and most expensive are Bach, Mozart, and Beethoven. It is not often they are offered for sale. More affordable are Gounod, Meyerbeer, Leonard Bernstein, and Andrew Lloyd Webber. Beginning with the late 19th Century it is possible to find signed photographs of such composers as Verdi, Wagner, Liszt, Brahms, and Tchaikovsky in addition to valuable autographed musical quotes and letters.

Among concert artists, collectors most frequently request examples of conductors Arturo Toscanini and Wilhelm Furtwingler, violinist Jascha Heifetz, and pianists Artur Rubinstein and Vladimir Horowitz. Pianists, in particular, have a tendency to start playing in public at an early age and continue at an advanced age. It is therefore possible to have signed photos of one artist spanning many decades. We once had a signed photo of Chilean pianist Claudio Arrau taken when he was a boy in knickers.

Actors and Actresses

Performers who led tragic, mysterious, and turbulent lives have always fascinated the public. The English actress Lily Langtry is remembered today more for her affairs with royalty than for her stage appearances. Her autographs sell while her contemporaries (with the exception of the ever-popular Sarah Bernhardt) are neglected by the public. Other performers were justly famed for their remarkable talents; Marilyn Monroe, Jean Harlow, Maria Callas, and Vaslav Nijinsky all fetch healthy prices.

Singers

Recordings have kept the memory of many opera singers alive. People are still held spell bound by the artistry of Adelina Patti, Enrico Caruso, Kirsten Flagstad, Claudia Muzio, Rosa Ponselle, Beniamino Gigli, Jussi Björling, and many others. We get many requests for these singers as well as many others each year. Among the most requested current singers are Luciano Pavarotti, Placido Domingo, Frederica von Stade, Kiri Te Kanawa, Jessye Norman, and Jose Carreras. Some collect material relating to only one singer and will buy any photo that they do not already have in their collections. We have customers who collect exclusively such singers as Mattia Battistini, Germaine Lubinf, Beniamino Gigli, Eva Marton, Mirella Freni, and Enrico Caruso.

Photographs

Celebrity photographers have become more and more collectable. Photos taken by Nadar, Sarony, Dupont, Falk, Mishkin, Hurrell, and Steichen are greatly appreciated today. Cabinet photos and *carte de visites* are particularly popular as are larger photos while some people prefer postcards.

Signed photos of Bessie Smith, Billie Holliday, Elvis Presley, and Judy Garland are in high demand and hard to come by. Among today's performers the most requested are Barbra Streisand and Frank Sinatra. It is particularly difficult to find a genuine signature of Frank Sinatra as his secretary often signed for him. So too is the case with Elizabeth Taylor. Bette Davis, Joan Crawford, and Gloria

Swanson always signed their own autographs. Others rarely signed at all, like Humphrey Bogart, Marilyn Monroe, Katharine Hepburn, Cary Grant, and of course Greta Garbo. Of particular interest are signed photos of actors costumed in roles they were particularly identified with but which rarely turn up. Vivien Leigh as Scarlett, Clark Gable as Rhett, and Bela Lugosi as Dracula come immediately to mind. Also popular are dance poses of Fred Astaire and Ginger Rogers.

Values Continue to Rise

Autographs increase in value. Some merchandise has doubled in the last ten years. In glancing through catalogs that we issued several years ago we are amazed at the appreciation in value of many items. In many cases we wish we had them back! We frequently purchase merchandise at higher prices than we sold them for several years ago. We always look for quality items and aim to meet the needs and requirements of our many customers, whatever they collect.

Bill Safka and **Arbe Bareis** are full-time dealers who feature classical music and cinema items, with specialization in opera and other performing arts. They issue a bimonthly catalog from **Safka and Bareis Autographs**, P.O. Box 886, Forest Hills, NY 11375 or call (718) 897-7275.

Operatic soprano Helen Traubel guested with George Sanders in Los Angeles in late 1958 on his "Sanders Meanders" show.

Chapter 10

FOR GOODNESS SAKE!

Collecting Clergy Autographs

by Frank and Ruth Ann Matthews

Among autograph dealers there is an apocryphal story making the rounds, regarding an old Bible found in an attic. A theological student selling books told a dealer that he had given the old book to the Scout paper drive because it "probably wasn't worth much since it was all in German and printed by someone by the name of Gute, or Guter, or Gutenberry, or something like that."

When, the astonished dealer regained his composure, he hastened to reply that the book was probably a priceless, early printing of a Gutenberg Bible. The student was not impressed. "Maybe so," he replied with a yawn, "but you wouldn't have wanted it anyway. Someone had scribbled all through it, and signed his name, 'Luther,' 95 times on the end papers under a bunch of paragraphs entitled 'Theses!'"

Collecting Clergy Only Now Coming Into Its Own

Until recently, collectible men of the cloth have elicited little more than a yawn, to collectors of the twentieth century. A sale in December, 1905, is a case in point. For three days an auction was held to dispose of the "concluding portion of the extensive and valuable collection of engraved portraits and autograph letters of John H. V. Arnold." The event was held by the Anderson Auction Company of West 29th St., New York, "successor to Bangs & Co., Est. 1833."

Scattered throughout the sale were a number of Clergy offerings. In the catalog now in our collection, the original owner noted by Lot 4, "American Clergy," that the 172 pieces sold as one lot for a total of $1.95. Lot 5, "American Divines," fared even worse; collectibles of Dwight L. Moody, and fifty others brought the grand sum of 25 cents total, an average of less than a half-cent each. (Of course, let it be noted that this was in an ancient age before auction BS—Buyer's Surcharge of 10%—and before the equally odious custom of sellers' auction reserves. But I digress . . .)

A year later, little had changed; no great strides had been made for the Clergy. In catalog #46 (November, 1906), Goodspeed's Book Shop carried a number of classic autograph pieces, among which were an ALS by Washington to John Hancock ($75.00, an LS of Lincoln ($20), and an equally amazing collection of Signers of the Declaration of Independence, from a Francis Hopkinson ALS at $1, to William Ellery at $12.50.

By comparison, anyone collecting Clergy, must have concluded "For goodness sake!" — A 1791 ALS by the Rev. Peter Thatcher, patriot, orator, and pastor of the Brattle Street Church of Boston, was offered for seventy-five cents. The same was true of the Rev. Theodore Parker—seventy-five cents as an ALS for a clergyman growing in interest to collectors today. The Rev. Henry F. Carey, translator of Dante, was listed as an ALS for $1.50, as was William Ellery Channing, famous Unitarian clergyman. A very interesting ALS of the Reverend Noah Webster, lexicographer and minister, written to Webster and the Federal Party, complaining about the high price of rye and corn, was offered for $3.

That perennial favorite, Ralph Waldo Emerson, former Unitarian minister of Second Church in Boston, was represented by a three page ALS to the Committee on Unitarian Festival; Emerson confesses, "I have been so long suffered to be a looker on and disengaged person in theological relations..."— all this and more for a mere $12.50.

Why Collect Clergy?

People collect Clergy for as many reasons as there are seemingly numberless saints, sinners, seers, sects, and sacred religions.

My interest began when I was eight years old, and our family had made something of a pilgrimage in the nineteen-thirties all the way from the Black Bayous of Louisiana to the White Temple of Aimee Semple McPherson in California. My father, ever after until the day he died, spoke of the blithe spirit of that angel in the wispy white gown. What I remember as a child, wide-eyed with wonder, was that I had never seen so much money in a church before, as the ushers took up the collection in shining wash tubs of silver. And I still have the autograph of Aimee Semple McPherson, purchased from an usher for 25 cents, one-tenth of my spending money on that vacation tip.

In the forties, the most charismatic member of the Clergy-circuit was Billy Graham. Those were the days of his red ties, college-stadium crusades, and first "Decisions for Christ" which could fill a football field with the penitent. Somewhere in my collection, there is a ticket from one of those crusades, and another Clergy autograph — from Graham, one of the notables. While there have been many other interesting evangelists since, I have not been attracted to those who seem predominantly an odd combination of the Ten Commandments and St. Vitus' Dance; nor have I had an abiding interest in the radio and television purveyors of the "Good News of Eternal Damnation." It's more a matter of theology than philography.

Some Significant Clergy of Modern Times

By the early fifties, I had enrolled in graduate studies at Boston University School of Theology. There as a chauffeur for notable guests who visited the University, I first met Paul Tillich. At the time, he was writing a book, *The Courage To Be*, an inscribed copy of which is in my library. With the publication of *The Shaking of the Foundations*, and other works in theology, Tillich became the giant of twentieth century Protestant theologians.

Another Clergy notable of those years was Bishop G. Bromley Oxnam who more than any other Methodist clergyman was responsible for making McCarthyism *McCarthywasm* in America by his appearances before the House Committee on Un-American Activities, and his ringing defense of religious freedom and civil liberties in a historic speech at Harvard Chapel. I was there to hear it all, and to collect yet another autograph of religious history.

Another seer of those days was a student at Boston University, as I was. His name was Martin Luther King, and he was somewhat responsible for my own pilgrimage from a person of provincial West Texas thought to that of a civil rights advocate and renaissance man. As a friend and colleague, I never thought to ask for his autograph, even in those civil rights days.

In most recent months, I have received a long-awaited letter from Elton Trueblood, Quaker saint, and mystic now in retirement. His brief ALS of one paragraph admonished me to buy his biography from "any bookseller of religious works."

No doubt I shall, and send it to him for the proper inscription and autograph!

Advantages of Collecting the Clergy

Collecting the Clergy has many advantages. For one thing, they are still relatively inexpensive. For another, they are readily available. Most importantly, they are, for the most part, men and women of courage and character who address the main issues of each new generation. From the nineteenth century, for example, Charles Spurgeon and Henry Ward Beecher come first to mind. Across the years I have gained much from a study of their lives, their victories and defeats, and their most interesting correspondence on almost every conceivable religious subject the 19th century had to offer. By all means, collect the Clergy — for goodness sake, if for no other!

This price guide includes new and revised prices on the Clergy to which we have contributed much new information. These prices can serve as a guide in your Clergy collecting endeavors.

In true Clergy form, we leave you with a benediction for your instruction and edification, a memorable extract translated from the will of Edmond de Goncourt:

> *My wish is that my Drawings, my Prints, my Curiosities, my Books in a word these things of art which have been the joy of my life shall not be consigned to the cold tomb of a museum, and subjected to the stupid glance of the careless passerby; but I require that they shall all be dispersed under the hammer of the Auctioneer, so that the pleasure which the acquiring of each one of them has given me shall be given again, in each case, to some inheritor of my own tastes.*

Frank and **Ruth Ann Matthews** are retired educators who in 1980 established **The Antique Paper Emporium**, affectionately known as "The Ape." Frank holds graduate degrees in English and American Literature, Theology, as well as an interdisciplinary Ph.D. in Intellectual History and American studies. Ruth Ann Matthews has received graduate degrees in Education and Music.

Dr. Matthews has published in the fields of fiction, nonfiction, and poetry, primarily in religion and the arts. He is a retired United Methodist minister. Ruth Ann has been prominent in civic and community service organizations, and has been recognized for many accomplishments in these areas. Frank and Ruth Ann are the parents of two daughters, who are career teachers in public education. The Matthews are now living in Tucson, Arizona.

The Matthews' have been serious students and collectors of clergy-related material since 1953. The autograph portion of their collection numbers several thousand clergy pieces.

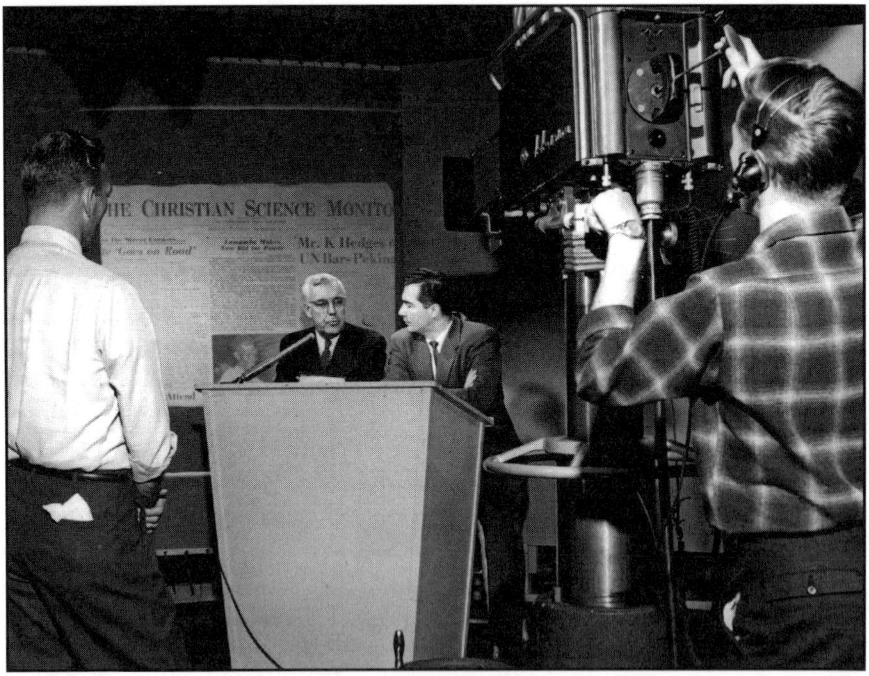

Erwin D. Canham, president of the Christian Science Church, is interviewed live on television in the early fifties by George Sanders. George was a pioneer television newscaster and reporter, and avidly collected the autographs of the celebrities he interviewed.

Chapter 11

MARILYN MONROE: HER FINAL AUTOGRAPH

by George Sanders

Did she commit suicide? Or was she murdered? Her final signature may be a clue!

As almost everyone is well aware, Marilyn Monroe has become a Hollywood icon—a screen legend among legends, but also an enigma within a mysterious puzzle of historic proportions. It happens only to those few beautiful ladies who enjoy liaisons with the rich, the famous, the politically powerful. Her personal dreams as a young girl became realities larger than life as a woman.

A Lonely Starlet

When we knew her she was just another lonely starlet attempting to find her way to stardom amongst the cruel, cynical power-brokers who used her like an inflatable doll. In the late forties, Marilyn would often stroll into our family's Los Angeles restaurant and cocktail lounge (for 30 years it was George Sanders' Lark on Third Street and Catalina) as her refuge from the dullness of her life and residency at the Studio Club apartment in Hollywood.

Wearing a camel-hair coat and a colorless scarf tied under her chin, she'd slide gracefully into a red-leathered booth and quietly sip a cup of coffee until our busy tiny mother, Grace Sanders, would find time to join her for some aimless chatter about life in the world of filmmaking. Marilyn seemed to enjoy those chats because she sensed that our mom was genuinely interested in any successes Monroe might report.

Frequently, we'd have a singer-pianist like Jess Stacy (even Liberace auditioned for a job at The Lark) or a loud Dixieland band like Kid Ory or Joe Darensbourg on the bandstand. Marilyn would show only mild interest in the music or dancing. Never requested a song and I know that I didn't dance with her. She seemed to need a modicum of serene companionship dusted with a few kind words of encouragement. She ignored the over zealous, male or female, and seemed content to simply spend her time with the "innkeepers."

"I Was Just Too Adult"

One night, following the broadcast of our "Sanders Meanders" syndicated radio show, I sat with her for several hours and found her to be surprisingly open and totally non glamourous. There was none of that gushy breathiness in her voice or sensuous twisting of her ample figure. The sexy affectations that ultimately were to become her trademarks simply were not on display in my company. She seemed weary, unattached, an unassuming woman seeking some straight talk about anything not pertaining to life in the fast track. We even discussed her feelings regarding religion which seemed fuzzy at best and surprisingly unsophisticated at worst.

Marilyn reluctantly discussed her school days at nearby Emerson Junior High in L.A. and Van Nuys High School out in the Valley where she said, "I was just too adult for the other girls. I filled out my sweaters and walked my walk until the

George Sanders and coauthor/publisher Ralph Roberts hold George's framed Marilyn Monroe check, nicely set off by photos of Marilyn. This check—a more routine one—is worth $5,000. Her last check, as we shall shortly see, is worth a whole lot more due to its significance.

By 1952—when this photograph was taken of Marilyn and actress Jane Russell placing their handprints in concrete at the famous Grauman's Chinese theater—Marilyn Monroe was on top of the world. Her film career was zooming upwards, millions of men dreamed of her, and the world, so it seemed, was hers merely for the asking.

boys all whistled and yelled. They were not ever happy days for me." She continued, "I was only 16 when I found out I was a bastard child and that news didn't make me too popular in school." It seemed there was nothing she wouldn't talk about. "I wasn't always sexy in school. In fact, when I first started junior high school, I was so skinny and sexless that I was called `Norma Jean, the Human Bean,' and even played a boy's part in my first school play and it wasn't any fun."

Final Visit

Later, when she made her fortune portraying breathless, naive, dumb broads, we remembered Monroe as being much smarter than her roles. As a fast-rising star, she'd saunter into the King's Restaurant on Santa Monica Boulevard where we did a disc jockey stint for George Jay or Larry Finley. She didn't come in to be interviewed but rather to rekindle those warm chats we'd had much earlier at The Lark. It wasn't possible because her sudden stardom had changed our perspective. She was now only attainable for the very powerful.

Our final visit with *la* Monroe came in the 1950s when she agreed to serve as a bat-girl in a Celebrity charity softball game. She refused to don the standard uniform (shorts and a team T-shirt) that the other female stars like Jane Russell, Marilyn Maxwell, Mona Freeman, Rhonda Fleming, Yvonne DeCarlo, Ava Gardner, Elizabeth Taylor, and Shelley Winters were happily wearing.

Marilyn popped out of the players' dugout on my arm attired in a sparkling, shocking pink, skintight dress that would have looked fine anywhere but on the pitchers' mound of a Hollywood baseball diamond. (We were playing at the old Gilmore Stadium that was torn down so that CBS

TV City could rest upon that hallowed pitchers' mound). Marilyn's ghost may still be searching for the long-gone dugout she once graced so spectacularly.

In any case, like some kind of glowing gypsy moth, she flitted from the center of the playing field to the sidelines oblivious to the glares she was receiving from the more cooperative, properly uniformed starlets and stars on that field. It was Van Nuys High School all over again. The scampering cameramen were of course delighted as Marilyn obligingly bowed low to exhibit voluminous cleavage surpassed only by her engaging toothy smile. No curve could be concealed in that costume and she looked so out of place, even in Hollywood!

Marilyn's Last Check

All of these memories came flooding back to us when a new friend in Dallas, Texas, autograph collector and sometime dealer Danny Cox telephoned to inform us that he had access to a very special Marilyn Monroe artifact owned by Ron Reedy, a CPA from Gainesville, Texas.

It has been reproduced on these pages and as you can see, it is a personal bank check made out to the Pilgrim Modern Furniture Company in Santa Monica for $228.80 worth of household furnishings plus a letter from her auditor that reads: "Dear Bryon, Hope that this suffices–the bank stamp is pale red and does not affect the signature at all. This undeniably is the last check and last time she signed her name as NO other checks were written that day–Because I had access to her account as auditor, I obviously would have pulled the only checks written that day (August 4, 1962) and there was only this one."

It is a matter of record that on August 4, 1962, according to the officials who investigated her death, she chatted with

Marilyn Monroe's last autograph was on this check (valued at $65,000.00 by the owner). It was written on August 4th, 1962. A few hours later, she was dead (just after midnight on August 5th). Would a woman enthusiastically shopping for and buying furniture for her new house commit suicide? It seems unlikely. She was still working, still a beautiful, voluptuous lady

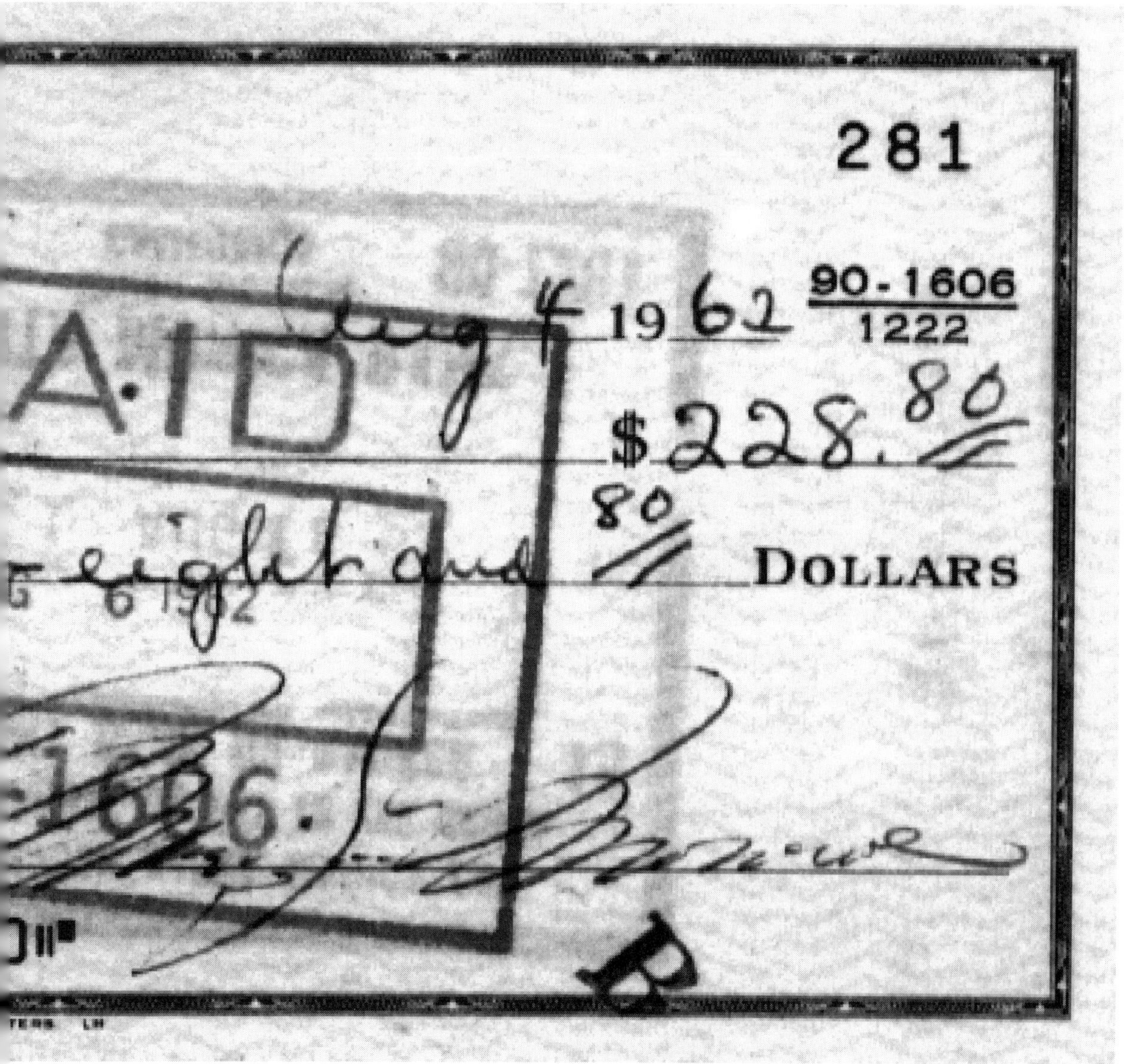

living the dream life. Evidence, such as this check, tends to say that Marilyn was not planning on ending her life but thinking about the future. This check adds credence to the theory that she was actually murdered. Was it because of her connection with the Kennedys (Robert and John)? There are several current conspiracy theories. Meanwhile, her last autograph disputes suicide.

actor Peter Lawford and asked him for the telephone number of his wife, Pat Kennedy Lawford, in Hyannisport, Massachusetts. Marilyn talked on the phone with Joe DiMaggio's son (by his first marriage to actress Dorothy Arnold) about his broken engagement. She had dinner in her new home at 12305 Fifth Helena Drive in Brentwood. Can we assume that the new furniture was for this new home?

At that informal dinner with her press agent, Pat Newcomb, she said she wanted to go to a movie the next day, a Sunday. Sometime on this Saturday, August 4th, she wrote the check you see here. A few hours later, shortly after midnight on August 5th she was dead.

What woman buys furniture and commits suicide on nearly the same day? Could this check be a clue adding a little bit of truth to the theories that Marilyn was killed? We think it might. If true, how very appropriate it would be that her still highly sought-after autograph is what finally brings her killers to justice or, at least, sheds light on the mystery and helps repair her personal honor.

The Marilyn Monroe we knew was never that mercurial and despite her early low self-esteem, not that desperate. Life wasn't always kind to her but she certainly loved every moment of her life as a movie star. She had no reason to end her life; certainly not before her furniture was delivered!

Helen and George Sanders with Ralph Roberts are the coauthors of the bestselling books **The 1994 Sanders Price Guide to Sports Autographs**, **The 1994 Price Guide to Autographs** (this book), **The Price Guide to Autographs** (1988 and 1991 editions), and **The Collectors Guide To Autographs**. The Sanders spent many years in Hollywood where, as part of the entertainment and broadcast business, they were privileged to meet and know many stars and other celebrities. The information and theory in this chapter is based in part on personal acquaintance with Marilyn Monroe.

(Above) The reverse of Marilyn Monroe's last check, showing cancellations.

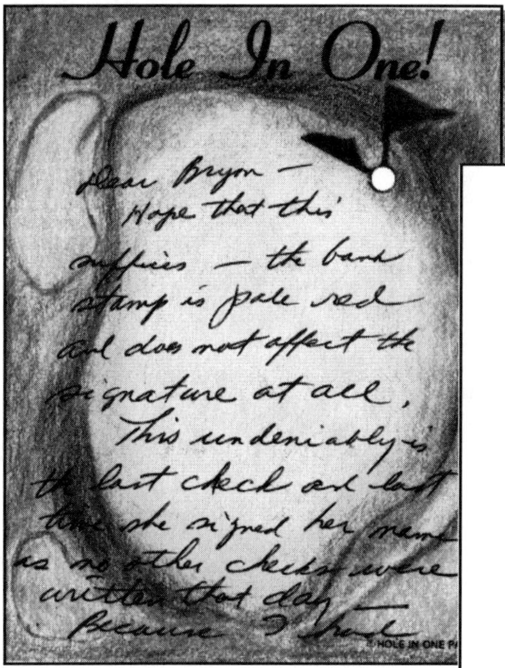
Hole In One!

Dear Bryon —
Hope that this
suffices — the bank
stamp is pale red
and does not affect the
signature at all.
This undeniably is
the last check and last
time she signed her name
as no other checks were
written that day —
Because I have

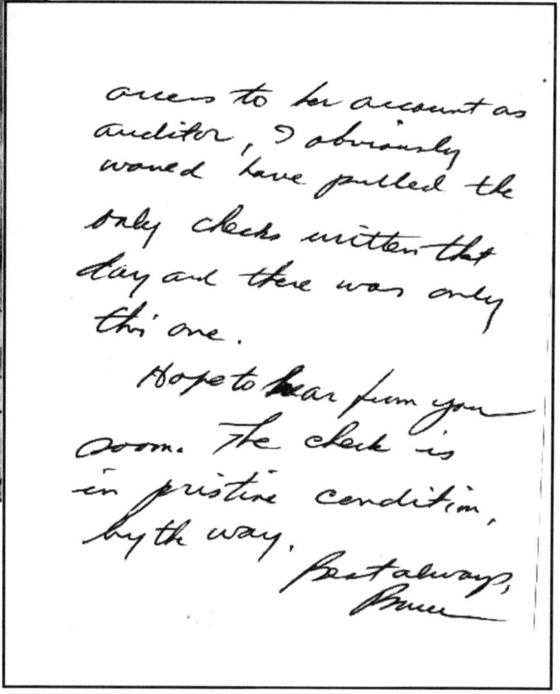
access to her account as
auditor, I obviously
would have pulled the
only checks written that
day and there was only
this one.

Hope to hear from you
soon. The check is
in pristine condition,
by the way.

Best always,
Bruce

(Above & right) the note from Marilyn's auditor attesting that this check is indeed the last signature of Marilyn Monroe (assuming no suicide note, at least one was not made public).

The glamourous Zsa Zsa Gabor was interviewed by George Sanders at the premiere of "Rear Window." George spent over 20 years in Hollywood as a radio and television personality, and as a movie actor himself. It was hard work, but someone had to do it. Zsa Zsa, the former wife of the late academy award-winner of the same name as George, loved to shout into this George's microphone, "This is the George Sanders I should have married."

Chapter 12

THE UNIVERSAL AUTOGRAPH COLLECTORS CLUB

by Al Wittnebert, Treasurer, U.A.C.C.

The Universal Autograph Collectors Club (UACC) has been serving the collector for over 25 years. Founded in 1965, the UACC began as just a small group of autograph collectors on New York's Long Island and has steadily grown to be the largest nonprofit collectors organization of its kind.

The UACC by its defined purpose is primarily an educational fellowship where knowledge and resources are shared with not only the membership, but the public at large.

By joining the UACC, you gain an introduction to the fastest growing hobby in the world today.

Autographs have been called "frozen moments in time" by some people. Probably the most personal thing that one person has to give is their signature.

In 1834, former President James Madison sent "an autographic specimen .... for a collection which the Princess Victoria is making." The future British Queen was only 15 years old at the time.

Financier J.P. Morgan, Sr., began collecting when he was 16, and his son continued adding to the father's collection. As the daughter of the Mayor of Boston, Rose Fitzgerald collected autographs, as did her son, John F. Kennedy. William Randolph Hearst, Franklin Roosevelt, Malcolm Forbes, Ray Bradbury and Glenn Ford were and are autograph collectors. By collecting autographs, you become a curator of history.

What Can I Collect?

Anything ink adheres to is fair game to be collected. Be it letters, documents, manuscripts, checks, notes, quotations, franked envelopes or signatures on album pages, photographs, visiting cards, first day covers, type scripts, baseballs, menus, programs, books and I am sure many other items.

Which Collecting Areas Should I Choose?

Choose an area or field that interests you. Some topics to consider are:

- Presidents
- Authors
- Scientists
- Composers
- Aviators
- Astronauts
- Royalty
- Explorers
- Entertainment
- Sports
- Military Leaders
- Nobel Prize Winners

There are countless other topics to choose; only your imagination is the limit.

How Can Autograph Collecting Be Interesting?

Imagine not only reading about history, but actually holding a piece of it in your hands?

Imagine a letter of Mark Twain's or Jefferson Davis, or a baseball signed by Yankee great Mickey Mantle or even a check written by Thomas Edison? These items and much more are available to collectors to own and care for.

Writing for autographs to noted individuals can also be interesting and profitable. You can write to celebrities for their autographs (if they are still alive, of course). The more interesting the letter, the better chance for an interesting reply.

Letters of content from people like George Bush and Stephen King are always desirable as collectibles because you have more than a signature—you have the person's thoughts at the time of the response.

How Can Autographs Be Profitable?

According to *Money Magazine*, investing in autographs is a rising market and for the last 20 years, bluechip autographs have increased in value between 200-500%.

Why Join the UACC?

As with all collectibles, there are things of which the new collector should be aware. Unscrupulous individuals have been known to take advantage of new collectors by offering them supposedly great deals on rare and desirable autographs at bargain prices.

The UACC affords the novice, as well as the experienced collector, numerous ways to become informed and educated as to what, how and where to buy genuine autographic materials, as well as how to write for autographs.

George and UACC Treasurer Al Wittnebert, author of *Signatures of the Stars,* at the Ft. Lauderdale UACC show.

Some of the best reasons to join the UACC include:

The UACC is the largest autograph organization in the world today with members in over 30 countries.

The UACC publishes the highly regarded *Pen & Quill*, a bimonthly journal featuring articles and news in all fields of autograph collecting.

The UACC offers its members the opportunity to purchase uncommon autographic material at below dealer prices.

The UACC publishes low cost reference works which are made available to the membership.

UACC members may utilize the Classified Ads in the *Pen & Quill* to express their wants, sell their excess, or just communicate with other members at no charge.

The UACC sponsors Autograph Shows all over the world featuring Educational Displays, Autograph Dealers who comply with the UACC Code of Ethics and celebrity guests.

The UACC sponsors seminars to educate collectors and

the public on all phases of collecting, preservation and identification of forgeries. (These are held in conjunction with our shows.)

The UACC sponsors literary and service awards as well as paying for articles published in the *Pen & Quill*.

The UACC has a Code of Ethics that all members are required to abide by, as well as an aggressive Ethics Board to mediate disputes and uphold standards.

The UACC sponsors autograph auctions where members can bid on and possibly win quality autographic material.

Once a member of the UACC, you will be included on our mailing list and will receive lists and catalogs of autographs for sale by dealer members.

The UACC also keeps you abreast of the current crop of:

- Facsimiles
- Rubber stamped signatures
- Secretarial signatures
- Autopen signatures
- Forgeries

These are all part of the hobby and as previously mentioned, the new collector is particularly susceptible to these items.

Remember, reputation is very important in our hobby! The *Pen & Quill* keeps UACC members aware of disreputable dealers and forgers, as well as the newest secretarial and autopen signatures in use.

How Do I Join the UACC

Simply send for an application: UACC, Dept. PG, P.O. Box 6181, Washington, D.C. 20044-6181.

King Mahendra of Nepal and his wife, Queen Ratna (according to the 1950s wire article accompanying this photograph) were to sit down to a full course American style Thanksgiving dinner at the Captain Cook Hotel in Anchorage. The royal couple was on an extended hunting expedition in Alaska. Each had bagged a Kodiak Bear. Oh. Yes, you're right. That *is* George Sanders in the background.

Chapter 13

THE MANUSCRIPT SOCIETY

The Manuscript Society was founded in 1948 as the National Society of Autograph Collectors, and has grown to an international membership of over 1,400, including dealers, private collectors, scholars, authors, and caretakers of public collections, such as librarians, archivists, and curators. There are also many institutional members, such as historical societies, museums, special libraries, and academic libraries.

Publications

The Society publishes a quarterly journal, *Manuscripts*, and a newsletter, which are sent to each member without charge. *Manuscripts* has an established reputation for excellent articles reflecting the diverse interests of the autograph field. Issues also have special departments giving news and views on the principal areas of historical and literary collecting, on new and important discoveries and acquisitions, and on auction results. Dealer and auctioneer advertisements publicize sources of autographs.

The newsletter also features news about the Society and its members.

Scholars seeking manuscript material are permitted to place their notices in a special section, and announcements of proposed editions of collected papers also may be made. Warnings of stolen material which may come into the market are faithfully published, as an aid to the victims and a deterrent to thieves.

Annual Meeting

The Society's chief activity is a three-day annual meeting, held in a community offering good manuscript resources for viewing.

The programs feature tours, exhibitions, panel discussions, speakers of note, and social occasions for fellowship and interchange of ideas. Major cities have alternated with smaller communities as the locales for these meetings, in order to provide a varied view of the manuscript riches available throughout the United States.

Three annual meetings have been held abroad: London in 1970 and 1986, and Ottawa in 1978.

Local Chapters

Local chapters in such areas as the Twin Cities, Washington, and Southern California offer members a chance to meet with others in their area. All members in good standing may belong to a chapter.

Reference Resource

A comprehensive monograph, entitled *Autographs and Manuscripts: A Collector's Manual*, was published under the auspices of The Manuscript Society by Charles Scribner's Sons in 1978. Its long definitive articles on many aspects of collecting, arranging, and preserving manuscript material, all of them written by experts in their fields, have caused the book to be hailed as a classic treatment of the subject. In 1984, Greenwood Press published *Manuscripts: The First Twenty Years*, an anthology of 50 memorable articles from the Society's journal.

To celebrate the bicentennial of the United States, in 1975 and 1976, a traveling exhibit was sponsored by the Society in cooperation with the Smithsonian Institution. It consisted of documents written during the early months of the Revolution, which were loaned for the purpose by members of the Society from their own collections.

Membership

The Manuscript Society welcomes new members. The annual individual membership fee is $25; institutional membership is $30. Contributing memberships at $50; sustaining memberships at $75; and life memberships at $600 help in furthering Society interests. Memberships are on a calendar year basis; new members joining after July I may pay half the annual rate. All moneys go to support the publication program, to aid in the defense of individuals against government agencies in replevin suits, and to maintain the expenses of management of Society affairs.

How to Join the Manuscript Society

To Join, Contact:

David R. Smith,
Executive Director
THE MANUSCRIPT SOCIETY
350 N. Niagara Street
Burbank, CA 91505
(818) 560-5424

George Sanders with the perky Miss Doris Day.

Chapter 14

THE COMPUSERVE AUTOGRAPH COLLECTORS CLUB

by Matt Mrowicki

CompuServe is a computer-based information service with over 600,000 members world-wide. It is based on areas called "Forums" where members can discuss topics ranging from sports to financial services to games and hobbies of all sorts. One such is the Collectibles Forum which contains sections devoted to collecting specialties including Sports Collectibles, Coins, Stamps, Rare Books and, yes, Autographs. All you need to use CompuServe is a computer and modem (any rate from 300 to 9600 bps). A starter kit can be purchased at most hardware or software stores or by calling 1-800-848-8199, ask for operator 132.

CompuServe Autograph Collectors Club

The CompuServe Autographs Collectors Club (CACC) has spent the early years of our existence building its membership from all fields of autograph collecting. Our members collect in all categories including Civil War, Entertainment (Movies and TV), Space, Aviation, Political, Historical, Auto Racing, Baseball, Novel Prize Winners, Authors, Cartoonists, U.S. Presidents, and just about every other field imaginable. Our members are on all levels of collecting expertise, from beginners (who wrote to their first celebrity using an address posted on the message board) to veterans who have large and important collections. All members are treated equally and all have the same access to CACC services.

Areas

The CACC is subdivided into two areas. The message board is an area when collectors can talk and exchange information on whatever topics they wish. Putting a message on the board (referred to as "posting") can be done by all members. Replying to a message is as simple as a few keystrokes and typing your reply. Messages that can be found on the board at any time include items for sale, want lists, addresses, auction news, club news, success stories, dealer information, addresses to avoid, and general chit-chat about the hobby (usually the best part). The message board is a place of constant change where conversations and discussions lasting many weeks are common.

The second area is the files library. The library is an area where informative files are stored for the use of all members. Information stored in the library remains there for as long as the uploader (a term meaning the person who put the file into the library or "uploads the file") desires. Our library contains over 250 files including address lists, want lists, listings of autograph dealers, items for sale, , special offers to CACC members and even pictures of autographs that can be shown on your computer!

Unlimited Potential

As I hope you can already see, the CACC has an unlimited potential for use by collectors. Each new member we get brings a wealth of new knowledge and insight to our club and since we are expanding our membership constantly, questions asked on the message board usually get an answer within 24 hours.

Access and Conferences

This brings me to the most fascinating part of the CACC (and CompuServe in general). Access is possible 24 hours a day, 365 days a year. News, autograph listings, successful addresses and other messages can be posted instantly. Immediately, collectors from all over the U.S. (and other nations, including England, Wales, Australia, Canada, Germany, and Belgium) have access to that information. This allows for second opinions on prices, questions about reference books or just general questions or comments to be quick and painless.

Every week, the CACC holds a real-time on-line conference, called AUTOCON. These events are open to all and invite members to discuss, live with other members from around the country, their favorite hobby. In the past, we have had special guests, news bits about the ACM's latest publications and a lot of success stories. Transcripts of these conferences are made available to members who cannot attend. The "Conference Rooms" are also available for members 24 hours a day to use on their own to hold their own meetings or even private one-on-one discussions.

The CACC has attempted to make itself a place where all autograph-related information can be exchanged. Our library has the capacity to hold files called GIF's. These are graphic files where pictures of autographs can be stored and displayed on the computer screen. While a special piece of hardware called a scanner (becoming quite common) is required to make a GIF file, any computer can view one with a simple program that can be found right in the Collectibles

Forum. The potential of GIF files is enormous. Not only can authentic autographs be shown (including photographs and documents), but autopen signatures and secretarial signatures can be put on-line for comparison. Members can even use GIF files to display unidentified signatures. One member who did this had an identification to his mystery autograph in less than 24 hours! Recently, autographs of all U.S. Presidents from Washington to Johnson were put into the Library in GIF form. An autopen example from President Clinton was available in the library long before it appeared in most other publications.

Dealers Encouraged

The CACC also encourages the sale and trade of autographs. Dealers can put their monthly listings into files (or messages) that will be read by all of our members. These listings can then be updated as often as the dealer desires. The message board (or private CompuServe Mail (C-Mail) services) makes inquiries about desired items very simple without the hassle of answering machines or busy signals. Dealers can even post GIF files of special items for potential customers to view. The CACC allows you to reach many collectors with a single file, saving money on postage and printing costs. Of course, requests for printed catalogues can be made instantly as well.

Collectors are also welcomed to offer items from their collection for sale or trade with other members. The CACC holds quarterly auctions, without any fees or commissions, where any CACC member can offer items for sale. The CACC simply acts as the means for buyers to be in contact with sellers, and does not interfere with any transactions.

The CACC is proud to have played a role in teh creation and success of *Autograph Times*. The publisher of AT, as well as all of the Contributing Editors, are all active CACC members. Each issue of the hobby's leading newspaper is filled with infromation provided by, or articles written by, CACC members. The CACC provides the opportunity to go into more detail about many topics, without the constraints placed on any publisher, of space and deadlines. Increasingly, CACC members have been active in trying to determine the authenticity of some famous questionable thru-the-mail signatures and this information is discussed publicly for any members to present their opinions.

Joining

Joining the CACC and finding your way around is very simple. CompuServe provides a toll-free number to assist in signing up with their service and once you join the Collectibles Forum, there are many SysOps (System Operators), SL's (Section Leaders) and friendly members who are willing to answer questions.

The CACC also allows members who do not live near cities where shows or club meetings are held to become part of a gathering of collectors. Since access to CompuServe is via a local phone call in almost every U.S. city, members can move around the country and still access the CACC. Since the CACC began, we have had many members who have moved and were able to resume participation in a few days. This is a handy feature for members who's business requires them to travel.

If you have a computer, all you need is a modem and a CompuServe Membership Kit. These kits can be purchased at hardware/software stores and many large bookstore chains and mail order outlets. Once you logged onto CompuServe, just type GO COLLECT at any "!" prompt and you will be in the Collectibles Forum. AUTOGRAPHS is Section 11.

CACC Awards for 1992

The CACC also presents awards in the field of philography (autograph collecting). Award winners are chosen by a vote of the CACC membership. Winners for 1992 were:

LIFETIME ACHIEVEMENT IN PHILOGRAPHY:
Mary A. Benjamin
PHILOGRAPHER OF THE YEAR:
George and Helen Sanders
DEALER OF THE YEAR:
R&R Enterprises
PUBLICATION OF THE YEAR: (tie)
The Autograph Collector's Magazine (50%)
The Pen & Quill (50%)
ORGANIZATION OF THE YEAR:
Universal Autograph Collector's Club
REFERENCE OF THE YEAR:
The Price Guide to Autographs (Second Edition)
(Sanders, Sanders and Roberts)

CACC Awards for 1993

LIFETIME ACHIEVEMENT IN PHILOGRAPHY:
George and Helen Sanders
PHILOGRAPHER OF THE YEAR:
Tom and Cordelia Platt
DEALER OF THE YEAR:
Star Shots
PUBLICATION OF THE YEAR:
The Pen & Quill
ORGANIZATION OF THE YEAR:
Universal Autograph Collector's Club
REFERENCE OF THE YEAR:
The Price Guide to Autographs (Second Edition)
(Sanders, Sanders and Roberts)

CACC Awards for 1994

LIFETIME ACHIEVEMENT IN PHILOGRAPHY:
Charles Hamilton
PHILOGRAPHER OF THE YEAR:
Stephen Koschal

DEALER OF THE YEAR:
Star Shots
PUBLICATION OF THE YEAR:
The Pen & Quill
ORGANIZATION OF THE YEAR:
Universal Autograph Collector's Club
REFERENCE OF THE YEAR:
The Sanders Price Guide to Sports Autographs
(Sanders, Sanders and Roberts)

Thanks, CACC!

For the past three years straight, the CACC has honored our price guides with the **Best Reference of the Year** awards. Also, they've been so kind as to name George and Helen as **Philographers of the Year** in 1992 and to present them with the **Lifetime Achievement** award in 1993. We'd just like to take this opportunity to say Thank you, CACC!" and thanks for helping to bring our wonderful hobby into the Information Age.

The CACC award for **Lifetime Achievement in Philography** (right) was presented to George and Helen Sanders in 1993 by a vote of the CACC membership on the CompuServe computer network. The CACC is in the forefront of modernizing the autograph collecting hobby and bringing it into the Information Age. Members are in daily contact with their computers and get first chance at a lot of good autographs, among many other advantages.

For the past three years (the history of the CACC awards), the Sanders autograph price guides have been chosen **Best Reference of the Year** evey year by a vote of the membership. We are very grateful and pleased that the CACC (and so many others) recognize our hard work. George and Helen Sanders and Ralph Roberts have been doing these price guides since 1988. We have been blessed by a combination of many friendly experts in the field of autograph collecting and by following the latest advances in computer technology. This has allowed us to put together price guides that are simply unrivaled in detail, comprehensiveness, and completeness. It gives us immense satisfaction to know that we are doing a good job, and that many of you, our loyal readers and users of our prices guides, get so much out of them.

Chapter 15

THE CARE AND PRESERVATION OF YOUR COLLECTION

by Ralph Roberts

Collecting autographs is an exciting and profitable hobby. Autograph values, as shown in this book continue to rise in value at a faster rate than most other collectibles, and are certainly a safer investment than, say, the stock market these days.

We have repeated the information in this chapter in every single price guide we have put out. It is being reproduced here because a) we already know that this price guide is reaching a much larger audience than our previous books and b) because the tips here cannot be repeated too often. The autographs we own are ours for only a brief time. It is our privilege and our honor to preserve them for future generations. To make sure the magic we hold endures and fulfilling our sacred obligation as guardians for this short but glorious time in which we own the piece.

Autograph items, normally being just pieces of paper such as letters and photographs, are also easy to store. A collection worth many thousands of dollars fits easily within an album, a safety deposit box or, for that matter, a plain old shoe box.

The potential for "buying low, selling high" is no less than astonishing in autographs. Just for getting a sports star or other celebrity to sign a piece of paper, you gain instant profit—immediate assets for you just by them signing their name. Whether you get their signature in person or an authentic one through the mail, the value is there.

Take celebrities as an example. Go to any major event featuring big names and, with a little luck, some great autographs are yours merely for politely asking. A very few years of perseverance on your part and the worth of your autograph collection is awesome for the effort expended. (By the way, just to repeat it, our price guides have grown so big that sports prices are now in a separate volume, **The Sanders Price Guide to Sports Autographs**).

Add in meticulous study of autograph dealers' catalogues, and the snatching up of the many bargains you will find in signatures of people both living and dead, and yet more profit accrues. Trade judiciously with fellow collectors, and even more profit comes.

Which brings us to the point of this chapter. A collector of sterling silver would not leave Paul Revere pieces out in the rain to tarnish, nor where light-fingered persons could make their own instant profit.

There are a number of considerations the autograph collector should keep in mind. These fall into two major areas. Preservation, safeguarding, and display, *and* bookkeeping. The latter, in these days of complicated taxes, can be extremely important, especially if you decide to sell, insure, or donate items. As in any business, in the case of an IRS audit or theft, proper record keeping is a necessity.

Record Keeping

Paper can deteriorate or be defaced easily if care is not taken. In past years, collectors often would take a pencil and write the source and purchase price of a letter or other document directly on it. Many thousands of pieces now have such markings on them, or dealers' prices and comments such as "very rare", and so forth.

Whatever you do, *do not* attempt to erase these penciled notes. They don't injure the paper and may be of considerable importance in establishing provenance. The handwriting of many old-time dealers and collectors are recognizable by many dealers and collectors who have handled large numbers of manuscripts, thus helping to prove authenticity.

Now, however, *nothing* should be written on an autograph item. Nor, for reasons we will discuss shortly, should other paper (unless absolutely known to be acid-free) come in contact with it. So records for your collection need to be kept physically separate in some manner.

The simplest way is by the use of index cards, which may be alphabetized by categories and easily filed. On the card for a specific autograph, the following minimum information should be recorded: author, the source of the autograph, date obtained, cost, and exact measurements as well as other identifying characteristics. This latter being important in identifying your piece in case of loss or theft.

If you store autographs in plastic sleeves stored in a three-ring binder (an excellent way of doing so), a good practice on more important pieces is to type up a page with yet more information that you can then place in a facing sleeve. This page can include a complete transcript of the document or letter (increasing your facility in learning how to decipher handwriting of all types).

Other facts about the autograph should also be recorded. Some of these are public exhibitions, other existing copies, repairs, known publications, the address of the dealer (if you bought the piece), etc. Having this data to hand with the autograph can save you a lot of fumbling about to find it later. Including a picture of the person and biographical information also enhances the display of your collection, its value, and (most importantly) *your* enjoyment of it.

If the autograph was purchased from a dealer, save the correspondence relating to it along with the bill of sale. Reputable dealers will provide a sales slip on which they list the piece and include a description. A statement to the effect that "all autographs are guaranteed genuine" is usually included. If not, ask for it! There is no logical reason for a dealer to refuse to guarantee authenticity, so don't be shy in demanding it. Otherwise, take your money elsewhere.

In purchasing a packet of letters from the same person, or a group of documents that are all related in some manner, record keeping can become a bit more complicated. In such cases, you should break the collection down and assign a *pro rata* value to each piece. This holds true also for unrelated items which you may purchase for one lump sum. Record keeping may seem onerous at the time, but doing it at the time of purchase is a *lot* easier than trying to reconstruct it years later. Especially when an IRS auditor is breathing hotly down your neck, with glistening fangs and little red eyes glowing in anticipation of an imminent feeding frenzy.

The Computer Age

There are other ways to keep records for an autograph collection, too. Ledger books and loose-leaf notebooks are two. However, the advent of the Computer Age is proving a boon to many collectors. Autograph collecting, being in essence the management of large amounts of data, lends itself well to record keeping via a personal computer.

The fact that a good IBM-compatible system, including printer and monitor, can now be had for under a thousand dollars, makes this option more and more attractive. Whether a hobby or a business, autograph collection should be and can be fun. A computer eliminates much of the bookkeeping drudgery.

A full explanation of the myriad of computerization benefits for collectors is beyond the scope of this brief chapter, but the basic three programs needed are a database manager, a word processing program, and a communications program (along with a modem, the piece of computer hardware used to connect it to your telephone).

Any large group of related facts, such as facts about autographs, is called a database. A database manager program allows you to enter and retrieve these facts quickly and easily. It will alphabetize and generate reports for you, giving a total of your holdings and what each individual piece is worth, either for a category like Artists, or for the collection in its entirety.

Going to an autograph show? Print out a list of what you have and avoid buying duplications. Found a listing in a dealer's catalogue for a football player you may or may not have? Don't thumb through your albums or card index looking when all you have to do is key it into the computer and have all the pertinent information pop up on the screen.

The second program you need, word processing, speeds up correspondence and allows neatly formatted and automatically spell-checked descriptions to be included in autograph albums. As already detailed, this enhances the value of your collection and increases enjoyment.

Finally, going back to the previous chapter, the one on the CompuServe Autograph Collectors Club, you can get a feel for the importance of quick, inexpensive computer age communications. We've been *on-line* (i.e. having a modem hooked up to computer) since 1986. The advantages to a collector would fill a book a lot bigger than this one. We encourage you to look into it if you're not already computerized and hooked up to the world.

Computers are just a tool, like a hammer. Properly used, they can enhance your hobby, and make it even more profitable and enjoyable.

Preservation

No matter how precise your record keeping may be, computerized or not, the actual autograph itself must be kept in the best condition possible. Proper preservation insures that your collection retains and increases its value.

There are several good books on this subject. Two of the better sources being the material included in *Autographs: A Collector's Guide* by Jerry E. Patterson (Crown, 1973) and *The Collector's Guide to Autographs* by the authors of this price guide (published by Wallace-Homestead, 1990).

Older documents suffer from being folded. Before the invention of the file cabinet, papers were usually tied up in bundles with string or ribbon for storage. The English government often used red tape instead of string, thus coining the term "red tape" as applied to bureaucracy.

It is not uncommon to find such bundles still tied and folded in this manner. Should you acquire one of these, immediately unfold each piece and place them between two pieces of acid-free paper and onto a flat surface for gradual unwrinkling. A weight, such as a book, may be placed on top as long as it does not come in contact with the document. All paper clips, pins, ribbons, etc. should be removed. Wax seals, if intact (which is rare) should be left in place.

Many pieces of paper carry the seeds of their own

destruction deep within, acid! Dealers and librarians can tell horror stories of autograph collections preserved in folders or framed in which the paper degenerated or was left with stains and other damage.

Acid occurs naturally in wood. One look at an old "pulp" magazine from the 1930's—pages yellowed, tattered, and crumbling—can immediately show you how this internal destructive process works. Or last year's newspaper, for that matter. Older paper, from the 19th century and earlier, usually had a higher rag content than modern papers and, thus, less acid content.

As a rule of thumb, the higher the pulp content of the paper, the greater the acid content. Newsprint, the cheapest kind of paper, has the most pulp content. Even newspapers, pulp magazines, and old comic books (also with a high pulp content) can be preserved, though. In fact, a good collectible comic book store can be of great benefit to the autograph collector. The better ones carry such preservation materials as acetate bags and deacidfication sashes. These latter actually remove acid from paper, dramatically increasing its life. For valuable pieces on cheap paper, these can be a very worthwhile investment.

The mistake some collectors make is to put a newspaper clipping in the same folder with an autograph piece. Even though the autograph might be on good paper, the acid in the newsprint can quickly stain, even ruin the autograph document. So put autograph items in an acetate folder, and protect it from contact with other paper!

Acetate folders are also available at most stationer's stores, as well as those specializing in stamp or photography supplies. Even if designed for comic books, stamps, or photographs, these are fine for autographs too. Always ask for "acid free" material.

We autograph collectors can learn a lot about preservation from stamp collectors. Stamps are usually more delicate and likely to fade than autograph documents. Pages sold for philatelists are just as useful to us.

Buying acetate folders already punched for a three-ring binder makes your storage problems a lot easier. You can have notebooks for each category of your collection; Civil War, Presidential, Sports, Vintage Movie Stars, etc.

If you have a manuscript of several pages, remove all paper clips and staples. These will rust and discolor the paper. The general rule here is to let nothing but the protective acetate come in contact with the piece. Engravings, newspaper clippings, even photographs (which are sometimes still coated with chemicals) should be stored in a separate sleeve or folder.

Acid is not the only enemy of paper, so too is humidity. Excessive humidity, such as storing papers in a basement or garage, can lead to mold. Some areas, such as the Southeastern U.S., are especially hazardous to the collectors of books, stamps, and autographs. If you have this problem, the purchase of a dehumidifier for the room autographs are stored in, is a very wise investment.

You may also place small packets of silica gel (the stuff that is packed with new cameras and radios) inside binders, etc. These soak up water vapor from the air, but must be replaced after a period of time. The relative humidity should never be more than 70 percent, and about 50 is the best. Cold is no problem.

Another enemy is light, especially the ultraviolet laden destructiveness of direct sunlight. If you display an autograph in a frame, ultraviolet shields are available which will protect them, both from the sun and artificial sources.

Dust can also be harmful. The shelves where you keep

your collection should be kept clean. The same for filing cabinets, if those are used. Dust can carry particles of various chemicals that deteriorate paper.

In general, there is nothing wrong with taking an autograph out of its storage place for an occasional airing, just as stamp collectors air stamps. In fact, air circulating around paper is usually beneficial. No autograph should be sealed up too tightly.

Framing, Matting, and Display

As we've just seen, light is an enemy of autographs. The simple fact of life is that light causes ink on paper to fade. Ultraviolet shields, non-reflective glass and the like can decrease this fading action, but nothing except total darkness forever will completely guard against light's harm.

So a really valuable autograph, such as a Shoeless Joe Jackson, should not be framed and displayed. A better choice might be a favorite actor, actress, football player, or whatever your interest runs to in current celebrities.

If you do frame and hang a piece (and they can look quite awesome in your living room), *never* place it where direct sunlight has a chance of hitting. Reflected daylight is also dangerous, causing fading, as is fluorescent lighting. The plastic ultraviolet shields already mentioned will help protect against the worst of light damage.

Framing or even matting (placing the autograph between two pieces of cardboard-like material with a hole in the top one to thus frame the item) takes a modicum of skill, tools, and materials. This craft, if you collect and/or sell a lot of autographs is well worth learning and will quickly pay for itself. Professional framers charge professional prices.

Still, for the occasional piece, most people go to a framing shop. When you entrust an autograph document or letter or signed photograph to a framer, some precautions are in order. First, you must insist that the matting board used should be "museum board", i.e. acid-free. The thickness of board chosen should be one which will keep the autograph from touching the glass of the frame, and also allow for some air circulation.

Explain vigorously to the framer that Scotch tape, masking tape, or any other kind of tape *should never* be used, nor should the autograph be pasted down in any manner, not even to prevent wrinkling or buckling. The framer, also, must not be allowed to cut or trim the piece in any way. Engravings or photographs framed with the autograph, must not be allowed to touch it either.

Conclusions

Autograph collecting is a wondrously exciting and potentially profitable hobby. Proper record keeping and care of your autographs greatly enhance this fascinating pursuit.

George R. Sanders, Sr. and Grace Sanders (George's parents), cowboy star Roy Rogers, and a youthful Helen and George Sanders in 1950.

Chapter 16

HOW TO USE THIS PRICE GUIDE

by Helen Sanders

Many hours have gone into preparing this price guide. We have made great efforts to be as accurate as possible and to set up our databases so that this and future editions will realistically reflect market changes.

Keep in mind, however, that the title of this volume has the words ***price guide*** in its title, not ***price bible***. A letter written by Abraham Lincoln to his grocer, deploring the condition of the last slab of bacon or barrel of flour delivered, is not going to be worth the same as a letter to a prominent senator discussing the Emancipation Proclamation. Yet both are Autograph Letters Signed (ALS). What I am trying to say is that this is not an exact science and that there are shades of gray and you must be prepared to use them.

Just as content and condition guide you as to the cost of a particular piece,the figures in this volume, which represent an average price, are there to ***GUIDE*** you in buying or selling autograph material.

Condition

Condition—as it is in the collecting of coins, stamps, antiques, vintage cars, and so on–is just one important consideration in autograph collecting as well. The prices quoted in this guide are for autographs in fine condition. Extra-fine letters, documents, cut signatures and so forth are worth more. Tattered paper, wrinkled signed photographs and the like, decrease the value.

Pricing

Considerable diligence and thoughtfulness have gone into estimating the prices that appear in this guide. We had the further advantage of having already put out two previous editions of this book and were thus able to hone our techniques.

We carefully studied all available retail and wholesale offerings, auction prices, and realized reports, and held discussions with many dealers and collectors in the field. We weighed these and other factors in determining the prices for each piece, within its category. The prices in this guide, therefore, represent the figures that we have calculated to be the average price for a fine item offered by an informed dealer to an informed buyer.

Sales, of course, are often made at lower prices due to bargaining, overstocking, changes in popularity, and lack of local interest. Conversely, prices can be higher if the celebrity whose signature is being offered has a local connection (such as Thomas Wolfe in his birthplace of Asheville, N.C.), or if the piece is in pristine condition or has exceptional content. Of course a Washington letter about Mt. Vernon or the conditions at Valley Forge, would naturally be more valuable than one containing a thank you note for a lovely dinner. Also, a collector in need of a particular item to complete a topical collection or a set might be willing to go well over book value just to obtain a rare autograph.

This edition still reflects average prices. We have, however, presented them in a slightly different manner. In most cases (with some exceptions) the numbers have been rounded off to the nearest multiple of five; i.e. raised or lowered to the nearest increment. $57.50 would be raised to $60.00 but $57.00 would be lowered to $55.00. The notable exceptions are found mostly in the Entertainment category where the more common lower priced material was basically unchanged and is found within a $1.00-$5.00 or $5.00 to $10.00 range.

Because the prices for all categories are averages, you must take into consideration a trading range. What I have discovered in this current edition is that even though the basic printed average for a specific piece may not have changed, the range in which it is now traded is considerably wider. The better quality material is higher due to an influx of more knowledgeable and affluent collectors. The lower prices at that low end of the range reflect the entrance of new collectors who, as beginners, are looking for and are willing to accept less quality until they are better informed at which time they can upgrade. These are frequently pieces that premium quality dealers have heretofore thought unmarketable.

The important thing to remember is that these averages in this edition give you a wider price range with which to work than before, even though the quoted price may have remained unchanged.

The prices given in this book are retail prices—that is, the ones you would *pay* to a dealer or at an auction. If you sell to a dealer, a legitimate offer to you would be about half of the retail price. Since the dealer may have to hold the piece for years before selling it, this is a fair markup. You may always, however, bargain and haggle.

While every effort has been made to ensure the accuracy

of the information in this book, the authors and publisher will in no event be liable for any loss of profit or any other damage, including but not limited to special, incidental, consequential, or any other damages.

Pricing Categories

Although there are more than four pricing categories in autographs, we have chosen the four most important ones for this guide. They will cover the vast majority of autograph items, and exceptions may be interpolated from these prices. Following are the definitions we shall use:

Signature (**SIG**). This is the price that a signature is worth—that is, just the actual signature itself on a card, cut out of a letter, a page from an autograph album; may or may not be accompanied by date and/or place, etc.

Letter Signed or Document Signed (**LS/DS**). An example of more recent pieces might be a typed letter or document signed by a celebrity. During the nineteenth century, before the invention of the typewriter, it was common for secretaries or clerks to prepare handwritten letters or documents for signatures. These also fall within the LS/DS category.

Autograph Letter Signed (**ALS**). Generally the most important category except in the entertainment field where a signed photograph seems to take priority. This is a letter (or document) completely written in the hand of and signed by the important personage.

Signed Photograph (**SP**). This Category can also include signed portrait engravings, woodcuts, photo reproductions. Signed original cartoon drawings are designated with an asterisk (*) after the cartoonist's name and are found in the SP column. Reproductions of works of art and signed by the artist are shown in the Comment column.

Major Autograph Categories

The new format for autograph categories will please many and upset some. We have maintained a column to identify the category of each entry. In many cases the person is notable in more than one classification. We have identified him or her with the category in which the person is most known or collected. In addition we have added a Comment column to further enhance the information.

In some cases we have included prices for special material that could not be included in the averages because they were outside the normal trading range.

All names are now in alphabetical order as opposed to dividing the chapters into individual categories containing Authors, Artists, Aviation, Composers, Civil War, and so forth.

We are doing this for a number of reasons, not the least of these being the fact that there was considerable duplication of names because of their entry in multiple categories.

There was also a problem for the collectors, who, with diversified collections, were finding it difficult to catalog their material by going back and forth between the different chapters. There was also a problem when the collector was unaware in which chapter the celebrity belonged.

We feel you will find the new format much faster and much easier to use.

Thanks and we hope you find our price guide an enjoyable tool to use and one that is of great benefit to you. As always, we welcome your suggestions on improving our autograph price guides. Please send your comments to us at:

Autograph House
P.O. Box 658
Enka NC 28728.

George with Countess Alexandra Tolstoy, daughter of the immortal Russian author, Leo Tolstoy. Countess Tolstoy was brought to Hollywood in the 1950s by Paramount Pictures to aid in the promotion of the motion picture adapted from her father's literary classic, "War and Peace."

Chapter 17

A FINAL WORD ON PRICING

by Helen Sanders

Every effort has been made to provide as accurate an accounting of prices as is humanly possible. We have retrieved thousands and thousands of figures, tabulated them, averaged them, and entered them into what has become our permanent database.

These raw numbers have come from every corner of our country as well as from Great Britain, France, Germany, Switzerland, and Scandinavia. We have selectively incorporated the prices of nonspecialized material. By that we mean letters, documents, and so forth that do not contain or illustrate important historical content.

Letters by composers discussing music, by scientists theorizing about their field of expertise, or by authors, artists, military personnel, aviators, politicians, and so on doing likewise would be some examples of specialized material. We cannot put a price on this type of content. Its importance could double, triple, or quadruple the value of an otherwise moderately priced item.

We have also excluded signed musical quotations, literary quotations, and signed manuscripts because these, too, have special added value. Space does not allow us to include them in this issue of Alexander Books' **The 1994 Sanders Price Guide to Autographs**.

Please note that the presidential entries included here are nonpresidential. Presidentially signed pieces have considerably more value (in most cases) than nonpresidential ones. That even extends to signed White House or Executive Mansion cards.

When possible, the Civil War letters and documents reported are, for the most part, pre or postwar. Some material is, of course, only available with war dates, and in the case of extreme rarity in any category, we have reported the price(s) available.

We have presented to you "The Market." We have not created this market; therefore you may find among these thousands of entries some incongruities, whereby an Autograph Signed Letter is priced lower than a Letter Signed/ Document Signed. Sometimes Signed Photographs are significantly more valuable in a specific category because of particular group interest.

You will find bargains available where certain autographs in a category are priced far below others of equal importance, rarity, and collectibility. These numbers have all been recorded to serve as guides. They are not set in cement. They are not constants.

Unlike stamps, every autograph is an original work of art. Each one is different, and consequently, the value of each piece varies. There is no standard price. These prices comprise an average of many prices and should be referred to accordingly, with the reader taking into account the possible range of a given price to determine the level of value that a particular item warrants.

The higher the printed price, the wider the fluctuation (both up and down) you can anticipate. The relative value among autographs will also be of interest and help. These figures are not reflections of a particular autograph personality's ability, talent, intelligence, greatness, or beauty. They represent material—presented to the public from all over the world—that a knowledgeable buyer should be able to purchase from a knowledgeable seller.

Because of the vastness and ad infinitum concept of this book, there may be errors. For these we apologize. Further, we take no responsibility for quoting others' published prices in the compilation of our data.

We can, however, sincerely hope that this book will be of assistance to you in either your hobby or your business and that subsequent volumes will keep you in touch with the autograph marketplace as we bring you additional entries and updated quotes.

George, oldest son Sandy, and Helen Sanders in the studios of KGBS in Los Angeles in 1951. George, at that time, was the nation's leading disc jockey. Young Sandy is now a 43-year-old executive with Union Pacific Railroad in the state of Oregon. We were all younger in those days.

Additional Autograph Reference Books

Finally, in the firm knowledge that you can never have *too much knowledge*, we offer you a list of recommeded reference sources. The more you know about autographs, the more fun this wondrous hobby gives!

Benjamin, Mary A. *Autographs: A Key to Collecting*, Privately Printed, 1963.

Berkley, Edmund Jr. *Autographs and Manuscripts*, Scribner's.

Burford, Thomas *Celebrity Access - The Directory*, 1994, Celebrity Access Publications

Carr, Paul *The Universal Autograph Collectors Club's Study of Machine Signed Signatures*, UACC, 1989.

Darvick, Herman N. *Collecting Autographs*, Julian Messner, 1981.

Hamilton, Charles *American Autographs*, U. of Oklahoma Press, 1983.

Hamilton, Charles *Signatures of America*, Harper & Row, 1977.

Hamilton, Charles, *Collecting Autographs and Manuscripst*, 1993, Modoc, Inc. Santa Monica, CA

Hayes, Jim *War Between the States, Autographs and Biographical Sketches*, Palmetto Publishing, 1989.

Koschal, Stephen *Collecting Books and Pamphlets Signed by the Presidents of the United States*, Patriotic Publishers, 1982

Koschal, Stephen, *The American Antiquarian*, 1992, Compiled and Reprinted by Stephen Koschal

Maran, M. Wesley *Sincerely Yours* Little, Brown and Company, Boston 1983

Mashburn, J.L. *The Artist-Signed Postcard Price Guide*, 1993, WorldComm

Patterson, Jerry E. *Autographs: A Collectors Guide*, Crown, 1973.

Rawlins; Ray *The Stein and Day Book of World Autographs*, 1978.

Reese, Michael *Autographs of the Confederacy*, Cohasco Publishing, 1981.

Sanders, Sanders, & Roberts *The Collector's Guide to Autographs*, Wallace-Homestead, 1988.

Seagrave, Ronald Roy *Civil War Autographs and Manuscripts Prices Current*, 1994, Self-Published, P.O. Box 7171, Fredericksburg, VA 22404

Searle, Charles *From the Inkwells of Hollywood* (3 volumes), Woodbine Press, 1989.

Sullivan, George *Making Money in Autographs*, Coward, McCann & Geoghegan Inc., New York, 1977.

Taylor, John M. *From the White House Inkwell*, 1968, Charles E. Tuttle, Rutland, Vermont. (just reissued)

Vrzalik, Larry F. and Michael Minor, *From the President's Pen, An Illustrated Guide to Presidential Autographs*, State House Press 1990, $15.95.

Wittnebert, Al, *Signatures of the Stars*, 1988, UACC

The 1994 SANDERS PRICE GUIDE to AUTOGRAPHS

Section II: PRICES

NUMBER 3

KEY

NAME	Name of a person or group
CATEGORY	Artist, entertainer, writer, etc.
SIG	Signature
DS/LS	A signed letter or other document.
ALS	Autograph Letter Signed, i.e. written entirely in the hand of the celebrity
SP	Signed photograph
*	Signed art instead of photograph

PRICES

A

NAME	CATEGORY	SIG	LS/DS	ALS	SP	COMMENT
AAlton, Alvar	Architect	110	250		125	Finnish Architect-Designer
AC/DC	Entertainment	25			95	Rock
Aadland, Beverly	Entertainment	4	6		10	
Aames, Willie	Entertainment	5	7		12	
Abba	Entertainment	25			50	
Abba, Marta	Entertainment	15		45	95	It. Actress
Abbado, Claudio	Entertainment	10			35	Symph. & Opera Conductor
Abbey, Edwin Austin	Artist	15	30	40		Am.Portraitist, Illustrator
Abbot, Charles Greeley	Science	15	50		25	Am. Astrophysicist
Abbott & Costello	Entertainment	550			950	
Abbott, Bessie	Entertainment	25			40	Opera
Abbott, Bud	Entertainment	220	245	295	450	
Abbott, George	Entertainment	15	20	35	50	Producer/Director/Playwright
Abbott, Henry Larcom	Civil War	25	45	70		Union Gen.
Abbott, Henry Livermore	Civil War	90	205			Union Gen.
Abbott, Lyman	Clergy	30	45	75	45	
Abbott. John	Entertainment	8			20	
Abdnor, James	Senate/Congress	5	15		10	Senator SD
Abdul, Paula	Entertainment	25		55	100	
Abel, I.W.	Labor	10	25		10	Pres. United Steel Workers
Abel, Walter	Entertainment	20	25	30	25	
Abercrombie, John Joseph	Civil War	50	75	115		Union Gen.
Aberdeen, Lord, 4th Earl	Head of State	35	40	85		Br. Prime Minister
Abernathy, Ralph D.	Clergy	30	75	120	60	Civil Rights Leader
Abernathy, Thomas Gerstle	Senate/Congress	5	10		10	Congressman MS
Abraham, F. Murray	Entertainment	10	15	35	30	
Abrahamson, James	Military-Astro.	10			30	
Abrams, Creighton W.	Military	15	30	45	45	Gen. WW II Tank Commander
Abrams, Elliott	Diplomat	10	20		20	State Dept.
Abruzzo, Ben A.	Aviation	32			80	
Abt, Franz	Composer	70		200		
Abzug, Bella	Politician	10	15	60	15	Lawyer, Congresswoman NY
Acheson, Dean	Cabinet	25	55		40	Sec'y State
Acheson, George R.	Military	5		20	15	
Acosta, Bert	Aviation	35	60	135	85	
Acquanetta, Burna	Entertainment	10			35	

NAME	CATEGORY	SIG	LS/DS	ALS	SP	COMMENT
Acton, Loren	Astronaut	5		35	25	
Acuff, Roy	Country Music	10			32	
Adair, Allen	Military	20		55		Br. Gen."Operation Mkt. Garden"
Adair, John	Governor	40	125	185		Early Gov. KY
Adair, Red	Celebrity	15	35		20	Oil Well Fires
Adam, Adolphe-Charles	Composer	40	120	325	90	Opera & Ballet (Giselle)
Adamic, Louis	Author	15	55	110	30	Am. Novelist. Born Yugoslavia
Adamowski, Timothee	Composer	10			20	AMusQS $45
Adams, Abigail	First Lady	505	1820	6875		
Adams, Alva	Governor	5		15	10	Gov. CO
Adams, Andrew	Revolutionary War	105	215	440		Continental Congress
Adams, Ansel	Artist	100	260	600	200	Photographer, TLS/Content $450
Adams, Brooke	Entertainment	5	10	20	12	
Adams, Bryan	Entertainment	20			50	Rock
Adams, Charles Francis	Author-Diplomat	35	65	190		Ambassador to G.B. in Civil War
Adams, Clara	Aviation	20	35		50	
Adams, Daniel W.	Civil War	150	270	825		CSA Gen.
Adams, Don	Entertainment	5	8	20	25	
Adams, Edie	Entertainment	5	5	8	10	
Adams, Harriet	Author	35	45	45		
Adams, Henry B.	Authors	110	385	520		Am. Historian
Adams, J. Q. and J. Monroe	Presidents		3080			Signed by Both Presidents
Adams, James S.	Business	10	35	45	25	
Adams, Joey	Entertainment	4	5	9	10	
Adams, John	Civil War	195	375			CSA Gen.
Adams, John 1735-1826	President	1950	3845	17400		Signer Decl. of Indepen.
Adams, John Couch	Astronomer	20	45	125		Discoverer of Neptune
Adams, John Q. & Monroe, James	Presidents		2500			Signed By Both Presidents
Adams, John Quincy	President	400	1215	5500		Engr.S $12,500.ALS/Cont.$25,000
Adams, Julie	Entertainment	4	5	9	15	
Adams, Louisa Catherine	First Lady	200	450	1115		Wife of John Q. Adams
Adams, Mason	Entertainment	3			5	
Adams, Maud (current)	Entertainment	8	9	20	25	
Adams, Maude (vintage)	Entertainment	35	50	100	125	
Adams, Nick	Entertainment	125			350	
Adams, Samuel	Revolutionary War	440	1795	3750		Signer Decl. of Indepen.
Adams, Sherman	Governor	25	75	110	45	Eisenhower Asst., Gov. NH
Adams, Stanley	Composer	15	25	40	25	Lyricist
Adams, William T. (Oliver Optic)	Author	15	25	55	40	Various Series Books For Boys
Adams, William Wirt	Civil War	275	525			CSA Gen.
Adamson, James C.	Astronaut	5	15		15	
Adamson, William C.	Senate/Congress	5	15		30	19th Cent. Congressman GA
Addams, Charles*	Cartoonist	50			800	Addams Family
Addams, Jane	Am. Social Worker	70	225	310	300	Social Reformer, Nobel Peace
Addinsell, Richard	Composer	10	25	45	30	Br. "Warsaw Concerto"
Addis, Don*	Cartoonist	10			25	
Addison, Joseph 1672-1719	Author	80	205	360		Br. Poet, Essayist, Playwright
Ade, George	Author	25	70	155	35	Am. Humorist, Dramatist
Adelaide, HRH Queen England	Royalty	40		105		Queen of William IV
Adenauer, Konrad ("der Alte")	Head of State	20	205	225	140	1st Chan. Fed. Rep. of Germany
Ader, Rose	Entertainment	20			95	Opera
Adler, Alfred	Science	110	270	750	175	ALS/Content $2,000
Adler, Larry	Entertainment	20			35	Harmonica Virtuoso
Adler, Luther	Entertainment	10	15	25	25	Vintage Actor-Stage & Film
Adler, Max	Business	9	26	40	20	Pr.Sears, Roebuck. Philanthropy
Adler, Richard	Composer	15	35	65	30	AMusQS $135

NAME	CATEGORY	SIG	LS/DS	ALS	SP	COMMENT
Adler, Stella	Entertainment	15	15	25	35	Drama Teacher & Coach
Adoree, Renee	Entertainment	25	40		70	
Adrian, Iris	Entertainment	8	10		20	
Adrian, Lord Edgar	Science	25	45	130		Nobel Physiology
Aerosmith	Entertainment	35			85	
Aga Khan III	Royalty	95	300			
Aga Khan IV	Royalty	15	40	110	35	
Agar, John	Entertainment	4	4	9	10	
Agassiz, Jean Louis	Science	85	150	295	625	Zoologist, Biologist
Agnew, Spiro (V)	Vice President	35	130	170	75	
Aguinaldo, Emilio	Head of State	75	140	165	140	Filipino Leader Againt Spain
Agutter, Jenny	Entertainment	5	6	15	15	
Aherne, Brian	Entertainment	15	20	30	55	
Ahidjo, Ahmadou	Head of State	15		120	25	(Cameroon)
Ahlfors, Lars V., Dr.	Science	10	25		25	
Aiello, Danny	Entertainment	10	25	30	25	
Aiken, Conrad	Author	30	72	155	40	Am.Novelist, Poet. Pulitzer
Aiken, George D.	Senate	20	25		30	Senator & Gov. VT
Aiken, William	Governor	10	15	30	20	Gov. & Congressman SC
Ainger, Alfred	Clergy	10	15	25	25	
Airy, George	Science	35	130	210		Br. Royal Astronomer
Aitken, Robert	Printer	75	180		300	!st English Bible Printed in Am
Aitken, Robert Grant	Science	10	20	45		Astronomer
Aitken, Robert Ingersoll	Artist	25	75	190		Am. Sculptor Military Statues
Akers Peter	Clergy	35	45	60		
Akers, Elizabeth	Author	5		20	10	
Akihito & Machiko (Both)	Royalty	410				Emperor & Empress of Japan
Akihito, Emperor of Japan	Royalty	475	540	675	350	
Akin, Susan	Celebrity	4	7	12	10	
Akin, Warren	Civil War	40	55	90		CSA Congress
Akins, Claude	Entertainment	6	10	14	15	
Akroyd, Dan	Entertainment	10	15	20	35	
Alabama (signed by all 4)	Country Music	35			75	
Alard, Nelly	Entertainment	4			10	
Albanese, Licia	Entertainment	35	40	55	65	It. Soprano. Opera, Concert
Albani, Emma, Dame	Entertainment	50	60	100	200	Canadian Soprano. Opera
Albee, Edward	Author	20	80	110	90	Am. Dramatist. Pulitzer
Alberghetti, Anna M.	Entertainment	3	5	6	10	
Albert I (Belgium)	Royalty	25	115	195	50	
Albert III (Rainier-Monaco)	Royalty	75	200	445	120	
Albert Victor, Duke of Clarence	Royalty	150		500	550	Eldest Son Edward VII
Albert, Carl	Senate/Congress	15		40	25	Speaker of the House. OK
Albert, Don	Entertainment	25			50	Trumpet & Bandleader
Albert, Eddie	Entertainment	10	15	20	20	
Albert, Eugen	Composer	130	190		150	Ger. Pianist.Opera Composer
Albert, Marv	Entertainment	5	7		10	TV Host
Albert, Prince (Monaco)	Royalty	15			25	
Albert, Prince (Victoria)	Royalty	125	310	490		Consort of Queen Victoria
Albert, Stephen	Entertainment	20			30	Pulitzer, AMusQS $75
Albertson, Frank	Entertainment	15	20		30	
Albertson, Jack	Entertainment	25	40		60	
Albertson, Joseph A.	Business	8	10	20	20	
Albright, Charles (C.W.)	Senate/Congress	15	20	30		Union Col. CW, Congressman PA
Albright, Lola	Entertainment	9	10	20	20	
Albritton, Louise	Entertainment	15	15	25	30	
Albury, Charles Donald, Capt.	Aviation	20	45	60	55	

NAME	CATEGORY	SIG	LS/DS	ALS	SP	COMMENT
Alcock, John William, Sir	Aviation	235	495	685	600	Pioneer Aviator/Brown
Alcorn, James Lusk	Civil War	55	145	210		CSA Gen.
Alcott, Amos Bronson	Author	40	85	135		Social, Civil, Education Reform
Alcott, Louisa May	Author	165	200	435		
Alda, Alan	Entertainment	15	15	30	30	
Alda, Frances	Entertainment	20			75	Opera. New Zealand Born Soprano
Alda, Robert	Entertainment	10	10	15	25	
Aldasoro, Eduardo	Aviation	15		55	35	
Aldasoro, J. Pablo	Aviation	15		55	35	
Aldington, Richard	Author	25	107	176		Br. Poet, Novelist,Biographer
Aldred, Joel	Aviation-WWII	18	38	55	45	Canadian ACE
Aldrich, Bess Streeter	Author	5	15	35		Am. Novelist,Short Story Writer
Aldrich, Nelson W.	Senate	10	15		15	Senator NY
Aldrich, Thomas Bailey	Author	20	30	45	200	Novels, Poetry, Editor
Aldridge, Kay	Entertainment	4			10	
Aldrin, Edwin 'Buzz'	Astronaut	40	150	300	310	Moonwalker Astro
Aler, John	Entertainment	10			40	
Alexander I (Rus)	Royalty	265	905	895		
Alexander II (Rus)	Royalty	225	775	1760		Assassinated
Alexander III (Pope)	Clergy		45000			
Alexander III (Rus)	Royalty		375	600		
Alexander, Barton S.	Civil War	45	65	95		Union Gen.
Alexander, Ben	Entertainment	40	50		125	
Alexander, Cecil Frances	Clergy	10	20	25	35	
Alexander, Clifford	Activist	10		25	15	Afro-Am Activist
Alexander, Edward Porter	Civil War	95	175			CSA General
Alexander, George	Entertainment	6	8	15	15	
Alexander, Harold R.L., Sir	Military	65	90	155	75	Alexander of Tunis, WW II
Alexander, Henry	Business	3	7	15	10	
Alexander, J. B.	Governor	20	25		25	Guam
Alexander, Jane	Entertainment	10	10	15	25	
Alexander, Joshua Wallis	Cabinet	20	40		25	Sec'y Commerce, Congress MO
Alexander, Robert	Revolutionary War	30	65			
Alexander, William (Lord Stirling)	Military-Rev. War	200	725	1000		Gen. in Continental Army
Alexander, William, Archbishop	Clergy	25	30	40	35	
Alexanderson, Ernst F. W.	Science	45	115	195		"Father of Television"
Alexandra (Edw VII)	Royalty	95		245	475	Queen of Edward VII (Eng.)
Alexandra (Nich. II Rus.)	Royalty	110	235	675		ALS/Content $5,000
Alexis, Kim	Entertainment	10			30	
Alfieri, Carlo	Entertainment	10		35	35	Opera
Alfono, Heradio	Aviation	10			35	
Alfonso XIII (Spain)	Royalty	140	500	625	500	
Alfonzo, Kristian	Entertainment	5			15	Pin-up $25
Alford, Henry	Clergy	10	20	25	25	
Alfred, Prince	Royalty	20	35	65		2nd Son of Queen Victoria
Alfven, Hannes	Science	20	30	45	30	Nobel Physics
Alger, Horatio	Author	150	190	340	240	Popular Books For Boys
Alger, Russell Alexander	Civil War,Cabinet	30	55	85	75	Union Gen., Gov. MI, Sec'y War
Algren, Nelson	Author	25	60	200	50	Am.Novelist.Naturalistic Novels
Alice, Princess	Royalty	15		65		2nd Daughter of Queen Victoria
Alicia, Ana	Entertainment	5	6	15	15	
Allan, Buddy	Country Music	5	10		12	
Allen, Adrienne	Entertainment	10	10	20	15	
Allen, Andrew	Astronaut	7	10		15	
Allen, Charles L.	Clergy	20	35	50	35	
Allen, Debbie	Entertainment	6	8	15	20	

NAME	CATEGORY	SIG	LS/DS	ALS	SP	COMMENT
Allen, Elizabeth	Entertainment	8	9	15	15	
Allen, Ethan	Military-Rev. War	650	1975	3200		Col. Green Mounain Boys
Allen, Frank A., Jr.	Military	10	20	45		
Allen, Fred	Entertainment	50	65	100	125	
Allen, Gracie	Entertainment	50	60	75	150	
Allen, Grant	Author	5	15	30	10	
Allen, Henry T.	Military	25	70	125	50	General WW I
Allen, Henry Watkins	Civil War	220	395			CSA Gen., ALS/Content $850
Allen, Horatio	Business	65		115		
Allen, Ira (Brother of Ethan)	Military-Rev. War					Rev. War Date LS $15,000
Allen, Irwin	Entertainment	5			12	
Allen, Joseph P.	Astronaut	10			25	
Allen, Karen	Entertainment	10	10	20	25	
Allen, Marty	Entertainment	3	3	6	10	
Allen, Peter	Composer	15	17	25	125	
Allen, Rex	Entertainment	10	10	15	30	
Allen, Robert	Civil War	30	55	90		Union Gen.
Allen, Roderick R.	Military	10	20	35		
Allen, Steve	Entertainment	10	10	15	15	Composer, Pianist,TV-Radio Host
Allen, Tim	Entertainment	20			80	
Allen, Valerie	Entertainment	4	4	9	10	
Allen, Viola	Entertainment	15	20	25	25	Vintage Stage Star
Allen, William M.	Business	20	40	55	30	
Allen, William Wirt	Civil War	190	375			CSA Gen., War Dte DS $510
Allen, Woody	Entertainment	20	30	45	45	
Allenby, Edmund	Military	30	95	150	75	Br.Fld Marshal, ALS/Cont.$750
Allende Gossens, Salvador	Head of State	35	120	285	60	1st Marxist Pres. Chile
Alley, Kirstie	Entertainment	10	15	25	45	
Allgood, Sara	Entertainment	10		35	25	
Allingham, Margery	Author	30	65	150		Br. Mystery Writer
Allison, Fran	Entertainment	10	12	15	25	Early TV Children's Show
Allison, May	Entertainment	15			40	
Allison, Mose	Composer	15			30	Jazz Pianist-Vocalist
Allison, W.B.	Senate	10	15	20	15	Senator IA
Allman, Greg	Entertainment	20			50	Rock
Allston, Washington	Artist	275	400	825		Pioneered Romantic Landscapes
Allyn, Kirk	Entertainment	10	12	20	25	
Allyson, June	Entertainment	5	6	15	25	
Alma-Tadema, Lawrence	Artist	20	55	150		Br. Painter of Roman Scenes
Almond, Edw. M.	Military	12	35	50		
Almonte, Juan Nepomuceno	Military	50	200			Mex. General, Politician
Alonso, Maria Conchita	Entertainment	10	15	25	22	
Alpert, Herb	Entertainment	8	10	12	10	Big Band Leader-Trumpet
Alphand, Nicole H.	Celebrity	8			15	
Alsop, Joseph	Author	5	10	30	10	Journalist, Synd. Columnist
Alsop, Stewart	Author	10	26	35	15	Journalist, Synd. Columnist
Alt, Carol	Entertainment	10	15	25	40	
Altgeld, John P.	Governor	15	50			Gov. IL
Altieri, Albert (Johnny)	Celebrity	4			10	Philip Morris Trademark
Altman, Robert	Entertainment	5	6	15	20	
Alvarez, Luis W., Dr.	Science	15	35	85	25	Nobel Physics
Alvarez, Roma	Entertainment	3	3	6	10	
Alvary, Lorenzo	Entertainment	10	12	25	35	
Alvord, Benjamin	Civil War	25	45	60		Union General
Amani, Giorgio	Designer	10		35	25	Fashion
Amara, Lucine	Entertainment	15		55	45	Opera

NAME	CATEGORY	SIG	LS/DS	ALS	SP	COMMENT
Amato, Pasquale	Entertainment	25			125	It. Baritone. Opera
Ambler, Eric Clifford	Author	45	150			Br.Novelist
Ameche, Don	Entertainment	20	25	40	65	
Ames, Adelbert	Civil War	55	65	110		Union Gen., CMH Bull Run
Ames, Ed	Entertainment	10	15		20	
Ames, Leon	Entertainment	15	15	20	35	
Ames, Nancy	Entertainment	5	6	15	10	
Ames, Oliver	RR Exec.-Mfg.	30	45	125		With Oakes, Union Pacific RR
Amherst, Jeffrey, Lord	Revolutionary War	455	850	1100		Gov. Gen. Br. No. Amer.Br.Gen.
Amin Dada, Idi	Heads of State	50	130	210	65	
Amis, Kingsley	Author	15	30	65	25	
Ammen, Daniel	Civil War	32	60	85	175	Union General
Ammen, Jacob	Civil War	20	35	80		Union Gen.
Amos & Andy (Corell & Gosden)	Entertainment	100	150		250	Signed by Both
Amos, Wally 'Famous'	Business	4	10	20	10	Afro-Am. Cookie King
Amparan, Belen	Entertainment	10			35	Opera
Ampere, Andre Marie	Science	170	420	1400		Fr. Physicist, Mathematician
Amsden, Ben	Aviation	10	22	38	28	Navy ACE WW II
Amsterdam, Morey	Entertainment	5			15	
Amundsen, Roald	Explorer	95	195	450	395	Nor. Polar Explorer
Ancerl, Karel	Entertainment	3	4	8	5	
Ancona, Sydenham E.	Senate/ Congress	15		45		Civil War Congressman PA
Anders, Luana	Entertainment	10	15		20	
Anders, Merry	Entertainment	5			15	
Anders, Pamela	Entertainment	20			35	
Anders, William A.	Astronaut	40			95	
Andersen, Hans Christian	Authors	350	650	1500	1300	AQS on CDV $1450
Anderson, 'Bronco Billy'	Entertainment	105	175	200	375	
Anderson, Bill	Country Music	4			12	
Anderson, Brad*	Cartoonist	15		35	40	Marmaduke
Anderson, C.E. "Bud"	Aviation	12	28	45	35	WW II ACE
Anderson, Carl David	Science	20	35		40	Nobel Physics
Anderson, Carl*	Cartoonist	15			60	Henry
Anderson, Clifford	Civil War	70	130	95		CSA Congress
Anderson, Clinton	Cabinet	15	20		25	Sec'y Agriculture. Senator NM
Anderson, Eddie "Rochester"	Entertainment	40			150	
Anderson, Elizabeth G.(Physician)	Science	55	150	175		1st Eng. Hospital for Women
Anderson, George Burgwyn	Civil War	235	425			CSA Gen., War Dte DS $525
Anderson, George Thomas "Tige'	Civil War	50	130	205	250	CSA Gen.
Anderson, George W.	Military	10	30	40	25	
Anderson, Harry	Entertainment	5	8	20	20	
Anderson, Jack	Author	3	5	15	15	Syndicated Newspaper Columnist
Anderson, James Patton	Civil War	80	185	365		CSA Gen.,ALS/Content $475
Anderson, John B.	Military	5	10	20		
Anderson, John Jr.	Governor	12	15		15	Governor KS
Anderson, Joseph	Revolutionary War	60	225	390		Early Senator TN
Anderson, Joseph Reid	Civil War	75	225	1125		CSA Gen.,ALS War Dte $825
Anderson, Judith	Entertainment	25	30	45	55	
Anderson, June	Entertainment	5			25	Opera
Anderson, Laurie	Entertainment	10	15		25	
Anderson, Leroy	Composer	25	75	195	45	AMusMsS $325
Anderson, Les 'Carrot-top'	Country Music	10	12		20	
Anderson, Loni	Entertainment	9	10	25	25	
Anderson, Lynn	Country Music	4			12	
Anderson, Marian	Entertainment	110	325	250	335	Concert, Opera
Anderson, Martin B.	Clergy	10	15	25		

NAME	CATEGORY	SIG	LS/DS	ALS	SP	COMMENT
Anderson, Mary (American)	Entertainment	30	45	50	100	
Anderson, Mary (English)	Entertainment	10	20	30	30	
Anderson, Maxwell	Author	30	70	140	50	Am. Dramatist. Pulitzer
Anderson, Melissa Sue	Entertainment	10	35		35	
Anderson, O.A.	Aviation	10	25	40	30	General
Anderson, Philip W.	Science	45		95	50	Nobel Physics
Anderson, Richard	Entertainment	4	5	10	12	
Anderson, Richard Dean	Entertainment	5	10	25	50	
Anderson, Richard Heron	Civil War	55	120	245		CSA Gen.,War Dte DS $375
Anderson, Robert	Author	10	20	45	15	
Anderson, Robert	Civil War	115	325	300	1950	Cmdr.Ft. Sumter,Wardte ALS$3500
Anderson, Robert B.	Cabinet	10	17	35	20	Sec'y Treasury
Anderson, Robert H.	Civil War	95	355	425		CSA Gen.,War Dte DS $550
Anderson, Roy A.	Business	5	15	20	10	
Anderson, Samuel	Military	40	130	220		Early Congressman PA 1827
Anderson, Samuel R.	Civil War	125	300	350		CSA Gen.
Anderson, Samuel E.	Military	5	10	20		
Anderson, Sherwood	Author	35	95	150	40	Novelist, Journalist, Poet
Anderson, W.R.	Military	15	35		50	Cmdr. N/S Nautilus
Anderson, Willie Y.	Aviation	10	22	35	30	WW II ACE
Andes, Keith	Entertainment	5	6		10	
Andre, John	Revolutionary War	1200	3500	7875		Br. Officer. Hanged as Spy
Andreotti, Guilio	Head of State	10	20	35	20	It. Journalist, Prime Minister
Andress, Ursula	Entertainment	15	20	30	35	
Andrew, A. Piatt	Senate/Congress	5	10		10	Congressman MA
Andrew, John A.	Governor	45	65	120		Civil War Gov. MA
Andrews Sisters (All Three)	Entertainment	70			170	
Andrews, Arkansas Slim	Entertainment	3	5	9	10	
Andrews, Christopher C.	Civil War	35	70	195		Union Gen.
Andrews, Dana	Entertainment	12	35		45	
Andrews, George Leonard	Civil War	35	55	90		Union Gen.
Andrews, Harry	Entertainment	7			25	
Andrews, Julie	Entertainment	9	12	20	40	
Andrews, Maxine	Entertainment	8	9	19	15	
Andrews, Patty	Entertainment	5			15	
Andrews, Roy Chapman	Science	60		135	125	Naturalist, Explorer, Author
Andrews, V.C.	Author	4			10	Novelist
Andrews, William Frederick	Business	4	10		10	CEO Scoville, Inc.
Andriola, Alfred*	Cartoonist	5			30	Kerry Drake
Andros, Edmund, Sir	Revolutionary War			7500		Only Reported Amount Shown
Andrus, Cecil D.	Cabinet	5	10	35	15	Sec'y Interior
Anfinsen, Christian	Science	15	25	45	20	Nobel Chemistry
Angel, Heather	Entertainment	10	12	15	35	
Angeli, Pier	Entertainment	40	55	195	100	
Angell, Norman, Sir	Author	25	80	95	65	Nobel Peace Prize
Angelou, Maya	Author	15	40		35	Am. Poet
Angelyne	Celebrity	10			20	
Anglesea, Marquis of	Military	15	35	60		
Angus, Joseph	Clergy	10	20	25		
Animals, The	Entertainment	50			150	Rock HOF
Anka, Paul	Composer	3	5	12	25	
Ankers, Evelyn	Entertainment	15	30	60	40	
Ann-Margret	Entertainment	6	8	15	25	
Anna Ivanovna (Rus)	Royalty	265	900	2250		Empress of Russia
Annabella	Entertainment	10	15	25	40	
Annaloro, Antonio	Entertainment	10		35	40	It. Tenor, Opera

NAME	CATEGORY	SIG	LS/DS	ALS	SP	COMMENT
Anne, Princess	Royalty	95	250		140	Daughter of Elizabeth II
Anne, Queen (Eng) 1665-1714	Royalty	365	1450	2150		
Annenberg, Walter H.	Business	10	25	40	35	Publisher
Annesley, H.N.	Law Enforcement	5	10		15	Northern Ireland
Annseau, Fernand	Entertainment	20			75	Opera
Anouilh, Jean	Author	30	95	220	40	Fr. Dramatist, Screenwriter
Ansara, Michael	Entertainment	6	8	15	25	
Anthonly, Robert N.	Nobel	15	25		25	Nobel
Anthony, HRH	Royalty	30	100			King of Saxony
Anthony, Henry	Senate/Congress	10	15	35		Editor, Gov., Senator RI
Anthony, Ray	Entertainment	6	10	13	12	Big Band Leader
Anthony, Susan B.	Woman Suffrage	230	385	975	650	Reformer, Women's Rights
Antokolski, Mark Matveyevich	Artist	30	65	155		Russ. Sculp. 1843-1902
Anton, Susan	Entertainment	7	8	10	20	
Antonelli, Laura	Entertainment	18	20	45	50	
Antonioni, Michelangelo	Entertainment	15			50	Film Director
Anwar, Gabrielle	Entertainment	20			65	
Aoti, Rocky	Business	6	15	30	15	Benihana Japanese Resaurants
Apollinaire, Guillaume	Author	125	400	1010		Avant Garde Poet, Critic
Apollo I	Astronauts				3000	Signed by All Three
Apollo II	Astronauts	250			575	Signed by All Three
Appleby, Ray	Entertainment	3	3	5	5	
Applegate, Christina	Entertainment	10	15		25	Actress-Model
Appleton, Edward, Sir	Science	25	35		55	Nobel Physics
Apt, Jay	Astronaut	5	10		15	
Aquino, Corazon	Head of State	20			45	Pres. Philippines
Arafat, Yassir	Head of State	95	195		150	PLO Leader
Araisa, Francisco	Entertainment	5			35	Opera, Concert, Mexican Tenor
Arambula, Roman*	Cartoonist	40			200	Mickey Mouse
Araujo, Arturo	Head of State	15	40		30	Salvador
Arber, Werner	Science	20	35		30	Nobel Medicine
Arbuckle, Maclyn	Entertainment	15	15	30	25	
Arbuckle, Roscoe 'Fatty'	Entertainment	335	400	750	775	
Archer, Anne	Entertainment	12	15	15	35	
Archer, James J.	Civil War	200	375	825		CSA Gen.
Archer, Jeffrey	Author	5	15		15	Novelist
Archer, Jules	Author	7			10	
Archi, Attila	Entertainment	10	15	40	45	Opera
Arden, Elizabeth	Business	30	65	145	40	Founder & Owner Eliz. Arden Co.
Arden, Eve	Entertainment	20	25	50	50	
Arden, Nicke	Entertainment	3	3	5	5	
Arena, Angelina	Entertainment	5		30	25	Australian Soprano
Argento, Dominick	Composer	10	30	65	20	Pulitzer, AMusQS $175
Argyll, 9th Duke, John D. Campbell	Head of State	30	45	60		Governor-General Canada
Arias Sanchez, Oscar	Head of State	35		65	50	Nobel Peace, Pres.Costa Rica
Arias, Harmodio	Head of State	25	50		30	
Arie, Raffaele	Entertainment	5			25	Bulgarian Basso
Ariyoshi, George R.	Governor	15			25	Governor Hawaii
Arkell, Bartlett	Business	5	27	45	15	
Arkell, W.J. (Judge Publ)	Business	5	15	30	10	
Arkin, Adam	Entertainment	5	7		10	
Arkin, Alan	Entertainment	5	6	15	25	
Arlen, Harold	Composer	50	65	95	55	AMusQS $1,600
Arlen, Richard	Entertainment	25	30	70	60	
Arletty	Entertainment	25			75	Fr. Actress
Arliss, Florence	Entertainment	15	30	40	35	

NAME	CATEGORY	SIG	LS/DS	ALS	SP	COMMENT
Arliss, George	Entertainment	40	45	70	100	
Armendariz, Pedro	Entertainment	30	35	45	65	
Armetta, Henry	Entertainment	25	30	50	65	
Armistead, Lewis Addison	Civil War	600				CSA Gen., Last recorded sale—
Armour, Philip D.	Business	50	225		75	Meat Packing. Armour & Co.
Arms, Russ	Entertainment	3	3	6	10	
Armstead, Henry Hugh	Artist	10	20	35		Br. Sculptor.Albert Memorial
Armstrong, Edw. R., Dr.	Science	30	75	150		Inventor Seadrome
Armstrong, Edwin H.	Science	75	250			Invented FM Broadcasting System
Armstrong, Frank Crawford	Civil War	290	365			CSA Gen.
Armstrong, Harry	Composer	80		195		"Sweet Adeline"AMusQS $365
Armstrong, John	Cabinet	45	125	270		Sec'y War
Armstrong, Louis "Satchmo"	Entertainment	190	405	695	525	
Armstrong, Martin	Author	5	10	15	10	
Armstrong, Neil A.	Astronaut	150	300	700	400	1st to walk on the Moon
Armstrong, Robert	Entertainment	55	60	75	350	
Armstrong, Robert	Military	175	450			Gen. TN Vols, Indian Fighter
Armstrong, Samuel Chapman	Civil War	55	120	350		Union Off. Cmdr. Black Regiment
Armstrong, William, Dr.	Science	20	50	110	35	
Arnaz, Desi	Entertainment	30	35	50	100	
Arnaz, Lucie	Entertainment	5	10	15	20	
Arness, James	Entertainment	15	15	25	40	
Arnett, Peter	TV News	5			10	CNN News
Arngrim, Alison	Entertainment	6	8	15	10	
Arno, Peter	Cartoonist	15	30	75	25	Drew for "The New Yorker"
Arno, Sig	Entertainment	10			25	
Arnold, Archibald	Military	20	62	102		
Arnold, Benedict	Revolutionary War	750	1975	6750		Am. Army Officer. Traitor
Arnold, Eddy	Country Music	10	30		30	
Arnold, Edward	Entertainment	30	40		60	
Arnold, Edwin, Sir	Author	50	90	170	80	Br. Poet, Journalist
Arnold, Fred	Aviation	20	35		50	ACE, WWII P-38
Arnold, Henry 'Hap'	Military	45	340	450	200	Air Force Gen. WW II
Arnold, Leslie P.	Aviation	10			30	
Arnold, Lewis Golding	Civil War	55	90	205		Union Gen.
Arnold, Matthew	Author	40	65	125		Br. Poet, Critic
Arnold, Richard	Civil War	40	95			Union Gen.
Arnold, Tom	Entertainment	20			50	
Arnot, William	Clergy	10	20	25		
Arnt, Charles	Entertainment	10			25	
Arp, Jean	Artist	75		275		Fr. DaDa Artist, Sculptor
Arquette, Cliff	Entertainment	20	25		40	
Arquette, Rosanna	Entertainment	15	15		35	
Arrhenuis, Svante August	Science	95	295	500		Nobel Chemistry 1903
Arrington, A. H.	Civil War	75	130			CSA Congress
Arriola, Gus*	Cartoonist	5			25	Gordo
Arrow, Kenneth J.	Economist	35	55			Nobel Economics
Arthur, Beatrice	Entertainment	5	10	20	20	
Arthur, Chester A.	President	310	1115	1275	625	ALS as Actg Pres $2,500
Arthur, Chester A. (As President)	President	375	1250	1350		
Arthur, Duke of Connought	Head of State	10	18	25		Prime Minister
Arthur, Ellen Lewis	First Lady	600	1000	1200		
Arthur, George K.	Entertainer	6		15	10	Comedian, Producer
Arthur, Jean	Entertainment	125	150	325	285	
Arthur, Julia	Entertainment	15			25	Pioneer Film Star
Arthur, Timothy Shay	Temperance Author	20	45			Am. "10 Nights In A Barroom"

NAME	CATEGORY	SIG	LS/DS	ALS	SP	COMMENT
Artot, Desiree	Entertainment	35		150	70	Opera, Concert
Arvin, Newton	Author	18	40	85		
Asboth, Alexander S.	Civil War	60	190			Union Gen.
Asbury, Francis, Bishop	Clergy	175	290	625		
Ash, Mary Kay						SEE Kay, Mary
Ash, Roy L.	Business	10	20	50	35	
Ashby, Hal	Entertainment	8	8	15	15	
Ashby, Turner	Civil War	250	645	1250	750	CSA Gen., War Date ALS $1750
Ashcroft, Dame Peggy	Entertainment	20	25	35	65	
Ashe, John	Revolutionary War	75	225	450		NC General
Ashe, William Shepperd	Senate/Congress	35	90			CW Blockade Runner
Ashford and Simpson	Entertainment	15			40	
Ashley, Elizabeth	Entertainment	6	8	15	15	
Ashley, John	Entertainment	5			15	
Ashley, William	Fur Trader	200	750			Pioneer. Route for Oregon Trail
Ashworth, Ernie	Country Music	10			20	
Asimov, Isaac	Author	25	175		110	Rus-Am Biochemist.Sci-Fi Writer
Askew, Reubin	Governor	12			15	Governor FL
Asner, Ed	Entertainment	4	4	10	15	
Aspin, Les	Cabinet	5			20	Clinton Sec'y Defense
Asquith, Herbert H.	Head of State	35	70	125	150	Prime Minister
Assad, Hafez Al	Head of State	15	40	105	65	
Assante, Armand	Entertainment	6	8	15	25	
Astaire, Fred	Entertainment	75	80	135	175	
Asther, Nils	Entertainment	25	35	65	120	
Astin, John	Entertainment	7	10	15	25	
Aston, Francis W.	Science	35	80	155		Nobel Chemistry 1922
Astor, Brooke	Author	5	15		10	
Astor, John J. Lord of Hever	Publisher	15	40	60	35	1st Baron of Hever 1886-1971
Astor, John Jacob 1763-1848	Business	300	1150			Fur Trader-Capitalist, Financier
Astor, John Jacob Jr.	Business	40	135	360	125	Union Gen., Financier
Astor, John Jacob Mrs.	Business	35	100	195		
Astor, Mary	Entertainment	30	35		120	
Astor, Nancy(Viscountess)	Celebrity	20	55	95	35	1st Woman To Sit As Br. M.P.
Astor, Vincent	Business	8	20	45	20	
Astor, Waldorf 1879-1952	Politics	15	35	80	55	Br. M.P., Publisher Observer
Astor, William Backhouse	Business	85	195	350		Administered Astor Estate
Astor, William Waldorf	Business	65	200	350		Journalist-Capitalist-Financier
Astronauts (Deceased)	Astronaut				1500	Chaffee, White, Grissom (All)
Asturias, Miquel Angel	Author	50	135	285		Guatamala. Nobel Literature
Atchison, David Rice	President	275	350	975		Pres.for a day.ALS/Cont $4500
Ates, Roscoe	Entertainment	25	30	60	65	
Athenagoras, Archbishop	Clergy	25	40	55	50	
Atherton, Gertrude	Author	30	55	150	75	Am. Novelist
Athlone, Earl, Prince Alex.of Teck	Head of State	15	25	40		Governor-General of Canada
Atkins, Chet	Country Music	5	15		20	Guitarist
Atkins, Christopher	Entertainment	6	8	15	15	
Atkins, Gaius Glenn	Clergy	15	30	45		
Atkinson, Brooks	Author	15	45		30	Theater Critic, Columnist
Atkinson, Joseph H.	Military	10	25	30		
Atlantov, Vladimir	Entertainment	20		75	55	Opera. Rus. Tenor
Atlas, Charles	Business	15	30	35	35	Mail Order Phys. Culture
Attenborough, Richard	Entertainment	25	30	35	45	Br. Actor-Director
Atterbury, William	Military	15	30			Gen. WW I, Pres. Penn. RR
Attlee, Clement	Head of State	40	180	250	75	Prime Minister
Atwill, Lionel	Entertainment	100			250	

NAME	CATEGORY	SIG	LS/DS	ALS	SP	COMMENT
Auber, Daniel Francois	Composer	40		130		Father of Fr.Opera, AMusQS $350
Auberjonois, Rene	Entertainment	5	5	10	20	
Aubert, Lenore	Entertainment	5	8	15	20	
Aubrey, M. E.	Clergy	10	15	20		
Aubry, Cecile	Entertainment	15			20	Fr. Actress
Auchincloss, Janet L.	Business	3	5	10	5	
Auchincloss, Louis	Author	15	35	75	30	U.S. Novelist, Short Story
Auchinleck, Claude J.E., Sir	Military	45	75		95	Br. Fld. Marshal WW II
Auckland, Baron (Geo.Eden)	Head of State	35	45	85		Gov-Gen India
Audemars, Edmund	Aviation	27			48	
Auden, W. H. (Wystan Hugh)	Author	75	335	625	700	Br.-Am. Poet, Pulitzer
Audran, Edmond	Composer	45	85	175		Fr. Operettas
Audubon, John J.	Artist	785	2500	3750		Ornithologist
Auel, Jean M.	Author	6	10	25	25	Novelist
Auer, Leopold	Entertainment	25	200		40	Hungarian Violinist
Auer, Mischa	Entertainment	25	30	45	40	
Auger, Arleen	Entertainment	25			55	Opera. Am Soprano
Auger, Christopher C.	Civil War	50	125	170		Union General
Augereau, P.F.C. de Castiglione	Military	100	305	525		Marshal of Napoleon
Augustus I, Duke of Saxony	Royalty	2000				1526-1586
Augustus III	Royalty	145	425	345		King Poland
Auld, Georgie	Entertainment	5	6	15	10	
Aumont, Jean Pierre	Entertainment	6	12	20	15	
Aurand, Henry S.	Military	5	10	20	15	
Auriol, Jacqueline	Aviation	15	35	70	45	
Auriol, Vincent	Head of State	45	60	85		1st Pres. 4th Republ. France
Ausensi, Maurel	Entertainment	15			50	Opera, Sp. Baritone
Auslander, Joseph	Author	25	125		50	Poet. Harvard Lecturer Poetry
Austen, Jane	Author	625	2250	7500		Br.Novelist."Pride & Prejudice"
Austin, Bobby	Country Music	10			20	
Austin, Horace	Governor	10			15	Governor MN
Austin, Karen	Entertainment	5	6	10	10	
Austin, Moses	Merchant	425	1425	2995		Orig. Founder of TX. Mine Owner
Austin, Stephen F.	Texas Colonizer	800	2050	6500		Sec'y State Repub. Texas
Austin, Teri	Entertainment	5	8	10	10	
Austin, Warren R.	Senate	5	10		20	Senator VT
Autry, Gene	Entertainment	25	30		60	
Avallone, Michael	Author	5	15		10	
Avalon, Frankie	Entertainment	6	8	15	25	
Avedon, Richard	Artist	40	65	90	45	Photographer
Average White Band	Entertainment	15			25	Rock
Averell, William Woods	Civil War	65	160	195		Union General
Avery, John, Jr.	Revolutionary War	40	77			
Avery, Margaret	Entertainment	3	3	6	10	
Avery, Sewell L.	Business	35	55	105	40	CEO Montgomery Ward
Avery, Tex*	Cartoonist	25			400	Annimator. (*Original Cell)
Avery, William W.	Civil War	75	140			CSA Congress
Avildsen, John G.	Entertainment	5			20	Film Director
Axelrod, Julius	Science	35	60	95	35	Nobel Medicine
Axtell, George	Aviation	12	25	45	35	Marine ACE
Axton, Hoyt	Country Music	10	25		25	
Ayckbourn, Alan	Author	10	15	30	25	Br. Prolific Playwright
Aykroyd, Dan	Entertainment	10	12	15	25	
Ayres, Agnes	Entertainment	60	75	150	125	Silent Film Star
Ayres, Lew	Entertainment	10	15	25	25	
Ayres, Romeyn Beck	Civil War	45	75	110		Union Gen.

NAME	CATEGORY	SIG	LS/DS	ALS	SP	COMMENT
Ayub Khan, General	Head of State	20	35	75	100	Afghan Prince. General
Aznavour, Charles	Entertainment	10			35	

B

NAME	CATEGORY	SIG	LS/DS	ALS	SP	COMMENT
B 52's	Entertainment	30			75	Rock
Babbage, Charles	Science-Math.	80	245	675		Br. Pioneer of Modern Computers
Babbitt, Bruce	Cabinet	10	20		15	Gov. AZ
Babbitt, Milton	Composer	25		70	30	AMusQS $150
Babcock, Barbara	Entertainment	4	4	9	10	
Babcock, Joseph W.	Senate/Congress	5		30		Congressman WI
Babcock, Orville E.	Civil War	30	55	85		LS as Grant ADC $385
Babcock, Tim	Governor	12	20	25	15	Governor MT
Babcock, Verne C.	Aviation	16			40	
Babilee', Jean	Entertainment	30	45		70	Ballet
Baby Peggy	Entertainment	5	6	15	15	
Bacall, Lauren	Entertainment	9	10	20	30	
Baccaloni, Salvatore	Entertainment	20	25	40	95	Opera, Concert, Films
Bach, Barbara	Entertainment	10	12	15	25	
Bach, Catherine	Entertainment	6	8	15	20	
Bach, Johann Sebastian	Composer	2500	22670	35000		Conservative Estimates
Bach, Richard	Author	25	100	175		
Bach, Sebastian	Entertainment	20			50	Rock
Bacharach, Burt	Composer	13	25	40	25	
Bacharach, Fabian	Artist	50	100	150	75	
Bache, Alexander D.	Science	25	50	110	40	1st Pres. Nat'l Acad. Science
Bache, Harold L.	Business	15	45	110	65	US Stockbroker. J.S.Bache & Co.
Bacheller, Irving	Author	25	60		75	Am. Novelist, Editor
Back, George, Sir	Explorer	20	105	140		Arctic Navigator
Backhaus, Wilhelm	Entertainment	30			100	Ger. Concert Pianist
Backhouse, James	Clergy	20	35	50		
Backus, Jim	Entertainment	15	18	25	35	Mr. McGoo
Baclanova, Olga	Entertainment	10			25	
Bacon, Edmund	Celebrity	10			15	
Bacon, Francis, Sir	Author	1500	3650	10500		Br. Philosopher, Statesman
Bacon, Frank	Entertainment	10	12	20	15	
Bacon, Kevin	Entertainment	9	10	20	30	
Bacon, Leonard	Clergy	10	15	20	25	
Bacon, Peggy	Artist	35	65	150		
Bacon, Robert	Senate/Congress	15	25		30	Congressman NY. Military
Bacon, Walter W.	Governor	10		25	15	Governor DE
Baddeley, Hermione	Entertainment	12	15	22	30	
Badeau, Adam	Civil War	35	60	125		Union General
Baden-Powell, Robert, Sir	Military	150	360	525	985	Br. Gen., Founder of Boy Scouts
Bader, Douglas, Sir	Aviation	45	70	205	70	

NAME	CATEGORY	SIG	LS/DS	ALS	SP	COMMENT
Badger, Charles J.	Military	15	45	70	30	
Badger, George E.	Cabinet	10	25	40		Sec'y Navy, Senator NC
Badham, John	Entertainment	10			20	Film Director
Badham, W.L.	Aviation	25	50	75	55	Bi-plane , WW I
Badler, Jane	Entertainment	5	8	20	25	
Badoglio, Pietro	Head of State	30		135	55	lt. Gen.,succeeded Mussolini
Baekeland, L. H. Dr.	Science-Inventor	30	50	125		Invented Bakelite. 1st Plastic
Baer, George F.	Business	10	25	45	30	Pres. Reading Railroad
Baer, John	Entertainment	5	6	15	15	
Baer, Max, Jr.	Entertainment	15		85	35	
Baez, Joan	Entertainment	10	12	20	25	
Bagian, James P.	Astronaut	5	10		15	
Baglioni, Bruna	Entertainment	10		45	35	Opera
Bailey, Buster	Entertainment	30			75	Jazz Clarinet, Sax
Bailey, Carl E.	Governor	10	15			Governor AR
Bailey, F. Lee	Legal	12	25	45	15	Noted Trial Attorney
Bailey, Jack	Entertainment	5	5	6	10	Early Radio-TV M.C.
Bailey, James Anthony	Circus	250	950	1100		Barnum & Bailey Circus
Bailey, Joseph	Civil War	115	195			Union Gen.
Bailey, Pearl	Entertainment	15	15	20	60	
Bailey, Razzie	Country Music	5			20	
Bailey, Temple	Author	30	45	110		
Bailey, Theodorus	Civil War	35	70	145		Union Naval Officer
Bailey, Walter R.	Business	10	35	45	20	
Baillie, Joanna 1762-1851	Author	15	50	95		Scottish Dramatist, Poet
Baillie, John	Clergy	35	75	110	50	
Bailly, Jean-Sylvain 1736-93	Astronomer	40	90	160		& Fr. Politician. Guillotined
Bain, Barbara	Entertainment	5	6	15	15	
Bain, Conrad	Entertainment	5			10	
Bainbridge, William	Military	150	375	550		US Naval Officer War 1812
Bainter, Fay	Entertainment	70	85	135	125	
Baio, Scott	Entertainment	5	6	15	15	
Baird, Absalom	Civil War	32	45	70		Union Gen.
Baird, John Logie	Science	150	295	525	600	1st TV Picture of Moving Object
Bairnsfather, Bruce	Cartoonist	15	30	110	25	Br. WW I "Old Bill" Cartoons
Bakaleinikoff, Constantin	Composer	200				
Baker, Alpheus	Civil War	135	275	475		CSA Gen.
Baker, Art	Entertainment	5	10		20	Early Radio-TV M.C.
Baker, Benny	Entertainment	5		15	10	Comic Actor
Baker, Blanche	Entertainment	5	8	15	20	
Baker, Bonnie "Wee"	Entertainment	6	8	15	15	Big Band Vocalist
Baker, Carroll	Entertainment	15	20	40	40	
Baker, Charles S.	Senate/Congress	5	10		5	Congressman NY.
Baker, Chauncey	Military	10		25	15	General WW I
Baker, Diane	Entertainment	3	3	6	10	
Baker, Edward D.	Civil War	85	160	200		Union Gen.
Baker, Ellen	Astronaut	5			25	
Baker, George*	Cartoonist	30			175	Sad Sack
Baker, Howard Henry, Jr.	Senate	5		25	10	Senator TN. WH Chief of Staff
Baker, James A., III	Cabinet	10	25		50	Bush Sec'y State
Baker, Janet, Dame	Entertainment	10	15		35	Opera. Br. Mezzo Soprano
Baker, Josephine	Entertainment	185	305	450	720	
Baker, Kenny	Entertainment	12	15	25	50	"Jack Benny Show" Vocalist
Baker, La Fayette Curry	Civil War	115	165	235		Union Gen.
Baker, LaVerne	Entertainment	10			25	Jazz Vocalist
Baker, Laurence Simmons	Civil War	60	135			CSA Gen.

NAME	CATEGORY	SIG	LS/DS	ALS	SP	COMMENT
Baker, Lucien	Senate	10		30		Senator KS
Baker, Mark	Entertainment	5	10		25	Opera
Baker, Michael	Astronaut	4	10		12	
Baker, Newton D.	Cabinet	15	135	190	55	Wilson Sec'y War
Baker, Royal N.	Aviation	25			50	
Baker, Samuel, Sir	Explorer	30	65	150		Br. Located Sources of Nile
Bakewell, William	Entertainment	10			25	Gone With The Wind (Cast)
Bakker, Jim	Clergy	20	25	35	40	
Bakst, Leon	Artist	95		650		Rus. Painter, Scenic Designer
Bakula, Scott	Entertainment	20			50	
Balanchine, George	Entertainment	125		250	200	Ballet-Choreographer
Balbo, Italo	Aviation	125	160	200	195	It. Air Marshal & Pioneer
Balch, Emily Greene	Social Scientist	10	30	60		Economist, Reformer, Pacifist
Balchen, Bernt	Aviation	30	40	75	45	
Balck, Hermann	Military	20			75	Ger. Panzer General
Baldridge, Howard Malcolm	Senate/Congress	10	15		20	Congressman NE
Baldwin, Abraham	US Senate		3750			Signer Constitution, Rare
Baldwin, Alec	Entertainment	12			50	
Baldwin, Faith	Author	15	25	45	20	Novelist
Baldwin, Henry (SC)	Supreme Court	25	40	110		
Baldwin, James	Author	50	200	500	230	ALS/Content $975
Baldwin, Judy	Entertainment	3	3	6	8	
Baldwin, Raymond E.	Governor	10	20		20	Governor, Senator CT
Baldwin, Roger Sherman	Senate	35		50		Early Gov.1844, Senator CT 1847
Baldwin, Stanley	Head of State	40	90	200	125	Br. Prime Minister
Baldwin, William E.	Civil War	385	750			CSA General
Balewa, A. T., Sir	Head of State	10	35	80	25	Nigeria
Balfe, Michael William	Composer	18	55	125		
Balfour, Arthur J.	Head of State	35	95	120	90	Br. Prime Minister
Ball, Albert	Aviation	125	225	330	275	Brit. RAF ACE WW I
Ball, Lucille	Entertainment	75	380		425	Full Signature
Ballard, Kaye	Entertainment	10	12	20	25	
Ballard, Robert, Dr.	Science	17	40	85	25	Oceanographer. Found Titanic
Ballentine, John J.	Military	15	35	60		
Ballew, Smith	Entertainment	15	20		40	
Ballinger, Richard A.	Cabinet	10	25	50	25	Sec'y Interior 1909
Ballou, Charles	Military	35	110			General WW I
Balsam, Martin	Entertainment	9	10	20	25	
Baltimore, David, Dr.	Science	15	25	40	15	Nobel Medicine
Balzac, Honore de	Author	600	1250	1950		Fr. Novelist
Bampton, Rose	Entertainment	20	35	45	50	Opera, Concert
Bananarama	Entertainment	20			50	
Bancroft, Anne	Entertainment	6	8	15	20	
Bancroft, George	Entertainment	19	25	45	45	
Bancroft, George	Cabinet-Author	30	85	140		Polk Sec'y Navy, Historian
Band, The	Entertainment					Rock HOF. No Price Available
Bandaranike, S.W.R.D	Head of State	10	25	45	30	Ceylon
Bangles, The (All)	Entertainment	40			85	Rock
Bangs, John Kedrick	Author	5	45		20	Humor Editor"Harper's Magazine"
Banisadr, A.	Head of State	10	30	80	40	Iran
Bank, C. D.	Cabinet	10	25			
Bankhead, Tallulah	Entertainment	80	195	220	265	
Banks, Billy	Entertainment	80			250	Jazz
Banks, Joseph, Sir	Science-Explorer	30	110	560		Br. Naturalist.Sailed/Capt.Cook
Banks, Leslie	Entertainment	20			35	
Banks, Michael A.	Author	4	10	25	10	

NAME	CATEGORY	SIG	LS/DS	ALS	SP	COMMENT
Banks, Nathaniel P.	Civil War	70	100	145		Gov. MA, MOC, Union Gen.
Banky, Vilma	Entertainment	45	75	190	160	
Banner, John	Entertainment	70			150	
Banning, Henry Blackstone	Civil War	30	65			Union Gen., Congressman OH
Banning, Margaret C.	Author	5	12	25	10	
Banting, Frederick G., Dr.	Science	600	1050	1650		Discoverd Insulin with Best
Bar-Lev, Chaim	Military	20	60		45	Israeli Military Leader
Bara, Theda	Entertainment	145		300	275	
Baraka, I.A.(LeRoi Jones)	Author	35	50	75	40	
Barbarin, Paul	Entertainment	25		65		Bandleader, Drummer
Barbarolli, John, Sir	Entertainment	30		55	150	Br. Conductor
Barbe-Marbois, Francois de	Napoleon Cabinet	30	75	250		Louisiana Purchase
Barbeau, Adrienne	Entertainment	6	8	15	15	
Barbee, John Henry	Entertainment	35				Blues Vocalist
Barbejacque, Prince	Entertainment	3	3	6	10	
Barber, Rex T.	Aviation	12	35	75	35	Am. ACE, Downed Yamamoto
Barber, Samuel	Composer	55	260	295	70	Opera, Songs, String Music
Barber, William	Military	25			70	Marine CMH Korea
Barbera, Joe	Entertainment	10	12	15	20	
Barbier, George	Entertainment	10	15	25	25	
Barbieri, Fedora	Entertainment	25			75	Opera, Concert
Barbour, Dave	Composer	15			40	Jazz Guitar
Barbour, Philip (SC)	Supreme Court					NRPA
Barbour, William Warren	Senate	10	35		15	Senator NJ
Barclay, Thomas	Revolutionary War	25	55			Adj.-Gen'l Nova Scotia
Barclay, William	Clergy	40	75	95	75	
Barcroft, Roy	Entertainment	50			150	
Bardeen, John	Science	25	50	95	35	Nobel. Signed Bio Card $55
Bardot, Brigitte	Entertainment	25	25	45	75	
Bardshar, F.A.		10	25	40	35	Navy ACE, WW II
Barere de Vieuzac, B.	Fr. Revolution	30	120	150		"Anacreon of Guillotine".Exiled
Baretti, Giuseppe	Author	25	80	155		Friend of Burke, Johnson
Bari, Lynn	Entertainment	5	8	15	15	
Baring, Francis, Sir	Business	25	35	95		Dir. East India Company
Baring-Gould, Sabine	Author	20	95	335	60	"Onward Christian Soldiers"
Barker, Bob	Entertainment	3	3	6	10	"The Price is Right"
Barker, Clive	Author	15	25		25	Br. Horror Novelist
Barker, Lex	Entertainment	65	75	130	200	
Barker, William George	Aviation	125	225	350	295	Canadian ACE, WW I
Barkhorn, Gerhard	Aviation	40	195		125	Ger. ACE, #2 Worldwide
Barkin, Ellen	Entertainment	15			60	
Barkley, Alben W. (V)	Vice President	30	95	175	65	Truman VP
Barks, Carl*	Cartoonist	20			300	Donald Duck, Scrooge
Barksdale, Ethelbert	Civil War	30	50	65		CSA Congress
Barksdale, William	Civil War	435				CSA General
Barlow, Francis C.	Civil War	55	85	145		Union Gen.
Barlow, Jane	Author	5	10	25		
Barlow, Joel	Diplomat	40	120	245		Author, Chaplain Rev. War
Barnabee, Henry Clay	Entertainment	6	8	15	15	Operatic Comedian
Barnaby, Ralph S.	Aviation	27			35	
Barnard, Christian, Dr.	Science	20	35	85	35	Heart Specialist
Barnard, Frederick A.P.	Educator	75	165	275		Barnard College.For Women's Ed.
Barnard, John Gross	Civil War	25	60	95		Union Gen.
Barne, Michael	Celebrity	12	35	90	40	
Barnes, Binnie	Entertainment	6	8	15	15	
Barnes, Demus	Senate/Congress	5	15	25		Congressman NY. Writer

NAME	CATEGORY	SIG	LS/DS	ALS	SP	COMMENT
Barnes, Djuna	Author	45	110	260	85	Am. Novelist-Short Story Writer
Barnes, James	Civil War	50	115	170		Union Gen.
Barnes, Joanna	Entertainment	5	6	15	15	
Barnes, Joseph K.	Civil War	150	205			Union Surgeon Gen.
Barnes, Priscilla	Entertainment	8	10	20	25	
Barnet, Charlie	Entertainment	15			30	Big Band Leader-Tenor Sax
Barnett, Ross R.	Governor	10		25	15	Governor MS
Barnette, Vince	Entertainment	15	20	35	45	
Barneveld, Jan Van Olden 1547-1619	Dutch Statesman			2000		Father of Dutch Independence
Barney, Natalie	Author	110	315	450		Am. Poet, Translator
Barnhart, George 'Eddie'	Aviation	16	35		50	
Barnum, Henry Alanson	Civil War	35	90	145		Union Gen.
Barnum, Malvern H.	Military	10		35	25	General WW I
Barnum, Phineas T.	Business-Circus	195	470	625	1135	ALS/Content $1,500, $2,000
Baronova, Irina	Entertainment	20			70	Rus.-Br. Ballerina
Barr, Candy	Stripper	10			55	Prison for Shooting Husband
Barr, Doug	Entertainment	3	3	6	8	
Barr, Joseph Walker	Cabinet	5	15	30	15	Sec'y Treasury, Congressman IN
Barr, Roseanne (Arnold)	Entertainment	20	25	50	60	
Barras, Paul-Francois-Jean	Fr. Revolution	85	250			Jacobin Club.Exiled From Paris
Barrault, Jean-Louis	Entertainment	40			125	
Barrett, John	Military	20		50		WW I Victoria Cross
Barrett, Lawrence	Civil War	20			45	Union Officer, Actor
Barrett, Majel	Entertainment	10			30	"Star Trek"
Barrett, Rona	Entertainment	6	8	15	15	
Barrett, Wilson	Entertainment	15		95	55	Br. Playwright, Actor, Manager
Barrie, Barbara	Entertainment	4	6	10	10	
Barrie, James M., Sir	Author	75	265	330	140	"Peter Pan" etc.
Barrie, Mona	Entertainment	15	15	35	30	
Barrie, Wendy	Entertainment	20	25	30	45	
Barrier, Edgar	Entertainment	4	7	10	15	
Barringer, Rufus	Civil War	70	190	210		CSA Gen.
Barrington, Shute	Clergy	10	15	25	20	
Barron, Clarence	Business	25			40	Editor, Publisher "Barron's"
Barrow, Edward G.	Business	100	300		150	Gen'l Mgr. NY Yankees
Barrow, John, Sir	Statesman	60	170	375		1st Lord of the Admiralty
Barrow, Robert H.	Military	10	30	50	20	
Barrows, Lewis O.	Governor	12		25	15	Governor ME
Barrows, Sydney Biddle	Celebrity	10			30	Mayflower Madame
Barry, Charles, Sir	Architect	20	45	125		Br. Houses of Parliament
Barry, Dan*	Cartoonist	10			100	Flash Gordon
Barry, Don 'Red'	Entertainment	22	25	35	60	
Barry, Gene	Entertainment	8	10	15	15	
Barry, John	Revolutionary War	1150	2000			Ir. Born US Naval Officer
Barry, John Decatur	Civil War	145		475		CSA Gen.
Barry, John Wolfe, Sir	Celebrity	6	12	35	20	
Barry, Marion	Politician	5	8	15	15	Mayor Washington, D.C.
Barry, Sy*	Cartoonist	10			50	Phantom
Barry, Thomas	Military	35		150		General WW I
Barry, Wesley	Entertainment	6	12	25	20	
Barry, Wm. Farquhar	Civil War	60	145	190		Union Gen.
Barrymore, Diana	Entertainment	25	35	45	30	
Barrymore, Drew	Entertainment	20			60	
Barrymore, Ethel	Entertainment	125	150		250	
Barrymore, John	Entertainment	215	250	300	550	

NAME	CATEGORY	SIG	LS/DS	ALS	SP	COMMENT
Barrymore, Lionel	Entertainment	80	350		175	
Barrymore, Maurice	Entertainment	15			50	
Bartato, Elisabeth	Entertainment	15			40	Opera
Barth, John	Author	35	40	85	30	Am. Novelist
Barth, Karl	Clergy	40	95	125	75	
Barthelmess, Richard	Entertainment	20	30	80	80	
Bartholdi, Frederic Auguste	Artist	620	725	875	750	Statue of Liberty Print S $1395
Bartholomew, Freddie	Entertainment	20	25	35	75	
Bartle, Joyce	Entertainment	5	6	10	10	
Bartlett, Bonnie	Entertainment	5	6	10	10	
Bartlett, Joseph Jackson	Civil War	45	110			Union Gen.
Bartlett, Josiah	Revolutionary War	225	595	1240		Signer Decl. of Indepen.
Bartlett, Paul Wayland	Artist	10	15	30		US Sculptor
Bartlett, Robert Abram	Explorer	50	175	275		Cmdr. Ship on Peary Arctic Exp.
Bartlett, Thomas	Clergy	15	20	35		
Bartlett, William F.	Civil War	45	80	170		Union Gen.
Bartoe, John David	Astronaut	7	20		30	
Bartok, Bela	Composer	475	675	1950	650	
Barton, Bruce	Business	10	30	40	20	Advertising Exec.. BBD&O
Barton, Clara	Humanitarian	155	560	1050	390	Founder Am. Red Cross
Barton, Derek H. R., Sir	Science	20	30	40	30	Nobel Chemistry
Barton, James	Entertainment	40			125	
Barton, Seth Maxwell	Civil War	75	205	380		CSA Gen.
Bartow, Francis Stebbins	Civil War	70		135		CSA Congress
Barty, Billy	Entertainment	6	10	20	15	
Baruch, Bernard M.	Statesman	40	150	225	135	Financier, Pres. Advisor
Baryshnikov, Mikail	Entertainment	65	85	130	150	Ballet
Barzun, Jacques	Author	7	12	25	15	
Basehart, Richard	Entertainment	6	10	20	15	
Basie, Wm. 'Count'	Composer	70	200		150	Big Band Leader-Pianist
Basinger, Kim	Entertainment	20	25	40	45	
Baskett, James	Entertainment	200			600	
Basov, Nickolay	Science	20	45		30	Rus. Nobel Physicist
Bassett, Angela	Entertainment	10			35	Singer
Bassett, Charles A.	Astronaut	40			65	
Bassett, Leslie	Composer	15	30	65		Pulitzer,AMusQS $100
Bassett, Richard	Revolutionary War	375	800			Signer Constitution
Bassi, Amedeo	Entertainment	35			150	Favorite Tenor of Toscanini
Bate, William Brimage	Civil War-Senate	45	150			CSA General-Also Gov. Tenn.
Bateman, Jason	Entertainment	15			25	
Bateman, Justine	Entertainment	15	15	25	30	
Bates, "Peg-Leg"	Entertainment	10			18	Dancer
Bates, Alan	Entertainment	5			20	
Bates, Arthur Laban	Senate/Congress	5	10		20	Congressman PA
Bates, Blanche	Entertainment	15	25	40	45	
Bates, Edward	Cabinet	35	125	250	450	Lincoln Att'y Gen.
Bates, John C.	Civil War	25		110		Union General
Bates, Katharine Lee	Author	50		300	125	AMsS"Am.The Beautiful" $6,500
Bates, Kathy	Entertainment	15			55	
Bates, Sanford	Law Enforcement	10	35			Commissioner of Prisons
Bates. Florence	Entertainment	10			25	
Bathurst, Henry	Clergy	15	25	40	30	
Batista, Fulgencio	Head of State	25	85	195	175	Dictator Cuba
Batiuk, Tom*	Cartoonist	5			25	Funky Winkerbean
Battaglia, Franco	Entertainment	15			50	Opera, Concert
Batten, Hugh	Aviation	10	25	40	30	Navy ACE, WW II

NAME	CATEGORY	SIG	LS/DS	ALS	SP	COMMENT
Batten, Jean	Aviation	30	75			Pioneer Aviatrix
Battle, Cullen Andrews	Civil War	200	405			CSA Gen.
Battle, Kathleen	Entertainment	20			50	Opera, Concert
Batz, Willhelm	Aviation	35			95	Ger. ACE, #7 Worldwide
Baucus, Bob	Aviation	10	20	35	25	
Baudelaire, Charles-Pierre	Author	300	1000	1950		Fr. Modernist Poet
Baudouin, King (Belg)	Royalty	35	100	250	125	King of Belgium
Baudry, Patrick	Astronaut	12	25		25	
Bauduc, Ray	Entertainment	10			25	Big Band Bassist
Bauer, Harold	Entertainment	45	80			Pianist
Bauer, Jaime Lyn	Entertainment	6	8	10	15	
Bauer, Steven	Entertainment	6	8	15	20	
Baulieu, Etienne	Science	20		45	40	Inventor RU486 Abortion Pill
Baum, L. Frank	Author	500	925	1175		The Wizard of Oz books
Baum, William W., Cardinal	Clergy	35	55	70	50	
Baumer, Steven	Entertainment	10	15	20	25	
Baur, Hans	Aviation	20	45	90	125	Hitler's Pilot
Bavier, Frances	Entertainment	55	60	95	150	
Baxley, Barbara	Entertainment	4	4	10	10	
Baxter, Anne	Entertainment	15	20	40	40	
Baxter, Henry	Civil War	35	95	160		Union Gen.
Baxter, James P. III	Author	5	15	30	10	
Baxter, Keith	Entertainment	3	3	6	10	
Baxter, Percival P.	Governor	12		25		Governor ME
Baxter, Warner	Entertainment	45	50		85	
Baxter-Birney, Meridith	Entertainment	6	8	15	20	
Bayard, George Dashiell	Civil War	45	170	290		Union Gen., ALS Wardte $675
Bayard, John	Revolutionary War	40	160	185		Continental Congress
Bayard, Richard Henry	Senate	20	40	85		Senator DE
Bayard, Thomas F., Sr.	Cabinet	15	35	80		Sec'y State, Senator DE
Bayard, William	Revolutionary War	85	220	450		
Bayh, Birch	Senate	10	25		20	Senator IN
Bayne, Barbara	Entertainment	20			55	
Bayne, Beverly	Entertainment	9	10	20	20	
Beach Boys (all)	Entertainment	200			450	
Beach, Amy M.	Composer	45		500		Pianist-Composer AMQS $75
Beach, Rex	Author	20	35	95	35	
Beacham, Stephanie	Entertainment	5	6	10	10	
Beadle, George Wells, Dr.	Science	20	30	45	40	Nobel Medicine
Beakley, Wallace M.	Military	5	15	25		
Beal, George Lafayette	Civil War	42	112	135	270	Union Gen.
Beal, John	Entertainment	10	15	25	25	
Beale, Richard Lee Turberville	Civil War	52	105	225		CSA Gen.
Beall, William N.R.	Civil War	175			700	CSA General
Beals, Jennifer	Entertainment	20	20	40	45	
Bean, Alan L.	Astronaut	15			95	Moonwalker Astro.
Bean, Roy, Judge	Frontier Judge	3950	4500			"The Law West of the Pecos"
Beane, Hilary	Entertainment	5	10	15	10	
Beard, Charles A.	Author	5	20	55		Am. Historian
Beard, Daniel	Author	25		105	55	Founder Boy Scouts of America
Beard. "Stymie"	Entertainment	75			175	
Bearden, Romare*	Artist	20			200	Am. Artist
Beardslee, Lester Anthony	Military	20		100		Admiral Spanish American War
Beardsley, Aubrey	Artist	175	375	675		Am. Illustrator. Art Nouveau
Beatles (all four)	Entertainment	2700			3050	
Beaton, Cecil	Photographer	35	150	190	195	Br.Portrait,Theatrical Designer

NAME	CATEGORY	SIG	LS/DS	ALS	SP	COMMENT
Beatrice, Princess	Royalty	20	125	115	120	Youngest Daughter Q. Victoria
Beatrix, Queen	Royalty	100		450		Netherlands
Beatty, Clyde	Business-Circus	40	95	175	150	
Beatty, David, Adm.	Military	30	78	115	100	
Beatty, Ned	Entertainment	7	10	15	12	
Beatty, Samuel	Civil War	25	45	70		Union Gen.
Beatty, Warren	Entertainment	30	40	65	85	
Beatty. John	Civil War	27	55	80		Union General
Beauharnais, Eugene de	Royalty	45	115	430		Stepson of Napoleon I
Beauharnais, Hortense de	Royalty	50		500		Wife of Louis Bonaparte
Beaumont, Hugh	Entertainment	75			150	
Beauregard, P.G.T.	Civil War	295	835	1025	2250	CSA Gen.,War Dte. ALS $15,000
Beauvoir, Simone de	Author	25	60	125		Fr. Novelist. Existentialist
Beaux, Cecilia	Artist	20	60			Am. Portrait Painter
Beaver, James A.	Civil War-Gov.	30	55	110		Union Gen., Gov. PA
Beaverbrook, Max, Lord						SEE MAXWELL. WM.
Beavers, Louise	Entertainment	60			150	
Bechet, Sidney	Entertainment	125	275		175	Jazz Clarinetist-Saxaphonist
Bechi, Gino	Entertainment	25			55	Opera
Beck, C.C*	Cartoonist	10			100	Captain Marvel
Beck, Dave	Labor Leader	20	35	50	30	Sent to Prison for Union Fraud
Beck, Jeff	Entertainment	35			75	Rock
Beck, John	Entertainment	3	3	6	8	
Becker, Barbara	Entertainment	3	3	6	8	
Beckett, Samuel	Author	155	185	475		Nobel Lit."Waiting for Godot"
Beckwith, Edward G.	Civil War	45				Union General
Beckwith, J. Carroll	Artist	35	80	145		
Becquerel, Henri	Science	175	450	520		Nobel Curies' Radioactivity
Beddoe, Don	Entertainment	8			20	
Bedelia, Bonnie	Entertainment	3	4	10	10	
Bedford, Gunning, Jr.	Revolutionary War	285	700			Signer of Constitution. Scarce
Bedford, Gunning, Sr.	Revolutionary War	175	325			Cousin of above, Scarce
Bee Gees (3)	Entertainment	35			85	
Bee, Barnard E.	Civil War	275	725	2075		CSA Gen., Sec'y War Rep. Texas
Bee, Carlos	Senate/Congress	10	20		20	Congressman TX
Bee, Hamilton Prioleau	Civil War	290				CSA Gen.
Bee, Molly	Country Music	6			20	
Beebe, Charles William	Explorer	25	60	125	40	Invented Bathysphere.Naturalist
Beebe, Marshall	Aviation	18	35	55	42	ACE, WW II
Beech, Olive Ann	Aviation	20	45		50	Beechcraft Airplane Mfg.
Beecher, Henry Ward	Clergy	60	120	185	100	Abolition, Temperance Activist
Beecher, Lyman	Clergy	40	55	65	45	Early Anti Slavery
Beems, Patricia	Entertainment	3	3	6	8	
Beene, Geoffrey	Business	10	25		25	Fashion Designer
Beerbohm, Max	Author	55	135	220	65	Humorist, Caricaturist
Beery, Noah	Entertainment	55	60	250	175	
Beery, Noah Jr.	Entertainment	15	20	25	35	
Beery, Wallace	Entertainment	95	130	350	300	
Beeson, Jack	Composer	15	35	95	20	
Beethoven, Ludwig van	Composer	4900	19250	25000		ALS/Content $35,000
Begin, Menachem	Head of State	90	200	245	150	Prime Minister Israel
Begley, Ed, Jr.	Entertainment	4	7	9	15	
Begley, Ed, Sr.	Entertainment	25	45	70	75	
Behan, Brendan F.	Author	160	400	645		Ir. Author-Playwright
Behrman, S. N.	Author	15	25	60	25	Am. Playwright, Screenplays
Beiderbecke, Bix	Entertainment	5000				Jazz Musician, Big Band Leader

NAME	CATEGORY	SIG	LS/DS	ALS	SP	COMMENT
Beinhorn, Elly	Aviation	10	22	40	30	
Beith, Ian Hay (John)	Author	10	30	60	20	Br. Novelist, Playwright
Beke, Charles Tilstone	Explorer	20	50	125		Br. Geographer. Nile Source
Bekins, Milo	Business	35	45	160	125	Bekins Van & Storage Co.
Bel Geddes, Norman	Artist	20	50	155	35	Scenic Designer Theater
Belafonte, Harry	Entertainment	10	15		30	
Belafonte, Shari	Entertainment	5	6	15	20	
Belasco, David	Entertainment	22	30	55	65	Theatrical Producer
Belaunde, Fernando T.	Head of State	10	20	50	25	
Belcher, Edward, Sir	Military-Navy	15	35	60		Arctic Exped.for J. Franklin
Belcher, Jonathan	Colonial America	205	325	650		Colonial Gov. MA, NH, NJ
Belita	Entertainment	15	25	45	45	
Belknap, George	Civil War	15		50		Union Naval Officer
Belknap, William W.	Civil War,Cabinet	50	160	175		Union General, Sec'y War
Bell, Alexander Graham	Science	525	1150	2125	2375	Inventor of Telephone
Bell, Charles H.	Civil War	50	95	140		Union Naval Captain
Bell, Digby	Entertainment	12			20	Vintage Actor
Bell, Eric Temple (John Taine)	Author	30		130	55	Scot., Math Books, Sci-Fi
Bell, Griffin	Cabinet	10			25	Att'y General
Bell, Henry H.	Civil War	60	150			Rear Adm under Farragut
Bell, Herbert A.	Business	15	20	75	50	
Bell, John	Cabinet	95	145			W.H. Harrison, Tyler Sec'y War
Bell, Lauralee	Entertainment	4			7	Soaps
Bell, Rex	Entertainment	50			125	
Bell, Terrel H.	Cabinet	5	15	26	15	Sec'y Education
Bell, Tyree Harris	Civil War	55	130	215		CSA Gen.
Bellamy, Edward	Author	25	75	150		Novelist
Bellamy, Elizabeth W.	Author	3	9	18		
Bellamy, Madge	Entertainment	10	15	40	35	
Bellamy, Ralph	Entertainment	10	15	25	25	
Bellanca, Giuseppe M.	Aviation	40	85	160	125	Bellanca Aircraft Designer-Mfg.
Beller, Kathleen	Entertainment	6	8	15	15	
Belleri, Marguerite	Entertainment	5		30	25	Metropolitan Opera 1917-20
Bellew, John Chippendall	Clergy	10	20	25	20	
Belli, Melvin	Law	10	15	35	20	Trial Attorney
Belliard, Augustin D. (Count)	Military	25	55	125		Fr. Gen. under Napoleon
Bellincioni, Gemma	Entertainment	35		150	100	It. Soprano
Bellini, Vincenzo	Composer	575		4050		It. Opera
Bellmer, Hans	Artist	55	160	350		Ger. Surrealist
Bellmon, Henry Louis	Senate	15	20		20	Senator OK, Gov. OK
Belloc, Hilaire	Author	25	75	150	50	Versatile Novelist, Poet,Critic
Belloc-Lowndes, Marie	Author	15	40	95	30	Author of Historical Works
Bellon, Leoncadia	Entertainment	16			45	Opera, Film
Bellonte, Maurice	Aviation	75	145	270	205	
Bellow, Saul	Author	20	35	85	35	Nobel Literature. Novelist
Bellows, George	Artist	95	225	635		Urban Scenes, Sports, Landscape
Bellson, Louis	Entertainment	25		55	70	Jazz Drummer
Bellwood, Pamela	Entertainment	6	8	15	15	
Belmont, August	Business	55	75	210	125	Banker, Diplomat
Belmont, August, Jr.	Business	45	120			
Belmont, August, Mrs.	Socialite	15	25	40		
Belsham, Thomas	Clergy	15	20	35	30	
Belushi, James	Entertainment	10	15	20	25	
Belushi, John	Entertainment	• 250			750	
Bemelmans, Ludwig	Author	45	105	255	50	Writer-Illustrator. Novelist
Ben-Gurion, David	Head of State	175	1050	1155	350	1st Prime Minister of Israel

NAME	CATEGORY	SIG	LS/DS	ALS	SP	COMMENT
Ben-Yehuda, Eliezer	Author	35	175	425		Jewish Scholar
Ben-Zvi, Itzhak	Head of State	75	185	225	80	2nd President Israel
Benacerraf, Baruj	Science	27	55		40	Nobel Medicine-Physiology
Benatar, Pat	Entertainment	20			70	
Benavidez, Roy	Military	10	25	40	20	
Benchley, Peter	Author	15	25	50	20	Sketch of "Jaws" S $15-$35
Benchley, Robert	Author	45	80	195	75	Am. Drama Critic, Humorist
Bendix, William	Entertainment	25	30	60	160	
Benederet, Bea	Entertainment	40			100	
Benedict XV. Pope	Head of State	125		450	550	
Benedict, Dick	Entertainment	9	10	20	30	
Benedict, Julius, Sir	Composer	15			25	Br. Pianist
Benedict, William	Entertainment	25			60	
Beneke, Tex	Entertainment	30			125	Sax for Glenn Miller. Big Band
Benes, Eduard	Head of State	75	90	145	200	Prime Minister, Czech.
Benet, Stephen Vincent	Author	80	140	155	150	Poet, Novelist. Pulitzer (2)
Benet, William Rose	Author	15	35	50	40	Poet, Editor. Pulitzer
Benham, Henry Washington	Civil War	35	50	135		Union General
Bening, Annette	Entertainment	10			55	
Benjamin, Judah P.	Civil War	300	885	1080		CSA Gen. & Sec'y of State
Benjamin, William, Jr.	Supreme Court	40			60	
Bennett, Arnold	Author	40	175			Br. Novelist
Bennett, Bruce	Entertainment	10	12	20	35	
Bennett, Constance	Entertainment	30	60	120	65	
Bennett, Floyd	Aviation	300	370	750	500	Pilot with Byrd over North Pole
Bennett, James Gordon	Publisher	45	195			Financed Stanley-Livingstone
Bennett, Joan	Entertainment	15	15	25	45	
Bennett, Johnstone	Entertainment	15			35	Actress with Mansfield
Bennett, Julie	Entertainment	3	3	6	10	
Bennett, Richard	Entertainment	15			35	Stage & Silent Films
Bennett, Samuel F.	Composer	30	75	150		"In the Sweet Bye & Bye"
Bennett, Spencer Gordon	Entertainment	10			25	
Bennett, Tony	Entertainment	5	10	20	30	
Bennett, Wallace F.	Senate	5	10	20	15	Senator UT
Bennett, William J.	Author-Cabinet	10	20	25	25	"Book of Virtues".Sec'y Ed.
Bennett, Wm. Andrew	Head of State	4	10	15	10	
Benning, Henry Lewis	Civil War	145	275	350		CSA Gen.
Benny, Jack	Entertainment	60	200		140	
Benois, Alexander	Artist	45	195	425		Rus. Designed Sets, Costumes
Benson, Edward Frederic	Author	15	35	75		Satirical, Macabre Novels
Benson, Edward W., Archbishop	Clergy	20	35	55	35	
Benson, Egbert	Revolutionary War	35	75	160		Continental Congress
Benson, Elmer A.	Governor	5	12	20	15	Governor & Senator MN
Benson, Ezra Taft	Cabinet	15	25	55	25	Sec'y Agriculture
Benson, Frank Robert, Sir	Entertainment	15	20	35	20	Vintage Br. Actor
Benson, George	Entertainment	15			25	
Benson, Jodi	Entertainment	10			35	
Benson, Richard Meux	Clergy	35	55	65	75	
Benson, Robbie	Entertainment	5	6	15	15	
Benson, William S.	Military	10	20	35	25	Adm. USN WW I
Bent, James Theodore	Explorer	5	10	25	10	Archaeologist
Benteen, Frederick W.	Civil War		3500		2500	
Benton, Barbi	Entertainment	5	6	15	15	
Benton, Robert	Entertainment	6			20	Film Director
Benton, Samuel	Civil War	345	540			CSA Gen.
Benton, Thomas Hart	Artist	150	250	875		ALS/Content $1,350

NAME	CATEGORY	SIG	LS/DS	ALS	SP	COMMENT
Benton, Thomas Hart 1782-1858	Senate/Congress	50	95	205		30-Year Senator From Missouri
Benton, William	Senate	10	30	65	20	Publisher, Statesman, Sen. CT
Benton, William Plummer	Civil War	95	130			Union Gen.
Bentsen, Lloyd	Senate-Cabinet	10	30		25	Senator TX, Sec'y Treas.
Benzell, Mimi	Entertainment	15			35	Opera
Berdyaev, Nikolai	Clergy	75	100	130	175	
Berenson, Marisa	Entertainment	9	10	15	25	
Berenstain, Stan*	Cartoonist	20			75	Berenstain Bear
Beresford, Charles, Lord	Military	15	35	100	75	Br. Admiral
Berfson, Henri-Louis	Author	30	80	155		
Berg, Alban	Composer	135	485	1425		Atonal Music. Orchestral, Songs
Berg, Gertrude	Entertainment	12	15	20	30	
Berg, Paul	Science	27	35	65	30	Nobel Chemistry
Berganza, Teresa	Entertainment	10			35	Opera
Bergen, Candice	Entertainment	10	15	25	35	
Bergen, Edgar	Entertainment	55	80	125	85	
Bergen, Frances	Entertainment	5	6	10	10	
Bergen, Polly	Entertainment	6	8	15	15	And Cosmetics Mfg.
Berger, Erna	Entertainment	10			30	Opera
Berger, Gottlob	Military	40	120	200	75	
Berger, Senta	Entertainment	15	15	35	30	
Bergere, Lee	Entertainment	4	4	9	10	
Bergeron, Marion	Beauty Queen	15			75	Miss America 1934
Bergh, Henry	Reformer	70		400		Founder ASPCA
Bergland, Bob	Cabinet	4	10	20	15	Sec'y Agriculture, Congress MN
Bergman, Ingmar	Entertainment	35	40	50	75	
Bergman, Ingrid	Entertainment	100	150	260	375	
Bergman, Sandahl	Entertainment	6	8	15	20	
Bergner, Elizabeth	Entertainment	20	35	60	30	
Bergonzi, Carlo	Entertainment	30			65	Opera
Berio, Luciano	Composer	20	30	75		
Berkeley, Busby	Entertainment	100	155	300	295	Dance Choreographer-Director
Berkowitz, David	Criminal	175	195	250		Son of Sam,Serial Murderer
Berle, Milton	Entertainment	15	15	25	35	
Berlier, Jean Baptiste	Science	15	27	45		Fr.Engineer. Undergr. RR System
Berlier, Theophile, Count	Fr. Revolution	50	150	295		
Berlik, Jan	Entertainment	25			50	Czech. Operatic Tenor
Berlin, Irving	Composer	230	1060	1420	1100	AMusQS $2,300
Berlioz, Hector	Composer	245	785	2190		AMusQS $3,900
Berlitz, Charles	Business	16	20		35	Language Educator
Berman, Eugene	Artist	40	105	185		Rus.-Born Painter-Designer
Berman, Pandro S.	Entertainment	5	10		15	Film Producer
Berman, Shelley	Entertainment	3	3	6	8	
Bernadotte, Jean-Baptiste	Royalty	120	420	650		Charles XIV John
Bernard, Claude	Science	145		975		Fr. Fndr. Experimental Medicine
Bernard, Crystal	Entertainment	10			45	"Wings"
Bernard, Francis, Sir	Colonial Governor	175	590	650		Col.Gov. Mass. Bay Colony
Bernard, John Henry, Archbishop	Clergy	30	45	50	40	
Bernard, Simon	Civil War	45	115			Fr. Engineer, Nap.& US Gen.
Berndt, Walter*	Cartoonist	10			50	Smitty
Bernhard, Sandra	Entertainment	4	6		10	Comedienne
Bernhardt, Sarah	Entertainment	135	275	375	525	"The Divine Sarah"
Bernie, Ben	Entertainment	20		25	25	Big Band Leader
Bernsen, Corbin	Entertainment	18	20	45	40	
Bernstein, Elmer	Composer	15	25	45	20	
Bernstein, Leonard	Composer	200	350	525	255	AMusMsS $1,600, $4,500

NAME	CATEGORY	SIG	LS/DS	ALS	SP	COMMENT
Berosini, Josephine	Entertainment	5	10	20	30	
Berrien, J. Macpherson	Cabinet	20	55	95		Jackson Att'y General
Berrigan, Daniel, Fr.	Clergy	15	30	65	25	
Berry, Chuck	Entertainment	50			155	
Berry, Halle	Entertainment	15			50	
Berry, Hiram G.	Civil War	325	680			Union Gen.
Berry, Ken	Entertainment	5	6	15	15	
Berry, Lucien	Military	15	50			General WW I
Berry, Sidney M.	Clergy	10	15	25		
Berryman, Clifford	Artist	55	75	95		The "Teddy Bear"
Bertelson, Richard L.	Aviation	10	22	38	28	Navy ACE, WW II
Berthier, L. Alexandre	Napoleonic Wars	75	210	425		Marshal of Napoleon
Berthold, Rudolf	Aviation	200	350	650	450	ACE, WW I, The Iron Knight
Berthollet, Claude-Louis, Count	Science	60	150	330		Fr. Chemist.Senator of Napoleon
Bertinelli, Valerie	Entertainment	6	8	15	20	
Bertolucci, Bernardo	Entertainment	15			35	Film Director
Berwick, Duke (J.Fitzjames)	Fr. Military	150	400			Gen. of Louis XIV, Marshal Fr.
Berzelius, Jons Jacob	Science	70	165	475		Swe. Chemist. Chemical Symbols
Besant, Annie Wood	Clergy	50	115	300		Radical Free-Thinker
Besant, Walter	Author	35	125	195		
Besch, Bibi	Entertainment	3	4	8	8	
Beser, Jacob	Aviation	50	100		100	Both Atomic Missions
Bess, Gordon	Cartoonist	5			25	Redeye
Bessemer, Henry, Sir	Metallurgist	35	60	150	90	Inventor "Blast Furnace".Steel
Besser, Joe	Entertainment	10	10	20	15	
Bessieres, Bertrand	Fr. Revolution	55	100			
Bessieres, Jean-Baptiste	Fr. Military	175	475			Marshal of Napoleon
Best, Charles H.	Science	125	225	310		Discovered Insulin/Banting
Best, Edna	Entertainment	15	15	30	45	
Best, James	Entertainment	5	6	15	15	
Best, Pete	Entertainment	40			150	Pre Ringo. Beatles Drummer
Best, Willie	Entertainment	50			150	Vintage Afro-Am. Film Actor
Beswick, Martine	Entertainment	5	6	15	10	
Betham-Edwards, Matilda	Author	5	10	22		
Bethe, Hans, Dr.	Science	35	55		45	Nobel Physics
Bethune, Mary McLeod	Clergy	125	325	500	175	
Betjeman, John, Sir	Author	40	85	125	50	Br. Poet Laureate
Bettelheim, Bruno	Science	35	65		150	Psychiatrist researched Autism
Bettger, Lyle	Entertainment	7			20	
Betz, Carl	Entertainment	40			75	
Beugnot, J.C., Count	Fr. Military	85	160			
Beverage, John	Civil War	30	85			Union Gen., Gov. IL
Bevin, Ernest	Statesman	25	55	125	45	Br. Powerful Union Leader
Bewick, Thomas	Artist	105	275	425		Br. Illustrator, Wood Engraver
Bey, Turhan	Entertainment	15	19	35	35	
Bhutto, Zullikar Ali	Head of State	20			90	Pres. Pakistan, Prime Minister
Biaggi, Mario	Senate/Congress	5	15		10	Congressman NY. NY Police MOH
Bialik, Chaim	Author	65	225	425	80	Jewish Poet
Biasini, Piero	Entertainment	10			35	Opera
Bibb, George M.	Cabinet	20	45	80		Early Sec'y Treas.,Senator KY
Bickersteth, Edward H., Bishop	Clergy	15	25	35	35	
Bickford, Charles	Entertainment	30	45	65	100	
Biddle, Clement	Revolutionary War	225	875			Revolutionary Officer, Merchant
Biddle, Francis	Cabinet	20	35	75		Att'y General
Biddle, George	Artist	26	85	210		
Biddle, Nicholas 1786-1844	Business	125	375	550		Pres. U.S. Bank, Financier

NAME	CATEGORY	SIG	LS/DS	ALS	SP	COMMENT
Biden, Joe	Senate/Congress	5	15		20	Senator DE
Bidwell, John	Western Pioneer	20	100			Calif. Pioneer, Pres. Candidate
Biehn, Michael	Entertainment	9	10	20	25	
Bierce, Ambrose	Author	285	670	870		Journalist, Short Stories
Bieri, Ramon	Entertainment	10			35	
Bierstadt, Albert	Artist	125	220	540		Of the Hudson River School
Biery, James S.	Senate/Congress	10	15		25	Congressman PA
Bigard, Barney	Entertainment	70			150	Jazz Clarinet, Ten. Sax
Bigelow, Erastus B.	Business-Inventor	100	290	595		Power Looms for Carpet Weaving
Bigelow, John	Publisher	5	10	25	15	Editor NY Evening Post
Bigge, Arthur, Sir	Military	10	30	65		
Biggers, Earl Derr	Author	150	210	365	350	Am. Novelist, Mystery Writer
Biggs, Asa	Civil War	25	60			CSA Judge, US Senator NC
Biggs, Ronnie	Criminal	25			95	Train Robber
Bikel, Theodore	Entertainment	5			15	
Bilbo, Theodore G.	Senate	20	30		25	Senator MS, Gov. MS
Bill, Max	Celebrity	8	20	40	15	
Bill, Tony	Entertainment	5			20	Actor, Film Director
Billings, Josh (H.W.Shaw)	Author	25	80	165	40	American Humorist
Billingsley, Barbara	Entertainment	3	3	6	10	
Billo, James D.	Aviation	10	22	38	28	Navy ACE, WW II
Billroth, Theodor 1829-94	Science	45	225	295		Ger. Surgeon. Use of Antisepsis
Binci, Mario	Entertainment	15			45	Opera
Bing, Herman	Entertainment	20			40	
Bing, Rudolph	Entertainment	15	20	35	35	Metropolitan Opera Leader
Bingham, Amelia	Entertainment	6	8	15	25	
Bingham, Henry	Civil War	85		160		Union Gen., CMH Wilderness
Bingham, John A.	Congress	20	35	90		Repr. OH, Lincoln Judge Adv.
Bingham, Judson David	Civil War	45	140	185		Union General
Bingham, William	Revolutionary War	120	315	340		Continental Congr. Senator PA
Binney, Thomas	Clergy	20	30	45	35	
Binnig, Gerd, Dr.	Science	20	60		45	Nobel Physics
Binns, Edward	Entertainment	4	4	9	9	
Bird, Jerry	Country Music	10			20	
Birdseye, Clarence	Business	100	340	550	150	Birdseye Frozen Foods
Birdwood, William, Sir	Military	45	145			Br. Fld. Marshal, WW I
Birendra, Bir B.	Head of State	10	15		20	Prime Minister Nepal
Birney, David	Entertainment	5	6	15	10	
Birney, David Bell	Civil War	225		775		Union General
Birney, William	Civil War	35	70	90		Union General
Bisbee, Horatio, Jr.	Civil War	25	45	105		Union Officer & MOC
Bishop, Barry	Celebrity	7	14			
Bishop, J. Michael, Dr.	Science	25	40		35	Nobel Medicine
Bishop, Jim	Author	15	35	45	20	Journalist. Best Selling Novels
Bishop, Joey	Entertainment	3	3	6	10	
Bishop, Julie	Entertainment	6	8	15	15	
Bishop, Stephen	Entertainment	4			10	Rock Star
Bishop, Wm. 'Billy'	Aviation	150	225	300	220	ACE, WW I, 72 Kills
Bismark, Prince Otto von	Royalty	250	550	745	950	"The Iron Chancellor"
Bispham, David	Entertainment	60	80	110	120	Opera
Bissell, Clayton L.	Aviation	25	40	100		
Bissell, Whit	Entertainment	7		15	18	
Bissell, William H.	Governor	10	28	60		Governor IL, MOC
Bisset, Jacqueline	Entertainment	15	20	30	35	
Bissit, J.E.	Br. Navy	10	25		15	Commander HMS Queen Eliz.
Bitter, Karl Theodore	Artist	25	75	155	100	Am. Sculptor

NAME	CATEGORY	SIG	LS/DS	ALS	SP	COMMENT
Bittrich, Wilhelm	Military	27	70	135	60	
Bixby, Bill	Entertainment	5	10	25	30	
Bizet, Georges	Composer	350	890	2100		"Carmen", L'Arlesienne Suite
Bjoerling, Jussi	Entertainment	500	650	1000	1100	
Bjornsen, Bjornstierne	Author	40	55	140		Nobel Literature
Bjornstad, Alfred	Military	10	20	35		General WW I
Black, Alexander	Author	5	10	20	5	
Black, Clint	Country-Western	20			50	
Black, Eugene R.	Business	5	20	30	15	
Black, Hugo (SC)	Supreme Court	55	120	285	95	
Black, Jeremiah	Cabinet	25	60	115		Att'y General (Buchanan)
Black, John Charles	Civil War	50	126	155		Union General, MOH
Black, Karen	Entertainment	6	8	15	18	
Black, Richard B.	Military	10	25	45		
Black, William	Military	20			45	General WW I
Blackburn, John T.	Aviation	12	24	38	30	ACE, WW II
Blackburn, Luke P.	Governor	15	35			Governor KY
Blackett, Patrick M.	Science	20	35	50	30	Nobel Physics. Cosmic Rays
Blackman, Honor	Entertainment	10	15	25	25	
Blackmer, Sidney	Entertainment	10	15	20	35	
Blackmon, Fred L.	Senate/Congress	10	20		15	MOC AL
Blackmore, Richard D.	Author	15	40	95		Br. Novelist. "Lorna Doone"
Blackmun, Harry A. (SC)	Supreme Court	40	105	270	75	
Blackstone, Harry	Entertainment	150	375	475	175	Self Sketch Signed $375
Blackstone, Harry, Jr	Entertainment	5	5	10	10	Magician
Blackwell, Alice Stone	Reformer	60		95		Woman's Suffrage
Blackwell, Mr.	Business	8	10		20	Fashion Critic
Blackwell, Otis	Composer	25	85	175		
Blaha, John E.	Astronaut	5	10		15	
Blaine, James G.	Cabinet	30	65	180	45	U.S.Sen. ME,Garfield Sec'y St.
Blaine, Vivian	Entertainment	5	6	15	25	
Blair, Charles	Aviation	45			60	
Blair, Francis P., Jr.	Civil War	45	80	145		Union General, U.S.Sen. MO
Blair, Frank	Entertainment	3	3	6	6	Radio-TV News
Blair, Janet	Entertainment	9	10	20	20	
Blair, John (SC)	Supreme Court	150	775	1200		Signer of Constitution
Blair, Linda	Entertainment	5	10	20	20	
Blair, Montgomery	Legal	75	205	545		Counsel to Dred Scott
Blake, Amanda	Entertainment	55	65	115	175	
Blake, Bud*	Cartoonist	4			25	Tiger
Blake, Eubie	Composer	60	105	175	125	AMusQS $385-$650
Blake, Eugene Carson	Clergy	50	95	150	70	
Blake, Madge	Entertainment	100			250	
Blake, Robert	Entertainment	6	10	10	15	
Blake, William	Artist					Content ALS $30,000
Blakely, Susan	Entertainment	6	8	15	20	
Blakeslee, Don	Aviation	10	25	38	30	ACE, WW II
Blanc, Louis	Author	12	25	45		Fr. Socialist, Journalist
Blanc, Mel	Entertainment	55	85	110	150	
Blanchard, Albert G.	Civil War	140	198			CSA Gen.
Blanchard, Nina	Entertainment	4			8	
Bland, Schuyler Otis	Senate/Congress	5	15	25		MOC VA
Bland, William T.	Senate/Congress	5	15	20		MOC MO
Blandick, Clara	Entertainment	200			650	
Blane, Sally	Entertainment	6	8	15	15	
Blanks, Mary Lynn	Entertainment	3	3	6	6	

NAME	CATEGORY	SIG	LS/DS	ALS	SP	COMMENT
Blanton, Leonard Ray	Governor	10			15	Governor TN, MOC TN
Blanton, Thomas L.	Senate/Congress	10	20		20	Senator TX, MOC TX
Blaschka, Rudolph	Artist	10	35	75		Bohemian Artist in Glass
Blasco-Ibanez, Vicente	Author	100			450	Sp. Novelist. Self Exiled
Blaslev, Lisabeth	Entertainment	10			25	Opera
Blass, Bill	Business	5	15		25	Fashion Designer
Blatchford, Samuel (SC)	Supreme Court	45	135	190		
Blatty, William Peter	Author	15	30	45	20	Novelist. "The Exorcist"
Bledsoe, Tempest	Entertainment	15	35		35	
Blenker, Louis	Civil War	100	210			Union Gen
Blennerhassett, Harman	Revolutionary War	115	330	575		Funds, Refuge-Burr Conspiracy
Bleriot, Louis	Aviation	250	500	595	450	1st To Fly Englist Channel
Bless, Frederick	Aviation	10	22	38	32	ACE, Korea
Bletcher, Billy	Entertainment	50			200	
Bligh, William, Capt.	Military	650	1300	2500		Br. Adm. Capt. HMS "Bounty"
Bliss, Arthur, Sir	Composer	25		175		Brit. Opera, Orch. works
Bliss, Cornelius	Cabinet	10	25	55	40	Sec'y Interior
Bliss, George Jr.	Civil War	8	15	25		MOC OH
Bliss, J. S.	Civil War	5	10	20		
Bliss, Tasker H.	Military	15	25	50	25	US Gen.1st Cmdr. War College
Bliss, William Wallace S.	Military	130	435	500		Pvt. Sec'y Zachary Taylor
Bliss, Zenas R.	Civil War	35	110	160		Union Officer
Blitzstein, Marc	Composer	80		250		Opera
Blixen, Karen (Isak Dinesen)	Author	110	500		200	Danish Novelist "Out of Africa"
Bloch, Ernest	Composer	80		525	205	Swiss-Am. Composer
Bloch, Ernst	Author	55	140	425	90	Ger. Philosopher.
Bloch, Felix	Science	25	40	100	30	Nobel Physics
Bloch, Konrad, Dr.	Science	20	30	45	30	Nobel Medicine
Bloch, Raymond	Composer	10	20	35	10	
Bloch, Robert	Author	15	50	60	20	Novelist. TMsS $450
Block, Henry W.	Business	20	45		30	H & R Block
Block, Herb*	Cartoonist	15			100	Herblock-political
Block, John R.	Cabinet	5	10	15	10	
Block, Joseph L.	Business	4	6	9	6	
Block, Richard	Business	20	35	90	25	H & R Block
Blocker, Dan	Entertainment	200			550	
Blodget, Samuel Jr.	Revolutionary War	285	750	1540		Inventor, Soldier, Judge
Bloembergen, Nicolaas Dr.	Science	20	35	40	30	Nobel Physics
Blomberg, Werner Von	Military	30	75	165	125	Ger. Fld. Marshal WW II
Blomfield, Ezekial	Clergy	35	45	60		
Blondell, Joan	Entertainment	35	40	65	55	
Blondin, Charles	Entertainment	30	70	175	60	Tightrope walker Niagara Falls
Blood, Robert O.	Governor	5		25		Governor NH
Blood, Sweat and Tears	Entertainment	35			80	
Bloom, Claire	Entertainment	6	8	15	20	
Bloom, Lindsay	Entertainment	8	9	12	15	
Bloomfield, Joseph	Revolutionary War	30	95	157		Officer, Attorney, Gov. NJ
Bloomfield-Zeisler, Fannie	Entertainment	25			75	Concert Pianist
Blore, Eric	Entertainment	20	25	65	60	
Blossom Rock	Entertainment	40			75	
Blough, Roger	Business	5	15	25	15	
Blount, James H.	Civil War	25	40			CSA Officer, MOC GA
Blount, William	Senate	320	900			Continental Congr. Senator TN
Blount, Winton M.	Cabinet	5	15	25	10	P.M. General
Bloustein, Edward J.	Celebrity	5	12	20	10	
Blucher, Gebhard L. von	Military	200	550	2200		Pruss. Fld. Marshal vs Napoleon

NAME	CATEGORY	SIG	LS/DS	ALS	SP	COMMENT
Blue, Ben	Entertainment	22	30	60	50	
Blue, Monte	Entertainment	19	25	45	65	
Bluford, Guion S. Jr.	Astronaut	10			30	
Blum, Leon (Fr)	Head of State	25	40	110	35	Pres. France WW II
Blum, Norbert	Statesman	5			10	German Minister & Statesman
Blumberg, Baruch S.	Science	20	30	55	25	Nobel Medicine
Blumenthal, Jacques	Composer	40		250		And Pianist
Blumenthal, W. Michael	Cabinet	5	10	15	10	
Blunt, James G., Dr.	Civil War	46	75			Union General
Blunt, John Henry	Clergy	15	25	35	25	
Blyden, Larry	Entertainment	3	3	6	6	
Blyth, Ann	Entertainment	5	6	15	15	
Blythe, Betty	Entertainment	35			175	Silent Star
Boardman, Eleanor	Entertainment	10	15	25	25	Vintage Actress
Boardman, Russell	Aviation	25	55	95	80	
Bob & Ray	Entertainment	25			50	
Bobbitt, John Wayne	Media Celebrity	25			50	Victim of Angry Wife
Bobbitt, Lorena	Media Celebrity					Penis Slasher. NRPA
Bobkins, Addie	Entertainment	5	6	9	8	
Bobko, Karol J.	Astronaut	7			15	
Bochco, Steven	Entertainment	10	15		20	TV Emmy Award Producer
Bochner, Lloyd	Entertainment	4	4	9	15	
Bock, Feodor von	Military	100	295		150	Ger.Gen. WW II. Failed
Bock, Jerry	Composer	5	16	35	10	
Bodenschatz, Karl	Aviation	30	75	150	95	
Bodwell, Joseph R.	Governor	8	12		10	Gov. ME
Boe, Nils A.	Governor	10	15			Governor SD
Boesch, Ruthilde	Entertainment	5	10		20	Opera
Bogard, Dirk	Entertainment	10		30	25	
Bogart, Humphrey	Entertainment	1000		1750	2750	
Bogdonavich, Peter	Entertainment	10	30		15	Controversial Film Director
Boggs, Charles	Civil War	45	90	115		Union Adm.
Boggs, Hale	Senate/Congress	10	25			MOC LA
Boggs, Lindy (Mrs. H.Boggs)	Congress	10	15		15	MOC LA
Bohay, Heidi	Entertainment	5	6	15	10	
Bohr, Aage Niels	Science	225	835		400	Nobel Physics
Boisrond-Canal	Haitian Statesman	30	95			
Boito, Arrigo	Composer	45	110	325		& Verdi Librettist. AMusQS $750
Bok, Edward W.	Author-Business	30	55	140	40	Editor, Curtis Publishing
Bokor, Margit	Entertainment	10			30	Hung. Soprano
Boland, Frederick	Celebrity	5	15	40	10	
Boland, Mary	Entertainment	25	75		70	
Bolcom, William	Composer	15	25	65		Pulitzer, AMusQS $75
Bolden, Charles F. Jr.	Astronaut	5			18	
Boles, John	Entertainment	20	30	45	40	
Bolger, Ray	Entertainment	55	60	135	150	
Bolingbroke, Henry (St.John)	Author	30	150	250		1st Viscount, Politician,Writer
Bolivar, Simon	Head of State	385	3075	4975		Statesman, Revolutionary Leader
Boll, Heinrich	Author	20	30	95	25	Nobel Lit., Novelist, Poet
Bolling, Tiffany	Entertainment	3	3	6	15	
Bolt, John	Aviation	12	30	50	35	ACE, WW II & Korea
Bolton, Frances Payne	Senate/Congress	10	25			MOC OH
Bolton, Guy	Author	15	100			Playwright
Bolton, Michael	Entertainment	125			150	Singer, Composer
Bolton-Jones, Hugh	Artist	10	25	45		Am. Landscape Painter
Bombeck, Erma	Author	5	15	25	10	Humorous Columnist

NAME	CATEGORY	SIG	LS/DS	ALS	SP	COMMENT
Bomford, George	Military Engineer	65	195			Invented Howitzer Bomb Cannon
Bomford, James Voty	Civil War	37	80	116		
Bon Jovi, Jon	Entertainment	10			60	Rock
Bonaduce, Danny	Entertainment	10			25	
Bonaparte, Caroline	Royalty	35	95	275		Marie-Annonciade
Bonaparte, Elisa (Maria Ana)	Royalty	400		500		Oldest Sister of Napoeon
Bonaparte, Eugene Napoleon	Royalty	75	200	435		Adopted by Napoleon
Bonaparte, Jerome	Royalty	60	135	240		Brother of Napoleon
Bonaparte, Joseph	Royalty	120	290	350		Elder Brother of Napoleon
Bonaparte, Letizia	Royalty		1500	2700		Mother of Napoleon
Bonaparte, Louis Napoleon	Royalty					SEE Napoleon III
Bonaparte, Lucien	Royalty	50	105	165		Brother. Opposed Nap., Exiled
Bonaparte, Marie Louise	Royalty	195	815	2795		Wife of Napoleon
Bonaparte, Napoleon	Royalty					SEE Napoleon I
Bonar, Horatius	Clergy	15	20	25		
Bonci, Alessandro	Entertainment	35			115	Opera
Bond, Carrie Jacobs	Composer	35	110	170	45	Am. Composer Art Songs
Bond, Charles	Aviation	10	28	40	30	ACE, WW II, Flying Tigers
Bond, Christopher "Kit"	Senate	5	10		10	Senator MO
Bond, Johnny	Country Music	10			20	
Bond, Julian	Politician	10	20	50	15	Afro-Am. Activist. Poet
Bond, Tommy "Butch"	Entertainment	10			25	
Bond, Ward	Entertainment	75	80	95	200	
Bond, William C.	Science	45	190	350		Am. Astronomer. Harvard Observ.
Bondi, Beulah	Entertainment	15	15	30	38	
Bondur, Roberta	Astronaut	10			20	Canadian Astro
Boner, Edmond 1500-69	Clergy	650				Appealed to Pope for Henry VIII
Bonerz, Peter	Entertainment	3	3	6	6	
Bonesteel, Charles H.	Military	11	35	58		
Bong, Richard	Aviation	500	1200	2000	1800	ACE, WW II, Top U.S. Ace
Bonham, Joe 'Bonzo'	Entertainment	75			125	
Bonham, Milledge L.	Civil War	175	255	300		CSA General
Bonheur, Rosa	Artist	110	155	300		Fr. "Horse Fair" & Rural Scenes
Bonnard, Pierre	Artist	105	280	675		Fr. Postimpressionist
Bonneville, Benj. L. E.	Military	225	600	1200		Pioneer Explorer NW Territory
Bonney, Barbara	Entertainment	15			30	Opera
Bono, Sonny	Entertainment	10			20	Mayor Palm Springs
Bonstelle, Jessie	Entertainment	25		40		Stage Actress, Producer
Bontemps, Arna	Author	20	175			Am. Novels, Non-Fiction, Poetry
Bonvalot, Gabriel	Celebrity				155	
Book of Love (4)	Entertainment	20			40	Rock Group
Book, Sorrell	Entertainment	3	3	6	6	
Boone, Daniel	Revolutionary War	2000	9300	21500		Am. Pioneer Cumberland Gap
Boone, Debbie	Entertainment	5	20		25	
Boone, Pat	Entertainment	3	3	6	8	
Boone, Richard	Entertainment	75	80	95	150	
Boone, Squire	Revolutionary War			1150		NC Farmer. Father of Daniel
Boosler, Elayne	Entertainment	15		35	35	Comedienne
Booth, Adrian	Entertainment	5			20	
Booth, Ballington	Clergy	24	75	150		Co-Cmdr. Salvation Army
Booth, Bromwell	Clergy	25	50	75		
Booth, Edwin	Entertainment	100		300	275	
Booth, Evangeline	Reformer	35	115	360	90	Salvation Army
Booth, John Wilkes	Civil War	1550	3050	4000	4500	Assassin of Lincoln
Booth, Maude	Reformer	35	80	225		Fndr. Vols. of Am. & PTA
Booth, Newell S., Bishop	Clergy	20	35	50	50	

NAME	CATEGORY	SIG	LS/DS	ALS	SP	COMMENT
Booth, Newton	Senator	15	25	60		Governor CA, Senator CA
Booth, Shirley	Entertainment	20	25	35	45	
Booth, William	Clergy	125	160	350	150	Founder & Gen'l Salvation Army
Booth, William Bramwell	Clergy	40	75	100	65	Eldest Son & Organizer
Boothe, Powers	Entertainment	5	6	15	15	
Boozer, Brenda	Entertainment	4	5	10	10	
Bor, Tadeusz	Military	15	45	75		
Borah, William E.	Senate	20	30		45	Senator ID
Borch, F.J.	Business	4	10		10	Pres. General Electric
Borchers, Adolf	Aviation	10	15	30	25	
Bordaberry, Juan M	Head of State	7	15	25	10	Uraguay
Bordelon, Guy	Aviation	8	20	35	25	ACE, Korea
Borden, Lizzy	Celebrity			15000		Alleged Ax Murderess
Borden, Olive	Entertainment	30	35	45	150	
Bordoni, Irene	Entertainment	15	15	35	30	
Borge, Victor	Entertainment	5	7	15	10	
Borghese, Camillo	Head of State					SEE Paul V, Pope
Borgia, Francesco Card'l	Clergy	3200	2200			
Borglum, Gutzon	Artist	225	375	535	925	Creator Mt. Rushmore Sculptures
Borglum, Lincoln	Artist	25	60	85		Son of Gutzon. Sculptor
Borglum, Solon	Artist	15		45		
Borgnine, Ernest	Entertainment	5	10	12	20	
Bori, Lucrezia	Entertainment	30	95		100	Opera
Boring, Wayne*	Cartoonist	30			400	Superman
Boris III	Royalty	120			185	King & Dictator Bulgaria
Bork, Robert A.	Jurist	5	20		30	
Borlaug, Norman, Dr.	Science	20	35	80	30	Nobel Peace Prize
Borman, F. & Lovell, J.	Astronaut	35			75	Signed by Both
Borman, Frank	Astronaut	10			30	
Bormann, Martin	Military	350	1160	1500	850	Nazi Private Sec'y to Hitler
Born, Max	Science	175	350	500		Nobel, Ger. Physicist
Borne, Hermann von Dem.	Military	20	45	90		
Borno, Louis	Head of State	15	75			Pres. Haiti
Borodin, Alexander	Composer	250	450	1100		Rus. Composer & Prof. Chemistry
Borowski, Felix	Composer	15	40	100	50	
Borso, Umberto	Entertainment	15			45	It. Tenor
Borzage, Frank	Entertainment	40			150	Film Director-Producer
Bosanquet, Helen D.	Author	8	15	22		
Bose, Jagadis, Sir	Science	27	40	150		Indian Physicist
Boshell, Louise	Entertainment	6	8	15	15	
Bosley, Tom	Entertainment	5	8	20	12	
Bosson, Barbara	Entertainment	5	5	10	15	
Bostwick, Barry	Entertainment	6	8	15	20	
Bostwick, George	Aviation	10	25	40	30	ACE, WW II
Boswell, Connie	Entertainment	10	10	25	30	
Boswell, James	Author	750		4545		Biographer of Sam'l Johnson
Bosworth, Hobart	Entertainment	25	30	40	55	
Botha, Louis	Head of State	50	70	95		S. Afr. Soldier, Statesman
Bottolfsen, C.A.	Governor	12		25	15	Governor ID
Bottome, Margaret	Author	15	45	100	25	Lecturer
Bottoms, Joseph	Entertainment	4	4	9	12	
Bottoms, Sam	Entertainment	6	8	15	12	
Bottoms, Timothy	Entertainment	7			15	
Boucher, V.	Military	5	25			
Boucicault, Dion	Entertainment	20	35	50	40	19th Cent. Am. Actor-Playwright
Bouck, William C.	Governor	15	25			Governor NY

NAME	CATEGORY	SIG	LS/DS	ALS	SP	COMMENT
Boudin, Eugene-Louis	Artist	105	280	575		Fr. Sea & Beach Scenes
Boudinot, Elias	Revolutionary War	95	250			Cherokee Leader. Murdered
Boudinot, Elias 1740-1821	Revolutionary War	240	1980	785		Washington's Att'y Gen.
Boulard, Georges	Aviation	15		60	35	
Boulez, Pierre	Composer	15	45	75	25	
Boulle, Pierre	Author	10	15	30	15	
Bourguiba, Habib	Head of State	15	40	100	25	Pres. Tunisia
Bourke-White, Margaret	Artist	55	95	165		Photograpic Essays. "Life" Mag.
Bourne, Francis, Cardinal	Clergy	35	45	60	40	
Bourrienne, L.A.F. de	Fr. Revolution	45	60	120		Pvt. Sec'y to Napoleon
Bouton, Chas. Marie	Artist	110	165	400		
Boutwell, George S.	Cabinet	15	45	150	40	Grant Sec'y Treasury
Bow, Clara	Entertainment	165	175	330	290	"It Girl"
Bowden, Doris	Entertainment	3	3	6	6	
Bowditch, Nathaniel 1773-1838	Science	100	310	610		Astronomer, Mathematician
Bowe, Rosemarie	Entertainment	4	4	9	10	
Bowen, Elizabeth	Author	25	75	170	30	Ir.-Br. Psychological Novelist
Bowen, George F., Sir	Head of State	10	25	35		Governor Australia, New Zealand
Bowen, Ira Sprague	Science	10	25	35	15	Dir. Mt.Wilson-Palomar Obs.
Bowen, John Stevens	Civil War	175	260	450		CSA Gen.
Bowen, Louise de Koven	Social Reformer	12	20			Pres. Hull House
Bowen, Thomas Meed	Civil War	45				Union General, Senator CO
Bower, Antoinette	Entertainment	3	3	6	8	
Bowers, George M.	Senate/Congress	10	20		10	MOC WV
Bowes, Major Edward	Entertainment	12	15	19	25	
Bowie, David	Entertainment	30			85	Rock
Bowie, James (Jim)	Military		15000			Co-Cmdr. Alamo. Bowie Knife
Bowie, Sydney J.	Senate/Congress	10	20	35		MOC AL
Bowker, Judy	Entertainment	6	8	15	19	
Bowler, Metcalf	Jurist	50	135	250		Opponent of The Stamp Act 1765
Bowles, Chester	Governor	10	25	85	40	Diplomat, Advertising Exec.
Bowlin, James B.	Senate/Congress	15	30	45		MOC MO
Bowman, Lee	Entertainment	15	20	25	30	
Boxcar Willie	Country Western	6	12		15	Singer
Boxleitner, Bruce	Entertainment	8	9	19	20	
Boy George	Entertainment	15	20	45	50	
Boyd, Alan S.	Cabinet	4			10	Sec'y Trans., CEO Amtrak
Boyd, Belle	Western Outlaw	1025			9650	Confederate Spy
Boyd, Linn	Senate/Congress	20	30	55		MOC KY
Boyd, Steven	Entertainment	25	29	70	70	
Boyd, William "Hopalong Cassidy"	Entertainment	175			300	
Boyer, Charles	Entertainment	35	40	75	90	
Boyer, Jean-Pierre	Head of State	35	125			Pres. Haiti
Boyesen, Hjalmar H.	Author	15	35	70	20	
Boyington, Gregory 'Pappy'	Aviation	65	155	215	145	ACE WW II Marine, #4 US, CMH
Boyle, John J.	Artist	5	10	20		
Boyle, Kay	Author	20	75	150	30	Am. Short Story Writer, Novels
Boyle, Lara Flynn	Entertainment	25			60	
Boyle, Peter	Entertainment	6	8	15	15	
Boynton, Henry Van Ness	Civil War	45	80	165		Union Officer & MOH winner
Brabazon-Moore, John T.	Aviation	25	60	85	50	1st Licensed. WW I Pilot
Bracken, Eddie	Entertainment	5	6	9	9	
Bradbury, James Ware	Senate/Congress	20	25	40		Senator ME 1847
Bradbury, Norris E.	Science	15		25		
Bradbury, Ray	Author	35	155	275	45	Am. Sci-Fi Writer
Bradford, Barbara P.	Author	5			10	

NAME	CATEGORY	SIG	LS/DS	ALS	SP	COMMENT
Bradford, William	Senate	125	350	590		Sen. RI 1793
Bradley, Bill	Senate/Congress	5	10		20	Sen. NJ., Pro. Basketball
Bradley, Ed	Entertainment	3	7	20	10	TV News
Bradley, James	Military	11	35	58		
Bradley, John H.	Military	35	95		50	Iwo Jima Flag Raiser FDC $200 S
Bradley, Joseph P. (SC)	Supreme Court	55	100	200		
Bradley, Kathleen	Entertainment	4			10	"Price is Right" Model
Bradley, Omar N.	Military	75	165	295	175	5 Star General WW II
Bradley, Tom	Political	6	15	30	15	Mayor Los Angeles
Bradna, Olympe	Entertainment	10	75		25	
Bradstreet, John	Colonial	60	140	295		Br. Soldier. Ticonderoga
Brady, Alice	Entertainment	90		95	175	
Brady, James B. 'Diamond Jim'	Business	185	340	715	385	Financier & Bon Vivant
Brady, James S.	Celebrity	20	65		30	
Brady, Mathew B.	Photographer	275	1050	2300		Presidential & Civil War Photos
Brady, Pat	Entertainment	100			250	
Brady, Scott	Entertainment	12	15	25	35	
Brady, William A.	Entertainment	25			65	
Braga, Sonia	Entertainment	10	15	30	30	
Bragg, Braxton	Civil War	300	445	675	900	CSA General
Bragg, Edward Stuyvesant	Civil War	45	85	135		Union Gen., Statesman, MOC
Bragg, Thomas	Civil War	135	225			CSA Att'y General
Bragg, Wm. Henry, Sir	Science	45	95			Nobel Physics with son Wm. L.
Bragg, Wm. Lawrence, Sir	Science	48	85			Nobel Physics with father W.H.
Brahms, Johannes	Composer	1000	1350	3375	6200	AMusQS $2,750-$12,500
Braithwaite, Wm. Stanley	Author	35	120	235	45	
Branagh, Kenneth	Entertainment	20			65	Br. Actor
Branch, John	Cabinet	25	75	225		Sec'y Navy, Gov. NC, Gov. FL
Branch, Lawrence O.	Civil War	340		1060		CSA Gen.
Brand, Christopher Q., Sir	Aviation	75	150	300	200	ACE, WW I, Only night Ace
Brand, Neville	Entertainment	75			150	
Brand, Vance D.	Astronaut	10	40		15	
Brandauer, Klaus Maria	Entertainment	15	15	30	35	
Brandegee, Augustus	Senate/Congress	15	35			MOC CT. Civil War Member
Brandeis, Louis D. (SC)	Supreme Court	150	615	1950		
Brandenstein, Daniel	Astronaut	5			15	
Brando, Marlon	Entertainment	200	675	365	650	
Brandon, Henry	Entertainment	5			10	
Brandt, Marianne	Entertainment	25		80	75	Opera
Brandt, Willy	Head of State	25	80	210	45	Ger.Chan. Nobel Peace Prize
Branigan, Laura	Entertainment	10			30	
Brann, Louis J.	Governor	5	15		10	Gov. ME
Brannan, Charles F.	Cabinet	10	15		15	Sec'y Agriculture
Branzell, Karin	Entertainment	40			145	Opera
Braque, Georges	Artist	420	675	1225		Developed Cubism with Picasso
Brattain, Walter	Science	25	50	90	45	Nobel Physics. Transistor
Bratton, John, Dr.	Civil War	95	135	330		CSA Gen.
Brauchitsch, Walter von	Military	75	155	210	125	Hitler Fld.Marshall
Braun, Eva	WWII Nazi	1000		2750		Hitler's Mistress-Wife
Braun, Wernher von	Science					see Von Braun
Brautigan, Richard	Author	45	150			"Counter-Culture" Classic
Braxton, Carter	Revolutionary War	275	550	1275		Signer Decl. of Indepen.
Brayman, Mason	Civil War	30	78			Union General, Gov. Idaho
Brayton, Charles Ray	Civil War	40	65	100		Union General
Brazzi, Rossano	Entertainment	8	9	19	20	
Brearley, David	Revolutionary War	375	800			Continental Congress

NAME	CATEGORY	SIG	LS/DS	ALS	SP	COMMENT
Breathed, Berke*	Cartoonist	20			175	Bloom County
Brecht, Bertolt	Author	375	1750	3100		Ger.-Jewish Playwright, Poet
Breckinridge, John Cabell	Civil War & VP US	160	400	750		CSA Gen., Sec'y War, US Congr.
Breckinridge, Joseph Cabell	Military	25	40			1842-1920
Breckinridge, Wm. C.	Civil War	110	250	275		CSA Officer
Breeding, J. Floyd	Senate/Congress	5	15		10	MOC KS
Breen, Bobby	Entertainment	10	15	35	25	
Breese, Lou	Entertainment	5	9	15	12	
Breese, Vance	Aviation	30	115		40	Aviator & Aircraft Designer
Brefoort, H. B.	Military	15	30			
Brendel, El	Entertainment	15			60	
Breneman, Tom	Entertainment	15	15	30	25	
Brennan, Eileen	Entertainment	4	4	9	15	
Brennan, Francis J., Cardinal	Clergy	30	45	55	50	
Brennan, Walter	Entertainment	125	150	300	225	
Brennan, William J., Jr. (SC)	Supreme Court	75	105	155	85	
Brennecke, Kurt	Military	15	35	60	35	
Brenner, Victor D.	Artist	85	240	575		
Brent, Charles H., Bishop	Clergy	25	40	55	40	
Brent, Evelyn	Entertainment	15	20	25	35	
Brent, George	Entertainment	25	30	35	60	
Brent, George Wm.	Civil War	100	210	300		
Brent, Joseph Lancaster	Civil War	90	145	190		CSA Gen.
Brent, Robert	Military	35	100	165		
Brereton, Lewis Hyde	Aviation	45	140		55	Cmdr. 1st Allied Airborne WW II
Bres, Edward S.	Military	10	30	50		
Breslau, Sophie	Entertainment	35			90	Opera
Breslin, Jimmy	Celebrities	5	15	40	10	Journalist, Novelist
Bresser-Gianoli, Clotilde	Entertainment	20			55	Opera
Breton, Andre	Author	60	175	325		Fr. Poet, Essayist, Critic
Breuer, Marcel	Architect	20	60	125	150	Bauhaus School/Gropius
Brewer, David J. (SC)	Supreme Court	75	95	160		
Brewer, Teresa	Entertainment	3	3	10	15	Big Band Singer
Brewster, Benjamin	Cabinet	10	35			Arthur Att'y General
Brewster, David, Sir	Science	30	55	140		Scot., Law of Polarization.
Brewster, Kingman Jr	Educator	5	15	25	15	Diplomat
Brewster, Ralph Owen	Senate	10	25	40	30	Senator, MOC ME
Brezhnev, Leonid I.	Head of State	375	975		400	Soviet Communist Party Leader
Brian, Mary	Entertainment	5	7	15	25	
Brice, Benjamin W.	Civil War	15	45			Union Paymaster General
Brice, Fanny	Entertainment	150	185	375	375	
Brickell, Edie	Entertainment	7			30	
Bricker, John W.	Senate	15	30		20	Gov. Ohio
Bridges, Beau	Entertainment	5	6	15	20	
Bridges, H. Styles	Senate	7	15		10	Senator NH
Bridges, Harry	Labor Leader	70	180		140	Pres. Longshoreman Union
Bridges, Jeff	Entertainment	5	6	15	15	
Bridges, Lloyd	Entertainment	5	6	15	15	
Bridges, Roy D. Jr.	Astronaut	7			25	
Bridges, Todd	Entertainment	15			40	
Bridgman, Laura D.	Celebrity	110		235		Blind, Deaf, Mute
Briggs, Austin*	Cartoonist	25			200	Flash Gordon
Briggs, Charles F.	Author	15	40	125		Editor NY Times
Briggs, Claire	Cartoonist	15			50	Mr. & Mrs.
Briggs, James E.	Military	10	25	50	20	
Brigham, Louis S.	Business	10	35	45	20	

NAME	CATEGORY	SIG	LS/DS	ALS	SP	COMMENT
Bright, John	Statesman	35	50	155		Radical Br. Orator.(Corn Laws)
Brimmer, Andrew F.	Government	10	15		12	Afro-Am. Gov. Fed. Res. Board
Brinegar, Paul	Entertainment	10	15	20	25	
Brinkley, Christie	Entertainment	10	15	25	45	
Brinkley, David	Entertainment	5			15	News Anchor-Commentator
Brinley, Wilford	Entertainment	5			20	
Brinson, Samuel Mitchell	Senate/Congress	10	20	45		MOC NC
Brisbane, Arthur	Author	15	35	100	30	Influential Editorial Writer
Brisebois, Danielle	Entertainment	3	3	6	6	
Brisson, Carl	Entertainment	10	15	25	15	Danish Actor
Bristol, Mark	Military	20	25			Admiral WW I
Bristow, Benjamin Helm	Cabinet	20	65	115		Civil War Commanded 25th KY
Britt, Mai	Entertainment	10			25	
Britt, Maurice L., Capt.	Military	18	30			WW II Hero CMH & Football Star
Brittany, Morgan	Entertainment	10	15	25	30	
Britten, Benjamin	Composer	115	405	650	195	Conductor
Britton, Barbara	Entertainment	6	8	15	25	
Britton, Sherry	Entertainment	5	6	15	15	
Brix, Herman	Entertainment	10	12	15	20	
Broadhead, James Overton	Law	25		75		Att'y Friend of Lincoln
Broccli, Cubby	Entertainment	3	3	6	12	
Brochler, Jan	Entertainment	10			35	Opera, Dutch Baritone
Brock, William	Clergy	15	25	40	25	
Brock, William G. Sen.	Business	20	70	125	40	
Broderick, Helen	Entertainment	25			70	
Broderick, Matthew	Entertainment	9	10	20	25	
Brodhead, James E.	Entertainment	5	6	15	15	
Brodhead, Richard	Senator	15	35	75		Senator from PA
Brody, Lane	Entertainment	4			10	
Broglie, Duke A-C-L-V	Statesman	135	270	540		Fr. Politician. Author
Broglie, Louis Victor de	Science	20	55	105	25	Nobel Physics
Brokow, Tom	Entertainment	5	12	25	15	TV News Anchor-Commentator
Brolin, James	Entertainment	15	15	30	25	
Bromberg, J. Edward	Entertainment	30			65	
Bromfield, John	Entertainment	8			15	
Bromfield, Louis	Author	35	75	170	55	Am. Novelist. Pulitzer
Bronk, Detlev W.	Science	10	22	40	20	Pres. Nat'l Adademy of Sci.
Bronson, Betty	Entertainment	35			75	
Bronson, Charles	Entertainment	10	15	25	28	
Bronte, Charlotte	Author			8250		Br. Novelist. "Jane Eyre"
Brook, Alexander	Artist	25	40	75		
Brook, Clive	Entertainment	40	55	75	75	
Brooke, Alan, Fld Marshal, Sir	Military	40	110	205	75	Cmdr. Br.II Corps WW II,Dunkirk
Brooke, Edward W.	Senate	10	15		25	Senator MA
Brooke, Hilary	Entertainment	10	15	25	25	
Brooke, John Rutter	Civil War	35	65	185		Union Gen.
Brooke, Rupert	Author	450	550	1045		Br. Poet
Brooke-Popham, Robert	Military	30	65	95	50	Br. Air Chief Marshal WW II
Brookhart, Smith W.	Senate	10	15		15	Senator IA
Brooks, A. Raymond	Aviation	35	60	90	75	Bi-Plane ACE, WW I
Brooks, Albert	Entertainment	5			10	
Brooks, Arthur	Aviation	15		30	35	
Brooks, Avery	Entertainment	30			100	"Star Trek"
Brooks, Foster	Entertainment	5	6	15	10	
Brooks, Fred Emerson	Author	10	15	35		Poet
Brooks, Garth	Country Western	15			55	

NAME	CATEGORY	SIG	LS/DS	ALS	SP	COMMENT
Brooks, Gwendolyn	Author	20	40		25	Afro-Am. Poet
Brooks, James L.	Entertainment	10			20	
Brooks, John	Military	55	125	275		Am. Revolution Gen., Gov. MA
Brooks, Leslie	Entertainment	10	12	15	15	
Brooks, Louise	Entertainment	150		425	595	
Brooks, Mel	Entertainment	10	15	25	30	
Brooks, Peter H.	Clergy	15	25	35		
Brooks, Phillips	Clergy-Author	90	120	175	75	"O Little Town of Bethlehem"
Brooks, Rand	Entertainment	10	15	30	35	
Brooks, Randi	Entertainment	6	8	15	15	
Brooks, Richard	Entertainment	20	10		60	Film Director
Brooks, William Thomas H.	Civil War	42	65	105		Union Gen.
Broom, Jacob	Revolutionary War	350	900	2000		Continental Congress
Broomall, John M.	Senate/Congress	10	15	40		MOC DE 1863. CW Officer
Brophy, Kevin	Entertainment	3	3	6	9	
Brophy, Theodore F.	Business	4	5		10	CEO GTE
Brosnan, Pierce	Entertainment	6	8	15	20	
Brothers, Joyce	Science	4	10	25	10	Early TV Psychiatrist
Brough, Candi & Randi	Entertainment	10			25	
Brough, Fanny	Entertainment	4	4	9	10	
Brough, Lionel	Entertainment	4	4	9	10	
Brougham, Henry, Lord	Law	35	95	245		Designed One Horse Brougham
Brougham, John	Entertainment	12			30	Am. Actor-Playwright
Broughton, Joseph M.	Senate/Congress	5	12		10	Senator/MOC NC
Broun, Heywood	Author	10	30	70	15	Journalist, Novelist, Columnist
Browder, Earl	Political	15	35	65	20	US Communist Party Leader
Brown, "Down Town" Julie	Entertainment	5			15	TV Host
Brown, Albert Gallatin	Governor	45	60	90		CSA Senator, Gov. Miss.
Brown, Alice	Author	15	35	100		Prolific Novelist, Poet
Brown, Arthur Witten	Aviation	300	395	575	575	Alcock & Brown
Brown, Blair	Entertainment	6	8	15	15	
Brown, Bo	Cartoonist	5			20	Magazine Cartoonist
Brown, Bothwell	Entertainment	10	15	25	25	
Brown, Charles Brockden 1771-1810	Author	975		6500		Father of the American Novel
Brown, Clarence	Entertainment	10			25	
Brown, Curt	Astronaut	7			15	
Brown, Edmund G. 'Jerry'	Governor	10	25		20	Governor CA, Pres. Candidate
Brown, Edmund G. 'Pat'	Governor	10	25		20	Governor CA
Brown, George	Military	25				
Brown, Harold, Dr.	Science-Cabinet	10	20		15	Sec'y Defense
Brown, Helen Gurley	Author	5	10	20	10	Editor, Publisher
Brown, Henry B. (SC)	Supreme Court	50	175	250		
Brown, Henry W.	Aviation	12	25	42	32	ACE, WW II
Brown, Herbert C., Dr.	Science	25	30	45	35	Nobel Chemistry
Brown, Jacob	Military	50	135			Gen. War 1812
Brown, James	Entertainment	5			15	Actor
Brown, James (Afro-Am.))	Entertainment	40			75	
Brown, Jim Ed	Country Music	5			15	
Brown, Joe E.	Entertainment	25	30	40	75	
Brown, John 1800-1859	Civil War	775	1700	3450	8500	Abolitionist-Hung for treason
Brown, John Calvin	Civil War	95	165			CSA Gen.
Brown, John George	Artist	10	30	45		
Brown, John Y.	Business	10	25	51	19	
Brown, Johnny Mack	Entertainment	60	75		125	Cowboy Actor
Brown, Joseph Emerson	Civil War	45	60	85		Civil War Gov. Georgia
Brown, Julie	Entertainment	4			10	Singer

NAME	CATEGORY	SIG	LS/DS	ALS	SP	COMMENT
Brown, Les	Entertainment	15			35	Big Band Leader
Brown, Lt. John	Revolutionary War	72	175	400		
Brown, Mark N.	Astronaut	5			15	
Brown, Moses	Revolutionary War	45		265		Naval Commander
Brown, Nicholas 1729-91	Revolutionary War	35	80	195		Supplied Army. Brown University
Brown, Norma	Military	10	20	30	15	
Brown, Norman	Entertainment	4			10	
Brown, Phyllis George	Entertainment	5	8	20	15	
Brown, Prentiss M.	Senate	10	25		15	Senator MI
Brown, Preston	Military	15	35			General WW I
Brown, Robert	Military	20		75		General WW I
Brown, Robert	Science	135		775		Scot. Living Cells Nucleus
Brown, Ron	Cabinet	7	20		10	Clinton Cabinet
Brown, Ruth	Entertainment	20			45	Rock & Roll HOF
Brown, Sam J.	Aviation	18	40	55	45	ACE, WW II
Brown, Tom	Entertainment	10	15	25	25	
Brown, William Wallace	Senate/Congress	10	15	30		MOC PA. CW Officer
Browne, Charles Farrar						SEE Ward, Artemus
Browne, Chris*	Cartoonist	20			75	Hagar
Browne, Coral	Entertainment	10	15	18	25	
Browne, Dik*	Cartoonist	20			60	Hi & Lois, Hagar
Browne, Hablot Knight	Artist	25	90	150		Watercolor. Illustrator Dickens
Browne, Jackson	Entertainment	20			55	Rock
Browne, Leslie	Entertainment	5	7	12	10	
Brownell, Herbert Jr.	Cabinet	10	18	40	20	Att'y Gen.
Browning, Eliz. Barrett	Author	400	1085	2750	2500	
Browning, George	Business	195	580			Browning Arms Mfg.
Browning, John B.	Business	50	160		75	Pres. Browning Arms Co.
Browning, John Moses	Inventor-Business	195	1200	575		Inventor, Designer of Fire Arms
Browning, Orville H.	Cabinet	25	125			Sec'y of Interior
Browning, Ricou	Entertainment	10			20	Creature, Olympic Swimmer
Browning, Robert	Author	280	470	950	685	Br. Poet
Browning, Tod	Entertainment	75			250	
Brownlee, John	Entertainment	10		45	30	Opera, Australian/Am. Baritone
Brubeck, Dave	Entertainment	10	15	25	25	Jazz
Bruce, Blanche K.	Senator	500				1st Afro-Am.Full Term Senator
Bruce, Carol	Entertainment	5	5	10	30	Vocalist
Bruce, David	Entertainment	10			20	
Bruce, Lenny	Entertainment	450	600		1200	
Bruce, Nigel	Entertainment	150	175	300	300	
Bruce, Thos.(7th Earl Elgin)	Diplomat	50	190	340		Conveyed "Elgin Marbles"
Bruce, Virginia	Entertainment	10			15	
Bruce, Wallace	Author	35		120		
Bruce, William Cabell	Senate	7	15	30	15	Senator MD
Bruch, Max	Composer	55	200	475	95	Ger. Opera,AMusQS $1,100
Bruckner, Josef Anton	Composer	1200	2500	5500	2500	Aus. 10 Symphonies.
Brummel, Geo. B. 'Beau'	Dandy	90	220	650		Br. Man of Fashion
Bruna Rasa, Lina	Entertainment	65			350	Opera
Brune, Guillaume M.A.	Napoleonic Wars	85	340	450		Marshal of Napoleon
Brunel, Marc Isambard, Sir	Science	70	145	315		Fr.-Br.Inventor, Engineer
Brunet, Isambard Kingdom	Science	40	145	325		Br. Engineer, Broad Gauge RR
Brunner, Emil	Clergy	45	75	110	50	
Bruscantini, Sesto	Entertainment	10			25	Opera
Bruson, Renato	Entertainment	10			30	Opera
Bry, Ellen	Entertainment	3	3	6	6	
Bryan, Charles W.	Governor	12	27			Governor NE

NAME	CATEGORY	SIG	LS/DS	ALS	SP	COMMENT
Bryan, George	Revolutionary War	120	350	750		Jurist. Proposed Abolition 1777
Bryan, Goode	Civil War	140		440		CSA Gen.
Bryan, Jane	Entertainment	5	10	20	15	
Bryan, William E.	Aviation	10	22	38	28	ACE, WW II
Bryan, William Jennings	Cabinet	95	250	610	350	"Cross of Gold" Speech
Bryant, Alys McKey	Aviation	35	60	140	75	
Bryant, Anita	Entertainment	5	6	10	10	
Bryant, William Cullen	Author	60	400	325	750	Am. Poet, ALS/Content $1,750
Brynner, Yul	Entertainment	40	55	70	135	
Buber, Martin	Clergy	75	175	250	90	
Buchan, John, Lord	Author	40	185			Gov. Gen. Canada, Novelist
Buchanan, Edgar	Entertainment	30	40	55	75	
Buchanan, Franklin	Civil War	160	210			CSA Admiral
Buchanan, James	President	325	1100	1280	750	Special SP $12,500
Buchanan, James M.	Economics	35	45	85	40	Nobel Economics
Buchanan, Patrick	Political	12	15		25	Political Commentator
Bucher, Lloyd	Military	30	80	150	90	Capt. of USS Pueblo
Buchli, James F.	Astronaut	5	15		25	
Buchman, Franklin	Clergy	20	35	65		
Buchwald, Art	Author	10	15	25	15	Syndicated Humor Column
Buck, Clayton Douglass	Senate	11	15	25	20	Senator-Governor DE
Buck, Frank	Hunter	40	65	145	85	"Bring 'Em Back Alive"
Buck, Paul H.	Author	4	10	15	5	
Buck, Pearl S.	Author	50	145	185	50	Am. Novelist. Nobel, Pulitzer
Buckingham, William A.	Governor	40	65	140		Civil War Gov. CT.
Buckland, Ralph Pomeroy	Civil War	130		265		Union Gen.
Buckle, Henry Thomas	Author	5	10	25		
Buckley, James	Senate/Congress	6	15		10	
Buckley, William F., Jr.	Author	7	15	45	20	Publisher "National Revue"
Buckner, Simon Bolivar	Civil War	200	400	510	295	CSA Gen. War Dte. LS $2,500
Budd, Julie	Entertainment	3	3	6	6	
Buell, Don Carlos	Civil War	70	155	175	150	Union General
Buffalo Bill Jr.	Entertainment	25			50	
Buffett, Jimmy	Entertainment	10			30	Rock
Buffington, Thomas Mitchell	Cherokee Chief	350	1350			Chief of Cherokee Nations
Buford, Abraham	Civil War	125	234	789		CSA Gen. 1990 Price Averages
Buford, John	Civil War	85	210			Union Gen. Price Estimated
Buford, Napoleon Bonaparte	Civil War	35	145	375		Union Gen.
Buhari, Mohammed	Head of State	15	50	130	25	
Buick, David D.	Business	170	675	885	275	Buick Motor Co.
Bujold, Genevieve	Entertainment	6	8	15	20	
Bulfinch, Charles	Architect	130	375			Fanueil Hall, Completed WH
Bulfinch, Thomas	Author	20	45	100		"Bulfinch's Mythology"
Bulkley, John D.	Military	20			35	Adm. USN WW II
Bull II, William	Governor	55	80			Governor SC
Bull, John S.	Astronaut	15			25	
Bull, Ole B.	Composer	15		125	125	Nor. Violin Virtuoso
Bull, William, II	Governor	60		240		Governor SC 1760
Bullard, Robert Lee	Military	20	75	130	100	General WW I
Bullard, William	Military	15	35			Admiral WW I
Buller, Redvers, Sir	Military	40	110	230	45	Cmdr-in-Chief South Africa
Bullet Boys (4)	Entertainment	10			40	
Bullitt, William P.	Diplomat	10	20		25	Ambassador To USSR
Bulloch, Terrence	Aviation	20			35	Br. Aviator WWII
Bullock, Walter	Author	3	4	7	5	
Bulow, Bernhard H.M.K. von	Head of State	15	35	90	40	Prussian Imperial Chancellor

NAME	CATEGORY	SIG	LS/DS	ALS	SP	COMMENT
Bultmann, Rudolph	Clergy	70	90	165	80	
Bulwer, Wm. Henry Lytton	Diplomat	15	40	85		Clayton-Bulwer Treaty. US & Eng
Bulwer-Lytton, Edward	Author	60	220	460		
Bumbry, Grace	Entertainment	10	15		40	Opera
Bumpers, Dale	Governor	12	15		20	Senator AR
Bunce, Francis M.	Military	25	55	125	65	Admiral Spanish-American War
Bunche, Ralph J.	Diplomat	50	95	225	125	Nobel Peace Prize
Bundy, McGeorge	Law	20	35	45	25	Director FBI
Bundy, Omar	Military	35	90		55	General WW I
Bunner, Henry C.	Author	65		135		Editor "Puck" Magazine
Bunny, John	Entertainment	100	130	160	200	
Bunsen, Christian K.J., Baron	Diplomat	15	45	110		Prussian Theologian, Scholar
Bunsen, Robert W.	Science	175	410	925		Ger. Chemist, Bunsen Burner
Bunting, Mary	Celebrity	10	28		15	
Bunting, William M.	Clergy	49	100	150		
Buntline, Ned	Author	140	185	250	75	Novelist,Adventurer,Dime Novel
Buono, Sonny	Entertainment	5	10		20	
Buono, Victor	Entertainment	30			75	
Burbank, Luther	Science	90	275	298	165	Pioneer, Experimental Botanist
Burder, George	Clergy	10	15	20	15	
Burdette, Robert J.	Author	20	55	135	40	
Burge, V.L.	Aviation	18			35	
Burger, Warren E. (SC)	Supreme Court	50	140	205	75	
Burgess, Anthony	Author	40	55		45	Br. Novelist."Clockwork Orange"
Burgess, Thomas, Bishop	Clergy	15	25	35		
Burgess, Thornton W.	Author	30	100	225		"Peter Rabbit"
Burghley, Wm. Cecil, Lord	Head of State	1725				Elizabeth I, Tudor Statesman
Burghoff, Gary	Entertainment	10			40	
Burgoyne, John	Revolutionary War	1100	2850	6600		Br. Gen. vs Am. Colonies
Burke, Arleigh	Military	15	25	40	35	Adm. USN WW II
Burke, Billie	Entertainment	150	165		250	
Burke, Delta	Entertainment	10	15	25	30	
Burke, Edmund	Senate/Congress	5	12	20		MOC NH
Burke, Edward A.	Celebrity	45			150	
Burke, Paul	Entertainment	5	6	15	15	
Burke, Selma	Artist	10	20	75	15	
Burke, Yvonne B.	Senate/Congress	10			20	Afro-Am 3 Term MOC CA
Burleigh, Harry Thacker	Composer	25		150		AMusQS $200, Spirituals
Burleson, Albert S.	Cabinet	10	25	35		P.M. General, MOC TX
Burleson, OmarTruman	Senate/Congress	5	15		10	MOC TX
Burmester, Willy	Entertainment	90		275		Ger. Violinist. AMusQS $350
Burne-Jones, Edward, Sir	Artist	125	235	650		Pre-Raphaelite Painter,Designer
Burnett, Carol	Entertainment	5	6	15	20	
Burnett, David	Head of State	275		1000		1st Pres. Republic TX
Burnett, Frances Hodgson	Author	40	145	285		"Little Lord Fauntleroy"
Burnett, Leo	Business	5	10	25	10	Advertising
Burnett, Peter H.	Governor	200		550		California Pioneer & 1st Gov.
Burnette, Smiley	Entertainment	30	35		75	
Burney, Cecil, Sir	Military	15	35			Br. Adm. WW I
Burnham, Hiram	Civil War	60	195			Union Gen.
Burns & Allen	Entertainment	100			200	
Burns, Bob	Entertainment	25	25	45	45	
Burns, Edmund	Entertainment	30			75	Silent Screen Star
Burns, Geo. & Gracie Allen		150			395	
Burns, George	Entertainment	10	18	30	25	
Burns, James MacGregor	Author	20	30			Educator, Political Science

NAME	CATEGORY	SIG	LS/DS	ALS	SP	COMMENT
Burns, John 1791-1872	Civil War	350			1250	Vet. War 1812. Vol. Gettysburg
Burns, John A.	Governor	12	15		15	Hawaii
Burns, Ken	Entertainment	5			15	Documentary Film Maker
Burns, Robert	Author	500	1450	3650		Scottish Poet
Burns, William J.	Business	35	10	175		Chief FBI 1921-24, Det. Agency
Burns, William Chalmers	Clergy	25	40	50	35	
Burns, William Wallace	Civil War	35	75	95	150	Union General
Burnside, Ambrose E.	Civil War	110	375	405	725	ALS war date $2,500
Burpee, David	Business	25	35	70	35	Burpee Seed Co.
Burpee, Jonathan	Business	10	25	50	20	Burpee Seed Co.
Burr, Aaron (V)	Vice President	330	925	1675		ALS's/Content $7,000-12,000+
Burr, Raymond	Entertainment	15	20	30	65	
Burritt, Elihu	Am. Linguist	20		125		
Burroughs, Edgar Rice	Author	250	570	675	625	Creator of Tarzan
Burroughs, John	Author	50	100	175	200	Am. Naturalist
Burroughs, John	Governor	10		25	15	Governor NM
Burroughs, Sherman Everett	Senate/Congress	5	15	30	10	MOC NH
Burrows, Abe	Author	10	15	25	20	Playwright, Pulitzer
Burrows, J. C.	Senate	10		25		Senator MI
Bursch, Daniel	Astronaut	7			15	
Burstyn, Ellen	Entertainment	6	8	15	15	
Bursum, Holm Olaf	Senate	5	15	25		Senator NM
Burton, Isabe, Ladyl	Author	25	85	180		
Burton, Charlotte	Entertainment	8	9	12	15	
Burton, Harold H. (SC)	Supreme Court	75	175	350	85	
Burton, LeVar	Entertainment	6	8	10	15	
Burton, Richard	Entertainment	100	300		275	
Burton, Richard F., Sir	Explorer	150	275	975		Orientalist, Linguist, Author
Burton, Theodore E.	Senate/Congress	7	10	35		Senator, MOC OH
Burton, Tim	Entertainment	15			45	Film Director
Busby, George Henry	Governor	11	15			Governor GA
Buscalia, Leo	Author	16	25	40	20	Educator, Author, Lecturer
Busch, Adolphus	Business	55		225		Anheuser-Busch Brewery
Busch, August A.	Business	25	90	175	50	Anheuser-Busch Brewery
Busch, Fritz	Entertainment	45			250	Ger. Conductor
Busch, Niven	Author	12		25		Dramatist, Screenwriter
Busey, Gary	Entertainment	6	8	15	20	
Bush, Barbara	First Lady	45	145		100	
Bush, George	President	160	415	1230	275	White House Cd. S $500
Bush, George W.	Business	4			10	Baseball Exec.
Bush, Owen	Entertainment	4			8	Character Actor
Bush, Prescott	Senate	25	75		90	Senator CT
Bush, Vannevar	Science	50	180	255	125	Pioneer In Analog Computers
Bushkin, Joe	Entertainment	6	8	10	12	
Bushman, Francis X.	Entertainment	40	70	110	100	Silent Star of Ben Hur
Bushmiller, Ernie*	Cartoonist	20			125	Nancy
Bushnell, David 1742?	Science	250	750	1250		Invented 1st Submarine
Bushnell, Horace	Clergy	25	35	45		
Bushyhead, D.W.	Celebrity	200		1500		
Busoni, Ferruccio	Composer	120		340	425	Pianist, AMusQS $175-$450
Busse, Henry	Entertainment	20			50	Big Band Leader
Bustamante, Jose Luis	Celebrity	9	35	60		
Butcher, Susan	Ididorod	5	10		15	Dog Breeder
Butenandt, Adolf F.J.	Science	20	30	45	25	Nobel Chemistry
Butler, Benjamin F.	Civil War	90	125	255		Union General, Politician
Butler, Carl & Pearl	Country Music	15			30	

NAME	CATEGORY	SIG	LS/DS	ALS	SP	COMMENT
Butler, Daws	Entertainment	15	15	20	40	
Butler, Dean	Entertainment	5	8	12	15	
Butler, John	Clergy	10	15	20	20	
Butler, John	Revolutionary War	75	185	375		Am. Loyalist."Butler's Rangers"
Butler, Matthew Calbraith	Civil War	90	160	200		CSA General, US Sen. SC
Butler, Nicholas Murray	Educator	15	35	90	30	Nobel Peace Prize
Butler, Pierce (SC)	Supreme Court	35	90	275	45	
Butler, Pierce 1744-1822	Revolutionary War	60	180	385		Signer of Constitution
Butler, Samuel 1835-1902	Author	20	60	125		Br. Author, Artist, Musician
Butler, Smedley D.	Military	15	35	75	35	Marine Corps Gen/2 CMH
Butler, Thomas S.	Senate/Congress	5	15			MOC PA
Butler, William Orlando	Military	45	210			Hero Battle of New Orleans
Butler, Zebulon	Military	70	200			Col. Revolutionary War
Butt Rumford, Clara	Entertainment	35			150	Opera
Butterfield, Billy	Entertainment	25			45	Jazz Trumpet, Bandleader
Butterfield, Daniel	Civil War	55	260	315	450	Union General .Composed TAPS
Butterworth, Charles	Entertainment					
Buttlar-Brandenfels, F.H.	Military	5	15	25	15	
Buttons, Red	Entertainment	5	7	15	20	
Buttram, Pat	Entertainment	10	10	15	25	
Buttrick, George A.	Clergy	25	45	75	45	
Butts, Alfred M.	Inventor	35	50			"Scrabble"
Butz, Earl L.	Cabinet	6	18	30	15	Sec'y Agriculture
Buzzi, Ruth	Entertainment	3	6	10	15	
Byers, Samuel Hawkins	Author	25	40	60		Union Soldier-Author
Byington, Spring	Entertainment	20			55	
Byner, John	Entertainment	3	3	6	8	
Byrd, Harry F., Jr.	Senate	10	25		25	Senator VA
Byrd, Ralph	Entertainment	100			350	
Byrd, Richard E.	Aviation-Explorer	75	235	560	235	Adm. USN, Polar Expl.
Byrd, Robert C.	Senate	15	30		25	Senator WV
Byrne, Jane	Politician	5	10	28	10	Mayor
Byrnes, Edd	Entertainment	5			15	
Byrnes, James F. (SC)	Supreme Court	50	110	235	55	
Byrns, Joseph Wellington	Senate/Congress	15	25		20	MOC TN
Byron, Arthur	Entertainment	15	15	20	35	
Byron, Geo. Gordon, Lord	Author	1200	2750	9350		Poet
Byron, Jean	Entertainment	5			15	

C

NAME	CATEGORY	SIG	LS/DS	ALS	SP	COMMENT
Caan, James	Entertainment	6	8	15	20	
Cabana, Robert D.	Astronaut	6			20	
Cabell, James Branch	Author	30	120	165		Novels Attacked for Immorality
Cabell, William L.	Civil War	175	405			CSA General
Cable, George Washington	Author	35	50	85	45	CSA Soldier, Short Story Writer

NAME	CATEGORY	SIG	LS/DS	ALS	SP	COMMENT
Cabot, Bruce	Entertainment	50	55	90	125	
Cabot, Sebastian	Entertainment	25	30	90	75	
Caceres, Andreas A.	Head of State	10	25	65	20	Peru
Cadbury, George	Business	35		170	50	Cadbury Chocolate Mfg.
Cadbury, Richard	Business	30	45	160	50	Cadbury Chocolate Mfg.
Cade, Robert, Dr.	Business	10	15		10	Inventor of Gatorade
Cadman, Chas. Wakefield	Composer	60	215	360	100	AMusQS $195
Cadman, S. Parkes	Clergy	20	35	50	35	
Cadmus, Paul	Artist	36	85	120		
Cadwalader, George	Civil War	50	110	160		Union General
Cadwalader, Lambert	Revolutionary War	55	140	335		Continental Congress
Cady, Daniel	Congress	20	35	50		MOC NY 1815
Caesar, Irving	Composer	26	55	90	.45	Lyricist (Tea for Two)
Caesar, Sid	Entertainment	5	6	15	15	
Cage, John M.	Composer	95	125	250	190	AMusQS $125-$200
Cage, Nicholas	Entertainment	15			45	
Cagney, James	Entertainment	40	60	100	275	
Cahier, Madame Charles	Entertainment	25			90	Early Opera
Cahn, Sammy	Composer	15	80	125	50	AMusQS $250
Cain, James	Author	40	55	90		Novelist. "Hard Boiled" Fiction
Caine, Michael	Entertainment	10	15	25	30	
Caine, Thos. Hall, Sir	Author	15	45	95	25	Br. Novelist
Calder, Alexander	Artist	125	225	475	150	Sculptor, Created the Mobile
Calderon, A. W. Gen.	Head of State	5	15	35	10	
Caldwell, Erskine	Author	40	135	210	75	
Caldwell, John Curtis	Civil War	35	75		95	Union Gen.
Caldwell, Sarah	Conductor	15			20	1st Woman Conductor NY Met.
Caldwell, Taylor	Author	35	150	225	50	Novelist
Caldwell, Zoe	Entertainment	5	6	15	15	
Calhern, Louis	Entertainment	19	25	45	45	
Calhoun, Alice	Entertainment	15	15	35	30	
Calhoun, Eleanor	Entertainment	3	3	6	8	
Calhoun, John C. (V)	Vice President	165	350	505	375	
Calhoun, Rory	Entertainment	7	10	12	15	
Calhoun, William Barron	Senate/Congress	10	15	35		MOC MA 1835
Calhoun, William M.	Senate/Congress	5	10			
Calkin, Dick*	Cartoonist	75			500	Buck Rogers
Callaghan, James	Head of State	40	75	140	45	Br. Prime Minister
Callahan, Laurence K.	Aviation	10	20	45	30	
Callas, Charlie	Entertainment	3	5	8	10	
Callas, Maria Meneghini	Entertainment	300	850	976	825	Opera, Concert
Calleia, Frank	Entertainment	19	25	45	45	
Calleia, Joseph	Entertainment	25			55	
Calley, William	Military	20	35	45	40	My Lai, Viet Nam
Calloway, Cab	Entertainment	25	30	50	120	Afro-Am. Big Band Leader
Calvert, Louis	Entertainment	5	6	15	15	
Calvert, Phyllis	Entertainment	5	15		15	
Calvet, Corinne	Entertainment	9	10	15	15	
Calvin, John	Clergy	5500	7500	10000		
Calvin, Melvin, Dr.	Science	25	35	55	35	Nobel Chemistry
Calvé, Emma	Entertainment	55	90	135	450	Opera
Camacho, Manuel Avila	Head of State	35		80	20	Pres. Mexico
Camargo, Alberto	Head of State	10	18	35	20	Columbia
Cambaceres, J.J.R.(Parma)	Napoleonic Wars	115	200			Prince & Duke
Cambell, James	Cabinet	35	80	120		Pierce P.M. General
Cambon, Jules	Diplomat	20	25	35		Fr. Ambassador to US

NAME	CATEGORY	SIG	LS/DS	ALS	SP	COMMENT
Cambridge, G.O.	Clergy	10	20	25		
Cambridge, Godfrey	Entertainment	40			80	
Cameron, Betsy	Author	5	10	20	10	
Cameron, George	Military	20		45		General WW I
Cameron, James D.	Cabinet	20	35	40		Senator PA. Sec'y War
Cameron, Kenneth	Astronaut	5			15	
Cameron, Kirk	Entertainment	15			20	
Cameron, Simon	Cabinet	100	200	225		Lincoln Sec'y War, Financier
Cammaerts, Emile	Author	10	20	40	15	Belgian Poet-Writer
Camp, Colleen	Entertainment	9	10	20	25	
Campanella, Joseph	Entertainment	3	3	6	6	
Campanini, Italo	Entertainment	65	80	175		
Campbell, Archibald	Revolutionary War	95	275			Br. General.
Campbell, Archie	Country Music	8			25	
Campbell, Beatrice	Entertainment	19	25	45	45	
Campbell, Charles Thomas	Civil War	35	80	110		Union General
Campbell, Colin, Sir	Military	16	45	60		Br. Gen. Vs U.S., War 1812
Campbell, Douglas	Aviation	38	65	80	95	ACE, WW I, Bi-plane Ace
Campbell, E. Simms*	Cartoonist	20			150	1st Black Mag. Cartoonist
Campbell, Ernest T.	Clergy	20	30	40	30	
Campbell, Geo.J.(8th Duke Argyll)	Statesman	25	60	130		Author. Br. Cabinet
Campbell, George W.	Cabinet	55	160	310		Sec'y Treas. Senator TN 1803
Campbell, Glen	Entertainment	5	6	15	20	
Campbell, Jack M.	Governor	10	20			Governor NM
Campbell, James E.	Governor	15	25	30		Governor OH, MOC
Campbell, John	Revolutionary War	62	175	290		Br. General
Campbell, John A. (SC)	Supreme Court	100	200	300		
Campbell, Naomi	Model	20			60	
Campbell, Patrick, Mrs.	Entertainment	35	60		80	Vintage Stage Actress
Campbell, R. L.	Military	5	15	20	10	
Campbell, William	Entertainment	5	5	10	12	
Campbell, William B.	Civil War	40	55	95		Union Gen., Congress TN
Campbell-Bannerman, Henry, Sir	Head of State	18	45	110		Prime Minister
Campora, Giuseppe	Entertainment	10			40	It. Tenor, Opera
Camus, Albert	Author	75	290	440		Nobel. AMsS (Poem) $595
Canby, Edward	Civil War	55	310	370		Union Gen.
Candler, Asa Griggs	Business	475	1275		595	Founder of Coca Cola
Candler, Warren Akin	Clergy	25	35	50		
Candlish, Robert Smith	Clergy	10	15	25	35	
Candy, John	Entertainment	4	4	9	25	
Canetti, Elia	Author	65	225	350		Bulg.-Br.Nobel Literature
Canfield, Dorothy (Fisher)	Author	50		300		Am. Novelist, Essayist
Canham, Erwin	Journalist	10	20			Christian Science Monitor
Caniff, Milton*	Cartoonists	25			150	Terry & Steve Canyon
Cannell, Stephen J.	Entertainment	6	10		10	TV Producer
Canning, Charles John	Head of State	15		65	45	1st Viceroy of India
Canning, Effie I.	Author	45		300		
Canning, George	Head of State	55	130	165		Prime Minister
Cannon, Dyan	Entertainment	6	8	15	20	
Cannon, Frank J.	Senate	5			10	Senator UT
Cannon, George Q.	Senate/Congress	50	140	200		Utah's 1st Congressman
Cannon, Howard W.	Senator	5	10	25	15	Senator NV
Cannon, John K.	Military	10	30	50		
Cannon, Jos. G.'Uncle Joe'	Senate/Congress	20	40	95	40	Speaker of the House
Cannon, Martha H., Dr.	Science	25	30	60	30	
Canova, Antonio	Artist	85	250	645		It. Sculptor. Classical Revival

NAME	CATEGORY	SIG	LS/DS	ALS	SP	COMMENT
Canova, Diana	Entertainment	3	3	6	10	
Canova, Judy	Entertainment	12	15	20	25	
Cantinflas	Entertainment	15	15	25	35	
Cantor, Eddie	Entertainment	100	155		165	
Cantrell, Lana	Entertainment	3	3	6	10	
Canutt, Yakima	Entertainment	10	15	25	25	
Capers, Virginia	Entertainment	3	3	6	6	
Caperton, William	Military	20			50	Adm. WW I
Capka, Carol	Entertainment	3	3	6	6	
Caplin, Mortimer	Celebrity	5	5	10	10	
Capon, Robert F.	Clergy	10	15	20	15	
Capone, Al	Criminal	1200	7500		3800	Gangster.Bootlegger & Vice King
Capote, Truman	Author	125	340	550	235	Novelist, Short Story Writer
Capp, Al*	Cartoonists	75			245	Li'l Abner
Capper, Arthur	Senate	12	25		30	Senator KS
Capra, Frank	Entertainment	25	35		70	Film Director.TLS Ltr/Poem $450
Capshaw, Kate	Entertainment	6	8	15	19	
Captain & Tennile	Entertainment	5	6	15	15	
Capucine	Entertainment	25	30	70	65	
Caraway, Hattie	Senate	25	50	35	40	1st Woman Senator, AR
Carberry, John J., Cardinal	Clergy	50	65	80	50	
Cardigan, 7th Earl Brudenell	Military	75	175	250	130	Br.Gen. Charge of Light Brigade
Cardinale, Claudia	Entertainment	10			35	
Cardozo, Benjamin N. (SC)	Supreme Court	150	350	875	840	
Carey, Harry Jr.	Entertainment	6	8	15	20	
Carey, Harry Sr.	Entertainment	100	110	175	250	
Carey, Hugh L.	Governor	10	15		15	Governor NY
Carey, Macdonald	Entertainment	5	5	8	8	
Carey, Mariah	Entertainment	30			65	Singer
Carey, Michele	Entertainment	5	6	15	25	
Carey, Ron	Entertainment	5	6	10	10	
Carias Andino, Tiburcio	Head of State	40	125		45	Pres. Honduras
Carl, Marion	Aviation	12	32	55	38	ACE, WW II, 1st Marine Ace
Carle, Frankie	Entertainment	15			35	Big Band Leader
Carleton, Guy, Sir (Baron)	Military-Rev. War	250	645	750		Br. Commander-in-Chief
Carleton, Will	Author	15	50	100	25	Ir. Novelist
Carlin, George	Entertainment	7	10	12	15	
Carlin, Lynn	Entertainment	3	3	6	6	
Carlisle, 7th Earl Geo.W.F. Howard	Author-Politician	20	45	115		Poet,Orator,Viceroy of Ireland
Carlisle, Belinda	Entertainment	20			50	
Carlisle, John Griffin	Senate-Cabinet	15	25	35	30	Speaker. Sen. KY,Sec'y Treas.
Carlisle, Kitty	Entertainment	8	9	12	15	
Carlisle, Mary	Entertainment	10	12	25	20	
Carlo Alberto 1798-1849	Royalty	45	150	375		King of Sardinia
Carlota (Marie-Charlotte-Amalie)	Royalty	340	770	1700		Empress of Mex. Became Insane
Carlsen, Capt. Kurt	Celebrity	20	55	125	45	
Carlson, Frank	Governor-Senate	10	18	25	20	Governor, Senator KS
Carlson, Richard	Entertainment	20			40	
Carlyle, Thomas	Author	90	225	450	85	Br. Philosopher, Social Critic
Carman, Tex J.	Country Music	10			20	
Carmen, Jean	Entertainment	4	4	9	10	
Carmer, Carl	Author	20	45	175		
Carmichael, Hoagy	Composer	45	200		110	AMusQS $250, $320
Carmichael, Oliver C.	Educator	20	35		25	Pres. Univ. Alabama
Carnarvon, Henry 4th Earl	Statesman	15	35	80		Created Fed. Dominion Canada
Carne, Judy	Entertainment	6	8	15	10	

NAME	CATEGORY	SIG	LS/DS	ALS	SP	COMMENT
Carnegie, Andrew	Business	150	750	750	1350	Industrialist, Philanthropist
Carnegie, Dale	Author	20	35		45	Teacher."How To Win Friends..."
Carney, Art	Entertainment	5	6	15	25	
Carney, Robert B.	Military	8	20	25		
Carnot, Lazare N.M.	Fr. Revolution	85	235	350		Min. of War. Exiled
Carnovsky, Morris	Entertainment	15		40	45	
Carol, Sue (Ladd)	Entertainment	5	6	15	15	
Caroline (Geo. IV-Eng)	Royalty	95	150	210		Estranged Queen
Caroline (Monaco)	Royalty	25			80	Princess. Daughter of Grace
Caroline of Anspach	Royalty	335	450	1000		Queen of George II (Eng.)
Caron, George R.	Aviation	35		100	90	"Enola Gay" Tail gunner
Caron, Leslie	Entertainment	15	15	30	30	
Carpenter, Carleton	Entertainment	5	6	10	10	
Carpenter, John	Entertainment	10			25	Film Director
Carpenter, Joseph Estlin	Clergy	40	50	60	75	
Carpenter, Karen	Entertainment	75	250		125	
Carpenter, Mary-Chapin	Entertainment	5			35	Singer-Composer
Carpenter, Matthew H.	Senate/Congress	10	15	30	35	Senator WI
Carpenter, Richard	Entertainment	4	4	9	10	
Carpenter, Scott	Astronaut	25	75	125	65	Mercury 7 Astro
Carpenter, W. Boyd, Bishop	Clergy	10	20	30		
Carpenter, William B.	Explorer	10	35	60		Br. Physiologist
Carpenter, William S.	Military	10	15	45	20	
Carr, Darleen	Entertainment	3	3	6	6	
Carr, Eugene Asa	Civil War	30	65		220	Union Gen. CMH
Carr, Gerald P.	Astronaut	5			15	
Carr, Jane	Entertainment	5			15	Actress
Carr, Tommy	Entertainment	20			35	
Carr, Vicki	Entertainment	3	3	6	6	
Carradine, David	Entertainment	7			20	
Carradine, John	Entertainment	65	70	150	150	
Carradine, Keith	Entertainment	7			20	
Carradine, Robert	Entertainment	7			25	
Carranza, Venustiano	Head of State	52	205	400		Revolutionary Pres.Mex.Murdered
Carrel, Dr. Alexis	Science	75	220	300	85	Nobel Medicine
Carreno, Terresa	Composer	20		135	90	Pianist. Pupil of Gottschalk
Carrera, Barbara	Entertainment	6	8	15	19	Pin-Up SP $25
Carrigain, Philip	Law	20	50			Surveyed NH, Named Granite St.
Carrillo, Leo	Entertainment	45	50	60	150	
Carroll, Charles (Of Carrollton)	Revolutionary War	275	565	765		Signer Decl. of Indepen.
Carroll, Daniel	Revolutionary War	175	685	710		Continental Congress
Carroll, Diahann	Entertainment	6	8	15	20	
Carroll, Earl	Entertainment	85	105	210	190	
Carroll, Georgia	Entertainment	5			15	Pin-Up SP $20
Carroll, John	Entertainment	10	15	20	20	
Carroll, John Lee	Governor	10		30		Governor MD
Carroll, Julian M.	Governor	10		35		Governor KY
Carroll, Leo G.	Entertainment	25			45	
Carroll, Lisa Hart	Entertainment	6	8	15	19	
Carroll, Madeleine	Entertainment	45	150		75	
Carroll, Mickey	Entertainment	10			30	"Wizard of Oz" Munchkin
Carroll, Nancy	Entertainment	10	15	20	35	
Carroll, William	Military	25		90		Gen. TN Militia, Gov. TN 1821
Carroll, William H.	Civil War	60	145			CSA Gen.
Carryl, Guy Wetmore	Author	4	15	25		
Cars, The	Entertainment	50			85	

NAME	CATEGORY	SIG	LS/DS	ALS	SP	COMMENT
Carson, Christopher "Kit"	Frontiersman	4500			3000	Scout, Indian Agt.,Trapper etc.
Carson, Jack	Entertainment	15			50	
Carson, John	Military	10			35	General WW I
Carson, Johnny	Entertainment	15	20	30	30	
Carson, Leonard "Kit"	Aviation	12	25	42	32	ACE, WW II
Carson, Rachel	Author-Science	70	130	285	100	ALS/Content $1,650
Carson, Sunset	Entertainment	20	25		45	
Carter, Ann S.	Aviation	25	40		45	1st Woman Helicopter Pilot
Carter, Ben	Entertainment	100			250	
Carter, Benny	Entertainment	40	60	100	90	
Carter, Betty	Entertainment	15			35	Lionel Hampton Vocalist
Carter, Billy	Celebrity	4	10	15	10	Pres. Carter's Brother
Carter, Boake	Radio	5	20	35	15	Radio Commentator-Vintage
Carter, Dixie	Entertainment	5	7	20	20	
Carter, Elliot	Composer	20		125		Pulitzer
Carter, Helen	Country Music	10			20	
Carter, Helena Bonham	Entertainment	20	30		40	
Carter, Hodding	Consultant	4	8	12	10	White House Aide
Carter, Howard	Science	125		425		Egyptologist, King Tut's Tomb
Carter, Janis	Entertainment	4	4	9	9	
Carter, Jimmy	President	145	410	1650	175	Pres. TLS/Content $3,000
Carter, Jimmy & Rosalyn	Pres. & 1st Lady	195			295	
Carter, Leslie, Mrs.	Entertainment	20	75	90	70	Vintage Stage & Early Films
Carter, Lillian	Celebrity	12	25		15	Pres. Carter's Mother
Carter, Lynda	Entertainment	6	8	15	20	Pin-Up SP $25
Carter, Mother Maybelle	Country Music	40			80	
Carter, Nell	Entertainment	5			15	
Carter, Robert	American Colonial		1400			
Carter, Rosalynn	First Lady	20	85	130	50	
Carter, Sonny	Astronaut	6			25	
Carter, Thomas H.	Senate	10		35	25	Senator MT. 1st Repr.from State
Carter, Tony	Entertainment	4	4	9	10	
Carter, Wilf	Country Music	10			20	
Carteri, Rosanna	Entertainment	10			30	
Cartland, Barbara	Author	15	50	70	75	Br. Novelist. Romantic Novels
Cartwright, Angela	Entertainment	5	6	15	15	
Carty, John J.	Science-Business	60	150	275	150	Telephone Pioneer. AT&T
Caruso, Anthony	Entertainment	25	29	70	65	
Caruso, Enrico	Entertainment	275	625	1250	1265	Caricature Self-Portr.$625-1350
Carvel, Elbert M.	Governor	10	15			Governor DE
Carver, Geo. Washington	Science	200	820	860		Hall of Fame, Botanist,Educator
Carvey, Dana	Entertainment	10			40	
Carville, Edward P.	Gov-Senate	12	15	40	20	Senator, Governor NV
Cary, Phoebe	Author	10	15			Am. Poet/Sister Alice
Cary, Samuel Fenton	Senate/Congress	10		30	25	MOC OH
Casadesus, Robert, Dr.	Composer	45		100	100	Fr. Concert Pianist-Composer
Casals, Pablo	Composer-Cellist	100	150	245	285	Spanish Cellist, AMusQS $300
Casanovo, Giacomo	Author	150	580	915		Adventurer, Gambler, Spy
Case, Clifford P.	Senate/Congress	5			10	Senator, MOC NJ
Case, Francis H.	Senate/Congress	10	25		15	Senator, MOC IA
Case, Jerome I.	Business	30	60	155		Case Tractors & Farm Implements
Case, Norman S.	Governor	10	25			Governor RI
Casella, Alfredo	Composer	35	130	250		Pianist, Conductor
Casellato, Renzo	Entertainment	5			20	Opera
Casey, Silas	Civil War	35	85	160		Union General
Cash, Johnny	Country Music	8			20	

NAME	CATEGORY	SIG	LS/DS	ALS	SP	COMMENT
Cash, June Carter	Country Music	6			15	
Cash, Kellye	Celebrity	8		12	12	
Cash, Rosanne	Entertainment	5	6	15	20	Pin-Up SP $25
Cash, Tommy	Country Music 5			10		
Casper, John H.	Astronaut	8		95	20	
Cass, Lewis	Cabinet	30	110	190		Jackson Sec'y War, Senator MI
Cass, Peggy	Entertainment	5			10	
Cassatt, Mary	Artist	225	475	975		ALS/Content $4,500, $5,000
Cassavetes, John	Entertainment	20	15	20	55	Actor, Film Director
Cassidy, David	Entertainment	5			15	
Cassidy, Jack	Entertainment	25			55	
Cassidy, Joanna	Entertainment	5	6	15	15	
Cassidy, Shaun	Entertainment	10			35	
Cassidy, Ted	Entertainment	175	220	300	425	
Cassin, Jimmy	Composer	10	40			Songwriter
Cassin, Rene	Statesman	30	75	175	45	Founder UNESCO, Nobel Peace
Cassini, Oleg	Business	10	25	40	15	Fashion Designer
Casson, Mel*	Cartoonist	10			20	Redeye
Castagna, Bruna	Entertainment	20			100	Opera
Castanzo, Jack	Entertainment	10			30	Jazz Musician
Castelnuovo-Tedesco, M.	Composer	65		300	125	Opera, Ballet, Orchestral, Film
Castle, Irene	Entertainment	20	40	65	45	
Castle, Irene & Castle, Vernon	Entertainment	100			425	Dance Couple
Castle, Lee	Entertainment	5	6	15	15	
Castle, Peggy	Entertainment	10			25	
Castle, Vernon	Entertainment	50			150	
Castle, William	Entertainment	40			100	
Castlereagh, R. Stewart, Viscount	Statesman	20	55	130		Powerful Minister War vs Napol.
Castro, Emilio	Clergy	25	30	35	35	
Castro, Fidel	Head of State	850	925	1350	1250	Communist Premier of Cuba
Castro, Raul H.	Governor	5			12	Governor AZ
Cates, Clifton B.	Military	10	25	50	18	
Cates, Phoebe	Entertainment	7	8	15	30	Pin-Up SP $35
Cathcart, Wm. Schaw Sir	Revolutionary War	65	130			Cmdr."British Legion"in America
Cather, Willa	Author	120	360	645	150	Novelist.ALS/Cont $2,250
Catherine I (Rus)	Royalty	520	2000	4500		
Catherine II (The Great)	Royalty	325	2325	3050		
Catherine de Medicis 1519-89	Royalty	270	800	1700		Queen of Henry II, France
Catherwood, Mary	Author	10	15	20		
Catlett, Walter	Entertainment	10	15	25	25	
Catlin, George	Artist-Author	100	310	640		Travel Books.Indian Scenes
Catlin, Isaac	Civil War	50	95			Union Gen., CMH
Catt, Carrie Chapman	Women's Rights	50	120	250		Suffragette
Catton, Bruce	Author	30	75	125	30	Historian, Editor. Pulitzer
Caulfield, Joan	Entertainment	10			30	Pin-Up SP $35
Cavalieri Muratore, Lina	Entertainment	50			220	Opera
Cavallaro, Carmen	Entertainment	15			35	Big Band Leader-Pianist
Cavanagh, Paul	Entertainment	7			20	
Cavanaugh, Hobart	Entertainment	15	18	20	35	
Cavell, Edith	Science	225	375	545		Br. Nurse.Court Martial.Shot
Cavett, Dick	Entertainment	3	6	10	10	
Cayce, Edgar	Author	70	225			Am. Rural Healer, Seer
Cayvan, Georgia	Entertainment	6	8	15	15	
Ceausecu, Nicolae	Head of State	40	120		90	Pres. Romania. Assassinated
Cech, Thomas R., Dr.	Science	20	35		30	Nobel Chemistry
Cecil, Edg. Algernon, Lord	Diplomat	20	30			Statesman. Nobel Peace Prize

NAME	CATEGORY	SIG	LS/DS	ALS	SP	COMMENT
Celler, Emanuel	Senate/Congress	5	20		10	MOC NY
Cellini, Benvenuto	Artist	1000	4800	13500		Florentine Goldsmith, Sculptor
Cello, Aldo	Business	3	9	10	10	TV Ad vertising
Cenker, Robert	Astronaut	5			15	
Cerf, Bennett	Author	15	20	30	10	Random House Editor
Cermak, Anton J.	Politician	15	40	95	125	Assassinated Mayor of Chicago
Cernan, Eugene A.	Astronaut	20			70	Moonwalker Astro.
Cervantes, Miguel de	Author	10000	15000			Sp.Novelist,Poet."Don Quixote"
Cesky, Charles J.	Aviation	10	22	38	28	ACE, WW II
Cetywago, King of Zulu	Afr. Leader	375				
Cezanne, Paul	Artist	1100	2300	8000		Fr. Impressionist to Cubism
Chabas, Paul Emile	Artist	35	60	135		
Chabot, Phillipe de Brion, Comte	Military	1750				1480-1543. Fr.Cmdr.In Chief
Chabrier, Emmanuel	Composer	70	255	450		Fr. Opera, Orchestral, Piano
Chadwick, James, Sir	Science	80	215	450		Nobel Phys. Discovered Neutron
Chaffee, Adna R.	Civil War	35	80	115		Union General
Chaffee, Roger	Astronaut	200			400	
Chagall, Marc	Artist	280	660	575	595	Color Repro S $125-$275
Chaka Kahn	Entertainment	10			30	
Chakiris, George	Entertainment	10	15	25	25	
Chalia, Rosalia	Entertainment	25	40	65		
Chaliapin, Feodor	Entertainment	200	260	500	820	Opera. Rus. Basso
Chalker, Jack	Author	10	20	40	10	
Chalmers, James R.	Civil War	130	346			CSA General
Chalmers, Thomas	Clergy	55	60	80	75	
Chamberlain, Austen, Sir	Statesman	20	85	100	100	Nobel Peace Prize
Chamberlain, Daniel	Governor	50	125			Carpetbag Gov. SC
Chamberlain, Joseph	Br. Politician	20		85	75	Statesman, Nobel Peace Prize
Chamberlain, Joshua Lawrence	Civil War	450	875	1150		ALS Re Gettysburg $3500
Chamberlain, Neville	Head of State	75	450	400	165	Prime Minister
Chamberlain, Owen, Dr	Science	25	35	75	30	Nobel Physics
Chamberlain, Richard	Entertainment	15	15	30	25	
Chamberlain, S.J.	Military	10	30	50		
Chamberlaine, William	Military	10		35	20	General WW I
Chamberlin, Clarence	Aviation	50	250	375	250	Record Non-Stop Flight NY-Ger.
Chambers Brothers (All)	Entertainment	50			200	Rock Group
Chambers, Marilyn	Entertainment	10	15	25	30	Pin-Up SP $50
Chambers, Robert Wm.	Author-Artist	10	15	20		Novelist."Life" Mag Illustrator
Chambers, Whittaker	Journalist	15	50	150	25	Charged Alger Hiss as Communist
Chaminade, Cecile	Composer	85	195	300	270	AMusQS $125
Champion, Gower	Entertainment	25	30	60	75	
Champion, Gower & Marge	Entertainment	50			75	Both Dancers
Champion, Marge	Entertainment	10	12	15	20	Dancer
Chan, Genie*	Cartoonist	10			35	Conan
Chancellor, John	News	15			20	Radio-TV News Commentator
Chandler, A.B. 'Happy'	Senate-Gov.	15	35		50	Sen., Gov. KY.Baseball Comm.
Chandler, Christopher	Celebrity	6		40		
Chandler, Dorothy 'Buff'	Business	8	20	45	25	"Buffums" Dept. Stores
Chandler, George	Entertainment					
Chandler, Helen	Entertainment	30			75	
Chandler, Jeff	Entertainment	60	75	150	120	
Chandler, Joseph Ripley	Senate/Congress	15		35		MOC PA 1843. Editor US Gazette
Chandler, Lane	Entertainment	20			40	
Chandler, Norman	Business	15	35	75	30	L.A. Times
Chandler, Otis	Business	20	45	95	40	Founder L.A. Times
Chandler, Raymond	Author	190	540	975		Novelist. Detective Fiction

NAME	CATEGORY	SIG	LS/DS	ALS	SP	COMMENT
Chandler, William E.	Cabinet-Senate	15	38	65		Senator NH, Sec'y Navy
Chandler, Zachariah	Cabinet-Senate	12	35	50		Senator NH, Sec'y Interior
Chandrasekhar, Subrahmanyan	Science	30	110	225		Nobel, Astrophysicist
Chandu the Magician	Entertainment	5	7	25	20	
Chanel, Coco	Business	50	110	235	85	Fashion Designer, Perfumer
Chaney, Lon, Jr.	Entertainment	375	410	500	650	
Chaney, Lon, Sr.	Entertainment	1225			2700	
Chang	Entertainment	15			45	Chinese Giant
Chang, Franklin R.	Astronaut	5			15	
Channing, Carol	Entertainment	4	4	9	10	
Channing, Stockard	Entertainment	4	4	9	10	
Channing, William Ellery	Clergy-Author	40	70	120		
Channing, William Henry	Clergy	35	45	65	50	
Chaparral, John and Paul	Country Music	20			40	
Chapin, Harry	Composer	100			285	Singer-Songwriter
Chaplin, Charlie	Entertainment	275	325	500	930	
Chaplin, Geraldine	Entertainment	10	15	28	30	
Chaplin, Lita Grey	Entertainment	15	20	30	25	
Chaplin, Sydney	Entertainment	15	15	35	30	
Chapman, Graham	Entertainment	15	20	25	30	
Chapman, Leonard, Jr.	Military	15	30		55	USMC General, WW II
Chapman, Marguerite	Entertainment	10			20	Pin-Up SP $25
Chapman, Mark David	Criminal	75	135			Murdered John Lennon
Chapman, Oscar L.	Cabinet	15	20	30	35	Sec'y Interior 1849
Chapman, Philip K.	Astronaut	6			20	
Chappell, Clovis G.	Clergy	20	25	30	30	
Chappell, William 1809-1888	Business	20	45	110	35	Music Publisher
Chaptal, Jean Antoine, Count	Napoleonic	135	200			Chemist.Min.Agri., Interior
Charcot, Jean Martin	Science	90	225	825		Fr. Neurologist and Teacher
Charisse, Cyd	Entertainment	5	6	15	20	Pin-Up SP $30
Charlemagne	Royalty	75000				Price Estimate Only
Charles Edw. Stuart	Royalty	110	350	815		"Bonnie Prince Charlie"
Charles Emmanuel I 1562-1630	Royalty	595	900			"The Great"
Charles I (Eng)	Royalty	625	2400	4000		Important DS (1642) $4500
Charles II (Eng)	Royalty	375	1585	2700		
Charles II (Sp)	Royalty	275	395			
Charles IV (Eng)	Royalty	245	1100			
Charles IV (Sp)	Royalty	185		600		
Charles IX (Fr)	Royalty	190	550	1700		
Charles V (Charles I {Sp})	Royalty	580	2000	5000		
Charles VI (Charles III {Sp})	Royalty	375	1200			Holy Roman Emperor 1711-1740
Charles X (Fr)	Royalty	150	450	725		
Charles XIV John (Swe)	Royalty	145	675	880		See also Bernadotte
Charles XV (Swe-Nor)	Royalty	45	140	320		
Charles, Ernest	Composer	20	80		45	
Charles, Prince of Wales	Head of State	675		1350	756	Philip Arthur George
Charles, Ray	Entertainment		200			Blind Afro-Am. Singer-Musician
Charles, Suzette	Entertainment	5	6	15	20	Miss American 1984
Charlotte Sophia	Royalty	145	275	546		Queen of George III (Eng)
Charlotte, Grand Duchess	Royalty	20	75	180	50	Luxembourg
Charo	Entertainment	3	3	6	10	
Charpentier, Gustave	Composer	100	250	370	300	AMusQS $450-$625
Charteris, Leslie	Author	20	55	135	85	"The Saint"
Chase, Charley	Entertainment	20			150	Vintage Film Comedian
Chase, Chevy	Entertainment	5	6	15	25	
Chase, Ilka	Author, Entertain	10	10	20	25	

NAME	CATEGORY	SIG	LS/DS	ALS	SP	COMMENT
Chase, Mary Ellen	Author	25	70	150	35	Educator, Essayist,Novelist
Chase, Salmon P. (SC)	Supreme Court	90	150	325	300	Chief Justice Supr. Ct.,Cabinet
Chase, Samuel	Revolutionary War	275	775	1550		Signer Decl. of Indepen.
Chase, William C.	Military	6	20	35		
Chateaubriand, Francois Rene de	Author	120	305	650		Fr. Novelist, Diplomat
Chatterton, Ruth	Entertainment	20			55	
Chauncey, Isaac 1772-1840	Military	20	45	90		Am. Naval Off. Tripoli, War1812
Chausson, Ernest	Composer	50	145	345		Fr. Opera, Symphonies
Chauvel, Henry, Sir	Military	25	75			Aussie General WW I
Chavez, Carlos	Composer	15	35	70	40	Mexican Conductor-Composer
Chavez, Cesar E.	Labor	40			55	Migrant Labor Organizer
Chavez, Dennis	Senate	10	25		30	NM. 1st Hispanic Rep & Senator
Chavez, George A.	Aviation	45	58	175	65	
Chayefsky, Paddy (Sidney)	Author	75	150	250	125	Plays, TV Dramas, Screenplays
Cheap Trick	Entertainment	35			40	
Cheatham, Benj. Franklin	Civil War	225	375			CSA General
Checker, Chubby	Entertainment	10	20	25	40	Rock
Cheek, John	Entertainment	10			25	Opera
Cheever, Charles A., Dr.	Science	40	100		75	
Cheever, John	Author	45	125	250	100	Subtle, Ironic Novels. Pulitzer
Chekhov, Anton	Author	560	1815	4225		Rus.Dramatist. Novelist
Chen, Tina	Composer	10	10		15	
Cheney, Dick	Cabinet	10			25	Sec'y Defense
Cheney, Sherwood	Military	5		25		General WW I
Chennault, Anna	Celebrity	10	20	50	25	Wife of Claire Chennault
Chennault, Claire L.	Aviation	200	350	660	650	Flying Tigers. USAAF Gen.
Cher	Entertainment	10	15	28	70	Pin-Up SP $80
Cherkassky, Shura	Entertainment	20			60	Opera
Chernov, Vladimir	Entertainment	10			30	Opera, Rus. Baritone
Cherry, R. Gregg	Governor	5	15		10	Governor NC
Cherubini, Luigi	Composer	175	375	595		It. 29 Operas, 15 Masses
Chesebrough, George M.	Science		750			
Chesebrough, Robert	Business	15	30	50		Vaseline Products
Cheshire, Leonard	Military	15	50	65	40	Br. RAF
Chester, Bob	Entertainment	20			40	Big Band Leader
Chester, Colby M.	Business	10			55	CEO General Foods
Chester, John	Revolutionary War	35	80			Continental Army. Judge
Chesterfield, Fourth Earl of						SEE STANHOPE, P.D.
Chesterton, Gilbert Keith	Author	50	175	325	190	"Father Brown, Detective"
Chestnut, James	Civil War	250				CSA Gen.
Chevalier, Albert	Composer	6	25	40		
Chevalier, Maurice	Entertainment	35			95	
Chevrolet, Louis	Business	750				Chevrolet Auto Mfg.
Chiao, Leroy	Astronaut	7			15	
Chicago	Entertainment	35			85	
Chichester, Francis, Sir	Celebrity	35	100	165	75	Aviator, Sailed Gypsy Moth IV
Child, Julia	Celebrity Chef	5	12	15	10	TV Chef. Cookbook Author
Child, Lydia Maria	Author	30	90	155		Abolitionist, Reformer, Editor
Childress, Alvin	Entertainment	50			125	
Childs, George Wm.	Publisher	10	15	25		
Chiles, Lawton Mainor, Jr.	Senate	10	15	20	15	Senator FL
Chiles, Lois	Entertainment	5	6	15	15	
Chilton, Kevin P.	Astronaut	4			12	
Chirac, Jacques	Head of State	25	75	185	35	Fr. Prime MInister, Mayor Paris
Chisholm, Shirley A.	Senate/Congress	5			12	Afro-Am. Congresswoman NY
Choate, Joseph H.	Diplomat	15	60	90	25	Prosecuted Tweed Ring

NAME	CATEGORY	SIG	LS/DS	ALS	SP	COMMENT
Choate, Rufus 1799-1859	Senate	20	35	55		Boston Statesman,Orator, NY Sen
Choiseul, Leopold C. de, Cardinal	Clergy	100	165			
Chong, Rae Dawn	Entertainment	6	8	15	20	
Chopin, Frederic	Composer	1200	3500	8000		ALS/Cont. $16,500
Chou En-Lai	Headsof State	1155	4000	10000	2500	Chinese Communist Premier
Chouteau, Rene Auguste	Revolutionary War	350	800	1515		American Pioneer. Fur Trader
Christian VII (Den & Nor)	Royalty	125	320	625		
Christian, George B.	Senate	5	20		10	Senator OH
Christians, Mady	Entertainment	25	30	65	60	
Christie, Agatha	Author	225	775		800	Classic Detective Novels
Christie, Julie	Entertainment	10	15	28	25	Pin-Up SP $60
Christina, Queen (Swe)	Royalty	250	1675	2300		
Christine, Virginia	Entertainment	4	4	9	15	
Christo	Artist	5	12	20	85	
Christophe, Henry	Head of State	1375	875			Haiti
Christopher, Dennis	Entertainment	3	3	6	6	
Christopher, Warren	Cabinet	15	35		25	Sec'y State
Christopher, William	Entertainment	5	6	15	15	
Christy, Howard Chandler	Artist	45	125	275		Illustrator, Portraitist. Books
Christy, June	Entertainment	10			20	Stan Kenton Vocalist
Chrysler, Walter P.	Business	150	500	750	420	Chrysler Auto Mfg.
Chun Doo-Hwan	Head of State	25		50		
Chung, Connie	News	5	10	20	15	TV News Anchor
Church, Benjamin 1734-38	Revolutionary War	195	530	1010		Am. Physician & Spy
Church, Frank	Senate/Congress	5	15		10	Senator ID
Church, Frederick Edwin	Artist	150	425	725		Painted Dramatic Landscapes
Church, Frederick S.	Artist	40	65	120		ALS/Sketch $500
Church, R.W.	Clergy	20	35	50		
Churchill, Clementine S.	Br. First Lady	75	200	235	160	Wife of Winston S.
Churchill, Jennie(Jerome)	Celebrity	15	75	235	95	W.S. Churchill's Mother
Churchill, John 1650-1722	Military	1100				1st Duke of Marlborough
Churchill, Mary	Celebrity	5		25		
Churchill, Randolph, Lord	Br. Statesman	45	95	285		Father of Winston S.
Churchill, Sarah	Entertainment	20	15	30	35	Actress-Daughter of Winston S.
Churchill, Thomas J.	Civil War	45	80	135		CSA Gen., Gov. AR
Churchill, Winston	Author	15	35	60	35	
Churchill, Winston S.	Head of State	750	3575	4500	3650	WW II Prime Minister
Ciannelli, Eduardo	Entertainment	20			45	
Ciano, Galeazzo, Conte	Royalty	65	295			Son-in-Law of Mussolini
Cicognani, A.G., Cardinal	Clergy	35	50	75	60	
Cigna, Gina	Entertainment	55	70			
Cimaro, Pietro	Entertainment	10	25	50		It. Conductor
Cimino, Michael	Entertainment	6	8	15	20	Film Director
Citroen, Andre	Business	75	350		325	Citroen Auto Mfg.
Civiletti, Benjamin	Cabinet	5	10	20	10	
Clairborne, Liz	Business	10			20	Clothing Designer
Claire, Ina	Entertainment	15	15	35	25	
Claire, Marion	Entertainment	10			25	Am. Soprano
Clamorgan, Jacques	Explorer-Trader		750			Missouri Co. 1795
Clancey, Tom	Author	5	15		10	Am. Novelist
Clanton, Jimmy	Entertainment	20			25	Rock
Clanton, N.H.	Celebrity	1100				
Clapton, Eric	Entertainment	30			90	Rock
Clark, Abraham	Revolutionary War	320	800	2750		Signer Decl. of Indepen.
Clark, Barzilla W.	Governor	5	12	20		Governor ID
Clark, Bruce C.	Military	6	20	35	15	

NAME	CATEGORY	SIG	LS/DS	ALS	SP	COMMENT
Clark, Buddy	Entertainment	10			25	40's Singer
Clark, Candy	Entertainment	3	3	6	6	
Clark, Carol Higgins	Author	5	15		20	"All Around the Town"
Clark, Charles	Civil War	110	275	350		CSA General, CW Gov. of Miss.
Clark, Clarence D.	Senate	10		35	15	Senator WY
Clark, Cottonseed	Country Music	15			30	
Clark, Dane	Entertainment	7	7	10	13	
Clark, Dick	Entertainment	6	8	15	19	
Clark, Francis E.	Clergy	10	15	25	20	
Clark, Frank	Senate/Congress	5	15		10	Congressman FL
Clark, Fred	Entertainment	25			50	
Clark, George Rogers	Revolutionary War	675	3280	4300		Frontier Leader
Clark, James B. "Champ"	Congress	60	120	145	95	Speaker of the House. MO
Clark, James, Sir	Medical	15	35	85		Phys.to Queen Victoria & Albert
Clark, L. Gaylord	Author	20	35	95		Editor Knickerbocker Magazine
Clark, Marguerite	Entertainment	20			50	Stage.Film Rival Mary Pickford
Clark, Mark W.	Military	35	215	275	110	Gen. WW II
Clark, Mary	Military	5	8	15	15	
Clark, Myron H.	Governor	10	20	35	15	Governor NY
Clark, Petula	Entertainment	7	9	11	13	Br. Singer
Clark, Ramsay	Cabinet	15	35	60	20	Att'y Gen.
Clark, Roy	Country Music	6			15	
Clark, Susan	Entertainment	5	10	12	15	Pin-Up SP $25
Clark, Tom C. (SC)	Supreme Court	40	100	125	75	
Clark, Walter J.	Aviation	10	22	38	28	ACE, WW II
Clark, William	Explorer	375	1650	2500		Lewis & Clark Expedition
Clark, William A.	Senate	35	135	195		Railroad & Mining Magnate
Clarke, Adam	Clergy	75	145	350		
Clarke, Annie	Entertainment	15	15	25	25	
Clarke, Arthur C.	Author	15	35	75	25	"2001"
Clarke, Charles Mansfield	Medical	20	65	140		Br. Obstetrician
Clarke, George	Colonial Gov. N.Y	85	350			
Clarke, Henri J.G. Duc de	Napoleonic Wars	50	275	345		Marshal of Napoleon
Clarke, James Freeman	Clergy	30	50	75	60	
Clarke, James McClure	Senate/Congress	5			10	MOC NC
Clarke, Mae	Entertainment	25			60	
Clarke, Robert	Entertainment	20			50	
Clarke, Thomas	Revolutionary War	165	550			
Clarkson, Mathew	Military-Rev. War	45	95	185		
Clary, Alice	Author	15	25		15	
Clary, B. A.	Military	5	15	20	10	
Clary, Robert	Entertainment	4	4	9	12	
Clavell, James	Author	10	25	55	15	Novelist
Clay, Cassius Marcellus	Civil War	80	220	450		Union Gen., Senate, Abolition.
Clay, Henry	Cabinet	100	290	550	250	Sec'y State, ALS Auct. $9,300
Clay, Lucius D.	Military	30	110	145	100	Gen. WW II
Clay, William L., Sr.	Senate/Congress	5			15	Afro-Am. Congressman MO
Clayburgh, Jill	Entertainment	5	6	15	15	
Clayton, Henry D.	Senate/Congress	5	10			MOC AL
Clayton, Jan	Entertainment	5	6	15	15	
Clayton, John M.	Cabinet	30	65	140		Taylor Sec'y State
Clayton, Joshua 1744-1798	Revolutionary War	220	425			1st Gov. DE. Senator DE
Clayton, Powell	Senate/Congress	10	25			Senator AR
Clayton, S. J.	Senate/Congress	5	10			
Cleave, Mary	Astronaut	12			25	
Cleaveland, Moses	Revolutionary War	170	850			Cleveland, Ohio Namesake

NAME	CATEGORY	SIG	LS/DS	ALS	SP	COMMENT
Cleburne, Patrick R.	Civil War	1050	1650			CSA General
Cleese, John	Entertainment	5	6	15	32	
Clem, John L. "Johnny"	Civil War	150	185	220		Union Drummer Boy, Chicamauga
Clemenceau, Georges	Head of State	110	140	175		Prime Minister France
Clemens, Orion (Brother of Samuel)	West	125		160		Sec'y of Nevada Territory 1861
Clemens, S. as Mark Twain	Author	875			4500	ALS/Content $19,500
Clemens, S.L. and Twain, Mark	Author	1025		4500		
Clemens, Samuel L.	Author	750	2085	4375	4465	ALS Content $19,000
Clement VIII, Pope	Head of State	550	1300			
Clement, Martin Withington	Business	3	8	16	6	Pres. CEO Pennsylvania RR
Clements, Stanley "Stash"	Entertainment	10			20	
Cleveland, Carleton A.	Business	10	35	45	20	
Cleveland, Charles	Clergy	20	25	45		
Cleveland, Frances F.	First Lady	50	80	245	250	
Cleveland, Grover	President	250	560	925	635	ALS/Content $3,500
Clewes, Henry	Business	25	45			Banker
Cliburn, Van	Entertainment	25	28	55	95	Am. Pianist
Clifford, Clark M.	Cabinet	10	15	25	15	Sec'y Defense
Clifford, John Henry	Governor	10	55	95		
Clifford, Nathan (SC)	Supreme Court	75	175	240	150	
Clifford, Rich	Astronaut	7			15	
Clift, Montgomery	Entertainment	275	355	600	750	
Clifton, Joseph C.	Aviation	15	35	60	40	
Cline, Patsy	Country Music	465			650	
Clinger, Debora	Entertainment	3	5	7	8	
Clingman, Thomas Lanier	Civil War	95	205	315		CSA General
Clinton, De Witt	Governor	65	175	225		Promoted Erie Canal. Statesman
Clinton, George (V)	V.P.-Military	120	330	385		Historical ALS $7,000
Clinton, Henry, Sir	Military-Rev. War	425	925	2200		Br. Soldier
Clinton, James	Military-Rev. War	200	490			General Revolutionary War
Clinton, William J. (Bill)	President	150	275		455	
Clive, Colin	Entertainment	250			525	
Clive, E.E.	Entertainment	20			50	
Clive, Robert	Military	250	600	1200		Baron Clive of Plassey
Cloggers, Stoney Mtn.	Country Music	30			60	
Clokey, Art*	Cartoonist	20			150	Gumby
Clooney, Rosemary	Entertainment	5	6	15	15	
Close, Glenn	Entertainment	10	15	20	30	
Clostermann, Pierre	Military	55	85	125	75	
Clover, Richardson	Military	35	125			USN Admiral
Clovio, Giorgio Guilio 1498-1578	Artist	650	1400	2000		It. Miniaturist
Clyde, Andy	Entertainment	50			150	
Clyde, June	Entertainment	8	9	15	20	
Clymer, George	Revolutionary War	125	660	725		Signer Decl. of Indepen.
Coase, Ronald	Economist	20	35		25	Nobel Economics
Coates, Eric	Composer	25	55	85	130	
Coates, Phyllis	Entertainment	10			20	
Coats, Bob	Aviation	10	22	38	30	ACE, WW II
Coats, Michael L.	Astronaut	10			25	
Cobb, Calvin H.	Military	15	40	75		
Cobb, Howell	Civil War	125	255	375		CSA Gen.
Cobb, Irvin S.	Author	35	115	150	95	Journalist-Humorist
Cobb, Jerrie	Aviation	5	10	19	21	
Cobb, Lee J.	Entertainment	35	50	75	85	
Cobham, Alan J., Sir	Aviation	25	65	85	45	Br. Aviation Pioneer
Cobham, Gov. Gen. NZ	Head of State	5	8	15	10	New Zealand

NAME	CATEGORY	SIG	LS/DS	ALS	SP	COMMENT
Cobo, Albert E.	Celebrity	10	15	45	15	Detroit's Cobo Hall
Coburn, Charles	Entertainment	40	90	155	125	
Coburn, James	Entertainment	10	15	25	25	
Coca, Imogene	Entertainment	10			25	
Cochran, Eddie	Entertainment	100			300	Star of Early Rock. Died at 22
Cochran, Jacqueline	Aviation	45	175		75	Speed record holder
Cochran, Robert L.	Governor	12	20	30	15	Governor NE
Cochran, Steve	Entertainment	15	15	30	28	
Cochrane, Basil, Sir	Military	15	25	30		
Cochrane, John	Civil War	30	45	100		Union Gen.
Cochrane, Ralph	Military	5	15	25	20	NRPA
Cockburn, George, Sir	Military	40	100	140		Br. Admiral War 1812
Cockcroft, John Douglas, Sir	Science	60	110	245	75	Nobel Physics
Cocker, Joe	Entertainment	20	40		35	Rock
Cockrell, Francis Marion	Civil War	50	110	225		CSA General, US Sen. MO
Cockrell, Ken	Astronaut	7			15	
Coco, James	Entertainment	15	20	25	35	
Cocteau, Jean	Author-Artist	100	175	535	450	Orig. Sketch S $795
Coda, Eraldo	Entertainment	5			25	Opera
Cody, Buck	Entertainment	3	3	6	6	
Cody, Iron Eyes	Entertainment	15	18	25	30	
Cody, John P., Cardinal	Clergy	25	35	50	45	
Cody, Lew	Entertainment	15	20	25	35	
Cody, William F.	Celebrity	675	1375	1250	1650	CW Scout, Pony Expr.,Showman
Cody, William F. & "Buffalo Bill"	Celebrity	785			6500	Signed both Ways
Coffin, Henry Sloane	Clergy	25	35	40	50	
Coffin, John 1756-1838	Revolutionary War	175	500			Loyalist General
Coffin, Tris	Entertainment	20			35	
Coffin, William Sloane	Clergy	25	30	35	50	
Coffyn, Frank	Aviation	40	65		95	
Coggan, Donald, Archbishop	Clergy	35	45	50	50	
Coghlan, Frank, "Jr."	Entertainment	5			20	
Coghlan, Joseph B.	Military	25			60	Adm USN-Spanish American War
Cogswell, William	Civil War	15	35			MOC MA
Cohan, Alexander	Entertainment					
Cohan, George M.	Composer	85	185	275	280	
Cohen, Octavus Roy	Author	15	30	45	25	Novels, Screenplays, Radio
Cohen, Stanley, Dr.	Science	20	35		25	Nobel Medicine
Cohen, Wilbur J.	Cabinet	5	7	12	10	Sec'y HEW
Cohen, William S.	Senate/Congress	10		25	20	Senator ME, MOC ME
Cohn, Harry	Business	35	85	165	65	Co-Founder Columbia Pictures
Cohn, Jack	Business	25	70	140	55	Co-Founder Columbia Pictures
Cohn, Roy	Lawyer	15	25	40	20	Legal Aide Sen. McCarthy
Coit, James Brolles	Civil War	25		125		Union General
Coke, Thomas, Bishop	Clergy	250	350	750		
Coker, Jack	Entertainment	6	8	15	20	
Colbert, Claudette	Entertainment	20	110		65	
Colby, Bainbridge	Cabinet	10	30	55		Sec'y State
Colby, Leonard	Military	40	90			General. Indian Fighter
Colden, Cadwallader	Revolutionary War	100	240			Am. Colonialist
Cole, Cornelius	Senate/Congress	15	25	40		MOC CA 1863, Senator CA
Cole, Edward N.	Business	5	12	30	10	Pres. General Motors
Cole, Michael	Entertainment	3	3	6	8	
Cole, Nat King	Entertainment	160	250		295	Am. Jazz Pianist, Singer
Cole, Natalie	Entertainment	15			40	Singer
Cole, Sterling	Congress/Senate	5	10			Congressman NY

NAME	CATEGORY	SIG	LS/DS	ALS	SP	COMMENT
Coleman, Cy	Composer	25			30	Arranger
Coleman, Dabney	Entertainment	5	6	15	15	
Coleman, Gary	Entertainment	5	7	12	15	
Coleman, Nancy	Entertainment	6	8	15	10	
Colenso, John W., Bishop	Clergy	20	25	35		
Coleridge, John Duke	Celebrity	6	12	25		
Coleridge, Samuel Taylor	Author	325	575	1290		Br. Poet, Critic
Coleridge-Taylor, Samuel	Composer	30	70	125	40	Choral, Musical Theatre, Songs
Colette, Sidonie-Gabrielle	Author	65	315	440	600	Fr. Novelist
Colfax, Schuyler (V)	Vice President	65	125	175	250	Speaker of House IN, Grant VP
Colgate. James C.	Business	10	25	50	40	Colgate University. Donor
Colgrass, Michael	Composer	20	35	85		Pulitzer, AMusQS $100
Collamer, Jacob	Cabinet	20	55	80		Taylor P.M. General
Collier, James W.	Senate/Congress	5	15		10	MOC MS
Collier, Peter F.	Business	14	35	70		
Collinge, Patricia	Entertainment	6	8	15	19	
Collingwood, Charles	Journalist	5	10		15	News Analyst, War Correspondent
Collins, Cardiss	Senate/Congress	5	15		10	MOC MO
Collins, Eileen	Astronaut	7			15	
Collins, J. Lawton	Military	15	50	80	35	General WW II
Collins, Jackie	Author	10	15	20	15	Novelist
Collins, Joan	Entertainment	15	15	30	25	Pin-Up SP $30
Collins, Judy	Entertainment	5	6	15	15	Singer
Collins, LeRoy	Governor	5	10		14	Governor FL
Collins, Lottie	Entertainment	15	15	25	25	
Collins, Michael	Astronaut	40	150	250	135	
Collins, Phil	Entertainment	30			55	Singer
Collins, Ray	Entertainment	50	60	150	175	
Collins, Wilkie	Author	110	309	530		Br. Novelist,Biography,Mystery
Collis, Charles	Civil War	25		60		Union Gen., CMH
Collishaw, Raymond	Aviation	75	175	375	225	Brit. ACE, WW I
Collyer, Robert, Dr.	Clergy	35	50	65		
Colman, Ronald	Entertainment	50	65	130	150	
Colombo, Scipio	Entertainment	10			30	Opera
Colonna, Jerry	Entertainment	8	9	19	15	
Color Me Badd	Entertainment	10			25	Rock
Colquitt, Alfred H.	Civil War	85	165	275	250	CSA Gen., US Sen. GA
Colson, Charles W. 'Chuck'	Clergy	35	50	85	45	
Colston, Raleigh E.	Civil War	70	425			CSA Gen.
Colt, Samuel	Business-Inventor	400	1875	3975		Founder Colt Firearms
Coltrane, John	Entertainment					Great Jazz Saxophonist. NRPA
Colum, Padraic	Author	30	150		40	Irish Poet & Playwright
Columbo, Russ	Entertainment	50	90	200	175	
Comden, Betty & Green, A.	Composers	10	45		30	Collaberators Broadway Musicals
Commager, Henry Steele	Civil War	25	60	105		Union General
Command Performance (5)	Entertainment	20			50	
Commodores	Entertainment	25			60	
Como, Perry	Entertainment	4	6	15	10	
Compson, Betty	Entertainment	25	30	60	70	
Compton, Arthur H.	Science	90	205	200	100	Nobel Physics
Compton, Fay	Entertainment	5			15	Br. Actress
Compton, Joyce	Entertainment	8	9	19	15	
Compton, Karl T.	Science	90	210		110	Physicist, Pres. M.I.T.
Conant, A. Roger	Aviation	10	22	38	28	ACE, WW II, Marine Ace
Conant, James Bryant	Diplomat	10	15	30	20	Educator, US Ambassador
Conati, Lorenzo	Entertainment	20			65	Opera

NAME	CATEGORY	SIG	LS/DS	ALS	SP	COMMENT
Conchita, Maria	Entertainment	4			10	
Condon, Eddie	Composer	40			60	Guitarist
Condon, Richard	Author	5	15	35	10	
Cone, Fairfax M.	Business	10	35	45	20	Foote,Cone & Belding, Adv.
Cone, Hutchinson	Military	25	35			Admiral WW I
Confalonieri, Carlo, Cardinal	Clergy	50	75	90	65	
Conforti, Gino	Entertainment	3	3	6	6	
Congreve, William 1670-1729	Author	190	575	1050		Br. Drama. Restoration Comedy
Congreve, William, Sir.2nd Baronet	Science	45	125	235		Artillerist, Invented Rocket
Coningham, Sir Arthur	Aviation	35	60			Cmdr. RAF 1st Tactical
Conklin, Chester	Entertainment	100	115	220		
Conkling, Roscoe	Senate	15	25		20	MOC, Senate NY Political Boss
Conlee, John	Entertainment	4			10	
Conley, Eugene	Entertainment	20	30		50	Opera
Conley, Joe	Entertainment	3	3	6	8	
Connally, John B.	Cabinet	15	40	70	30	Gov. TX, Sec'y Treasury
Connally, Tom	Senate	15	25		20	Senator TX
Connelly, Jennifer	Entertainment	15			37	
Connelly, Marc	Author	20	40	75	30	Am. Dramatist. Pulitzer
Connelly, Matthew J.	White House Staff	10	25	35	15	Pres. Truman Aide
Conner, James	Civil War	90	210	270		CSA General
Conner, Nadine	Entertainment	10			35	
Connery, Sean	Entertainment	40	50	65	125	
Conness, John	Senate	45	85			Civil War Senator CA
Connick, Harry, Jr.	Entertainment	25	45		75	Big Band Leader-Singer-Pianist
Conniff, Ray	Entertainment	25	35	65	45	
Connolly, Walter	Entertainment	70		90	85	
Connor, Harry P.	Aviation	15	30	45	50	
Connor, James	Civil War	95	205	260		CSA General
Connor, John T.	Cabinet	7	20	35	20	Sec'y Commerce
Connor, Patrick Edward	Civil War	35	58			Union General
Connors, Chuck	Entertainment	20	25	30	35	
Connors, Mike	Entertainment	5	5	7	14	
Connors, Norman	Entertainment	4			10	
Connors, Patti	Entertainment	3	3	6	6	
Conover, Harry	Business	10	17	25	15	Top Modeling Agency
Conquest, Ida	Entertainment	15	15	25	30	
Conrad, Charles Magill	Cabinet	15	30	65		Sec'y War
Conrad, Charles, Jr.	Astronaut	10			35	
Conrad, Gerhard	Aviation	10	25	45	25	
Conrad, Joseph	Author	230	1125	1450	2000	Br. Novelist. "Lord Jim" etc.
Conrad, Michael	Entertainment	15	20	40	35	
Conrad, Robert	Entertainment	7	10		20	
Conrad, William	Entertainment	5	6	15	15	
Conried, Hans	Entertainment	15	20	40	40	
Conroy, Kevin	Entertainment	3	3	6	6	
Constable, John	Artist	155	610	1430		Br. Landscapes, Rural Life
Constantino, Florencio	Entertainment	75			365	Opera
Conte, John	Entertainment	4	5	9	12	
Conte, Richard	Entertainment	7	10	15	15	
Conti, Bill	Composer	60	85	100	40	
Conti, Joseph	Entertainment	4			10	
Contino, Dick	Entertainment	3			8	Accordianist
Conway, Henry Seymour 1721-95	Military	25	60	85		Br. Fld. Marshal. Politician.
Conway, Rose A.	Cabinet	3	5	10	5	
Conway, Thomas	Revolutionary War	65	105	250		Maj. Gen. Rev. War

NAME	CATEGORY	SIG	LS/DS	ALS	SP	COMMENT
Conway, Tim	Entertainment	5	6	15	15	
Conway, Tom	Entertainment	50			150	
Conwell, Russell H.	Clergy	35	45	60		
Cony, Samuel	Governor	30	45	60		Civil War Gov. ME
Conyers, John	Senate/Congress	3	12		5	Afro-Am. Congressman MI
Coogan, Jackie	Entertainment	20	25	30		
Coogan, Richard	Entertainment	5	6	15	15	
Cook, Ann T.	Model	10			25	Model For Gerber Baby Products
Cook, Elisha Jr.	Entertainment	15	20	25	40	
Cook, Everett R.	Aviation	10	30		50	ACE WW I
Cook, Francis Augustus	Military	25		55	30	Spanish American War
Cook, Frederick Albert, Dr.	Explorer	75	145	175	150	Claimed 1st at North Pole
Cook, James, Capt.	Br.Naval Explorer	3800	8850	27000		"Captain Cook"
Cook, Joseph, Sir	Politician	10	20	40		Australian Statesman
Cook, Robin	Author	5			10	Novelist
Cook, Thomas	Business	35	110	545		Founder British Tourist Company
Cook, Walter V.	Aviation	8	20	38	28	ACE, WW II
Cooke, Alistair, Sir	Author	20	95	140	75	TV Host. Masterpiece Theatre
Cooke, Jack Kent	Business	10	22		15	
Cooke, Jay	Business	100	225	375	175	Banker, Financier
Cooke, Nicholas	Revolutionary War		1100			Rev. War Gov. Rhode Island
Cooke, Sam	Entertainment	175			350	
Cooke, Terence J., Cardinal	Clergy	60	75	100	95	
Cool, Harry	Entertainment	4	4		6	
Cooley, Denton A., Dr.	Science	20	40	90	40	Heart Specialist
Cooley, Lyman E.	Science	10		35		Civil Engineer
Cooley, Spade	Country Music	15			35	King of Western Swing
Coolidge, Calvin	President	200	510	3900	675	
Coolidge, Calvin (As President)	President	225	700		675	
Coolidge, Grace	First Lady	65	220	275	165	
Coolidge, John	Celebrity	40	65			Father Of Pres. Coolidge
Coolidge, Rita	Entertainment	15			25	
Coolidge, T. Jefferson	Statesman	4	10	20		
Coolidge, William David, Dr.	Science	35	85	165	125	Dir. Research G.E., Inventor
Coombs, Patricia	Artist	10	20	35	15	
Cooper, Alfred Duff	Statesman	10	25	60	15	1st Viscount Norwich. Author
Cooper, Alice	Entertainment	15		35	40	Rock
Cooper, Emil	Composer	30	45	80	50	Rus.Internat'l Cond.-Violinist
Cooper, Gary	Entertainment	165	415	375	635	
Cooper, Gladys, Dame	Entertainment	30	35	65	55	
Cooper, Gordon	Astronaut	25			80	Mercury 7 Astro.
Cooper, Jackie	Entertainment	15	15	35	30	
Cooper, James Fennimore	Author	90	215	890		Am. Novelist.ALS/Cont.$1,750
Cooper, John Sherman	Senate/Congress	10	25			Senator KY, Statesman, Diplomat
Cooper, Leon N., Dr.	Science	20	35	60	30	Nobel Physics
Cooper, Merian C.	Entertainment	100			250	King Kong, Four Feathers
Cooper, Miriam	Entertainment	35			75	
Cooper, Peter	Industrialist	45	200	310	175	Am. Inventor, Philanthropist
Cooper, Prentice	Governor	10	16			Governor TN
Cooper, Samuel	Civil War	120	230	445		CSA Ranking Gen.
Cooper, Thos. Sidney	Artist	10	20	35		
Coors, W. K.	Business	20	60	95	50	Coors Brewery
Coots, J. Fred	Composer	35	45	100	40	AMusQS $150
Copas, Cowboy	Country Music	100			225	
Copeland, C.C.	Clergy	30	80	225		
Copeland, L. du Pont	Business	20		50		

NAME	CATEGORY	SIG	LS/DS	ALS	SP	COMMENT
Copeland, Royal S., Dr.	Senate	15	70			Senator NY. Author
Copeland, William John	Clergy	20	25	35		
Copland, Aaron	Composer	75	165	285	155	AMusQS $225, $750
Copley, John Singleton 1738-1815	Artist	350	710	4875		Outstanding Am. Portraitist
Copley, Teri	Entertainment	5			15	Pin-Up SP $20
Copmpanari, Giuseppe	Entertainment	35			125	Opera
Coppens, Willy (Baron de H)	Aviation	20	40	75	50	
Copperfield, David	Entertainment	10	15		20	Illusionist
Coppola, Francis Ford	Entertainment	20	40		50	Director
Coppée, Francois	Author	15	45	115		Fr. Poet, Novelist, Dramatist
Coquelin, Benoit-Constant(Aine')	Entertainment	15	60	90		Fr. Actor-Manager, Cyrano
Coquelin, Ernest-Alex.-H.(Cadet)	Entertainment	15	30	50		Comedie-Francaise. Author
Corbett, Boston	Civil War	965		1800		Shot John Wilkes Booth
Corbett, Henry Winslow	Senate/Congress	10	15	25	20	Senator OR
Corbett, Michael	Entertainment	4			10	Actor "Young and the Restless"
Corbin, Henry Clarke	Civil War	50		115		Union General
Corbusier, Le	Architect	85	415		100	Jeanneret, Charles Edouard
Corby, Ellen	Entertainment	10			20	
Corcoran, William W.	Business	20	50			Banker, Philanthropist
Corden, Henry	Entertainment	25	55		40	Fred Flintstone (Voice)
Corea, Chick	Entertainment	15			35	
Corelli, Franco	Entertainment	25	35	100	105	Opera
Corelli, Marie	Author	20	55	65	70	Eng. Novelist
Corena, Fernando	Entertainment	20			45	Opera
Corey, Elias	Science	20	35		30	Nobel Chemistry
Corey, Jeff	Entertainment	5			15	
Corey, Wendell	Entertainment	35	45	80	75	
Cori, Carl F.	Science	15	25	47	20	Nobel Medicine
Corio, Ann	Entertainment	12	15	20	30	
Corlett, Irene	Entertainment	3	3	6	6	
Cormack, Allan M.	Science	20	35	50	25	Nobel Medicine
Corman, Roger	Entertainment	5			20	
Cornbury, Edward Hyde, Lord	Colonial Gov.	200	450			1st Colonial Gov. NJ, Gov. NY
Corneliano, Mario N. di	Clergy	35	45	60	50	
Cornelius, Peter (Carl August)	Composer	55		325		Opera, Choral Works, Song Cycle
Cornell, Ezekiel	Military	60	200			Brig. Gen. American Rev.
Cornell, Ezra	Business	30	80	165	75	Financed Western Union Telegr.
Cornell, Joseph	Artist	135	470	700		Am. Surrealist Sculptor
Cornell, Katharine	Entertainment	25		75	75	
Cornell, Lydia	Entertainment	3	3	10	10	Pin-Up SP $30
Corner, George W.	Science	75	150		100	
Cornfeld, Bernard	Business	10	20	55	35	
Cornforth, J. W.	Science	15	25	45	20	
Corning, Erastus 1794-1872	Business	70	175	295		1st Pres. NY Central Railroad
Cornwallis, Charles E.	Revolutionary War	175	365	750		Br. General Am. Revolution
Corot, J.B. Camille	Artist	212	490	990	3000	Barbizon School. Impressionist
Corrigan, Douglas	Aviation	30	80	125	100	"Wrong Way"
Corrigan, Mairead/B. William	Irish Activists	30			50	Nobel Peace Prize
Corrigan, Michael A.	Clergy	10		30	20	Bishop
Corrigan, Ray "Crash"	Entertainment	40			150	
Corse, John Murray	Civil War	35	50	80		Union General
Corson, Fred P., Bishop	Clergy	20	30	50	45	
Cortelyou, George B.	Cabinet	50	150	220		Served two Presidents.
Cortes, Hernando (Cortez)	Explorer		44300			Sp. Conqueror of Mex.
Cortez, Ricardo	Entertainment	25			40	
Cortina, Juan	Military		1500			Mexican General

NAME	CATEGORY	SIG	LS/DS	ALS	SP	COMMENT
Corwin, Thomas	Cabinet	30	55	125		Fillmore Sec'y Treasury
Cosby, Bill	Entertainment	9	10	20	25	
Cosby, George B.	Civil War	60	130	200		CSA General
Cosby, N. Gordon	Clergy	20	30	45		
Cosgrave, William T.	Head of State	85	140	275		Sinn Fe'in Easter Uprising.
Coslow, Sam	Composer-Author	50	200	300	350	Academy Award 1943
Cosmovici, C. B.	Astronaut	12			25	
Cossotto, Fioranza	Entertainment	10			30	Opera
Cossutta, Carlos	Entertainment	5			25	Opera
Costa Lo Giudice, Silvio	Entertainment	40			100	Opera
Costa, Michael, Sir	Composer	15	40	95	25	Br. Conductor.Opera, Ballet
Costa-Gavras, Constantin	Entertainment	20			40	Film Director
Costas, Bob	TV Host	5			10	TV Host & Sports Commentator
Coste, Dieudonne	Aviation	125	235	385	275	
Coste, Dieudonne & Bellonte, M.	Aviation	210			365	
Costello, Delores (Barrymore)	Entertainment	28	35	65	60	
Costello, Elvis	Entertainment	10			30	
Costello, Lou	Entertainment	200	225		400	
Costner, Kevin	Entertainment	25			65	
Coswell, Henry T.	Aviation	55	105	150		1st Balloon ascent 1844
Cotten, Joseph	Entertainment	6	10	15	25	
Cotton, Carolina	Country Music	15			30	
Coty, Francois	Business	100	300	475		Coty Perfume & Cosmetics
Couch, Darius Nash	Civil War	65	80	145		Union General
Couch, Virgil	Urban Designer	10	20	15		Dir. National Civil Defense
Coue', Emile 1857-1926	Science	175		850		Fr. Psychotherapist, Hypnotism
Cougar, John	Entertainment	10			35	
Coughlin, Charles	Clergy	25	50	60		
Coulter, Jessie	Country Music	6			15	
Coulter, Richard	Civil War	42	75	95		Union Bvt. General
Courbet, Jean D. Gustave	Artist	225	600	1090		Leader of Realist School
Couric, Katie	TV Host	5			16	Host "Today"
Court, Hazel	Entertainment	10			35	
Courtney, Inez	Entertainment	15			35	
Cousins, Norman	Author	10	25	40	15	Saturday Review Editor, Author
Cousins, William E., Archbishop	Clergy	20	35	45	35	
Cousteau, Jacques	Science-Author	50		175	100	Underwater Explorer, Films
Cousteau, Jim (Son of Jacques)	Science	25			150	Underwater Explorer (Deceased)
Couter, John B.	Military	15	47			
Couve de Murville, M.	Celebrity	5	12	20	15	
Couzens, James	Senate/Congress	10	30		15	Senator MI
Covarrubias, Miguel	Artist	150	325			Mex. Book & Magazine Illustr.
Covey, Richard O.	Astronaut	5			15	
Cowan, Edgar	Senate	15	25	35		Civil War Senator PA
Cowan, Jerome	Entertainment	10			35	
Coward, Noel, Sir	Author-Composer	165	210	380	375	AMusQS $275,Playwright,Actor
Cowl, Jane	Entertainment	22		35	45	
Cowles, Gardner	Business	12		25	15	Publisher Des Moines Register
Cox Family, The	Entertainment	25			45	Bluegrass
Cox, Archibald	Cabinet	15	35	55	20	Att'y Gen., Watergate
Cox, George H.	Author	5	15	30		Br. Historical Writer
Cox, James M.	Governor	15	60	75	25	Pres. Candidate,MOC,Gov. OH
Cox, Palmer*	Cartoonist	50	140	275	225	Author, Illustrator "Brownies"
Cox, Samuel S.	Senate/Congress	20		35		Civil War MOC OH
Cox, Wally	Entertainment	25			40	
Cox, William R.	Civil War	60	85	105		CSA Gen.

NAME	CATEGORY	SIG	LS/DS	ALS	SP	COMMENT
Coxe, Tenche	Revolutionary War	40	100	170		Continental Congress
Coxey, Jacob S.	Reformer	20	55	140	30	Led "Coxey's Army" to Wash. D.C
Coyote, Peter	Entertainment	10			35	
Crabbe, Buster	Entertainment	10	15	40	45	
Crabtree, Lotta (Charlotte)	Entertainment	25	70	125	130	Am. Musical Comedy Actress
Craddock, Crash	Country Music	5	8	20	18	
Craig, James, Sir	Head of State	60	185			1st Prime Minister No. Ireland
Craig, Edward Gordon	Entertainment	15	40	95	190	Br. Stage Designer, Actor
Craig, James	Entertainment	15			35	
Craig, James	Civil War	45	75	95		Union General
Craig, Jenny	TV Personality	4			10	Talk Show Host
Craig, Malin	Military	6	15	30		
Craig, Yvonne	Entertainment	10			25	Pin-Up SP $30
Crain, Jeanne	Entertainment	15	20	40	45	Pin-Up SP $50
Cram, Donald J., Dr.	Science	20	35		30	Nobel Chemistry
Cramer, Floyd	Country Music	5			12	Pianist
Cramer, Grant	Entertainment	6	8	15	15	
Crane Frank	Clergy	15	20	35		
Crane, Bob	Entertainment	150			200	Murdered TV Star Hogans Heroes
Crane, Charles Henry	Civil War	25		80		Union General-Surgeon
Crane, Cheryl	Celebrity	30			40	Killed Mother's "Friend"
Crane, Daniel (Scandal)	Congress	5		25	20	MOC IL
Crane, Frank	Clergy	15	25	45		
Crane, Fred	Entertainment	15			35	
Crane, Hart	Author	130	600	1500	350	Am. Poet, "The Bridge"
Crane, Henry Hitt	Clergy	25	30	50	35	
Crane, John	Military	100	250			Gen. Revolutionary War
Crane, Richard	Entertainment	20			45	
Crane, Roy*	Cartoonists	30			200	Wash Tubbs, B. Sawyer
Crane, Stephen	Author	370	1100	4350		Died at 28."Red Badge of......"
Crane, Walter	Artist - Poet	45	140	215		Br. Painter-Illustrator
Crane, William H.	Entertainment	30	45	90	55	
Crane, Winthrop M.	Senate-Business	10	25		35	Crane Stationery, Gov., Sen. MA
Cranston, Alan	Senate	15	20		22	Senator CA
Crass, Franz	Entertainment	5			25	Opera
Craven, Wes	Entertainment	10			25	Director
Cravens, Jordan E.	Civil War	25		80		CSA Officer, MOC AR
Crawford, Broderick	Entertainment	15	20	40	75	
Crawford, Christina	Author	6	10	20	15	Daughter of Joan Crawford
Crawford, Cindy	Model	10			35	Pin-Up SP $50
Crawford, Francis M. 1854-1909	Author	12	15	25		Am. Novelist
Crawford, J. W. "Capt. Jack"	Author	35		95		
Crawford, Joan	Entertainment	35	125	170	175	Pin-Up SP $200
Crawford, Johnny	Entertainment	15			30	
Crawford, Michael	Entertainment	20		35	65	
Crawford, Samuel W.	Civil War	48	85	210		Union Gen.
Crawford, William H.	Cabinet	40	140	205		Madison Sec'y War
Crawford-Frost, Wm. A.	Business	15	25	70	20	
Cream	Entertainment	35			75	
Creedence Clearwater Revival	Entertainment	40			90	
Creeley, Robert	Contemp. Poet	5	12		10	American
Cregar, Laird	Entertainment	115	120	200	310	
Creighton, John O.	Astronaut	5			15	
Creighton, Mandell	Clergy	10	15	20		
Cremer, Peter Erich	Military	75		120		
Crenna, Richard	Entertainment	5	6	15	15	

NAME	CATEGORY	SIG	LS/DS	ALS	SP	COMMENT
Cresap, Mark	Business	4	6	15	7	
Crespin, Régine	Entertainment	10			35	Opera
Creston, Paul	Composer	10			35	
Creswell, John A. J.	Cabinet	20	25	40		Senator MD,CW MOC. P.M. Gen.
Crews, Laura Hope	Entertainment	150			350	Aunt Pittypat-"Gone With the.."
Crichton, Michael	Author	20	150		25	"Jurassic Park", etc.
Crick, Francis, Dr.	Science	50	75			Nobel in Medicine, DNA
Crier, Katherine	TV News	5			10	TV Commentary, Special Analysis
Crippen, Hawley Harvey	Criminal		415	450		Murdered Wife.Executed in Eng.
Crippen, Robert L.	Astronaut	7			30	
Cripps, Richard Stafford, Sir	Statesman	30	90	210		Br.Economist, King's Counsel
Crisp, Charles Frederick	Senate/Congress	20		35		CSA Officer,' Speaker of House
Crisp, Charles Robert	Senate/Congress	12	20		15	MOC GA
Crisp, Donald	Entertainment	55	60	90	150	
Cristal, Linda	Entertainment	15	15	30	20	Pin-Up SP $25
Crittenden, John J.	Cabinet	25	60	105		Sen.,MOC KY, Att'y General
Crittenden, Thomas Leonidas	Civil War	40	135	285	250	Union Gen.
Croce, Benedetto	Author-Philos.	25	35	80		It.Statesman, Critic, Historian
Crocker, Charles	Business	20	55	100		Am.Financier. Pres. S.P. RR
Crockett, David	Military	6000	10000	29500		Am. Frontiersman.Died at Alamo
Crockett, Samuel R.	Author	7	15	35		Scot.Abandoned Ministry
Croft, Dwayne	Entertainment	5			25	Opera
Croghan, George	Colonial America	195	420	850		Trader,Indian Agt,Treaty Maker
Croker, Richard "Boss"	Politician	20	45	80		Tammany Hall Leader
Croly, George	Clergy	15	25	40		
Crompton, Richmal	Author	15	40	80	30	
Cromwell, Oliver	Head of State	1200	5300	10225		Named Lord Protector
Cromwell, Richard	Entertainment	7	9	20	15	
Cronenberg, David	Entertainment	10			25	Film Director
Cronin, A. J.	Author	25	85	170	30	Br. Physician-Novelist.
Cronin, James W.	Science	15	25	35	20	Nobel Physics
Cronkite, Walter	TV News	10	20	35	20	TV News Anchor, Commentator
Cronyn, Hume	Entertainment	10	15	25	25	
Crook and Chase	Entertainment	5			10	Lorianne & Charlie
Crook, George	Civil War	125	275	375	400	Union General & Indian Fighter
Crookes, William, Sir	Science	45	125	265		Br.Physicist, Chemist, Inventor
Crooks, Richard	Entertainment	19	25	45	50	Opera
Crosby, Bing	Entertainment	75	360	395	220	
Crosby, Bob	Entertainment	15			25	Big Band Leader
Crosby, Cathy Lee	Entertainment	9	10	20	25	Pin-Up SP $30
Crosby, Gary	Entertainment	3	3	6	6	
Crosby, Howard	Clergy	15	20	25		
Crosby, J.T.	Aviation	10	22	38	28	ACE, WW II, Navy Ace
Crosby, Kathryn	Entertainment	10	15	25	25	
Crosby, Mary	Entertainment	3	5	10	15	
Crosby, Norm	Entertainment	5	6	15	10	
Crosby, Percy*	Cartoonist	40	90		200	Skippy
Crosley, Powel Jr.	Business	20	75	95	35	Crosley Radio Corp.
Crosman, Henrietta	Entertainment	10			25	40 Years on Stage. Silent Films
Cross, Christopher	Entertainment	5			10	Composer, Singer
Cross, Wilbur L.	Governor	4	10			Gov. CT
Crossfield, A. Scott	Aviation	15	30	45	55	1st U.S. Test Pilot of X-15
Crothers, Rachel	Author	7	25	45	15	Am. Playwright. "Susan & God"
Crothers, Scat Man	Entertainment	25	30	45	55	
Crouse, Lindsay	Entertainment	15	15	30	30	
Crouse, Russell	Author	10	15	45	60	Playwright. "Life With Father"

NAME	CATEGORY	SIG	LS/DS	ALS	SP	COMMENT
Croves, H. (B.Traven)(Torsvan)	Author	250	800			Ger. Novelist, Actor, Pacifist
Crowe, William	Military	15	45		25	Admiral U.S. Navy
Crowley, Leo	Cabinet	3	5	10	5	Chm. FDIC. 9 Gov't Posts
Crowley, Pat	Entertainment	5	6	15	15	
Crowninshield, Benj. W.	CabinetP	30	85	185		Sec'y Navy 1814
Crozier, William	Military	35			60	General WW I, Inventor
Cruikshank, George*	Artist	160	270	345	375	Illustrator,Caricaturist,Etcher
Cruise, Tom	Entertainment	20	25	60	95	
Crumb, George	Composer	25		375		Pulitzer, AMusQS $200, $320
Crumb, Robert*	Cartoonist	25			260	Underground Cartoons
Crume, Dillard	Entertainment	5			20	Blues Bassist/Koko Taylor
Crummit, Frank	Entertainment	5			15	Vintage Radio/Julia Sanderson
Cruz-Romo, Gilda	Entertainment	5			30	Opera
Cruzen, Richard H.	Explorer	20		50	75	Adm. Arctic-Antarctic/Byrd
Crystal, Billy	Entertainment	20			55	
Cuberli, Lella	Entertainment	10			35	
Cudahy, Michael F.	Business	25	65	135	50	Meat Packer. Refrigeration
Cuellar, Javier P.	Diplomat	5			15	Sec'y Gen. UN
Cugat, Xavier	Entertainment	20	30	35	45	Big Band "Rhumba King"
Cui, Cesar	Composer	95	200	450		And Russian Military Engineer
Cukor, George	Entertainment	25	95		75	Stage and Screen Director
Culbertson, Frank L. Jr.	Astronaut	6			20	
Culkin, Macaulay	Entertainment	20			50	Child Actor
Cullen, Countee	Author	280	410	600		Am. Black Poet
Cullom, Shelby	Senate	10	20			MOC 1865, Senator, Gov. IL
Culp, Julia	Entertainment	35			150	Opera
Culp, Robert	Entertainment	9	10	25	25	
Culver, Roland	Entertainment	10	15	25	25	
Culverhouse, Hugh	Business	10		15		
Cummings, Homer	Cabinet	15	35	75	125	FDR Att'y Gen.
Cummings, Robert	Entertainment	15			50	
Cummings, e.e.(Edw. Estlin)	Author	200	350	500		Am. Poet, Painter
Cunard, Samuel, Sir	Business	90	130	210		Br. Shipowner.Cunard Line
Cunningham, E.V. (Howard Fast)	Author	20			35	Suspense Novels & Sci-Fi
Cunningham, John W.	Clergy	10	15	20	35	
Cunningham, R. Walter	Astronaut	10	20	30	25	
Cunningham, Randy	Aviation	12	25	45	38	ACE, Nam, Only Navy Ace
Cuomo, Mario	Governor	15	35		65	Governor NY
Curie, Marie	Science	550	3360	3000	1800	Curie Laboratory DS $9,500
Curie, Pierre	Science	440	895	1975		Content ALS $9,000
Curless, Dick	Country Music	10			20	
Curley, Michael J., Archbishop	Clergy	45	55	65		
Currie, Donald, Sir	Business	10	20	40		Scot. Shipowner. Castle Line
Currier, Moody	Governor	4			10	Gov. NY
Currier, Nathaniel	Artist	225	800			Currier & Ives, Lithographers
Curry, B.	Civil War	30	75			CSA Officer
Curry, Charles Forrest	Senate/Congress	10	15	35		MOC CA
Curry, George	Military	30	105			1st Territorial Gov. NM
Curry, John Steuart	Artist	65		370		Orig. Ink Sketch S $750,Murals
Curry, Tim	Entertainment	15			45	"Rocky Horror Show"
Curtin, Andrew G.	Governor	30	45			Civil War Gov. PA.
Curtin, Jane	Entertainment	10	15	20	25	
Curtis, Alan	Entertainment	15	15	35	30	
Curtis, Benjamin R. (SC)	Supreme Court	35	150	250		Resigned. Protest of Dred Scott
Curtis, Charles (V)	Vice President	75	125	175	90	
Curtis, Cyrus H. K.	Business	35	55	140	95	Curtis Publishing Co.

NAME	CATEGORY	SIG	LS/DS	ALS	SP	COMMENT
Curtis, Edward Sheriff	Artist		1000			Photographer, Native Americans
Curtis, George Wm.	Author	20	32	50		Man of Letters.Editor,Lecturer
Curtis, Jamie Lee	Entertainment	9	10	20	25	Pin-Up SP $30
Curtis, Ken	Entertainment	25			45	And Country Music
Curtis, Robin	Entertainment	6	8	15	15	
Curtis, Samuel Ryan	Civil War	45	60	235		Union General
Curtis, Tony	Entertainment	8	10	20	25	
Curtis, Verna Maria	Entertainment	10			30	Am. Soprano
Curtis, Wilfred A.	Aviation	10	25	40	25	
Curtiss, Glenn	Aviation	285	400	650	850	Am. Inventor. Pioneer Aircraft
Curtiz, Michael	Entertainment	30			100	Film Director
Curzon, Robert (Zouche)	Br. Explorer	10		25		
Cusack, John	Entertainment	15			35	
Cushing, Caleb	Cabinet	25	55	100		Pierce Att'y Gen., Diplomat
Cushing, Harvey, Dr.	Science	165	475	675		Specialist in Neurosurgery
Cushing, Peter	Entertainment	15	19	38	40	
Cushing, Richard, Cardinal	Clergy	35	60	80	55	
Cushing, Thomas 1725-1788	Colonial Am.	565	1100			Patriot.Prominent in Col.Congr.
Cushman, Charlotte S.	Entertainment	15	20	35	80	19th Century Stage
Cushman, Samuel	Senate/Congress	10	20	35		MOC NH 1835
Custer, Elizabeth	Author-Civil War	80	200	775	360	Wife of George A. Custer
Custer, George A.	Civil War	3380	12500	15000	13000	Union Gen., Indian Fighter
Custine, Adam Philippe, Count de	Revolutionary War	100	350			Fr.Gen.Fought in Am. Revolution
Cutler, Lysander	Civil War	90	185	260		Union General
Cutler, Manasseh 1742-1823	Revolutionary War	425	550			Am.Clergyman, Botanist, Pioneer
Cuvier, Georges, Baron	Science	70	215	365		Fr. Comparative Anatomy
Cuyler, Theodore L.	Author	10	15	35		
Cyrus, Billy Ray	Country Music	25			55	
Czerny, Carl	Composer	75	255	460		Master of Liszt. Etudes
Czerny, Vincenz	Science	110		900		Ger. Leader Abdominal Surgery
Czerwenka, Oskar	Entertainment	5			25	Opera
Céline, Louis Ferd. (Destouches)	Author	175		1275		Fr. Physician, Novelist

D

NAME	CATEGORY	SIG	LS/DS	ALS	SP	COMMENT
D'Abo, Maryan	Entertainment	10			20	Pin-Up SP $25
D'Abo, Olivia	Entertainment	20			35	
D'Albert, Eugene F.C.	Composer	55	75	130		Ger. Opera, Piano Concertos
D'Amato, Alfonse	Senate/Congress	4			10	Senator NY
D'Angelo, Beverly	Entertainment	10			30	
D'Annunzio, Gabriele	Author	75	175	365	375	It. Writer, Pro-Fascist Soldier
D'Arclee', Hariclee'	Entertainment	100				Fr. Soprano
D'Artagnan, Comte de	Military			6500		Capt.Louis XIV Musketeers
D'Arville, Camille	Entertainment	15			45	Actress-Vintage
D'Eon, Charles de Beaumont	Adventurer	100		400		Louis XV's secret agent to Russ

NAME	CATEGORY	SIG	LS/DS	ALS	SP	COMMENT
D'Estaing,V. Gistard	Head of State	15	40	100	60	Pres. France
D'Indy, Vincent	Composer	40	125	360	200	Fr.Opera,Orchestral,Vocal Music
D'Orsay, Alfred, Count	Society Leader	25	65	175		Fr.Wit, Fashion Arbiter, Artist
D'Orsay, Fifi	Entertainment	15	20	25	35	
D'Oyly Carte, Rupert	Entertainment	20	70	125	135	Producer of Gilbert & Sullivan
D'Oyly, George	Clergy	15	20	35		
Dache', Lilly	Business-Designer	55	70	130	150	Coutourier.Specialty-Hats
Daddi, Francesco	Entertainment	5	8	15		
Dafoe, Allan Roy, Dr.	Science	25	75	135	225	Delivered Dionne Quintuplets
Dafoe, Willem	Entertainment	8	11	40	35	
Dagmar	Entertainment	20			35	
Daguerre, Louis	Science	150	490	1250		Fr. Inventor Daguerreotype
Dahl, Arlene	Entertainment	5	6	15	15	Pin-Up SP $25
Dahl, Perry	Aviation	10	22	38	28	ACE, WW II
Dahl, Roald	Author	12	20	35	15	Br. Short Stories, Children's
Dahlberg, Edward	Author	15	25	35	20	Am. Writer & Critic
Dahlberg, Ken	Aviation	15	30	50	40	ACE, WW II
Dahlgren, John Adolphus B.	Civil War	85	295	415		Adm. Union Navy. Dahlgren Gun
Dailey, Dan	Entertainment	20	25	45	45	
Dailey, Janet	Author	5	10		10	
Dailey, Peter F.	Entertainment	6	8	15	15	
Dal Monte, Toti	Entertainment	25			95	Opera
Daladier, Edouard	Head of State	30	85	150	50	Premier Fr.Arrested-Liberated
Dalai Lama XIV	Head of State	75	160	200	100	Tibetan Religious Leader
Daley, Cass	Entertainment	7	9	20	15	
Daley, Richard J.	Political	15	40	85	40	Mayor Chicago.Last Big City Bos
Daley, Richard M.	Political	5			10	Mayor Chicago
Dali, Salvador	Artist	200	425	650	250	Sp. Surrealist
Dallapozza, Adolf	Entertainment	5			25	Vienna Operettas
Dallas, Alexander J.	Cabinet	30	75	185		Madison Sec'y Treasury
Dallas, George M. (V)	Vice President	50	200	300		Dallas, Texas Named for Him
Dalmores, Charles	Entertainment	25			85	Opera
Dalton, Abby	Entertainment	5	6	15	15	
Dalton, Charles	Entertainment	5	6	10	10	
Dalton, Dorothy	Entertainment	20	25	65	60	
Dalton, Emmett	Outlaw	600	1875	4050	1625	Western Train Robber
Dalton, Frank	Lawman	850	2500			U.S.Marshal-Old West
Dalton, John	Science	135	400	750		Br. Chemist & Philosopher
Dalton, Lacy J.	Entertainment	5			15	
Dalton, Timothy	Entertainment	20			50	
Daltry, Roger	Entertainment	15			45	Rock
Daly, James	Entertainment	5	6	15	15	
Daly, John Charles	Entertainment	5			10	Broadcaster, News Commentator
Daly, Tyne	Entertainment	9	10	20	25	
Damita, Lili	Entertainment	35	40	65	70	Fr. Film Star. Mrs. Errol Flynn
Damon, Cathryn	Entertainment	5	6	15	15	
Damone, Vic	Entertainment	5			10	Singer
Damrosch, Walter	Composer-Cond.	50	75	115	200	Pioneer of Symphonic Broadcasts
Dana, Charles A.	Publisher	20	35	70	35	Owner & Editor NY Sun
Dana, James D.	Science	15		45		Scientific Observer Antarctic
Dana, James Jackson	Civil War	40	140			Union General
Dana, Richard Henry	Author	50	200	215		Sailor,Law. Prosecutor J.Davis
Danaher, John A.	Senate/Congress	5	15		10	Senator CT
Dandridge, Ruby	Entertainment	35			90	
Dandrige, Dorothy	Entertainment	45	50	75	125	
Dane, Karl	Entertainment	10			15	Actor

NAME	CATEGORY	SIG	LS/DS	ALS	SP	COMMENT
Dane, Nathan	Revolutionary War	25	65	130		Continental Congress
Danenhower, John Wilson	Explorer	15	45	115		De Long Arctic Expedition 1879
Danforth, John C.	Senate	5			10	Senator MO
Danforth, Thomas 1622-1699	Colonial America	390	470			Deputy Governor MA
Dangerfield, George	Author	5	10	25		
Dangerfield, Rodney	Entertainment	10	15	25	25	
Daniel, John W.	Senate	10	25			Senator VA, Disabled in CW
Daniel, Peter Vivian (SC)	Supreme Court	40	125	230		
Daniel, Price	Senate/Congress	15	40		20	Senator, Gov. TX
Daniell, Henry	Entertainment	50			150	
Daniels, Bebe	Entertainment	20	25	65	75	
Daniels, Billy	Entertainment	10			20	Vocalist
Daniels, Charlie	Country Music	6			12	
Daniels, Josephus	Cabinet	25	75	160	125	Sec'y Navy 1913
Daniels, William	Entertainment	5			20	
Daniloff, Nick	Celebrity	20		25		
Danilova, Alexandra	Entertainment	20	35	60	75	Rus-Am Ballerina, Teacher
Dannay, Frederick	Author	50	160	300		ELLERY QUEEN
Danner, Blythe	Entertainment	5	6	15	15	
Dannihill, Albert	Entertainment	3	3	6	8	
Danning, Sybil	Entertainment	9	10	20	25	
Dano, Royal	Entertainment	9	10	20	25	
Danova, Cesare	Entertainment	6	8	15	18	
Danson, Ted	Entertainment	15			60	
Dantine, Helmut	Entertainment	12	15		30	
Danton, Georges-Jacques	Fr. Revolution	1080	2800			Guillotined Leader of Revolution
Danton, Ray	Entertainment	7			15	
Danza, Tony	Entertainment	10	15	28	30	
Darby, Kim	Entertainment	15			35	
Darcy, Emery	Entertainment	15			65	
Darin, Bobby	Entertainment	50			150	
Darion, Joe	Composer	10			30	AMusQS $50
Darling, J.N. 'ding'*	Cartoonist	25			150	Political Cartoonist
Darnell, Linda	Entertainment	45	145		175	
Darrah, Thomas	Military	35	50			General WW I
Darrall, Chester B.	Senate/Congress	10	30	55		MOC LA. Union Surgeon CW
Darrell, Johnny	Country Music	10			20	
Darren, James	CelebrityEntertainment	10			20	
Darro, Frankie	Entertainment	50			150	
Darrow, Clarence	Celebrity	550	1750	2275	650	Scopes Trial, Loeb & Leopold
Dart, Justin	Business	50	100	250	75	
Darville, Camille	Entertainment	10			20	Actress
Darwell, Jane	Entertainment	100	120	195	250	
Darwin, Charles	Science	540	2250	4050		Br. Naturalist
Dassin, Jules	Entertainment	20			45	Film Director
Daubigny, Charles Francois	Artist	95	280	410		Fr. Landscape Painter
Daudet, Alphonse	Author	35	80	175		Fr. Stories, Novels, Plays
Daugherty, Harry M.	Cabinet	25	55	125	50	Att'y Gen.Tried-Acquitted Fraud
Daumier, Honore	Artist	240	630	1470		Fr. Caricaturist & Serious Art
Dauphin, Claude	Entertainment	7			20	
Dausset, Jean, Prof.	Science	20	45		30	Nobel Medicine
Dauvray, Helen	Entertainment	3	3	6	6	
Daval, Danny	Entertainment	5	6	15	15	
Dave, Red River	Country Music	10			20	
Davenport, Addington	Revolutionary War	140	350	500		
Davenport, Fanny	Entertainment	20			50	

NAME	CATEGORY	SIG	LS/DS	ALS	SP	COMMENT
Davenport, Harry	Entertainment	100			250	
Davenport, Homer C.	Cartoonist	25	60	135		Political Cartoons, "Uncle Sam"
David, Felicien-Cesar	Composer	100	500			AMusMsS $650
David, Ferdinand	Composer	45		225		Ger. Violinist
David, Hal	Composer	20	30	65	35	
David, Jacques Louis	Artist	175	440	610		Fr. Classical Painter
David, Mack	Author	20			40	Lyricist
Davidson, Allen Turner	Civil War	25	80	125		CSA Congress. Lawyer, Banker
Davidson, Jo	Artist	40	75	135		Am. Sculptor
Davidson, John	Entertainment	3	6	6	10	
Davidson, Loyal	Military	35	60			
Davidson, Randall T., Archbishop	Clergy	25	35	45		
Davies, Gail	Entertainment	4			10	Singer
Davies, Marion	Entertainment	35	50	185	125	C. Bull Original SP $275
Davies, Rhys	Author	5	20	35	10	Welch. Novels, Stories
Davies, Ronald N.	Law	25		60	30	Nazi War Trials Jurist
Davies, Thomas F., Bishop	Clergy	30	35	45		
Davies, William	Revolutionary War	35		170		
Davis, Angela	Activist	10	15	25	30	Afro-Am. Activist
Davis, Ann B.	Entertainment	10			25	
Davis, Benjamin O. Jr.	Aviation	20	35	75	40	ACE, WW II, Afro-Am. Pioneer
Davis, Bette	Entertainment	65	190	350	200	
Davis, Brad	Entertainment	20			35	
Davis, Charles Henry	Civil War	30	65	105		Union Adm.
Davis, Clifton	Entertainment	5			15	
Davis, Cushman K.	Senate	12	25		30	Senator MN
Davis, David (SC)	Supreme Court	75	295	315		Sen. IL. Pres Pro Tem
Davis, Dwight F.	Cabinet	25	80	170	65	Sec'y War
Davis, Ewin L.	Senate/Congress	4	10			MOC TN
Davis, Fay	Entertainment	4	4	9	9	
Davis, Gail	Entertainment	15	20	25	35	
Davis, Geena	Entertainment	10	15	25	40	
Davis, Henry Greene	Civil War	55	130			Union General
Davis, James J.	Cabinet	20	50	95	75	Sec'y Labor, Founder Moose
Davis, Jefferson	Civil War	600	1990	3750	3500	CSA Pres. ALS/Content $15,000
Davis, Jefferson Columbus	Civil War	50	80	95		Union General
Davis, Jim	Entertainment	45	50	70	85	
Davis, Jim*	Cartoonist	35	50	225	175	Garfield
Davis, Jimmie	Governor	30	45		60	Gov. LA, "You Are My Sunshine"
Davis, Jo	Entertainment	3	3	6	8	
Davis, Joan	Entertainment	30			60	
Davis, John 1761-1847	Author	30	175	290		Historian, Comptroller US Treas
Davis, John 1787-1854	Governor	25	50	70		Gov. MA
Davis, John William	Congr.-Diplomat	20	35	70	25	Dem. Presidential Candidate
Davis, Johnny 'Scat'	Entertainment	10	10	12	15	
Davis, Mack	Country Music	10			20	
Davis, Meyer	Entertainment	15			35	Big Society Band
Davis, Miles	Entertainment	165			450	Jazz Trumpet
Davis, Nancy	Entertainment	50			150	
Davis, Nancy (Reagan)	First Lady	80			170	
Davis, Nelson H.	Civil War	25	60	78		Union Gen.
Davis, Noah	Senate/Congress	10	25	60		MOC NY 1869, Jurist
Davis, Ossie	Entertainment	10			25	
Davis, Patti (Reagan)	Entertainment	5	6	15	25	
Davis, Phil*	Cartoonist	30			250	Mandrake the Magician
Davis, Phyllis	Entertainment	10	15	20	25	

NAME	CATEGORY	SIG	LS/DS	ALS	SP	COMMENT
Davis, Rich'd Harding	Author	10	25	40	20	Correspondent 6 Wars, Novelist
Davis, Robert	Military	5		25		General WW I
Davis, Rufe	Entertainment	25			55	
Davis, Sammy, Jr.	Entertainment	40	50	80	210	
Davis, Varina	CSA First Lady	150	290	600	750	Mrs. Jeff. Davis.ALS/Cont $6000
Davison, Bruce	Entertainment	5			10	
Davison, Wild Bill	Entertainment	30			75	Jazz Cornet-Bandleader
Davisson, Clinton Joseph	Science	25	75			Nobel Physics.Bell Laboratories
Davout, Louis Nicolas, Duke	Fr. Revolution	45	210	248		Marshal of Napoleon
Davy, Humphry, Sir	Science	90	270	585		ALS Content $8,500,AMsS $2500
Dawber, Pam	Entertainment	9	10	20	25	
Dawes, Charles G. (V)	Vice President	30	150	295	275	
Dawes, William 1745-99	Revolutionary War	3500				Patriot. Rode with Paul Revere
Dawson, George	Clergy	20	35	60		
Dawson, John L.	Congress	20		70		Governor Kansas Terr. ,MOC PA
Day, Chon*	Cartoonist	10	35		50	Brother Sebastian
Day, Dennis	Entertainment	10	15	25	30	Vocalist-Comedian. Jack Benny
Day, Doris	Entertainment	10	12	15	25	Pin-Up SP $30
Day, Frank	Celebrity	10		25		
Day, J. Edward	Cabinet	4	5	15	10	P.M. General
Day, Jeremiah	Clergy	15	20	35		
Day, Laraine	Entertainment	10			25	
Day, Linda (George)	Entertainment	6	8	15	19	
Day, William R. (SC)	Supreme Court	40	95	135	65	
Day-Lewis, Daniel	Entertainment	25			85	
Dayan, Moshe	Military	50	185	220	215	Israeli Soldier, Politician
Daymond, Gus	Aviation	12	25	55	40	ACE, WW II, Eagle Squadron
Dayne, Taylor	Entertainment	5			35	Rock
Dayton, Elias	Revolutionary War	90	210	395		General. Continental Congress
Dayton, Jonathan	Revolutionary War	175	450	900		Continental Congress
Dayton, William	Senator	25	40	110		John C. Fremont Running Mate
De Acosta, Mercedes	Author	10	25	45		Intimate of Greta Garbo
De Beauvoir, Simone	Author	35	95	145		Fr. Writer,Philosopher,Feminist
De Bono, Emilio	Military	75	225		375	It. Fascist Politician & Gen.
De Corsia, Ted	Entertainment	20	25		40	
De Falla, Manuel	Composer	425	1200			Sp.Opera, Orchestral, Songs
De Forest, Lee, Dr.	Science	350	1050	2000	1200	ALS Scientific Content $12,500
De Gaulle, Charles	Head of State	275	695	950	875	Gen.,Statesman, Pres. France
De Havilland, Geoffrey	Aviation	70	140	205	125	De Havilland Aircraft Co.
De Kooning, Elaine*	Artist	50			275	Willem's Wife.Artist on her own
De Kooning, Willem	Artist	75	200	450	125	Repro "Two Women" S $285
De La Beckwith, Byron	Activist	12		35	28	White Supremicist
De La Cierva, Juan	Aviation	90		295	350	Inventor Autogyro
De La Mare, Walter	Author	20	65	90	30	Br. Poet."Songs of Childhood"
De La Pena, George	Entertainment	3	3	6	6	
De La Renta, Oscar	Business	10	15	35	20	Fashion Designer.Elegant Gowns
De Lancey, Stephen	Revolutionary War	75	180	225		Loyalist. Lawyer. Imprisoned
De Luca, Giuseppe	Entertainment	25	35	95	175	Opera
De Mornay, Rebecca	Entertainment	7	10		35	
De Palma, Brian	Entertainment	15		30	30	Film Director
De Paul, Saint Vincent	Clergy	1100	1600	4500		
De Peyster, John W. Jr.	Civil War	10	20	55		Aide to Gen.Kearny
De Quincey, Thomas	Author	145	310	650		AMs $650-$2,250
De Reszke, Edward	Entertainment	40			150	Opera-Vintage
De Reszke, Jean	Entertainment	100	120	250	345	Opera-Vintage
De Ridder. Anton	Entertainment	10		45	35	Opera

NAME	CATEGORY	SIG	LS/DS	ALS	SP	COMMENT
De Rita, Joe	Entertainment	15			35	
De Russy, Gustavus A.	Civil War	45	250			Union General
De Smet, Pierre 1801-73	Jesuit Missionary	225		800		Missionary to Western Indians
De Toth, Andre'	Entertainment	10			20	Film Director
De Valera, Eamon (Ire)	Head of State	35	45	325	110	Pres. Irish Free State, P.M.
De Vere, Aubrey T.	Author	20	60	140		Ir. Poet,Critic,Hymns
De Wilde, Brandon	Entertainment	100			300	
De Windt, Harry	Celebrity	5	15	40	25	
De Witt, Alexander	Senate/Congress	5		20		MOC MA
DeBeck, Billy*	Cartoonist	30			260	Barney Google, S.Smith
DeBlanc, Jeff	Aviation	12	28	52	38	ACE, WW II, CMH
DeBroglie, Louis-C-V- Maurice	Science	35	90			Physicist. Pioneer in X-Rays
DeButts, John D.	Business	10	35	45	20	
DeCarlo, Yvonne	Entertainment	8	9	20	25	
DeCasseres. Benjamin	Author	5	15	25		Columnist, Editorials NY Mirror
DeCisneros, Eleanora	Entertainment	40			185	Opera
DeCordova, Fred	Entertainment	5	8	15	15	
DeFore, Don	Entertainment	10			15	
DeHart, John	Revolutionary War	30	65	140		
DeHaven, Gloria	Entertainment	6	8	15	15	
DeHaven, Robert	Aviation	10	20	40	30	ACE, WW II
DeHavilland, Olivia	Entertainment	15	25	30	40	As Melanie, SP $150 in GWTW
DeKoven, Reginald	Composer	25	45	150	95	Versatile American Composer
DeLaCroix, Raven	Entertainment	3	3	6	8	
DeLand, Margaret	Author	12	25	75	25	Am. Novelist."Old Chester"Tales
DeLiagre, Alfred	Entertainment	5	7	12	10	
DeLong, Phillip C.	Aviation	12	25	40	30	ACE, WW II
DeLuise, Dom	Entertainment	5	6	15	15	
DeMille, Agnes	Entertainment	45	110	190	55	Dancer,Innovative Choreographer
DeMille, Cecil B.	Entertainment	65	110	395	275	Director, Producer, Film Giant
DeMille, Katherine	Entertainment	10	12	15	25	
DeMille, William C.	Entertaiment	15	45		50	Early Dir.,Playwright,Producer
DeMonvel, Boutes	Artist	25	70	125		
DeNiro, Robert	Entertainment	15	25	40	85	
DeSilva, Howard	Entertainment	10	12	20	25	
DeTreville, Yvonne	Entertainment	20			85	Opera, Light Opera
DeVane, William	Entertainment	10	5	10	30	
DeVito, Danny	Entertainment	8	10	20	25	As "The Penguin" $75
DeVries, William, Dr.	Science	15	25	40	20	
DeWitt, Joyce	Entertainment	5	8	15	25	
DeWolf, Billy	Entertainment	25	40	45	50	
DeWolf, H.G.	Military	5	15		20	Canadian Adm. WW II
DeYoung, Russell	Business	5			10	CEO Goodyear Tire & Rubber Co.
Deacon, Richard	Entertainment	25			50	
Dean, Billy	Country Music	5			12	
Dean, Donald J.	Military	15	45			WW I Victoria Cross
Dean, Eddie	Country Music	10	10	20	25	
Dean, James	Entertainment	3125	4050	3250	10750	
Dean, Jimmy	Country Music	5			12	Sausages & CW Singer
Dean, John W.	Law	5	15	25	20	Counsel to Nixon. Watergate
Dean, Julia	Entertainment	6	8	15	15	
Dean, Maureen	Author	10	35			(Mrs. John Dean)
Dean, William F.	Military	15	35	45	35	Gen. WW II
Deane, Silas	Revolutionary War	230	550	1050		Diplomat. Negotiated Treaties
Dearborn, Henry (1751-1829)	Cabinet	120	385	575		Jefferson's Sec'y War.
Dearborn, Henry A.S.1783-1851	Senate/Congress	55	175	250		Collector Port Boston 1812-29

NAME	CATEGORY	SIG	LS/DS	ALS	SP	COMMENT
Dearden, John, Cardinal	Clergy	30	35	45	40	
Debakey, Michael, Dr.	Science	20	35		30	1st Coronary Artery Bypass Op.
Debar, William J.	Senate	10	15			Senator KY
Debeck, Billy*	Cartoonist	25			165	Barney Google & Snuffy Smith
Debre, Michael	Head of State	5	20	50		
Debs, Eugene	Labor	70	225	255	135	U.S. Socialist Leader.Organizer
Debussy, Claude	Composer	350	1000	1375		AMusQS $7,500
Debye, Peter J.W.	Science	55	110	175		NobelChemistry-Discovered Rayon
Decamp, Rosemary	Entertainment	5			15	
Decatur, Stephen	Military	1100	3100	5710		American Naval Hero, War 1812
Dee, Francis	Entertainment	5	6	15	25	
Dee, Ruby	Entertainment	5	6	15	20	
Dee, Sandra	Entertainment	6	8	15	20	Pin-Up SP $25
Deems, 'Cousin'	Country Music	4			15	"And His Goat Herders"
Deems, Charles Force	Celebrity	5	10	20		
Deere, Allan Christopher	Aviation-Ace	15	40	50		N.Z. Ace WWII, 22 confirmed
Deere, John	Business	300		1350		John Deere Tractor & Plow
Deering, James	Business	10	25	45	25	
Deering, Olive	Entertainment	15			35	
Dees, Rick	Country Western	3	5	15	10	Singer
Defoe, Daniel 1660-1731	Author	1500	7500			Br. Journalist, Novelist
Defore, Don	Entertainment	5			15	
Degas, Edgar (Hilaire Germain)	Artist	250	760	2450		Fr.Impressionist. Ballet Scenes
Dehmelt, Hans G., Dr.	Science	20	35		30	Nobel Physics
Dehner, John	Entertainment	10		10	15	
Dekker, Albert	Entertainment	6			10	
Del Fuegos, The	Entertainment	20			50	
Del Monaco, Mario	Entertainment	45	65	125	175	Opera
Del Rio, Delores	Entertainment	30	35	55	65	
Del Tredici, David	Composer	15	35	80		Pulitzer, AMusQS $100
Delacroix, F.V. Eugene	Artist	175	385	840		Brilliant Colorist.Great Murals
Delafield, Richard	Civil War	38	65	95		Union General. Engineer
Delaney, Dana	Entertainment	10		25	35	
Delaney, Kim	Entertainment	4	5	10	10	
Delbridge, Del	Entertainment	10			15	Radio Announcer
Deledda, Grazia	Author	45	105	320		Nobel Literature 1926
Delibes, Leo	Composer	85	220	340		Light Opera, Ballet
Delius, Frederick	Composer	120	395	770		Br.Orchestral, Concerti, Songs
Dell, Gabriel	Entertainment	15	20	25	35	
Dell, Myrna	Entertainment	5	6	10	10	Pin-Up SP $15
Della Casa, Lisa	Entertainment	10			40	Swiss Soprano. Opera
Della Chiesa, Vivian	Entertainment	5	6	15	15	Soprano
Dello Joio, Norman	Composer	35	115	240	55	Pulitzer, AMusQS $175
Dellums, Ronald B.	Senate/Congress	10	15		15	Afro-Am. Congressman CA
Delna, Marie	Entertainment	25			90	Fr. Contralto. Opera
Deluise, Dom	Entertainment	10			30	
Demarest, William	Entertainment	12	15	25	35	
Dempsey, Patrick	Entertainment	10			15	
Demslow, W.W.*	Cartoonist	50			175	Illustrator Of Wizard Of Oz
Denby, Edwin	Cabinet	20	50	75	45	Sec'y Navy
Deneuve, Catherine	Entertainment	10	15	25	35	Pin-Up SP $40
Denfeld, Louis E.	Military	10	25	40	25	Adm.Chief Naval Operations WWII
Denison, Charles S.	Senate	5	10	15		Senator IL
Denison, John H.	Clergy	10	15	25		
Denman, G. "Tony"	Aviation	10	20	35	25	ACE, WW II, Navy Ace
Denman, Thomas, 3rd Baron	Head of State	7	15	35		Gov. General Australia

NAME	CATEGORY	SIG	LS/DS	ALS	SP	COMMENT
Dennehy, Brian	Entertainment	15	35		25	
Denning, Richard	Entertainment	6	8	15	15	
Dennis, Sandy	Entertainment	25	30	45	85	
Dennison, Jo Carroll	Entertainment	5	6	10	10	
Dennison, William	Cabinet	145		600		Lincoln P.M. Gen. CW Gov. OH
Dent, Elliott	Aviation	10	22	38	30	ACE, WW II
Dent, Frederick T.	Civil War	35	90	225		Union Gen.
Dent, S. Hubert	Senate/Congress	5	15		15	MOC AL
Denton, Jeremiah A., Jr.	Military-Congress	10	20	30	20	Admiral WW II, MOC AL
Denver, Bob	Entertainment	7	7	10	20	
Denver, James W.	Civil War	100	210	450		Denver, CO. Union Gen.
Denver, John	Country Music	5	6	15	25	
Depardieu, Gerard	Entertainment	10			45	
Depew, Chauncey M.	Senate	15	30	65	70	Orator, Business, U.S. Sen.NY
Depp, Johnny	Entertainment	10	14	40	75	
Derain, Andre'	Artist	125	210	425		Repro "Femme Nu Assise" $285
Derby,14thEarl (Edward Stanley)	Head of State	15	35	95		Br. Prime Minister
Derek & Dominoes (all)	Entertainment	50			150	
Derek, Bo	Entertainment	10	15	25	40	Pin-Up SP $50
Derek, John	Entertainment	6	8	15	25	
Deringer, Henry	Arms Mfg.	450		2500		Invented "Derringer Pistol"
Derleth, August	Author	20	75			
Dern, Bruce	Entertainment	6	8	15	15	
Dern, George H.	Cabinet	10	20	35		Sec'y War, Mining Exec.,Gov. UT
Dern, Laura	Entertainment	5	8	25	25	
Dershowitz, Alan M.	Law	16	20		20	Trial Attorney
Desai, M.R.	Head of State	5	15	25		Prime Minister India
Desanto, "Sugar Pie"	Entertainment	15			35	James Brown Vocalist
Descartes, Rene	Philosopher	950	4035	10000		Mathematician.Analytic Geometry
Desmond, Johnny	Entertainment	3	5		8	Singer
Destinn, Emmy	Entertainment	100		225		Czech Soprano
Deutekom, Cristina	Entertainment	10			35	Dutch Coloratura Soprano. Opera
Deutsch, Patti	Entertainment	3	3	6	8	
Devens, Charles, Jr.	Military -Cabinet	34	90	150	150	Union Gen.-Att'y Gen.
Devereux, James P.S.	Military	35	70	90	150	Gen. WW II, Congress MD
Devers, Jacob L.	Military	10	20	35	35	General WW II
Devine, Andy	Entertainment	30	35	50	75	
Devo	Entertainment	30			60	
Dew, William, Bishop	Clergy	20	30	45		
Dewey, George	Military-Civil Wa	80	125	200	300	Civil War & Span. American War
Dewey, John	Author	60	155	250	75	Philosopher, Educator, Psychol.
Dewey, Orville	Clergy	15	20	25		
Dewey, Thomas E.	Governor	40	80	165	90	Presidential Candidate,Gov.NY
Dewhurst, Colleen	Entertainment	10		35	40	
Dexter, J.M.	Clergy	10	15	20		
Dey, Susan	Entertainment	9	10	20	25	
Di Stefano, Giuseppe	Entertainment	25		65	75	It. TenorOpera
Diamond, David	Composer	25		35		AMusQS $200
Diamond, Neil	Entertainment	5	6	15	15	Composer-Singer
Diamond, Selma	Entertainment	30	40	55	75	
Diaz, Armando Vittorio	Military	35	100	175	120	It. General WW I
Diaz, Porfirio	Head of State	100	250	250	225	Dictatorial Pres. of Mexico
Dibrell, George Gibbs	Civil War	110	365	488		CSA General, MOC TN
Dick, Fred	Aviation	10	22	40	30	ACE, WW II
Dick, Samuel	Revolutionary War	50	170	225		Continental Congress NJ
Dickens, Charles	Author	550	1100	2400		Br. Novelist.

NAME	CATEGORY	SIG	LS/DS	ALS	SP	COMMENT
Dickens, Jimmy	Country Music	5			10	
Dickenson, Don M.	Cabinet	15	20	45	20	P.M. General 1888
Dickerson, Mahlon	Cabinet-U.S. Sen.	25	85	125		Jackson Sec'y Navy. Gov. NJ
Dickey, James	Author	15	30	65	45	Am.Poet, Novelist" Deliverance"
Dickinson, Angie	Entertainment	6	8	15	20	Pin-Up SP $30
Dickinson, Anna Eliz.	Author	25	70	125		
Dickinson, Clement C.	Senate/Congress	5			15	MOC MO
Dickinson, Daniel S.	Senate/Congress	15	25			Senator from NY
Dickinson, Don M.	Cabinet	10	20			P.M. Gen. 1888
Dickinson, Emily	Author	615	2560	6275		
Dickinson, Jacob M.	Cabinet	30	45	110		Taft Sec'y of War
Dickinson, James S.	Civil War	25	40	75		CSA Congressman
Dickinson, John P.	Revolutionary War	200	575			Continental Congress
Dickison, J. J.	Civil War	75	155	195		CSA Cav'ry Off.,Florida's Mosby
Dickman, Joseph	Military	50				General WW I
Dicks, Jacob	Governor	15	25	40		Governor NY
Diddley, Bo	Entertainment	20			60	Rock
Didier-Pouget, W.	Artist	30	65	95		
Diefenbaker, John	Head of State	15	35	110	20	Prime Minister Canada
Diemer, Louis	Composer	25			45	Fr. Pianist. AMusQS $100
Diemer, Walter E.	Business	20		75	90	Inventor Dubble Bubble Gum
Dies, Martin	Senate/Congress	15	50		25	MOC TX. Un-American Activities
Diesel, Rudolf	Science	900		3250		Ger. Mech. Engineer. Diesel Eng
Diesenhofer, Johann, Dr.	Science	20	25		40	Nobel Chemistry
Dieterle, William	Entertainment	30			75	Film Dirctor
Dietrich, Dena	Entertainment	5			10	"Mother Nature" (Commercial)
Dietrich, Marlene	Entertainment	30	40	175	125	ALS/Content $400
Dilke, Charles W. 2d Baronet	Author	10	25	45		Br. Travel Books, Politician
Dillards	Entertainment	25			60	Herb, Dean, Rodney, Merle
Diller, Phyllis	Entertainment	8	9	19	20	
Dillman, Bradford	Entertainment	8	9	15	15	
Dillon, C. Douglas	Cabinet	10	20	30	20	Ambassador, Diplomat
Dillon, Matt	Entertainment	10	15	20	35	
Dillon, R. Crawford	Clergy	15	45	60		
Dimitrova, Ghena	Entertainment	10			35	Opera
Dinesen, Isak (Karen Blixen)	Author	110	500		200	Danish. "Out of Africa"
Dingley, Nelson, Jr.	Senate/Congress	10	20	35		Governor, MOC ME
Dinkins, David	Political	10	35		15	Mayor NYC
Dinning Sisters (3)	Entertainment	10			15	Jean, Jayne, Ginger
Dior, Christian	Fashion	110	400		225	Fashion Designer
Dippel, Andreas	Entertainment	35			125	Ger. Tenor. Impresario. Opera
Dire Straits	Entertainment	30			75	
Dirks, Rudolph*	Cartoonists	70			400	Katzenjammer Kids
Dirksen, Everett M.	Senate	20	80		50	Senator, MOC IL
Disney, Roy E.	Business	20	55		30	Brother of Walt. Disney Exec.
Disney, Walt*	Cartoonist				19300	M.Mouse, D.Duck, etc.
Disney, Walter "Walt" Elias	Business	1375	2760	3650	4185	Animated Film Producer
Disraeli, Benjamin, (Beaconsfield)	Head of State	175	350	1050		Prime Minister, Novelist
Disraeli, Isaac	Author	25	80	160		Br. Man of Letters. Novels
Divine	Entertainment	35			75	Rock
Divine, M.J., 'Father'(Geo. Baker)	Clergy	150	525	700	200	Founded Communal Religious Soc.
Dix, Dorothea L.	Civil War	100	250	425		Union Superintendent of Nurses
Dix, Dorothy (Eliz. Gilmer)	Author	15	30	45	25	Am. Journalist, Editor, Advice
Dix, John Adams	Civil War-Cabinet	60	110	170	500	Union Gen., Sec'y Treasury
Dix, John Adams (CW Date)	Civil War	115		600		Union Gen.
Dix, Morgan	Clergy	25	35	50		Abolitionist

NAME	CATEGORY	SIG	LS/DS	ALS	SP	COMMENT
Dix, Richard	Entertainment	25	40	65	5	
Dixey, Henry E.	Entertainment	10	20	30	25	
Dixon, Donna	Entertainment	9	10	20	25	
Dixon, Jeane	Celebrity	10			15	Forecasts the Future
Dixon, Julian C.	Senate/Congress	10	15		12	Afro-Am MOC CA
Dixon, Thomas	Author	15	30	50		"The Clansman".Social Critic
Dixon, Willie	Entertainment	50			100	Rock HOF. Late Blues Man
Dizengoff, Meir	Celebrity	48	150			
Dmytryk, Edward	Entertainment	20			40	Film Director
Doane, G.W.	Clergy		20	25	35	
Dobbin, James C.	Cabinet	25	75	125		Pierce Sec'y Navy
Dobbin, John F.	Aviation	20	40	65	45	ACE, WW II, Marine Ace
Dobehoff, F.L.	Aviation	15	150		75	
Dobie, Charles Cald.	Author	5	10	15	5	
Dobie, J. Frank	Author	20	50	130	75	Folklorist & Western Author
Dobrinyin, Anatole	Head of State	40	130	375	75	U.S.S.R. Political Power
Dobson, Kevin	Entertainment	5	6	15	15	
Dockery, Thomas	Civil War	275	600			CSA Gen.
Docking, Robert	Governor	5	12	20		Governor KS
Dockstader, Lew	Entertainment	75				
Doctorow, E. L.	Author	15	35	90	30	Am. Novelist. "Ragtime"
Dodd, Christopher J.	Senate/Congress	5	15		10	Senator, MOC CT
Dodd, Thomas J.	Senate & Congress	20	40	65	30	Chief of Counsel at Nuremberg
Dodd, William E.	Historian	15	60	75	25	Ambassador to Nazi Germany
Dodderidge, Philip	Clergy	25	35	45		
Dodge, Grenville M.	Civil War	70	160	200		Union General, MOC IA
Dodge, Jerry	Entertainment	3	3	6	6	
Dodge, Joseph M.	Business	10	25	50		Banker, Built Jap. Economy
Dodge, Mary Mapes	Author	15	40	75	30	Children's Books.
Dodge, William Earl	Business	10	25	50		Phelps, Dodge & Co. YWCA
Dodge, William G.	Civil War	25	55	85		
Dodgson, Charles L.(Lewis Carroll)	Author	210	715	1450		"Alice in Wonderland"
Dods, Marcus	Clergy	40	45	60		
Dodson, Jack	Entertainment	6	8	15	15	
Doenitz, Karl	Military	75	315	350	140	Ger. Adm., Signed Peace Treaty
Doerflinger, Joseph	Aviation	10		75	45	
Doering, Arnold	Aviation	10	20	35	25	
Dohanos, Stevan	Illustrator	5	15			
Doherty, Shannen	Entertainment	25			50	
Dohnanyi, Erno	Composer	50	135	220		AMusQS $350
Doi, Takao	Astronaut	15	25		25	
Doig, Andrew Wheeler	Senate/Congress	10	20			MOC NY 1839, Banker, Mining
Doisy, Edward A.	Science	20	45	70	30	Nobel Medicine. Vitamin K
Dolby, Ray	Science	20	35			Inventor Dolby Sound
Dolby, Thomas	Entertainment	20			40	
Dole, Charles F	Clergy	10	15	20		
Dole, Elizabeth	Cabinet	6	15	30	20	Sec'y Labor. Head Red Cross
Dole, James D.	Business	55	145	235	75	Fdr.Hawaiian Pineapple Industry
Dole, Robert	Senate	10	20		20	Senator KS
Dole, Sanford B.	Business	45	245	390	100	Financier, Pres. Repub. Hawaii
Dolenz, Mickey	Entertainment	10		25	35	Monkees
Dolin, Anton	Entertainment	25	40	95	75	Ballet
Dollar, Robert	Business	20	55	130	50	Dollar Steamship Line.
Dolliver, Jonathan P.	Senate & Congress	20	35		25	Senator, MOC IA 1889
Domenici, Pete	Senate	5			15	Senator NM
Domerque, Faith	Entertainment	10			35	

NAME	CATEGORY	SIG	LS/DS	ALS	SP	COMMENT
Domingo, Placido	Entertainment	20		40	50	Opera, Concert
Dominick, Fred H.	Senate & Congress	5	15		10	MOC SC 1917-33
Domino, Fats	Entertainment	20	25	35	65	Rock
Donahue, Al	Entertainment	15			40	Big Band Leader
Donahue, Archie	Aviation	12	25	50	35	ACE, WW II, Ace in one day
Donahue, Elinor	Entertainment	5	6	15	15	Pin-Up SP $20
Donahue, Phil	Entertainment	5			15	TV Talk Show Host
Donahue, Troy	Entertainment	5	6	15	25	
Donaldson, Jesse M.	Cabinet	10	15	35	15	1st Postman Becomes P.M. Gen.
Donaldson, Sam	TV News	7			16	TV News Anchor, Commentator
Donat, Peter	Entertainment	5	6	15	15	
Donat, Robert	Entertainment	65	75	155	250	
Donat, Zdislawa	Entertainment	5			25	Opera
Doniphan, Alexander William	Military	120	250	475		Fought Mex.,Indians,Mormans
Donizetti, Gaetano	Composer	500	800	2150		AMusQS $2,750,AMusMs $3,000
Donlan, Roger	Military	10	25	40	15	
Donlevy, Brian	Entertainment	20			100	
Donnell, Jeff	Entertainment	5	6	10	10	
Donnelly, Ruth	Entertainment	10	15	25	25	
Donner, Richard	Entertainment	10			20	
Donovan, Hedley	Editor	5	6	15	10	Time-Life Editor
Donovan, King	Entertainment	15			35	
Donovan, Raymond J.	Cabinet	8	15	35	16	Sec'y Labor
Donovan, Wm. J."Wild Bill"	Military	80	225	325	95	"Fighting 69th",OSS-CIA
Doobie Brothers	Entertainment	40			80	
Doohan, James 'Scotty'	Entertainment	10	12	20	25	"Star Trek"
Dooley, Paul	Entertainment	5	6	15	15	
Dooley, Thomas A., Dr.	Science	125	185	400	150	Jungle Physician, SE Asia
Doolittle, Hilda	Author	75	205	475		Imagist Poet. Ed."The Egoist"
Doolittle, James A.	Aviation	70	170	275	150	Gen. WW II, Test Pilot
Doolittle, James Rood	Senate	15	25	40		Civil War Senator WI
Doors & Jimmie Morrison	Entertainment	475			1000	Rock
Doors, The (3)	Entertainment	100				Rock
Doran, Ann	Entertainment	15	15	25	22	
Dore', Paul Gustave	Artist	55	170	395		
Dornberger, Walter R.	Military	40	100	120	75	Rocket Engineer. Bell Aircraft
Dorr, Julia C. R.	Author	3	5	15		
Dors, Diana	Entertainment	20			150	
Dorsey, Jimmie	Entertainment	30	150		100	Big Band Leader-Saxophone
Dorsey, Tommy	Entertainment	55	140		140	Big Band Leader-Trombone
Dortch, William T.	Civil War	25	40	75		CSA Senator NC
Dos Passos, John	Author	20	35	90	30	Am. Novelist
Dostoevsky, Fyodor	Author	1500	5700	13800		Rus.Novelist."Crime & Punishmen
Doubleday, Abner	Civil War	285	675	1670		Union Gen.-Credit for baseball
Doubleday, Frank Nelson	Business	65	185	375		Book Publisher
Doucette, John	Entertainment	6	8	15	15	
Dougherty, Dennis, Cardinal	Clergy	35	40	50	40	
Douglas, Beverly B.	Civil War	30	40	55		CSA Officer, MOC VA
Douglas, Donald W. Jr.	Business	25	60		45	Douglas Aircraft
Douglas, Donald W. Sr.	Aviation	150	295	450	360	Pioneer Aircraft Mfg.
Douglas, Donna	Entertainment	6	8	10	15	Pin-Up SP $20
Douglas, Helen Gahagan	Entertainment	30	60	120	55	MOC CA, Opera, Actress
Douglas, Kirk	Entertainment	10		15	25	
Douglas, Leon	Country Music	10			20	
Douglas, Lloyd C.	Author	25	50	65	30	Retired Minister. "The Robe"etc
Douglas, Melvyn	Entertainment	18	20	25	40	

NAME	CATEGORY	SIG	LS/DS	ALS	SP	COMMENT
Douglas, Michael	Entertainment	15		25	45	
Douglas, Mike	Entertainment	4	5	9	9	Singer. Early TV Host
Douglas, Paul	Entertainment	10	12		25	
Douglas, Paul H.	Senate	10	20		15	Senator IL
Douglas, Paul P.	Aviation	10	22	42	32	ACE, WW II
Douglas, Robert	Entertainment	10			25	
Douglas, Stephen A.	Senate	120	290	510	270	Statesman, Pres. Candidate
Douglas, William O. (SC)	Supreme Court	75	200		200	
Douglas, William Taylor	Clergy	15	20	25		
Douglass, Frederick	Abolitionist	125	410	700		Author, Lecturer, Editor
Douglass, Robyn	Entertainment	4	4	9	10	
Doulton, Henry, Sir	Potter-Inventor	20	35	70		Royal Doulton China
Dove, Billie	Entertainment	15	15	35	30	
Dow, Neal	Civil War	44	75	105		Union Gen., Temperance Reformer
Dow, Tony	Entertainment	4	6	10	15	
Dowden, Edward	Author	10	15	25		Ir. Critic, Editor, Professor
Dowling, Eddie	Entertainment	20	25	45	45	
Down, Lesley-Anne	Entertainment	5	6	15	15	
Downey, Morton	Entertainment	10	15	20	25	
Downey, Robert, Jr.	Entertainment	20			70	Actor
Downey, Sheridan	Senate	10	25		20	Senator CA 1938-50
Downing, Big Al	Entertainment	3	3	6	6	
Downing, George, Sir 1623-84	Diplomat	850				2nd Graduate Harvard College
Downs, Hugh	TV Host	10		25	30	TV Co-Host 20/20
Downs, Johnny	Entertainment	10			35	
Doyle, Arthur Conan, Sir	Author-Physician	425	700	2400	875	Br. Novelist. "Sherlock Holmes"
Dozier, James	Military	12	30	45	15	
Dr. Seuss*	Cartoonists	25			450	Cat In The Hat-early
Dragonette, Jessica	Entertainment	18	20		35	Soprano
Dragoni, Maria	Entertainment	10			30	Opera
Drake, Alfred	Entertainment	7			10	Musical Theatre
Drake, Betsy	Entertainment	5			15	
Drake, Frances	Entertainment	8	9	15	20	
Drake, Francis M.	Governor	5	15			Gov. IA
Drake, Michele	Entertainment	4			15	Pin-Up SP $20
Drake, Samuel Adams	Civil War	45		75		Union General, Author
Drake, Stan*	Cartoonist	20			100	Blondie
Drake, Tom	Entertainment	3	3	6	10	
Draper, Eben S.	Governor	5	12			Governor MA
Draper, Rusty	Country Music	5			12	
Draper, Ruth	Entertainment	10	30	70	50	Am. Monologuist
Draper, William H.	Clergy	20	35	40		
Drayton, Gracie*	Cartoonist	20			250	Created Campbell Soup Kids
Drees, Willem	Head of State	20	35	100		Survivor Buchenwald
Dreiser, Theodore	Author	70	200	300		"American Tragedy"
Dresser, Louise	Entertainment	25			55	Stage. Major Silent Film Star
Dressler, Marie	Entertainment	130			250	
Drew, Ellen	Entertainment	4	6	9	10	
Drew, John 1853-1927	Entertainment	60	75	125	100	
Drexel, Anthony	Banker	45	65	145		Philanthropist
Drexel, J. A.	Aviation	43	60	100	65	
Dreyfus, Alfred	Military	140	310	1250	750	Framed for Treason, Devil's Isl
Dreyfus, Julie Louis	Entertainment	10			20	Actress, Seinfeld
Dreyfuss, Richard	Entertainment	10	15	25	40	
Dribrell, George G.	Civil War	95	250	300		
Drinan, Robert, Father	Senate/Congress	4			15	Catholic Activist Priest

NAME	CATEGORY	SIG	LS/DS	ALS	SP	COMMENT
Drinkwater, John	Author	20	50	75	25	Poet
Driscoll, Bobby	Entertainment	125	155	190	250	
Driver, Samuel Rolles	Clergy	85	100	125		
Drouet, Robert	Entertainment	25	30	60	68	
Dru, Joanne	Entertainment	4	4	9	12	
Druckman, Jacob	Composer	20	50	95		Pulitzer, AMusQS $250
Drum, Hugh A. Lt.Gen	Military	25	55	120	50	General WW I, WW II
Drum, Richard C.	Civil War	27	50	80		
Drummond, Henry	Clergy	50	60	80		
Drummond, James	Clergy	25	35	50		
Drury, Allen	Author	10	30	65	35	
Drury, Frank	Aviation	10	25	40	30	ACE, WW II, Marine Ace
Drury, James	Entertainment	10			30	
Dryer, Fred	Entertainment	10		25	25	
Du Barry, Jeanne, Comtesse	Royal Mistress	285	950	1200		Banished, Arrested, Guillotined
Du Chaillu, Paul B.	Explorer	50	80	125		Brought 1st Gorillas out of Afr
Du Maurier, Daphne, Dame	Author	45	140	185	50	Br. Novelist. "Rebecca"
Du Maurier, George	Author	15	45	125		And Illustrator of "Punch"
Du Pont, Elizabeth H	Business	20	75	110	30	
Du Pont, Henry A.	Business	55	240			1838-1926, CW, CMH
Du Pont, Lammot	Business	20			50	CEO Du Pont Chemical
Du Pont, Pierre S.	Governor	15	35		50	Governor DE, Du Pont Chemical
Du Pont, Pierre-Samuel 1739-1817I	Economist	45	110	240		Progenitor of Du Pont Lineage
Du Pont, R.	Aviation	40	110			Am Aviation Exec.
Du Pont, Samuel Francis	Civil War	80	135	350		1803-1865, Union Adm.
Du Vigneaud, Vincent	Science	25	55	145	45	Nobel, Synthesized Penicillin
DuBois, W. E. B.	Author	300	675		425	Black Rights, Educator-Writer
DuBridge, Lee, Dr.	Science	30	100	145	50	Pres. Cal-Tech
DuPonceau, Pierre	Military	25	60	140		
Duane, James	Revolutionary War	100	270	540		1st Continental Congress
Dubcek, Alexander	Head of State	80	130			Czech. Reformer
Dubose, Dudley	Civil War	95	275			CSA Gen., MOC GA
Dubuffet, Jean	Artist	150	400			Swiss proponent of "raw art"
Dubuque, Julien	Am. Pioneer	600	2500			1st White Settler Near Dubuque
Duchamp, Marcel	Artist	125	350	600		Fr. Avante Garde Artist
Duchin, Eddie	Entertainment	25	40		120	Big Band Leader, Pianist
Duchin, Peter	Entertainment	5	6	15	15	Pianist, Band Leader
Duckworth, John T., Sir 1748-1817	Military	55	180			Br. Admiral, Gov. Newfoundland
Ducos, Jean Francois	Fr. Revolution	36	100	205		
Dudicoff, Michael	Entertainment	10	12		25	
Dudley, Dave	Country Music	6			15	
Dudley, Joseph 1647-1720	Colonial America	450	895	1500		Col.Gov.MA.Philos.Scholar,Divin
Dudley, Paul 1675-1751	Colonial America	115	310			Jurist. Religious Activist
Dudley, Thomas V., Bishop	Clergy	35	50	45	50	
Duesenberg, Frederick S.	Business	550	1350			
Duff, Arthur, Sir	Military	15	45	70		Br. Admiral
Duff, Howard	Entertainment	5	6	15	25	
Duff, James H.	Senate	5	15		10	Governor, Senator PA
Duffer, Candy	Entertainment	20			45	Rock
Duffie, Alfred Napoleon Alex.	Civil War	35	50	85		Union Gen. Cavalry
Duffy, Brian	Astronaut	5			15	
Duffy, Francis P.	Clergy	15	20	25		
Duffy, Julia	Entertainment	9	10	20	20	
Duffy, Patrick	Entertainment	7			20	
Dufy, Raoul	Artist	300	450	820	500	Fr. Impressionist, Fauvism
Duggan, Andrew	Entertainment	15			25	

NAME	CATEGORY	SIG	LS/DS	ALS	SP	COMMENT
Dukakis, Michael S.	Governor	15			20	Governor MA
Dukakis, Olympia	Entertainment	15	25	35	30	
Dukas, Paul	Composer	55	160	400		Fr. "Sorcerer's Apprentice"
Duke, Basil Wilson	Civil War	50	170	275		CSA Gen. War dte. SP $5,000
Duke, Charles M., Jr.	Astronaut	20			40	Moonwalker
Duke, Clarence	Celebrity	4	10	25	5	Sports Announcer
Duke, David	Activist	40			95	Ex KKK Grand Wizard
Duke, Patty	Entertainment	8	9	15	20	
Duke, Vernon	Composer	20	50	145		AMusQS $175
Dulbecco, Renato	Science	20	35	60		Nobel Physiology-Medicine
Dullea, Keir	Entertainment	8	12	15	20	
Dulles, Allen W.	Diplomat	30	165	225	75	State Dept., OSS, CIA
Dulles, John Foster	Cabinet	25	115	150	75	Sec'y State, Diplomat, UN
Dumas, Alexandre (Fils)	Author	55	105	175	425	Fr. Dramatist, Novelist
Dumas, Alexandre (Pere)	Author	110	225	390	750	Fr. Novelist."Three Musketeers"
Dumbrille, Douglass	Entertainment	40			75	
Dummar, Melvin E.	Celebrity	20	30	45		Fraudulent H. Hughes Heir
Duna, Steffi	Entertainment	10		15	25	
Dunagin, Ralph	Cartoonist	5			20	The Middletons
Dunaway, Faye	Entertainment	10	15	25	30	
Dunbar, Bonnie J.	Astronaut	5			15	
Dunbar, Charles E., Sr.	Bureaucrat	10	25			Chm. US War Trade Board 1914-18
Dunbar, Dixie	Entertainment	6	8	15	15	
Dunbar, Paul Lawrence	Author	250				Afro-Am. Poet, Novelist etc.
Duncan, Charles T.	Celebrity	4	10	25	10	
Duncan, Isadora	Entertainment	400		1150	825	Am. Interpretive Dancer
Duncan, Johnny	Country Music	10			20	
Duncan, Sandy	Entertainment	5			15	
Duncan, Thomas	Civil War	20	50			Union General
Duncan, Todd	Entertainment	25			100	First "Porgy"
Dundas, Henry 1742-1811	Statesman	25	40	85		Br. Sec'y War.Pro War with Am.
Dunlap, John	Am. Printer	150	575			1st To Print Decl. of Ind. etc.
Dunlop, John T.	Cabinet	5	10	15	15	Sec'y Labor
Dunn, Emma	Entertainment	20			35	
Dunn, Holly	Country Music	10			25	
Dunn, James	Entertainment	60	60	120	125	
Dunn, William	Civil War	25	40	70		Union Gen.(Judge, Adv. Gen.'75)
Dunne, Irene	Entertainment	15	15	30	35	
Dunne, Phillip	Author	5	20	35	15	Novelist
Dunnock, Mildred	Entertainment	7			20	
Dunsany, Lord	Author					see Plunkett
Durais, C.	Artist	10	20	50		
Duran Duran	Entertainment	60			100	
Durand, Asher B.	Artist	85	175	500		Hudson River School. Engraver
Durant, Ariel (Ida)	Author	25	50	115	35	Historian with Husband Will
Durant, Will	Author	30	50	135	45	Historian with Wife Aerial
Durant, William Crapo	Business	250		900		Durant Motor Car. GM, Chevrolet
Durante, Jimmy	Entertainment	25			70	
Durbin, Deanna	Entertainment	15			30	
Durenberger, David	Senate	5			15	Senator MN
Durer, Albrecht	Artist	3000	8200	21000		Foremost Ger.Renaissance Artist
Durham, Bobby	Country Music	10			20	
Durning, Charles	Entertainment	5	6	15	25	
Duroc, Geraud C.M.	Military	25	65	185		Napol. Grand Marshal-Diplomat
Durrell, Lawrence	Author	25	70	190	40	Br-Ir Poet,Playwright,Travel
Duryea, Charles E.	Science-Business	195	625		650	Built 1st Am.Gasoline Motor Car

NAME	CATEGORY	SIG	LS/DS	ALS	SP	COMMENT
Duryea, Dan	Entertainment	15	15	30	35	
Duse, Eleanora	Entertainment	200	400	990	850	
Dussault, Nancy	Entertainment	3	3	6	10	
Dussek, Jan L 1760-1812	Composer	30	90	145		Marie Antoinette was Patron
Dustinn, Emmy	Entertainment	30			170	Opera
Dutra, Enrico Gaspar	Head of State	10	20	50	35	Pres. Brazil.Outlawed Communist
Duval, Gabriel (SC)	Supreme Court	45	115	245		
Duvalier, Francois	Head of State	75	145		150	"Papa Doc". Haitian President
Duvall, Robert	Entertainment	10	15	25	30	
Duvall, Shelley	Entertainment	6	8	15	18	
Duvé, Christian de, Dr.	Science	20	35		30	Nobel Medicine
Duyckinck, Evart A.	Editor	40		150		Literary World
Dvorak, Ann	Entertainment	6	8	15	15	
Dvorak, Antonin	Composer	400	895	2500		Czech.Slavonic Dances,Symphonie
Dwan, Allan	Entertainment	15			35	
Dwight, Timothy 1752-1817	Author-Clergy	20	55			"Harvard Wit", President Yale
Dyer, Eliphlet	Revolutionary War	50	155			Continental Congress
Dyer, George C.	Military	15	40	60		Admiral USN
Dyer, Leondidas Carstarphen	Senate/Congress	5			10	MOC MO 1915-1933
Dyke, Leroy Van	Country Music	5			15	
Dylan, Bob	Entertainment	125	225	400	340	Songwriter, Poet, Folksinger
Dymally, Mervyn M.	Senate/Congress	5			15	Afr-Am. Congressman CA
Dysart, Richard	Entertainment	10	15	25	18	

E

NAME	CATEGORY	SIG	LS/DS	ALS	SP	COMMENT
Eadie, Betty J.	Author	5			10	Non-Fiction
Eadie, John	Clergy	10	15	25		Scot. Theologian & Scholar
Eads, James Buchanan	Civil War	105	330	500		Engineer, Shipbuilder for Union
Eagleburger, Lawrence	Diplomat	4			10	State Dept., Ambassador
Eagles	Entertainment	40			80	
Eagleston, Glenn	Aviation	20	42	70	45	ACE, WW II
Eagleton, Thomas F.	Senate	20	50		10	Senator MO
Eaker, Ira	Aviation	20	60	95	80	WW II Air Force Cmdr
Eakins, Thomas	Artist	375		3250		Am. Painter-Sculptor
Eames-Story, Emma	Entertainment	85			145	Opera
Earhart, Amelia	Aviation	530	1125		1380	TLS/Content $2,495
Earle, George H.	Governor	10	15			Governor PA
Earle, Virginia	Entertainment	6	8	15	15	
Early, Jubal	Civil War	260	400	825		CSA General
Earp, Virgil	Lawman	500	4500	6800		US Marshal. S Auction $8,250
Earp, Wyatt B.S.	Lawman	3875		25000		Legendary Gambler, Gunfighter
East, James	Lawman	250	750			Western Cowboy
East, John	Senate	10	20	40	35	Senator NC, Suicide
Eastlake, Charles L., Sir	Artist	50	150	350		Pres. of Royal Academy, Critic
Eastland, James	Senate/Congress	10			15	Senator MS 1943-78

NAME	CATEGORY	SIG	LS/DS	ALS	SP	COMMENT
Eastman, George	Business	140	465	825	400	Eastman Kodak Co.
Eastman, Max	Author	35	80	115		Editor-Fdr. "The Masses"
Easton, Florence	Entertainment	45			175	Opera
Easton, Sheena	Entertainment	12	15	25	45	
Eastwood, Clint	Entertainment	20			95	
Eaton, Amos Beebe	Civil War	25	50	90		Union General
Eaton, Dorman 1823-99	Reformer	10	25	55		Jurist, Nat'l Civil Service Act
Eaton, John Henry	Cabinet	20	55	90		Senator TN 1818, Sec'y War
Eaton, William 1764-1811	Military-Diplomat	30		75		U.S.Consul Tunis,Tripoli Action
Eban, Abba	Diplomat	15	35	75	65	Israeli Diplomat, Ambass. UN
Ebb, Fred	Composer	10		35	20	AMusQS $50 "New York, NY.."
Ebbets, Charles H.	Business	150			175	Orig. Brooklyn Dodgers Field
Eben Emael	Military	30	85	140	60	
Eberhart, Adolph O.	Governor	5	22			Governor MN
Eberhart, Richard	Author	10	20	45	15	Major Poet 20th Cent.,Pulitzer
Eberly, Bob	Entertainment	3	3	10	15	
Ebsen, Buddy	Entertainment	5	6	15	25	
Eccles, John C.	Science	20	30	40	30	Nobel Medicine
Echols, John	Civil War	90	195	315		CSA General
Echols, Leonard Sidney	Senate/Congress	5	15			MOC WV 1919
Eckels, James H.	Entertainment					
Eckener, Hugo von	Aviation	200	525	650	450	Ger. Aeronaut, Built G.Zeppelin
Eckstine, Billy	Entertainment	20			50	Vocalist-Trumpet-Bandleader
Ed, Carl	Cartoonist	10			30	Harold Teen
Eddington, Arthur Stanley, Sir	Science	25	140	185		Mathematician, Astrophysicist
Eddy, Duane	Entertainment	30			45	Rock Guitarist. HOF
Eddy, Mary Baker	Clergy	975	2125	3890		
Eddy, Nelson	Entertainment	50	175		110	
Eden, Anthony, Sir	Head of State	55	140	190	75	Prime Minister
Eden, Barbara	Entertainment	10	15	25	25	Pin-Up SP $30
Ederle, Gertrude "Trudy"	Entertainment	25			60	And Showgirl
Edeson, Robert	Entertainment	20			45	Silent Star. "Ten Commandments"
Edge, Walter E.	Senate/Congress	15	25		20	Gov.NJ 1917, Senator PA, Ambass
Edison, Charles	Cabinet	55	75	110	60	Sec'y Navy. Son of Thos. A.
Edison, Thomas Alva	Science	475	1225	3050	1725	
Edmonds, Walter Dumanx	Author	5	25	40	20	
Edmunds, George Franklin	Senate	10	15	30		Senator VT 1866-91
Edmundson, Henry A.	Civil War	40	55	80		CSA Officer, MOC VA
Edward IV (England)1442-83	Royalty	25000				
Edward VII (England)	Royalty	110	350	400	625	Albert Edw., Q.Vict. Eldest Son
Edward VIII	Royalty	250	1700	900	750	As King
Edward VIII, as Prince of Wales	Royalty	150		645	675	
Edward and Wallis	Royalty	550			950	Duke and Duchess of Windsor
Edward, Duke Windsor	Royalty	200	775	1950	655	
Edward, Duke of Kent	Royalty	40	135	350		
Edwards, Anthony	Entertainment	9	10	20	25	
Edwards, Blake	Entertainment	10			25	Film Producer-Director
Edwards, Clarence	Military	35				General WW I
Edwards, Cliff (Ukele Ike)	Entertainment	50	70	100	125	
Edwards, Douglas	News	3	3	6	15	Radio-TV News
Edwards, Edward Irving	Senate	10	15			Senator, Governor NJ
Edwards, Elaine S.	Senate	7	20		10	Senator LA, 8/1/72-11/13/72
Edwards, Gail J.	Entertainment	5	6	15	15	
Edwards, Gordon	Business	4			10	Business Exec., U.S. Steel
Edwards, James B.	Cabinet	10	15	35	10	Governor SC, Sec'y Energy
Edwards, Joan	Entertainment	5			10	

NAME	CATEGORY	SIG	LS/DS	ALS	SP	COMMENT
Edwards, Jonathan	Clergy-Author	110	350	380		Great Theologian Am.Puritanism
Edwards, Oliver	Civil War	25	60	100		Union General
Edwards, Ralph	Entertainment	4	4	9	10	"This Is Your Life"
Edwards, Vince	Entertainment	5			15	
Egan, Richard	Entertainment	5	6	15	15	
Egan, William A.	Governor	5	12		10	Governor AK
Egbert, H.C.	Military	45				Gen. Spanish-Am. War
Egbert, Sherwood	Business	3	14	35	15	
Eggar, Samantha	Entertainment	6	8	15	19	
Eggleston, Benjamin	Senate/Congress	7	10	15		MOC OH
Eggleston, Edward	Author	5		30		Am. Regional Classic Novels
Eglevsky, Andre'	Entertainment	40	55	110	75	Rus-Am Ballet Teacher-Dancer
Ehrlich, Paul, Dr.	Science	150	275	450		Nobel. Diphtheria, Syphillis
Eichelberger. Robert L.	Military	20	45	70	40	Gen. WW II. Cmdr I Corps
Eichelbrenner, E. A.	Science	45	95	225		
Eichmann, Adolf	Military	275	500	1250	750	ALS/Cont.Offered $50,000-60,000
Eick, Alfred	Military	26		50		
Eiffel, Alexandre-Gustave	Arch.-Engineer	275	525	750	1200	ALS/Content $1,750
Eigen, Manfred	Science	20	35	80	40	Nobel Chemistry
Eilers, Sally	Entertainment	15	15	30	38	
Eilshemius, Louis Michel	Artist	35	60	145		Am. Landscape Expressionist
Einstein, Albert	Science	1400	3925	6375	3660	ALS/Sci. Content $25,000
Eisele, Donn F.	Astronaut	50			85	
Eisenberg, Maurice	Entertainment	10			20	Cellist
Eisenhower, Arthur B.	Business	5	15		10	Brother to Ike. Banker
Eisenhower, Barbara	Celebrity	5	15		10	Daughter-in Law to Ike
Eisenhower, Dwight D.	President	285	595	4300	530	ALS/Content $8,500-$17,500
Eisenhower, Dwight D.(As President)	President	315	1450			
Eisenhower, Edgar N.	Law	5	20		15	Brother & Lawyer to Ike
Eisenhower, John S. D.	Military	10	20	35	15	General & Only Son of Ike
Eisenhower, Julie Nixon	Celebrity	5	10	25	25	Daughter & Inlaw Two Presidents
Eisenhower, Mamie Doud	First Lady	60	115	165	100	White House Card S $65
Eisenhower, Milton	Educator	10	30		20	Brother. Pres. Penn. State U.
Eisenman, Robin G.	Entertainment	4	4	9	10	
Eisenstaedt, Alfred	Photographer	15	40		125	Celebrity Photographer
Eisley, Anthony	Entertainment	7			12	
Eisner, Michael O.	Business	25			40	CEO Walt Disney Co.
Eisner, William J.	Business	10	35	45	20	
Eizenstat, Stuart E.	Government	4	10	15	12	White House Staff
Ekberg, Anita	Entertainment	10			20	
Ekland, Britt	Entertainment	10	12	25	30	Pin-Up SP $35
Ekwall, William A.	Senate/Congress	5	10		10	MOC OR
Elam, Jack	Entertainment	5	6	15	15	
Elder, Ruth	Aviation	100	190	310	300	Pioneer Aviatrix
Elder, Will*	Cartoonist	30			400	Annie Fanny
Elders, Joycelyn	Cabinet	15	30		20	Clinton Surgeon General
Eldridge, Louise	Reformer	10	15	30		"Aunt Louisa" AQS $25
Electric Light Orchestra	Entertainment	35			75	
Eleniak, Erika	Entertainment	10			25	Actress-Model
Elgar, Edward, Sir	Composer	95	345	585	525	AMusQS $1,500
Elgin,7th Earl (T.Bruce)	Diplomat					SEE Bruce, Thomas
Elijah, Muhammad	Celebrity	385			425	Religious Activist
Elion, Gertrude, Dr.	Science	20	65		35	Nobel Medicine
Eliot, Charles W.	Educator	15	50	80		Pres. Harvard
Eliot, George (Pseud.)	Author	160	625	1250		Br. Novelist. (Mary Ann Evans)
Eliot, T.S.	Author	165	525	1100		Br. Poet, Critic, Editor, Nobel

NAME	CATEGORY	SIG	LS/DS	ALS	SP	COMMENT
Elizabeth I	Royalty	3400	19500			
Elizabeth II & Philip	Royalty		530		1185	
Elizabeth, II	Royalty	350	795	800	705	
Elizabeth, Queen Mother	Royalty	80	225	350	500	Queen of George VI
Elkins, Stephen B.	Cabinet	15	25	60	25	Sec'y War, Senator WV
Ellender, Allen J.	Senate	4	5		10	Senator LA
Ellerbee, Linda	TV News	10	35		15	TV News, Commentator
Ellery, William	Revolutionary War	180	460	770		Signer Decl. of Indepen.
Ellicott, Andrew	Revolutionary War	60	185	320		Surveyor, Mathematician
Ellington, Buford	Governor	10	12	20		Governor TN
Ellington, Duke	Composer	125	325		400	AMusQS $300-$1,200
Elliott, Bob	Entertainment	3	3	6	10	
Elliott, Carter	Composer	40	125	280		
Elliott, Cass (Mama)	Entertainment	175	375			Rotund, Sweet-Voiced Singer
Elliott, Maxine	Entertainment	30	40	75	70	
Elliott, R.W.B., Bishop	Clergy	25	35	40	40	
Elliott, Robert B.	Senate/Congress	10	15		15	MOC SC
Elliott, Sam	Entertainment	9	10	20	25	
Elliott, Wild Bill	Entertainment	50			150	Vintage Cowboy
Ellis, F. H.	Aviation	15	35		30	
Ellis, Havelock	Science	35	100	350		Br. Pioneer Advocate Sex Ed.
Ellis, Robert H.	Military	10	25	45		
Ellison, James	Entertainment	10		15	25	
Ellison, Ralph	Author	65	285			"The Invisible Man"
Ellsberg, Daniel	Activist	20	35	50	25	Leaked Pentagon Papers
Ellsworth, Ephriam Elmer	Civil War	540	1500	2500		
Ellsworth, Oliver (SC)	Supreme Court	100	400	450		Chief Justice Supreme Ct.
Ellul, Jacques	Clergy	25	30	45		
Elman, Mischa	Entertainment	40	225		80	Rus. Violinist
Elman, Ziggy	Entertainment	25			75	Trumpet
Elmore, E.C.	Civil War	55	105			Treas. CSA. ALS $3,500
Elrod, Jack*	Cartoonist	10			35	Mark Trail
Elson, Edward L.R.	Clergy	15	20	25		
Elssler, Fanny 1810-84	Entertainment	250				Austrian Ballerina
Elston, John A.	Congress	5	15			Congressman CA
Eltinge, Julian	Entertainment	15	20	35	40	Female Impersonator,Silent Film
Eluard, Paul	Author	110	225	375		Fr. Poet. Exponent Surrealism
Elvira	Entertainment	8	9	19	25	Pin-Up SP $35
Ely, Joseph Buell	Governor	15	35	70		Gov. MA, Anti New Dealer
Ely, Paul, General	Military	65		140	90	Fr. Cmdr. Indochina.Dienbienphu
Ely, Ron	Entertainment	10	12	15	25	
Emberg, Kelly	Model	10			25	Pin-Up SP $40
Emerson, Faye	Entertainment	5			10	
Emerson, Hope	Entertainment	15			35	
Emerson, Lake and Palmer	Entertainment	35			80	
Emerson, Ralph Waldo	Author-Clergy	190	275	850		ALS/Content $3,500
Emma, Queen (Neé Rooker)	Royalty	150				Wife of King Kamehameha IV
Emmett, Daniel D.	Composer	300	425	600		1st Minstral Show. "Dixie"
Emmons, Ebenezer 1799-1863	Science	25	40	70		Early Prof. of Natural History
Emory, William Hemsley	Civil War	65	170	300		Union General
Enders, John Franklin, Dr.	Science	25	60	110	45	Nobel Medicine.
Endicott, William C.	Cabinet	15	25	35	20	Sec'y War
Enesco, Georges	Composer	100	275	550		AMusQS $850
Enevoldson, Einer	Astronaut	10			20	
Engel, Georgia	Entertainment	5	6	15	15	
England, Anthony W.	Astronaut	5			15	

NAME	CATEGORY	SIG	LS/DS	ALS	SP	COMMENT
Engle, Frederick	Civil War	45				Union Commodore
Engle, Joe Henry	Astronaut	5			15	
English, Thomas Dunn	Author	10	30	45		"Ben Bolt".Dr.,Lawyer, Poet
Englund, Robert	Entertainment	10			35	Horror Movies
Enos, Roger 1729-1808	Military	55	175	295		General, Honored VT Citizen
Enriquez, Rene	Entertainment	12	15	30	35	
Ensley, F. Gerald, Bishop	Clergy	20	35	50	25	
Ensor, James Sydney, Baron	Artist	50	160	390		Belg. Painter, Etcher. Bizarre
Epp, Franz Xaver von	Military	15	40		75	Gen. WW I. Sturmabteilung Army
Epstein, Brian	Entertainment	275	1500			"Beatles" Manager & Promoter
Epstein, Jacob, Sir	Artist	150	210	475		Controversial Br. Sculptor
Erdrich, Louise	Author	5			10	Novelist. "The Bingo Palace"
Erhard, Ludwig	Head of State	20	70	170	50	Chancellor W. Germany
Erickson, Leif	Entertainment	20			40	
Ericsdotter, Siw	Entertainment	25			60	Opera
Ericsson, John	Civil War	75	195	725		Designed & Built "Monitor"
Erni, Hans	Artist	65		225		ALS=FDC/sig'd art
Ernouf, Manuel L.J(Baron)	Fr. Revolution	35	85	160		
Ernst, Max	Artist	235	355	900		Surrealist-Dada Movement
Errol, Leon	Entertainment	35			65	
Erskine, Graves B.	Military	15	35	65	40	Led US Marines at Iwo Jima
Erskine, John	Author	40	125	190		Novelist, Pres. Juilliard
Erte'	Artist	80	210	350	90	
Ervin, Sam J.	Senate/Congress	10	20		15	MOC, Senator NC
Ervine, St. John	Author	15	50			Br. Controversial Drama Critic
Erwin, Durward	Country Music	10			20	
Erwin, James	Military	45				General WW I
Erwin, Stuart	Entertainment	20			45	
Esaki, Leo	Science	20	35	50	30	Nobel Physics
Escobedo, Mariano	Military	50	225			Captured Maximillian
Eshkol, Levi	Head of State	70	250	560	120	Israeli P.M., Fndr. Histadrut
Esperian, Kalen	Entertainment	10			30	Opera
Essame, Hubert	Military	25	41			
Estaing, Charles Hector T. de	Revolutionary War	175	500	750		Fr.Gen-Adm. Pro American Hero
Este, Isabella d' 1474-1539	Royalty			10000		(Mantua) Art Patron, Diplomat
Estefan, Gloria	Entertainment	10			45	
Esterhasy, Gunt A.	Head of State	20	70			Austria
Estes, Billy Sol	Celebrity	5	20	45	15	Grain Storage Scandal
Estevez, Emilio	Entertainment	10	15	25	30	
Estil, Benjamin	Congress	15	25			Congressman VA 1825
Estrada, Erik	Entertainment	4	4	9	15	
Etter, Philippe	Head of State	15	50			Switzerland
Eubanks, Bob	Entertainment	4	4	9	10	
Eugenie, Empress(Nap.III)	Royalty	195	305	470		Influenced Nap. Fashion Leader
Euler (-Chelpin), Ulf Svante von	Science	20	35	60	40	Nobel Medicine
Eurythmics	Entertainment	30			60	
Eustis, Abraham	Military	40		350		War 1812. Promoted to Br. Gen.
Eustis, William	Cabinet	35	90	175		Sec'y War, MOC MA 1801
Evans, Dale	Entertainment	10	12		25	
Evans, Daniel J.	Senate-Gov.	15	18		20	Gov., Senato Washington
Evans, De Lacy	Military	150	220			Br. Col. Who Burned White House
Evans, Edith, Dame	Entertainment	15	35		35	
Evans, Edw. R.G.,Lord Mountevans	Explorer	35			75	Admiral, Arctic Explorer
Evans, Gene	Entertainment	5	6	15	30	
Evans, Geraint, Sir	Entertainment	10			35	Opera
Evans, Joan	Entertainment	7	10	15	15	

NAME	CATEGORY	SIG	LS/DS	ALS	SP	COMMENT
Evans, John V.	Governor	10	15			Governor ID
Evans, Linda	Entertainment	9	10	20	25	
Evans, Lt. Col. D. M	Civil War	15	25	40		
Evans, Madge	Entertainment	15	15	35	30	
Evans, Maurice	Entertainment	20	25	35	55	
Evans, Nathan G. "Shanks"	Civil War	175		575		CSA Gen.
Evans, Ray	Composer	15	35	45	40	
Evans, Robley D.	Civil War	30	65	110	150	Capt. USN, "Fight'n Bob"
Evans, Ronald E.	Astronaut	40			100	
Evarts, William M.	Cabinet	30	85	175	45	Att'y Gen., Sec'y State, Sen NY
Everest. F.K. 'Pete'	Aviation	15	30	45	35	
Everett, Chad	Entertainment	5	6	15	15	
Everett, Edward	Sen.-Cab.-Clergy	75	165	170	95	Fillmore Sec'y State, Sen. MA
Everly Brothers	Entertainment	30			75	
Evers, Charles	Celebrity	5	20	40	10	
Evigan, Greg	Entertainment	3	3	6	10	
Ewell, I.R.L.	Civil War	190	395			
Ewell, Tom	Entertainment	6	8	15	25	
Ewing, James	Military	45	142			Officer Am. Revolution
Ewing, Thomas 1789-1871	Cabinet	40	110	245		Sen. OH,Sec'y Treas. & Interior
Exelmans, Rene' J.I., Count	Fr. Revolution	20	35			Marshal of France
Exile (4)	Entertainment	20			50	Rock
Exon, J. James	Senator-Gov.	5	10		10	Senator, Governor NE
Eythe, William	Entertainment	10	15	20	20	
Eytinge, Rose	Entertainment	25		50	45	19th Cent./Laura Keene, Booth

F

NAME	CATEGORY	SIG	LS/DS	ALS	SP	COMMENT
Fabares, Shelley	Entertainment	7	10	15	20	
Faber, John Eberhard	Business	134	500	725		Eberhard Faber Pencil Co.
Fabian	Entertainment	5			20	
Fabian, John M.	Astronaut	10			15	
Fabio	Model	22			30	Fashion Model
Fabray, Nanette	Entertainment	5	6	15	15	
Factor, Max	Business	25	125	175	60	Cosmetic Mfg.
Factor, Max Jr.	Business	10	30	55	45	Cosmetic Mfg.
Fagan, James F.	Civil War		1625			CSA Gen.& U.S.Marshal
Fagoaga, Isidodo	Entertainment	15			50	Opera
Fair, James G.	Senate	30	50	110		Mining, Financier, CA Developer
Fairbank, Calvin	Abolitionist	40	85	150		Freed Fugitive Slaves
Fairbanks, Charles W. (V)	Vice President	50	100	275	150	T. Roosevelt VP
Fairbanks, Douglas, Jr.	Entertainment	20	75		35	
Fairbanks, Douglas, Sr.	Entertainment	150	165		245	
Fairbanks, Erastus 1792-1864	Governor	35		80		CW Gov. VT. Mfg.Platform Scales
Fairchild, Charles S.	Cabinet	20	35	55	40	Sec'y Treasury 1887
Fairchild, David G.	Science	5	10	20	10	Am. Botanist. Books on Plants

NAME	CATEGORY	SIG	LS/DS	ALS	SP	COMMENT
Fairchild, Lucius	Civil War	20	45	65		Union Gen., Gov. WI, Statesman
Fairchild, Morgan	Entertainment	10	15	20	25	Pin-Up SP $30
Fairchild, Sherman	Business	25	60	115	40	Fairchild Camera & Equipment Co
Fairfax, George Wm. 1787	Post Rev. War	75	210	395		Companion of Geo. Washington
Fairfax, Thomas Lord 1691-1782	Colonial America	220	600			Historically Important Family
Fairfield, John 1797-1847	Gov.-Senate	15	20	30		Senator, Gov. ME
Fairless, Benjamin F.	Business	35	95	190	70	CEO US Steel
Faisal, King	Royalty	25	50	95	125	King Saudi Arabia
Faith, Percy	Composer	15			150	Conductor-Arranger
Faithfull, Emily	Reformer	25	45	55		Br.Printer-Publisher Q.Victoria
Falck, Wolfgang	Aviation	20	45	60	40	
Falk, Peter	Entertainment	5	6	15	20	
Falkenburg, Jinx	Entertainment	5	6	10	12	
Fall, Albert B.	Cabinet	40	85	150	60	Sec'y Interior.Teapot Dome
Falla, Manuel de	Composer	175	510		850	AMusQS $1,200
Fallon, Walter A.	Business	4			10	CEO Eastman Kodak Co.
Falstaff, John, Sir	Military		8000			Model for Shakespeare's Play
Falwell, Jerry	Clergy	15	20	25	35	
Faneuil, Peter	Revolutionary War	125	225	555		Faneuil Hall, Boston
Fang, Wu Ting, Dr.	Statesman	10			20	Chinese Statesman
Fantin-Latour, Henri	Artist	35	90	175		Fr. Illustrator, Lithographer
Far, Frances	Composer	4	13	30	10	
Faraday, Michael	Science	160	400	700	650	Br. Physicist, Chemist
Fargo, Donna	Country Music	6	10		15	
Fargo, James C.	Business	150	695			Pres. Wells, Fargo & Co.
Fargo, William G.	Business	200	875	1250		Wells-Fargo, American Expr.
Farina, Dennis	Entertainment	15	35		25	
Farinelli, Patricia	Model	4			15	Pin-Up SP $20
Farley, James A.	Cabinet	15	35	70	25	FDR P.M. General
Farman, Henri	Aviation	60	110	175	165	Pioneer Aviator. Airplane Mfg.
Farman, Maurice	Aviation	75		190		Pioneer Aviator. License #6
Farmer, Art	Entertainment	10			25	Jazz Fluegelhorn-Trumpet
Farmer, Fannie Merritt	Author	190			250	Cookery Expert
Farmer, Frances	Entertainment	175	190	250	650	
Farnsworth, Charles	Military	25			65	General WW I
Farnsworth, John F.	Civil War	45	110			Union Gen.
Farnsworth, Philo T.	Inv.1st TV Camera					Rare NRPA
Farnsworth, Richard	Entertainment	8	9	15	20	
Farnum, Dustin	Entertainment	35	45	90	130	Silent Star. "The Virginian"
Farnum, William	Entertainment	40			150	
Farquhar, John Hanson	Senate/Congress	10	20	30		MOC IN, Capt. Union Army
Farr, Jamie	Entertainment	6	8	15	15	
Farragut, David G.	Civil War	100	290	750	1500	Union Adm. LS/Cont. $1,300
Farrar, Frederick W.	Clergy	25	35	50	50	
Farrar, Geraldine	Entertainment	65		120	130	Opera, Concert
Farrell, Charles	Entertainment	15	20	30	40	
Farrell, Eileen	Entertainment	10			35	Opera
Farrell, Glenda	Entertainment	25	30		75	
Farrell, Mike	Entertainment	5	6	15	15	
Farrimond, Richard	Astronaut	10			25	
Farrow, Mia	Entertainment	10	30		25	
Fassbaender, Brigitte	Entertainment	10			25	Ger. Mezzo Soprano,Opera
Fast, Howard (E.V.Cunningham)	Author	15	30		20	Historical Novels, Screenplays
Faster Pussy Cat	Entertainment	25			50	Rock
Fauber, Ben	Business	5	10		10	Pres. K Mart
Faubus, Orval E.	Governor	35		70	50	Gov. AR, Blocked Integration

NAME	CATEGORY	SIG	LS/DS	ALS	SP	COMMENT
Faulkner, Charles J., Jr.	Senate	15	25			Sen. WV. Battle of New Market
Faulkner, William	Author	350	1500	2500	750	Nobel Lit., Pulitzer Fiction
Fauquier, Francis	Colonial Gov. VA	200	575			Colonial Administrator
Faure', Gabriel	Composer	75	220	350	550	Fr.over 100 Songs,Chamber Music
Fausto, Cleva	Entertainment	30			65	Opera
Faversham, William	Entertainment	15			35	
Fawcett, Edgar	Author	45	105	225		
Fawcett, Farrah	Entertainment	9	10	20	25	Pin-Up SP $35
Fawcett, Millicent, Dame	Reformer	15	35	100		Br. Women's Suffrage Leader
Fay, Frank	Entertainment	15	25	45	45	
Faye, Alice	Entertainment	10	15	25	25	
Faye, Julia	Entertainment	4	6	10	12	
Faylen, Frank	Entertainment	45			75	
Fazenda, Louise	Entertainment	25			75	
Featherston, Winfield Scott	Civil War	62	160	375		CSA Gen.
Fegelein, Hermann Otto	Military	500				Ger. SS Gen. WWII
Feiffer, Jules	Cartoonist	10			50	Mag. Cartoonist
Feinhals, Fritz	Entertainment	30			50	Ger. Baritone, Opera
Feinstein, Diane	Senate	5	12	25	20	Senator CA
Feld, Fritz	Entertainment	8	9		20	
Feldany, Eric	Entertainment	3	3	6	10	
Felder, Rodney Dr.	Celebrity	5	8	17	5	
Feldman, Charles K.	Business	10	20	40	15	Fndr. Famous Artists Corp.
Feldman, Marty	Entertainment	35			85	
Feldon, Barbara	Entertainment	5	6	15	15	
Feldshuh, Tovah	Entertainment	5	6	10	12	
Feliciano, Jose	Entertainment	5	6		15	Guitar-Vocalist
Felix, Maria	Entertainment	10			30	
Fellini, Frederico	Entertainment	25	40		85	Film Director-Producer
Fellows, Edith	Entertainment	10			25	
Fels, Joseph	Business	95	210	490		Fels Naptha Soap
Felt, Harry, Adm.	Military	10	30	50	25	
Felton, Cornelius Conway	Educator	10	25	50		President Harvard 1860-62
Felton, Rebecca L.	Senate	25	45	150		Sen. GA For 1 Day 11/21-11/22
Fenn, Sherilyn	Entertainment	10			30	Pin-Up SP $45
Fenneman, George	Entertainment	10			20	
Fenton, Ruben E.	Governor	30	50	80		Civil War Gov. NY
Fenwick, B.J., Bishop	Clergy	20	25	30		
Fenwick, Millicent	Senate/Congress	10	20		15	MOC NJ. Ambassador UN
Ferber, Edna	Author	110	350	425		Novelist, Screenplays,Pulitzer
Ferdinand I 1503-1564	Royalty	400	1235			Holy Roman Emperor
Ferdinand I 1793-1875	Royalty	70	245			Emperor of Austria
Ferdinand I, III, IV, 1751-1825	Royalty	5200				King of Naples, Two Sicilies
Ferdinand II, The Catholic	Royalty	450	1700	4385		Spain
Ferdinand VII (Sp)	Royalty	125	330			
Ferebee, Thomas	Aviation	50	125	250	100	
Ferenczi, Sandor	Science	70	180	350		Hung.Psychoanalyst.Freud Friend
Ferguson, Homer	Senate/Congress	5	15		10	Senator MI. Ambass. Philippines
Ferguson, Maynard	Entertainment	10			30	Trumpet Player
Ferguson, Miriam A. 'Ma'	Governor	60	150			Governor TX
Ferguson, Samuel W.	Civil War	120	340	515		CSA Gen.
Ferkauf, Eugene	Business	7	10	14	10	
Ferlinghetti, Lawrence	Author	20	75	90	25	Am.Poet,Publisher.Beat Movement
Fermi, Enrico	Science	475	1375			Nobel Phys.Nuke Chain Reaction
Ferrar, Geraldine	Entertainment	35			130	Opera. Famous for Puccini Roles
Ferrara, Franco	Entertainment	45			250	Conductor

NAME	CATEGORY	SIG	LS/DS	ALS	SP	COMMENT
Ferrare, Cristina	Entertainment	6	8	15	15	Model. TV Host
Ferrari, Enzo	Business	300	850		250	Auto Mfg.
Ferraro, Geraldine	Congress	20	35	55	25	Congresswoman NY
Ferrer, Jose	Entertainment	20	25	40	45	
Ferrer, Mel	Entertainment	5			20	
Ferrero, Edward	Civil War	45	105	230		Union General
Ferrigno, Lou	Entertainment	5		10	12	
Ferris, Scott	Senate/Congress	12	15		15	MOC OK
Ferry, Orris S.	Civil War	45	70	105		Union Gen., U.S. Sen. NY
Ferry, Thomas White	Senate	60	95			Senate MI,Pres. Pro Tem Senate
Fersen, Hans-Axel, Count de	Revolutionary War		1250			With Rochambeau at Yorktown
Fesch, Cardinal	Clergy		220	450		Married Napoleon & Josephine
Fess, Simeon Davison	Senate/Congress	10	15	25		MOC, Senator MI
Fessenden, Francis	Civil War	25	50	80		Union Gen.
Fessenden, James	Civil War	20	52	70		Union Gen.
Fessenden, William P.	Cabinet	30	50	125		Lincoln Sec'y Treasury
Fetchit, Stepin	Entertainment	30			70	Early Afro-Am. Actor
Few, William	Revolutionary War	200	450	750		Continental Congress.1st GA Sen
Feynman, Richard P.	Science	25	40	85	30	Nobel Physics.
Fiderkiewicz, Alfred J., Dr.	Statesman	25	50			Polish Statesman
Fidler, Jimmy	Entertainment	5	6	15	15	Hollywood Gossip Columnist
Fiedler, Arthur	Entertainment	15			55	Conductor "Boston Pops"
Fiedler, John	Entertainment	3	3	6	10	
Field, Charles E	Clergy	20	35	45	25	
Field, Cyrus W.	Business	50	350	275		Atlantic Cable, Financier
Field, Eugene	Author	110	230	425	200	Children's Poet, Journalist
Field, Kate	Author	10	15			
Field, Marshall, III 1893-1956	Business	95	160	350		Communications Empire
Field, Marshall, Jr.1916-1965	Business	30	110	170	75	Pres.,CEO Field Entertprises
Field, Marshall, Sr.1834-1906	Business	125	245	550		Marshall Field & Co.
Field, Mary French	Author	5	15	20	15	
Field, Rachel	Author	20	100			Am. Novelist, Children's Books
Field, Sally	Entertainment	10	15	28	25	Pin-Up SP $30
Field, Stephen J. (SC)	Supreme Court	60	150	300	225	
Field, Virginia	Entertainment	5	6	15	15	
Fielder, James F.	Governor	10	15	25	15	Governor NJ
Fields, Debbi	Entertainment	2			4	
Fields, Gracie	Entertainment	15	35	55	80	Br. Singer & Comedienne
Fields, Shep	Entertainment	15			40	Big Band Leader
Fields, Stanley	Entertainment	15	15	35	30	
Fields, W. C.	Entertainment	450		765	1450	
Fieseler, Gerhard	Aviation	25	55	85	85	
15	Entertainment	15	15	30	45	Rock
Figueres, Jose	Head of State	15	45	110	20	
Filacuridi, Nicola	Entertainment	15			45	Opera
Filippeschi, Mario	Entertainment	25			85	Opera
Fillmore, Caroline	First Lady	600	950	800		
Fillmore, Millard	President	295	870	925	10000	LS as President $1,800
Finch, Peter	Entertainment	50	65	110	165	
Findlay, William 1768-1846	Governor	45	60	115		Gov. PA 1817, Sen. 1821
Fine, Larry	Entertainment	125			350	
Finegan, Bill (William J.)	Entertainment	20			40	Big Band Leader
Finlay, Frank	Entertainment	5	6	15	15	
Finletter, Thomas A.	Cabinet	5	12	30	15	Sec'y Air Force. Ambassador
Finley, Jesse J.	Civil War	65	115	220		CSA Gen.
Finley, John	Astronaut	5			15	

NAME	CATEGORY	SIG	LS/DS	ALS	SP	COMMENT
Finney, Albert	Entertainment	9	10	20	25	
Finney, Charles G.	Clergy	50	75	110		
Finnie, Linda	Entertainment	10			30	Opera
Finston, Nat W.	Composer-Author	10			20	Conductor-Violinist
Fio-Rito, Ted	Entertainment	15			35	Big Band Leader
Fiorella, Pascal A.	Rev.War Era	20	55	125		
Firestone, Harvey S.	Business	135	1500	1550	350	Founder Firestone Tire & Rubber
Firestone, Jr., Harvey S.	Business	25	50	85	35	Pres. CEO Firestone Tire....
Firestone, Leonard K.	Business	15	40	70	25	
First Ladies (Four Repub.)	First Ladies	250			900	Nixon, Ford, Reagan, Bush
Fischer, Bobby	Celebrities	40	85	200	75	
Fischer, Edmond H., Dr.	Science	20	45		30	Nobel Medicine
Fischer, Harold E.	Aviation	10	25	45	35	ACE, Korea, Double Ace
Fischer, Siegfried	Aviation	10	15	25	15	
Fish, Hamilton	Cabinet	20	75	100		Gov., Senator,Grant Sec'y State
Fish, Nicholas	Revolutionary War	40	120	245		Aide-de-Camp Gen. Scott
Fish, Preserved	Colonial	45	165			Merchant Banker
Fisher, Amy	Criminal	20		155		Shot alleged lover's wife.
Fisher, Anna L.	Astronaut	10			25	
Fisher, Bud* (Harry C.)	Cartoonist	75	95		425	Mutt & Jeff
Fisher, Carrie	Entertainment	5	10	20	20	Pin-Up SP $35
Fisher, Cindy	Entertainment	4			10	
Fisher, Eddie	Entertainment	5	10	20	15	
Fisher, Ham*	Cartoonist	100			250	Joe Palooka
Fisher, Harrison	Artist	40				Orig. Art as Illustrator S $700
Fisher, John S.	Governor	10	15	35		Governor PA
Fisher, Lawrence P.	Business	90	150	410		Co-Founder Fisher Body (GM)
Fisher, William F.	Astronaut	5			20	
Fisk, Clinton B.	Civil War	55	70	95		Union Gen. Founded Fisk Univ.
Fisk, James 1834-1872	Business	50	115	190	95	Financier, Stock Manipulator
Fisk, Minnie Maddern	Entertainment	15			35	Stage. Silent Films
Fiske, Bradley	Military	15		35		Admiral WW I
Fitch, Val L., Dr.	Science	20	35		30	Nobel Physics
FitzGerald, Edward	Author	90	250	760		Poet.Translator "Rubaiyat...."
Fitzgerald, Barry	Entertainment	125	135	195	250	
Fitzgerald, Ella	Entertainment	30	35	80	85	
Fitzgerald, F. Scott	Author	375	1635	2575	750	ALS/Content $4,850
Fitzgerald, Geraldine	Entertainment	6	8	15	15	
Fitzgerald, John	Revolutionary War	35	90	190		
Fitzgerald, John F.(Honey Fitz)	Political	20	55	95		Mayor Boston. JFK Grandfather
Fitzhugh, Gilbert	Business	2	5	12	5	
Fitzsimmons, Frank E.	Celebrity	3	8	25	10	
Fitzsimons, Thomas	Revolutionary War	200	315	375		Continental Congress
Fix, Paul	Entertainment	25			80	
Fixx, Jim	Author-Runner	15	35			
Flack, Roberta	Entertainament	15			35	Rock
Flagg, Fannie	Entertainment	5	10	20	15	Also Author, Playwright
Flagg, James Montgomery	Artist	60	190	450	175	Self Caricature S. $950
Flagler, D. W.	Military	15	20	25	20	
Flagstad, Kirsten	Entertainment	100			315	Nor. Soprano
Flahaut, A.C.J., Count	Fr. Revolution	15		25		Gen. Exploits in Gallantry
Flahiff, George B., Cardinal	Clergy	35	40	60	40	
Flake, Floyd H.	Congress	4	10			Congressman NY
Flammarion, Nicolas-Camille	Science	40	65	165		Fr. Astronomer
Flamsteed, John 1646-1719	Clergy-Science	800	975			Br. 1st Astronomer Royal
Flanagan, Edward, Father	Clergy	40	100		150	"Boy's Town"

NAME	CATEGORY	SIG	LS/DS	ALS	SP	COMMENT
Flatt, Earl Scruggs & Lester	Country Music	50			125	
Flaubert, Gustave	Author	175	635	1500		Fr. Novelist. Realist School
Flavin, James	Entertainment	4	4	9	10	
Fleetwood Mac	Entertainment	50			100	
Fleischer, Charles	Entertainment	10			15	Voice of Roger Rabbitt
Fleischer, Leonore	Author	15		40	30	"Shadowlands"
Fleischer, Max	Cartoonist	50			400	Animator
Fleischer, Richard	Entertainment	5			20	Film Director
Fleischmann, Charles L.	Business	95	450			Fleischmann's Yeast
Fleiss, Heidi	Business	10			50	"Oldest Biz", Hollywood Madame
Fleming, John Ambrose, Sir	Science	25	65	145		Br. Electrical Engineer
Fleming, Alexander, Sir	Science	225	300	1120	800	Nobel for Penicillin
Fleming, Eric	Entertainment	225	250		350	Original "Rawhide"
Fleming, Francis	Aviation	10	22	38	28	ACE, WW II
Fleming, Ian	Author	300	550	1100	1400	1st Ed. Signed $5,000
Fleming, Rhonda	Entertainment	8	12	25	20	Pin-Up SP $25
Fleming, Victor	Entertainment	150			450	Veteran Film Director
Fleming-Sandes, Alfred	Military	10	50			WW I Victoria Cross
Fleta, Miguel	Entertainment	45			250	Opera
Fletcher, Bramwell	Entertainment	30			75	
Fletcher, Frank Jack	Military	25	60	120	60	
Fletcher, James	NASA	10	20	35		Whistle Blower
Fletcher, James Cooley	Clergy	5		25		Missionary
Fletcher, John Gould	Author	15	30	100		Pulitzer Poet
Fletcher, Louise	Entertainment	6	8	15	25	
Flint, Austin 1812-86	Physician	70	215	400		Eminent Physician-Teacher
Flint, Lawrence	Aviation	10	16	35	25	
Flippen, Jay C.	Entertainment	25			60	
Floege, Ernest	Military		45		70	"Commandant Paul".Fr.Resistance
Florence, William J., Mrs.	Entertainment	10		25	15	Appeared With Husband
Florence, William Jermyn 1831-91	Entertainment	15	25	40	75	Actor, Songwriter, Playwright
Florey, Howard Walter	Science	25	40	75	35	Nobel Medicine, Penicillin
Florey, Robert	Entertainment	15			35	
Flory, Paul J., Dr.	Science	20	35	70	30	Nobel Chemistry
Flotow, Frederich von	Composer	75	220	425		Ger. Opera, Ballet, Concertos
Flower, R.P	Governor	10	15			Governor NY
Flower, Wm.Henry, Sir	Science	10	25	50		Br.Zoologist
Flowers, Bess	Entertainment	6	8	15	15	
Flowers, Wayland	Entertainment	12	15		23	
Floyd, John B.	Civil War	200	290	485		Gov. VA. Sec'y War, CSA General
Floyd, William	Revolutionary War	400	1295	1500		Signer Decl. of Indepen.
Fluckey, Gene	Military	45		110	90	Top US Submarine Cmdr.
Flunger, Anna	Entertainment	6	8	15	15	
Fluster, Lafayette	Senate	40				Pres. Pro Tem of Senate
Flynn, Edward J.	Political	5	10	25	10	Democratic "Boss" NY
Flynn, Errol	Entertainment	275	300	450	700	Warner Bros. DS $1,500
Flynn, James	Entertainment	4	5	9	9	
Flynn, Joe	Entertainment	50	60	110	125	
Flynt, Larry	Publisher	3			5	Hustler Magazine
Foale, Mike	Astronaut	4			12	
Foch, Ferdinand	Military	50	125	280	125	Fr. General WWI, Marshal
Foch, Nina	Entertainment	5	5	10	15	
Fogelberg, Dan	Entertainment	6			20	
Fogerty, John	Entertainment	15			40	Rock
Fokker, Anthony	Aviation	200	295	530	500	Am. Aircraft Designer-Builder
Foley, Red	Country Music	30			85	

NAME	CATEGORY	SIG	LS/DS	ALS	SP	COMMENT
Folger, Charles J.	Cabinet	7	15	30		Sec'y Treasury
Follett, Ken	Author	4	10		15	Br. Mystery Novelist
Folsom, Marion B.	Cabinet	15	25		20	Sec'y HEW. Drafter Soc.Sec.Adm.
Folsom, Nathaniel	Revolutionary War	125		450		Am. Gen., Continental Congress
Foltz, Frederick	Military			45	100	General WW I
Fonck, Paul-Rene'	Aviation	1000	1900			ACE, Fr. WW I. Top Allied Ace
Fonda, Bridget	Entertainment	25			65	
Fonda, Henry	Entertainment	35	40		75	
Fonda, Jane	Entertainment	6	10	30	25	Pin-Up SP $35
Fonda, Jelles	Revolutionary War	50	155	225		Colonial Leader,Rev.War Officer
Fonda, Peter	Entertainment	6	8	15	20	
Fonda, Ten Eyck H.	Civil War	50		95		Military Telegrapher Hero
Fong, Benson	Entertainment	25			40	
Fong, Hiram L.	Senate	5	10		10	Senator HI
Fonseca, Roberto A.	Head of State	5	16	40	20	
Fontaine, Joan	Entertainment	12	15	30	35	Pin-Up SP $45
Fontanne, Lynn	Entertainment	15			40	
Fonteyn, Margot	Entertainment	40	45	135	200	Premier Ballerina
Foot, Solomon	Senate/Congress	15	30	45		MOC VT 1843, CSA Congress
Foote, Andrew Hull	Civil War	45	110			Union Adm.War Dte ALS $3,500
Foote, Arthur	Composer	30	85	195		Organist. Church Music, Songs
Foote, Henry S.	Civil War	25	40	70		US Senator, CSA Congress
Foote, Horton	Author	5		20	15	Civil War
Foote, Shelby	Author	15	35			
Foraker, Joseph B.	Senator-Gov.	10	35			Governor, Senator OH
Foran, Dick	Entertainment	15	20	35	45	
Foray, June	Entertainment	5			10	Voice of Rocky & Bullwinkle
Forbes, Bertie Charles	Business	35	100	175	65	Founder Forbes Magazine
Forbes, Malcolm S.	Business	30	70	175	75	Publ., Motorcyclist,Balloonist
Forbes, Ralph	Entertainment	15	15	30	25	
Forbes-Robertson, John	Entertainment	19	25	45	50	Shakespearean Roles. Films
Ford, Benson	Business	5	15	30	15	Ford Motor Car
Ford, Betty	First Lady	35	175		50	
Ford, Edsel	Business	250	1350		500	Ford Motor Co.
Ford, Edsel B. II	Business	5	10	20	10	Ford Motor Co.
Ford, Eileen	Business	5	30		10	Ford Modelling Agency
Ford, Elaine	Business	24			30	
Ford, Gerald & Ford, Betty	Pres.-1st Lady				225	FDC S. $250
Ford, Gerald R.	President	150	330	825	175	Content: ALS $5,500,TLS $1,500
Ford, Glenn	Entertainment	20			35	
Ford, Harrison	Entertainment	50			200	
Ford, Henry	Business	950	2350	4500	2450	Pioneer Auto Designer-Mfg.
Ford, Henry II	Business	10	15	30	50	Ford Motor Co.
Ford, John	Entertainment	150			300	Classic Western Film Director
Ford, John Anson	Business	5	10	20	10	
Ford, John Thompson	Theatre Owner	475	600	750		Ford's Theater, Wash. D.C.
Ford, Lita	Entertainment	15			45	Singer
Ford, Paul	Entertainment	15			35	
Ford, Tennessee Ernie	Country Music	12			35	
Ford, Wallace	Entertainment	20			50	
Fordney, Joseph W.	Senate/Congress	15		30		MOC MI. Lumber, Banking
Forester. C[ecil] S[cott]	Author	75	260	90	95	Br.Novelist."Horatio Hornblower
Forman, Milos	Entertainment	20			60	Academy Award Director
Forman, Thomas M.	Revolutionary War	45	100			
Formes, Karl	Entertainment	5	6	15	15	
Formica, Fern	Entertainment	10			30	

NAME	CATEGORY	SIG	LS/DS	ALS	SP	COMMENT
Forney, William H.	Civil War	55	135	297		CSA Gen. MOC AL
Forrest, Edwin	Entertainment	35	80	125	150	Early Great Am. Actor
Forrest, French	Civil War	85	140	195		CSA Naval Commander
Forrest, Hal*	Cartoonist	25			125	Tailspin Tommy
Forrest, Nathan Bedford	Civil War	275	2030	3165		CSA General
Forrest, Sally	Entertainment	5			12	
Forrestal, James	Cabinet	55	150		100	1st Sec'y Defense. Suicide
Forslund, Constance	Entertainment	5	6	15	15	
Forster, Edw. Morgan	Author	65	265	440		Br. Novelist. "Howard's End"
Forster, John 1812-76	Author	20	25	50		Br. Historian, Biographer
Forsyth, Frederick	Author	10	40	80	20	Br., Master of Spy Novels
Forsyth, James William	Civil War	35	105	175		Union Gen., Wounded Knee
Forsyth, John	Cabinet	25	55	120		Sec'y of State (Jackson)
Forsythe, James W.	Civil War	40	120	185		Un. Gen. TLS/Cont. $250
Forsythe, John	Entertainment	9	10	20	25	
Fort, George F.	Governor	15	35	50		Governor NJ 1850
Fort, John Franklin	Governor	5	15			New Jersey
Fort, Luigi	Entertainment	20			45	Opera
Fortas, Abe (SC)	Supreme Court	40	90	200		Resigned from Court
Forte, Fabian (Fabian)	Entertainment	5	8	25	20	
Forti, Carmen Fiorella	Entertainment	25			60	Opera
Forward, Walter	Cabinet	15	45	80		Sec'y Treasury 1841
Fosdick, Harry Emerson	Clergy	35	50	75	50	
Foss, Joe	Aviation	30	75	85	55	ACE, WW II, Medal of Honor
Foss, Sam Walter	Author	5	10	20	10	
Fosse, Bob	Entertainment	35	45	90	55	Choreographer-Film Director
Foster, Abiel 1735-1806	Clergy-Political	120	345			Cont. Congress. 1st MOC NH '89
Foster, Charles	Cabinet	20	55	100		Gov. OH, Sec'y Treas.
Foster, Hal*	Cartoonist	100			600	Prince Valiant
Foster, Hal*	Cartoonist	100			500	Tarzan
Foster, Jodie	Entertainment	40			120	
Foster, John Gray	Civil War	45	90	120		Union General
Foster, John W.	Cabinet	25		0	125	Sec'y State 1892
Foster, Lafayette S.	Senate	25	60	100		Civil War Senator CT
Foster, Lawrence	Entertainment	3	5	8	10	
Foster, Myles B.	Artist	17	40	70		
Foster, Norman	Entertainment	15	15	35	45	
Foster, Preston	Entertainment	20	85		55	
Foster, Stephen	Composers	1000	3500	10000		
Foster, Susanna	Entertainment	10	15		25	
Foucauld, Charles E.	Explorer-Clergy	300		975		Fr. Priest & Explorer
Fouche', Jos. Duc d'Otrante	Fr. Revolution	125	400	680		Politician, Advisor Nap.
Fountain, Pete	Entertainment	6	10	20	25	Jazz-Dixieland Clarinetist
Four Tops	Entertainment	40			95	Rock Singing Group
Fournier, G.	Military	55	85			
Fowler, Gene	Author	20	90		30	Journalist, Biographer,Novelist
Fowler, Henry H.	Cabinet	5	20	35	15	Sec'y Treas.
Fowler, William, Dr.	Science	20	30	45	30	Nobel Physics
Fowles, John	Author	30	55	66	35	Br.Novelist."Fr. Lieut's Woman"
Fowley, Douglas	Entertainment	10			30	
Fox, Charles 1749-1806	Statesman	30	65	175		Br.Reformer, Orator, Libel Bill
Fox, Fontaine T.	Cartoonist	35	50		200	Toonerville Trolley
Fox, Michael J.	Entertainment	20	25	40	45	
Fox, Samantha	Entertainment	10			45	
Fox, Samuel	Clergy	15	20	25	35	
Fox, William	Business	185	550		375	Founder Fox Film Corp.

NAME	CATEGORY	SIG	LS/DS	ALS	SP	COMMENT
Foxworth, P. E.	Celebrity	5	15	35		
Foxworth, Robert	Entertainment	4	4	9	10	
Foxx, Redd	Entertainment	20	30		35	
Foy, Eddie, Jr.	Entertainment	20	25	40	45	
Foy, Eddie, Sr.	Entertainment	25			60	
Foy, Maximilian S., Count	Fr. Revolution	15	35	80		Statesman, General. Waterloo
Fradona, Ramon*	Cartoonist	15			50	Brenda Starr
Frakes, Jonathan	Entertainment	8	9	19	20	"Star Trek"
France, Anatole	Author	50	130	175	300	Fr.Novels, Poetry,Critic. Nobel
Franchetti, Alberto	Composer	35		130	90	Wrote 9 Operas
Franchi, Sergio	Entertainment	3	5	10	15	
Franciosa, Anthony	Entertainment	4	4	9	10	
Francis I 1494-1547	Royalty	500	750			France. Special DS $2,750
Francis II (1768-1835)	Royalty	95	300	425		Last Holy Roman Emperor(Aus)
Francis V (1819-75)	Royalty	40	100			Duke of Modena
Francis, Anne	Entertainment	5	6	15	15	
Francis, Arlene	Entertainment	5	6	15	10	
Francis, Connie	Entertainment	3	5	12	15	Singer
Francis, David R.	Cabinet	15	30	50	25	Sec'y Interior 1896
Francis, Dick	Author	25	175	80	40	Jockey Turned Author. Mysteries
Francis, Genie	Entertainment	5	6	15	15	
Francis, Kay	Entertainment	25	30	70	95	
Franciscus, James	Entertainment	10	12	15	20	
Franck, Cesar	Composer	340	1100	890		AMusMsS $5,000
Franco, Francisco	Head of State	175	750	1300	275	Sp. Soldier & Dictator
Frank, August	Military	10	30	45		
Frank, Hans	Nazi Lawyer	275	500			Nazi Administrator of Poland
Frank, Otto	Celebrity WWII		1500			Ann Frank
Franken, Rose	Author	10	25	40		Playwright
Frankenheimer, John	Entertainment	10		30	25	Film Director
Frankfurter, Felix (SC)	Supreme Court	145	550	795	750	Founder Am. Civil Liberties Un.
Franklin, Benjamin	Revolutionary War	3275	10700	25100		Rev. War Dte. DS $25,000
Franklin, Bonnie	Entertainment	4	5	12	20	
Franklin, Jane	Author	65		300		Wife of John Franklin,Traveller
Franklin, John, Sir	Explorer	125	320	610		Proved NW Passage
Franklin, William	Colonial & Revol.	145	410	865		Brit. Gov. NJ, Son of Benj.
Franklin, Wm. Buell	Civil War	65	150	180	195	Union Gen.
Frann, Mary	Entertainment	5	6	15	15	
Frantz, Charton C.	Business	10	35	45	20	
Franz Josef II	Royalty	30	75	140	45	Liechtenstein
Franz Joseph I (Aus)	Royalty	155	550	875		
Franz, Arthur	Entertainment	10			20	
Fraser, Douglas A.	Labor	10	15		15	Union President
Fraser, James Earle	Artist	540				Am. Sculptor of Buffalo Nickel
Fraser, Peter	Head of State	10	25		20	Prime Minister New Zealand
Frawley, William	Entertainment	225	250		450	
Frazer, John Wesley	Civil War	165	255			CSA General
Frazer, Joseph W.	Business	275	600			Kaiser-Frazer Auto Mfg.
Frazetta, Frank*	Cartoonist	50			450	Johnny Comet
Freddy & The Dreamers (All)	Entertainment	95				
Frederic, Harold	Author	10	35	70		Am. Novelist, Correspondent
Frederic, Prince (Hohenz.)	Royalty	10	25			
Frederick I (Wurttemburg)	Royalty	25	95			
Frederick II, The Great (Prussia)	Royalty	400	1360	2185		
Frederick III 1831-1888	Royalty	65	260	550	500	Prussia
Frederick IV 1671-1730	Royalty		320	805		Denmark

NAME	CATEGORY	SIG	LS/DS	ALS	SP	COMMENT
Frederick IX 1899-1972	Royalty	50	170	350		Denmark
Frederick V 1723-66	Royalty	90	270	500		Denmark
Frederick VII	Royalty	80	240			King of Denmark
Frederick VII 1808-63	Royalty	45	150			
Frederick Wm. I 1688-1740	Royalty	145	420			Prussia
Frederick Wm. III 1797-1840	Royalty	65	229	475		Prussia
Frederick Wm. IV 1840-61	Royalty	100	325	750		Prussia. Insane
Frederick, Pauline	Entertainment	15	30		80	Silent Cinema Star
Fredericks, Fred*	Cartoonist	10		85	50	Mandrake The Magician
Freed, Bert	Entertainment	5	6	15	15	
Freeland, Paul van	Head of State	5	16	40	20	Prime Minister
Freeman, Kathleen	Entertainment	7	10		15	
Freeman, Mona	Entertainment	6	8	15	18	
Freeman, Morgan	Entertainment	15		50	40	
Freeman, Orville	Cabinet	7	15	25	10	Sec'y Agriculture
Freeman, Samuel	Revolutionary War	15	45	100		Rev. War Patriot
Freeman, Ted	Astronaut	10			48	
Fregeville, C.L.J.Marquis	Fr. Rev. War	15	35	75		
Freleng, Frizz	Cartoonist	30			50	Animator, Crazy Cat
Frelinghuysen, Frederick T.	Cabinet	20	59	105	40	Sec'y State, Senator NJ
Frelinghuysen, Joseph S	Senate/Congress	5	15			Senator NJ
Fremont, Jessie Benton	Author	35	80	270		Wife of John C.
Fremont, John C.	Civil War	230	700	1025		Union Gen.-Content ALS $6,500
Fremstad, Olive	Entertainment	95			375	
French, Daniel Chester	Artist	95	200	395	125	Sculptor, Lincoln Memorial
French, Samuel Gibbs	Civil War	125	275	370		CSA General
French, Victor	Entertainment	15			40	
French, William H.	Civil War	40	125	250		Union General
Freni, Mirella	Entertainment	10			40	Opera
Freron, Louis M.S.	Fr. Revolution	20	45	90		Revolutionist
Freud, Anna	Science		570	750		Daughter of Sigmund Freud
Freud, Sigmund	Science	1400	3200	6250	4000	ALS/Content $7,500-$22,500
Frey, Richard	Aviation	25	50	100	65	
Friant, Louis, Count	Fr. Revolution	30	75	150		
Frick, Henry Clay	Business	95	215	320		Carnegie Steel.Frick Art Museum
Fricke, Janie	Entertainment	5			10	Singer
Fricke, Richard I.	Business	10	35	45	20	
Fricker, Brenda	Entertainment	20	35	65	100	
Friedan, Bette	Feminist	15		25	20	
Friedgen, A.E.	Business	10	35	45	20	
Friedkin, William	Entertainment	7	10		20	
Friedman, Herbert	Science	15	35	55	20	
Friedman, Jerome I.	Science	20	35		30	Nobel Physics
Friedman, Milton	Economist-Author	20	35		25	Nobel Economics
Friganza, Trixie	Entertainment	4	4	9	10	
Friml, Rudolf	Composer	100	250	325	250	AMusS $750
Frisch, Karl von	Science	15	30	40	25	Nobel Medicine
Fritchie, Barbara (Frietschie)	Civil War	12500				Patriotic Heroine
Frith, William P.1819-1909	Artist	25	45	110		Crowded Scenes Contemporay Life
Fritsch, Werner von	Military	55	150	210	175	
Frizzell, Lefty	Country Music	25			65	
Frobe, Gert	Entertainment	30			80	
Frohman, Daniel	Entertainment	15		40	35	Dean of Am.Theatrical Producers
Froman, Jane	Entertainment	15	15	20	25	
Fromm, Erich	Science	45	150		75	Psychoanalist-Social Philosophe
Fromme, Lynette 'Squeaky'	Assassin	45	120	210	60	Charles Manson Follower

NAME	CATEGORY	SIG	LS/DS	ALS	SP	COMMENT
Frondizi, Arturo	Head of State	15	35	75	55	President Argentina
Frontenac, Louis, Comte 1620-1698	Statesman			5400		Gov. La Nouvelle France(Canada)
Frontiersmen, The	Country Music	25			50	
Frost, A.B.*	Cartoonist	40			250	Illustrator
Frost, Daniel Marsh	Civil War	170	245	450		CSA General
Frost, David	Entertainment	5			15	
Frost, Edwin B.	Science	10	25	45		Am. Astronomer
Frost, Robert	Author	150	415	1625	735	Poet. Pulitzer 1924,'31,'37,'43
Frothingham, Octavius B.	Clergy	25	35	45		
Fry, Christopher	Author	20	95	150		
Fry, Elizabeth	Clergy-Philanthro	40	125	185		Br. Quaker Philanthropist
Fry, Franklin C.	Clergy	20	25	35		
Fry, James Barnet	Civil War	35	50	100		Union General
Frye, Dwight	Entertainment	650			1750	
Frye, Wm. P. (Actg V.P.)	Acting V.P.	15				
Fuchida, Mitsuo	Military-Aviation	300	300	500		Led Attack on Pearl Harbor 1941
Fuchs, Rutger	Military	40	125	195	95	
Fuchs, Vivian E. Sir	Explorer	30	75	150		
Fukuda, Takeo	Head of State	15		50	30	Prime Minister Japan
Fukui, Kenichi	Science	20	30	45	25	Nobel Chemistry
Fulbright, James W.	Senate/Congress	10	15		15	Senator AR
Fulford, Millie Hughes	Astronaut	10			15	
Fulgham, Robert	Author	5			15	
Fuller, Alfred C.	Business	125		195	150	Founder Fuller Brush Co.
Fuller, Alvan T.	Governor	15	25		20	Governor, MOC MA
Fuller, Eduard	Author	6	20	40		
Fuller, John G.	Celebrity	10	16			
Fuller, Loie	Entertainment	50	124		350	Am. Dancer
Fuller, Margaret 1810-1850	Reformer-Author	140	250	450		Feminist, ALS/Content $2,500
Fuller, Melville W. (SC)	Supreme Court	50	150	275	175	
Fuller, R. Buckminster	Architect	30	85	140	75	Engineer, Geodesic Dome
Fuller, Robert	Entertainment	4	4	9	9	
Fuller, Sam	Entertainment	35			80	Film Director
Fullerton, Chas. Gordon	Astronaut	10	30	35		
Fulton, Fitz	Astronaut	10		15	25	
Fulton, Robert	Inventor	325	925	3625		Submarine, Steamboat
Funicello, Annette	Entertainment	10	15	20	25	Pin-Up SP $30
Funk, Casimer	Science	25	65		30	Biochemist Discovered Thiamin
Funk, Isaac K.	Publisher	25	80	135		Funk & Wagnalls Dictionary
Funston, Frederick	Military	75	195	300		Cuba, Span.-American War. CMH
Furcolo, Foster	Governor	10	25			Governor MA
Furnas, Robert W.	Governor	5	10			Governor NE
Furness, Betty	Entertainment	10	15	25	25	
Furness, William H.	Clergy	10	15	20		
Furstenberg, Betsy von	Entertainment	5	10		10	Fashion Designer
Furtwangler, Wilhelm	Entertainment	175			250	Conducted Orchestras World-Wide
Fuseli, Henry 1741-1825	Artist	200	525			Br.-Swiss Romantic Painter
Futrell, J.M.	Governor	5	12		10	Governor AR

G

NAME	CATEGORY	SIG	LS/DS	ALS	SP	COMMENT
Gabet, Sharon	Entertainment	5	6	15	15	
Gable, Clark	Entertainment	300		850	975	
Gable, Kay	Entertainment	8	9	25	25	
Gabor, Eva	Entertainment	10	12	25	20	
Gabor, Zsa Zsa	Entertainment	5	6	15	15	Pin-Up SP $20
Gabreski, Frances	Aviation	35	95	125	75	ACE, WW II, #3 US
Gabriel, Peter	Entertainment	15			50	Rock
Gabrielle, Monique	Entertainment	10			25	Pin-Up SP $35
Gabrilowitsch, Ossip	Entertainment	110	195	240	115	Rus.-Am. Pianist, Conductor
Gadsden, James	Diplomat-Business	110	350	625		Gadsden Purchase
Gadski-Tauscher, Johanna	Entertainment	25		50	65	Opera
Gaffney, Drew	Astronaut	4			12	
Gagarin, Yuri	Astronaut	150	350		550	First Man To Travel In Space
Gage, Lyman J.	Cabinet	12	25	50	30	Sec'y Treasury 1897
Gage, Nicholas	Author	10	25		15	
Gage, Thomas	Revolutionary War	225	885	950		Br. General. Commander-in-Chief
Gagnon, Rene' A.	Military	25	30		40	Iwo Jima Flag Raising FDC $225
Gail, Max	Entertainment	3	5	10	15	
Gainsborough, Thomas	Artist	270	760	1850		Br. Portraitist. Landscapes
Gajdusek, D. Carleton, Dr.	Science	20	35		30	Nobel Medicine
Galanos, James	Business	12	30	50	25	
Galard, Genevieve de	Celebrity	40			50	
Galbraith, John Ken.	Economist	15	35		20	Author Books Economics
Gale, Zona	Author	10	20	40	15	Novelist
Galella, Ron	Photographer	5	10		10	Celebrity Photographer
Galileo 1564-1642	Science	5000		25000		It. Astronomer
Gall, Bob	Business	4			10	Business Exec.
Galland, Adolf	Aviation	40	75	150	105	ACE, Ger. WW II, Luftwaffe Head
Gallatin, Albert	Cabinet	75	285	360		Served both Jefferson & Madison
Galle, Emile	Artist	100	325	615		Fr. Artist in Glass Mfg.
Galli-Curci, Amelita	Entertainment	85	190	385	200	Opera
Gallian, Ketti	Entertainment	8	9	19	19	
Gallico, Paul W.	Author	15	110		35	Am.Novelist."Poseidon Adventure
Galligan, Zach	Entertainment	4			10	
Gallinger, Jacob Harold	Senate/Congress	10	20	35	15	MOC, Senator NH 1891-1919
Gallo, Ernest & Julio	Business	40			65	Gallo Winery, Sonoma, CA
Gallo, Gustavo	Entertainment	20			50	Opera
Gallo, Robert, Dr.	Science	20	35			Research Scientist
Gallup, Benadam	Military	25	75			Colonel French-Indian War
Gallup, George, Jr.	Pollster	10	20		15	"Gallup Poll"
Galsworthy, John	Author	30	85	175	225	Br. Novelist, Playwright
Galvan, Elias G., Bishop	Clergy	20	25	35	35	

NAME	CATEGORY	SIG	LS/DS	ALS	SP	COMMENT
Galvin, Robert	Business	12	17	25	15	
Gam, Rita	Entertainment	5	6	15	15	
Gandhi, Indira	Head of State	150	245	385	520	Prime Minister India
Gandhi, Mohandas K. (Mahatma)	Political Leader	550	1375	2125	1250	Spiritual Leader India
Gandhi, Rajiv	Head of State	40		85	150	P.M. of India, Assasinated
Gandier, D.M., Rev.	Clergy	10	20	35		Temperance Advocate
Gann, Ernest K.	Author	10	20	35		
Gannett, Frank E.	Business	20	55	140	35	Newspaper, TV, Radio Empire
Garber, Jan	Entertainment	15			35	Big Band Leader
Garbo, Greta	Entertainment	2150	4700		10000	Internat'l Film Star ALS$16,500
Garcelon, Alonzo	Governor	5	12			Governor ME
Garcia, Andy	Entertainment		10		45	
Garcia, Jerry	Entertainment	30			50	
Garcia-Robles, Alfonso, Dr.	Diplomat	35		130	60	Nobel Peace Prize, Disarmament
Gardanne, Gaspard A.	Fr. Revolution	40	115	250		
Garden, Mary	Entertainment	20	30	45	85	Opera
Gardiner, Reginald	Entertainment	10			35	
Gardner, Ava	Entertainment	30	45	110	100	Pin-Up SP $150
Gardner, Dale A.	Astronaut	10			25	
Gardner, Erle Stanley	Author	85	210	275	175	Lawyer & Detective Novelist
Gardner, Franklin	Civil War	120	215			CSA General
Gardner, Guy S.	Astronaut	10			25	
Gardner, John W.	Cabinet	5	15	30	10	Sec'y HEW. Fndr. Common Cause
Gardner, O. Max	Governor	15	20	35	20	Gov. NC. Lawyer, Industrialist
Garfield, James A.	President	300	810	975	2250	Union Gen.,DS/War Dte $2,500
Garfield, James R.	Cabinet	15	35	70	35	Sec'y Interior 1907
Garfield, John	Entertainment	75	90		375	
Garfield, Lucretia R.	First Lady	75	180	350		
Garfunkel, Art	Entertainment	5			10	
Gargan, William	Entertainment	15	15	35	50	
Garibaldi, Giuseppe	Head of State	135	370		585	It. Nationalist Leader, Soldier
Garland, Augustus H.	Cabinet & CW	50	145	215		U.S. Cab. & CSA Congress,Gov.
Garland, Beverly	Entertainment	5	10			
Garland, Hamlin	Author	20	35	50	85	Pulitzer. Novelist, Essayist
Garland, Judy	Entertainment	500			1500	Special DS $950
Garn, Jake	Senate-Astronaut	15	40		30	Senator UT
Garneau, Marc	Astronaut	15			35	
Garner, Erroll	Entertainment	75			150	Jazz Pianist
Garner, Francoise	Entetainment	10			35	Opera
Garner, James	Entertainment	5	10	20	25	
Garner, John Nance (V)	Vice President	50	125	300	175	
Garner, Peggy Ann	Entertainment	30			75	
Garnett, Francis H.	Author	20	60	125		
Garnett, Richard Brooke	Civil War	215	535	615		CSA Gen. RARE. 1991 Prices
Garr, Terri	Entertainment	10	15	25	25	
Garrard, Kenner	Civil War	45	75	160		Union Gen. War Date ALS $575
Garrett, Betty	Entertainment	4			10	
Garrett, Finis J.	Senate/Congress	10	15	25	20	MOC TN 1905
Garrett, Patrick R. (Pat)	Western Lawman	2700	3350	3500		Killed Billy the Kid
Garrett, Thomas	Emancipation	100	250	395		Chief Engineer Underground RR
Garriott, Owen I.	Astronaut	5			20	
Garrison, Lindley M.	Cabinet	35	85	140	50	Sec'y War 1913
Garrison, Vermont	Aviation	12	25	45	35	ACE, WW II & Korea
Garrison, Wm. Lloyd	Abolitionist	80	120	250		Reformer, Abolitionist
Garros, Roland	Aviation	125			425	Fr.ACE.1st To Fly Mediterranean
Garroway, Dave	Entertainment	10			25	

NAME	CATEGORY	SIG	LS/DS	ALS	SP	COMMENT
Garson, Greer	Entertainment	20	35	45	55	Pin-Up SP $65
Garvey, Marcus	Black Nationalist		1160			"Back to Africa" Movement
Gary, Elbert Henry	Business	25	90	175	35	U.S.Steel, "Gary", Ind., Lawyer
Gary, James Albert	Cabinet	15	25	40		P.M.Gen.Owned Cotton Mills 1897
Gasdia, Cecilie	Entertainment	10	15			35 Opera
Gasser, Heber S.	Science	20	35	60	50	Nobel Medicine
Gassman, Vittorio	Entertainment	25			85	
Gately, George	Cartoonist	5			20	Heathcliff
Gates, Daryl	Law Enforcement	15			30	Chief Police of L.A.
Gates, Horatio	Revolutionary War	250	475	1050		General, Continental Army
Gates, Seth	Senate/Congress	25	40	80		Anti-Slavery MOC from NY
Gatling, Richard J.	Inventor	285	565	1365		Gatling Gun."Gat" Slang Gun
Gatti-Casazza, Giulio	Entertainment	90	150	250		It. Impresario. Opera Director
Gatty, Harold	Aviation	75	275		175	Australian Wiley Post Navigator
Gaugin, Paul	Artist	585	1235	3450		Fr. Post-Impressionist
Gautier, Dick	Entertainment	5			12	
Gavarni, Paul	Artist	85		300		
Gavassi, Father Allesandro	Clergy	75	100	150		
Gavin, James M.	Military	45	100	275	125	Gen. WW II, Diplomat,Ambassador
Gavin, John	Entertainment	5			15	Ambassador to Mexico
Gavin, Leon	Senate/Congress	5	10		10	MOC PA 1943
Gaxton, William	Entertainment	10	15	25	25	
Gay, Enola	Aviation	150			350	Tibbets,Van Kirk,Ferebee
Gay, George A.	Civil War	15	25	45		Nat'l Commander GAR 1934
Gay, Sydney Howard	Author	3	10	20		
Gaye, Marvin	Entertainment	75			125	
Gayle, Crystal	Country Music	5			15	
Gayle, John	Governor	10	35			Statesman, Jurist
Gaynor, Janet	Entertainment	25	35	55	65	
Gaynor, Mitzi	Entertainment	10			20	Pin-Up SP $25
Gaynor, William J.	Celebrity	20	55	115	30	
Gazzara, Ben	Entertainment	5			15	
Ge'ricault, Theodore 1791-1824	Artist			3000		Broke Classical Tradition.
Gear, John Henry	Senate	10	20	25		Senator IA 1887
Geary, Anthony 'Tony'	Entertainment	6	8	15	15	
Geary, John W.	Civil War	55	125	275	250	Un.Gen.,1st Mayor San Francisco
Gedda, Nicolai	Entertainment	15		35	40	Swe. Tenor, Opera
Gee, Edwin A., Dr,	Business	5	10		10	CEO International Paper Co.
Geer, Will	Entertainment	25			55	
Geezinslaw, Sam & Dewayne	Country Music	15			30	
Geffrard, Nicholas Fabre	Head of State	35	125			Pres. Haiti
Gehlen, Reinhard	Military	15	40	45		
Geiger, Johannes H.1882-1945	Science	125	350	750		Ger. Physicist. Geiger Counter
Geisel, Ernesto	Head of State	12	20	25	15	
Geisel, Ted	Author					SEE Dr. Seuss
Gell, William, Dr.	Science	25	40			Br. Archaeologist
Gelston, David	Revolutionary War	85	170			
Gemar, Charles	Astronaut	4			12	
Gene't, Jean	Author	175	295	450		Fr. LS/Content $1,275
Geneen, Harold S.	Business	5	10	25	10	
Genesis	Entertainment	40			85	
Genet, Edmond C.	Fr. Revolution	55	150	285		
Genn, Leo	Entertainment	10	15	25	25	
Gentilini, Amerigo	Entertainment	15			45	Opera
Gentry, Bobbie	Country Music	5			12	
Gentry, Jerauld R.	Astronaut	5	25		15	

NAME	CATEGORY	SIG	LS/DS	ALS	SP	COMMENT
George I (Eng)	Royalty	230	975	2700		Created Cabinet System of Gov.
George I (Gr)	Royalty	45	85	130		
George II (Eng)	Royalty	325	730	1515		
George II (Greece)	Royalty	35	80	195	400	
George III (Eng)	Royalty	195	805	3500		
George IV (Eng)	Royalty	110	1145	695		13 pp. Warrant 1815 $3,500
George V (Eng)	Royalty	110	490	710	600	
George V And Queen Mary (Teck)	Royalty	250			1165	
George VI (Eng)	Royalty	190	355		630	
George, Chief Dan	Entertainment	20			45	
George, Christopher	Entertainment	20	25	65	75	
George, Gladys	Entertainment	20	25	40	40	
George, Grace	Entertainment	25			60	
George, Harold L.	Military	35	90	170	75	
George, Henry	Economist	30	105	170	35	Author, Reformer, Editor
George, Phyllis	Entertainment	4	4	9	10	Miss America
George, Susan	Entertainment	6	8	15	15	
George, Walter F.	Senate	15	35		20	Senator GA 1922-57
Gerard, Francis R.	Aviation	10	22	38	28	ACE, WW II
Gerard, Gil	Entertainment	9	10	20	20	
Gerard, Richard	Composer	50	95	165		AMusQS $235
Gerardy, Jean	Entertainment	125			190	Belg. Violin-Cellist
Gere, Richard	Entertainment	20	25	55	85	
Gerlache de Gomery, Adrien V.J.	Explorer	85	180	300		Belg. Naval Off'r., Antarctic
Gerland, Alfred	Aviation	15	35	55	40	
German, Edward, Sir	Composer	35	105	175	85	Incidental Music for Plays
Gernreich, Rudi	Business	10	15	40	25	Fashion Designer
Geronimo	Apache Chieftain	6085			4500	
Gerri, Toni	Entertainment	4	4	9	9	
Gerry, Elbridge (VP)	Revolutionary War	265	675	2760		Signer Decl. of Ind.
Gerry, Peter G.	Senate	10	15		20	MOC, Senator RI 1913
Gersel Cemal	Head of State	20	65	170	35	Turkey
Gershwin, George	Composer	900	1700	4650	4075	
Gershwin, George & Gershwin, Ira	Composer		4850			
Gershwin, Ira	Composer	85	250	1375	180	Lyrics AQS $880
Gessendorf, Mechthild	Entertainment	10			25	Opera
Getty, Estelle	Entertainment	5	9	20	15	
Getty, J. Paul	Business	195	360	875	350	Billionaire Oil Magnate
Getz, J. Laurence	Senate/Congress	10		20		MOC PA 1867. Publisher
Getz, Stan	Entertainment	85			225	Am. Jazz Saxophonist
Ghiaurov, Nicolai	Entertainment	10			25	Opera
Ghostley, Alice	Entertainment	5			15	
Giannini, A. P.	Business	150	290	500		Bank of America Founder
Gibb, Cynthia	Entertainment	5	6	15	15	Pin-Up SP $20
Gibbon, Edward	Author	300	885	1800		Br. Decline & Fall Roman Empire
Gibbon, John	Civil War	50	185	330		Union Gen., Indian Fighter
Gibbons, Cedric	Art	95	225	450		Hollywood Art Dir. 11 Awards
Gibbons, Floyd	Aviation	75	175	320	155	
Gibbons, Herbert Adams	Celebrity	10	20	45		
Gibbons, James, Cardinal	Clergy	45	115	150	175	Established Washington Univ.,DC
Gibbs, Addison C.	Governor	10	40			Governor OR
Gibbs, Georgia	Entertainment	15			35	Big Band Vocalist
Gibbs, Marla	Entertainment	6	8	15	10	
Gibran, Kahlil	Author-Artist	125	325	750	150	Syrian Poet, Novelist, Essayist
Gibson, Charles Dana	Artist	65	250	275		Illustrator-Gibson Girl
Gibson, Charles H.	Senate/Congress	5		15		MOC, Senator MD 1885

NAME	CATEGORY	SIG	LS/DS	ALS	SP	COMMENT
Gibson, Debbie	Entertainment	10			35	
Gibson, Edward G.	Astronaut	10			35	
Gibson, George	Military	5	15	25		
Gibson, Henry	Entertainment	5			12	
Gibson, Hoot	Entertainment	120	145		225	
Gibson, James	Military	75	230	425		Officer War 1812. Wounded, Died
Gibson, Mel	Entertainment	30			125	
Gibson, Randall Lee	Civil War	90	360	675		CSA General, US Sen. LA
Gibson, Robert L.	Astronaut	5			20	
Giddings, De Witt C.	Senate/Congress	15	25	40		MOC TX. Served in CSA Army
Gide, Andre	Author	175	350	590		Nobel Lit.,Moralist,Philosopher
Gielgud, John, Sir	Entertainment	15	45		30	
Gies, Miep	Celebrity	40	125	250		Befriended Anne Frank's family
Gieseking, Walter	Entertainment	10			50	Concert Pianist
Giesler, Jerry	Law	10	20	40	15	Brilliant Trial Lawyer
Gifford, Francis	Entertainment	5	7	12	10	
Gifford, Kathie Lee	Entertainment	5			20	Pin-Up SP $25
Gifford, Walter S.	Business-Diplomat	5	15	25	10	Pres. AT&T 1925-48, Chm.-'50
Gigli, Beniamino	Entertainment	50	90	300	275	Opera, Concert
Gilbert, A. C.	Business	60	95	175		Inventor Erector Set.
Gilbert, Billy	Entertainment	20	25	45	45	
Gilbert, Cass	Architect	20	60		35	Woolworth Bldg., Supr. Court...
Gilbert, H. E.	Celebrity	5	11	28	8	
Gilbert, John	Entertainment	70	85	275	250	
Gilbert, L. Woolfe	Composer	20	50	95	25	
Gilbert, Lynn	Entertainment	3	3	6	10	
Gilbert, Melissa	Entertainment	15			25	
Gilbert, William. S., Sir	Composer	165	365	775	400	Gilbert & Sullivan Operettas
Gilbreth, Lillian	Engineer	30		100		1st Woman Engineer
Gilder, Richard Watson	Civil War	125				Editor Century Magazine
Giles, William Branch	Senate	30	80	115		Early, influential VA Sen. 1801
Gilford, Jack	Entertainment	15			35	
Gill, Eric	Artist	20	70	150		Br. Sculptor, Engraver
Gill, Vince	Country Music	15			50	
Gillespie, Dizzy	Entertainment	25			65	
Gillett, Frederick H.	Speaker of House	15	35	95		MOC, Senator MA
Gillette, Anita	Entertainment	3	3	6	10	
Gillette, Francis	Senate	20	60			Free-Soiler Senator CT
Gillette, King Camp	Business	40	115	250	75	Gillette Co. (Safety Razor)
Gillette, William	Entertainment	35	115	215	150	Portrayed Sherlock Holmes
Gillis, J. H.	Military	5	15	25		
Gillmore, Joseph A.	Governor	35	90			Civil War Gov. NY
Gillmore, Quincy A.	Civil War	55	140	185		Union Gen.
Gilman, Nicholas	Revolutionary War	110	285	550		Continental Congress
Gilmer, John H.	Civil War	20		85		CSA Congress from NC
Gilmore, Gary	Celebrity	15	27	35		
Gilmore, P.S.	Composer-CW	35	80	180		"When Johnny Comes Marching...
Gilmore, Virginia	Entertainment	10	15	30	28	
Gilpin, Henry D.	Cabinet	25	50	75		Van Buren Att'y Gen. 1840
Gilruth, Robert R.	Astronaut	10			20	
Gimbel Brothers (6)	Business	475				Gimbel Department Stores
Gimbel, Bernard F.	Business	60	175	375	90	Gimbel Bros. Dept. Stores
Giminez, Eduardo	Entertainment	10			30	Opera
Gingold, Hermione	Entertainment	10			25	
Gingrich, Newt	Senate/Congress	5	15		15	MOC GA Since 1973
Ginsberg, Allen	Author	30	200	225	75	Beat Poet

NAME	CATEGORY	SIG	LS/DS	ALS	SP	COMMENT
Ginsberg, Ruth Bader	Supreme Court	30	40		40	Clinton Appointment to S.C.
Giordano, Umberto	Composer	250	400		400	Opera Composer. AMusQS $450
Girard, Stephen 1750-1831	Revolutionary War	125	350	440		Philanthropist, Merchant
Gisborne, Thomas	Author	30				
Gish, Dorothy	Entertainment	40			125	
Gish, Lillian	Entertainment	25	110		110	Silent Star. "Birth of a Nation
Gissing, George Robert 1857-1903	Author	50	175	345		Br. Novelist.
Given, Robin	Entertainment	10			25	
Givenchy, Hubert de	Business	35	70	95		Fashion Designer
Givens, Edward G. Jr.	Astronaut	10			25	
Glad, Gladys	Entertainment	10	12		20	
Gladden, Adley H.	Civil War	495	1215			CSA Gen. Civil War Dates Only
Gladden, Washington	Clergy	30	40	55		
Gladstone, William, Sir	Head of State	70	95	240	100	Prime Minister
Glaser, Donald A.	Science	20	35	70	30	Nobel Phys. Inv. Bubble Chamber
Glaser, Lulu	Entertainment	10	12	20	20	
Glaser, Paul Michael	Entertainment	5			20	
Glasgow, Ellen	Author	40	180			Novelist. Pulitzer. VA Life
Glashow, Sheldon Lee, Dr.	Science	20	35		30	Nobel Physics
Glaspell, Susan	Author	25	65	110		Am. Playwright. Pulitzer
Glass, Carter	Cabinet	15	45	65	25	Sec'y Treas., Sen. VA 1902
Glass, Philip	Composer	20	50		25	Am.Orchestra, Opera, Film,Stage
Glass, Ron	Entertainment	5			15	
Glassman, Alan	Entertainment	5			25	Opera
Glazer, Tom Paul	Country Music	15			30	
Glazunov, Alexander	Composer	225	365	675		Rus. AMusQS $1,000-$2,750
Gleason, Jackie	Entertainment	50	65	90	125	
Gleason, James	Entertainment	40			75	
Gledhill, Arthur	Business	4			10	Stanley Works
Glenn, John (As Astronaut)	Astronaut	40	150	450	90	1st To Orbit Earth
Glenn, Scott	Entertainment	8	12	35	30	
Glennon, John, Cardinal	Clergy	40	50	65	45	
Gless, Sharon	Entertainment	8	9	19	20	
Glossop, Peter	Entertainment	10			30	Opera
Gloucester, Henry Wm.Fred, Duke	Royalty	10	20	50	30	Son Geo. V., Gov-Gen. Australia
Glover, Danny	Entertainment	5	6	15	25	
Glover, John	Revolutionary War	240	610	1250		Gen. Continental Army. Active
Glubb, John, Sir "Pasha"	Military	20	45	55	30	Br. General
Gluck, Alma	Entertainment	20	35	45	60	Opera
Glueck, Nelson	Archaeologist	10	25	50	20	Uncovered 1500 Ancient Artifact
Glyn, Elinor	Author	20	70	165	45	Br. Novelist, Film Scenarios
Gnys, Wladek	Aviation	40			150	Shot Down 1st Plane in WW II
Goard, Nona	Aviation	10	15	25	15	
Gobbi, Tito	Entertainment	20			75	It. Baritone, Opera
Gobel, George	Entertainment	10			20	
Godard, Benjamin	Composer	75	120	225	150	Fr. Opera Jocelyn "Berceuse"
Godard, Louis	Aviation-Balloon	200	575			ALS/Content $6,500
Goddard, Paulette	Entertainment	35	45	80	125	
Goddard, Robert H.	Science	355	800	1425	600	Am. Physicist. Rocket Pioneer
Godden, Rumer	Author	15		65		
Goderich, Fred. John Robinson	Head of State	15	40	95		Viscount Goderich. Br. P.M.
Godey, Louis A.	Publisher	40	95	180		Godey's Ladies Book
Godfrey, A. Earl	Aviation	30	60	110	75	
Godfrey, Arthur	Entertainment	15	35	55	25	
Godoy, Manuel de 1767-1851	Head of State	295				Sp. Politician, Prime Minister
Godt, Eberhard	Military	15		70		

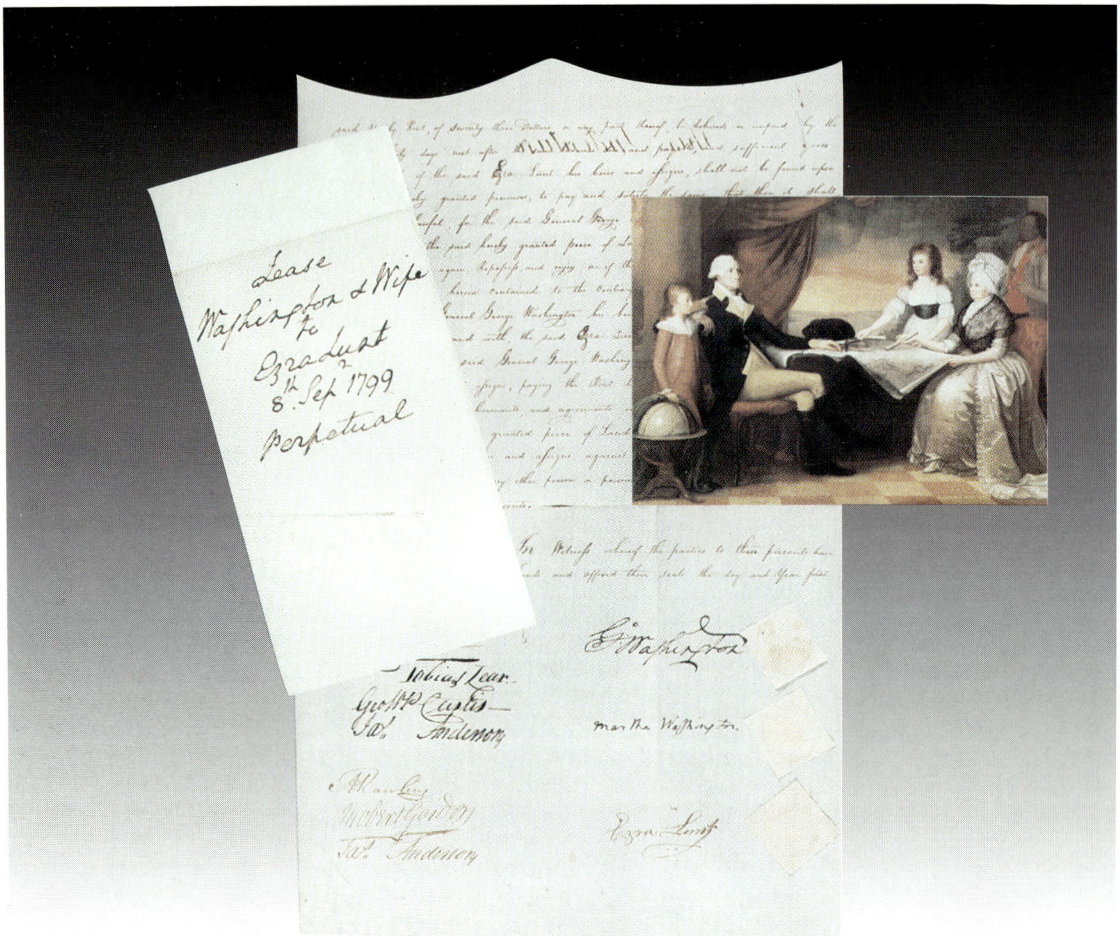
Lease
Washington & Wife
to
Perpetual

NAME	CATEGORY	SIG	LS/DS	ALS	SP	COMMENT
Godwin, Linda	Astronaut	5			15	
Goebbels, Joseph	Nazi Leader WWII	350	1025	1250	1250	Nazi Minister of Propaganda
Goebel, Arthur	Aviation	40			110	Pioneer Aviator
Goering, Hermann W.	Military	450	1265	2425	1475	Marshal of the Reich
Goethals, George W.	Military-Science	175	585			Panama Canal.TLS/Cont. $1,750
Goethe, Johann W. von	Author	1200	2550	5670		Ger. Poet, Dramatist, Novelist
Goettheim, F.	Business	10	20	45		
Goff, Nathan Jr.	Cabinet	15	25	50		Hayes Sec. of Navy
Gogh, Vincent van	Artist	2000	4500	13000		Dutch Painter. Individual Style
Gogol, Nicholai	Author	500	3350	6500		Father of Rus. Realistic Lit.
Golan, Menahem	Entertainment	5	6	15	15	Film Producer
Gold, Missy	Entertainment	5			15	
Gold, Tracy	Entertainment	5			15	
Goldberg, Arthur J. (SC)	Supreme Court	50	145		115	Resigned. Became Ambass. UN
Goldberg, Reiner	Entertainment	10			30	Opera
Goldberg, Rube*	Cartoonists	35			175	Ike & Mike, Boob McNutt
Goldberg, Stan*	Cartoonist	10			50	Archie
Goldberg, Whoopi	Entertainment	10	15	28	30	
Goldblum, Jeff	Entertainment	6	8	15	15	
Golden Girls, The	Entertainment	20			45	All Four
Golden, Charles, Bishop	Clergy	15	25	30	30	
Goldenson, Leonard H.	Business	10	20	30	15	TV Broadcasting Exec.
Golding, Louis	Author	55	85	125	50	Br. Verse, Stories, Novels
Golding, William	Author	55	90	150	65	Nobel Lit.,"Lord of the Flies"
Goldman, Edwin Franco	Composer	25	50	75		Bandmaster
Goldman, Emma	Anarchist	60	240	640	75	Deported. Author-Editor
Goldman, Michael	Author	5	10	15	10	
Goldman, Nahum	Zionist	15		50		Pres. World Zionist Org.
Goldmark, Peter C.	Science	25		40		Inventor. LP Records
Goldsboro, Bobby	Country Western	4			10	Singer
Goldsborough, Louis M.	Civil War	65	135	200		Rear Admiral USN
Goldschmidt, Neil E.	Cabinet	4	10	25	15	Sec'y Transportation
Goldsmith, Jerry	Entertainment	4			10	
Goldwyn, Sam	Business	100	124	255	195	Goldwyn Studios
Golonka, Arlene	Entertainment	4	4	9	15	
Gombell, Minna	Entertainment	25	30	55	55	
Gomes, Francisco	Head of State	15	55	135	25	
Gomez, Aurea	Entertainment	5			20	Opera, Brazilian Soprano
Gomez, Thomas	Entertainment	20			50	
Gompers, Samuel	Labor Leader	175	275	450		Founder & 1st Pres. A.F.of L.
Good, James W.	Cabinet	25	50		30	Hoover Sec'y of War
Goodman, Benny	Entertainment	45	200		135	Big Band Leader-Clarinetist
Goodman, Dody	Entertainment	4	4	9	10	
Goodman, John	Entertainment	15			25	
Goodpaster, Andrew	Military	15	35	50	25	Gen. WW II
Goodwin, E. S.	Aviation	3	5	10		
Goodwin, Hugh H.	Military	25	65	126	50	
Goodwin, Nat C.	Entertainment	20			30	Vintage Actor
Goodyear, Charles	Inventor	300	1750	2800		Developed Rubber Vulcanization
Goodyear, Charles Jr.	Business	20	60	150	30	Goodyear Tire & Rubber Co.
Gookin, Dan	Author	10		35	20	"Dos For Dummies"etc.
Goosens, Eugene	Composer	15	45	90	25	Br.Conductor. Orchestral Works
Gorbachev, Mikhail (USSR)	Head of State	500		895	1200	Instituted Perestroika,Glasnost
Gorbachev, Raisa	Rus. 1st Lady	50			125	
Gorcey, Leo	Entertainment	90	100		155	
Gordon, Alex., 4th Duke of	Revolutionary War	20		35		

NAME	CATEGORY	SIG	LS/DS	ALS	SP	COMMENT
Gordon, Charles G.	Military	110	350	650	600	"Chinese Gordon","Gordon Pasha"
Gordon, Charles W.	Clergy	20	25	30		
Gordon, George H.	Civil War	35	65	95		Union General
Gordon, George W.	Civil War	200	380	410		CSA General
Gordon, Huntley	Entertainment	9	10	20	25	
Gordon, John Brown	Civil War	155	215	295		CSA Gen., Gov. & US Sen. GA
Gordon, John F.	Business	4	6	15	5	
Gordon, Mack	Composer	30	60	130	40	Lyricist
Gordon, Richard F. Jr.	Astronaut	20			35	
Gordon, Ruth	Entertainment	10	15	30	30	
Gore, Albert A., Jr.	Vice President	15	25		80	Vice President
Gore, Albert A., Sr.	Senate	15	45			MOC, Senator TN 1939-44, 53-71
Gore, Christopher	Senate	85	205	350		Gov. MA, Senator MA 1813
Gore, Tipper	2nd Lady	5	12		10	
Gorgas, William C., Dr.	Science	125	225	325		Eradicated Yellow Fever
Gorham, George H.(cont)	Senate/Congress	10	20	35		
Gorham, Nathaniel	Revolutionary War	375	425	1100		Pres. Continental Congress
Goritz, Otto	Entertainment	30			85	Opera
Gorky, Maxim	Author	400	1200	1500	1050	Rus.Novels, Dramas, Stories
Gorman, Arthur P.	Senate	10	15	25		Senator MD 1881-99
Gorney, Karen Lynn	Entertainment	3	3	6	6	
Gorshin, Frank	Entertainment	10	15	20	25	
Gosse, Aristid V.	Science	30		80		
Gosse, Edmund, Sir	Author	20	35	50	30	Br. Poet, Man of Letters
Gossett, Louis, Jr.	Entertainment	30	80		100	
Gottfrederson, Floyd*	Cartoonist	100			500	Mickey Mouse Strip Art
Gotti, John	Crime	20			75	Mafia Boss
Gottschalk, Louis Moreau	Composer	500	1200	2000		Pianist , AMusQS $4500
Goudal, Jetta	Entertainment	9	10	20	40	
Goudsmit, Samuel A.	Science	15	25	40	20	Dutch Born Atomic Physicist
Gough, John B.	Clergy	20	45	60	25	Temperance Advocate, Reformer
Gould, Charles L.	Business	10	35	45	20	
Gould, Chester*	Cartoonist	50			450	Dick Tracy
Gould, Elliott	Entertainment	5	6	15	15	
Gould, George	Business	10	15	25	15	Son of Jay. Lost Inheritance
Gould, Gordon	Inventor	15	40			Commercial Laser Inventor
Gould, Harold	Entertainment	5	6	15	15	
Gould, Jay	Business	230	1050	1125		Financier, Railroad Pres.
Gould, John	Science	110		750		Br. Ornithologist
Gould, Morton	Composer	20	45	70	25	AMusQS $200
Gould, Robert Simonton	Civil War	25	65	90		CSA Cmdr. "Gould's Battalion"
Gould, Samuel B.	Celebrity	4	8	20	10	
Goulding, Ray	Entertainment	3	3	6	10	
Gounod, Charles	Composer	150	260	430	560	AMusQS $650-$2,500
Gouraud, Henri-Joseph E.	Military	40	150		75	Fr. Gen. WW I
Gowdy, John	Clergy	15	15	25		
Goya, Francisco	Artist	2200	7900	18750		Sp.Painter,Etcher,Lithographer
Goz, Harry	Entertainment	6	8	15	18	
Grabe, Ronald J.	Astronaut	5			20	
Grable, Betty	Entertainment	50			285	GI's WW II #1 "pin-up girl"
Grace and Prince Rainier	Royalty	175			350	PC SP $225
Grace de Monaco (Grace Kelly)	Royalty	130	375	425	250	As Princess
Grace, Eugene G.	Industrialist	25	65	140	40	Pres.,Chmn. Bethlehem Steel
Grace, William R.	Business	15	30	45	30	Mayor NYC. W.R. Grace & Co.
Gracen, Elizabeth Ward	Entertainment	5			10	Miss America '82, Pin-Up SP $25
Grady, Don	Entertainment	5			12	

NAME	CATEGORY	SIG	LS/DS	ALS	SP	COMMENT
Graf, Herman	Aviation	35			85	Ger. ACE. #9 Worldwide
Graham, Billy	Clergy	15	25	60	45	Evangelist
Graham, Donald	Business	10	25	40	15	
Graham, Elizabeth Candler	Author	5	7	10	15	Books about Coca-Cola
Graham, George 1772-1830	Cabinet	20	50	75		Monroe Sec. War (ad int)
Graham, John 1774-1820	Diplomatist	65	215	430		Aided Jefferson, Madison,Monroe
Graham, Katherine	Publisher	15	30	60	20	Chm. CEO Washington Post
Graham, M. Gordon	Aviaton	25			50	ACE WW II
Graham, Martha	Entertainment	65	210	235	250	Dancer, Teacher, Choreographer
Graham, Sheila	Author	25		40	35	Journalist, Gossip Columnist
Graham, William A.	Cabinet	20	40	75		Fillmore Sec. Navy 1850
Grahame, Gloria	Entertainment	50			150	
Grahame, Kenneth	Author	75	110	195		Br.Writer "Wind in the Willows"
Grahame-White, Claude	Aviation	62	100	250	120	1st Br. School of Aviation
Grahm	Entertainment	5			15	
Grainger, Percy	Composer	45	110	215	110	Pianist
Gramegna, Anna	Entertainment	45			95	Opera
Gramm, Phil	Senate	7			18	Senator TX
Grammer, Kelsey	Entertainment	10			35	TV Series-"Frasier"
Gran, Tryggve	Celebrity	12	30			
Granados, Enrique	Composer			700		Sp. Pianist. Piano Works, Opera
Grandi, Dino, Count	Political	25	45	90	40	Mussolini Cabinet
Grandy, Fred	Entertainment	5	10		10	Congressman IA- "Love Boat"
Grange, E. R.	Aviation	10	25	45	35	
Granger, Farley	Entertainment	5	7	12	20	
Granger, Francis	Cabinet	10	35	50		Wm. H. Harrison P.M. General
Granger, Gideon	Cabinet	65	100	300		P.M. General 1801
Granger, Gordon	Civil War	45	95	145		Union General
Granger, Stewart	Entertainment	20			50	
Granit, Ragnar	Science	20	45	110	35	Nobel Medicine
Grant, Amy	Entertainment	5	6	15	15	
Grant, Cary	Entertainment	200	350		450	
Grant, Frederick Dent	Military	125				Son Of U.S. Grant
Grant, Gogi	Entertainment	3	5	10	10	
Grant, Julia Dent	First Lady	140	375	575		
Grant, Kirby	Entertainment	15		25	35	
Grant, Lee	Entertainment	10	30		30	
Grant, U.S. III	Military	10	30	50		
Grant, Ulysses S.	President	745	1585	2250	4024	ALS War Dte $7,500-15,000 + -
Grant, William T.	Business	50	175	350	275	W.T. Grant Stores
Granville, Bonita	Entertainment	12	15	20	35	
Grapewin, Charles	Entertainment	150			350	
Grass, Gunter	Author	40	135	260	130	Ger. Novelist. Nazi Era
Grasse, Francois-Jos., Comte de	Revolutionary War					Kept Aid From Cornwallis. NRPA
Grasser, Hartmann	Aviation	14	25	50	30	
Grassi, Rinaldo	Entertainment	35	95			Opera
Grassle, Karen	Entertainment	4	4	9	10	
Grasso, Ella	Governor	10	35		20	1st Woman Governor CT
Grateful Dead (All)	Entertainment	100			250	Rock HOF
Gratiot, Charles	Military	150	205			War 1812. General 1828
Gratz, Barnard	Revolutionary War	75	212	400		
Graue, Dave*	Cartoonists	10			65	Alley Oop
Grauman, Sid	Entertainment	30	45	90	75	Owner of Opulent Theaters
Gravatte, Marianne	Entertainment	4	4	9	10	
Gravel, Maurice "Mike"	Senate	5			20	Senator Alaska
Graveline, Duane E.M.D.	Astronaut	5			20	

NAME	CATEGORY	SIG	LS/DS	ALS	SP	COMMENT
Graves, Peter	Entertainment	9	10	20	25	
Graves, Robert	Author	65	175	365	110	Br. Poet, Novelist, Critic
Graves, William	Military	50				General WW I
Gray, "Jack" Stearns	Aviation	150				TLS/Content $950. AVIATRIX
Gray, Asa	Science	35	60	175		Am. Botanist.Supporter Darwin
Gray, Billy	Entertainment	8			20	
Gray, Bowman	Business	7	15	35	15	
Gray, Colin	Aviation	35		90		Top New Zealand ACE
Gray, Colleen	Entertainment	15	25	45	35	
Gray, Elisha	Inventor	50		1125		Founder Western Electric Mfg.
Gray, Erin	Entertainment	9	10	20	25	
Gray, George	Senate	10			30	Senator DE
Gray, Gilda	Entertainment	40			125	
Gray, Glen	Entertainment	15			35	Big Band Leader
Gray, Harold*	Cartoonists	100			500	Little Orphan Annie
Gray, Harry Jack	Business	5	10	20	10	CEO United Technologies
Gray, Horace (SC)	Supreme Court	30	75	170	40	1882
Gray, Isaac P.	Governor	10	15			Governor IN
Gray, Linda	Entertainment	6	8	12	15	Pin-Up SP $20
Gray, Oscar L.	Senate/Congress	5	15		10	MOC AL 1915
Gray, Thomas 1716-71	Author	700	2005	5100		Br. Poet
Grayco, Helen	Entertainment	3	3	6	12	Vocalist & Wife Spike Jones
Grayson, Kathryn	Entertainment	8	10	20	25	
Greco, Jose	Entertainment	10	15		40	Dance
Greeley, Andrew, Rev.	Clergy	4	15		10	
Greeley, Horace	Journalist	65	200	295	1000	"Go West, Young Man..."
Greely, Adolphus W.	Explorer	75	225	350	150	Union General, Arctic Explorer
Green, Adolph	Composer	10	15		20	Collaborated/Betty Comden
Green, Al	Entertainment	10			20	
Green, Anna Katherine.	Author	35	50	65		Am. Detective Fiction
Green, Charles 1785-1870	Aeronaut	40	100	250		Br. Balloonist
Green, Dorothy	Entertainment	5	6	15	15	
Green, Dwight H.	Governor	10	15			Governor IL
Green, Herschel	Aviation	12	28	48	35	ACE, WW II, Triple Ace
Green, John(ny)	Composer	25	80	145	35	AMsS $250, $150, $350
Green, Mitzi	Entertainment	10	15	25	25	
Green, Richard	Entertainment	30			75	
Green, Theodore	Senate	10		20	15	Gov., Senator RI
Green, Thomas	Civil War	125	750			CSA Gen. LS/Content $3,250
Green, William F.	Labor Leader	40	95	195	125	Pres. A.F.of L.
Greenaway, Kate	Artist	1000				Orig. Pencil Drawing S $1,200
Greene, Frank L.	Senate/Congress	10		20	15	MOC, Senator VT
Greene, George S.	Civil War	30	70			Union Gen.
Greene, Graham	Author	95	425	615	135	Br. Novelist, Dramatist, Critic
Greene, Lorne	Entertainment	25			55	
Greene, Michele	Entertainment	5	8	25	22	
Greene, Nathanael	Military-Rev. War	600	1500	3065		Am.Revolutionary War Gen.
Greene, Shecky	Entertainment	5	6	15	15	
Greenleaf, John	Clergy	30	50	85		
Greenspan, Alan	Economist	15	30		35	Chairman Fed. Reserve Bd.
Greenstreet, Sidney	Entertainment	250		450	500	
Greenwood, Charlotte	Entertainment	15			30	
Greenwood, Edward D.	Science	10	15	35		
Greenwood, G.(Lippincott)	Author	10	30	75	15	
Greenwood, Lee	Country Music	5			10	
Greer, Dabbs (Bill)	Entertainment	10			20	

NAME	CATEGORY	SIG	LS/DS	ALS	SP	COMMENT
Greer, Jane	Entertainment	5	6	15	15	
Gregg, Andrew 1755-1835	Senate/Congress	40	155			Sen., MOC PA ALS/Content $475
Gregg, David M.	Civil War	35	65	155	125	Union Gen.
Gregg, John R.	Business	30	75	130	40	Inventor Gregg Shorthand System
Gregg, Virginia	Entertainment	10	12	20	25	
Gregory, Bill	Astronaut	7			15	
Gregory, Dick	Entertainment	8	9	19	20	
Gregory, F. H.	Civil War	60	95	115		Union Naval Captain
Gregory, Frederick D.	Astronaut	5	15		15	
Gregory, James	Entertainment	5	6	15	15	
Greico, Richard	Entertainment	10			45	
Grell, Mike*	Cartoonist	10			75	Tarzan
Grenfell, Wilfred T.	Physician-Clergy	35	50	75	130	Medical Missionary, Author
Grenville, George	Head of State	200	750			Br. P.M., Author of "Stamp Act"
Grenville, Wm. W., Baron 1759-1834	Statesman	95	285	585		Br. Pro Rom.Cath. Emancipation
Gresham, Walter Q.	Cabinet-CW	25	55	75		Union Gen., Sec'y Treas.
Gretchaninoff, Alexander T.	Composer	65	180	395		AMsS $350
Grew, Joseph C.	Diplomat	10	25		35	Ambassador Japan 1931-41
Grey, Chas. 2nd Earl of	Head of State	50	75	160		Prime Minister
Grey, George Sir 1799-1882	Diplomat	5	25	55		Br. Statesman
Grey, Joel	Entertainment	6	8	15	20	
Grey, Nan	Entertainment	4	8	12	15	
Grey, Virginia	Entertainment	10	15	15	20	
Grey, Zane	Author	60	250	620	200	Dentist Turned Western Writer
Gridley, Chas. Vernon	Military	235	410	895		Cmdr. of Adm. Dewey Flagship
Gridley, Richard 1711-96	Revolutionary War	170	450	790		Gen.Continental Army, Artillery
Grieg, Edvard	Composer	350	600	1125	1750	AMusQS $1,800-$2,800-$3,250
Grier, Pam	Entertainment	5	6	15	15	Pin-Up SP $20
Grier, Robert C. (SC)1794-1870	Supreme Court	80	235	420		
Grierson, Benjamin Henry	Civil War	120	235	330		Union General
Griesbach, Franz	Military	20			50	Ger. Infantry General
Griffes, Charles T.	Composer	175	380			ALS/Content $3,000
Griffin, Chris	Entertainment	10			25	Jazz Trumpet
Griffin, Cyrus	Revolutionary War	360	765			Continental Congress
Griffin, Merv	Entertainment	5			15	
Griffin, S. Marvin	Governor	10		30		Governor GA
Griffin, W.E.B.	Author	5			10	Fiction
Griffith, Andy	Entertainment	15	20	30	35	
Griffith, Corinne	Entertainment	35	45	90	100	
Griffith, D.W.	Entertainment	400	665	875	1025	
Griffith, Hugh	Entertainment	225	275		450	
Griffith, Melanie	Entertainment	20	30	55	55	
Griggs, John W.	Cabinet	15	45	110		Politician-Jurist, Gov. NJ
Griggs, S. David	Astronaut	60	150		140	
Grillo, Joann	Entertainment	4			10	
Grimes, Tammy	Entertainment	4	5	9	15	
Grimm, Jacob	Author	565	1840	3760		Grimm's Fairy Tales
Grimm, Wilhelm	Author	500	1425	3150		Grimm's Fairy Tales
Grinnell, Moses H.	Business	25	60	120		MOC NY. Merchant Prince NY
Grisham, John	Author	20			45	"The Firm", "The Pelican Brief"
Grisi, Giulia	Entertainment	250		300	195	It. Ballerina
Grissom, Virgil I.'Gus'	Astronaut	275	375		350	Merc. 7. FDC S $750 (Deceased)
Griswald, O.W.	Military	15	35			
Griswold, John A.	Senate/Congress	10		25		MOC NY 1869
Griswold, Matthew	Senate/Congress	12	20	25		MOC PA 1891
Griswold, Putnam	Entertainment	20			50	Opera

NAME	CATEGORY	SIG	LS/DS	ALS	SP	COMMENT
Grizzard, George	Entertainment	5	6	15	15	
Grizzard, Lewis	Author	20				Southern humorist
Grodin, Charles	Entertainment	6	8	15	15	
Groening, Matt*	Cartoonist	35			140	Simpsons
Grofe, Ferde	Composer	100	140	245	125	AMusMsS $1,850, AMusQS $360
Gromyko, Andrei A.	Statesman	125	160	295	150	Rus.Diplomat. Ambass. to US
Gronau, Wolfgang von	Aviation	75	135	235	195	
Groom, Victor	Aviation	20	45	75	55	
Gropius, Walter	Architect	125	285	600	375	Co-Founder of the Bauhaus
Gropper, William	Artist	30	80	200		Am. Social Protest Artist
Gross, Calvin	Celebrity	8	20		15	
Gross, Chaim	Artist	50	85	165		
Gross, Clayton K.	Aviation	8	16	28	22	ACE, WW II
Gross, Courtlandt	Business	5	10	15	10	
Gross, Milt*	Cartoonist	20			100	Nize Baby
Grossinger, Jennie	Business	23	60	135	35	Grossinger's Hotel,Catskill Mts
Grossmith, George 1874-1935	Entertainment	10			25	Br Musical Comedy,Films, Revues
Grosvenor, Charles H.	Civil War	25	40	55		Union Gen., MOC OH
Grosvenor, Gilbert H.	Business	135		195	95	Pres.National Geographic.Editor
Grosz, George	Artist	55	150	250		Expressed Hatred of Bourgeoisie
Grouchy, Marquis E. de	Napoleonic Wars	100	250			Marshal of Napoleon. Exiled
Grover, Cuvier	Civil War	30	65	85		Union General
Groves, Leslie R.	Military	55	145	220	85	Gen.WW II. Manhattan Project
Grow, Galusha A. 1822-1907	Celebrity	10	20	45	35	MOC PA, Speaker of the House
Gruberova, Edita	Entertainment	15			40	Opera
Gruelle, Johnny	Cartoonist	35			250	Raggedy Ann & Andy
Gruen, George John	Business	30	80	150	55	Chm. Gruen Watch Co.
Gruenther, Alfred M.	Military	15		30	25	Gen. WW II, Pres. Am. Red Cr.
Grumman, Leroy R.	Business	50	145		70	Grumman Aircraft
Guardia, R.A.C.	Head of State	15	50		25	Costa Rica
Guardino, Harry	Entertainment	6	8	15	20	
Guden, HIlde	Entertainment	25		75	50	Opera
Guderian, Hans	Military	30	55	100	45	
Guderian, Heinz	Military	50	175	285	500	Ger. Panzer Gen. WW II
Gudger, V. Lamar	Senate/Congress	10	30		15	MOC NC
Gudin de la Sablonniere	Fr. Revolution	120	235			
Gudunov, Alexander	Entertainment	15		40	35	Rus. Ballet
Guelfi, Piero	Entertainment	10			25	Opera
Guest, Edgar A.	Author	20	75	165	50	Am.Journalist-Poet of the Peopl
Guest, Lance	Entertainment	6	8	15	19	
Guest, Winston Mrs.	Business	5	10	15	10	
Guevaro, Ernesto Che	Revolutionary	340	895			Aide to Fidel Castro in Cuba
Guffey, Joseph F.	Senate/Congress	5	10		10	Senator PA
Guggenheim, Daniel	Business	20	45	85	35	Guggenheim Foundation
Guggenheim, Peggy	Business	15	25	70	20	Patron of Arts. Collector
Guggenheim, William	Business	55	125		75	Industrialist, Philanthropist
Guilbert, Yvette	Entertainment	40	65	130	150	
Guild, Curtis Jr.	Governor	12	15			Governor MA
Guild, Nancy	Entertainment	6	8	15	15	
Guilfoyle, Paul	Entertainment	10	15	35	30	
Guillaume, Robert	Entertainment	5	10	18	20	
Guillemin, Roger C.L.	Science	20	55	110	35	Nobel Medicine
Guillotin, Joseph-Ignace	Science	275	1650			Fr. Doctor Supported Guillotin
Guinan, Texas (Mary Louise)	Entertainment	25	70	90	40	Actress, Hostess of Speakeasies
Guiney, Louise Imogen	Author	50		300		Poet-Essayist
Guingand, Francis	Military	15	35	50		Fr. General

NAME	CATEGORY	SIG	LS/DS	ALS	SP	COMMENT
Guinness, Alec, Sir	Entertainment	9	10	30	45	
Guinness, Benjamin L. 1798-1868	Business	30	50	110		Guinness Brewing Co.
Guinness, Edward C. 1847-1927	Business	15	25	45	20	Guinness Brewing Co.
Guisewite, Cathy*	Cartoonists	25			85	Cathy
Guiteau, Charles	Assassin	460	850	2000		Shot Pres. Garfield
Gulager, Clu	Entertainment	6		15	20	
Gumbel, Bryant	Entertainment	5			10	
Guns 'N Roses (all)	Entertainment	45			135	
Gunsche, Otto	Military	50		85	55	
Gurie, Sigrid	Entertainment	20	25	60	45	
Gurrag-gchaa,Jugderdemidij	Astronaut	15	50		35	Mongolian Astro.
Gusmeroli, Giovanni	Entertainment	5			15	Opera
Gustavus II Adolphus(Swe)	Royalty	350	1100	2300		
Gustavus III (Swe)	Royalty	115	700	985		
Gustavus IV Adolphus(Swe)	Royalty	150				
Gustavus V (Swe)	Royalty				275	
Guthrie, Arlo	Country Music	5	6	15	15	
Guthrie, James 1792-1869	Cabinet-Senate	20	45	80		Pierce Sec'y Treas. Sen. KY
Guthrie, Thomas	Clergy	15	20	25		
Guthrie, Woody	Entertainer	300				Folksinger, Poet, Songwriter
Gutierrez, Sid	Astronaut	5			15	
Guttenberg, Steve	Entertainment	5		30	20	
Guy, Thomas	Celebrity	15	40	105		
Guynemer, Georges	Aviation	225	400	650	500	ACE, WW I. A French Legend
Guyot, Arnold H.	Author	25	45	160		Educator
Guyot, Pierre	Fr. Revolution	25	55	125		
Guyton-Morveau,L.B.Baron 1737-	Science	20	50	95		Fr. Chemist
Gwenn, Edmund	Entertainment	75	105		175	
Gwin, William M. 1805-1885	Senate/Congress	20	45	60		MOC MS, Senator CA
Gwinnett, Button	Revolutionary War	15000	165000			Rare Signer Decl. Independence
Gwynn, Fred	Entertainment	20			45	
Gwynne, Anne	Entertainment	6	8	15	15	
Gye, Albani	Entertainment	10			25	

H

NAME	CATEGORY	SIG	LS/DS	ALS	SP	COMMENT
Haab, Robert	Head of State	25	70			Switzerland
Haakon VII (Nor)	Royalty	120	205			1st King Independent of Sweden
Habberton, John	Author	10	15	25		
Habersham, Joseph 1751-1815	Revolutionary War	95	260	540		Continental Army,Cont.Congress
Hack, Shelley	Entertainment	4	7	12	15	Pin-Up SP $20
Hackett, Bobby	Entertainment	20			45	Cornet/Benny Goodman
Hackett, Buddy	Entertainment	5	10	20	25	Comedian
Hackett, James K.	Entertainment	12	15		30	Vintage Actor
Hackett, Joan	Entertainment	10	15	25	25	

NAME	CATEGORY	SIG	LS/DS	ALS	SP	COMMENT
Hackman, Gene	Entertainment	15	15	35	45	
Hadley, Jerry	Entertainment	10			35	Concert, Opera
Hadley, Reed	Entertainment	15			30	
Haenschen, Gus	Entertainment	15		25	30	Big Band
Hagar, Sammy	Entertainment	15			50	Rock
Hagen, Jean	Entertainment	5			10	
Hagen, Johannes 1847-1930	Science	15	40	100		Austr. Astron."Hagen's Clouds"
Hagen, Uta	Entertainment	10	12	20	20	
Haggard, Henry Rider, Sir	Author	90	130	160	270	"King Solomon's Mines"
Haggard, Merle	Country Music	10			30	
Haggerty, Dan	Entertainment	5	6	15	15	
Haggin, James Ben Ali	Business	35	205			Am Financier, Anaconda Copper
Hagman, Larry	Entertainment	6	8	15	15	
Hagood, Johnson	Civil War	125	250	310		CSA General
Hague, Frank	Politician	10	25	40	15	Headed Major Dem. "Machine"
Hahn, Jessica	Playboy Cover	4			15	Pin-Up SP $20
Hahn, Otto	Science	140	345	520	165	Ger.Nobel Chem. Nuclear Fission
Hahn, Reynaldo	Composer	70	160			Ven. Critic, Dir. Paris Opera
Haider, Michael	Business	15			40	Pres. Standard Oil NJ
Haig, Alexander M.	Military	20	45	50	40	Gen. WW II, Sec'y State
Haig, Douglas. 1st Earl	Military	25	75	130	60	Br.Gen., Boer War, India, WW I
Hailey, Arthur	Author	25	40	65	35	Am. Novelist."Hotel","Airport"
Haines, Connie	Entertainment	20			50	Big Band Vocalist
Haines, Daniel 1801-1877	Governor	30	45	90		Governor NJ
Haines, William	Entertainment	15	15	35	30	
Hairston, Jester	Entertainment	10			30	
Haise, Fred W. Jr.	Astronaut	10			30	
Halaby, Najeeb	Celebrity	10	30		15	
Halban, H.H., Dr.	Science	30	65			Fr. Pioneer Of Uranium Fission
Haldeman, George W.	Aviation	30	55	105	75	
Haldeman, H. R.	Political	10	20	45	15	Nixon-Watergate
Halder, Franz	Military	55	95	160	115	Ger.Gen.Opposed Hitler.Prison!
Hale, Alan Jr.	Entertainment	40	55	75	100	
Hale, Alan Sr.	Entertainment	50	55	95	100	
Hale, Barbara	Entertainment	10	15	25	25	Pin-Up SP $30
Hale, Edward Everett	Clergy	45	120	255	240	
Hale, Eugene	Senate	10	15	30		MOC 1869-75, Senator ME
Hale, George E.	Science	20	100			Invented Spectroheliograph
Hale, John Parker 1806-1873	Senate/Congress	15	45	100		Abolitionist, MOC, Senator NH
Hale, Monte	Entertainment	6	10	20	25	
Hale, Richard	Entertainment	6	8	15	15	
Hale, Robert	Entertainment	10			30	Opera
Hale, Sarah J. B.	Author	50	155	225		Editor."Mary Had A Little Lamb"
Halevy, Jacques 1799-1862	Composer	45	80	135		Opera. Taught Gounod, Bizet
Halevy, Ludivic	Author	25	70	165		Novels, Libretti For Operas
Haley, Alex	Author	30	100	150	135	Autobio. "Roots", "Malcom X"
Haley, Bill	Entertainment	225			450	
Haley, Jack	Entertainment	175			300	
Halifax, 1st Earl (C Wood)	Statesman	15	35	50	25	Diplomat, Ambassador to U.S.
Hall and Oates	Entertainment	20			40	
Hall, Abraham Oakey	Journalist	4	7	15	10	NY Mayor & Tweed Ring
Hall, Alvin W.	Celebrity	5	10		35	
Hall, Arsenio	Entertainment	10			20	TV Talk Show Host
Hall, Charles M.	Clergy	10	15	20		
Hall, David	Governor	12			15	Governor OK
Hall, Deidre	Entertainment	10			35	Soaps

NAME	CATEGORY	SIG	LS/DS	ALS	SP	COMMENT
Hall, Fawn	Entertainment	5	15	50	25	Pin-Up SP $30
Hall, Gus	Communist	30	55	150	30	US Communist Party Leader
Hall, Harry	Entertainment	3	3	6	6	
Hall, Huntz	Entertainment	10	15	25	40	
Hall, Jerry	Entertainment	10			30	Pin-Up SP $35
Hall, Jon	Entertainment	35	45	85	50	
Hall, Josephine	Entertainment	6	8	15	15	
Hall, Joyce C.	Business	50	600		90	Hallmark Greeting Cards
Hall, Juanita	Entertainment	30			75	
Hall, Lyman	Revolutionary War	2200	2950			Signer Decl. of Indepen.
Hall, Monty	Entertainment	3	3	6	10	
Hall, Nathan	Cabinet	20	35	110		Fillmore P.M. General
Hall, Pauline	Entertainment	10			30	Vintage Actress
Hall, Robert	Clergy	25	30	35	35	
Hall, Tom T.	Country Music	5			12	
Hall, William	Civil War	40		100		Union Gen., CW Gov. MO
Hallam, Henry	Author	35	115	175		Br. Historian
Halle, Wilhelmine	Entertainment	6	8	15	15	
Halleck, Fitz-Greene 1790-1867	Poet	25	80			Member of Knickerbocker Group
Halleck, Henry Wager	Civil War	150	300	530	200	Union Gen.ALS War Dte $4,500
Hallett, Mal	Entertainment	20			35	Big Band Leader
Halliburton, Richard	Explorer-Author	40	165		50	World Traveller, Lecturer
Halop, Billy	Entertainment	55	75	120	150	
Halpern, Seymour	Congress	5			15	MOC NY
Halpine, Charles G.	Author	20	35	90		
Halsey, Wm. F. 'Bull'	Military	75	150	210	200	Adm. WW II
Halstead, Murat	Editor	5	20	35		Journalist
Halston	Business	15	20	40	30	Designer
Halstrom, Holly	TV Model	5			10	"Price is Right" Model
Hamblen, Stewart	Country Music	15			30	
Hamel, Veronica	Entertainment	5	10	20	20	
Hamer, Frank	Military	110	465			
Hamer, Rusty	Entertainment	35		55	75	
Hamill, Mark	Entertainment	8	9	20	25	
Hamilton, Alex. Jr.	Military	15	40	65		Officer War 1812
Hamilton, Alexander	Cabinet	1125	3065	3500		Washington's Sec'y Treasury
Hamilton, Charles Smith	Civil War	32	65	110		Union Gen.ALS/Content $575
Hamilton, Donald	Author	7	15	30	10	
Hamilton, Emma, Lady	Celebrity	150		575		Mistress of Lord Nelson
Hamilton, George	Entertainment	5			20	
Hamilton, George Alexander, Sir	Diplomatist	75	540			Archaeologist, Husband Emma H.
Hamilton, James	Colonial Am.	65	160			Colonial Gov. PA
Hamilton, Lee	Congress	5	20		10	Congressman IN
Hamilton, Linda	Entertainment	20			50	Pin-Up SP $50
Hamilton, Margaret	Entertainment	75			150	SP Wicked Witch of West $300
Hamilton, Neil	Entertainment	25		65	75	
Hamilton,Ian, Sir	Military	50				Br. General WW I
Hamlin, Hannibal (V)	Vice President	55	285	320		Lincoln VP
Hamlin, Harry	Entertainment	10	15	28	30	
Hamlin, V.T.*	Cartoonist	50			325	Alley Oop
Hamlisch, Marvin	Composer	10		65	35	
Hammarskjold, Dag	Head of State	95	650	725		Sec'y General United Nations
Hammer	Entertainment	25			45	Rap
Hammer, Armand	Business	50	185	275	150	Occidental Petroleum
Hammerstein II, O. & Kern, Jerome	Composer		1200			
Hammerstein II, Oscar	Composer	240	515		260	Lyricist

NAME	CATEGORY	SIG	LS/DS	ALS	SP	COMMENT
Hammett, Dashiell	Author	450	1070	1750	575	"Hard-Boiled" Detective Fiction
Hammond, Jay S.	Governor	10	15			Governor AK
Hammond, L. Blaine	Astronaut	5			15	
Hammond, William A.	Civil War	50	120	400		Union Gen. /Surgeon Gen.Author
Hampden, Renn D.	Clergy	10	25	30		
Hampden, Walter	Entertainment	20		45	45	
Hampson, Thomas	Entertainment	10			40	Opera
Hampton, Hope	Entertainment	4	5	15	20	
Hampton, Lionel	Entertainment	25			45	Big Band Leader-Vibes
Hampton, Wade	Civil War	240	375	635		CSA General, Gov., US Sen. SC
Hamsun, Knut (Pedersen)	Author	45	80	135	75	Nobel Lit. Neo-Romantic Novels
Hanami, Kohei	Military	80	250			
Hancock, Herbie	Composer	10	15	45	20	
Hancock, John	Revolutionary War	2265	5500	9500		First Signer Decl. of Ind.
Hancock, Winfield Scott	Civil War	150	245	250		Union Gen.
Hand, Edward	Revolutionary War	185	525	1000		Gen. Cont. Army. MOC PA 1784
Handel, George Frederick	Composer	1000	5800	22000		
Handelman, Stanley M.	Entertainment	3	3	6	6	
Handler, Ruth	Business	40	75			Founder Mattel Toys
Handy, W. C.	Composer	275	420	500	750	Bandleader, Music Publisher
Hanks, Tom	Entertainment	15			50	
Hanna & Barbera	Cartoonists	30			100	Animators
Hanna, Marcus A.	Senator	25	70	145	35	Senator OH
Hannah, Daryl	Entertainment	10			45	Pin-Up SP $60
Hannah, John A.	Educator	7			10	Pres. Michigan State Univ.
Hansbrough, Henry Clay	Senate	10	15	30		MOC, Senator ND
Hansen, William	Entertainment	6	8	15	15	
Hanson, Howard	Composer	15	35	80		Pulitzer. Dir.Eastman Sch. Musi
Hanson, John	Revolutionary War	2250				Pres. Continental Congress
Harbach, Otto	Entertainment	125	245		175	Playwright,Lyricist, Music Publ
Harbaugh, Gregory J.	Astronaut	5			15	
Harbison, John	Composer	20		75		Pulitzer, AMusQS $150
Harbord, James G.	Military	60	145	185	125	Chief of Staff AEF WW I, RCA
Harburg, E. Y. 'Yip'	Composer	100	175	375		"Over the Rainbow"
Harcourt, Edward Venables	Clergy	25	30	40		
Hardee, William J.	Civil War	225	875	1150	950	CSA General (War Date)
Hardenberg, K.A.von Furst	Statesman	15	60	125		Prussian Politician
Hardie, James Allen	Civil War	55	205	245		Union General
Hardie, Russell	Entertainment	10	15	25	25	
Hardin, Clifford M.	Cabinet	5	10	18	15	Sec'y Agriculture
Hardin, Gus	Entertainment	4			10	Female Singer
Hardin, John Wesley	Outlaw	2900	6500			
Hardin, Ty	Entertainment	6	8	15	19	
Harding, Ann	Entertainment	15	15	35	30	
Harding, Florence Kling	First Lady	69	180		75	White House Card S $85
Harding, Warren G.	President	225	530	1675	635	
Harding, Warren G. (As President)	President		575	15000		White House Card S $400
Hardinge, Chas., 1st Baron	Diplomat	10	15	35	25	Br.Viceroy India, Ambass.Russia
Hardwicke, Cedric, Sir	Entertainment	35	65	90	95	
Hardy, Oliver	Entertainment	250	300	500	500	
Hardy, Thomas	Author	310	625	1205	1400	Br. Novelist, Poet, Dramatist
Hardy, Thomas Masterman, Sir	Military	70	195			1769-1839 Br. Adm./Nelson
Hare, John, Sir	Entertainment	20	30		50	
Hare, WIllam Hobart	Clergy	35	50	65	50	
Haring, Keith	Artist	25	40	95	120	
Harkins, Paul	Military	15	30	50	30	

NAME	CATEGORY	SIG	LS/DS	ALS	SP	COMMENT
Harkness, Georgia	Clergy	35	50	95	65	
Harlan, James A.1820-	Cabinet	20	55	100		A. Johnson Sec'y Interior 1865
Harlan, John Marshall 1833-1911	Supreme Court	55	95	175		
Harland, Marion	Author	7	15	20		
Harlfinger II, Frederick J.	Military	10			25	
Harlow, Jean	Entertainment	1000	1400	3000	2500	
Harlow, Jean (Mama)	Entertainment	25	30		45	
Harman, Fred*	Cartoonist	25			250	Red Ryder
Harmon, Judson	Cabinet	10	25	40	20	U.S. Att'y Gen., Gov. OH
Harmon, Mark	Entertainment	9	10	20	25	
Harmonica Rascals	Entertainment	10			25	Borah Minovitch and the......
Harned, Virginia	Entertainment	15			35	Vintage Actress, Mrs. Sothern
Harper, Joseph W.	Celebrity	10	30	80		
Harper, Robert G.	Revolutionary War	65		150		Gen. Rev. War, Statesman
Harper, Tess	Entertainment	9	10	20	25	
Harper, Valerie	Entertainment	5	6	15	15	
Harrell, Costen J., Bishop	Clergy	20	25	40	35	
Harrelson, Woody	Entertainment	15			45	"Cheers"
Harries, George	Military	20	35	80		General WW I
Harriman, Edw. Henry	Business	35	55	90	45	U.S. Railroad Magnate
Harriman, Edward Roland	Business	20	55	120	35	CEO Union Pacific RR. Banker
Harriman, W. Averell	Governor	25	65	100	50	Gov. NY, Statesman, Diplomat
Harrington, Pat	Entertainment	4	5	10	15	
Harris	Cartoonist	5			18	"The Better Half"
Harris, Arthur T., Sir "Bomber..."	Military	30	85	110	150	Cmdr.-in-Chief RAF WW II
Harris, Barbara	Entertainment	5			12	
Harris, Bernard A., Jr.	Astronaut	10			20	Afro-Am. Astronaut
Harris, Cecil	Aviation	14	25	50	40	ACE, WW II
Harris, Ed	Entertainment	5	6	15	15	
Harris, EmmyLou	Entertainment	10			35	
Harris, Fred R.	Senate/Congress	3	10			Senator OK
Harris, George E.	Senate/Congress	5	10			CSA Officer. MOC NC
Harris, Isham	Civil War	20	50			Civil War Gov. TN
Harris, Jean	Criminal	40	70	375		Murdered Dr. Herman Tarnower
Harris, Joel Chandler	Author	175	390	630		Books on Black Folklore
Harris, John	Frontier Leader	125	265			Founder Harrisburg, PA
Harris, John A.	Senate/Congress	3		15		
Harris, Julie	Entertainment	6	8	15	15	
Harris, Neil Patrick	Entertainment	10			35	
Harris, Patricia Roberts	Cabinet	5	15	25	20	Sec'y Health & Human Services
Harris, Paul Percy	Business	20	45		25	Fndr. & Pres. Emeritus Rotary
Harris, Phil	Entertainment	5			20	
Harris, Richard	Entertainment	15		35	40	
Harris, Robert H.	Entertainment	3	3	6	10	
Harris, Thomas S.	Aviation	15	45			ACE WW II, Test Pilot
Harris, William L., Bishop	Clergy	15	25	35		
Harrison, Albertis S. Jr.	Governor	10	20			Governor VA
Harrison, Anna Symmes	First Lady	500		2500		
Harrison, Benj.& Harrison Caroline	Pres.-1st Lady	600				Together
Harrison, Benjamin	President	290	855	1125	1875	
Harrison, Benjamin (As President)	President	345		1900		
Harrison, Benjamin 1726-91	Revolutionary War	450	750	1500		Signer Decl. of Indepen.
Harrison, Byron Patton 'Pat'	Senate/Congress	5	15		10	MOC, Senator MS
Harrison, Caroline Scott	First Lady	160	250	1000	900	
Harrison, Carter H.	Mayor	15	35	45		Mayor Chicago 1897
Harrison, George	Entertainment	200	575	275	300	

NAME	CATEGORY	SIG	LS/DS	ALS	SP	COMMENT
Harrison, Gregory	Entertainment	9	10	20	20	
Harrison, Helen	Aviation	40	125			Am Aviatrix
Harrison, Henry B.	Governor	12		20		Governor CT 1885
Harrison, Jenilee	Entertainment	4	4	9	12	Pin-Up SP $15
Harrison, Mary Lord	First Lady	70	120	195		
Harrison, Noel	Entertainment	5			15	
Harrison, Rex	Entertainment	40	55	70	100	
Harrison, Robert Hanson	Revolutionary War	210	400	750		Sec'y to G. Washington
Harrison, William Henry	President	670	1700	4025		
Harrold, Kathryn	Entertainment	8	9	19	20	Pin-Up SP $25
Harry, Debbie	Entertainment	25			75	Rock
Harry, Jackee	Entertainment	5			15	
Harryhausen, Ray	Entertainment	10			35	Film Director
Harshaw, Margaret	Entertainment	10	12	40	25	
Hart, Corey	Entertainment	6	8	15	15	
Hart, Dolores	Entertainment	4	4	15	20	
Hart, Dorothy	Entertainment	15		25	35	
Hart, Gary W.	Senate/Congress	5			15	Senator CO
Hart, John	Entertainment	10			25	
Hart, John 1708-1880	Revolutionary War	320	825	1300		Signer Decl. of Indepen.
Hart, Johnny*	Cartoonist	20			200	B.C. & Wizard Of Id
Hart, Lorenz	Composer	500	7500			Rogers & Hart
Hart, Mary	Entertainment	5	8	15	15	Pin-Up SP $15
Hart, Moss	Authors	20	55	105	30	
Hart, Paul	Entertainment	6	8	15	15	
Hart, Terry J.	Astronaut	5	15		30	
Hart, Thomas C.	Military	40			65	Adm. WW II
Hart, Veronica	Entertainment	10	15	35	35	Pin-Up SP $40
Hart, William S.	Entertainment	145	180	325	605	
Harte, Francis Brett	Author	75	185	415		Frontier Life, CA Mining Camps
Hartford, George L.	Business	40	175	280		Great Atlantic & Pacific Tea Co
Hartford, Huntington	Business	15	30	45	20	Patron of the Arts. Playboy
Hartford, John	Composer	10	45	70		AMusQS $95
Hartley, Fred A.	Congress	20		50		Congressman NJ
Hartley, Mariette	Entertainment	5	6	15	15	
Hartley, Nina	Entertainment	20			45	
Hartley, Roland H.	Governor	5	12		10	Governor WA
Hartline, Haldan K.	Science	25	80	140	35	Nobel Medicine
Hartman, David	Entertainment	4	8	12	10	Early Host "Good Morning Am."
Hartman, Lisa	Entertainment	10	15	25	20	Pin-Up SP $40
Hartmann, Erich	Aviation	40	105	190	120	Ger.Ace WW II. #1 Worldwide
Hartranft, John F.	Civil War	80		165		Union Gen., CMH Bull Run
Harts, William	Military	10		35		General WW I
Hartsfield, Henry W. Jr	Astronaut	10	40		15	
Hartsuff, George L.	Civil War	45	75	95		Union General
Hartwell, Alfred S.	Civil War	24	50	95		Union General
Harvey, George B. M.	Journalist-Dipl.	20	70		100	Fostered W. Wilson Nomination
Harvey, Lawrence	Entertainment	65	75		150	
Harvey, Lilian	Entertainment	5	6	15	25	
Harvey, Paul	Journalist	10	25		15	
Harvey, William 1578-1657	Science	750	3750	11000		1st Theory Blood Circulation
Hasbrouck, Robert W.	Military	50	165		75	Am. Gen. WW II
Hasen, Irwin	Cartoonist	5			20	Dondi
Haskell, James K.	Entertainment	10	15	30	25	
Haskin, Joseph Abel	Civil War	50				Union General
Hassam, Childe 1859-1935	Artist	150	350	480		Foremost in Am. Impressionism

NAME	CATEGORY	SIG	LS/DS	ALS	SP	COMMENT
Hassam, Crown Prince	Royalty	15	35	80	50	Morocco
Hassan, Crown Prince	Royalty	10	15	50	20	
Hassan, al Bakr, Ahmad	Head of State	10	35	90	18	Last Price Availble
Hasselhoff, David	Entertainment	6	8	15	19	
Hasso, Signe	Entertainment	5			20	
Hastings, Daniel H.	Governor	10	25			Governor PA
Hastings, Warren 1732-1818	Head of State	70	155	235		Gov. Gen. India. Colonial Adm.
Haswell, Charles H.	Civil War	25	35	55		Union Naval Architect
Hatch, John Porter	Civil War	30	50	80	75	Union Gen. CMH
Hatch, Orrin	Senate	5			10	Senator UT
Hatcher, Richard G.	Mayor	5	10		15	Afro-Am. Mayor, Gary IN
Hatcher, Teri	Entertainment	10			40	
Hatfield, Hurd	Entertainment	15	20	30	35	
Hatfield, Mark O.	Senate	10	15		15	Senator OR, Governor Oregon
Hathaway, Henry	Entertainment	40			95	
Hatlo, Jimmy	Cartoonist	10	90		80	Little Iodine
Hatton, Raymond	Entertainment	50			125	
Hatton, Robert	Civil War	125	265	365		No Current Price
Hatton, Rondo	Entertainment	450			1200	
Hauck, Frederick H.	Astronaut	10			25	
Hauer, Rutger	Entertainment	10			30	
Haught, Helmut	Aviation	10	15	30	20	
Hauptman, Herbert A., Dr.	Science	20	35		30	Nobel Chemistry
Hauptmann, Bruno Richard	Kidnapper	425				Convicted Killer Lindbergh Baby
Hauptmann, Gerhart	Author	90	295	575	375	Nobel Prize Literature 1912
Hausner, Jerry	Entertainment	4	4	9	9	
Haven, Annette	Entertainment	9	10	20	25	Pin-Up SP $40
Havens, Beckwith	Aviation	18	40	55	50	
Haver, June	Entertainment	3	3	10	12	Pin-Up SP $25
Havoc, June	Entertainment	6	8	15	15	
Hawes, Elizabeth	Artist	10	20	35		
Hawke, Ethan	Entertainment	15			50	
Hawke, Robert	Head of State	15	40	130	25	Prime Minister Australia
Hawkins, Anthony Hope, Sir	Author	10	35	70	30	Br.Novelist."Prisoner of Zenda"
Hawkins, Coleman	Entertainment	125			250	Jazz Tenor Sax
Hawkins, Jack	Entertainment	45			100	
Hawkins, John	Civil War	35		125		Union Gen.
Hawkins, Paula	Senate/Congress	3	10		10	Senator FL
Hawkins, William 1770-1819	Governor	35	85			Governor NC. War 1812
Hawks, Frank Monroe	Aviation	75	135	325	275	Pioneer Aviator
Hawks, Howard	Entertainment	85			150	
Hawley, Joseph R.	Civil War	45	90	120		Union General, Gov. CT, Sen CT
Hawley, Steven A.	Astronaut	5			20	
Hawn, Goldie	Entertainment	10	15	30	35	Pin-Up SP$65
Haworth, Jill	Entertainment	4	4	9	10	
Hawthorn, Alex. Travis	Civil War	155	295	445		
Hawthorne, Nathaniel	Author	400	850	2080		Novelist, Short Story,US Consul
Hay, Bill (Announcer)	Entertainment	10	1625	20		
Hay, John H.	Military	5		15		
Hay, John Milton	Cabinet	40	150	240	95	ALS/Content $950 War Dte
Hay, William Henry	Military	5	15	30		
Hayakawa, Sessue	Entertainment	125			250	
Hayden, Carl	Senate/Congress	10	25		20	MOC, Senator AZ. 42 Years
Hayden, Mellisa	Entertainment	5	6	15	15	
Hayden, Russell	Entertainment	25			75	
Hayden, Sterling	Entertainment	25			50	

NAME	CATEGORY	SIG	LS/DS	ALS	SP	COMMENT
Hayden, Tom	Senate/Congress	5	15		20	MOC CA
Haydn, Joseph	Composer	2200	15500	24000		
Hayes, George 'Gabby'	Entertainment	150	165		450	
Hayes, Helen	Entertainment	25	35	45	70	
Hayes, Ira H., Corporal	Military	400				Iwo Jima Flag Raising FDC $550
Hayes, Isaac	Entertainment	6	8	15	20	
Hayes, Isaac Israel	Explorer-Civil Wa	95	190	275		ALS/Content $1,500
Hayes, Joseph	Civil War	55	95	170	150	
Hayes, Lucy Webb	First Lady	230		400	700	
Hayes, Margaret	Entertainment	9	10		15	
Hayes, Patrick, Cardinal	Clergy	35	45	75	50	
Hayes, Roland	Entertainment	80			250	Am. Tenor, Spingarn Medal '25
Hayes, Rutherford B.	President	210	815	995	2730	ALS/Cont. $7,500, WH Cd. $300
Hayne, Paul Hamilton	Author	65		850		ALS/Literary Content $2,500
Haynes, Linda	Entertainment	4	4	9	9	
Hays, Frank A.	Aviation	35	55	95	65	ACE, SS II
Hays, Harry Thompson	Civil War	110	450			CSA General
Hays, Robert	Entertainment	6	8	12	12	
Hays, Wayne L.	Senate/Congress	5	20		15	MOC OH
Hays, Will H.	Motion Pic. Exec.	30	50		40	Film Czar
Hayward, George	Science	10	20	35	15	
Hayward, Louis	Entertainment	10	15	25	35	
Hayward, Susan	Entertainment	150	200	525	575	
Haywood, Thomas	Military	5	8	15	10	
Hayworth, Rita	Entertainment	150		390	435	
Hazelwood, John 1726-1800	Revolutionary War	75	190	370		Commodore Continental Navy
Hazelwood, Joseph	Navy Captain	20			45	Capt. Exxon Valdez-Oil Spill
Hazen, Wm. Babcock	Civil War	25	45	95		Union Gen.
Head, Edith	Entertainment	25			125	8 Academy Awards
Headle, Marshall	Aviation	25	70		85	Lockheed Chief Test Pilot
Healey, George	Artist	125	310	725		Eminent 19th Cent. Portraitist
Healey, Robert C.	Author	10	15	25		
Healy, Ted	Entertainment	25		40	45	
Hearnes, Warren E.	Governor	4	10		15	Governor MO
Hearst, George 1820-1891	Business-Senate	200		490		Fathered Newspaper Dynasty. CA
Hearst, Patricia	Celebrities	275				Kidnapped daughter
Hearst, Phoebe A.(Mrs. George..)	Business	20	40	90		Philanthropies
Hearst, Wm. Rand. Jr.	Business	10	20	45	20	
Hearst, Wm. Randolph	Business	180	350	575	695	MOC NY.Newspaper Chain
Heart	Entertainment	35			125	Rock
Heath, Edward	Head of State	30	90	115	45	Prime Minister
Heath, William	Revolutionary War	95	295	375		General Continental Army
Heatherton, Joey	Entertainment	9	10	20	25	
Heber, Reginald	Clergy	85	100	200		
Hebert, Paul O.	Civil War	105	200	260		
Hecht, Ben	Author	15	45		30	Playwright, Novelist, Newsman
Heckart, Eileen	Entertainment	5	6	15	15	
Heckerling, Amy	Entertainment	5	6	15	15	
Hedin, Sven	Explorer	55		200	125	Swe-Asian Explorer
Hedison, David	Entertainment	4	4	9	10	
Hedl, Walter	Composer	15	55	90		AMusQS $175
Hedman, Duke	Aviation	20	45	75	50	ACE, WW II, Flying Tigers
Hedouville, G.M.T.J,Count	Fr. Revolution	70	125			
Hedren, Tippi	Entertainment	5	6	15	22	
Hedrick, Roger	Aviation	12	25	40	32	ACE, WW II
Heflin, Howell	Senate	5	15	15		Senator AL

NAME	CATEGORY	SIG	LS/DS	ALS	SP	COMMENT
Heflin, James Thomas	Senate/Congress	10	20		15	MOC, Senator AL
Heflin, Van	Entertainment	35	40	95	100	
Hefner, Christie	Business	5	10	30	20	Publisher "Playboy Magazine"
Hefner, Hugh	Business	8			10	Founder "Playboy Magazine"
Hefti, Neal	Composer	15			40	AMusQS $195
Hegel, George Wilhelm F.1770-1831	Philosopher	550	2900			Ger. Idealist Philosopher
Heggie, O.P.	Entertainment	300			750	
Heidt, Horace	Entertainment	20			40	Big Band Leader.Musical Knights
Heifetz, Jascha	Entertainment	85			395	Violin Virtuoso
Heimlich, Henry Jay, Dr.	Science	20		45	40	Created "Heimlich Maneuver"
Heine, Heinrich 1797-1856	Author	570	1810	5890		Ger. Poet, Critic
Heinlein, Robert A.	Author	50	165	350		Sci-Fi Fiction
Heinrich, Albert H.	Aviation	35		120		
Heintzelman, Samuel P.	Civil War	50	95	115		Union General
Heinz, Henry John	Business	110		800	350	A Founder H.J. Heinz Co.
Heinz, John	Senate	10			22	Senator PA
Heinze, Karl	Astronaut	35			75	
Heisenberg, Werner, Dr.	Science	50	225	650		Nobel Physics,ALS/Cont. $950
Helbig, Joachim	Aviation	10	20	35	25	
Held, Anna	Entertainment	65	80	135	140	Mrs. Florenz Ziegfield
Held, John, Jr.*	Cartoonist	50			500	Illustrator Created The Flapper
Heldy, Fanny	Entertainment	40			110	Opera
Helena, Princess	Royalty	10	20	50	30	Third Daughter Queen Victoria
Helgenberger, Marg	Entertainment	15			35	Pin-Up SP $50
Heller, John R., Dr.	Science	12	20		15	
Heller, Joseph	Author	15	30	45	15	
Heller, Walter E.	Business	5	15		15	Fndr.,Chm. Walter E. Heller
Heller, Walter W.	Cabinet	5	15	30	15	
Helletsgruber, Luise	Entertainment	25			75	Opera
Hellinger, Mark	Author	35	105	225	40	Columnist, Playwright
Hellman, Lillian	Author	40	135		100	Am. Dramatist, "Little Foxes"
Hellyer, Paul T.	Celebrity	15	30			
Helm, Ben Hardin	Civil War	195	250			CSA General
Helmond, Katherine	Entertainment	5	6	15	15	
Helms, Jesse	Senate & Congress	5	15		15	Senator NC
Helms, Richard	Celebrity	5	15	45	20	
Helmsley, Leona	Business	10			35	Hotel Magnate
Heloise	Author	4			10	Columnist.
Helps, Arthur, Sir 1817-75	Author	10	15	40		Historian Re America
Helton, Percy	Entertainment	20			65	
Hemingway, Ernest	Author	965	3250	5200	2650	Nobel Literature
Hemingway, Margaux	Entertainment	20			25	Daughter E. Hemingway
Hemingway, Mariel	Entertainment	10			30	Daughter E. Hemingway
Hemingway, Mary	Author	20	45	80		Mrs. Ernest Hemingway
Hempel, Frieda	Entertainment	20			70	Ger. Soprano, Opera
Hemsley, Sherman	Entertainment	6	8	15	20	
Hench, Philip S.	Science	20	45	90	25	Nobel Medicine
Henderson, Archibald	Military	65	195			Marine General War 1812
Henderson, Florence	Entertainment	3	3	10	10	
Henderson, J. Pinckney	Statesman	390	525			Gen. TX Army, Gov. Texas
Hendon, Bill	Senate/Congress	3	5		5	Congressman NC
Hendricks, Barbara	Entertainment	10			30	Opera
Hendricks, Thomas A. (V)	Vice President	50	200	375	75	Cleveland VP, U.S. Sen. IN
Hendrix, Jimi	Entertainment	1040				
Hendrix, Wanda	Entertainment	10	15		35	
Heney, Hugh	Explorer	325	750			Scout for Lewis & Clark

NAME	CATEGORY	SIG	LS/DS	ALS	SP	COMMENT
Henie, Sonja	Entertainment	30			125	Gold in Olympic Figure Skating
Henize, Charles G.	Astronaut	10	15		15	
Henley, Don	Entertainment	15			35	Composer, Singer "The Eagles"
Henner, Marilu	Entertainment	6	8	15	25	Pin-Up SP $60
Henreid, Paul	Entertainment	20			95	
Henri, Robert	Artist	80	175	215		Portr. Painter, Ashcan School
Henricks, Terence T.	Astronaut	5			15	
Henry II	Royalty	295	1050	2460		France
Henry III	Royalty	250	1065	1325		France
Henry IV	Royalty	180	600	1725		France, Henry of Navarre
Henry IV (Sp)	Royalty		1600			King of Castile"The Impotent"
Henry V (Fr)	Royalty	40	65	150		Pretender to Throne
Henry VI	Royalty	195	525	1350		England
Henry VII (Eng)	Royalty	875	7200	10000		
Henry VIII (Eng)	Royalty	2150	12000	17500		
Henry, Bill	Entertainment	15	15	35	30	
Henry, Bill	Aviation	10	25	40	30	ACE, WW II, Navy Ace
Henry, Buck	Entertainment	6	6	10	12	
Henry, Gloria	Entertainment	5	7	10	15	
Henry, John 1750-1798	Revolutionary War	35	135	220		Continental Congress. Sen. MD
Henry, Joseph	Science	55	130	245		1st Electric Motor
Henry, Mike	Entertainment	10			35	
Henry, O.	Author					SEE W.S. Porter
Henry, Patrick	Revolutionary War	1025	1450	2175		Rev. War ALS $7,800,LS $4500
Henschel, George, Sir	Composer	70			150	Br. Conductor, Singer
Henshaw, David	Cabinet	20	60	105		Tyler Sec'y Navy
Henson, Jim	Entertainment	75			240	Created the Muppets
Henson, Matthew A.	Explorer	130	350			Afro-Am. Arctic Explorer
Henze, Hans Werner	Composer	45			165	Ger. Opera, Theater Works
Henze, Karl	Aviation	16	37	71	45	
Hepburn, Audrey	Entertainment	75	220	300	150	
Hepburn, Katharine	Entertainment	125	360		795	
Hepworth, Barbara, Dame	Artist	70	190			Br. Sculptor."Reclining Figure"
Herbeck, Ray	Entertainment	5			15	Big Band Leader-Sax
Herbert, F. Hugh	Author	12	20	30	20	Am. Playwright, Producer
Herbert, Frank	Author	15	20	35	20	Am. Sci-Fi. "Dune" Trilogy
Herbert, Geo.E. (Carnarvon)	Archaeology	20	45	90		With Carter, King Tut Tomb
Herbert, Hilary A.	Cabinet	10	20	35	20	Cleveland Sec'y Navy
Herbert, Hugh	Entertainment	30	45	70	75	
Herbert, P.O.	Civil War	100		375		CSA General
Herbert, Sidney	Entertainment	15	25	30	25	
Herbert, Victor	Composer	95	220	420	360	AMusQS $275-$475
Herford,Oliver	Cartoonist	10	25			
Hergesheimer, Joseph	Author	25	65	145	30	Am. Psychological Novels
Herget, Wilhelm	Aviation	20		50		
Hering, Constantine	Science	15	25	50		1st Homeopathic School
Herkimer, Nicholas	Revolutionary War		3700			General of Militia.
Herkomer, Hubert von, Sir	Artist	20	85	125		Br. Portrait Painter
Herman, Jerry	Composer	15	40	65	30	AMusQS $85 "Hello Dolly"
Herman, Pee Wee	Entertainment	12	15		30	
Herman, Woody	Entertainment	20	90		50	Big Band Leader-Clarinetist
Hermann, Hajo	Aviation	25	50		60	
Hern, James A.	Entertainment	15	15	30	28	
Herndon, William	Legal	160	450	925		Law Partner of Abraham Lincoln
Herres, Bob	Astronaut	5			16	
Herrick, Myron T.	Diplomat	30	135			Ambassador, Gov. OH

NAME	CATEGORY	SIG	LS/DS	ALS	SP	COMMENT
Herriman, George*	Cartoonist	50			600	Krazy Kat
Herring, Clyde L.	Senate	7			10	Senator IA
Herriot, Edouard	Head of State	25	80	175		Premier of Fr., Nazi Prisoner
Herriot, James	Author	15	40	75	25	"All Creatures Great & Small"
Herrmann, Adelaide & Alexander	Magic	50			75	Magicians
Herron, Francis J.	Civil War	45	80	125		Union Gen.
Herschbach, Dudley, Dr.	Science	25	35		40	Nobel Chemistry
Herschel, John Fred. Wm., Sir	Science	75	170	380		Br. Astronomer, Mathematician
Herschel, William, Sir	Science	150	475	675		Br.Astronomer,Discovered Uranus
Hersey, John	Author	20	50	125	25	Am."Bell for Adano" Pulitzer
Hershey, Alfred D., Dr.	Science	20	30	45	25	Nobel Medicine
Hershey, Barbara	Entertainment	5			20	
Hershey, Lewis B.	Military	15			25	Gen., Selective Service Adm.
Hersholt, Jean	Entertainment	20			65	
Herter, Christian	Cabinet	15	25		25	Sec'y State
Hertz, Alfred	Entertainment	25			120	Conductor
Hervey, Irene	Entertainment	15			35	
Herzberg, Gerhard, Dr.	Science	25	65		30	Nobel Chemistry
Herzl, Theodor	Zionist	150	900	1200	250	Important DS $8,000
Herzog, Chaim	Head of State	25	65	175	40	Pres. Israel
Hesburgh, Theodore M., Rev.	Clergy	15	30	45	25	
Hess, Myra, Dame	Entertainment	20	40	65	35	Br. Pianist
Hess, Rudolf	Military-Politici	155	450	775	750	Nazi WW II
Hess, Victor F.	Science	20	30	55	25	Nobel Physics
Hess, Walter R.	Science	20	30	50	25	Nobel Medicine
Hesse, Hermann	Author	90	565	550	175	Ger. Author, Artist, Poet
Hesseman, Howard	Entertainment	5	6	15	15	
Heston, Charlton	Entertainment	10			35	
Heth, Henry	Civil War	140	260	310		CSA General
Hewes, Joseph	Revolutionary War	1200	3250	8500		Signer Decl. of Indepen.
Hewes,Joseph & John Penn	Revolutionary War		25000			Signers Decl. of Indepen.
Hewett, Charlston	Entertainment	4			10	
Hewish, Anthony	Science	20	40	85	30	Nobel Physics. Pulsars
Hewitt, Abram S.	Business	35	60	85		Iron Manufacturing/Peter Cooper
Hewitt, H.K.	Military	20	50	85		
Hewlett, William R.	Business	25	70	145	30	Hewlett-Packard
Hexum, Jon-Erik	Entertainment	60			125	
Heydrich, Reinhard	Military	200	576	1350	600	Specialist in Nazi Terror
Heydt, Louis Jean	Entertainment	35			80	
Heyerdahl, Thor	Explorer	25	40	95	35	Nor. Ethnologist, Adventurer
Heyman, Edward	Entertainment	3	3	6	6	
Heyman, Edward 'Eddie'	Author	5	10	25	10	
Heyse, Paul	Author	45	135	350		Ger. Novelist, Nobel Literature
Heyward, Dorothy	Author	55	325			Co-writer of "Porgy"
Heyward, DuBose	Author	50	400			"Porgy...."LS/Cont. $2,250
Heyward, Thomas Jr.	Revolutionary War	175	465	1400		Signer Decl. of Indepen.
Heywood, Eddie	Entertainment	35			100	Big Band Leader-Piano
Hichens, Robert S.	Author	15	40	150		Br. Novelist."Garden of Allah"
Hickel, Walter J.	Cabinet	10	15	30	15	Governor Alaska, Sec'y Interior
Hickenlooper, Andrew	Civil War	30	55	80		Union Gen., Military Engineer
Hickenlooper, Bourke B.	Senate	10	15		15	Governor, Senator IA
Hickman, Darryl	Entertainment	5			15	
Hickman, Dwayne	Entertainment	5			15	
Hicks, Catherine	Entertainment	8		25	20	
Hicks, Frederick Cocks	Senate/Congress	10	15			MOC NY
Hidalgo, Miguel y Costilla	Clergy	1525				Mexican Revolutionist & Priest

NAME	CATEGORY	SIG	LS/DS	ALS	SP	COMMENT
Hieb, Richard	Astronaut	4			12	
Higgins, Andrew Jackson	Business	25		50		Bldr.WW II Higgins Landing Boat
Higgins, Charles	Science	15	35			
Higginson, Henry L.	Business	10	20	35		
Higginson, Thomas W.	Civil War-Clergy	30	55	110		Antislavery Writer, Military CW
Hildebrand, Samuel	Civil War		1750			Quantrill Raider-Murderer
Hildegarde	Entertainment	5	6	15	10	
Hill, Ambrose Powell	Civil War	525	4200		1350	CSA General
Hill, Annie	Entertainment	6	8	15	10	
Hill, Archibald V.	Science	25	45		35	Nobel Medicine 1922
Hill, Arthur	Entertainment	5	6	15	15	
Hill, Benjamin H.	Civil War-Senate	45	165	230		Signed CSA Constitution
Hill, Benny	Entertainment	25			30	
Hill, Dana	Entertainment	6	8	15	15	
Hill, Daniel Harvey	Civil War	285	485	620		CSA General
Hill, David B.	Senate	10	15			Governor NY, Senator
Hill, David Lee "Tex"	Aviation	12	30	42	35	ACE, WW II, Flying Tigers
Hill, Edwin C.	Commentator	10	20		15	Radio Commentator
Hill, George Roy	Entertainment	5			15	
Hill, George Washington	Business	80	220			American Tobacco Co.,Pres.
Hill, Grace Livingston	Author	25	40	75		Am. Novelist
Hill, Isaac 1789-1851	Senate/Congress	20	35	60		Governor, Senator NY
Hill, James J.	Business		225		950	Railrd. Exec., Financier
Hill, John F.	Governor	5	15			Governor ME
Hill, Rowland	Clergy	50	75	195		
Hill, Rowland, 1st Viscount	Military	35	80	170		Cmdr. in Chief. England
Hill, Rowland, Sir	Inventor	145	340	785		Originator of Penny Postage
Hill, Thomas	Clergy-Educator	15	20	35		Pres. Harvard, Antioch
Hill, Tiny	Entertainment	6	8	15	15	
Hill, Walter	Entertainment	5			20	Film Director
Hill, William	Entertainment	3	3	6	6	
Hillary, Edmund, Sir	Mt. Climber	70	150	285	125	1st To Climb Mr. Everest
Hillegas, Michael	Revolutionary War	225	645			U.S. Treasurer 1777
Hillegess, C.K. "Cliff"	Author	10			20	"Cliff's Notes" Study Helps
Hiller, Frank, Jr.	Aviation	75	150	330	160	
Hiller, Arthur	Entertainment	5			15	Film Director
Hiller, Ferdinand	Composer	40	85	125		Conductor, Pianist
Hiller, Wendy	Entertainment	15		35	25	
Hillerman, John	Entertainment	9	10	20	25	
Hilliard, Harriet	Entertainment	20			35	
Hilliard, Henry W.	Civil War	35	80	105		Conf. Commissioner to TN
Hilliard, Robert	Entertainment	20			40	
Hillig, Otto	Aviation	40	85	150	115	
Hillis, Marjorie	Author	5	10	15		
Hills, Carla A.	Cabinet	7	20	35	15	Sec'y HUD
Hilmers, David C.	Astronaut	5			20	
Hilton, Barron	Business	10	15	25	15	
Hilton, Conrad	Business	60	90	190	110	Fndr. Hilton Hotel Dynasty
Hilton, James, Sir	Author	35	120	205	35	"Lost Horizon"
Himmler, Heinrich	Military	250	750	1170	775	Nazi Head of the Gestapo
Hinchingbrooke, Alex	Celebrity	10	20	45	15	
Hinckley, John, Jr.	Assassin	35	150	200		Attempt on Pres. Reagan
Hincks, Edward W.	Civil War	50	185			Union General
Hindemith, Paul	Composer	100	295	425		Ger. Teacher, Theorist, Critic
Hindenburg, Paul von	Head of State	150	490	590	425	2nd Pres. Weimar Rep. of Ger.
Hindman, Thomas Carmichael	Civil War	200	385			CSA General

NAME	CATEGORY	SIG	LS/DS	ALS	SP	COMMENT
Hines, Duncan	Business	65	225		80	"Duncan Hines" Cake-Cookie Mix
Hines, Earl K. "Fatha"	Entertainment	125			250	Pianist, Composer, Bandleader
Hines, Gregory	Entertainment	9	10	25	30	
Hines, Herm	Entertainment	10			25	Jazz Sax
Hines, Jerome	Entertainment	20			90	Opera, Concert
Hines, John E.	Clergy	10	15	15		
Hingle, Pat	Entertainment	5	6	15	15	
Hinshelwood, Cyril Norman, Sir	Science	20	45		35	Nobel Chemistry
Hinton, Walter	Aviation	40	85	130	90	Pilot of NC-4
Hirohito	Head of State	2000	8000		12000	
Hirsch, Judd	Entertainment	5	6	15	15	
Hirschfeld, Al	Caricaturist	35			250	Repro S $145-$175-$250
Hirshfield, Harry	Cartoonist	10			125	Abie The Agent
Hiss, Alger	Diplomat	40	65	95		Figure in Sensational Spy Case
Hitchcock, Alfred	Entertainment	225	400	575	430	Self-Caricature S $350-$650
Hitchcock, Ethan Allen	Civil War	50	150	200		Union Gen., Also Author
Hitchcock, Frank H.	Cabinet	15	30	35	30	Sec'y Interior 1898
Hitchcock, Gilbert M.	Senate/Congress	10	20		15	Governor NE
Hitchcock, Raymond	Entertainment	20			35	
Hitchings, George, Dr.	Science	20	30	70	30	Nobel Medicine
Hite, June	Research	5	15	25		Hite Research
Hite, Les	Entertainment	75			275	Saxophone. "Hold Tight"
Hitler, Adolf	Head of State	1500	3150	17000	2070	Special DS $9,500-$18,500
Hittorff, Jacques 1792-1867	Architect	5	20	30		Fr.
Hitz, John	Celebrity	10	35	90		
Hitzfeld, Otto Maximilian	Military	20			50	Ger. Infantry General
Ho Chi Minh	Head of State	225	525	1500	600	Vietnam (Pr. Guide II Prices)
Ho, Don	Entertainment	5	6	10	12	Singer
Hoag, R. C., Major	Astronaut	5			15	
Hoar, Ebenezer R.	Cabinet	10		35		U.S. Att'y Gen 1869
Hoar, George F.	Senate	10		15		MOC, Senator MA 1877
Hoban, James 1762	Revolutionary War	255	675			Architect White House, Wash.D.C
Hobart, Garret A. (V)	Vice President	65	200	310	200	
Hobart, John Sloss 1738-1805	Senate/Congress	25	40	70		Delegate & Senator NY
Hobart, Rose	Entertainment	10			25	
Hobby, Oveta Culp	Cabinet	16	25	40	30	1st Sec'y HEW
Hobson, Richmond P.	Military	75	260	385	150	Adm.CMH. Blew up USS Merrimac
Hobson, Valerie	Entertainment	25			75	
Hoche, Lazare	Fr. Revolution	205	515			General French Republic
Hock, Robt C.	Astronaut	5			15	Skylab
Hockney, David	Artist	60		75		
Hodes, Art	Entertainment	10			25	Pianist-Bandleader
Hodes, H. I.	Military	5	15	25		
Hodge, Al	Entertainment	25			200	
Hodges, Courtney	Military	15	40		25	Gen. WW II
Hodgkin, Dorothy C.	Science	25		35		Nobel Chemistry
Hodgson, John	Clergy	20	25	35		
Hodiak, John	Entertainment	20	25	45	45	
Hoe, Richard	Business	30	55	95		Improved Hoe Rotary & Art Press
Hoe, Richard M.	Industrialist	90	310	395		Invented Rotary Press
Hoegh, Leo A.	Governor	5			12	Governor IA
Hoest, Bill	Cartoonist	10			40	The Lockhorns
Hoey, Clyde R.	MOC-Sen.-Gov.	10	25		15	MOC, Senator, Governor NC
Hoey, Dennis	Entertainment	75			200	
Hofer, Andreas	Military		3000			Tyrolean Patriot,executed
Hoff, Philip H.	Governor	5	15			Governor VT

NAME	CATEGORY	SIG	LS/DS	ALS	SP	COMMENT
Hoffa, James R.	Labor Leader	275	310		400	Teamsters Union (disappeared)
Hoffer, Eric	Celebrity	5	10	25	10	Self Made Philosopher
Hoffgen, Marga	Entertainment	10			35	
Hoffman, Dustin	Entertainment	10	15	30	35	
Hoffman, Harold Giles	Governor	12	30			Governor NJ
Hoffman, Jeffrey A.	Astronaut	5			15	
Hoffman, John Thompson	Governor	10	20	35		Governor NY 1868
Hoffman, Kurt-Caesar	Military	25			65	
Hoffman, Maud	Entertainment	3	5		8	
Hoffman, Paul G.	Business	10	20	35	20	Auto Mfg.-Studebaker Cars
Hoffmann, Oswald C.J.	Clergy	10	20	25		
Hoffmann, Peter	Entertainment	15			55	Opera
Hoffmann, Roald, Dr.	Science	20	30	45	25	Nobel Chemistry
Hofmann, Josef	Entertainment	40	100	140	125	Pianist, Composer AmusQS $200
Hofstadter, Robert	Science	20	30	45	25	Nobel Physics
Hogan, Hulk	Entertainment	5			10	Wrestler
Hogan, Paul	Entertainment	10	15	20	25	"Dundee"
Hogarth, Burne*	Cartoonist	25			250	Tarzan-2nd Artist
Hogarth, Wm. 1697-1764	Artist	450	1665	3500		Br. Painter-Engraver.
Hoiris, Holger	Aviation	40	85	155	95	
Hoke, Robert Frederick	Civil War	75				CSA General
Hokinson, Helen	Cartoonist	20			100	Mag. Cartoonist-the Ladies
Holbrook, Hal	Entertainment	6	8	15	15	
Holden, Fay	Entertainment	20			50	
Holden, William	Entertainment	40	60		175	
Hole, Jonathan	Entertainment	3	3	6	6	
Holiday, Billie	Entertainment	625	1350		1525	Legendary Jazz Singer
Holladay, Ben	Business	135	475	925		Indian Trade, Army Contracts
Holland, Edmund M.	Entertainment	15			45	Vintage Stage Actor
Holland, John Philip	Inventor	70	160	325		1st Sub/Internal Combustion Eng
Holland, Josiah Gilbert	Author	15	30	75		pseud. Timothy Titcomb
Holland, Spessard L.	Senate	10	20			Governor, Senator FL
Hollen, Andrea Lee	Military	10	20	35	15	
Holley, Marietta 1836-1926	Author	10	15	35		Am. Humorist
Holley, Robert, Dr.	Science	15	20	35	20	Nobel Chemistry
Holliday, Judy	Entertainment	125			325	
Holliday, Polly	Entertainment	5	6	15	15	
Holliman, Earl	Entertainment	5	8	10	15	
Holliman, John	TV News	5			15	TV News Commentator
Hollings, Ernest 'Fritz'	Senate	10			15	Senator SC
Hollins, Geo. Nichols	Civil War	275	520			Commodore CSA Navy
Holloway, Stanley	Entertainment	20			60	
Holloway, Sterling	Entertainment	15			50	
Hollowell, George	Aviation	10	22	38	30	ACE, WW II, Marine Ace
Holly, Buddy	Entertainment	1340	1725	3250	2800	Rock Singer-Songwriter
Holm, Celeste	Entertainment	5	6	15	15	
Holm, Eleanor	Entertainment	10			30	
Holman, William Steele	Senate/Congress	12	20	30		MOC IN 1859
Holmes, Burton	Author	12	20	40	25	In 1894 Originated"Travelogues"
Holmes, Christopher	Astronaut	15	25		25	
Holmes, D. Brainerd	Celebrity	10			25	
Holmes, John Haynes	Clergy	15	20	30		
Holmes, Oliver W., Jr. (SC)	Supreme Court	150	310	1975	300	
Holmes, Oliver W., Sr.	Author	65	205	400		HOF, ALS/Content $1,800
Holmes, Robert D.	Governor	5	10		5	Governor OR
Holmes, Theophilus Hunter	Civil War	125	245			CSA General

NAME	CATEGORY	SIG	LS/DS	ALS	SP	COMMENT
Holmquest, Donald L.	Astronaut	10	15		20	
Holshouser, James E.	Governor	5		20	15	Governor NC
Holst, Gustav	Composer	35	105	250		AMusQS $275-$625
Holstrom, E.W. 'Brick'	Military	15	35	70	25	
Holt, Jack	Entertainment	40	60	100	100	
Holt, Jennifer	Entertainment	5			10	
Holt, Joseph	Cabinet-Civil War	65	180	215		Prosecuted Lincoln Assassins
Holt, Rush D.	Senate/Congress	5	10			Senator WV 1935
Holt, Tim	Entertainment	45			120	
Holt, Victoria	Author	4		15	12	
Holton, Linwood	Governor	7			15	Governor VA
Holyoake, Keith, Sir	Head of State	45	95	125	50	NZ Prime Minister, Gov. General
Home, A. Douglas-	Head of State	45	70	150	135	Br. Prime Minister
Homer, Louise	Entertainment	20			45	Opera. Am Contralto
Homer, Winslow	Artist	235	480	1100		Remarkable
Seascapes,Landscapes						
Homesteaders, The	Country Music	25			50	
Homma, Masaharu	Military	75	205	340	180	Jap.Gen.Invasion of Philippines
Homolka, Oscar	Entertainment	25	30	50	55	
Honnegger, Arthur	Composer	45	130	290	50	AMusQS $575
Hood, Alexander Sir 1758-1798	Military	55	135	245		Accompanied Capt. Cook
Hood, John Bell	Civil War	685	1625		1000	CSA General
Hood, Samuel, Sir 1762-1814	Military	35	80	135		Br. Adm. with Lord Nelson
Hood, T. 'Tom' (Younger)	Author	15	30	70		
Hood, Thomas (Elder)1799-1845	Author	40	140	275		Br. Humorist, Poet
Hooft, W.A. VIsser't	Clergy	15	20	25	20	
Hooker, John Lee	Entertainment	20			50	Jazz Musician
Hooker, Joseph M.	Civil War	180	400	675		Union Gen. ALS/Content $4,500
Hooks, Benjamin L.	NAACP	5	15	25	10	NAACP Exec. Director
Hooper, Dennis	Entertainment	20			50	
Hooper, William	Revolutionary War	450	1300	7260		Signer Decl. of Indepen.
Hooper, William Henry	Senate/Congress	10	15	35	30	MOC UT 1859
Hooten, Ernest A.	Science	25	65	140		Am. Anthropologist.Harvard Prof
Hoover, Herbert	President	95	230	3100	340	Content TLS $2,500
Hoover, Herbert (As Pres)	President	375	490	3000	500	Historic TLS/Content $7,500
Hoover, J. Edgar	Criminologist	40	190	220	110	Director of F.B.I. for 48 Years
Hoover, Lou Henry	First Lady	60	185	245	250	
Hope, Bob	Entertainment	10		50	55	
Hopf, Hans	Entertainment	25			65	Opera
Hopkins, Anthony	Entertainment	20		45	50	
Hopkins, Bo	Entertainment	5	6	10	10	
Hopkins, Claude	Entertainment	30			60	Pianist-Bandleader-Composer
Hopkins, Frederick G., Sir	Science	45	120	200		Nobel Medicine 1929
Hopkins, Johns	Business	175	500	3250		Financier, Philanthropist
Hopkins, Mark 1802-87	Educator	40	105	255		Inspired Teacher, Lecturer
Hopkins, Miriam	Entertainment	35	40	75	110	
Hopkins, Samuel 1750-1819	Revolutionary War	90	280	530		Officer Cont'l Army.
Hopkins, Stephen	Revolutionary War	250	690	750		Signer Decl. of Indepen.
Hopkinson, Francis	Revolutionary War	250	1015	1365		Signer, Author, Composer
Hopkinson, Joseph 1770-1842	Judge-Author	90	200			MOC PA. "Hail Columbia"
Hopper, DeWolf	Entertainment	20	40	50	85	Major Stage Star for 50 Years
Hopper, Dennis	Entertainment	25			55	
Hopper, Hedda	Entertainment	15		30	35	
Hordern, Michael, Sir	Entertainment	10	20	35		
Horenstein, Jascha	Entertainment	60			375	Conductor
Horina, Louise	Entertainment	15			45	Opera

NAME	CATEGORY	SIG	LS/DS	ALS	SP	COMMENT
Hormel, Jay C.	Business	45	95		60	Chm. George A. Hormel & Co.
Hornberger, H. Richard	Author	20	30	45	25	
Horne, L. Donald	Business	5			10	CEO Mennen Co.
Horne, Lena	Entertainment	10	25		35	Afro-Am Film & Record Vocalist
Horne, Marilyn	Entertainment	15			40	Opera, Concert
Horner, H. Mansfield	Business	5			10	Aircraft Exec.
Horner, Henry	Governor	10			20	Governor IL
Horowitz, David	Celebrity	3	7	16	5	
Horowitz, Vladimir	Entertainment	65	150		250	Piano Virtuoso
Horrocks, Gen. Sir Brian	Military	15	25	40	25	Cmdr. XIII Corps WW II
Horsford, Eben N. 1818-74	Science	15	25	60		Am. Analytical Chemist
Horsley, Lee	Entertainment	6	8	15	19	
Horthy, Miklos, Adm.1868-1957	Head of State	55	190	485	150	Hungarian Admiral & Politician
Horton, Edw. Everett	Entertainment	20	25	65	75	
Horton, Edward A.	Clergy	15	20	25		
Horton, Peter	Entertainment	8	11	40	30	
Horton, Robert	Entertainment	3	3	6	15	
Hosmer, Titus 1736-80	Revolutionary War	35	95	200		Continental Congress. Judge
Hotchkiss, Benjamin J.	Inventor-CW			995		Union Arms Supplier
Houdini, Harry (E.Weiss)	Entertainment	800	1550	1785	2285	Am. Magician, Escape Artist
Hough, Lynn Harold	Clergy	15	20	35		
Houghton, Katharine	Entertainment	27			30	
Hounsfield, Godfrey	Science	20	30	40	25	Nobel Medicine
House, Edw. M.'Colonel'	Diplomat	35	100	310	45	Confidant of Pres. Wilson
Houseman, John	Entertainment	20			45	
Housman, Alfred Edward	Author	65	225	495		Br. Poet, Scholar
Houssay, Bernando A., Dr.	Science	65	135	250	100	Nobel Medicine 1947. Activist
Houston, David	Country Music	5			10	
Houston, George	Senate	35	85			Civil War Senator AL
Houston, Sam	Military	620	1750	4275		Pres. TX, Soldier, Statesman
Houston, Temple	Lawyer-Outlaw	375		1750		Son of Sam Houston
Houston, V. S. K.	Senate/Congress	10	25	40		MOC HI 1927
Houston, Whitney	Entertainment	35			75	Singer
Hovey, Alvin	Civil War	25	55	70		Union Gen., Gov. IN
Hovhaness, Alan	Composer	70		375		Noted for Orchestral Works
Hovis, Larry	Entertainment	5			15	
How, William Walsham, Bishop	Clergy	15	20	25		
Howard, Curley	Entertainment	400	500	900	1000	
Howard, Edward, Cardinal	Clergy	35	50	75		
Howard, James H.	Aviation	15	30	55	45	ACE, WW II, CMH; Flying Tiger
Howard, John	Entertainment	15	20	40	38	
Howard, Ken	Entertainment	6	8	15	15	
Howard, Leslie	Entertainment	200			440	
Howard, Moe	Entertainment	200		650	450	
Howard, Oliver Otis	Civil War	120	185	285	270	Union Gen. CMH
Howard, Robert, Sir 1626-98	Author	95	325			Br. Restoration Dramatist/Dryde
Howard, Ron	Entertainment	10		40	35	
Howard, Shemp	Entertainment	200	220	400	595	
Howard, Sidney	Author	50	175	375	75	Am. Playwright. Pulitzer
Howard, Trevor	Entertainment	10			35	
Howard, Willie	Entertainment	8	9	20	18	
Howe, Albion P.	Civil War	30	55	80		Union General
Howe, Elias	Science	200	400	900		Invented Sewing Machine
Howe, James Wong	Entertainment	10			30	Award Winning Cinematographer
Howe, Julia Ward	Author	85	150	275		"Battle Hymn" AQS $1,475-$3000
Howe, Richard, Earl	Revolutionary War	100	285	580		Br. Adm. Fought in Am. Rev. War

NAME	CATEGORY	SIG	LS/DS	ALS	SP	COMMENT
Howe, Samuel Gridley	Humanitarian-Mil.	10	35	80		Philanthropist, Doctor, Clergy
Howe, William, Sir	Revolutionary War	200	850			Cmdr-in-Chief Br. Forces in Am.
Howell, C. Thomas	Entertainment	5		25	20	
Howells, William Dean	Author	25	75	245		Novelist, Critic, Editor
Howes, Barbara	Author	7	10	20	10	
Howland, Beth	Entertainment	5	6	15	15	
Howley, William	Clergy	10	10	15		
Howlin, Olin	Entertainment	20			40	
Hoxie, Al	Entertainment	20			35	
Hoxie, Jack	Entertainment	20			50	
Hoyle, Edmond 1671-1769	Author	130	675	820		Card Games. Established Rules
Hoyt, John W.	Governor	50	85			Gov. WY Terr.,1st Pres. U.WY
Hruska, Roman	Senate & Congress	5	15			MOC, Senator NE
Hubbard, Elbert	Author	50	160	275	145	Roycrofters,"Message to Garcia"
Hubbard, Gardiner G.	Celebrity	25	55	170		Fndr. Nat'l Geographic Society
Hubbard, L. Ron	Author	100	600			Religious Activist
Hubble, Edwin P.	Science	15	80			Am. Astronomer.
Hubel, David H., Dr.	Science	20	30	45	25	Nobel Medicine
Huber, Oscar, Fr.	Celebrity	20		30		
Hubley, Adam	Revolutionary War	75	300			Officer Cont. Army. Politician
Huddleston, George	Senate/Congress	10	20		15	MOC AL 1915-1937
Hudson, George	Financier	10	20	35		Controlled 1,000 Miles Railrd
Hudson, Rochelle	Entertainment	25	30	50	45	
Hudson, Rock	Entertainment	25	30	80	65	
Huemer, Dick*	Cartoonist	15			100	Disney Artist
Huerta, Victoriano	Revolutionist	75	250	625	120	Mex. General, Politician.Exiled
Hufstedler, Shirley	Cabinet	5	10	15	10	Sec'y Education
Hug-Messner, Regula	Aviation	15	30	50	35	
Huger, Benjamin	Civil War	70	150			CSA General
Huger, Isaac 1742-97	Revolutionary War	100	215	450		General Continental Army
Huggins, Charles, Dr.	Science	25			35	Nobel Medicine
Huggins, Roy	Entertainment	15			25	TV Producer "Fugitive"
Huggins, William, Sir	Science	35	100	210	45	Br.Astron. Stellar Spectroscope
Hughes, Charles E. (SC)	Supreme Court	40	210		235	Chief Justice, Sec'y of State
Hughes, Chas. E. & Court	Supreme Court				4500	
Hughes, Edwin H., Bishop	Clergy	20	25	40	35	
Hughes, Howard	Business	1500	2450	7250	2500	Hughes Aircraft, Oil Tool. RKO
Hughes, Hugh Price	Clergy	15	20	25	20	
Hughes, Langston	Author	240	525			Poet, Short Story Writer
Hughes, Mary Beth	Entertainment	9	10	20	15	
Hughes, Richard	Military-Rev. War	25	60			Br. Adm. during Rev. War
Hughes, Richard J.	Governor	5	15			Governor NJ
Hughes, Rupert	Author	15	50	95		Poet, Author, Historian
Hughes, Thomas	Author	40		110		"Tom Brown's School Days"
Hughes. Sarah T.	Law	10	20	30	15	Swore In L.B. Johnson 1963
Hugo, Victor	Author	245	350	1175	525	Novelist-Politician-Poet
Huidekoper, Henry	Civil War	60				Union Col., "Bucktails"
Hull, Cordell	Cabinet	50	150		125	Nobel, Father Fed.Income Tax
Hull, Henry	Entertainment	25	30		65	
Hull, Isaac	Military	190	490	565		Cmdr. "Constitution"
Hull, J.E.	Military	25				General
Hull, Josphine	Entertainment	150		200	275	
Hull, Warren	Entertainment	25			45	
Hull, William	Military	145	370	770		Revolutionary War Gen.
Hulse, Tom	Entertainment	9	10	20	25	
Humbard, Rex	Clergy	10	15	15	15	

NAME	CATEGORY	SIG	LS/DS	ALS	SP	COMMENT
Humboldt, Alexander, Baron von	Science	70	125	300		Ger. Naturalist and Traveller
Hume, Benita	Entertainment	10			25	
Hume, Joseph 1777-1855	Politician	10	30	80		Br.Physician.Radical Politician
Hume, Mary-Margaret	Entertainment	5			12	Pin-Up SP $20
Humes, William Young C.	Civil War	140	235	435		CSA General
Hummel, Johann Nepomuk	Composer	60	190	400		Child Prodigy Piano Virtuoso
Humperdinck, Engelbert	Composer	95	225	375	250	AMusQS $450-$675
Humperdinck, Engelbert	Entertainment	5	7	20	25	Contemporary Vocalist
Humphrey, George M.	Cabinet	10	20			Sec'y Treasury
Humphrey, Hubert H. (V)	Vice President	35	100		45	
Humphrey, Muriel	Senate/Congress	10	20		15	Senator MN
Humphreys, Andrew A.	Civil War	85	180	255		
Humphreys, David	Revolutionary War	55	150	200		ADC Washington. Poet,Diplomat
Hunnicutt, Arthur	Entertainment	15			35	
Hunt, E. Howard	Gov't Official	15	25	90	25	21 Yr. Vet./CIA. Watergate
Hunt, Earl, Bishop	Clergy	20	25	35	25	
Hunt, George W. P.	Governor					Governor AZ
Hunt, H. L.	Business	90	310	580	175	TX Oil King. Arch Conservative
Hunt, Helen	Entertainment	10			35	
Hunt, Henry J.	Civil War	70		100		Union Gen. Artillery Gettysburg
Hunt, James B. Jr.	Governor	5	10			Governor NC
Hunt, James Bunker	Business	5	15	35	10	Son of Oil Magnate H.L.Hunt
Hunt, John, Sir	Celebrity	10	20	50		
Hunt, Linda	Entertainment	10	15		50	
Hunt, Marsha	Entertainment	8	9	19	20	
Hunt, Nelson Bunker	Business	8	20	40	15	Son of Oil Magnate H.L.Hunt
Hunt, Pee Wee	Entertainment	15			30	Trombone-Vocalist
Hunt, WIlliam Morris	Artist	50	215	500		American Portraitist
Hunt, Ward (SC)	Supreme Court	65	80	175		1872
Hunt, Washington	Governor	30		60		MOC 1842, Governor NY 1850
Hunt, William H.	Cabinet	15	30	60	25	Sec'y Navy 1881
Hunt, William Holman	Artist	55	165	330		Br. Pre-Raphaelite Painter
Hunter, David	Civil War	55	130	170	250	Union General
Hunter, Holly	Entertainment	20			55	
Hunter, Jeff	Entertainment	25	35	65	60	
Hunter, Kim	Entertainment	5	6	15	15	
Hunter, R. M. T.	Civil War	95	170	250		CSA Sec'y State. US Senator VA
Hunter, Rachel	Cover Girl	20			45	Pin-Up SP $100
Hunter, Robert	Revolutionary War	220	508	1035		Br. Gen. Colonial Gov. VA,NY
Hunter, Tab	Entertainment	8	9		35	
Hunter, William 1774-1849	Diplomat	55	80	125		Statesman, Senator RI
Huntington, Benjamin	Revolutionary War	60	175	280		Continental Congress
Huntington, Collis P.	Business	85	200			Pioneer Am. Railroad Builder
Huntington, Daniel	Artist		155	250		Portrait Painter
Huntington, Ebenezer	Revelutionary War	110	250	380		Statesman, Army General
Huntington, Henry E.	Business	65	125	200		Railroad Magnate
Huntington, Jabez W.	Senate/Congress	25	30	45		MOC 1829, Senator CT 1840
Huntington, Jedediah	Military	60	125	230		Gen. Revolutionary War
Huntington, Samuel	Revolutionary War	190	850	1225		Signer Decl. of Indepen.
Hunton, Eppa	Civil War	115	285			CSA General
Huppert, Isabelle	Entertainment	15			35	
Hurd, Peter	Artist	85	225	370		
Hurlbut, Stephen A.	Civil War	45	105			Union Gen., MOC
Hurley, Charles F.	Governor	12	25			Governor MA
Hurley, Patrick	Cabinet	15	46	60	25	Sec'y War
Hurst, Fannie	Author	15	45	70	40	Popular, Sentiment Novels

NAME	CATEGORY	SIG	LS/DS	ALS	SP	COMMENT
Hurt, John	Entertainment	9	10	20	30	
Hurt, Mary Beth	Entertainment	6	8	15	15	
Hurt, William	Entertainment	20	25	50	60	
Husa, Karel	Composer	15	30	65		Pulitzer, AMusQS $150
Husky, Ferlin	Country Music	5			15	
Hussein, King	Royalty	70	135	385	80	King of Jordan
Hussey, Olivia	Entertainment	5	8	12	15	
Hussey, Ruth	Entertainment	4	6	12	15	
Huston, Anjelica	Entertainment	8			40	
Huston, John	Entertainment	30		50	65	Film Director-Actor
Huston, Walter	Entertainment	100		170	225	
Hutchence, Michael	Entertainment	20			50	
Hutchins, Will	Entertainment	10	15		15	
Hutchinson, Frederick Sharpe	Civil War	35		130		Union General
Hutchinson, John W.	Composer	15		50		
Hutchinson, Josephine	Entertainment	10	15	25	25	
Hutchinson, Thomas	Colonial	185	450			Royal Gov. MA. Exiled
Hutton, Betty	Entertainment	8	9		18	Pin-Up SP $20
Hutton, Gunilla	Country Music	5			10	
Hutton, Ina Ray	Entertainment	20			45	All Girl Big Band
Hutton, Jim	Entertainment	40	70	110	100	
Hutton, Lauren	Entertainment	9	10	20	25	Pin-Up SP $25
Hutton, Robert	Entertainment	20	40	110	100	
Hutton, Timothy	Entertainment	9	10	20	25	
Huxley, Aldous	Author	65	200	400		Br. Novelist.TLS/Content $1,200
Huxley, Julian Sorell	Science-Author	30	60	175		Br. Biologist
Huxley, Thomas Henry	Science	55	150	255		Br. Biologist
Hyams, Leila	Entertainment	20	25	50	40	
Hyde, Arthur W.	Cabinet	7	15	30	10	Sec'y Agriculture 1929
Hyde, Edgar R.	Clergy	10	10	15		
Hyde-White, Wilfrid	Entertainment	15	15	35	35	
Hyer, Martha	Entertainment	6	8	15	15	Pin-Up SP $15
Hylton, Lord	Politician	7	15	25		Chief Whip Unionist Party
Hyman, Earle	Entertainment	5			10	Afro-Am. Actor
Hynde, Chrissie	Entertainment	25			40	Rock
Hyndman, Henry Mayers	Socialist	75		350		Br. Marxist-Socialist

I

NAME	CATEGORY	SIG	LS/DS	ALS	SP	COMMENT
Iacocca, Lee A.	Business	15	50		35	CEO Chrysler Motors
Ian, Janis	Entertainment	10	40		20	
Ibert, Jacques-Francois	Composer	75		325		AMusQS $450
Ibsen, Henrik	Author	205	600	1250	1500	Nor. Poet & Dramatist

NAME	CATEGORY	SIG	LS/DS	ALS	SP	COMMENT
Ickes, Harold L.	Cabinet	15	35	60	25	Roosevelt Sec'y Interior
Idol, Billy	Entertainment	10			25	Rock
Iglesias, Julio	Entertainment	15			50	
Ihlefedl, Herbert	Aviation	25	55		60	
Ikeda, Hayato	Head of State	15		65		Japan
Iman	Model	25			60	Model
Imboden, John Dan'l	Civil War	145	225	310		CSA Gen.
Immelmann, Max	Aviation	200	425	700	500	ACE, WW II, 1st German Ace
Impellitteri, Vincent	Celebrity	3	10	25	5	
Ince, John	Entertainment	40			125	
Ince, Ralph	Entertainment	40			125	
Ince, Thomas H.	Entertainment	40			125	Film Dir. Civil War Epics
Indiana, Robert	Artist	45	95	170	120	
Ingalls, John James	Senate/Congress	10	15			Senator KS
Inge, William	Author	55	120	180		Am. Playwright. Pulitzer
Inge, William R.	Clergy	50	80	150		Dean St. Paul's Cath., Writer
Ingels, Marty	Entertainment	10			35	
Ingersoll, Charles J. 1782-1862	Senate/Congress	15	25	40		MOC PA 1813
Ingersoll, Charles R.	Governor	5	15	25		Governor CT
Ingersoll, Jared	Revolutionary War	75	200	450		Continental Congress
Ingersoll, Robert Green	Civil War	30	60	85	40	Agnostic Lecturer, Orator
Ingersoll, Robert H.	Business	80	175	300	225	Ingersoll $1 Watch
Ingham, Samuel D.	Cabinet	35	70	145		Sec'y Treasury 1829
Ingle, Red	Entertainment	15			25	
Ingle, Robert P.	Business	5	15	25	10	Ingles Grocery Chain
Ingram, Rex	Entertainment	50			125	
Ingram, Rex	Entertainment	100			300	Vintage Afro-Am. Actor
Ingres, Jean-Auguste-Dominique	Artist	205		1050		Fr. Leader Among Classicists
Ingrid, Victoria (Fred. IX)	Royalty	15	40			
Ink Spots, The (4)	Entertainment	85			200	Vintage Singing Group
Inman, Henry	Artist	110	305	650		American Portraitist
Inman, Jerry	Country Music	10			20	
Innes, Roy	Celebrity	7	15		10	
Inness, George 1824-94	Artist	75	180	405		Content ALS $950
Inouye, Daniel K.	Senate	5			15	Senator HI
Inskeep, Jonathan	Revolutionary War	80	175			
Insull, Samuel	Financier	65	95	185		Pvt. Sec'y Thos. Edison
Ionesco, Eugene	Author	35	125	195		Fr. Dramatist.Theatre of Absurd
Ireland, Jill	Entertainment	25			60	Pin-Up SP $75
Ireland, John	Entertainment	10			35	
Ireland, Kathy	Cover Girl	10			25	Pin-Up SP $50
Irish, James M.	Military	10	30	50		
Irons, Jeremy	Entertainment	8		25	30	
Irvine, James 1735-1819	Revolutionary War	55	130	250		Gen. Militia. Cmdr. Fort Pitt
Irvine, William 1741-1804	Revolutionary War	55	160	300		Gen., Continental Congress
Irving, Amy	Entertainment	9	10	20	25	
Irving, Clifford	Author	16	60	124	25	
Irving, Henry, Sir	Entertainment	35	60	105	70	Vintage Actor-Manager
Irving, John	Author	5	15	29	10	Am."The World According to Garp
Irving, Washington	Author	110	385	885		"Rip Van Winkle"
Irwin, David	Celebrity	10	20	45	15	
Irwin, James B.	Astronaut	50	125	350	150	Deceased Moonwalker
Irwin, May	Entertainment	25		35	45	Vintage Stage. 1st Film Kiss
Isabella I, Of Castile	Royalty	850	3250	6500		Queen Spain.Columbus' Patron
Isabella II	Royalty	145	405	730		Spain. Strife, Intrigue
Ish Kabibble	Entertainment	15			25	Novelty Singer, Kay Kyser Band

NAME	CATEGORY	SIG	LS/DS	ALS	SP	COMMENT
Isherwood, Christopher	Author	38	140	225	300	Br. Novelist, Playwright
Ishiguro, Kazuo	Author	15			35	"Remains of the Day"
Ismay, Hastings Lionel	Military	20	35	60		Churchill Chief-of-Staff WW II
Israels, Jozef	Artist	55	180	350		Dutch. Hague School Genre Art
Ito, Hirobumi (Prince)1841-1909	Statesman	55	140			Japan. Prime Minister 1886
Ivan IV, The Terrible	Royalty	35000				No Current Price
Ives, Burl	Entertainment	10	30		25	
Ives, Charles E.	Composer	250	1250	1500	425	Tonal Experimentation. Pulitzer
Ivey, Judith	Entertainment	10			35	
Ivins, Marsha S.	Astronaut	5			15	
Ivogun, Maria	Entertainment	45			175	Opera
Izak, Edouard	Military	20	45			WW II CMH

J

NAME	CATEGORY	SIG	LS/DS	ALS	SP	COMMENT
Jabotinsky, Vladimir	Zionist	45	120	310	60	Zionist Leader WW I
Jacks, L.P.	Clergy	15	20	45		
Jackson, Alan	Country Music	10			30	
Jackson, Alfred Eugene	Civil War			950		CSA General
Jackson, Andrew	President	450	3710	4660	250	
Jackson, Anne	Entertainment	6	8	15	15	
Jackson, Glenda	Entertainment	10	20		30	
Jackson, Helen Hunt	Author	12	35	50	25	Am.Novelist, Poet. "Ramona"
Jackson, Henry M. "Scoop"	Senate/Congress	5	15			MOC, Senator WA
Jackson, Howell E. (SC)	Supreme Court	50			110	U.S. Senator 1881, Supr.Ct.1893
Jackson, James C., Dr.	Science	7	12		10	
Jackson, Janet	Entertainment	25			70	Rock
Jackson, Jesse	Clergy	20	65	80	55	
Jackson, Joe	Entertainment	20			35	
Jackson, Kate	Entertainment	10	15	25	20	
Jackson, LaToya	Entertainment	20		45	50	Pin-Up SP $150
Jackson, Mahalia	Entertainment	90			175	Gospel Singer
Jackson, Maynard	Entertainment	5	10	20	15	Trumpet
Jackson, Michael	Entertainment		800		340	
Jackson, Rachel	First Lady	575				
Jackson, Robert H. (SC)	Supreme Court	50	295		125	Chief Prosecutor at Nuremberg
Jackson, T.J. "Stonewall"	Civil War	2350	9730	10300		CSA-War Date ALS $27,500 + -
Jackson, Thomas	Clergy	25		40		
Jackson, Victoria	Entertainment	5			10	
Jackson, Wanda	Country Music	10			20	
Jackson, William 1759-1828	Revolutionary War	120	350	750		Gen. Washington Aide. Diplomat
Jackson, William Henry 1843-1942	Photographer	40	110			Indians, Union Pac. RR Route
Jackson, Wm. Hicks 'Red'	Civil War	90	185	240		CSA General
Jacob, Francois	Science	20	30	55	30	Nobel Medicine 1965
Jacob, John C.	CORE	10	15		15	Afro-Am. Leader CORE
Jacob, John J.	Governor	12	20			Governor WV

NAME	CATEGORY	SIG	LS/DS	ALS	SP	COMMENT
Jacobi, Derek	Entertainment	5		12	15	
Jacobi, Lou	Entertainment	5			15	
Jacobs, Josef	Aviation	30	40	80	55	
Jacobs, Lou	Entertainment	50	100		100	Clown
Jacobsen, Fritz	Aviation	10	20	35	25	
Jacquet, "Illinois" Jean	Entertainment	35			70	Jazz Sax, Bandleader
Jadlowker, Hermann	Entertainment	95			245	Opera
Jaeckel, Richard	Entertainment	4	5		15	
Jaeger, James A.	Aviation	10		30		
Jaehnert, Erhard	Aviation	5	10	20	15	
Jaffe, Sam	Entertainment	25			55	Gunga Din
Jagger, Bianca	Entertainment	10			25	
Jagger, Dean	Entertainment	15	25	30	35	
Jagger, Mick	Entertainment	50			145	
Jahn, Sigmund	Astronaut	15			35	
Jakes, John	Author	5			20	
James I & VI (Eng)	Royalty	800	1450	4475		
James II (Eng)	Royalty	530	1175	1700		
James, Daniel, Jr. "Chappie"I	Military	20	35	85	45	AF Gen. 1st Black 4 Star Gen.
James, Etta	Entertainment	20			40	Rock
James, Frank	Outlaw	775	2100	4100		
James, Harry	Entertainment	20		40	45	Big Band Leader-Trumpet
James, Henry 1811-82	Author	75		200		Theological & Social Scholar
James, Henry 1843-1916	Author	110	360	1315		Novelist, ALS/Content $5,500
James, Manley	Miitary	10		45		WW I Victoria Cross
James, Sonny	Country Music	10			30	
James, Thomas L.	Cabinet	15	25	45		P.M. General 1881
James, Will	Author	75	250	410	750	Illustrated own Western Novels
James, William	Science	90	250	470	125	Psychologist, Pragmatist
Jan & Dean	Entertainment	20			45	Rock
Janis, Conrad	Entertainment	5			12	
Janis, Elsie	Entertainment	25		50	55	Stage, Screen Comedienne
Janney, Leon	Entertainment	35			75	Member Original "Our Gang"
Jannings, Emil	Entertainment	150			375	1st Academy Award Winner
Janowitz, Gundula	Entertainment	10			35	Opera
Jansen, Marie	Entertainment	15			40	Opera
Janssen, David	Entertainment	50	55	75	90	
January, Lois	Entertainment	4	5	10	15	
Jardine, William	Cabinet	10	25	55	20	Sec'y Agriculture 1925
Jarman, Claude, Jr.	Entertainment	10			35	
Jarman, Maxie	Business	15			55	Jarman Shoes
Jaroff, Serge	Entertainment	5	6	15	15	Jaroff Ballet
Jarreau, Al	Entertainment	20			40	
Jarrett, Art	Entertainment	5			10	Jazz Vocalist
Jarriel, Tom	Entertainment	4	10	15	10	TV News
Jarvik, Robert, Dr.	Science	12	35	60	35	Inventor Artificial Heart
Jarvis, Anna M.	Promoter	65	175			Campaigned for "Mother's Day"
Jarvis, Gregory B.	Astronaut	100	600		275	
Jarvis, Howard	Tax Reformer	5	12	30	15	Sponsor Proposition 13
Jason, Sybil	Entertainment	5	6	15	15	
Javits, Jacob J.	Senate/Congress	5	20		25	MOC 1947, Senator NY 1957
Jaworski, Leon	Law	10	20	45	15	Dir.Watergate Prosecution Force
Jay, James, Sir	Science	90	275	400		Phys. to G. Washington,Inventor
Jay, John (Grandson)	Diplomat	15	25	40		Active Opposition to Slavery
Jay, John (SC)	Supreme Court	390	1785	2500		ALS at Auction $6,600
Jean, Gloria	Entertainment	5		20	25	

NAME	CATEGORY	SIG	LS/DS	ALS	SP	COMMENT
Jean, Norma	Country Music	10			20	
Jeans, James, Sir	Science	12	30	65	20	Br. Physicist, Astron., Author
Jedlichka, Ernest	Entertainment	45			200	Rus-Pol Pianist
Jeffers, Robinson	Author	65	295	450	90	Prize Winning Poet, Dramatist
Jeffers, William M.	Business	25	70	135	50	Union Pacific RR
Jefferson Airplane	Entertainment	125			300	Rock-The San Francisco Sound
Jefferson, Charles E.	Clergy	20	25	40		
Jefferson, Joe	Entertainment	25	70	125	65	Am.Vintage Actor
Jefferson, Martha Wayles	First Lady					Rare. Only 2 Known
Jefferson, Thomas	President	2585	8100	18010		Content ALS's $101,000-$200,00
Jefferson, Thomas & Madison,James	President		8000			Special Doc. S $30,000
Jefferson, Thomas (As President)	President	4000		20000		
Jeffreys, Anne	Entertainment	10	12	15	25	
Jellicoe, John R.	Military	20	65	120	50	Br.Adm.WW I,P.M. New Zealand
Jenckes, Joseph 1656-1740	Colonial Am.	90	250	520		Colonial Governor RI
Jenkins, "Butch"	Entertainment	10			25	
Jenkins, Allen	Entertainment	25			45	
Jenkins, Thornton Alex.	Military	10	25	35		Chief-of Staff Farragut Squad.
Jenner, Bruce	Entertainment	3	3	6	6	Olympic Decathlon Winner
Jenner, Edward	Science	325	850	1950		Smallpox Vaccination
Jenner, William E.	Senate	10	20			Senator IN
Jenner, William, Sir	Science	35	110	295		Phys. to Queen Victoria
Jennings, Al	Celebrity	450		308		
Jennings, Peter	Entertainment	5	15	35	15	Broadcast Journalist, Anchor
Jennings, Waylon	Country Music	10			20	
Jennison, Ralph D.	Business	10	35	45	20	
Jenrette, John W. Jr.	Senate/Congress	5	20		10	Congressman SC
Jenrette, Rita	Entertainment	4	6	15	10	Pin-Up SP $25
Jensen, Karen	Entertainment	4	4	9	10	
Jepson, Helen	Entertainment	10			40	Opera, Concert
Jergens, Adele	Entertainment	5	6	10	10	
Jeritza, Maria	Entertainment	25			125	Opera, Operetta, Films
Jernigan, Tamara E.	Astronaut	8			20	
Jernstedt, Ken	Aviation	10	25	40	30	ACE, WW II, Flying Tigers
Jerome III, Wm. Travers	Education	20	40		35	Pres. Bowling Green
Jerome, Jerome K.	Author	35	70	95		Humorist, Playwright
Jerusalem, Siegfried	Entertainment	15			40	Opera
Jessel, George	Entertainment	10	80		15	
Jesup, Thomas S.1788-1860	Military	45	125	190		Gen. LS/Content $950
Jesup, William H.	Military	5	15	25		
Jeter, Michael	Entertainment	5			20	
Jethro Tull	Entertainment	30			75	
Jethro, Homer and	Country Music	30			125	
Jett, Joan	Entertainment	20			50	Rock
Jewell, Marshall	Governor-Cabinet	40	75	195		ALS/Cont. $400
Jewett, Sarah Orne	Author	45		300		New England Life & Folklore
Jewison, Norman	Entertainment	5			20	Film Director
Jillian, Ann	Entertainment	6	8	15	20	Pin-Up SP $25
Jimenez, Enrique A.	Head of State	8	15	25	10	Panama
Jimenez, Marcos P.	Head of State	10	25	50	15	Venezuela
Joachim, Joseph	Composer	70	150	275	150	Hung.ViolinistAMusQS $250-$575
Jodl, Alfred	Military	150	435	550	250	Chief-of-Staff To Keitel WW I
Joel, Billy	Composer	15			55	Singer, Songwriter
Joffre, Joseph Jacques Cesaire	Military	65	155	250	225	Marshal of France WW I
Johann, Zita	Entertainment	15			35	
John II, (King Castile) 1406-1454	Royalty	4700	6000			Patron of Literature & Arts

NAME	CATEGORY	SIG	LS/DS	ALS	SP	COMMENT
John XXIII, Pope	Clergy	595			650	Angelo Giuseppe Roncalli
John of Austria (Don John)	Royalty	150				1629-1679
John, Augustus	Artist	50	135	330		Welch. Portraits, Landscapes
John, Elton	Entertainment	70	130	225	95	Br. Singer-Songwriter
Johns, Glynis	Entertainment	15	15	30	30	
Johns, Jasper	Artist	20	90		30	Am. Pop Artist
Johnson, Amy (Mollison)	Aviation	70	85	135	200	Br. Aviation Pioneer
Johnson, Andrew	President	460	1570	7000	2500	ALS/Content $19,500
Johnson, Art	Aviation	10	22	38	30	ACE, WW II, USAAF Ace
Johnson, Ben	Entertainment	8	10	19	20	
Johnson, Ben 1572-1637	Author	450	1500			Br. Poet, Playwright
Johnson, Betty	Entertainment	3	3	6	6	
Johnson, Bradley T.	Civil War	75	265	270		CSA Gen.,ALS/Content $4,500
Johnson, Bunk	Entertainment	200			550	Jazz Trumpet
Johnson, Bushrod Rust	Civil War	115	300			CSA General
Johnson, Cave	Cabinet	50	110	195		P.M.Gen. 1st US Postage Stamps
Johnson, Chic	Entertainment	30			55	(Olsen & Johnson)
Johnson, Crockett*	Cartoonist	50			500	Barnaby
Johnson, Don	Entertainment	15			40	
Johnson, Eastman	Artist	40		180		Am. Portrait & Genre Artist
Johnson, Eliza M.	First Lady	750	1500			
Johnson, Fred*	Cartoonist	10			35	Moon Mullins
Johnson, Gerald	Aviation	15	30	50	40	ACE, WW II
Johnson, Harold K.	Military	12	35	50	30	WW II. Prisoner. 4 Star Gen.
Johnson, Henry A.	Business	5			15	CEO Spiegel Inc.
Johnson, Herschel	Civil War	40	110			Gov. GA, CSA Senator
Johnson, Hiram W.	Senate	25	60			Senator CA
Johnson, Howard B.	Business	80				Howard Johnson Inns
Johnson, Howard S.	Business	12	30		24	
Johnson, Hugh S.	Cabinet	20	90	150	25	Gen., Administrator NRA
Johnson, James "Johnnie"	Aviation	30	65	120	85	ACE, WW II, Br. RAF Top Ace
Johnson, James K.	Aviation	10	25	38	32	ACE, Korea, Double Ace
Johnson, James Weldon	Author	30	100	225		NAACP, Spingarn Medal
Johnson, Jesse G.	Military	35	85	170		Adm. WW II
Johnson, Jonathan Eastman	Artist	25	150			Am. Portrait, Genre Painter
Johnson, Keen	Governor	5	15		10	Governor KY
Johnson, L.B. & Johnson, Lady Bird	Pres.-1st Lady				600	
Johnson, Lady Bird	First Lady	40	105		95	
Johnson, Leon W.	Military	10	20	35		
Johnson, Louis	Cabinet	10	45	55	20	Sec'y Defense 1949
Johnson, Lyndon B.	President	165	435	3365	550	TLS as Pres. $1,250
Johnson, Lynn	Cartoonist	7			25	For Better Or Worst
Johnson, Lynn-Holly	Entertainment	5	7	12	15	
Johnson, Martin	Explorer-Photogr.	15	40			With Osa, Wild Animal Films
Johnson, Nunnally	Author	15	75		40	Am. Playwright
Johnson, Oliver	Celebrity	5	15	30		
Johnson, Osa	Explorer-Photogr.	15	15	35	30	With Martin, Wild Animal Films
Johnson, Philip	Architect	25			125	Early Skyscrapers
Johnson, Reverdy	Cabinet	20	50	95		Statesman, Att'y Gen.
Johnson, Richard L.	Aviation	15	20	30	20	
Johnson, Richard M. (V)	Vice President	70	200	300		Van Buren Vice Pres.
Johnson, Robert S.	Aviation	20	25	45	80	ACE, WW II, #5 US
Johnson, Russ	Entertainment	3	3	6	6	
Johnson, Samuel C.	Business	5			10	Pres. Johnson's Wax
Johnson, Samuel, "Dr.Johnson"	Author	1750	4080			Lexicographer, Critic
Johnson, Van	Entertainment	7			20	

NAME	CATEGORY	SIG	LS/DS	ALS	SP	COMMENT
Johnson, William B.	Business	5			10	CEO Railway Express
Johnson, William Cost	Senate/Congress	10	20	35		MOC MD 1833
Johnson, William Samuel	Revolutionary War	130	375	675		Continental Congress
Johnston, Albert Sidney	Civil War	260	620	1730		CSA Gen.,TX Sec.War DS $9500
Johnston, Harriet Lane	Acting First Lady	200		625		Buchanan's Niece
Johnston, J. Lawson	Business	15	35	60		
Johnston, Johnny	Aviation	20	45		55	
Johnston, Joseph E.	Civil War	240	600	1000		CSA ALS/Cont $6,000-12,000
Johnston, Lynn*	Cartoonist	20			75	For Better or Worse
Johnston, Mary	Astronauts	5			15	
Johnston, Olin D.	Senate/Congress	5	15			Senator SC 1945
Johnston, Richard M.	Author	5	10	20		
Joliot-Curie, Irene	Science	40		205		
Jolley, I. Stanford	Entertainment	20			50	
Jolson, Al	Entertainment	150	485		460	
Jones, Allan	Entertainment	10	15	35	30	
Jones, Anne	Country Music	10			20	
Jones, Annisa	Entertainment	150			325	
Jones, Anson	Am. Politician	350		1200		Physician, Pres. Texas Repub.
Jones, Anthony Armstrong	Country Music	10			20	
Jones, Bob	Clergy	15	25	60	25	
Jones, Buck	Entertainment	200	230	300	350	
Jones, Carolyn	Entertainment	30	35	65	75	
Jones, Casey	Aviation	45	90	175	150	
Jones, Chuck*	Cartoonist	25			175	Animator
Jones, Claude A.	Military	40	65			
Jones, David (Davy)	Entertainment	7			40	"The Monkies"
Jones, Dean	Entertainment	9	10	20	25	
Jones, Dick	Entertainment	10			35	
Jones, E. Stanley	Clergy	35	50	75	50	
Jones, Edward F.	Civil War	50	110	155	150	Union Gen.
Jones, George	Country Music	10			25	
Jones, Grace	Entertainment	10	15	30	30	Pin-Up SP $75
Jones, Grandpa	Country Music	5			12	
Jones, Gwyneth	Entertainment	15			40	Opera
Jones, Henry	Entertainment	5			15	
Jones, Howard	Entertainment	10			20	
Jones, Isham	Entertainment	15			40	Vintage Big Band
Jones, J. Carey	Military	20	45			Admiral WW II
Jones, Jack	Entertainment	5			10	
Jones, James	Author	50	240			"..Here To Eternity"
Jones, James Earl	Entertainment	10			20	
Jones, Janet	Entertainment	10	15	28	30	Pin-Up SP $30
Jones, Jennifer	Entertainment	150	225		275	
Jones, Jenny	Entertainment	10			20	TV Host
Jones, Jesse H.	Cabinet	5	10	15	10	Sec'y Commerce 1940
Jones, Jim	Clergy	250	375	650	850	
Jones, John Marshall	Civil War	225	650			CSA General
Jones, John Paul	Military-Rev. War	5000				Naval Hero
Jones, John Percival	Senate/Congress	10		25		Senator NV 1873
Jones, L.Q.	Entertainment	5			15	
Jones, Louis R.	Military	10	30			
Jones, Maj. Gen. David M.	Astronaut	10			20	
Jones, Marcia Mae	Entertainment	5	6	15	15	
Jones, Mary H. 'Mother'	Labor	60	195	430		Agitator, Speaker, Organizer
Jones, Quincy	Composer	12	20	35	30	AMusQS $50

NAME	CATEGORY	SIG	LS/DS	ALS	SP	COMMENT
Jones, Rickie Lee	Entertainment	20			35	
Jones, Samuel	Civil War	90	375			CSA General
Jones, Samuel Porter	Clergy	20	25	35		
Jones, Shirley	Entertainment	10	30		25	Pin-Up SP $30
Jones, Spike	Entertainment	25			65	Big Band Leader
Jones, Thomas	Astronaut	7			15	
Jones, Thomas V.	Business	15	30		25	
Jones, Tom	Entertainment	8	9	19	20	
Jones, Tommy Lee	Entertainment	20			35	
Jones, William E. "Grumble"	Civil War	110	315			CSA General
Jong, Erica	Author	10	12	20	15	Best Selling Bawdy Autobiograph
Jongkind, Johan 1819-1891	Artist	200	450	860		Dutch.Master of Rendering Light
Jonson, Ben 1572-1637	Author	2850				Br. Playwright, Poet
Jope, Bernhard	Aviation	10	25	40	30	
Joplin, Janis	Entertainment	500	600	900	1000	
Joplin, Scott	Composer	650	980	2000		Rag Time Composer
Jordan, Barbara	Senate/Congress	12			30	Afr-Am.Congresswoman TX
Jordan, Dorothy	Entertainment	15	15	35	30	
Jordan, Hamilton	Gov't Official	5	15	20	15	Chief of Staff Carter Admin.
Jordan, Jim (Fibber)	Entertainment	15	20	35	25	
Jordan, Louis	Entertainment	20			50	Big Band Leader
Jordan, Thomas	Civil War	135	255	350		CSA General
Jordan, Vernon	Cabinet	5	16			
Jordon, Richard	Entertainment	10		15	20	
Jorgensen, Christine	Celebrities	10	20	45	30	1st To Undergo Sex Change
Jorn, Carl	Entertainment	30			85	Opera
Jory, Victor	Entertainment	30	40		90	
Joseffy, Raphael	Entertainment	25			125	Pianist, Pupil of Llszt
Joseph II 1741-1790	Royalty	125	350	875		King Ger. & Holy Roman Empire
Josephine, Empress	Royalty	1200	1510	2400		Fr. Wife of Napoleon
Joslyn, Allyn	Entertainment	25			55	
Joswig, Wilhelm	Aviation	10			30	
Jouett, James	Civil War	25	55	125		Union Naval Officer/Farragut
Jouhaux, Benjamin 1879-1954	Reformer	25	60	140	50	Nobel Peace Prize 1951
Jourdan, Jean B., Count	Napoleonic Wars	55	260	290		Marshal of Napoleon
Jourdan, Louis	Entertainment	9	10	20	25	
Journey	Entertainment	25			50	
Jowett, Benjamin	Scholar	10	22	35		One of Greatest Teachers
Jowett, Charles	Clergy	15	20	25		
Joy, Leatrice	Entertainment	12			30	
Joyce, Alice	Entertainment	15	25		60	Silent Star
Joyce, Elaine	Entertainment	4	4	9	12	
Joyce, James	Author	400	590	2875		Ir. Novelist, Poet, Playwright
Joyce, Richard	Military	40	100	175		
Juan Carlos, King	Royalty	55	120	245	150	Spain
Juarez, Benito 1806-1872	Head of State	350	2950		1500	Pres. Mexico. Revolutionary
Judd, Naomi & Wynona	Country Music	20			40	
Judd, Walter H.	Senate/Congress	10	15			Congressman MN
Judge, Arline	Entertainment	15	15	35	30	
Julian, George	Woman Suffrage	15	30	75		One Founder of Free Soil Party
Juliana, Queen	Royalty	100	250	710	150	Netherlands
Jump, Gordon	Entertainment	5	6	15	15	
Jung, Karl Gustav	Science	510	1950	3400		Swiss Psychiatrist-Psychologist
Junkers, Hugo	Science	50		355		Ger. Airplane Engineer-Designer
Junot, Andache,Duc Abrantes	Military	70	235			Fr. Gen., Sec'y to Napoleon
Junot, Jean Androche	Fr. Revolution	30	90	185		

NAME	CATEGORY	SIG	LS/DS	ALS	SP	COMMENT
Jurgens, Curt	Entertainment	15			40	
Jurgens, Dick	Entertainment	20			45	Big Band Leader
Justice, Bill*	Cartoonist	25			250	The Chipmunks
Justin, A.G.	Civil War	10	25			CW Gov. PA

K

NAME	CATEGORY	SIG	LS/DS	ALS	SP	COMMENT
Kabaiwanska, Raina	Entertainment	10			35	Opera
Kabalevsky, Dmitri	Composer	32	100	233		
Kadar, Janos	Head of State	50	130			
Kafka, Franz	Author	850		16400		Ger. Novelist. Visionary Tales
Kahn, Julius	Senate/Congress	5	15			MOC CA 1899
Kahn, Madeline	Entertainment	5	6	15	15	
Kahn, Otto H.	Business	25	50	95	30	Banker, Philanthropist, Arts
Kahn, Yahya	Head of State	30			50	Pakistan
Kahoutek, Lubos	Science	5	15	30	15	Am. Astronomer
Kai-Shek, Chiang	Head of State	100	220	450	450	Republic of Charles
Kai-Shek, Mayling Soong	Head of State	50	120		100	Madame Chiang
Kaiser, Henry J.	Industrialist	90	150		225	S.F.Bay Bridge.Grand Coulee Dam
Kalakaua, David	Royalty	100	425	775	450	King Hawaii
Kaltenborn, H. V.	Radio	5	15	30	15	Radio Commentator
Kaltenbrunner, Ernst	Military	150	500		175	Perpetrator of Nazi Atrocities
Kamehameha II, Liholiho 1797-1824	Royalty	960		3850		King Hawaii
Kamehameha III, Kauikeaouli	Royalty	750	1585			King Hawaii
Kaminsky, Max	Entertainment	10			30	Dixieland Jazz Bandleader
Kamio, Mitsuomi	Military	110		225		
Kammhuber, Josef	Aviation	20	30	65	25	
Kanaly, Steve	Entertainment	6	8	15	20	
Kander, John	Composer	5	20	35	10	
Kandinski, Vasili	Artist	200	715			Rus. Painter, Designer
Kane, Bob*	Cartoonist	100			1150	Batman
Kane, Carol	Entertainment	10	12	20	25	
Kane, Elisha Kent	Explorer	95	215	450		Grinnell Arctic Expedition
Kane, Helen	Entertainment	25			60	Boop-Boop-a-Doop Girl
Kane, Richard	Military	20			90	
Kane, Thomas L.	Civil War	48	105	160		Union Gen.
Kangaroo, Captain	Entertainment	5	6	15	25	
Kanin, Garson	Author	10	20	50	45	Playwright, Director, Screen.
Kansas	Entertainment	30			60	
Kant, Immanuel 1724-1804	Author	1005	3950	7375		Ger. Philosopher, Professor
Kantor, MacKinlay	Author	15	30	65	25	"Andersonville", Pulitzer
Kantrowitz, Adrian, Dr.	Science	25	70	145	30	
Kantrowitz, Arthur, Dr.	Science	15		30		
Kaper, Bronislaw	Composer	10	30	55	15	

NAME	CATEGORY	SIG	LS/DS	ALS	SP	COMMENT
Kaplan, Gabe	Entertainment	5			15	
Kappel, Frederick R.	Business	3	6	15	8	
Karas, Anton	Composer	25	40	85	100	
Karloff, Boris	Entertainment	250	415	500	650	
Karman, Theodore von	Industrial	25	60	110	50	Designer Karman-Ghia VW
Karns, Roscoe	Entertainment	30			75	
Karpis, Alvin "Creepy"	Criminal	65	195	300	100	30's Public Enemy #1
Karras, Alex	Entertainment	5	6	15	15	
Karsavina, Tamara	Entertainment	50			300	Rus.-Br. Dancer
Karsh, Yousuf	Photographer	35	90	225	70	Portraits, Royalty,World Famous
Kasavubu, Joseph	Head of State	20	75	185	40	1st Pres. Dem. Repub. of Congo
Kasem, Casey	Entertainment	5	8		12	Disc Jockey
Kasem, Jean	Entertainment	5	8		15	
Kasha, Al	Composer	15			45	
Kashfi, Anna	Entertainment	10		30	35	
Kassebaum, Nancy Landon	Senate	5	15		15	Senator KS
Kastler, Alfred, Dr.	Science	15	35		40	Nobel Physics 1966
Katchinsky, Victorin	Aviation	20			45	
Katz, Bernard, Sir	Science	15	30	45	35	Nobel Medicine 1970
Katzenbach, Nicholas	Cabinet	10	20		15	Att'y General 1965
Katzenberg, Jeffrey	Business	15	20			Disney CEO
Katzir, Ephraim	Head of State	10			35	Pres. Israel
Kaufman, Andy	Entertainment	25			60	
Kaufman, George S.	Author	30	85	175	35	Dramatist, Critic, Director
Kaunda, Kenneth	Head of State	40	150	350	70	1st Pres. Zambia
Kawato, Masajiro "Mike"	Aviation	40	100		150	Ace WW II, Downed Boyington
Kay, Beatrice	Entertainment	10			20	
Kay, Dianne	Entertainment	3	3	6	6	
Kay, Mary (Ash)	Business	5	15	30	10	Cosmetics Empire
Kaye, Celia	Entertainment	4	5	10	12	
Kaye, Danny	Entertainment	35			65	
Kaye, Sammy	Entertainment	15			40	Big Band Leader
Kaye, Stubby	Entertainment	10			25	
Kazan, Elia	Entertainment	10	10	20	25	Director, Producer, Author
Keach, Stacy	Entertainment	8	9		20	
Kean, Jane	Entertainment	5	6	15	12	
Keane, Bil*	Cartoonists	10			45	The Family Circus
Keane, Edward	Entertainment	10			25	
Kearny, Philip	Civil War	360	650	850		Union General
Kearny, Stephen	Military-Governor	85	195	380		War of 1812, 1st Gov. of CA
Keating, Kenneth B.	Senate/Congress	5	15		10	Gen. WW II, MOC Senator 1947-65
Keaton, Buster	Entertainment	180	225		400	Great Film Comedian
Keaton, Diane	Entertainment	10			65	
Keaton, Michael	Entertainment	10			45	As "Batman" SP $75
Keble, John	Clergy	75	125	350		
Kedrova, Lila	Entertainment	10	15	25	25	
Keeble, John	Author	10	30	75		
Keel, Howard	Entertainment	5	6	25	30	
Keeler, Ruby	Entertainment	25			55	
Keene, Carolyn	Author	5	15	30	10	Publisher Pseud.(5 Authors)
Keene, Charles S.	Entertainment	10			25	
Kefauver, Estes	Senate	15	40		35	Senator TN
Keifer, Joseph W.	Civil War	25	45	60		Union Gen.& Speaker
Keillor, Garrison	Author	15	25	35	20	Humorist
Keirstead, Wilfred C.	Clergy	10	15	20	15	
Keisha	Model	5			15	Pin-Up SP $25

NAME	CATEGORY	SIG	LS/DS	ALS	SP	COMMENT
Keitel, Harvey	Entertainment	10			25	
Keitel, Wilhelm	Military	350	600	1500	650	Ger. Fld. Marshal WWII
Keith, Arthur, Sir	Author	10		35		Anthropologist, Origins of Man
Keith, Brian	Entertainment	5	8	15	20	
Keith, David	Entertainment	5	6	15	10	
Keith, George Keith E., Viscount	Military	45	135	155		Br. Admiral. 1746-1823
Keith, Rosalind	Entertainment	10			75	
Keith, William, 1680-1749	Revolutionary War	135		700		Colonial Lt. Governor PA & DE
Kekkonen, Urho	Head of State	15	45			Finland
Kelcey, Herbert	Entertainment	10			20	Vintage Stage Actor
Kelland, Clarence Buddington	Author	20	55	150	30	Am. Novelist, Short Stories
Kellar, Harry	Entertainment	15			35	Vintage Stage Actor
Kellard, Ralph	Entertainment	10			25	
Kellaway, Cecil	Entertainment	25			75	
Keller, Helen	Author	195	425	2100	875	Blind, Deaf, Mute Author
Keller, Helen & A. Sullivan	Author-Teacher	535			1750	
Kellerman, Annette	Entertainment	45		165	175	Aussie Dancer & Swimming Star
Kellerman, Sally	Entertainment	10			25	
Kellerman,FC,Duke Valmy	Military	75	285	405		7 Years' War. Marshal of Nap.
Kelley, Clarence M.	Celebrity	5	15	35	20	
Kelley, Deforest	Entertainment	10	15	25	35	
Kelley, Kitty	Author	12			20	Celebrity Biography
Kelley, Patrick Henry	Senate/Congress	5	10		10	MOC MI 1913
Kellogg, Charlotte	Philanthropist	7	20			Mrs. Vernon Kellogg
Kellogg, Frank B. 1856-1937	Cabinet	20	50	95	35	Nobel Peace Prize 1929
Kellogg, John Harvey, Dr.	Food Business	15	30	75		Became W.K. Kellogg Co.
Kellogg, W. K.	Business	110	150	325	200	Fndr. W.K. Kellogg Co.
Kellogg, William P.	Senate/Congress	50				U.S. Senator 1868, Gov. LA 1873
Kelly, Emmett, Sr.	Entertainment	60	150		325	Circus Clown
Kelly, Gene	Entertainment	15	15	35	40	
Kelly, Grace (as actress)	Entertainment	200	325	1500	400	
Kelly, Howard A., Dr.	Science	20	35	60	40	Orig. Faculty Johns Hopkins U.
Kelly, Jack	Entertainment	15			45	
Kelly, John H.	Civil War	475	975			CSA Gen., Youngest Killed
Kelly, Nancy	Entertainment	10	20		25	
Kelly, Patsy	Entertainment	28	35	65	60	
Kelly, Paul	Entertainment	25			55	
Kelly, Paula	Entertainment	5		12	15	Pin-Up SP $18
Kelly, Thomas W.	Military	10	20		15	Gen. Desert Storm
Kelly, Walt*	Cartoonists	50			425	Pogo
Kelsey, Linda	Entertainment	5	6	15	15	
Kelton, Pert	Entertainment	15			45	
Kelvin, William T., Lord	Science	75	195	300	175	Kelvin Scale, Atlantic Cable
Kemble, E.W.*	Artist-Cartoonist	25			250	Am. Illustrator Huck Finn, etc.
Kemble, Frances A."Fanny"	Entertainment	20	75	90		
Kemp, Hal	Entertainment	15			40	Big Band Leader
Kemp, Jack	Cabinet	15			25	Sec'y HUD
Kemper, John M.	Celebrity	3	7	15	10	
Kendal, Madge	Entertainment	10			25	
Kendall, Amos	Cabinet	20	50	95		Jackson P.M. General,Journalist
Kendall, Cy	Entertainment	25			50	
Kendall, Edward C., Dr.	Science	30	55	100	35	Nobel Medicine 1950
Kendall, Henry W.	Science	20	35		30	Nobel Physics 1990
Kendall, Paul	Military	10	30			
Kendren, John C.	Science	15	20	30	20	
Keneally, Thomas	Author	10			20	"Schindler's List"

NAME	CATEGORY	SIG	LS/DS	ALS	SP	COMMENT
Kenellopoulos, Panayotis	Head of State	15	35	90		Greece
Kennan, George F.	Author	15	45			Am.Diplomat, Historian.Pulitzer
Kennedy, Anthony M.	Supreme Court	30			50	
Kennedy, Arthur	Entertainment	30	40	95	75	
Kennedy, Edgar	Entertainment	125			250	
Kennedy, Edward M."Ted"	Senate	35	55	150	90	Senator MA 1962
Kennedy, Ethel	Celebrity	15	50	75	35	Mrs. Robert Kennedy
Kennedy, George	Entertainment	5	6		40	
Kennedy, George C.	Aviation	45			250	
Kennedy, Gerald, Bishop	Clergy	25	40	50	40	
Kennedy, Jacqueline	First Lady	280	785	1995	550	
Kennedy, Jacqueline (As 1st Lady)	First Lady	850	1350	2650		
Kennedy, Jayne	Entertainment	6	8	15	15	
Kennedy, John F.	President	900	3000	7500	4000	TLS/Cont. As Pres.$19,500
Kennedy, John F., Jr.	Attorney	25			50	
Kennedy, John P.	Cabinet	35	50	95		Fillmore Sec'y Navy 1852
Kennedy, Joseph P.	Business	75	165	300	120	Boston Financier, Father of JFK
Kennedy, Joseph Patrick II	Congress	15	30		70	MOC MA 1987
Kennedy, Madge	Entertainment	10			30	
Kennedy, Martin John	Senate/Congress	5	15			MOC NY 1930-45
Kennedy, Robert F.	Cabinet	175	605		835	Att'y Gen. Brother of JFK
Kennedy, Rose Fitzgerald	Celebrity	25	165	200	50	Kennedy Family Matriarch
Kennedy, Tom	Entertainment	50			125	
Kenney, George	Military	25	60	110	40	USAAF Gen. WW II
Kenny, Bill	Entertainment	25			75	Leader of Ink Spots
Kenny, Elizabeth, Sister	Science	175			275	Pioneer Polio Treatment
Kent, A. Atwater	Inventor	20	45	90	35	Radio Mfg., Philanthropist
Kent, E.A., Duke of	Royalty	15	75			
Kent, J. Ford	Military	90	195			Gen., Took San Juan Hill
Kent, Jack	Cartoonist	10			35	King Aroo
Kent, James 1763-1847	Revolutionary War	80	140	250		Legal Reporting System
Kent, Rockwell	Artist	35	170	300	75	Am. Landscape, Figure Painting
Kent, Walter	Composer	40	105			AMusQS $200(Be Home for Xmas)
Kent, William	Senate/Congress	5	12		10	MOC CA 1911
Kenton, Simon 1755-1836	Pioneer	420	1350			Hunter, Trader, Spy, General
Kenton, Stan	Entertainment	35			100	Big Band Leader-Pianist
Kenyatta, Jomo	Head of State	125	220	525	150	Prime Min. Kenya
Kenyon, Doris	Entertainment	15	25	45	45	
Kenyon, William S.	Senate/Congress	10	15	35		MOC NY 1859
Kepford, Ira	Aviation	15	30	48	42	ACE, WW II
Kepner, Wm. E.	Military	15	35	60	25	
Keppel, Francis	Celebrity	5	15	20	15	
Keppler, Joseph 1838-1894	Publisher	15		45		Founder "Puck" Magazine
Kerbs, Edwin G., Dr.	Science	20	30	55	35	Nobel Medicine
Kercheval, Ken	Entertainment	5			25	
Kerensky, Alexander	Head of State	205	850	1250	475	Rus. Revolutionary Politician
Kern, Jerome	Composer	450	875	2100	2250	AMusQS $685-$2,500
Kern, Paul B., Bishop	Clergy	20	25	35	25	
Kernan, Francis	Senate/Congress	10		35		MOC 1863, Senator NY 1875
Kerns, Joanna	Entertainment	5		10	15	
Kerouac, Jack	Author	290	650	895		Representative Beat Generation
Kerr, Clark	Celebrity	5	10	20	10	
Kerr, Deborah	Entertainment	8	9	20	25	Pin-Up SP $35
Kerr, Robert S.	Senate/Congress	5	15		10	Senator, Gov. OK
Kerr, Ruth	Business	25	35	150	100	Kerr Glass Co.
Kerrigan, J. Warren	Entertainment	25			60	

NAME	CATEGORY	SIG	LS/DS	ALS	SP	COMMENT
Kerry, Robert	Senate	10			20	Senator
Kershaw, Joseph Brevard	Civil War	160		390		CSA General
Kerwin, Joseph P.	Astronaut	7			25	
Kesey, Ken	Author	30	40	55	30	"One Flew Over the Cukoo's...."
Kesselring, Albrecht	Military	95	525		175	Ger. Field Marshal WW II
Kestnbaum, Meyer	Business	20	30		25	Pres. Hart, Schaffner & Marx
Ketchum, Hank*	Cartoonist	20			55	Dennis The Menace
Kettering, Charles F.	Inventor	100	160	325	125	Engineer. Sloan-Kettering Inst.
Kevorkian, Jack, Dr.	Science	25			150	Euthanasia. "Dr. Death"
Key, David M. 1824-	Cabinet	15	25	35		P.M. General. CSA Officer
Key, Francis Scott	Lawyer-Author	500	825	1275		Special ADS $2,500
Key, Philip Barton 1857-1815	Senate/Congress	10	30	40		MOC MD 1807
Key, Ted*	Cartoonist	10			75	Hazel
Keyes, Erasmus	Civil War	47	120	275		Union General
Keyes, Evelyn	Entertainment	15			90	SP in GWTW Costume $75
Keyes, Irwin	Entertainment	4			10	Character Actor
Keyes, Roger J.B.1st Baron	Military	15	30	55	25	Br. Adm.Fleet. Boxer Rebellion
Keynes, John Maynard	Economist	75	680	585	230	Br. Economist-Author
Keys, Ancel	Science	5	15	30	10	
Keys, Henry W.	Governor	10	20	35		Governor NH
Keyser, Ralph S.	Military	30	55			
Keyserling, Hermann	Philosopher	15	35	60	50	Ger. Social Philosopher
Khalid, King	Royalty	20	65	135	60	Saudi Arabia
Khambatta, Persis	Entertainment	10		30	25	
Khan, Chaka	Entertainment	15			30	
Khan, Mohammad Ayub	Head of State	30	95			
Khanh, Nguyen, Gen.	Head of State	20	60	175	35	
Khatchaturian, Aram	Composer	150		675	650	AMusQS $300, $575, $625
Khomeini, Ruhollah, Ayatollah	Religious Leader	500				Iranian Moslem Leader
Khorana, Har G., Dr.	Science	15	25	45	20	Nobel Medicine 1968
Kiam, Victor	Business	10	25		15	Remington Electric Razor Co.
Kibbee, Guy	Entertainment	20			40	
Kidder, Margot	Entertainment	10			25	Pin-Up SP $30
Kidman, Nicole	Entertainment	20			45	
Kiel, Richard	Entertainment	5			15	
Kielmansegg, Graf J.A.	Military	15			35	Gen. German Army
Kiepura, Jan	Entertainment	30			125	Opera, Concert
Kilban, B.*	Cartoonist	10	25		100	Cat Cartoons, The New Yorker
Kilbride, Percy	Entertainment	100			350	
Kilby, J. S. "Jack"	Science	15	35	60	30	Inventor of Micro Chip
Kiley, Richard	Entertainment	6	8	15	20	
Kilgore, Harley, M.	Senate/Congress	5	15		15	Senator WV 1941
Kilgore, Merle	Country Music	10			20	
Kilham, Hannah	Clergy	50	75	100		
Kilian, Victor	Entertainment	10		20	25	
Killinger, John W.	Senate/Congress	10	15	30		MOC PA 1859
Kilmer, Joyce	Author	205	550			Poet. "Trees"
Kilpatrick, Hugh Judson	Civil War	120	245	355	415	Union Gen. Cavalry
Kimball, Dan	Cabinet	20	30	40	25	Sec'y Navy. Aerojet General
Kimball, Spencer W.	Clergy	25	25	35	30	Morman Leader
Kimball, Ward	Cartoonist	25			75	Musician-Discny Cartoonist
Kimberly, John W., 1st Earl	Statesman	20	30	110		Br.Colon'l Sec'y. Kimberly S.A.
Kimberly, R. Lewis	Civil War	25	40	50		Union General
Kimbrough, Emily	Author	10	20	45	15	"Our Hearts Were Young & Gay"
Kimmel, Husband E.	Military	70	165	250	150	US Adm. Cmdr.At Pearl Harbor
Kindelberger, James H. "Dutch"	Business	45			75	Pres. No. American Aviation

NAME	CATEGORY	SIG	LS/DS	ALS	SP	COMMENT
Kindermann, K. B.	Aviation	5	10	15	10	
King, Alan	Entertainment	5	6	15	15	
King, B.B.	Entertainment	20			70	R & B Singer, Guitarist
King, Ben E.	Composer	10			25	"Stand by Me"
King, Cammie	Entertainment	15		35	30	GWTW
King, Carole	Entertainment	15			25	
King, Charles	Entertainment	20			50	
King, Charles	Civil War	50		175		Soldier-Author
King, Coretta Scott	Celebrity	20	40	95	20	Mrs. Martin Luther King, Jr.
King, Edward J., Bishop	Clergy	25	35	50		
King, Ernest J.	Military	30	100		125	Fleet Adm. WW II
King, Frank*	Cartoonist	35			165	Gasoline Alley
King, Henry	Entertainment	30			75	Film Director
King, Horatio 1811	Cabinet	40	175			P.M. General 1861
King, John 'Dusty'	Entertainment	20	30	45	55	
King, John Alsop	Governor	10		35		Gov. NY, a Founder Repub. Party
King, Larry	Celebrities	10	20	35	15	Talk Show Host
King, MacKenzie	Head of State	25	55	90	55	Prime Minister Canada
King, Martin Luther, Jr.	Clergy	1150	1535	2600	1750	Advocate Peaceful Nonviolence
King, Martin Luther. Sr.	Clergy	35	45	60	65	
King, Pee Wee	Country Music	5			15	
King, Perry	Entertainment	6	8	15	18	
King, Preston	Senate/Congress	15	45	105		MOC 1843, Senate NY 1849
King, Rodney	Celebrity	100				Afro-Am. L.A. Vicitim
King, Rufus	Revolutionary War	250		355		Continental Congress
King, Rufus	Civil War	35	100			Union General
King, Stephen	Author	95	125	175	70	Master of Horror and Suspense
King, Thomas Starr	Clergy	25	35	95	40	
King, Walter Woolf	Entertainment	12		25	35	
King, Wayne	Entertainment	15			20	Big Band Leader
King, William R. (V)	Vice President	200	340			Pierce VP. Died after 45 days
Kingman, Dong	Artist	25	50	100		
Kingsford-Smith, Charles	Aviation	45	250		200	FDC Trans-Tasman Fl. $175
Kingsley, Ben	Entertainment	9	10	20	25	
Kingsley, Charles 1819-75	Author-Clergy	45	95	150		Br. Novelist, Clergyman
Kingston, William H.	Author	25		100		Br. Boy's Adventure Books
Kinks	Entertainment	40			85	
Kinsey, Alfred C., Dr.	Science	140	230	375	95	Am. Sexologist Researcher
Kinskey, Leonid	Entertainment	7			25	
Kinski, Klaus	Entertainment	20		35	45	
Kinski, Natassia	Entertainment	15	20	90	40	
Kinstler, E.R.*	Cartoonist	10			150	Illustrator
Kintner, Robert	Business	5	10	30	10	
Kip, William I., Bishop	Clergy	50	85	125		
Kipling, Rudyard	Author	170	995	825	1500	Nobel Lit., Novelist, Poet
Kiplinger, Austin	Business	10	20	45	15	Kiplinger Washington Newsletter
Kipnis, Alexander	Entertainment	35	75		120	Opera
Kirby, George	Entertainment	5			15	
Kirby, Jack*	Cartoonist	25			170	Captain America
Kirby, Rollin*	Cartoonist	20			90	
Kirby-Smith, Edmund	Military	65	185	295		CSA General
Kirk, Claude Jr.	Governor	7	15			Governor FL
Kirk, Eddie	Country Music	10			20	
Kirk, Florence	Entertainment	10			30	Opera
Kirk, George	Aviation	10	22	38	30	ACE, WW II
Kirk, Phyllis	Entertainment	20		95	45	

NAME	CATEGORY	SIG	LS/DS	ALS	SP	COMMENT
Kirk, Tommy	Entertainment	10			20	
Kirkby-Lunn, Louise	Entertainment	30			95	Opera
Kirkconnell, Clare	Entertainment	4	5	9	10	
Kirkham, Ralph W.	Civil War	27	55	75		Union General
Kirkland, Lane	Labor	8	15	30	15	Labor Leader. AFL-CIO
Kirkland, Sally	Entertainment	5			20	
Kirkpatrick, Jean J.	Cabinet	12		25	20	Ambassador U.N.
Kirkwood, Joe, Jr.	Entertainment	45	75	150	100	And Golfer
Kirkwood, Samuel J.	Cabinet	15	25	55	30	Sec'y Intertior, Gov,Senator IA
Kirman, Richard, Sr.	Governor	10		30		Governor NV
Kirsten, Dorothy	Entertainment	20			50	Am. Soprano, Opera, Concert
KISS	Entertainment	35			125	Rock
Kissinger, Henry A.	Cabinet	20	125		50	Sec'y State
Kistiakowsky, G.B., Dr.	Science	40	135			Nobel Chemistry
Kitchener, Horatio H. of Khartoum	Military	85	205	335	200	Ir.-born Br. Field Marshal
Kitt, Eartha	Entertainment	10			25	Pin-Up SP $25
Kittinger, Joe	Aviation	25	45			
Kittredge, Walter	Composer	30				"Tenting Tonight..."AMQS $300
Kleber, Jean-Baptiste	Fr. Revolution	145	410	855		One of France's Greatest Gen'ls
Klee, Paul	Artist	205	615	1850		Swiss Surrealist Painter
Klein, Calvin	Business	5	15	35	25	Fashion-Accessory Designer
Klemperer, Otto	Entertainment	50			170	German Conductor
Klemperer, Werner	Entertainment	15	25		25	
Kleppe, Thomas S.	Cabinet	5	15	30	10	MOC ND, Sec'y Interior
Klerk, F.W. de	Head of State	75	150		90	Nobel Peace, Pr.Minister S.A.
Klimt, Gustav 1862-1918	Artist	165	575	1250		Austrian. Allegorical Murals
Kline, Kevin	Entertainment	10	12	45	35	
Kluge, Hans Gunther von	Military	75		250		Ger. Gen.l WW II, Suicide
Klugman, Jack	Entertainment	10			25	
Klutznick, Philip M.	Cabinet	5	12		8	Sec'y Commerce
Kmentt, Waldemar	Entertainment	10			30	Opera
Knern, H.H.*	Cartoonist	25			180	Katzenjammer Kids
Knibb, William	Clergy	45	60	75		
Knievel, Evel	Celebrity	5	15	35	30	Daredevil Motorcycle Rider
Knight, Fuzzy	Entertainment	50			150	
Knight, Gladys	Entertainment	15	15	35	40	Rock
Knight, Goodwin J.	Governor	10	15		15	Governor CA
Knight, John S.	Business	10	35	45	20	Publisher
Knight, Jordan	Entertainment	10			45	
Knight, June	Entertainment	8	9	20	25	
Knight, Laura, Dame	Artist	60	140	200		
Knight, Phil	Business	20	30	45	25	Nike Athletic Shoes Etc.
Knight, Shirley	Entertainment	9	10	20	25	
Knight, Ted	Entertainment	15		35	35	
Knopf, Alfred A.	Business	7	20	35		Knopf Publishing
Knote, Heinrich	Entertainment	20			50	Opera
Knott, Walter	Business	150			475	Founder Knott's Berry Farm
Knott, Walter And Cordelia Knott	Business	25	70		75	Co-Founders Knott's Berry Farm
Knotts, Don	Entertainment	10			25	Self Sketch S $35
Knowland, William F.	Senate	10	20		25	Senator CA, Publisher
Knowles, James S.	Author	10	25	50		
Knowles, Patrick	Entertainment	10			25	
Knox, Alexander	Entertainment	10	15	30	30	
Knox, Elyse	Entertainment	15	20	35	35	
Knox, Frank	Cabinet	50	75	95	40	Sec'y Navy. TLS/Cont $275
Knox, Henry	Cabinet-Military	150	720	700		Rev. War Dte. ALS $4,500

NAME	CATEGORY	SIG	LS/DS	ALS	SP	COMMENT
Knox, James, Cardinal	Clergy	30	30	35	35	
Knox, Philander C.	Cabinet	12	25	70	30	Att'y Gen., Senator PA
Knudsen, William S.	Business	20	35	85	45	Pres. GM. WW II War Prod. Dir.
Knutson, Harold	Senate/Congress	5	10		10	MOC MN
Kobayashi, Takeji	Author	20		60	45	Proletarian Literary Movement
Koch, Edward I.	Political	10	20	35	15	Mayor NYC
Koch, Heinrich H. Robert	Science		1500	2259	1500	Nobel Bacteriology-Medicine'05
Koch, Howard W.	Entertainment	10			25	
Kodaly, Zoltan	Composer	125	290	685		
Koehl, Herman	Aviation	75			250	1st East-West Crossing Atlantic
Koehler, Armin	Aviation	10	20	35	25	
Koening, Walter	Entertainment	20			45	
Kohl, Hannelove	Celebrity	5			10	Mrs. Helmut Kohl
Kohl, Helmut	Heads of State	15	30	65	25	Chancellor Germany
Kohner, Susan	Entertainment	5			15	
Kokoschka, Oskar	Artist	100			275	PC Repro Painting S $180
Kolker, Henry	Entertainment	10			20	
Kollo, Rene	Entertainment	10		35	25	Opera
Komarov, Vladimir	Astronaut	125			190	
Konetzni, Anny	Entertainment	25			65	Opera
Kook, Abraham Isaac	Clergy	45	145			Palestinian Rabbi
Koontz, Dean	Author	25	65		70	Horror
Koop, C.Everett, Dr.	Military	7			20	Adm., US Surgeon General
Kopell, Bernie	Entertainment	5			15	
Koppel, Ted	TV News	10	15	30	20	
Korda, Alexander	Entertainment	40	45	90	85	
Koren, Edward*	Cartoonist	10			75	New Yorker Cartoonist
Korman, Harvey	Entertainment	5	6	15	15	
Kornberg, Arthur	Science	20	30	45	25	Nobel Medicine
Kornby, Arthur	Science	15		20		
Korngold, Erich W.	Composer	75	200	285	90	Opera, Orchestral, Film Scores
Korvin, Charles	Entertainment	4	4	9	10	
Kosciusko, Thaddeus	Revolutionary War	300	750	2500		Polish Patriot.
Kosleck, Martin	Entertainment	15			35	
Kossa, Frank R.	Military	7	9	12	10	
Kossuth, Lajos	Head of State	110	240	325	90	Hungarian Patriot
Kostal, Irwin	Composer	3	10	20	10	
Kostelanetz, Andre	Entertainment	15	25		25	Conductor
Koster, Henry	Entertainment	15	35		40	Film Director
Kosygin, Aleksei	Head of State	275	350	875	480	Premier of Soviet Union
Kovack, Nancy (Mehta)	Entertainment	4	4	9	10	
Kovacs, Ernie	Entertainment	200			400	
Kovansky, Anatol	Artist	15		40	25	
Kove, Martin	Entertainment	6	8	15	15	
Kowarski, L.	Science	10	25	60		
Kozky, Alex*	Cartoonist	10			20	Apt. 3-G
Kraft, Chris	Astronaut	15			25	
Kraft, James L.	Business	30	95	175	50	Founder Kraft Foods Co.
Kragen, Ken	Business	5	10	20	20	Entertainment Business Mgr.
Kral, Roy	Celebrity	10	25		15	
Kramer, Stanley	Entertainment	16	35		35	Film Producer, Director
Kramer, Stephanie	Entertainment	5			20	
Krantz, Judith	Author	25		40	35	Novelist
Kraus, Alfredo	Entertainment	15			35	Opera
Kraus, Clemens	Entertainment	65			220	Austrian Conductor
Kraus, Robert	Artist	10	25	50	25	

NAME	CATEGORY	SIG	LS/DS	ALS	SP	COMMENT
Krebs, Hans Adolf, Sir	Science	15	26	40	20	Nobel Medicine
Kreisler, Fritz	Composer	135	170	300	170	Violinist, AMQS $275
Kremer, Andrea	TV News	5			12	ESPN News
Krenek, Ernst	Composer	15	35	90	55	AMusQS $95-$225
Krenn, Fritz	Entertainment	15			35	Opera
Kreps, Juanita M.	Cabinet	4	10	15	12	Sec'y Commerce
Kresge, S. S.	Business	150	250	305	100	Kresge Stores
Kretschmer, Otto	Military	45	140		185	Highest Scoring U Boat Cmdr.
Kreutzer, Conradin	Composer	125	300	650		Ger. Composer/Conductor
Krige, Alice	Entertainment	4	4	9	10	
Kristel, Sylvia	Entertainment	20			45	
Kristofferson, Kris	Entertainment	10		35	30	
Kroc, Mrs. Ray (Joan)	Business	5	15	35	15	"McDonalds"
Kroc, Ray A.	Business	30	90	150	100	"McDonalds"
Krock, Arthur	Author	7	20	40	15	Bureau Chief,Columnist NY Times
Kroesen, Fred J.	Military	4	15	20	10	
Krol, John, Cardinal	Clergy	35	40	75	50	
Kropotkin, Peter A.	Revolutionist	30	75	180		Geographer, Philosopher
Krug, J. A.	Cabinet	10	20	30	15	Sec'y Interior
Kruger, Kurt	Entertainment	8	9	15	35	
Kruger, Otto	Entertainment	20			65	
Kruger, Paul	Head of State	75	350		175	Pres. So. Afr., Kruger Nat'l Pk
Kruger, Stephanus J.P.	Head of State	125	450			Krugerrand Named For Him
Krupa, Gene	Entertainment	35	195		75	Big Band Leader-Drums
Krupinski, Walter	Aviation	15	30	55	35	
Krupp, Alfred	Business	180	450	500		Founder Krupp Works
Krupp, Friedrich Alfred	Business	125	350			Arms Manufacturer
Kruschchev, Nikita S.	Head of State	300	410	550	450	Premier Soviet Union
Krylov, Ivan A.	Author	15	40	75	20	Russion Fabulist. Fables
Kubelik, Jan	Composer	40	115	240	225	Violinist, AMQS $200, $475
Kubitschek,Juscelino	Head of State	10	35	90	25	Brazil
Kubrick, Sidney	Entertainment	5	5	10	15	
Kubrick, Stanley	Entertainment	10			20	
Kuchta, Gladys	Entertainment	10			30	Opera
Kuhlman, Katherine	Clergy	35		50		Radio Evengelist
Kung, Hans	Clergy	35	50	75	60	
Kunstler, William	Law	10	25		15	Noted For Defense of Radicals
Kupka, Frantisek	Artist	110	225	450		Czech.Abstract Art, Illustrator
Kuralt, Charles	TV News	10	20	35	15	Commentator
Kusch, Polykarp, Dr.	Science	20	50		25	Nobel Physics
Kwan, Nancy	Entertainment	6	8	15	15	
Ky, Nguyen Cao	Head of State	30	100	250	75	
Kyne, Peter B.	Author	5	15	30	10	Homsey Family Novels
Kyser, Kay	Entertainment	15			30	Big Band Leader

L

NAME	CATEGORY	SIG	LS/DS	ALS	SP	COMMENT
L A Guns	Entertainment	15			40	Rock
L'Amour, Louis	Author	50	375	490	125	Novels Re The Old West
L'Enfant, Pierre Charles	Aviation	400	850	1500		
La Belle, Patti	Entertainment	15			35	Singer
La Forge, Frank	Composer	15			45	
La Marr, Barbara	Entertainment	300			800	
La Revelliere-Lepaux,L.	Fr. Revolution	25	70	145		Politician
La Rocque, Rod	Entertainment	20		45	55	
La Rue, Jack	Entertainment	10			25	
La Verne. Lucille	Entertainment	75			150	
LaDelle, Jack	Entertainment	3	3	6	6	
LaFarge, John	Artist	40	95	240		Am. Landscape & Figure Painter
LaFollette, Philip	Governor	15	35		20	Governor WI
LaFollette, Robert Jr.	Senate/Congress	10	25		20	Senator WI
LaFollette, Robert M.	Senate/Congress	35	95		40	Senator WI
LaFontaine, Henri Marie	International Law	10	20	30		Nobel Peace Prize
LaGuardia, Fiorello	Congress	20	90	145	175	Fiery Mayor NYC
LaLanne, Jack	Entertainment	10	15	30	25	TV Body Builder
LaMarck, Jean Baptiste de	Science	400	950	1050		Forerunner of Darwin
LaMarr, Hedy	Entertainment	35			65	
LaMartine, Alphonse de	Author	90	205	365		Fr. Poet-Statesman
LaMotta, Vikki	Celebrity	3		10	5	
LaPlace, P.M.,Marquis de	Science	535				Fr. Astronomer, Mathematician
LaRocca, D.J. "Nick"	Musician-Composer	50			225	AMusQS $250
LaRosa, Julias	Entertainment	5			10	Singer Arthur Godfey Show
LaRoushe, Lyndon, Jr.	Pres. Candidate	20		35	25	Tax Evader
LaRue, Lash	Entertainment	5	6	15	20	
Labouisse, Eve Curie	Science	15	45	90	35	
Lacepede, Bernhard de	Science	30	75	145		Fr. Naturalist & Politician
Laciura, Anthony	Entertainment	5			25	Opera
Ladd, Alan	Entertainment	60	85		160	
Ladd, Cheryl	Entertainment	8	9	20	20	Pin-Up SP $30
Ladd, Diane	Entertainment	5	6	15	15	
Ladd, Sue Carol	Entertainment	5	6	15	15	
Laemmle, Carl	Business	125	225	825	750	Film Pioneer, Founder Universal
Laennec, Rene T.H.	Science	3500	4000			Fr. Phys., Invented Stethoscope
Lafayette, Marquis de	Revolutionary War	400	1435	1650		Gilbert Motier
Lagerkvist, Pär F.	Author	30	70	175	100	Nobel Literature 1951
Lagerlöf, Selma	Author	95	305		125	Nobel Literature 1909
Lagge, James	Clergy	20	25	35		
Lahm, Frank	Aviation	35	75	140	90	
Lahr, Bert	Entertainment	225	340		450	Comedian, Cowardly Lion of OZ
Lahti, Christine	Entertainment	6	8	15	15	

NAME	CATEGORY	SIG	LS/DS	ALS	SP	COMMENT
Laidlie, D. A.	Clergy	15	20	25		
Laine, Frankie	Entertainment	5			15	
Laine, J.L.J.,Viscount	Fr. Revolution	30	85	175		
Laingen, Bruce	State Dept.	5			15	Iran Hostage
Laird, Melvin	Cabinet	7	20	25	15	Sec'y Defense
Lake, Arthur	Entertainment	15	25	50	35	
Lake, Simon	Science-Engineer	110	350	1225		Inv. Even-Keel Type Submarine
Lake, Veronica	Entertainment	100			255	
Lakes, Gary	Entertainment	10			30	Opera
Lamar, Joseph R. (SC)	Supreme Court	35	95	225		
Lamar, Lucius Q.C. (SC)	Supreme Court	125		235		CSA Officer
Lamar, Mirabeau B.	Head of State	95	300			Pres. Repub. of TX,Cavalry Cmdr
Lamas, Fernando	Entertainment	20	25	45	45	
Lamas, Lorenzo	Entertainment	9	10	20	25	
Lamb, Charles	Author	115	350	750		Br. Essayist, Critic
Lambert, Ray	Celebrity	5	14		10	
Lambert, William C.	Aviation	75	135	175	150	ACE, WW I, 2nd Leading Ace
Lamond, Frederic	Composer	20		100	100	Scot. Pianist & Composer
Lamont, Daniel S.	Cabinet	15	25	40		Sec'y War, Journalist, Politici
Lamont, Forrest	Entertainment	25			65	Opera
Lamont, Robert P.	Cabinet	25	60	95		Sec'y Commerce
Lamont, Thomas	White House	15	30	45		Lincoln Pvt. Sec'y
Lamont, Thomas S.	Business	8	25	40	10	Banker. Morgan Guaranty
Lamour, Dorothy	Entertainment	9	10	20	25	Pin-Up SP $25
Lampton, Mike	Astronaut	7			15	
Lamson, C.M.	Clergy	10	10	20		
Lana,Cosmo Gordon	Clergy	10	15	25		
Lancaster, Burt	Entertainment	25	150		65	
Lance, Bert	Business	3	5	15	10	Banker
Lanchester, Elsa	Entertainment	15	20	40	45	
Land, E. S.	Military	25	65		35	Adm. Maritime Comm. WW II
Land, Edwin H.	Business	75	225		175	Polaroid Camera
Landau, Martin	Entertainment	5			15	
Lander, Frederick West	Civil War	180	225	475		Union Gen.
Landers, Ann	Columnist	8	20	30	10	Advice Column
Landers, Audrey	Entertainment	6	8	15	15	
Landers, Judy	Entertainment	5	6	15	15	Pin-Up SP $25
Landesberg, Steve	Entertainment	5			20	
Landi, Bruno	Entertainment	15			35	Opera
Landi, Elissa	Entertainment	25	30	60	70	
Landis, Carole	Entertainment	90			125	Suicide at 29
Landis, Jessie Royce	Entertainment	25			75	
Landis, John	Entertainment	15			25	Film Dirctor
Landis, Kenesaw Mountain	Jurist	300			525	Baseball Commissioner
Landon, Alfred M.	Governor	25	55	110	45	Rep. Pres. Candidate vs FDR
Landon, Michael	Entertainment	100			250	
Landowska, Wanda	Entertainment	110			275	Pol-Fr Harpsichordist
Landrieu, Moon	Cabinet	6		15	10	Sec'y HUD
Landseer, Charles	Artist	30		75		R.A. & Keeper of Royal Academy
Landseer, Edwin H., Sir	Artist	30	65	150		Extraordinary Landscape Painter
Landseer, John	Artist	25		125		Father of Edwin H.
Landseer, Thomas	Artist-Engraver	25	40	75		Brother of E.H.
Landsteiner, Karl, Dr	Science	50	90	210		Nobel Medicine
Lane, Abbe	Entertainment	6			10	Mrs.Xavier Cugat. Pin-Up SP $15
Lane, Allan "Rocky"	Entertainment	65			250	
Lane, Christy	Entertainment	5	6	15	15	Gospel Singer

NAME	CATEGORY	SIG	LS/DS	ALS	SP	COMMENT
Lane, Diane	Entertainment	10	20		15	
Lane, Franklin K.	Cabinet	25	40		25	Sec'y Interior
Lane, Harriet	First Lady, Actg.	100	250	375		Actg. 1st Lady, Buchanan
Lane, James H. 1814-1866	Civil War	80	135	210		US Sen. KS, Union Gen.,Suicide
Lane, James Henry 1833-1907	Civil War	65	200	335	950	CSA General
Lane, Joseph	Governor	40	75	130		Gov. OR Terr.& 1st US Sen.
Lane, Lola	Entertainment	15	15	30	25	
Lane, Priscilla	Entertainment	10	15	25	25	
Lane, Rosemary	Entertainment	15	15	35	35	
Lang, Anton	Entertainment	18	25	45	40	
Lang, Cosmo Gordon	Clergy	25	35	45	35	
Lang, Fritz	Entertainment	50	375		150	Ger. Innovative Film Director
Lang, K D	Country Music	20	20		75	
Lang, Rosa	Entertainment	4	4	9	10	
Lang, Sebastian	Entertainment	19	25	45	45	
Lang, Walter	Entertainment	20			45	Film Director. 40 Year Vet.
Langan, Glenn	Entertainment	10	15	35	30	
Langdon, Harry	Entertainment	100			225	
Langdon, John	Revolutionary War	210	615	1575		Continental Congress, Gov. NH
Lange, David	Head of State	5	15	30	15	New Zealand
Lange, Hope	Entertainment	10			30	Pin-Up SP $30
Lange, Jessica	Entertainment	10			60	
Lange, Ted	Entertainment	5			15	
Langella, Frank	Entertainment	15	20		45	
Langer, Will	Senate	10	35			Senator ND
Langford, Frances	Entertainment	12			20	
Langley, Samuel P.	Aviation	205	260	500	350	1890's Aeronautical Pioneer
Langlie, Arthur	Governor	12	20		15	Governor Washington
Langmuir, Irving	Science	30	75	145		Nobel Chemistry 1932
Langtry, Lillie	Entertainment	325		465		Actress & Mistress of Edw. VII
Langtry, Lily	Entertainment	20	25	60	45	
Lanier, Sidney	Author	300	590	1165		Most Important So. Poet of Time
Lannes, Jean	Fr. Revolution	675				Marshal of France
Lanphier, Thomas G., Jr.	Aviation	40	70	120	85	ACE, WW II, Yamamoto Mission
Lansbury, Angela	Entertainment	5	6	15	25	
Lansing, Robert	Cabinet	40	125			Sec'y State
Lantieri, Rita	Entertainment 5	5			20	Opera
Lantz, Walter*	Cartoonist	40			250	Woody Woodpecker
Lanza, Mario	Entertainment	110			675	
Lapoype, J.F.C., Baron	Fr. Revolution	20		125		
Larch, John	Entertainment	6	8	15	10	
Larcom, Lucy	Author	15	25	45		
Lardner, Dionysius	Author	45	175			Irish writer on Sci. & Math.
Lardner, James L.	Civil War	35	85	125		Union Naval Commodore
Lardner, Ring	Author	65	140	310	75	Am. Humorist, Social Satirist
Lardner, Ring Jr.	Author	10	20	35	15	
Laredo, Ruth	Entertainment	15	15	30	35	
Larmouth, Kathy	Entertainment	4	4	9	9	
Larrey, Dominick Baron	Fr. Revolution	45	155	310		
Larroquette, John	Entertainment	10			30	
Larsen-Todsen, Nanny	Entertainmnt	20			50	Opera
Larson, Gary*	Cartoonist	20			100	Far Side
Larson, Leonard, Dr.	Science	5	15	30	10	
Lasker, Mary	Business	5	10	15	10	
Lasky, Jesse L.	Business	40	75	150	75	Pioneer Film Producer
Lasser, Louise	Entertainment	6			25	

NAME	CATEGORY	SIG	LS/DS	ALS	SP	COMMENT
Laswell, Fred*	Cartoonist	25			150	B.Google & Snuffy Smith
Latham, Hubert	Aviation	25	35	90	75	
Lathrop, George P.	Author	20	50	150		Am. Journalist, Writer
Latour-Maubourg,M.V.N.F.	Napoeonic Wars	20		75		Cavalry Gen.
Latourette, Kenneth Scott	Clergy	20	30	45	30	
Lattimore, Richard	Author	10	15	25	15	
Laubach, Frank C.	Clergy	35	50	90	60	
Lauder, Harry, Sir	Entertainment	60	90	145	70	Vintage Scottish Comedian
Laughton, Charles	Entertainment	80			275	
Lauper, Cyndi	Entertainment	25	35	85	60	Rock
Laurance, John	Revolutionary War	15		90		
Laurants, Arthur	Author	5			20	
Laurel, Stan	Entertainment	130	400		375	
Laurel, Stan & Hardy, Oliver	Entertainment	890			1025	
Lauren, Ralph	Business	10	15	40	25	Fashion Designer.
Laurencin, Marie	Artist	125		590		Fr. Painter & Printmaker
Laurens, Henry	Revolutionary War	1250	1550	1975		Pres. Continental Congress
Laurie, Piper	Entertainment	6	8	15	20	Pin-Up SP $30
Lausche, Frank J.	Governor	12	20		15	Governor OH
Lauter, Harry	Entertainment	5			20	
Lauterbach, Johann Christoph	Entertainment		95	195		Ger. Violinist
Lavi, Daliah	Entertainment	4			10	Pin-Up SP $10
Lavin, Linda	Entertainment	5	6	15	15	
Lavoisier, Antoine L. de	Science	400	2965			Fr. Founder Modern Chemistry
Law, Andrew Bonar	Head of State	30	80	135		Br. Prime Minister
Law, Evander McIvor	Civil War	100	225			CSA General
Law, George H.	Clergy	10		15	20	
Law, John Phillip	Entertainment	5			15	
Law, Ruth	Aviation	30			100	
Lawden, Frank O.	Celebrity	4	12	30		
Lawes, Lewis E.	Law Enforcement	20	40	120	25	Prison Warden. Sing Sing
Lawford, Peter	Entertainment	20			55	
Lawrence, 1st Baron	Head of State	10	30	75		India
Lawrence, Barbara	Entertainment	5			20	
Lawrence, Carol	Entertainment	5	6	15	15	
Lawrence, David Herbert	Author	225	590	2590		Br. Novelist
Lawrence, David L.	Governor	17	20			Governor PA
Lawrence, Elliot	Entertainment	20			40	Big Band Leader
Lawrence, Ernest O.	Science	95	275	400	200	Nobel Physics
Lawrence, Gertrude	Entertainment	20	50		45	1st Star of "King and I"
Lawrence, Herbert A., Sir	Military	10	30	50	25	
Lawrence, Jacob	Artist	13	25			Afro-Am. Painter
Lawrence, John	Revolutionary War	35	90	175		CT Statesman, Rev. War Leader
Lawrence, Marc	Entertainment	10	15	25	25	
Lawrence, Marjorie	Entertainment	10			35	Opera, Concert
Lawrence, Steve	Entertainment	6	8	10	15	
Lawrence, Thomas Edw.	Author-Soldier	650	1250	2865		Lawrence of Arabia
Lawrence, Thomas, Sir	Artist	150	225	500		
Lawrence, Vicki	Entertainment	5	6	15	15	
Lawson, James M.	Clergy	20	25	35	25	
Lawson, Ted	Aviation	15	30		40	
Lawton, Alexander R.	Civil War	110	270	320		CSA Gen.
Laxalt, Paul	Senate/Congress	4	10		15	Governor, Senator NV
Lay, Herman W.	Business	10	25	50	30	Lay's Potato Chips
Layard, Austin Henry, Sir	Archaeologist	10	25	50		Br. Diplomat
Lazarus, Mel*	Cartoonist	5			20	Miss Peach, Momma

NAME	CATEGORY	SIG	LS/DS	ALS	SP	COMMENT
Lazarus, S. Ralph	Business	4	7	10	5	Pres.Benrus Watch.Philanthropis
Lazenby, George	Entertainment	10	15	28	25	
Lazzari, Virgillo	Entertainment	15			45	
LeBrock, Kelly	Entertainment	10	15		35	Pin-Up SP $40
LeCarre, John (David Cornwell)	Author	20	45	75	30	Br. Realistic Spy Novels
LeGallienne, Eva	Entertainment	5	25	50	35	
LeGallienne, Richard	Author	20	50	65		Brit. Man of Letters
LeGarde, Tom and Ted	Country Music	10			20	
LeHand, M. A. (Missy)	Gov't Exec. Aide	20	65	95	40	FDR Personal Sec'y 20 Years
LeMay, Curtis S.	Military	25	125		75	AF Gen. WW II
LeRoy, Hal	Entertainment	7			15	Film Director
LeRoy, Mervyn	Entertainment	25			75	Film Director
Lea, Homer	Military	55	175			Predicted US-Jap. War/HI as Key
Leachman, Cloris	Entertainment	6	8	15	20	
Leadbetter, Danville	Civil War	150	475			CSA General
Leahy, Patrick	Senate/Congress	5	15		10	Senator VT
Leahy, William Daniel	Military	35	145	105	195	Chief of Staff-FDR & Truman
Leake, J. B.	Civil War	20	55	75		
Leakey, Louis B.	Science	45	125	225	65	Anthropologist, Archaeologist
Leakey, Mary D.	Science	15	25	70	30	Anthropologist, Archaeologist
Leakey, Richard, Dr.	Science	125				Br. Anthropologist
Lean, David, Sir	Entertainment	45			70	Film Director
Lear, Edward	Artist	130		550		Br. Painter & Nonsense Poet
Lear, Norman	Business	10	15	45	20	TV Film Producer
Lear, Tobias	Revolutionary War	75	240	325		Pvt. Secretary to G. Washington
Lear, William P. Sr.	Business	30	115	175	100	Lear Jet Aircraft
Learned, Michael	Entertainment	9	10	20	25	
Leary, Timothy, Dr.	Activist-Educator	15	35		20	Drug Cult Leader Psychologist
Lease, Mary Elizabth	Reformer	15	20	40		Orator, Writer Woman Suffrage
Leavenworth, Henry	Military	250		750		Frontier Soldier, General
Lebrun, Albert	Head of State	20	50	125	35	Last Pres. 3rd French Repub.
Lebrun, Charles F. Duc de	Napoleonic Wars	35	90	190		3rd Consul/Bonaparte
Lecuona, Ernesto	Composer	150			375	AMusQS $400-$600
Led Zeppelin (all-org.)	Entertainment	250			700	
Lederer, Francis	Entertainment	10			25	
Lederman, Leon M., Dr.	Science	15	25	50		Nobel Phyics
Ledoux, Harold*	Cartoonist	5			25	Judge Parker
Lee, Alfred	Clergy	10	15	35		
Lee, Anna	Entertainment	5			15	
Lee, Bernard	Entertainment	15			25	
Lee, Brenda	Country Music	5			12	
Lee, Bruce	Entertainment	375	700		900	
Lee, Canada	Entertainment	50			125	
Lee, Charles (1731-82)	Military			4500		Turncoat Gen. Rev. War
Lee, Charles (1758-1815)	Cabinet	110	250	550		Washington's Att'y Gen.
Lee, Christopher	Entertainment	15			50	
Lee, Dixie (Mrs Bing Crosby)	Entertainment	10	15	25	25	
Lee, Dr. Tsung-Dao	Science	20	30	45	25	Nobel Physics
Lee, E. Hamilton	Aviation	10	25	50	35	
Lee, Edwin G.	Civil War	165	290	410		CSA Gen.
Lee, Fitzhugh	Civil War	125	190	665	480	CSA General
Lee, Francis Lightfoot	Revolutionary War	660	1050	4250		Signer Decl. of Indepen.
Lee, Geo. Wash. Custis	Civil War	150	375	785		CSA General
Lee, Gypsy Rose	Entertainment	35			75	
Lee, Harper	Author	110	350			"To Kill a Mocking Bird"
Lee, Henry	Revolutionary War	200	525	625		"Light-Horse Harry"

NAME	CATEGORY	SIG	LS/DS	ALS	SP	COMMENT
Lee, Lila	Entertainment	5	6	15	15	
Lee, Mark C.	Astronaut	5			20	
Lee, Mary Custis	Civil War	150		450	475	Mrs. Robert E. Lee
Lee, Michele	Entertainment	5	6	15	15	
Lee, Peggy	Entertainment	10			25	Singer-Composer
Lee, Pinkie	Entertainment	15			35	
Lee, Richard Henry	Revolutionary War	275	700	3350		Signer Decl. of Indepen.
Lee, Robert E.	Civil War	3100	5370	14700	7500	CSA Gen. Auction $23K-$36,000
Lee, Ruta	Entertainment	4	4	9	10	Pin-Up SP $10
Lee, Samuel P.	Civil War	60	210	275		Union Adm.
Lee, Spike	Entertainment	10	25		30	Afro-Am Film Director
Lee, Stephen Dill	Civil War	100	345	450		CSA General
Lee, Tommy	Entertainment	20			50	Rock
Lee, William H.	Civil War	140		375		CSA Gen.,Nephew of R.E. Lee
Lee, William Raymond	Civil War	15	45	70		Union General
Lee, Yuan T., Dr.	Science	20	35	45	30	Nobel Chemistry
Leeb, Wilhelm R. von	Military	20		135		
Leech, John	Artist	70	125	165		Br. Caricaturist $875
Leech, Richard	Entertainment	15			35	Opera
Leeds, Andrea	Entertainment	10			25	
Leese, Oliver, Sir	Military	20	50		35	Br. Gen. WW II
Leestma, David C.	Astronaut	5			15	
Lefebvre, F.J., Duke	Fr. Revolution	160	300			Marshal of Napoleon
Lefevre, Edwin	Financial Writer	4	8	15		Panamanian Ambass. to Spain
Leftwich, John W.	Senate/Congress	10	15	30		MOC TN 1866
Leger, Fernand	Artist	80	240	575		Fr. Abstract Painter.AMsS $2750
Leggett, Mortimer Dormer	Civil War	20	40	65		Union General
Legrand, Michel	Composer	5	45	25	20	
Lehar, Franz	Composer	80	170	535	375	"The Merry Widow"
Lehman, Herbert H.	Governor	15	30			Gov. NY, Senator NY
Lehmann, Ernst August	Aviation	175		365		
Lehmann, Lilli	Entertainment	175		100		Ger. Soprano
Lehmann, Lotte	Entertainment	45	60	175	125	Opera
Lehmann, Marie	Entertainment	50			175	Ger. Prima Donna. Mother Lilli
Lehr, Lew	Entertainment	15	15	35	30	
Leibman, Ron	Entertainment	5	6	15	15	
Leider, Frida	Entertainment	35			135	Opera
Leiferkus, Sergei	Entertainment	10			25	Opera
Leigh, Janet	Entertainment	5	9	15	20	Pin-Up SP $25
Leigh, Jennifer Jason	Entertainment	7			70	
Leigh, Vivien	Entertainment	780	550	950	990	
Leigh, Vivien (As Scarlett O'Hara)	Entertainment				7750	
Leigh, Vivien and Laurence Olivier	Entertainment		475		925	
Leighton, Frederic	Artist	25		100		Pres. Royal Academy
Leighton, Margaret	Entertainment	15			40	
Leinsdorf, Erich	Entertainment	15			45	Austro-Amer Conductor
Leisure, David	Entertainment	5			10	
Lejeune, John Archer	Military	35	75	150	75	Commandant US Marine Corps
Leland, W. C.	Business	20	55	140	40	
Leloir, Luis Frederico	Science	20	30	45	25	Nobel Chemistry
Lelouch, Claude	Entertainment	9	10	20	25	
Lemass, Sean	Head of State	10	25	60	30	Prime Minister Ireland
Lembeck, Harvey	Entertainment	30			75	
Lembeck, Michael	Entertainment	3	3	6	10	
Lemmon, Jack	Entertainment	6	8	15	25	
Lemnitz, Tiana	Entertainment	40			125	Opera

NAME	CATEGORY	SIG	LS/DS	ALS	SP	COMMENT
Lemnitzer, Lyman L.	Military	30	40	90	35	Supreme Allied Commd'r WW II
Lenin, Vladimir Ilyich (N.Lenin)	Head of State					ALS/Content $29,000
Lennon Sisters, The (4)	Entertainment	20			50	
Lennon, John	Entertainment	640	2250		1350	Assassinated Beatle
Lennon, Julian	Entertainment	20			40	
Lennox, Vera	Entertainment	12			20	Br. Actress
Leno, Jay	Entertainment	10			35	Self Caricature S $75
Lenoir, William B.	Astronaut	7			20	
Lenox, Lucie	Entertainment	15			40	
Lenske, Rula	Entertainment	4	4	9	15	
Lenya, Lotte	Entertainment	20	60		150	Cabaret Singer, Character Actr.
Leonard, Elmore	Author	5			15	
Leonard, George	Jurist	40	100			Colonial Am. Jurist
Leonard, Gloria	Entertainment	5	6	15	15	
Leonard, Sheldon	Entertainment	5	6	15	15	
Leoncavallo, Ruggiero	Composer	175	500	475	700	AMusQS $850
Leone, Sergio	Director-Movies	55			400	Master of Spaghetti Western
Leonov, Aleksei	Astronaut	130			275	Rus. Cosmonaut, 2nd in Space
Leontif, Wassily, Dr.	Economist	20	35		40	Nobel Economics
Leontovich, Eugenie	Entertainment	15		30	45	
Leopardi, Giacomo	Author	80	350	475		Physically Deformed Italian Poe
Leopold I	Royalty	105	475			Belgium
Leopold I	Royalty	75	375	625		Hungary
Leopold II	Royalty	65	325	540		Belgium
Leopold, Nathan F.	Criminal	150	385	575	150	Loeb & Leopold Case
Lermontov, Mikhail 1814-1841	Author	540	2300	4625		Novelist, Poet. Killed in Duel
Lerner, Alan Jay	Composer	45	95	175	135	Am. Lyricist, Librettist
Lerner, Max	Author	5	30	40	10	
Leslie, Frank, Mrs.	Publisher	20		75	75	Leslie's Magazine
Leslie, Joan	Entertainment	6	8	15	19	
Leslie, Preston H.	Governor	10	15			Governor KY
Lesseps, Ferdinand, Comte de	Diplomat	110	225	415		Engineer. Promoted Suez Canal
Lester, Buddy	Entertainment	3	4	10	15	
Lesters, The (5)	Entertainment	10			25	Gospel Singers
Leszczynski, Stanislaus	Royalty	575				Stanislaw I, King of Poland
Letcher, John	Civil War	65	265			CW Gov. VA, ALS/Cont. $2,500
Letterman, David	Entertainment	20			50	
Letterman, Jonathan	Civil War	95	175			Med. Services for CW Union Army
Leutze, Emanuel	Artist	75		320		"Washington Crossing Delaware"
Levant, Oscar	Entertainment	20			45	Pianist, Humorist, Actor
Levene, Sam	Entertainment	10			20	
Levenson, Sam	Entertainment	10	35		15	Radio, TV Comic
Lever, Asbury	Senate/Congress	5	10		5	MOC SC
Lever, Lord (Wm. Hesketh)	Business	30	100	190	60	Br. Soap Mfg. Lever Brothers
Leverett, John 1662-1724	Colonial	50	130	275		President of Harvard, Judge
Levi, Edward H.	Cabinet	7	25	45	10	Att'y General
Levi-Montalcini, Rita, Dr.	Science	20	65			Nobel Medicine
Levin, Ira	Author	25	35		30	"Rosemary's Baby"
Levine, David	Cartoonist	15			100	Caricaturist
Levine, Irving R.	TV News	4	10		5	Commentator
Levine, Jack	Artist	10	15	30		
Levine, James	Entertainment	7	10	35	25	Conductor
Levinson, Barry	Entertainment	5			15	
Lewellyn, Anthony	Astronaut	5	16		15	
Lewis, Al	Entertainment	10			30	
Lewis, C(live) S(taples)	Author	240	575	1750		Br. Medievalist, Philosopher

NAME	CATEGORY	SIG	LS/DS	ALS	SP	COMMENT
Lewis, David 'Duffy'	Aviation	15	30	55	40	
Lewis, Drew	Cabinet	10		20	15	Sec'y of Transportation
Lewis, Edwin	Clergy	15	20	30		
Lewis, Emmanuele	Entertainment	6	8	15	15	
Lewis, Francis	Revolutionary War	375	1250	2500		Signer Decl. of Indepen.
Lewis, Gwilym H.	Aviation	20	45	80	55	
Lewis, Huey (And the News)	Entertainment	12			30	Rock
Lewis, J.C.	Entertainment	12			25	Blues Drummer
Lewis, James	Entertainment	15	15	30	25	
Lewis, Jerry	Entertainment	5	6	15	25	
Lewis, Jerry Lee	Country Music	30			70	And Rock
Lewis, Joe E.	Entertainment	15	25	45	40	
Lewis, John	Activist	5	15			Civil Rights Leader
Lewis, John L.	Labor	40	60	195	55	AFL-CIO Labor Leader
Lewis, Juliette	Entertainment	25			45	
Lewis, Meriwether	Explorer	4500	5000			Lewis & Clark Expedition
Lewis, Monica	Entertainment	5			10	Singer-Actress
Lewis, Morgan	Revolutionary War	50	70	110		Gen.Gates Chief of Staff. Gov.
Lewis, Ramsey	Entertainment	25			50	Pianist-Composer
Lewis, Shari	Entertainment	6	8	15	18	
Lewis, Sinclair	Author	100	350	750	240	1st Am. Awarded Nobel for Lit.
Lewis, Ted	Entertainment	20	25		75	
Lewis, William Arthur, Sir	Science	20	25	40	25	Nobel Economics
Lewis, William H.	Aviation	10	22	40	28	ACE, WW II
Lewishon, Ludwig	Author	20		25		Ger.-Born Author of 31 Books
Lewisohn, Adolph	Business	20	45	65	25	Mining, Investment
Lewitt, Sal	Artist	25			100	
Ley, Bob	TV News	5			10	ESPN News
Ley, Willy	Science	25	75	145	35	Rocker Expert, Sci-Fi Writer
Libby, Willard F.	Science	20	35	55	25	Nobel Chemistry
Liberace	Entertainment	50	200		135	
Liberace, George	Entertainment	6	8		10	
Liberman, Evsei, Prof.	Celebrity	15	35		20	
Lichtenberg, Byron, Dr.	Astronaut	7			20	
Lichtenstein, Roy	Artist	30	65	140	50	Repro S $175
Liddell, Henry George	Clergy	20	35	40	45	
Liddy, G. Gordon	Gov't Official	5	20	50	10	Lawyer, Watergate,Convicted
Lie, Jonas	Author	15	40	60		Nor. Novelist, Dramatist
Lie, Trygve	Head of State	50	145	250	175	1st Sec'y Gen'l United Nations
Lieber, Fritz	Entertainment	35			100	
Liebig, Justus von, Baron	Science	150		750		Ger. Chem. ALS/Content $1,750
Lienart, Archille, Cardinal	Clergy	30	40	50	40	
Liggett, Huntcr	Military	15	45	60	35	Gen. WW I
Liggett, Louis Kroh	Business	85	170	350		Liggett's Drug Store Chain
Light, Judith	Entertainment	12	15	25	30	
Lightner, Candy	Celebrity	12	30		20	1st Pres. MADD
Lightner, Winnie	Entertainment	19	25	45	45	
Ligi, Josella	Entertainment	5			25	Opera
Liles, Brooks	Aviation	8	20	38	22	ACE, WW II, USAAF Ace
Lilienthal, David E.	Business	15	30		20	Co-Fndr. I.J. Fox, Furriers
Liliuokalani, Lydia K.	Royalty	140	460	955	475	Queen Hawaii
Lillie, Beatrice	Entertainment	25		65	35	
Lillie, Gordon W. (Pawnee Bill)	Entertainment	100	360	435	400	Buffalo Bill Contemporary
Liman, Arthur	Celebrity	4	12		18	
Limbaugh, Rush	Radio/TV	10			25	Radio/TV Commentator
Lin, Y. S. Maya	Artist	25	100			Designed Viet Nam Wall

NAME	CATEGORY	SIG	LS/DS	ALS	SP	COMMENT
Lincke, Paul	Composer	70	185	325		AMusQS $675, "Glow Worm"
Lincoln, Abraham	President	2950	7440	12500	10000	Brady SP $50,000
Lincoln, Benjamin	Cabinet-Military	100	380	500		Gen. Revolutionary War
Lincoln, Benjamin (b.1700)	Justice of Peace	45	160			Father of Gen. Lincoln
Lincoln, Elmo	Entertainment	475			1500	
Lincoln, Evelyn	Gov't Official	15	25		20	Presidential Sec'y
Lincoln, Joseph	Author	13	20	30		Writer of Cape Cod Stories
Lincoln, Levi	Cabinet	35	85	130		Memb. Continental Congr
Lincoln, Mary Todd	First Lady	300	985	7685	3000	FF on Mourning Env. $3,900
Lincoln, Robert Todd	Cabinet	90	310	350		Capt. CW, Arthur Sec'y of War
Lincoln, Rufus	Revolutionary War		1650			Present at Burgoyne Surrender
Lind, Don L.	Astronaut	6			20	
Lind, Jenny (Goldschmidt)	Entertainment	65	125	285	500	Concert, Opera
Lindberg, Charles W.	Military	25	85			Iwo Jimo Flag Raiser
Lindbergh, Anne Morrow	Author	15	45	120	30	Am. Writer-Poet.
Lindbergh, Charles A.	Aviation	1000	1475	2560	3050	ALS/Content $7,500
Linden, Hal	Entertainment	5			15	
Lindfors, Viveca	Entertainment	9	10	20	25	
Lindholm, Berit	Entertainment	10			25	Opera
Lindley, Audra	Entertainment	4			10	
Lindsay, E. "Lin"	Aviation	10	22	38	30	ACE, WW II, USAAF Ace
Lindsay, Howard	Entertainment	10	15	25	25	Theatrical Producer
Lindsay, John	Politician	4	8		10	Lawyer, Author, Mayor NYC
Lindsay, Margaret	Entertainment	15	25	45	45	
Lindsay, Vachel	Author	50	185	575	125	Poet, Artist, "Prairie Troubado
Lindsey, George	Entertainment	6	8	15	19	
Linkletter, Art	Entertainment	7			15	
Linn-Baker, Mark	Entertainment	5			15	
Linnaeus, Carolus von	Science	925	2250			Swe. Botanist.
Linville, Larry	Entertainment	10			25	
Liotta, Ray	Entertainment	25			50	
Lipchitz, Jacques	Artist	130	210	408		Lith-Am. Cubist Sculptor
Lipfert, Helmut	Aviation	35			70	#15 World Highest ACE. Ger.
Lipkovska, Lydia	Entertainment	75			325	Rus. Soprano
Lipman, Clara	Entertainment	12			20	Stage Actress
Lipmann, Fritz A.	Science	25	45	70	30	Nobel Medicine 1953
Lipovsek, Marjana	Entertainment	10			30	Opera
Lippman, Walter	Author	25	75		30	Journalist, Editor, Pulitzer
Lipscomb, William N., Dr.	Science	20	35		30	Nobel Chemistry
Lipsner, B.B.	Aviation	30	65		90	Pioneer Air Mail Pilot
Lipton, Peggy	Entertainment	4	4	9	15	
Lipton, Thomas, Sir	Business	120	425		250	Br. Tea Merchant-Yachtsman
Lisa, Manuel	Celebrity	763				
List, Emanuel	Entertainment	35			95	
Lister, Joseph, 1st Baron	Science	225	420	685		Pioneer of Antiseptic Surgery
Liston, Robert 1794-1847	Science	15	30	50		Skilled Scottish Surgeon
Liszt, Franz	Composer	400	650	1685	1815	AMuQS $3,800,AMMsS $16,750
Litel, John	Entertainment	15	15	35	30	
Lithgow, John	Entertainment	5	6	15	15	
Litjens, Stefan	Aviation	7	15	25	20	
Little Richard	Entertainment	18	20	45	50	Rock
Little River Band	Entertainment	25			50	
Little, Cleavon	Entertainment	13			35	
Little, Little Jack	Entertainment	15			35	Big Band Leader
Little, Rich	Entertainment	3			10	
Little, Royal	Business	22		55		

NAME	CATEGORY	SIG	LS/DS	ALS	SP	COMMENT
Littlejohn, Abram N.	Clergy	10	20	35		
Littlejohn, Dewitt C.	Civil War	40	85	120		Union General
Litvak, Anatole	Entertainment	20			45	Film Director
Litvinov, Maksim M.	Diplomat	50		95	65	Soviet Foreign Minister
Liu-Li Pei	Entertainment	10			25	Chinese Opera Star
Livermore, Dan'l P.	Clergy	15	20	45		
Livermore, Mary A.	Reformer	60	75	125		Woman Suffrage, Temperance
Liverpool, 2nd Earl	Head of State	120	135	200		Robt. Banks Jenkinson, P.M.
Livingston, Edward	Cabinet	30	85	150		Sec'y of State 1831
Livingston, Henry B. (SC)	Supreme Court	100	310			
Livingston, Jay	Composers	15	40	85	40	AMusQS $100-$300
Livingston, Margaret	Entertainment	10			25	
Livingston, Mary	Entertainment	15	25	45	40	
Livingston, Philip	Revolutionary War	375	1080	1175		Signer Decl. of Indepen.
Livingston, Robert	Entertainment	20			45	
Livingston, Robert 1742-94	Revolutionary War	170	350	400		Dir. Bank of the U.S. (1792)
Livingston, Robert R. 1746-1813	Revolutionary War	195	440	1250		Continental Congress
Livingston, William	Revolutionary War	300	1300	1750		Continental Congr. Gov. NJ
Livingstone, David	Explorer-Clergy	225	885	1465		Missionary, Explorer of Africa
Llewellyn, Anthony	Astronaut	10			30	
Lloyd, Christopher	Entertainment	10	15	28	30	
Lloyd, Emily	Entertainment	10			40	
Lloyd, Harold	Entertainment	135			300	
Lloyd, James 1769-1831	Senate/Congress	30	65	90		Senator MA 1808
Lloyd, Kathleen	Entertainment	4	4	9	15	
Lloyd, Norman	Entertainment	4	4	9	10	
Lloyd-George, David, 1st Earl	Head of State	80	240	435	265	Prime Minister
Lo Giudici, Franco	Entertainment	40			150	Opera
LoBianco, Tony	Entertainment	6	8	15	19	
Loan, Nguyen Ngoc	Military	75			100	Gen. Viet Nam
Locke, John	Author	700	1950	5000		Br.Philosopher. LS/Cont.$12,500
Locke, Sandra	Entertainment	9	10	20	25	
Locke, William John	Author	20	35	75	30	Br. Novelist
Lockhart, Gene	Entertainment	25			50	
Lockhart, June	Entertainment	5	6	15	15	
Lockheed, Alan	Aviation	80	150	300	150	Pioneer Aviator, Plane Designer
Locklear, Heather	Entertainment	10	15	25	28	Pin-Up SP $35
Lockwood, Belva A.	Women's Rights	225	325	875		1st Woman to Practice Supr. Ct.
Lockwood, Chas.W, Capt	Civil War	95				1st MN to Enlist,Last Survivor
Lockwood, Margaret	Entertainment	15	20	40	35	
Lockyer, Herbert	Clergy	25	35	45		
Lodge, Henry Cabot	Senate	40	160	200	55	MOC 1887, Senator MA 1893
Lodge, Henry Cabot, Jr.	Senate	20	60	95	25	Ambassador UN, Diplomat
Lodge, Oliver J., Sir	Science	90	130	225		Br. Physicist
Loeb, William	Business	10	26	55	35	
Loew, Marcus	Business	30	40	65	35	
Loewe, Frederick	Composer	35	65	145	50	AMusQS $220
Loewy, Raymond	Business	35	90	140	75	Designer
Loftus, Cissie	Entertainment	25	55			Br. Actress
Logan, Benjamin 1752-1802	Military	350	560			Pioneer Hero, Indian Fighter
Logan, Ella	Entertainment	8	9	19	15	
Logan, John Alexander (CMH)	Civil War	80	215	275		Union Gen.,Father Memorial Day
Logan, Josh	Entertainment	25			45	Director
Logan, Olive	Author	25	35			
Loggia, Robert	Entertainment	6	8	15	18	
Loggins and Messina	Entertainment	25			50	

NAME	CATEGORY	SIG	LS/DS	ALS	SP	COMMENT
Loggins, Kenny	Entertainment	10			25	
Loisy, Alfred	Clergy	20	25	35		
Lolobrigida, Gina	Entertainment	10	15	25	30	Pin-Up SP$30
Lom, Herbert	Entertainment	10			30	
Lomax, Lunsford Lindsey	Civil War	100	270	370		CSA General
Lombard, Carole	Entertainment	300		950	1200	DS $750
Lombardo, Guy	Entertainment	15	75	120	85	Big Band Leader
London, Charmian	Celebrity	40			175	2nd Wife of Jack London
London, George	Entertainment	35			70	Opera, Concert
London, Jack	Author	215	670	1050	585	Am. Novelist, Adventurer
London, Julie	Entertainment	4	4	9	15	
London, Tom	Entertainment	50			100	
Long, Earl K.	Governor	20	30		25	Governor LA,
Long, Huey P.	Senate	85	175			Sen., Gov. LA. Assassinated
Long, John D.	Cabinet	12	30	40	20	Sec'y Navy, Governor MA
Long, Johnny	Entertainment	10			25	Big Band Leader
Long, Pierse 1739-89	Revolutionary War	30	75	180		Continental Congress
Long, Richard	Entertainment	25			65	
Long, Russell	Senate/Congress	5	15		10	Senator LA
Long, Shelley	Entertainment	9	10	20	25	Pin-Up SP $25
Longacre, James B.1794-1869	Engraver	110		400		Chief Engraver of the U.S. Mint
Longet, Claudine	Entertainment	10	15	35	35	
Longfellow, Henry W.	Author	145	475	825	715	Poet, Harvard Prof.
Longfellow, Samuel	Clergy	40	50	75	55	
Longfellow, Stephen 1775-1849	Senate/Congress	20	50	145		MOC ME 1823
Longley, James B.	Governor	9	15			Governor ME
Longstreet, James	Civil War	365	740	975	850	CSA General
Longworth, Alice Roosevelt	Pres. Daughter	15	25	95	30	
Longworth, Nicholas	Senate/Congress	15	40	85		Speaker of the House, OH
Loo, Richard	Entertainment	20			55	
Loomis, Gustavus	Civil War	28	65	95		Union General
Loos, Anita	Author	17	30	70	30	Am. Novelist, Film Scripts
Loos, Walter	Aviation	10	20	35	25	
Loper, Don	Business	5	15	35	10	Fashion Designer
Lopez, Vincent	Entertainment	20			55	Big Band Leader-Pianist
Loraine, Robert	Aviation	15		55		
Lorca, Frederico Garcia	Author	435	1240	3125		Sp. Poet, Dramatist
Lord, Daniel, Rev.	Clergy	10			35	
Lord, E.J.	Senate	10		35		Senator CA
Lord, Jack	Entertainment	6	8	15	15	
Lord, John Wesley, Bishop	Clergy	20	35	40	45	
Lord, Marjorie	Entertainment	6			25	"Danny Thomas Show"
Lord, Walter	Author	3	5	10	5	
Lords, Traci	Entertainment	5	15	30	30	Pin-Up SP $65
Loren, Sophia	Entertainment	15			50	Pin-Up SP $50
Lorengar, Pilar	Entertainment	10			35	Opera
Lorillard, Peter	Business	125	260	475		Tobacco Industry
Loring, Gloria	Entertainment	5	8	15	18	
Loring, Israel	Clergy	25	75	125		
Loring, Wm. Wing	Civil War	145	205	315	425	CSA General
Lorne, Marion	Entertainment	100			225	
Lorre, Peter	Entertainment	200			450	
Losigkeit, Fritz	Aviation	10	15	30	20	
Lossing, Benson	Author	15	30	60		Historian, Engraver
Lott, Felicity	Entertainment	15			35	Opera
Loughlin, Lori	Entertainment	5			12	

NAME	CATEGORY	SIG	LS/DS	ALS	SP	COMMENT
Louis Philippe (Fr)	Royalty	65	215	275		"Citizen King"
Louis XII (Fr)	Royalty	800	1750	4200		King of France
Louis XIII (Fr)	Royalty	875	1475	3590		King of France
Louis XIV (Fr)	Royalty	450	1000	3750		The "Sun King"
Louis XV	Royalty	750	1700	5500		King of France
Louis XVI	Royalty	375	1305			King of France. Guillotined
Louis XVIII (Fr)	Royalty	205	475	1680		Louis Stanislas Xavier
Louise Caroline Alberta, Princess	Royalty	25		65	175	4th Daughter of Queen Victoria
Louise Vict.(Alex. Dagmar)	Royalty	15		105	195	Princess Royal
Louise, Anita	Entertainment	15			45	
Louise, Tina	Entertainment	9	10	20	25	Pin-Up SP $25
Lounge, John M.	Astronaut	10			20	
Lousma, Jack F.	Astronaut	10	20		35	
Love, Bessie	Entertainment	35			70	Vintage
Love, John A.	Governor	5	12		10	Governor CO
Love, Montagu	Entertainment	20			50	
Love, Mother	Entertainment	4			10	Comedienne
Lovecraft, H. P.	Author	165	290	475	425	Reclusive Horror Story Writer
Lovejoy, Frank	Entertainment	25			55	
Lovejoy, Owen	Clergy-Congress	15	30	45		MOC IL 1857-64
Lovelace, Linda	Entertainment	25			60	Porn Queen
Loveless, Patty	Entertainment	15			35	Singer
Lovell, Bernard Dr.	Science	15	25	40	20	
Lovell, James	Revolutionary War	75	195	450		Continental Congress
Lovell, James A. Jr.	Astronaut	15			45	
Lovell, Mansfield	Civil War	100	250	335		CSA Gen.
Loverboy	Entertainment	25			50	
Lovett, John 1761-1818	Senate/Congress	40		135		War 1812. ALS/Content $300
Lovett, Lyle	Country Music	25			75	
Lovett, Robert	Cabinet	5	10	25	10	Sec'y Defense
Lovkay, John	Business	3			7	CEO Hamilton Standard
Lovrenich, Rodger T.	Business	4	9	207		Inventor of electronic ignition
Low, David, Sir*	Cartoonist	15	45	110	140	NZ-Br Political."Colonel Blimp"
Low, Frederick F.	Governor	45		175		Gov, MOC CA 1860, Diplomat
Low, G. David	Astronaut	5			15	
Low, Nicholas	Revolutionary War	90	245	450		Prominent NY, Backed Revolution
Low, Seth	Mayor NYC	10	25	45		Merchant, Pres. Columbia Univ.
Lowe, Ed	Inventor	20			45	Kitty Litter
Lowe, Edmund	Entertainment	25	30	60	45	
Lowe, Hudson, Sir	Military		1000	500		Last custodian of Napoleon
Lowe, Rob	Entertainment	20			45	
Lowe, Thaddeus S. C.	Civil War	195	325	500		Aeronaut,Inventor,CW Balloonist
Lowell, Amy	Author	35	125	250		Am. Poet,Critic.,Imagist School
Lowell, Carey	Entertainment	5			20	
Lowell, James Russell	Author	40	145	315	350	Hall of Fame, Educator, Editor
Lowell, John H.	Aviation	12	25	40	32	ACE, WW II
Lowell, Percival	Science	15	40	65		Am. Astronomer, Author
Lowell, Robert	Author	30	150			Pulitzer Poetry
Lowery, John	Senate/Congress	10	15		15	
Lowery, Robert	Entertainment	30			65	
Lowry, Robert	Governor	10	25			Governor MS
Loy, Myrna	Entertainment	20			35	
Lubbers, Bob*	Cartoonist	10			70	Tarzan
Lubbock, Francis R.	Civil War	150	185	295	350	CSA Governor TX
Lubbock, Sir John 1834-1913	Statesman	10	15	35		Br. Banker.Author Science Books
Lubin, Arthur	Entertainment	25			65	Film Director

NAME	CATEGORY	SIG	LS/DS	ALS	SP	COMMENT
Lubitsch, Ernst	Entertainment	55			120	Vintage Film Director
Lubke, Heinrich	Head of State	10		25		Pres. Ger. Fed. Repub.
Lucas, Edward Verrall	Author	3	5	15	5	
Lucas, George	Entertainment	20	25	60	60	Film Director
Lucca, Pauline	Entertainment	30	70	130		Opera
Lucci, Susan	Entertainment	6	8	15	20	
Luccock, Halford E.	Clergy	20	35	50	40	
Luce, Clare Boothe	Author	30	100	175	40	Ambassador, Playwright
Luce, Cyrus G.	Governor	5	15	25		Governor MI
Luce, Henry R.	Publisher	40	115	205	50	Time, Life, Fortune, Sports Ill
Luce, Stephen Bleecker, Adm.	Military	10	35	60	30	Am. !st Pres. Naval War College
Lucid, Shannon W.	Astronaut	5			25	
Luckinbill, Laurence	Entertainment	5			15	
Luckner, Felix Count von	Military	195	205	280	85	The "Sea Devil" WWII
Luckner, Nicholas	Fr. Revolution	225	675			Marshal of Fr. Guillotined
Lucon, L. J., Cardinal	Clergy	45	55	75	60	
Ludendorff, Erich von	Military	100	225	350	275	Ger. Gen. WW I, Politician
Ludin, Hanns	Military	130	350			Ger. Gen.-Storm Trooper WW II
Ludlington, Marshall I.	Civil War	65	135	195		Union General
Ludlum, Robert	Author	10	20	35	20	Super Spy novels
Ludwig I	Head of State	65	200	450		King of Bavaria
Ludwig II	Head of State	55	255	470		King of Bavaria
Ludwig, Christa	Entertainment	5			30	Opera
Ludwig, Emil	Authors	40	120	200		
Lufbery, Raoul	Aviation	125	350	590	400	ACE, WW I, Lafayette Escadrille
Luft, Lorna	Entertainment	5		10	10	Singer Sister of Liza Minelli
Lugosi, Bela	Entertainment	275	375	700	1275	
Luhan, Mabel Dodge	Author			225		
Lujan, Albert	Artist	20		45		
Lukas, Paul	Entertainment	40			100	
Luke, Frank	Aviation	150	400	600	500	ACE, WW I, CMH, #3 U.S. Ace
Luke, Keye	Entertainment	15			45	
Luks, George Benjamin	Artist	20	55	135		Member Ashcan Shool.
Lum & Abner	Entertainment	25			65	
Lumet, Sidney	Entertainment	10			35	TV Director-Dramatist
Lumholtz, Carl	Celebrity	3	8	20		
Lumiere, Louis	Inventor	175		950	375	Cinematographe Projector
Lumley, Joanna	Entertainment	5	6	15	15	
Luna, Barbara	Entertainment	4			10	
Lunceford, Jimmie	Entertainment	35			140	Big Band Leader-Arranger
Lund, John	Entertainment	5	6	15	15	
Lunden, Joan	TV Host	12			20	TV Host
Lundgren, Dolph	Entertainment	5			15	
Lundigan, William	Entertainment	20			40	
Lunney, G.	Astronaut	5			15	
Lunt, Alfred & Fontanne, Lynne	Entertainment	60			125	DS For "Idiot's Delight" $650
Lupino, Ida	Entertainment	15	95	30	35	
Lupino, Stanley	Entertainment	15			35	
Lupton, John	Entertainment	10			20	
Luria, Salvador F.	Science	20	35	55	25	Nobel Medicine
Lurie, Bob	Business	10	25	45	15	
Luse, Harley	Country Music	10			20	
Luther, Hans	Head of State	40	55	85		Chancellor Ger., Ambass. US
Luther, Martin	Clergy	10000	30000	38375		LS/Extremely Rare $49,500
Lutzow, Gunther	Aviation	175		445	450	
Lyautey, Louis	Military	10	35	90	35	Marshal of Fr.,Statesman

NAME	CATEGORY	SIG	LS/DS	ALS	SP	COMMENT
Lyell, Charles, Sir	Science	95		425		Br. Founder of Modern Geology
Lyman, Charles Edwin	Clergy	15	25	50	30	
Lynch, David	Entertainment	20			50	TV Director "Twin Peaks"
Lynch, Kelly	Entertainment	10			50	Pin-Up SP $75
Lynch, Thomas Jr.	Revolutionary War	5565				Rare Signer
Lynde, Paul	Entertainment	10	15	25	25	
Lynen, Feodor	Science	20	40		25	Nobel Medicine
Lynley, Carol	Entertainment	15	15	35	35	Pin-Up SP $40
Lynn, Diana	Entertainment	15	15	35	30	
Lynn, Jeffrey	Entertainment	9	10	20	25	
Lynn, Loretta	Country Music	6			15	
Lyon, Ben	Entertainment	15			35	
Lyon, Mary Mason	Educator	55	165	340		
Lyon, Nathaniel	Civil War	350		1245		Union General
Lyon, Sue	Entertainment	9	10	20	25	
Lyons, Lord, Adm.	Military	25		130		
Lyons, Richard B.P.,1st Earl Lyons	Diplomat	20		65		Br. Minister to US in Civil War
Lyons, William	Business	40	80	175		
Lytell, Bert	Entertainment	35	45	90	60	
Lytton, E. George Bulwer	Author	30	95	205		Novelist, Poet, Colonial Sec'y

M

NAME	CATEGORY	SIG	LS/DS	ALS	SP	COMMENT
Mabley, Jackie "Moms"	Entertainment	65			200	
MacArthur, Arthur	Military	45	90	125	70	CW Off'r, Sp.-Am. War. General
MacArthur, Charles	Author	15	30	50	25	Playwright Husband Helen Hayes
MacArthur, Douglas	Military	200	790	870	670	5 Star Gen. WW II
MacArthur, Douglas II	Military	10	15	20	15	
MacArthur, James	Entertainment	6	8	15	25	
MacArthur, Jean	Military	15	20	25	15	Mrs. Douglas MacArthur
MacChesney, Nathan Wm.	Celebrity	10	20	85		
MacCracken, Henry M.	Clergy	20	35	45	30	
MacDonald, Charles H.	Aviation	15	30	52	3	ACE, WW II
MacDonald, Cordelia H.	Entertainment	40	75	120		1st Eva in "Uncle Tom's Cabin"
MacDonald, George	Clergy	20	30	45		
MacDonald, J. Farrell	Entertainment	25			50	
MacDonald, J. Ramsey	Head of State	30	130	170	265	Prime Minister
MacDonald, J.E.J.A.	Fr. Revolution	30	100	175		Marshal of Napoleon
MacDonald, Jeanette	Entertainment	50	200	275	175	
MacDonald, John Alexander	Head of State	35	90			Premier 1857, 1st P.M. Canada
MacDonald, Ross	Author	45	145	250		Mystery Writer
MacDonough, Thomas 1783-1825	Military	95	290	490		Am. Naval Off'r. Tripoli, 1812
MacDougall, Clinton	Civil War	35	60			Union General
MacDowell, Andie	Entertainment	15			40	
MacDowell, Edward	Composer	130	290	650	400	Songs, Concertos, Piano Pieces
MacDowell, Melbourne	Entertainment	15			40	Vintage Actor

NAME	CATEGORY	SIG	LS/DS	ALS	SP	COMMENT
MacGraw, Ali	Entertainment	8	9		20	Pin-Up SP $25
MacInnes, Helen	Author	5	15	20		Am Best Selling Novelist
MacKay, Charles	Clergy	20	25	35		
MacKaye, Percy	Author	35	90	150		Am. Poet, Dramatist
MacKenzie, Gisele	Entertainment	3	5	6	15	
MacLachlan, Kyle	Entertainment	10			20	
MacLagan, William D., Bishop	Clergy	15	25	35		
MacLaine, Shirley	Entertainment	15	15	35	45	Pin-Up SP $45
MacLaren, Donald M.	Military	25	40	95	75	
MacLean, Steve	Astronaut	7	15		16	
MacLeay, Lachlan	Astronaut	7			15	
MacLeish, Archibald	Author	30	115	135	40	Am. Poet, Lawyer. 3 Pulitzers
MacLeod, Gavin	Entertainment	6	8	15	15	
MacMahon, Aline	Entertainment	20			60	
MacMahon, Marie E.P.	Head of State	35	110	225		Fr.Soldier, Politician, Marshal
MacMillan, Harold	Head of State	25	85	150	50	Br. P.M.
MacMurray, Fred	Entertainment	20	95		45	
MacNee, Patrick	Entertainment	10			35	
MacNelly, Jeff*	Cartoonist	30			200	Shoe
MacNider, Hanford	Military	3	9	15		
MacPherson, James B.	Civil War	117	240	335		Union General
MacRae, Gordon	Entertainment	15			30	
MacRae, Meredith	Entertainment	5			15	
MacRae, Sheila	Entertainment	3			12	
MacReady, George	Entertainment	20			40	
MacVeagh, Franklin	Cabinet	10	25	60	20	Sec'y Treasury
MacVeagh, Wayne	Cabinet	30	40	65		Att'y Gen.
Macartney, Clarence E.	Clergy	15	20	25	20	
Macartney, George	Head of State	10	35	85		
Macaulay, (Emilie) Rose, Dame	Author	10	20	35		Br. Novelist, Critic, Verse
Macaulay, Thos. B., Lord	Author	45	62	115		Historian & Poet. Politician
Macbeth, Florence	Entertainment	20			50	Am. Soprano
Macchio, Ralph	Entertainment	7			20	
Macdonald, Jacques E.J.A.	Fr. Revolution	75		250		Marshal of Napoleon
Macdonogh, P. M. W.	Military	6	17	22		
Macfadden, Bernarr	Business	15	45	96	35	Physical Culturist, Publisher
Macfadyen, Dugald	Clergy	45	45	50	50	
Machado, Anesia Pinheiro	Aviation	35	55	80	65	
Machiavelli, Niccolo 1469-1527	Author	500	1250	4500		
Mack, Connie III	Senate	7	10		15	Senator FL
Mack, Helen	Entertainment	10			30	
Mack, Marion	Entertainment	10			35	
Mack, Ted	Entertainment	8			15	
Mackaill, Dorothy	Entertainment	25	30	70	60	Vintage Film Actress
Mackall, William W.	Civil War	250	350			CSA General
Mackay, John William	Business	40	100	215		Founder Postal Telegraph Co.
Mackensen, August von	Military	12	25	40	55	Ger. Gen. Fld. Marshal WW I
Mackenzie, Morell, Sir	Science	60	165	350		Larygologist. Misdiagnosed
Mackie, Bob	Business	5	10	25	15	Fashion Designer
Maclane, Barton	Entertainment	50			125	
Macleay, Lachlan	Astronaut	5			15	
Macleod, George F.	Clergy	20	25	30		
Macmillan, Donald B.	Explorer	25	65	170		Am./Peary at North Pole
Macnelly, Jeff*	Cartoonist	5			100	Shoe
Macpherson, Elle	Cover Girl	10			25	Pin-Up SP $40
Macy, Bill	Entertainment	4			15	

NAME	CATEGORY	SIG	LS/DS	ALS	SP	COMMENT
Madden, Charles Edw.	Military	45	120	215	100	
Maddox, Lester	Governor	25	40		30	Georgia Anti-Civil Rights Gov.
Madeira, Jean	Entertainment	15			40	Am. Contralto
Madigan, Amy	Entertainment	10			40	
Madison, Dolley Payne	First Lady	750	1825	2550		
Madison, Guy	Entertainment	6			25	
Madison, James	President	400	2390	4100	2500	
Madison, James & Monroe, James	Presidents		3535			
Madonna	Entertainment	50			240	
Madriguera, Enric	Entertainment	15			30	Big Band Leader
Madsen, Chris	Pioneer Lawman		2250			Outlaw & Indian Fighter
Madsen, Virginia	Entertainment	10			25	Pin-Up SP $35
Maeterlinck, Maurice, Count	Author	35	115	205		Nobel Literature
Maffett, Debbie Sue	Entertainment	4	5	9	9	
Magee, John A.	Senate/Congress	10		35		MOC NY 1827. Banker, RR
Magee, Patrick	Entertainment	10			35	
Magg, Alois	Aviation	4	9	16	15	
Magilton, Jerry	Astronaut	4			12	
Magnani, Anna	Entertainment	300			650	
Magritte, Rene'	Artist	200	350	840		Belgian Surrealist Painter
Magruder, John B.	Civil War	250	525	540		CSA General
Magsaysay, Ramon	Head of State	20	55	155	35	Pres. Philippines
Maguire, W.A. Cpt.	Military	25	50	75	60	
Mahan, Alfred Thayer	Military	50	75	100		US Navy Off'r-Historian. CW
Maharis, George	Entertainment	10	15	25	20	
Mahen, Robert A.	Business	15	30	70	40	
Mahendra Bir Bikram	Royalty	35	50	135	50	King, Leader Nepal
Mahler, Alma	Author	20		125		Author & Wife Gustav Mahler
Mahler, Gustav	Composer	550	1200	2560	1475	Austrian Composer
Mahone, William	Civil War	120	205	535		CSA General, US Senator VA
Mahoney, Jock	Entertainment	20	35	55	45	
Mahurin, Walker M. "Bud"	Aviation	15	35	55	40	ACE, WW II, Legendary Ace
Maiakovski, Vladimir V.	Author	300	795	2200		
Maikl, George	Entertainment	5			20	Opera
Mailer, Norman	Author	35	125	200	75	
Maillol, Aristide	Artist	200	460	800		Fr. Sculptor, Painter, Tapestry
Main, Majorie	Entertainment	100			250	
Maintenon, Francoise, Marquise de	Royalty			975		2nd Wife Louis XIV
Maison, Nicholas J. Marquis de	Fr. Revolution	35	150	195		Marshal of France
Maison, Rene'	Entertainment	30			60	Opera
Maitland, Lester J.	Aviation	20		40		
Major, John	Head of State	5			20	Br. Prime Minister
Majors, Lee	Entertainment	5	6	15	15	
Makarios III, Mikhail, Archbishop	Clergy-Head State	50	65	140	75	Cyprus
Makarova, Natalia	Entertainment	10			15	Ballet
Mako	Entertainment	6			20	
Malamud, Bernard	Author	25	40	105	30	Am. Novelist, Pulitzer
Malcom X	Black Leader	200	3950	4565		TLS/Content $10,000
Malden, Karl	Entertainment	9			25	
Malenkov, Georgi M.	Head of State	175	350	800	250	Union Sov. Russia
Malet, C. Francois de	Fr. Revolution	120	240			Gen'l. Court-martialed, Shot
Malher, J.P.F.	Fr. Revolution	25	80			
Malik, Charles	Head of State	7	15	35	10	
Malis, David	Entertainment	10			25	Opera
Malko, NIcolai	Entertainment	75			225	Rus. Conductor
Malkovich, John	Entertainment	10			40	

NAME	CATEGORY	SIG	LS/DS	ALS	SP	COMMENT
Malle, Louis	Entertainment	15		30	25	
Mallick, Don	Astronaut	5			15	
Mallory, Charles M.	Aviation	10	22	38	30	ACE, WW II
Mallory, Stephen R.	Civil War	105	225	240		CSA Sec'y of Navy
Malmesbury, Ist Earl 1746-1820l	Br. Diplomat	15	30	45		James Harris. Minister, Ambass.
Malo, Gina	Entertainment	3	3	6	6	
Malodva, Milada	Entertainment	7	9	20	15	
Malone, Dorothy	Entertainment	15	75		50	
Malone, Dumas	Author	10	30	75	15	
Maloney, Francis T.	Senate/Congress	10	20	40		Senator, MOC CT 1933-45
Malthus, Thomas Robert	Br. Economist	310	1100	2800		Educator, Author
Mamas and the Papas	Entertainment	350	900			(Four)
Mamas and the Papas, The (NEW)	Entertainment	10			20	(Four)
Mamet, David	Entertainment	10			25	Film Director
Mamoulian, Rouben	Entertainment	10	35		35	Film Director
Man Ray	Artist					SEE Ray, Man
Manchester, Melissa	Entertainment	10			25	
Manchester, William	Author	5	10	20	15	
Mancini, Henry	Composer	20			50	Conductor-Pianist
Mandel, Howie	Entertainment	6	8	15	15	
Mandel, John	Entertainment	5	6	15	10	
Mandel, Marvin	Governor	10	15		22	Governor MD
Mandela, Nelson	Afr. Statesman	80	170		100	Leader African Nat'l Congress
Mandell, Howie	Entertainment	5	8	20	15	
Manderson, Charles	Civil War	70	105	150		Union Gen. , U.S. Sen. NE
Mandrell, Barbara	Country Music	6			15	
Manet, Edouard	Artist	350	1945	2500		"Impressionist" School Founder
Manfrini, Luigi	Entertainment	40			125	Opera
Mangano, Silvana	Entertainment	25	35	60	50	
Mangione, Chuck	Entertainment	5	6	15	15	
Manhattan Transfer	Entertainment	35			80	
Manilow, Barry	Entertainment	15	45		55	Composer, Vocalist, Pianist
Manke, John	Astronaut	5			15	
Mankiewicz, Joseph L.	Entertainment	20		55	50	Film Director
Manley, N. W.	Head of State	12		25	20	Prime Minister Jamaica
Mann, Daniel	Entertainment	10			35	
Mann, Delbert	Entertainment	20			45	Film Director
Mann, Heinrich	Author	35	145	275		Ger. Novelist. Exiled, Interned
Mann, Horace	Educator	35	135	275		Reformer, Abolitionist
Mann, Manfred (All)	Entertainment	125				
Mann, Orrin L.	Civil War	20	35	60		Union General
Mann, Thomas	Aviation	12	25	48	35	ACE, WW II, Double Ace
Mann, Thomas	Author	125	520	1000	570	Ger. Novelist, Nobel Prize
Mann, Thomas Clifton	Celebrity	3			10	
Mannering, Mary	Entertainment	15			25	Vintage Stage Actress
Manners, David	Entertainment	10			35	
Manners-Sutton, Charles	Clergy	25	35	40		
Manning, Daniel	Cabinet	18	35	65		Sec'y Treasury
Manning, Henry E., Cardinal	Clergy	40	60	95	50	
Manning, Irene	Entertainment	6	8	15	10	
Manning, Stephen H.	Civil War	30	55	110		Union General
Manning, Timothy J., Cardinal	Clergy	35	40	50	45	
Manning, William T., Bishop	Clergy	20	35	75	25	
Manoff, Dinah	Entertainment	5			20	
Manone, Wingy	Entertainment	10			50	Jazz Trumpet-Vocalist
Mansfield, Jayne	Entertainment	165			500	

NAME	CATEGORY	SIG	LS/DS	ALS	SP	COMMENT
Mansfield, Joseph K.F.	Civil War	150	330	410		Union General
Mansfield, Mike	Senate/Congress	10	25	40	15	MOC, Senator MT
Mansfield, Richard	Entertainment	50		175		Vintage Stage Actor
Manship, Paul Howard	Artist	40	275	450		Am. Sculptor Prometheus Fount.
Manson, Charles (Buglioni)	Criminal	75	215	455	175	Murderer, Cult Figure
Manstein, Erich von, General	Military	20	60	95	75	Planned Assault vs France WW II
Mantell, Gideon A 1790-1852.	Science	10	25	40		Paleontologist. 4 Dinosaurs
Mantell, Robert B.	Entertainment	12			25	Vintage Shakespearean Actor
Mantelli, Eugenia	Entertainment	25			60	Opera
Manteuffel, Edwin F. von	Military	75		420		Prussian Fld. Marshal
Manteuffel, Hasso von	Military	40	85	190	90	Ger. Tank Commander
Mantovani	Entertainment	8	12		20	Conductor-Arranger
Manville, Tommy	Business	20		35		Much Married Asbestos Heir
Mao Tse Tung	Head of State	3000				Chinese Communist Leader
Maphis, Joe and Rose Lee	Country Music	10			20	
Mapleson, James H.	Entertainment	75				Opera
Mara, Adele	Entertainment	5	8		10	
Maragliano, Luisa	Entertainment	5			15	
Marat, Jean-Paul	Fr. Revolution			4500		Leader-Doctor-Author.Murdered
Marbot, J.B.A.M.	Fr. Revolution	25	70	125		Napoleonic General
Marceau, Marcel	Entertainment	20			95	Mime
Marcellino, Muzzy	Entertainment	10	15	25	25	
March, Fredric	Entertainment	35		95	80	
Marchesi, Mathilde	Entertainment	50		160	175	Ger. Mezzo-Sopr. Teacher
Marcinkus, Paul C., Archbishop	Clergy	45	65	100	50	
Marconi, Guglielmo	Science	160	450	2050	975	It. Physicist-Inventor. Nobel
Marcos, Ferdinand E.	Head of State	50	135		130	Pres. Philippines
Marcovicci, Andrea	Entertainment	10			20	
Marcus, Rudolph A., Dr.	Science	20	35		30	Nobel Chemistry
Marcus, Stanley	Business	25	75	160	55	Merchant. Nieman-Marcus
Marcy, William L.	Cabinet	40	175	235		Sec'y War, State. Senator NY
Maren, Jerry	Entertainment	15			35	
Marescot, Armand S.	Fr. Revolution	30	80	170		
Maressyev, Alexei	Aviation	135				Rus. ACE & Soviet Hero
Maret, Hugues B., Duke	Fr. Revolution	75	210			Napoleon Confidential Advisor
Maret, Hugues B., Duke de	Napoleonic Wars	90	200			Diplomat-P.M.-Advisor Napoleon
Marey, Etienne	Science	50		700		Fr. Physiologist. Sphygmograph
Margie*	Cartoonist	20			250	Little Lulu
Margo (Mrs Ed Albert)	Entertainment	15	15	35	30	
Maria (Castile)	Royalty		2500			Queen of Alfonso V of Aragon
Maria Theresa	Royalty	185	650	980		Archduchess, Qn Hung.-Bohemia
Marie Amelie (Queen of Fr.)	Royalty	170	240			Queen of Louis Phillippe I
Marie Antoinette (Fr)	Royalty	1200	4850			Queen of Louis XVI France
Marie of Modena (Queen Gr. Brit.)	Royalty	335	530			Queen of James II
Marie of Naples	Royalty	15		85		Queen of King Louis-Phillipe I
Marie of Romania	Royalty	85	115	240	100	
Marin, John	Artist	60	225	550		Am. Watercolorist, Etching
Marinaro, Ed	Entertainment	6	8	15	15	
Marion, Francis	Rev. War		6500	8500		"The Swamp Fox"
Mariscal, Don Ignacio	Statesman	20	35	55		V.P. Mexico
Maritain, Jacques	Clergy	40	45	95	75	
Maritza, Sari	Entertainment	8	9		20	
Markham, Albert H., Sir	Celebrity	5	20	45		
Markham, Clements, Sir	Geographer	10	25	55		Historian,Pres.Royal Geogr.Soc.
Markham, Edwin	Author	30	115	140	65	"The Man With The Hoe"
Markham, William	Colonial America	135	450			Colonial Gov. PA

NAME	CATEGORY	SIG	LS/DS	ALS	SP	COMMENT
Markova, Alicia	Entertainment	20			50	Ballet
Markowitz, Harry M., Dr.	Economics	20	35	45		Nobel Economics
Marks, Johnny	Composer	35	90	125	50	AMusQS $175
Marks, William, Jr. 1778-1858	Senate	35	140			PA Senator, ALS/Content $400
Marlborough,John Churchill,1stDuke	Military	220	765			Br. General and Statesman
Marley, Bob	Entertainment	50			100	Rock HOF. Reggae King
Marlin, Mahlon F.	Business	40	115	225		Pres-Treas. Marlin Firearms Co.
Marlow, Lucy	Entertainment	5	6	15	15	
Marlowe, Hugh	Entertainment	25			50	
Marlowe, Julia	Entertainment	25	35	70	60	Major Stage Star/E.H. Sothern
Marly, Florence	Entertainment	4	4	9	9	
Marmont, A.F.L.V., Duke	Fr. Revolution	45	90			Marshal of Fr.,Napoleon A-D-C
Marney, Carlyle	Clergy	20	25	35	35	
Marquand, John P.	Author	40	120	165	45	Am. Novelist. Pulitzer
Marques, Antonio	Entertainnment	35			85	Opera
Marriott, J.	Business	20	35	70	30	Marriott Hotel Chain
Marryat, Frederick 1792-1848	Military-Author	30	100	225		Br. Naval Cmmdr. Novelist
Marsala, Joe	Entertainment	20			65	Clarinet, Sax, Composer
Marsalis, Branford	Entertainment	10			25	Conductor, Sax
Marsalis, Wynton	Entertainment	15			30	Trumpet Virtuoso. Classic-Jazz
Marsden, Jason	Entertainment	10			25	"The Munsters"
Marsh, Jean	Entertainment	7			20	
Marsh, Joan	Entertainment	15	20	40	35	
Marsh, Mae	Entertainment	30	40	75	40	
Marsh, Marion	Entertainment	15			40	
Marsh, Ngaio, Dame	Author	20	35	50	40	New Zealand Mystery Writer
Marshall, Catherine	Author	20	60	150	25	
Marshall, Cathy	TV News	7	20		10	CNN News
Marshall, Christopher	Revolutionary War	100				Am. Patriot & Diarist
Marshall, E.G.	Entertainment	10			25	
Marshall, George	Entertainment	35			75	Film Director. 400+ Films
Marshall, George C.	Military	100	250	550	375	WW II Chief Staff. Nobel Peace
Marshall, Herbert	Entertainment	6	75		35	
Marshall, Humphrey	Civil War	80	195			CSA General
Marshall, John (SC)	Supreme Court	435	1725	5000		Chief Justice
Marshall, John, Sir	Head of State	10	20	35	20	Prime Minister New Zealand
Marshall, Margaret	Entertainment	10			25	Opera
Marshall, Penny	Entertainment	8			20	And Film Director
Marshall, Peter	Clergy	45	75	100	75	
Marshall, Thomas Riley (V)	Vice President	75	175	400	175	Wilson VP
Marshall, Thurgood (SC)	Supreme Court	115	145	200	175	
Marshall, Tully	Entertainment	20			50	
Marshall, William	Entertainment	15			25	Film Director
Marshall, William	Civil War	25	40	75		Union Gen., Gov. MN
Marshall. Catherine	Clergy	25	30	50	30	
Marterie, Ralph	Entertainment	10			20	Big Band Leader
Martin, Charles H.	Governor	10	25			Governor OR
Martin, Chris Pin	Entertainment	50			100	
Martin, Clarence D.	Governor	5	15		10	Governor WA
Martin, Dean	Entertainment	5		30	25	
Martin, Dean & Lewis, Jerry	Entertainment	125				Vintage SP (Both) $275
Martin, Dean Vincent	Entertainment	5	6	15	15	
Martin, Dick	Entertainment	6	8	15	20	
Martin, Freddie	Entertainment	35			65	Big Band Leader-Pianist
Martin, Glenn L.	Aviation	75	170	265	250	Aeronautical Pioneer.
Martin, James Green	Civil War	80	165			CSA General

NAME	CATEGORY	SIG	LS/DS	ALS	SP	COMMENT
Martin, John A.	Governor	12		30		Governor KS
Martin, John C.	Senate/Congress	5	10			MOC IL
Martin, Joseph W. Jr.	Senate/Congress	20	35		25	Speaker of the House
Martin, Luther	Revolutionary War	70	175	360		Continental Congress
Martin, Mary	Entertainment	16			40	
Martin, Pamela Sue	Entertainment	6		15	15	Pin-Up SP $20
Martin, Ricardo	Entertainment	15			45	Opera
Martin, Ross	Entertainment	10	20	40	30	
Martin, Steve	Entertainment	5			25	
Martin, Struther	Entertainment	35			80	
Martin, Theodore, Sir	Author	5	15	25	10	
Martin, Thomas S.	Senate	12	25			Senator VA 1893. CSA Army
Martin, Tony	Entertainment	10			25	
Martin, William C., Bishop	Clergy	15	25	30	35	
Martin, William Thompson	Civil War	125	295	525		CSA General
Martine, James E.	Senate/Congress	5	15		10	Senator NJ
Martinelli, Giovanni	Entertainment	40	50		225	Opera
Martinez, Luis, Cardinal	Clergy	30	45	55	50	
Martini, Steve	Author	5	10		10	Novelist
Martino, Al	Entertainment	3	5		8	
Martino, Donald	Composer	20	35	90		Pulitzer, AMusQS $180
Martinu, Bronislaw	Composer					Czech. Composer AMusQS $900
Martiny, Philip	Artist	25	40	80	30	
Marton, Eva	Entertainment	20			50	Opera
Marvel, Ik	Author	10		30		Pseud. Donald G. Mitchell
Marvin, Lee	Entertainment	85			225	
Marx Brothers (3)	Entertainment	750			1500	
Marx Brothers (4)	Entertainment	950			2650	
Marx, Arthur	Author	10	15		15	
Marx, Chico	Entertainment	125	170	325	325	
Marx, Groucho	Entertainment	150	300		225	
Marx, Harpo	Entertainment	400				
Marx, Karl	Author	540	1500	14750		Ger. Political Philosopher
Marx, Richard	Entertainment	20			50	Singer
Marx, Zeppo	Entertainment	90			125	
Mary (of Teck)	Royalty	125		205	370	Queen of George V (Eng.)
Mary Adalaide (Dchs. Teck)	Royalty	25	70	195		Queen Mary's Mother
Mary I 1516-58	Royalty	900	3000	7500		Queen England, Bloody Mary
Mary II (Eng)	Royalty	370	1240	3100		Queen William II (NRPA)
Mary of Modena	Royalty					SEE Marie of Modena
Masaryk, Jan	Head of State	95	155	275		Pres. Czechoslavakia
Masaryk, Thomas G.	Head of State	150	250	575	550	Czech.Philosopher,1st President
Mascagni, Pietro	Composer	165	375	675	515	AMusQS $650-1250
Mascherini, Enzo	Entertainment	15			50	Opera
Masefield, John	Author	25	95	200	40	Br. Poet Laureate
Maskelyne, Nevil	Science	85	250	385		Br. Astronomer Royal
Mason, Alfred Edw. W.	Author	10	30	45	15	Br. Novelist
Mason, George	Revolutionary War	1775	4500			Am. Planter & Rev. Statesman
Mason, James	Entertainment	20	45	65	60	Actor-Film Director
Mason, James M.	Civil War	50	115	145		US Sen. VA, CSA Diplomat
Mason, LeRoy	Entertainment	50			150	
Mason, Marsha	Entertainment	5	10		25	
Mason, Sully	Entertainment	5	6	15	10	
Mason, William E.	Senate/Congress	12	20		15	MOC, Senator IL
Massen, Osa	Entertainment	4	6	10	10	
Massena, Andre, Duke	Fr. Revolution	95	305	450		Marshal of Fr.

NAME	CATEGORY	SIG	LS/DS	ALS	SP	COMMENT
Massenet, Jules	Composer	65	145	240	295	AMusQS $650-$800-$1500
Massey, Gerald	Author	25	70	95		Br. Poet, Journalist, Editor
Massey, Illona	Entertainment	20		30	30	
Massey, Raymond	Entertainment	25			55	
Massie, Paul	Entertainment	5	6	15	10	
Massine, Leonide	Entertainment	20			105	Ballet Dancer,Choreographer...
Masson, Andre	Artist	40	55	95		
Masters and Johnson	Sex Researchers	20			40	Wm. H. and Virginia
Masters, Edgar Lee	Author	50	150	250	65	Am. Poet, Biographer
Masters, Frankie	Entertainment	5			25	Big Band Leader
Masterson, Mary Stuart	Entertainment	10			40	
Masterson, Wm. B. "Bat"	Lawman	500		3850		Scout, Sheriff, Gambler
Mastroantonio, Mary	Entertainment	10	15	25	30	
Mastroianni, Marcello	Entertainment	20			45	
Mata Hari (M.G. Zelle)	Spy	350	1100	2850		Executed Secret Agent WW I
Mather, Cotton	Rev. War-Clergy	825	1950	3500		Author, Published 382 Books
Mathers, Jerry 'Beaver'	Entertainment	25			45	
Matheson, Tim	Entertainment	10			25	
Mathews, George 1739-1812	Revolutionary War	85	190			Statesman, General
Mathias, Bob	Senate/Congress	10	15		15	MOC CA
Mathis, Johnny	Entertainment	9	10	20	25	
Mathiuci, Franca	Entertainment	5			15	
Matisse, Henri	Artist	510	820	2040		Fr. Painter, Sculptor, Fauvist
Matlack, Timothy	Revolutionary War	85	275	450		Continental Congress
Matlin, Marlee	Entertainment	10		45	40	Pin-Up SP $100
Matsushita, Konosuke	Business	25	65	145	40	Japanese Electronic Giant
Mattea, Kathy	Country Music	5			15	
Mattern, Jimmie	Aviation	15	25	60	35	
Matthau, Walter	Entertainment	5		15	25	
Matthews, Frank Arnold	Clergy	20	25	35	25	
Matthews, Jessie	Entertainment	20			35	Br.Vintage Film Actress
Matthews, Stanley (SC)	Supreme Court	45	150	250		
Mattingly, Thos. Ken	Astronaut	15			40	
Mattson, Conrad	Aviation	8	15	28	22	ACE, WW II
Mature, Victor	Entertainment	9	10	20	25	
Maubourg, Lafayette	Celebrity	5	12	20		Nephew
Mauch, Billy	Entertainment	10	15	25	25	
Mauch, Bobby	Entertainment	30			65	
Maugham, W. Somerset	Author	90	330	275	315	Br. Novelist and Playwright
Mauldin, Bill*	Cartoonist	25			225	Willie & Joe
Maupassant, Guy de	Author	325	795	1185		Fr. Master of Short Story
Maura, Antonio	Head of State	110	165			Sp. P.M. Provoked Rif War
Maurey, Pierre	Clergy	10	15	30	25	Pres. Reform Church France
Mauro, Ermanno	Entertainment	15			40	Opera
Maurois, Andre (Emile Herzog)	Author	35	75	120		Fr. Biographer, Novelist
Maury, Dabney H.	Civil War	150	200	350		CSA General
Maury, Matthew Fontaine	Civil War	105			1550	CSA Naval Cmdr., Hydrographer
Mawson, Douglas, Sir	Explorer	50	160	375		Australian Polar Explorer
Max, Peter	Artist	90	350			Am. Contemporary Art.
Maxey, Samuel Bell	Civil War	165	210	265		CSA General, US Sen. TX
Maxey, Virginia	Entertainment	5			10	
Maxim, Hiram Percy	Science	40	265			Inventor Maxim Gun Silencer etc
Maxim, Hiram Stevens	Science	95	190	285	300	Inventor Maxim Machine Gun
Maxim, Hudson	Science	60	115	175	175	Inventor Smokeless Powder
Maximilian II (Bohemia-Hung.)	Royalty	110	415	770		Holy Roman Emperor
Maximilian, Ferdinand	Royalty	310	785	1250		Emperor Mexico

NAME	CATEGORY	SIG	LS/DS	ALS	SP	COMMENT
Maxon, R.*	Cartoonist	20			100	Tarzan
Maxwell, Elsa	Columnist	8	25	35	15	Hostess & Professional Party
Maxwell, Lois	Entertainment	10			25	
Maxwell, Marilyn	Entertainment	8	10		35	
Maxwell, Robert	Aviation	12	25	28	22	ACE, WW II
Maxwell, Robert	Publisher	45			120	Died Mysteriously
Maxwell, William (Ld. Beaverbrook)	Publisher	25	110	180		Newspaper Proprietor, Statesman
May, Edna	Entertainment	18		30	28	Vintage Stage & Film
Mayall, John	Entertainment	10			30	
Maybank, Burnet R.	Governor	10	18		15	Governor, Senator SC
Maye, Carolyn	Entertainment	10			25	
Mayer, Louis B.	Business	65	190	275	200	MGM Film Studio
Mayer, Maria, Dr.	Science	30	85		50	Nobel Physics
Mayfair, Mitzi	Entertainment	4			10	
Maynard, Ken	Entertainment	100		145	175	
Mayo, 6th Earl(Rich.Bourke)	Head of State	10		30		Br. Politician.Viceroy of India
Mayo, Charles H., Dr.	Science	150	290	380	475	Co-Founder Mayo Foundation
Mayo, Charles W., Dr.1898-1968	Science	65	140	235	350	Surgeon Mayo Clinic.Prof. Surg.
Mayo, Henry Thomas	Military	15	40	75	40	Adm. Cmdr. Atlantic Fl. WW I
Mayo, Virginia	Entertainment	5			25	Pin-Up SP $40
Mayo, William J., Dr.	Science	105	290	380	475	Co-Founder Mayo Foundation
Maytag, Frederick L.	Business	95	275	600	150	Maytag Electric Appliances
Mazurki, Mike	Entertainment	5	6	15	15	
Mazurski, Paul	Entertainment	5			20	Film Director
Mazzini, Joseph (Giuseppe)	Revolutionary	55	155	645		Italian Patriot
Mazzoleni, Ester	Entertainment	50			190	Opera
McAdoo, William G.	Cabinet	25	100	165	50	Wilson Sec'y Treasury
McAllister, Ron	Entertainment	15			30	
McArdle, Andrea	Entertainment	5	6	15	15	
McArthur, Kim	Playboy Bunny	4			8	Pin-Up SP $10
McArthur, William	Astronaut	7			15	
McAuliffe, Anthony A.	Military	45	175	225	250	WW II Gen'l. Replied "Nuts"
McAuliffe, S. Christa	Astronaut	450			650	
McBain, Diane	Entertainment	5	6	15	10	
McBain, Ed	Author	10	20	50	15	
McBride, George W.	Senate	5	15			Senator OR
McBride, Jon A.	Astronaut	5	15		30	
McCaffrey, Anne	Author	5			10	Novelist
McCain, John S., Jr.	Military-Senate	5	30	45	20	Senator AZ
McCall, Tom	Governor	5	10		15	Governor OR
McCalla, Irish	Entertainment	10		25	25	Pin-Up SP $35
McCallister, Lon	Entertainment	10			30	
McCallum, David	Entertainment	5	6	15	15	
McCambridge, Mercedes	Entertainment	40			75	
McCampbell, David S.	Aviation	15	25	45	75	ACE, WW II, Top Navy Ace, MOH
McCandless, Bruce II	Astronaut	10		90	24	
McCann, Chuck	Business	5	15	30	10	
McCarey, Leo	Entertainment	35			65	Academy Award Director, Prod.
McCarthy, Eugene J.	Senate	25			30	Senator MN. Pres. Candidate
McCarthy, Joe	Senate/Congress	50	150		95	Senator WI
McCarthy, Kevin	Entertainment	10			25	
McCarthy, Mary	Author	45	135		50	Novelist
McCarthy, Michael W.	Business	3	5	10	5	
McCartney, Paul	Entertainment	100			475	
McCaulay, Rose, Dame	Br. Author	20			45	
McCay, Winsor*	Cartoonists	50			600	Little Nemo

NAME	CATEGORY	SIG	LS/DS	ALS	SP	COMMENT
McClanahan, Rue	Entertainment	10	10		25	
McClellan, George B.	Civil War	200	275	395		Union General
McClellan, John L.	Senate/Congress	10	20		25	MOC, Senator AR
McClernand, John A.	Civil War	65	95	175		
McClintic, James V.	Senate/Congress	5	10		7	MOC OK
McClintock, Francis Leopold	Explorer	45	115	200		Br. Adm., Arctic Navigator
McClintock, John	Astronaut	5	15		20	
McClinton, Delbert	Country Music	10			25	Singer-Musician. TX Blues Man
McCloskey, John, Cardinal	Clergy	95	125	250	100	
McCloskey, Lee	Entertainment	5	6	15	15	
McClosky, Pete	Senate/Congress	5	10		10	
McClung, J.T.M.	Senate/Congress	5	15		10	
McClure, Doug	Entertainment	5			15	
McClurg, Alexander C.	Civil War	50	85			Union General
McColpin, Carroll W.	Military	25	45	75	45	ACE WW II
McConnell, Calvin D., Bishop	Clergy	20	25	30	30	
McConnell, Francis J., Bishop	Clergy	20	25	50	30	
McConnell, James, Bishop	Clergy	20	25	35	30	
McConnell, Joseph, Jr.	Aviation	75	140	175	150	ACE, Korea, Top Korea Ace
McCoo, Marilyn	Entertainment	5	6	15	15	
McCook, Alex. M. D.	Civil War	35	65	90		Union Gen.
McCook, Anson	Civil War	30	55			Union Gen., MOC
McCook, Henry C.	Clergy	10	10	15		
McCormack, John	Entertainment	40	155	265	170	
McCormack, John W.	Speaker of House	10	25	75		Speaker of the House
McCormack, Patty	Entertainment	5	8	15	15	
McCormick, Anne O'Hare	Author	30	45	110	35	1st Pulitzer Woman Journalist
McCormick, Cyrus H.	Science-Business	190	705	1025		Invented the Reaper
McCormick, Myron	Entertainment	15	25	45	40	
McCormick, Nettie Fowler	Business	25		90		Mrs. Cyrus McCormick
McCormick, Robert R., Col.	Business	35	140	165	60	Editor Chicago Tribune
McCoy, Charles B.	Business	5			10	Pres. DuPont Co.
McCoy, Clyde	Entertainment	6	8	15	15	
McCoy, Tim	Entertainment	45			155	
McCoy, Wilson*	Cartoonist	15			75	Phantom
McCrea, Joel	Entertainment	15	95		40	
McCreery, Richard L., Sir	Military	30	75		40	Br. Gen. WW II
McCudden, James T.B.	Aviation	135	225	350	300	ACE, WW I, RAF
McCullers, Carson	Author	60	195	375	75	Am. Novelist
McCulley, Michael J.	Astronaut	5			15	
McCulloch, Ben	Civil War	130	310	370		CSA General
McCulloch, Henry E.	Civil War	145	350			CSA General
McCulloch, Hugh	Cabinet	40	70	135		Lincoln, Johnson Sec'y Treas.
McCullough, Colleen	Author	35	105	225	40	Austr. Novelist."Thorn Birds"
McCullough, John	Entertainment	10			35	Vintage Stage Actor
McCullough, Julie	Entertainment	7			20	Pin-Up SP $35
McDaniel, Hattie	Entertainment	750			2500	
McDermott, Dylan	Entertainment	15			50	
McDevitt, Ruth	Entertainment	10			20	
McDivitt, James A.	Astronaut	10			35	
McDonald, A. J. (Al)	Astronaut	20			30	NASA Whistleblower
McDonald, Marie	Entertainment	35	45	90	85	
McDonald, Richard J.	Business	90	225	450	175	MacDonald's
McDonald, Skeets	Country Music	10			20	
McDonnell, James S.	Business	20	45	95	35	Founder, McDonnell Aircraft
McDonnell, Mary	Entertainment	20			50	

NAME	CATEGORY	SIG	LS/DS	ALS	SP	COMMENT
McDougall, Alexander	Revolutionary War	90	200	415		Gen. Cont. Army,Cont. Congress
McDowell, Andre	Entertainment	5			30	
McDowell, Irvin	Civil War	125	235	525	1250	Union Gen.Special DS $400
McDowell, Malcolm	Entertainment	10			35	
McDowell, Roddy	Entertainment	15			25	
McElroy, Neil H.	Cabinet	15	35		25	Sec'y Defense. Pres. P & G
McEnery, S.D.	Governor	12	25			Governor LA
McEntire, Reba	Country Music	15			30	
McEntyre, Joe (New Kids)	Entertainment	10			45	
McFadden, Gates	Entertainment	5			15	"Star Trek"
McFadden, Obadiah B.	Senate/Congress	15	30	40		MOC WA 1873
McFarland, Spanky	Entertainment	25			60	
McGarru. William D.	Aviation	15	30	45	40	ACE, WW II, Flying Tigers
McGavin, Darren	Entertainment	25			50	
McGee, Gale	Senate/Congress	5	15		10	Senator WY
McGill, John	Clergy	90		450		CW Bishop of Richmond
McGillis, Kelly	Entertainment	10		20	35	
McGinley, Phyllis	Author	10	30	45	20	Am Poet. Pulitzer
McGoohan, Patrick	Entertainment	20			45	
McGovern, Elizabeth	Entertainment	5			20	
McGovern, George	Senate	10			25	Senator SD, Pres. Hopeful
McGovern, John	Author	25	40			
McGranery, James P.	Cabinet	10	15	25		Att'y General
McGrath, J. Howard	Cabinet	5	20	35	15	Att'y General
McGuffy, William H.	Educator	95	475			McGuffy's Reader
McGuigan, James, Cardinal	Clergy	5	10	15	12	
McGuire Sisters	Entertainment					Singing Group
McGuire, Barry	Entertainment	5	6		25	New Christy Minstrels
McGuire, Dorothy	Entertainment	15			30	
McGuire, Phyllis	Entertainment	4	15		10	McGuire Sisters
McGuire, Thomas B.	Aviation	150	300	650	450	ACE, WW II, #2 U.S. Ace
McHenry, James	Cabinet-Military	180	280	895		Signer Constitution, Sec'y War
McHugh, Frank	Entertainment	20	25	65	60	
McHugh, Jimmy	Composer	25	75			AMusQS $825
McHugh, Joseph	Artist	5			10	
McIntire, John	Entertainment	20			50	
McIntosh, Lachlan	Revolutionary War	550	855	1375		Killed Button Gwinnett. Duel
McIntyre, James F., Archbishop	Clergy	40	65	75	60	
McIntyre, Marvin H.	Cabinet	3	10	15		Sec'y to FDR
McIntyre, O. O.	Author	15	25	40	20	Journalist, Synd. Columnist
McKay, Douglas	Cabinet	15	25		20	Governor OR, Sec'y Interior
McKay, Gardner	Entertainment	6	8	15	20	
McKean, Thomas	Revolutionary War	175	470	910		Signer Decl. of Ind.
McKee, Thomas H.	Senate/Congress	10	20			
McKeldin, Theodore R.	Governor	5	17		10	Governor MD
McKellar, Kenneth	Senate	10	30			Senator TN
McKenna, Joseph (SC)	Supreme Court	35	50	80	40	Att'y General
McKenna, Siobhan	Entertainment	15			35	
McKenzie, Fay	Entertainment	5		15	15	
McKeon, Nancy	Entertainment	4	6		20	
McKeon, Phillip	Entertainment	5			20	
McKinley, Ida S.	First Lady	400	625	975	450	
McKinley, William	President	295	750	965	1075	Assassinated by Anarchist
McKinly, John	Revolutionary War	65	180			First Gov. DE, Captured by Br.
McKinstry, Addis E.	Business	10	25	50	20	
McKone, John R.	Military	10	20	40	30	

NAME	CATEGORY	SIG	LS/DS	ALS	SP	COMMENT
McKuen, Rod	Author	10	20	35	50	Poet
McLaglin, Andrew V.	Entertainment	10		25		
McLaglin, Victor	Entertainment	150			275	
McLain, Raymond S.	Military	30			45	Gen. WW II
McLains, The	Country Music	20			45	
McLane, Louis	Business	35	150			Pres. Wells Fargo & Co.
McLane, Louis 1786-1857	Cabinet	15	45	60		Jackson Sec'y Treasury
McLane, Robert	Diplomat-Gov.	35	80	135		Gov. MD, U.S. Minister to Jap.
McLaughlin, E.A.	Business	10	35	45	20	
McLaughlin, James C.	Senate/Congress	10	15		15	MOC MI
McLaughlin, Kyle	Entertainment	20			75	
McLaws, Lafayette	Civil War	75	155	230		CSA General
McLean, Don	Entertainment	20			45	Rock
McLean, George P.	Senate	10	15	25		Gov., Senator CT
McLean, John (SC)	Supreme Court	55	200	200		Dissented Dred Scott Opinion
McLean, Nathaniel C.	Civil War	60	80	170		Union General
McLeod, Archibald Norman	Fur Trader		2500			Hudson's Bay Co. vs NW Co.
McLeod, Catherine	Entertainment	6	9		15	
McLintock, Francis Sir	Celebrities	10	30	75		
McMahon, Brien	Senate	10	40		15	Senator CT
McMahon, Ed	Entertainment	5			15	
McMahon, Horace	Entertainment	20			50	
McManus, George*	Cartoonist	40			200	Bringing Up Father,Panel $1,500
McMichael, Morton	Journalist	45	95			1st Editor Saturday Eve'g Post
McMillan, Edwin M.	Science	20	35	69	30	Nobel Chemistry 1952
McMillan, James	Senate	12	20	35		Senator MI 1889
McMillan, James Winning	Civil War	40				Union General
McMillan, Kenneth	Entertainment	5	6	15	15	
McMillan, Terry	Entertainment	3	4	10	8	
McMonagle, Donald	Astronaut	4			12	
McMullen, Clements	Military	50	150			WW I Aviator, WW II General
McMullen, Richard C.	Governor	5	10			Governor DE
McNair, Leslie J.	Military	35	95	165	80	WW I, General, WW II KIA
McNair, Robert	Governor	5	15		10	Governor SC
McNair, Ronald E.	Astronaut	85			275	Died in Challenger Crash
McNally, Stephen	Entertainment	10			20	
McNally, W.	Entertainment	5	6	15	15	
McNamara, Robert S.	Cabinet	15	50		30	Sec'y Defense, Pres. World Bank
McNamara, William	Entertainment	5	8	25	25	
McNarney, Joseph T.	Military	20	50			General WW II
McNary, Charles L.	Senate	15	35			Senator OR. McNary Dam
McNaughton, Kenneth	Military	4	9	15	10	
McNee, Patrick	Entertainment	10			25	
McNeill, Don	Entertainment	10			20	
McNichol, Kristy	Entertainment	10			30	Pin-Up SP $35
McNutt, Paul V.	Governor	15	30			Governor IN
McPartland, Jimmy	Entertainment	30	55		85	Jazz Trumpet
McPhatter, Clyde	Entertainment	400		800		Classic Rocker
McPherson, Aimee Semple	Clergy	100	300	495	350	
McPherson, Craig	Artists					
McPherson, Isaac V.	Senate/Congress	5	15			MOC MO
McPherson, James B.	Civil War	150		1125		Union General
McPherson, John R.	Senate	12	20	30		Senator NJ
McQuade, James	Civil War	20	40	65		Union General
McQueen, Butterfly	Entertainment	15	30		45	
McQueen, Steve	Entertainment	200	295	400	325	

NAME	CATEGORY	SIG	LS/DS	ALS	SP	COMMENT
McRaney, Gerald	Entertainment	5			25	
McReynolds, James C. (SC)	Supreme Court	50	125	145	100	Wilson Att'y Gen.
McShane, Ian	Entertainment	9	10	20	25	
McShann, Jay	Entertainment	50			125	Jazz Pianist,Vocalist, Bandlead
McWhorter, Hamilton	Aviation	12	25	45	35	ACE, WW II
McWilliams, Caroline	Entertainment	4	6	9	9	
Mcaffee, Johnny	Entertainment	3	3	6	6	
Mead, Margaret	Science	50		170	65	Anthropologist,Lecturer, Author
Meade, Carl J.	Astronaut	5			16	
Meade, George Gordon	Civil War	245	345	765	350	Union Gen. DS $1,750 War Dte
Meadowlarks	Entertainment	3			6	
Meadows, Audrey	Entertainment	15			40	Pin-Up SP $45
Meadows, Jayne	Entertainment	5			10	
Meaney, Colm	Entertainment	15			25	"Star Trek"
Meany, George	Labor Leader	15	30		45	Pres. AFL-CIO
Meara, Anne	Entertainment	4	4		15	
Meat Loaf	Entertainment	5		25	45	Rock
Mecham, Edwin L.	Senate	5	15		12	Governor, Senator NM
Medawar, Peter B., Sir	Science	20	30	60	25	Nobel Medicine 1960
Medeiros, Humberto, Cardinal	Clergy	35	50	60	50	
Medici, Cosimo I, de	Royalty	375	1500			"The Great". Duke of Florence
Medici, Fernando de 1549-1609	Royalty	370	1250	3125		Son of Cosimo I. Gr. Duke
Medici, Leopoldo de, Cardinal	Clergy	300	385	550		Cardinal. Son of Cosimo II
Medicis, Francesco de	Royalty	100	200	500		NRPA
Medicis, Marie de	Royalty	350	950			Queen of Henry IV (Fr)
Medill, Joseph	Journalist	125		250		A founder Repub. Party
Medina, Harold R.	Jurist	10	25		15	
Medina, Patricia	Entertainment	4	5		15	
Medjugorje (Jugo) Children of	Religious	300				2 Who Saw Vision Virgin Mary
Medley, Bill	Country Music	6			20	
Meeker, Ralph	Entertainment	25			40	
Meese, Edwin III	Cabinet	5	20	35	25	Att'y General
Mehta, Zubin	Entertainment	10			25	International Conductor
Meier, Waltraud	Entertainment	15			35	Opera
Meighan, Tom	Entertainment	35			85	
Meigs, Montgomery C.	Civil War	70	140	195	250	Union Quartermaster General
Meigs, Return J., Jr.	Military-Cabinet	80	205	360		Monroe P.M. General
Meiklejohn, G.D.	Cabinet	15	40			Ass't Sec'y War
Meinl, Tanaka	Entertainment	30			75	Opera
Meir, Golda	Head of State	90	375	605	225	TLS/Content $1,500-$2,500
Melba, Nellie	Entertainment	70	135	205	215	Australian Soprano
Melbourne, Wm. Lamb, Lord	Head of State	50	70	110		Q.Victoria's 1st Prime Minister
Melchoir, Lauritz	Entertainment	60			210	Opera
Melis, Carmen	Entertainment	35			85	Opera, Teacher
Mellencamp, John	Entertainment	35			50	Rock
Mellnik, Steve	Military	5	25	35		
Mellon, Andrew	Business	60	295	410	150	
Melnick, Bruce E.	Astronaut	5			16	
Melton, James	Entertainment	10			50	
Melvill, Thomas	Revolutionary War	90	250	550		Memb. Boston Tea Party
Melville, George W.	Military	40	105	170		Union Adm.
Melville, Herman	Author	500	1820	5000		ALS's/Content $20,000-$40,000
Memminger, Christopher G.	Civil War	165	460	535		CSA Sec'y of Treasury
Mencken, Henry L.	Author	95	310	365	450	Satirist, Editor, Critic
Mendel, Gregor Johann	Science	400	850	2000		Laws of Biological Inheiritance
Mendelssohn-Bartholdy, F.	Composer	600	1250	2650		ALS/Content $6,500

NAME	CATEGORY	SIG	LS/DS	ALS	SP	COMMENT
Mendes, Abraham Caulle	Author	15	35	100		Fr. Poet.Plays, Verses,Libretti
Mendez, Arnaldo Tamayo	Astronaut	6			15	
Mengelberg, Willem	Entertainment	85			210	Dutch Conductor
Menjou, Adolphe	Entertainment	20	25		75	
Menk, Louis W.	Business	5			10	CEO International Harvester
Menken, Helen	Entertainment	15	15	30	25	
Menkes, Sara	Entertainment	20			55	Opera
Mennin, Peter	Composer	10		65		AMusQS $75
Menninger, Karl	Science	35	95	120	65	Menninger Clinic & Foundation
Menninger, Roy	Science	10	25	55	30	
Menninger, William C., Dr.	Science	15	40	70	35	Psychiatrist, Pres. Foundation
Menocal, Mario G.	Head of State	25			40	Pres. Cuba 1913-21
Menon, V. Krisna	Diplomat	20		25		Ambassador Gr. Britain
Menotti, Gian Carlo	Composer	150	250	495	350	
Menuhin, Yehudi	Entertainment	30			65	Concert Violinist
Menzies, Robert, Sir	Head of State	15	55	125	25	Australian Prime Minister
Merbold, Ulf	Astronaut	10	25		25	
Mercadante, Saverio 1795-1870	Composer	150		450		Dir. Royal Conservatory, Naples
Mercer, Frances	Entertainment	5	8		15	
Mercer, Hugh W.	Civil War	90	170			CSA General
Mercer, John Francis	Revolutionary War	70		250		Aide-de-Camp Gen Lee
Mercer, Johnny	Composer	50			135	Vocalist, Pianist
Mercer, Marian	Entertainment	10			35	
Mercier, D. Joseph, Cardinal	Clergy	35	45	75		
Mercouri, Melina	Entertainment	20	30	45	50	
Meredith, Burgess	Entertainment	10	15	25	30	
Meredith, Edwin T.	Cabinet	5	20	30	15	Sec'y Agriculture 1920
Meredith, James H.	Activist	35	90	185	60	Afro-Am. Activist
Meredith, Samuel	Cabinet	70	165	220		Rev. War Gen.,1st US Treasurer
Meredith, Solomon	Civil War	125		450		Union Gen. "Iron Brig. of West"
Meriam, Ebenezer	Science			225		Meteorologist
Merivale, Philip	Entertainment	5		25	20	Vintage Br.Actor
Meriwether, Lee	Entertainment	5	10	12	15	
Merkel, Una	Entertainment	10			25	
Merli, Francesco	Entertainment	25			65	Opera
Merli, Gino J.	Military	5	25			WW II Hero CMH
Merlin de Douai, P.A.	Fr. Revolution	40		200		Revolutionist. Min. of Justice
Merman, Ethel	Entertainment	20			50	
Merriam, Frank F.	Governor	5	15		10	Governor CA
Merrick, David	Entertainment	20	20	70	60	Theatrical Producer
Merrick, Samuel Vaughan	Business	40	175			Financier
Merrill, Dina	Entertainment	6	8	15	15	
Merrill, Frank D.	Military	225				Gen.WW II."Merrill's Marauders"
Merrill, Gary	Entertainment	15	20	45	40	
Merrill, Henry T.	Aviation	30	45	100	100	
Merrill, Lewis	Civil War	60	175			Union General
Merrill, Richard "Dick"	Aviation	30	55	105	75	
Merrill, Robert	Entertainment	30			50	Metropolitan Opera Co. Baritone
Merrill, Stuart	Author	30		125		Am. Poet. Wrote in French
Merrimon, Augustus S.	Senate	22	35			Senator NC
Merritt, Chris	Entertainment	10			30	Opera
Merritt, Wesley	Civil War	80	250	175		Union Gen., Indian Fighter
Merton, Thomas	Clergy	375	1135			Priest-Writer, Poet
Mesmer, F. Anton	Science	115	285	535		Ger. Dr."Mesmerise"
Messerschmitt, Wilhelm	Aviation	125			395	Ger. Aircraft Designer-Mfg.
Messiaen, Olivier	Composer	70	200			Fr. Organist

NAME	CATEGORY	SIG	LS/DS	ALS	SP	COMMENT
Messick, Dale*	Cartoonists	15			105	Brenda Starr
Messmer, Otto*	Cartoonists	55			400	Felix The Cat
Mesta, Perle	Business	25	30	70	35	Washington Hostess
Metcalf, Victor H.	Cabinet	20	70			Sec'y Navy
Metcalfe, Ralph H.	Senate/Congress	5	15		22	MOC IL
Metchnikoff, Elie	Science	60	95		150	Nobel Physiology 1908
Metternich, Prince Clemens W. von	Head of State	70	245	480		Austrian Statseman
Metzenbaum, Howard	Senate	10			20	Sentator OH
Meusel, Lucille	Entertainment	10			25	Soprano
Mewman, Larry	Aviation	25			75	
Meyer, Albert G., Cardinal	Clergy	35	40	50	40	
Meyer, E. C.	Military	6	10	30	20	
Meyer, George von L.	Cabinet	15	20	35	20	P.M. General 1907
Meyerbeer, Giacomo	Composer	115	235	440	300	Ger. Composer of Fr. Operas
Michael, George	Entertainment	20	30	95	100	
Michaels, Barbara	Author	5		25	15	
Michaels, Bret	Entertainment	10	20	50	45	
Michaels, Lorraine	Playboy Model	4			8	Pin-Up SP $10
Michaels, Marilyn	Entertainment	5		25	20	
Michel, Frank Curtis	Astronaut	5			15	
Michelangelo (Buonarroti)	Artist	2250	10000	25000		NRPA
Michele, Denise	Entertainment	3	3		8	
Michelson, Albert A.	Science	120		450		Nobel Physics 1907
Michelson, Charles	Political	12	15			Speech Writer New Deal
Michener, James A.	Author	50	265	340	115	Am. Novelist. Pulitzer
Middleton, Arthur	Revolutionary War	1100	3300	3850		Signer Decl. of Indepen.
Middleton, Charles	Entertainment	75			250	
Middleton, Robert	Entertainment	50			150	
Middleton, Thomas Fanshaw	Clergy	30	50	80		
Middleton, Velma	Entertainment	30			70	Jazz Vocalist
Midler, Bette	Entertainment	15			55	Singer-Actress
Midori	Entertainment	15			50	
Mielziner, Jo	Entertainment	15		40	35	Film Director
Mifflin, Thomas	Revolutionary War	150	825			Pres. Continental Congress
Mifune, Toshiro	Entertainment	15	25	65	40	
Migenes, Julia	Entertainment	15			35	Opera
Milano, Alyssa	Entertainment	20			50	
Milanov, Zinka	Entertainment	20			65	
Milch, Erhard	Aviation	80	250	400	175	WW I, Insp. Gen.Luftwaffe WW II
Miles, Josephine	Author	7	15	25	10	
Miles, Nelson A.	Civil War	85	160	230		Union General, CMH
Miles, Sarah	Entertainment	9	10	25	25	Pin-Up SP $35
Miles, Sylvia	Entertainment	5	6	15	15	
Miles, Vera	Entertainment	6	8	15	20	Pin-Up SP $25
Milestone, Lewis	Entertainment	35			85	Film Director
Milhaud, Darius	Composer	100	250	315	300	AMusQS $500
Mill, James	Author	65	250	515		Scot.Philosopher,Historian,Econ
Mill, John Stuart	Author-Editor	150	400	850		Br. Economist, Philosopher
Mill, William Hodge	Clergy	20	25	30		
Millais, John Everett, Sir	Artist	45	85	185		Pre-Raphaelite Painter
Milland, Ray	Entertainment	30			70	
Millay, Edna St. Vincent	Author	140	325	1200	200	Am. Poet, Dramatist. Pulitzer
Miller, Alice Duer	Author	15	25	45		Novelist, Poet
Miller, Ann	Entertainment	10			20	Pin-Up SP $30
Miller, Arjay R.	Business	3	10	25	5	
Miller, Arthur	Author	40	90	160	75	Am. Playwright. Pulitzer

NAME	CATEGORY	SIG	LS/DS	ALS	SP	COMMENT
Miller, Caroline	Author	10	20			Pulitzer
Miller, Denny	Entertainment	5			20	
Miller, Eddie	Entertainment	20			45	Big Band Tenor Saxophonist
Miller, Frederick	Business	12	32	64	25	
Miller, G. William	Cabinet	5	15	25	12	Sec'y Treasury
Miller, Glenn	Entertainment	175	275	450	525	Big Band Leader-Trombonist
Miller, H.G.	Business	10			15	
Miller, Henry	Entertainment	35	40	75	70	Henry Miller Theatre
Miller, Henry V.	Author	55	160	345	150	"Tropic of Cancer"
Miller, Joaquin	Author	50		125		Am. Poet, Journalist
Miller, John F.	Civil War	35	50	60		Union Gen., U.S. Sen. CA
Miller, Leslie A.	Governor	10	20			Governor WY
Miller, Marilyn	Entertainment	110		240	215	Ziegfield Follies Dancing Star
Miller, Marvin	Entertainment	10			25	
Miller, Mitch	Entertainment	5			15	Conductor, Arranger
Miller, Nathan L.	Governor	15	25		20	Governor NY
Miller, Patsy Ruth	Entertainment	25			45	
Miller, Penelope Ann	Entertainment	25			60	
Miller, Roger	Country Music	35			60	Composer
Miller, Samuel F. (SC)	Supreme Court	95	185	290		
Miller, Stanley	Science	15	35	65	20	
Miller, Stephen	Civil War	95	195	295		Union General
Miller, Taylor	Entertainment	4	4	9	10	
Miller, Warner	Senate	10	20	35		MOC, Senator NY
Miller, William H. H.	Cabinet	10	30	50	20	Att'y General 1889
Millerande, Alexandre	Head of State	25	45	60	35	Socialist Pres. France
Milles, Carl	Artist	30	55	90		Am. Sculptor
Millet, Francis Davis	Artist	25	45	145		Medal Winning Art. Journalist
Millet, Jean Francois 1814-75	Artist	200	450	1200		Fr.Religious,Classical,Peasant
Milliken, John	Military	9	30	50	20	
Milliken, Robert A., Dr.	Science	85	290	425	200	Nobel Physics,Educator,Author
Milliken, William G.	Governor	5	15		10	Governor MI
Millinder, Lucky	Entertainment	40			125	Bandleader
Millo, Aprile	Entertainment	10			35	Opera
Mills Brothers (4)	Entertainment	100			200	
Mills, Darius Ogden	Business	150	450			Merchant,Banker, Philan.
Mills, Donna	Entertainment	9	10		25	Producer. Pin-Up SP $25
Mills, Earle W.	Military	12	30			
Mills, Hayley	Entertainment	10	15	25	30	Pin-Up SP $28
Mills, John, Sir	Entertainment	20			35	
Mills, Juliette	Entertainment	10			20	
Mills, Ogden L.	Cabinet	10	35	45	15	Sec'y Treasury 1932
Mills, Roger Q.	Civil War	25	35	50		CSA Colonel, MOC TX
Mills, Wilbur	Senate/Congress	25			30	Congressman AR
Milne, A. A.	Author	240	450	1000	300	"Winnie-the-Pooh"
Milner, Martin	Entertainment	4	6		15	
Milnes, Rich.M.(Baron of Houghton)	Celebrity	5	10	25	10	Man of Letters.Oxford Movement
Milnes, Sherrill	Entertainment	10			25	Opera. Am. Basso
Milosz, Czeslaw, Dr.	Author	45	125		50	Nobel Literature
Milsap, Ronnie	Country Music	5	6	15	15	
Milstein, Nathan	Entertainment	40			75	Rus. Violinist
Miltonberger, Butler	Military	35	60			
Mimieux, Yvette	Entertainment	5	8		21	Pin-Up SP $25
Mindszenty, Jozef, Cardinal	Clergy	50	75	135	95	
Miner, Jan	Entertainment	5	6	15	10	
Mingus, Charlie	Entertainment					Jazz Musician-No Price Availabl

NAME	CATEGORY	SIG	LS/DS	ALS	SP	COMMENT
Minh, Duong Van Gen.	Military	15	40	75	40	
Minich, Peter	Entertainment	5			20	Opera, Light Opera
Mink, Patsy T.	Senate/Congress	5	15		10	MOH HI
Minnelli, Liza	Entertainment	9	10	20	30	Pin-Up SP $35
Minnelli, Vincent	Entertainment	30			65	Film Director
Minor, Ruediger, Bishop	Clergy	25	40	45	50	
Minow, Newton N.	Law	12			15	Chairman FCC
Minter, Mary Miles	Entertainment	90	115	230	200	
Minton, Sherman (SC)	Supreme Court	40	165	250	100	
Minton, Yvonne	Entertainment	5			25	Opera
Minvielle, Gabriel	Fr. Revolution	850				NRPA
Miollis, S.A.F.	Fr. Revolution	100	215			
Mirabeau, Gabriel H.R 1749-91.	Fr. Revolution	95	275	575		Statesman, Diplomat,Politician
Mirabehin (M. Slade)	Celebrity	25		45		Companion-Follower of Gandhi
Miramon, Miguel (Mex)	Military	20	85	140		Cmdr. Army vs Juarez.
Miranda, Carmen	Entertainment	125			285	
Miranda, Isa	Entertainment	35			85	Fr. Actress
Mirisch, Walter	Entertainment	6	8	15	20	Motion Picture Producer
Miro, Joan	Artist	175	505	700		Repro "The Hare" S $250,$325
Miroslava	Entertainment	25	30	70	65	
Mister, Mister	Entertainment	15			55	
Mistral, Frederic	Author	30	75	130	50	Nobel Literature 1904
Mistral, Gabriela	Author	20	35	60	25	Nobel Lit.'43(Godoy Alcayaga)
Mitchel, Ormsby M.	Science-Civil War	125		475		Union Gen., Astronomy Prof.
Mitchell, Billy	Aviation	200	595	850	525	Gen. WW I
Mitchell, Cameron	Entertainment	15			40	
Mitchell, Charles E.	Business	20	35	65	25	Chmn. National City Bank
Mitchell, Edgar D.	Astronaut	10			75	Moonwalker
Mitchell, Grant	Entertainment	35			80	
Mitchell, James P.	Cabinet	12	20	30		Sec'y Labor
Mitchell, John	Cabinet	25			75	Att'y General.TLS/Cont $200
Mitchell, John Grant	Civil War	30	50	140		Union General
Mitchell, John Inscho	Civil War	44	60			Union Gen., MOC PA
Mitchell, John W.	Aviation	12	25	42	32	ACE, WW II
Mitchell, Joni	Entertainment	20			35	Singer
Mitchell, Maggie	Entertainment	10			20	
Mitchell, Margaret	Author	550	3835	2500		TLS/Content $15,000
Mitchell, Maria	Science	70	185	375		Astronomer, Mathematician
Mitchell, Martha	Celebrity	35	100		45	Wife Att'y Gen.-Watergate
Mitchell, Silas Weir	Science-Civil War	25	95			Civil War Surgeon
Mitchell, Stephen Mix	Revolutionary War	65	185			Continental Congress.
Mitchell, Thomas	Entertainment	250			550	
Mitchell, William D.	Cabinet	5	25	30	10	Att'y General
Mitchelson, Marvin	Law	13	25		20	Trial Att'y. Specialty Divorce
Mitchum, Robert	Entertainment	5	10	20	25	
Mitford, Jessica	Author	10	15	20	15	
Mitropoulous, Dimitri	Composer	20	50	95	135	Greek Conductor
Mitscher, Marc A.	Military	375			450	Adm. WW II (RARE)
Mitterand, Francois	Head of State	15	25	40	20	Pres. France
Mittford, Mary Russell	Author	15	20	40		Br. Poet. Historical Drama
Mix, Tom	Entertainment	75			400	
Mix, Victoria	Entertainment	8	9	15	10	
Mizell, Wilmer D.	Senate/Congress	5	15			MOC KS, Prof. Baseball Pitcher
Mobley, Mary Ann	Entertainment	5	8	15	12	
Model, Walter	Military			500		NRPA
Modesti, Giuseppe	Entertainment	15			35	Opera

NAME	CATEGORY	SIG	LS/DS	ALS	SP	COMMENT
Modigliani, Amedeo	Artist	275	840	1750		It. Planar, Asymmetric Style
Modine, Matthew	Entertainment	5			20	
Modjeske, Helena	Entertainment	15	25	35	30	
Moeur, Benjamin B.	Governor	12	15	25		Governor AZ
Moffat, Robert	Clergy	50	90	100		
Moffett, W.A., Adm.	Military	15		50	55	MOH. With Adm. Dewey. FDC $90
Moffo, Anna	Entertainment	15			35	Opera, Concert
Mohler, A. L.	Business	8	20	40	15	
Mohnke,Wllhelm	Military	35			150	Ger. Gen. SS
Moholy-Nagy, Laszlo (Hungarian)	Artist	80	250			Painter,Designer,Photographer
Mohr, Gerald	Entertainment	35			75	
Mohri, Momoru	Astronaut	12	25		25	
Mojica, Jose	Entertainment	60			225	Opera
Molders, Werner	Aviation	175	275	400	325	ACE, WW II, !st to 100 Kills
Molitor, G.J.J.	Fr. Revolution	75	155	250		Distinguished in Napoleonic War
Moll, Kurt	Entertainment	15			35	Opera
Moll, Richard	Entertainment	6	8	15	15	
Mollet, Guy	Head of State	20	40	65		Socialist Premier France
Molnar, Ferenc	Author	70	160	250		Playwright,Novelist, Journalist
Moltke, H. Johann L.von	Military	15	30	60	30	Nephew Helmuth.
Moltke, Helmuth von, Count	Military	90	220	400	295	Prussian Field Marshal
Moltmann, Jurgen	Clergy	50	75	100	80	
Momaday, N. Scott	Author	10	15	25	15	
Momo, Giuseppe	Entertainment	10			35	Opera
Monaghan, Tom	Business	10			20	Domino's Pizza
Moncey, Bon-Adrien J. de	Fr. Revolution	45	135	160		Marshal of France
Mondale, Walter (V)	Vice President	25	185		75	
Mondell, Franklin W.	Senate/Congress	10	15		15	MOC WY
Mondrian, Piet	Artist	225	675	1500		Dutch.Traditional-Cubism
Monet, Claude	Artist	300	1275	2845		Fr. Impressionist
Money, Hernando De Soto	Senate/Congress	10	25	45		MOC, Senator MS. CSA Army
Money, Ken	Astronaut	5	15		15	
Monk, Thelonious	Entertainment	50			150	Jazz Musician
Monroe, Elizabeth	First Lady					Rare 10-12 Known
Monroe, James	President	405	1300	2900		
Monroe, James & Adams, John Q.	President					SEE Adams, John Quincy
Monroe, James & Madison, James	President		3535			SEE Madison
Monroe, Marilyn	Entertainment	2250	5500	7500	7000	ALS/Cont. $15,000
Monroe, Marilyn	Entertainment			15000		Signed Norma Jean
Monroe, Vaughn	Entertainment	10	15		30	
Montagu, Edwin Samuel	Politician	15	50	80	35	Br. Statesman
Montagu, John (Earl of Sandwich)	Celebrity	65	205	450		"Sandwich" Named For Him
Montague, Andrew J.	Senate/Congress	5	15	35		MOC, Senator VA
Montalban, Ricardo	Entertainment	10	15	25	25	
Montalivet, J.P.B. Count	Fr. Revolution	35	100	225		
Montana, Bob*	Cartoonist	40			175	Archie
Montana, Bull	Entertainment	25			50	
Montana, Monte	Entertainment	5			15	
Montana, Patsy	Country Music	15			35	
Montand, Yves	Entertainment	10			25	
Montcalm, Louis J. Marquis de	Military	575	1765	3077		Cmdr. Fr.Troops in North Am.
Montefiore, Moses, Sir	Philanthropist	30	70			Jewish Philan.Sherrif of London
Montenegro, Conchita	Entertainment	8	9	19	19	
Montessori, Maria	Educator	175		1050		1st Italian Woman Doctor
Monteux, Pierre	Entertainment	10			35	Conductor
Monteverde, Alfred de	Aviation	25	50	85	55	

NAME	CATEGORY	SIG	LS/DS	ALS	SP	COMMENT
Monteverde, George de	Aviation	25	50	85	55	
Montez, Lola	Adventuress	200		500		
Montez, Maria	Entertainment	50	55		100	
Montgolfier, Jacques-E.	Aviation			1800		With Joseph,1st hot air Balloon
Montgolfier, Joseph	Aviation					Special Content ALS $63,000
Montgomery, Bernard Law, Sir	Military	85	425		300	Special DS $2,500
Montgomery, Douglass	Entertainment	10	15	25	25	
Montgomery, Elizabeth	Entertainment	6	8		20	Pin-Up SP $25
Montgomery, George	Entertainment	6	8	15	19	
Montgomery, James Shera	Clergy	50	65	75		Chaplin U.S. Congress
Montgomery, M., Lady	Celebrity	5	10	20		Mother of Bernard L. Montgomery
Montgomery, Melba	Country Music	10			20	
Montgomery, Robert	Entertainment	10	30	60	25	
Monti, Carlotta	Entertainment	15			35	W.C. Fields Paramour
Monti, Nicola	Entertainment	35			85	Opera
Montoya, Carlos	Entertainment	10	10	25	25	Classical Guitarist
Moody Blues	Entertainment	125			275	60's Rock Group
Moody, Dwight L.	Clergy	55	110	195	125	Evangelist, LS/Content $500
Moody, William H. (SC)	Supreme Court	45	125	175	50	
Moody, William V.	Author	30	85	125		Poet, Playwright
Moog, Bob	Science	50	70	110	65	Inventor. Synthesizer
Mooney, Art	Entertainment	10			20	Big Band Leader
Mooney, Edward, Cardinal	Clergy	30	40	50	40	
Mooney, Tom	Labor Activist	25	60	180	50	Bombed Parade. TLS/Cont.$550
Moore, Francis D., Dr.	Science	10	30	55	20	
Moore, Alfred	Supreme Court	3000				
Moore, Arch A. Jr.	Senate/Congress	5	15			Governor, MOC WV
Moore, Arthur J., Bishop	Clergy	20	25	40	40	
Moore, Barbara, Dr.	Celebrity	5		20		Br. Marathon Walker
Moore, Clayton	Entertainment	10	10		25	The Lone Ranger
Moore, Clement C.	Author	135	460	950		"'Twas the Night Before ...."
Moore, Colleen	Entertainment	8	9		20	
Moore, Constance	Entertainment	10			20	
Moore, Dan K.	Governor	5	15	30		Governor NC
Moore, Demi	Entertainment	20			70	
Moore, Dick	Entertainment	8			15	
Moore, Dudley	Entertainment	8	9		20	
Moore, Edward C.	Clergy	10	20	30		
Moore, Foster*	Cartoonist	15			50	Napoleon
Moore, Gary	Entertainment	12			25	
Moore, George	Author	45	150	125		Irish Novelist
Moore, Grace	Entertainment	65	90		150	Opera. Films
Moore, Henry	Artist	60	255	550	105	Br. Sculptor. "The Thinker"
Moore, Jeremy, Sir	Military	5	15	25	15	General
Moore, Joanna	Entertainment	10			25	
Moore, John Bassett	Law-Jurist	65		250		International Lawyer
Moore, John, Sir	Military	60	180	350		Br. General. KIA 1809
Moore, Marianne C.	Author	60	185		75	Am. Poet. Pulitzer
Moore, Mary Tyler	Entertainment	10	15		25	Pin-Up SP $25
Moore, Ray*	Cartoonist	25			190	Phantom
Moore, Roger	Entertainment	10			75	
Moore, Roy D.	Business	10	25		20	Fndr. Newspaper-Radio Chain
Moore, Samuel P.	Civil War	595	725			Surgeon General CSA
Moore, Sara Jane	Radical	30	80	200		Attempted Assassination Ford
Moore, Sydenham	Congress-CW	40	55	90		MOC AL. CSA Officer
Moore, Terry	Entertainment	5	6	15	15	Pin-Up SP $20

NAME	CATEGORY	SIG	LS/DS	ALS	SP	COMMENT
Moore, Thomas	Author	45	105	250		Irish Poet
Moore, Thomas O.	Civil War		440			CSA Gen., CW Gov. LA
Moore, Victor	Entertainment	25			55	
Moore, William	Colonial	90	225			Colonial Am. Statseman-Jurist
Moorehead, Agnes	Entertainment	25			95	
Moorer, Thomas	Military	70	145		100	Adm. Survivor—Twice
Moores, Dick*	Cartoonists	10			30	Gasoline Alley
Morales, Ramon V.	Head of State	15	30			Ecuador
Moran, Lois	Entertainment	5	5	10	15	
Moran, Thomas	Artist	80	225	350		Specialized in American West
Moranis, Rick	Entertainment	5			25	
Moranville, H. Blake	Aviation	10	22	40	30	ACE, WW II, Navy Ace
More, Thomas, Sir	Author	19750				NRPA
Moreau, Jean-Victor	Fr. Revolution	90	275	300		Fr. General under Napoleon
Morehead, James B.	Aviation	10	22	38	28	ACE, WW II, USAAF Ace
Morehead, John M.	Governor	10	25			Governor NC
Morehouse, A.P.	Governor	10	20		25	Governor MO
Moreland, Mantan	Entertainment	100	125		200	
Moreno, Anthony	Entertainment	3	3	6	6	
Moreno, Bertha	Entertainment	20			95	Opera
Moreno, Rita	Entertainment	9	10	25	25	Pin-Up SP $30
Morgan, Barbara	Astronaut	5	35		15	
Morgan, Charles L.	Author	20	65	80		Br. Novelist, Drama Critic
Morgan, Dennis	Entertainment	8		15	20	
Morgan, Edward J.	Entertainment	10	12		25	
Morgan, Edwin Barber	Senate/Congress	40	75			MOC NY, Merchant,Philanthropist
Morgan, Edwin Dennison, Jr.	Civil War	40		65		Union Gen.,CW Gov., Senator NY
Morgan, F. Crossley	Clergy	10	15	15	15	
Morgan, Frank	Entertainment	400	600		650	
Morgan, G. Campbell	Clergy	20	30	45		
Morgan, George	Country Music	15			35	
Morgan, George	Revolutionary War	125	425	675		Indian Agent, Speculator
Morgan, Harry	Entertainment	5	10	20	15	
Morgan, Helen	Entertainment	50	175		200	1st Julie in "Show Boat"
Morgan, Jaye P.	Entertainment	5			15	
Morgan, John Hunt	Civil War	800	995	1750		CSA Gen. Wardte. DS $12,500
Morgan, John Pierpont, Jr.	Business	85	185	280	95	Banker,Financier
Morgan, John Pierpont, Sr.	Business	280	985	1500	950	Banker, Financier
Morgan, John Tyler	Civil War	115	250	795	240	CSA Gen., US Sen. AL
Morgan, Michele	Entertainment	10			25	
Morgan, Ralph	Entertainment	35			65	
Morgan, Sydney, Lady	Author	15	35	60		Ir.Author."The Wild Irish Girl"
Morgan, Thomas H.	Science	95	200	425	125	Nobel Medicine 1933
Morgan, Thos. Jeff.	Civil War	70	90	125		Union General
Morgan, Wm. H.	Civil War	25	55	75		
Morganna	Entertainment	5	8	20	15	Pin-Up SP $30
Morgenthau, Henry Jr.	Cabinet	35	75	145	60	FDR Sec'y Treasury
Moriarty, Michael	Entertainment	10			30	
Morini, Erica	Entertainment	20			50	Austrian-born Violinist
Morison, Patricia	Entertainment	15	15	30	25	
Morita, Pat	Entertainment	10		25	25	
Morland, Mantan	Entertainment	25			50	
Morley, Christopher	Author	30	90	145		Am. Writer, Editor
Morley, Robert	Entertainment	25			65	
Morrill, Justin Smith	Senate/Congress	45	60	110		MOC, U.S. Senate VT 1855-98
Morrill, Lot M.	Cabinet	15	30	60		Sec'y Treas., Gov., Senator ME

NAME	CATEGORY	SIG	LS/DS	ALS	SP	COMMENT
Morris, Anita	Entertainment	6	8		20	
Morris, Charles	Military	20	60			Commodore USN
Morris, Chester	Entertainment	35	40		70	
Morris, Felix J.	Entertainment	15			40	Vintage Stage Actor
Morris, Gouverneur	Revolutionary War	190	585	760		Continental Congr., Diplomat
Morris, Harrison Smith	Publisher	30	55			Magazine Editor
Morris, James	Entertainment	5			25	Opera
Morris, Lewis	Revolutionary War	305	1025	1525		Signer Decl. of Indepen.
Morris, Lewis, Sir	Author	5	10	20		
Morris, Robert	Revolutionary War	300	720	1470		Signer, Auction LS $22,000
Morris, Robert & J. Nicholson	Revolutionary War					Content DS $45,000
Morris, Robert Page W.	Senate/Congress	5	10			MOC MN
Morris, Wayne	Entertainment	25			60	
Morris, William	Artist	125	275	650		Br.Poet,Artist,Designer,Printer
Morris, William Walton	Civil War	25	55	80		Union General
Morrison, Harold	Country Music	10			20	
Morrison, Henry Clay	Clergy	25	35	50	40	
Morrison, Herb	Aviation	40	85	160	100	Announcer of Hindenburg Crash
Morrison, Jim	Entertainment	850	2800		1375	Composer.Lead Singer "The Doors
Morrison, Samuel E.	Author	12	20			Historian
Morrison, Toni	Author	20	35		25	Afro-Am. Nobel Literature
Morrison, Van	Entertainment	15			45	
Morrison, William Ralls	Civil War	25		80		Union Officer, MOC IL
Morrow, Dwight W.	Diplomat	10	35			Lawyer, Banker, Amb. to Mex.
Morrow, Jeff	Entertainment	5	6	15	15	
Morrow, Rob	Entertainment	15			30	
Morrow, Vic	Entertainment	100				
Morse, Carleton E.	Writer-Producer	20	25		30	"One Man's Family" Vint. Radio
Morse, Samuel F. B.	Science-Artist	360	1500	2495	2000	Telegraph, Pioneer Photographer
Morse, Wayne	Senate	10	25		55	Senator OR
Mortier, Edouard A.C.J.	Fr. Revolution	35	115	230		Marshal of Fr., Statesman
Mortimer, Charles	Business	5	15	25	10	CEO General Foods
Morton, J. Sterling	Cabinet	25	50	145	75	Father Arbor Day, Sec'y Agri.
Morton, John	Revolutionary War	375	885	1100		Signer Decl. of Indepen.
Morton, Levi P. (V)	Vice President	55	175	240	240	
Morton, Oliver P.	Senate	10	25			Governor, Senator IN
Morton, Wm. Thos. Green	Science	170	450	825		1st To Us Ether as Anesthetic
Mosby, John S.	Civil War	490	1100	1575	3250	CSA Off., Content ALS $12,500
Moscona, Nicola	Entertainment	30			60	Opera
Moscone, George R.	Celebrity	80		95		
Mosel, Tad	Author	5	15	30	10	Am. Dramatist
Moser, Edda	Entertainment	5			25	Opera
Moses, Anna Mary R. (Grandma)	Artist	175	550	860	250	ALS/Content $1,500
Moses, George H.	Senate/Congress	7	15	35		Senator NH. Diplomat
Moses, Robert	Public Official	3	7	15	5	Dominated NY Politics
Mosher, Terry	Celebrity	5		10		
Mosley, Jack*	Cartoonists	25			105	Smilin' Jack
Mosley, Oswald, Sir	Political	25	65	180	140	Founder Br. Union of Fascists
Moss, Kate	Model	4			15	Pin-Up SP $25
Moss, Ralph W.	Senate/Congress	10	15	25		MOC IN 1909
Mossadegh, Muhammad	Head of State	40	75	165		Premier Iran. Nationalized Oil
Mossbauer, Rudolf L.	Science	25	55	90	45	Nobel Physics
Mostel, Zero	Entertainment	25			65	
Moszkowski, Moritz	Composer	50		200		Ger. Pianist
Motherwell, Robert	Artist	45	150	325		Am. Abstract Expressionist
Motley Crue (4)	Entertainment	30			95	

NAME	CATEGORY	SIG	LS/DS	ALS	SP	COMMENT
Motley, John Lothrop	Author	30	50	125		Historian,Diplomat,Hall of Fame
Mott, Frank L.	Journalist	10		35	20	Educator, Pulitzer
Mott, John R.	Clergy	30	45	75	100	Nobel Peace Prize
Mott, Lucretia	Women's Rights	70	150	375	250	Reformer, Abolitionist
Mott, Neville F. Dr.	Science	20	35	50	25	Nobel Physics
Moulton, Louise Chandler	Author	25	70	125		American Poet
Moulton, William	Revolutionary War	20	60145			
Moultrie, William	Governor-Military	160	485			Revolutionary War Gen.
Mount, James A.	Governor	30	100			Gov. IN
Mountbatten, Earl Louis, Lord	Military	110	220	315	200	Of Burma. Adm. of Fleet
Mountbatten, Edwina, Lady	Celebrity	10	35			Wife of Louis Mountbatten
Mountevens,Baron (E Evans)	Military	20	45		50	Br. WW I Naval Hero
Moutrie, Alexander	Revolutionary War	35		200		
Mowbray, Alan	Entertainment	20			75	
Mowbray, H. Siddons	Artist	25	40	70		Murals. J.P. Morgan Library etc
Mower, Joseph A.	Civil War	35	95	115		Union General
Moyers, Bill	Author	5	15	45	15	TV Host
Moynihan, Daniel Patrick	Senate/Congress	10	20		20	Senator NY
Mozart, Wolfgang A.	Composer	2500	8000	30000		
Mubarak, M. Hosni	Head of State	50	110	275	80	President Egypt
Mucha, Alphonse	Artist	60		400		Czech Painter & Illustrator
Muck, Karl, Dr.	Conductor	10			50	
Mudd. Roger	News	5	10	30	10	Radio-TV News
Mueller, Frederick H.	Gov't Official	5	15	30		
Mueller, Reuben H., Bishop	Clergy	20	25	35	25	
Mueller-Stahl, Armin	Entertainment	4			10	
Muench, Aloisius J., Cardinal	Clergy	35	50	65	50	
Mugabe, Robert G.	Head of State	20	60	145	40	
Muggeridge, Malcolm	Clergy	30	40	50	40	
Muhammed, Elijah	Muslim Leader	115	345			
Muhlenberg, John Peter Gabriel	Revolutionary War	125	260	550		Clergy, Patriot, Gen. Cont. Arm
Muhlenberg, W. Augustus	Clergy	25	40	60		
Muir, Jean	Entertainment	8	9		20	
Muir, John	Science	450	1450	2400	500	Am. Naturalist, Explorer
Mukai, Chiaki	Astronaut	10	25		27	
Muldaur, Diana	Entertainment	6	8	15	20	
Muldaur, Maria	Entertainment	5			15	
Muldoon, Robert	Head of State	10	20	30	20	Prime Minister New Zealand
Mulgrew, Kate	Entertainment	5	6	15	15	
Mulhare, Edward	Entertainment	15			40	
Mulheen, R.J.	Business	3	5		8	CEO Boston & Maine RR Corp.
Mull, Martin	Entertainment	5	6		20	
Mullane, Richard M.	Astronaut	5			10	
Muller, Herman J.	Science	20	35	75	25	Nobel Medicine 1946
Mullican, Moon	Country Music	10			20	
Mulligan, Jerry	Entertainment	12			25	Baritone Sax. Arranger-Composer
Mulligan, Richard	Entertainment	5	5		15	
Mulligan, Robert	Entertainment	5			20	
Mulliken, Robert S., Dr.	Science	30	40	65	35	Nobel Chemistry
Mullin, Willard	Cartoonist	10			30	Sports Cartoonist
Mullowney, Deborah	Entertainment	4	6	10	15	
Mumy, Bill	Entertainment	5	6	15	15	
Munch, Charles	Entertainment	10			35	Ger. Conductor
Munch, Edvard	Artist	55	350			Painter-Printmaker
Mundelein, George Wm., Cardinal	Clergy	65	110	225	90	
Mundt, Karl E.	Senate	10	25		35	MOC, Senator SD, Educator

NAME	CATEGORY	SIG	LS/DS	ALS	SP	COMMENT
Muni, Paul	Entertainment	75	90	120	135	
Munro, Caroline	Entertainment	5	6	15	15	
Munro, Leslie K., Sir	Diplomat	10	15		25	Pres. UN Assembly
Munro, Peter Jay 1767-1833	Jurist	30	65	155		Nephew of John Jay.
Munsel, Patrice	Entertainment	10	20	50	50	Met. Debut at 18
Munsey, Frank A.	Editor	15		35		Muncey's Magazine
Munson, Ona	Entertainment	100			200	
Munster, Earl of	Military	10	25	40		
Munteanu, Petre	Entertainment	35	110	165		Opera
Muntz, Earl 'Madman'	Business	13	18	25	20	Pioneer TV Advertiser-Owner
Murat, Joachim	Fr. Revolution	135	470	590		Marshal of Napoleon
Murchison, Clint	Business	10	15	25	20	TX Oil Entrepreneur Millionaire
Murchison, Clint, Jr.	Business	5	10	20	12	
Murdoch, Rupert	Business	10	35	55	40	International Newspaper Publ.
Murphy, Audie	Military	60	175	325	400	CMH, Film Star
Murphy, Ben	Entertainment	5	6	15	15	
Murphy, Eddie	Entertainment	25			75	
Murphy, Edward, Jr.	Senate	6	12			Senator NY
Murphy, Frank (SC)	Supreme Court	50	200	350	150	
Murphy, Franklin	Governor	5	10		10	Governor NJ
Murphy, George	Entertainment	12	20	25	25	And Senator from CA
Murphy, John Cullen*	Cartoonist	5			45	Big Ben Bolt & Prince Valiant
Murphy, Turk	Entertainment	20	40		50	Bandleader, Composer, Trombone
Murphy, William P., Dr.	Science	30	75	120	35	Nobel Medicine 1934
Murray, Anne	Entertainment	5			20	
Murray, Arthur	Business	10	15	30	15	Ballroom Dance Studios
Murray, Bill	Entertainment	20			65	
Murray, Bob	Aviation	12	24	42	30	ACE, WW II
Murray, Don	Entertainment	5			15	
Murray, Eli	Civil War	30	65			Union Gen., Gov. UT Territory
Murray, George, Bishop	Clergy	25	40	50		
Murray, Jan	Entertainment	4			10	
Murray, Jim	Journalist	5			20	Sports Writer, L.A. Times
Murray, John C., S.J.	Clergy	10	15	35	20	
Murray, Joseph E., Dr.	Science	20	30		25	Nobel Medicine
Murray, Ken	Entertainment	5	6	15	15	
Murray, Mae	30	25	35	70	60	
Murray, Philip	Labor Leader	35	45	70	50	Pres. CIO, United Steel Workers
Murray, Stuart S.	Military	25	75		45	
Murray, William Vans	Revolutionary War	25	40	90		Diplomat, Lawyer, MOC MD
Murrow, Edward R.	Journalist	105	175		250	"You Can Hear(See) It Now"
Musante, Tony	Entertainment	4	4		15	
Musgrave, Story, Dr.	Astronaut	15			25	
Muskie, Edmund	Cabinet	10	20	40	20	Sec'y State
Mussolini, Benito	Head of State	390	700	3250	950	Fascist Italian Dictator
Muybridge, Eadweard	Photographer	150		400		Br.-Am Pioneer Motion Pictures
Muzio, Claudia	Entertainment	200			640	
Myers, Mike and Dana Carvey	Entertainment				75	"Wayne's World"
Myers, Russell*	Cartoonists	10			65	Broom Hilda
Myerson, Bess	Celebrities	10	20		25	Miss America. NYC Official
Myrt and Marge	Entertainment	20			60	Vintage Radio Series

N

NAME	CATEGORY	SIG	LS/DS	ALS	SP	COMMENT
Nabakov, Vladimir	Author	325	1250			and Researcher of Butterflies
Nabors, Jim	Entertainment	5	6	15	15	
Nache, Maria Luise	Entertainment	20			45	Opera
Nadar (F. Tournachon)	Artist-Author	80	175	300		Fr. Caricaturist, Photographer
Nader, George	Entertainment	15		45	40	
Nagel, Anne	Entertainment	25			55	
Nagel, Conrad	Entertainment	20	25	45	45	
Nagel, Steven R.	Astronaut	4			12	
Nagy, Imre	Head of State	50	150			Premier Hungary. Executed
Naish, J. Carrol	Entertainment	25			85	
Nakasone, Y.	Head of State	25	35	85	35	Japan
Naldi, Nita	Entertainment	20			35	
Nansen, Fridtjof	Explorer	85	140	260	450	Nor. Zoologist, Statesman
Napavilova, Zofie	Entertainment	25			65	Opera
Napier, Alan	Entertainment	30			55	
Napier, Charles	Entertainment	4	4	9	9	
Napier, Chas. James, Sir	Military	15	30	80		Br. Gen. vs U.S. War 1812
Napier, McVey 1776-1847	Law	10	15	30		Editor 4-7th Encyclo.Britannica
Napier, Robert C., Sir	Military	15	35	125		Field Marshal,Gov.Gen. India
Napier, Sir Wm. F.P.	Military	20	40	70		Br. General
Napoleon I	Royalty	670	2950	15000		Emperor of France
Napoleon II (Duke Reichstadt)	Head of State	260	800	2200		Francois-Charles-Jos. Bonaparte
Napoleon III, Emperor of France	Royalty	75	425	525		Louis Napoleon, Nephew of Nap.
Nasby, Petroleum (D. Locke)	Author	50	75	145		Outstanding Humorist
Nash, Clarence	Entertainment	100			150	
Nash, Graham	Entertainment	10			25	Rock
Nash, Ogden	Author	30	65	150	35	Poet-Humorous, Unorthodox
Nash, Walter	Head of State	10	40	85	20	Prime Minister New Zealand
Nasser, Gamal Abdel	Head of State	75	400	350	275	President Egypt
Nast, Thomas*	Cartoonist	135	350		825	Political Cartoonist.CDV S $400
Nathan, George Jean	Author	10	15	30	15	Powerful Drama Critic
Nathans, Daniel, Dr.	Science	25	35	45	30	Nobel Medicine
Nation, Carry	Reformer	75	185	215		Temperance Agitator
Natta, Giulio	Science	25	35	80		Nobel Chemistry 1963
Natwick, Mildred	Entertainment	10			25	
Nazimova, Alla	Entertainment	60			100	Russian Stage & Screen Star
Ne'meth, Maria	Entertainment	20			60	Opera
Neagle, Anna, Dame	Entertainment	10	15		30	
Neal, Bob	Aviation	15	35	45	40	ACE, WW II, Flying Tigers
Neal, Patricia	Entertainment	6	8		25	
Neal, Tom	Entertainment	10			20	
Nebel, Rudolf	Science	40	125			
Neblett, Carol	Entertainment	5			20	Opera

NAME	CATEGORY	SIG	LS/DS	ALS	SP	COMMENT
Necker, Jacques	Fr. Revolution	125	350			Fr. Financier & Statesman
Needham, Hal	Entertainment	10			20	Film Director-Stunt
Neel, Louis Eugene Felix	Science	20	30	40	25	Nobel Physics
Neely, Thomas B., Bishop	Clergy	15	25	35		
Neeson, Liam	Entertainment	35			80	
Neff, Francine I.	Cabinet	4	10	25	10	
Neff, Pat Morris	Governor	10	15			Governor TX, Pres. of Baylor U.
Negley, James S.	Civil War	40	65	90		Union Gen., MOC
Negri, Pola	Entertainment	50	75		135	
Neher, Fred*	Cartoonist	10			95	
Nehru, B.K.	Diplomat	10	15		20	Ambassador
Nehru, Jawaharlal	Head of State	95	350	700	200	Assassinated Prime Minister Ind
Neidlinger, Gustav	Entertainment	15			40	Opera
Neil, Stephen, Bishop	Clergy	10	15	35	20	
Neil, Vince	Entertainment	20			50	Rock
Neill, James	Entertainment	15			35	Vintage Stage Actor
Neill, Noel	Entertainment	10			20	
Neill, Sam	Entertainment	15			60	
Neiman, LeRoy	Artist	40	175	245	50	Repro Paintings S $125-$150
Nell, Stephen, Bishop	Clergy	10	15	35		
Nelligan, Kate	Entertainment	5	8	25	20	
Nelson, Bill	Astronaut	6			22	MOC FI
Nelson, Craig T.	Entertainment	10			25	
Nelson, Gaylord	Senate	10	25	40		Gov., Senator WI
Nelson, Gene	Entertainment	10			25	
Nelson, George D.	Astronaut	5			15	
Nelson, Harriet Hilliard	Entertainment	25			50	Band Singer-Actress
Nelson, Horatio	Military	875	3500	4500		Br. Admiral, Naval Hero
Nelson, Jimmy	Entertainment	3	3	6	6	
Nelson, John	Cabinet	20	50	95		Tyler Att'y General
Nelson, Knute	Senate	5	15		10	Senator MN
Nelson, Lori	Entertainment	5	6	15	15	Pin-Up SP $15
Nelson, Ozzie	Entertainment	35			75	Big Band Leader, Actor
Nelson, Ozzie & Nelson, Harriet	Entertainment		250			Contract Signed By Both
Nelson, Rick	Entertainment	100	425	475	250	
Nelson, Samuel (SC)	Supreme Court	50	150	250		
Nelson, Thomas Jr.	Revolutionary War	510	1550	3100		Signer Decl. of Indepen.
Nelson, William L.	Senate/Congress	5	15			MOC MO
Nelson, Willie	Country Music	12			35	
Nemerov, Howard	Author	10		35	25	3rd Poet Laureate US, Teacher
Nero, Peter	Entertainment	6	8	15	15	Jazz Pianist
Nesbit, Evelyn	Entertainment	50			100	"Girl in the Red Velvet Swing"
Nesbitt, Cathleen	Entertainment	15			30	
Nesmith, Michael	Entertainment	20			45	Rock
Ness, Eliot	Law Enforcement	174	750		600	
Nethersole, Olga	Entertainment	15			45	Vintage Stage Actress
Nettleton, Lois	Entertainment	5	6	15	15	
Neubert, Frank	Aviation	25	75			Scored 1st Air Victory 9/1/39
Neumann, Theresa	Religious	65	175	395	150	Confirmed Stigmata Bearer
Neurath, Constantin von 1873-1956	Diplomat	45	80	150	115	Ger.Imprisoned For "War Crimes"
Nevelson, Louise	Artist	50	80	155	90	Am. Sculptor.Large Scale Pieces
Neville, Aaron	Entertainment	4			10	
Neville, Henry	Entertainment	4	4	9	10	
Nevin, Ethelbert	Composer	55	140	450	85	Short Piano Pieces & Songs
Nevins, Allan	Author	12	30			Am.Historian, Editor, Professor
New Kids on the Block	Entertainment	50			175	

NAME	CATEGORY	SIG	LS/DS	ALS	SP	COMMENT
New, Harry	Cabinet	15	20	50	20	P.M. Genera 1923
Newberry, Truman H.	Cabinet	15	20	35		Sec'y Navy 1908
Newcomb, Simon 1835-1909	Science	60	195	305		Am. Astronomer, Mathematician
Newell, Frederick B., Bishop	Clergy	20	25	50	30	
Newhart, Bob	Entertainment	6	8	12	15	
Newhouse, Samuel	Business	15	25	60	25	Newspaper-Radio-TV Empire
Newley, Anthony	Entertainment	5			15	
Newman, Barry	Entertainment	4	6		10	
Newman, Edwin	Celebrity	4	10	20	5	
Newman, John Henry, Cardinal	Clergy	125	275	700	395	Leader Oxford Movement
Newman, Paul	Entertainment	80	150		175	
Newman, Randy	Entertainment	10			20	
Newmar, Julie	Entertainment	9	10	20	25	Pin-Up SP $30
Newton, Huey P.	Activist	100			350	Afro-Am. Activist
Newton, Isaac, Sir	Science	1100	2000	4000	850	LS/Cont. $16,500
Newton, John	Civil War	50		325		Union General
Newton, Juice	Entertainment	6	8	15	17	
Newton, Robert	Clergy	35	45	45	60	
Newton, Robert	Entertainment	50	65	90	75	
Newton, Wayne	Entertainment	9	10		35	
Newton-John, Olivia	Entertainment	15			50	Singer-Actress
Ney, Michael	Fr. Napoleon	125	295	650		Marshal of France.
Ney, Richard	Entertainment	15			35	
Ngor, Haing S.	Entertainment	10	15	50	55	
Niarchos, Stavro	Business	45	110	190	75	Gr.Millionaire Shipping Magnate
Nicholas I	Royalty	175	560			Czar of Russia
Nicholas II	Royalty		2860	9500		Czar of Russia
Nicholas, Denise	Entertainment	5	5		15	
Nicholas, Prince & King 1841-1921	Royalty	25	60	150		Greece
Nicholls, Francis R. T.	Civil War	70	105	170		CSA General, Gov LA
Nichols, Barbara	Entertainment	10			25	
Nichols, John Anthony	Senate/Congress	5		15		MOC NC
Nichols, Michelle	Entertainment	6	8	15	15	
Nichols, Mike	Entertainment	35			100	Film Director
Nichols, Red	Entertainment	35			60	Jazz Instrumentalist
Nichols, Ruth Roland	Aviation	125	295		250	Holder of Flying Records
Nicholson, Jack	Entertainment	15			45	
Nicholson, John 1783-1846	Military	30	75	190		Commodore U.S. Navy
Nicholson, Meredith	Author	20	50	125	30	
Nickerson, Francis Stillman	Civil War	25	50	65		Union General
Nicks, Stevie	Entertainment	20			50	
Nicolai, Elena	Entertainment	25			65	Opera
Nicolay, John G.	Civil War	35	150	275		Lincoln Personal Sec'y. Author
Nicollet, Joseph N.	Explorer	105	225	345		1st Expedition Headwaters Miss.
Nicollier, Claude	Astronaut	15			30	
Niebuhr, H. Richard	Clergy	35	60	95	50	
Niebuhr, Reinhold	Clergy-Author	55	120	135	85	
Nielsen, Alice	Entertainment	35			150	Opera-Operetta
Nielsen, Asta	Entertainment	20			50	Opera
Nielsen, Brigitte	Entertainment	5			20	Pin-Up SP $30
Nielsen, Carl	Composer	180	480	1100		Danish Composer, Conductor
Nielsen, Gertrude	Entertainment	10			25	
Nielsen, Terry	Entertainment	8	9		15	
Nielson, Leslie	Entertainment	5			25	
Niemack, Horst	Military	20			50	Ger. General Major
Niemoller, Martin	Clergy	60	175	350	200	In Concentration Camp WW II

NAME	CATEGORY	SIG	LS/DS	ALS	SP	COMMENT
Nietzsche, Friedrich	Author	470	775	7765		Ger.Poet, Philosopher,Philology
Nigh, William	Entertainment	10			30	Actor-Director
Nightingale, Florence	Science	625	975	1050		Br. Nurse, Hospital Reformer
Nijinsky, Vaslav	Entertainment	440			3250	Ballet
Nikisch, Arthur	Entertainment	25	65	85		Hung. Conductor.AMusQS $100
Nikolayev, Andryan G.	Astronaut	150			185	Russian Cosmonaut
Nillson, Christine	Entertainment	45		175		Opera
Nilssen, Anna Q.	Entertainment	15	20		45	
Nilsson, Birgit	Entertainment	15			45	Swe. Soprano, Opera
Nilsson, Harry	Entertainment	50			100	
Nimersheim, Jack	Author	5	8	20	20	Campbell Award nominee
Nimitz, Chester W.	Military	115	305	450	435	SP Japanese Surrender $1250
Nimoy, Leonard	Entertainment	35			80	"Star Trek"
Nin, Anais	Author	40	125	225	50	Content ALS $395
Nina	Model	4			15	Pin-Up SP $20
Nirenberg, Marshall W.	Science	15	25	45	20	Nobel Medicine 1968
Nisbit, Eugenius Aristides	Senate/Congress	20	80	150		MOC GA 1839
Nissen, Greta	Entertainment	10			25	
Niven, David	Entertainment	25	50	130	75	
Nivernais, Louis Mancini-. Duc de	Military			725		French Soldier-Diplomat
Nixon, John 1733-1808	Revolutionary War	125	320			Proclaimed Decl.Ind. 1st Time
Nixon, Marion	Entertainment	15			40	
Nixon, Patricia	First Lady	40	140	325	195	
Nixon, Richard M.	President	185	395	6250	315	
Nizer, Louis	Law	25	75	215	35	Noted Trial Attorney
Nkomo, Joshua	Head of State	55	125	275	85	African Nationalist, Zimbabwe
Nobel, Alfred	Science	250	426	1180	450	ALS/Content $3,500
Nobile, Umberto	Aviation	65	145	335	175	It.Aeronautical Arctic Engineer
Noble, James	Entertainment	5	6	15	15	
Noble, John W.	Cabinet	20	50	120	95	Union Gen. CW. Sec'y Interior
Noe, Sydney P.	Numismatist	5	15			
Noel, Baptist W.	Clergy	20	35	50		
Noel-Baker, Philip	Statesman	20	40	130	25	Nobel Peace Prize
Noguchi, Isamu	Artist	25		65		Am. Sculptor, Designer
Noguchi, Thomas T.	Celebrity	10	30		20	
Nolan, Jeanette	Entertainment	5	6	15	15	
Nolan, Kathleen	Entertainment	8			15	
Nolan, Lloyd	Entertainment	10	95		35	
Nolan, Mae E.	Senate/Congress	10	18			MOC CA 1923
Nolte, Nick	Entertainment	10			40	
Nomura, Kichisaburo	Diplomat	275				Japanese Ambassador 12/7/41
Noone, Peter	Entertainment	20			50	
Noor, Queen	Head of State	15	40	125	40	Queen of Hussein (Jordan)
Norblad, Albin W.	Senate/Congress	15	30		20	MOC OR.Intelligence Off'r WW II
Nordau, Simon Max	Science	50	105	225	60	Hung. Phys.-Writer,AMsS $1750
Nordenskjold, Nils Adolf E.	Explorer	200			340	Navigated North-East Passage
Nordenskjold, Nils Otto	Explorer	215			300	Led Antarctic Exped'n, Rescued
Nordhoff, Charles	Author	20	35	60		Collaborator"Mutiny— —Bounty"
Nordica, Lillian	Entertainment	60			400	Am. Soprano
Nordsieck, Kenneth	Astronaut	6			16	
Norgay, Tenzing	Celebrity	40	110	255	50	Sherpa Guide. Mt. Everest
Noriega, Manuel A.	Head of State	100	100			Gen., Notorious Pres. Panama
Normand, Mabel	Entertainment	150			575	
Norris, Chuck	Entertainment	8	10		25	
Norris, Frank 1870-1902	Author	125	275	525		Novelist, War Correspondent
Norris, George W.	Senate/Congress	15	30		40	MOC,Sen. NE. Fathered TVA

NAME	CATEGORY	SIG	LS/DS	ALS	SP	COMMENT
Norris, J. Frank Dr.	Clergy	5	15	25	10	Fundamentalist Baptist Pastor
Norris, Kathleen	Author	20	40	65	25	Prolific Am. Novelist
Norstad, Lauris	Military	20	50		40	Gen. WW II
North, Brownlow	Clergy	15	25	40		
North, Frederick, Lord 1732-92	Head of State	95	290	595		Br. P.M. During Am. Revolution
North, Jay	Entertainment	10			35	
North, John Ringling	Business	30	70	135	60	Ringling Brothers Circus
North, Luther	Celebrity	28	83	225		NRPA
North, Oliver L.	Military	35	100	175	75	Col. Marine
North, Sheree	Entertainment	5	6	15	15	Pin-Up SP $20
North, William 1755-1836	Military	75	185	350		Gen. Cont. Army. US Senator NY
Northbrook,Lord (Thos. Baring)	Head of State	15	25	55		Br. Statesman, Gov.-Gen. India
Northrop, John K.	Business	45	125	275	95	Founder Northrup Aircraft
Northrup, John H.	Science	40	150		100	Nobel Chemistry 1946
Northumberland, 2nd Duke	Revolutionary War	50	145	250		Hugh Percy. Br. General vs Am.
Norton, Daniel Sheldon	Senate/Congress	7	10	25		Senator MN 1865
Norton, Mary Teresa	Senate/Congress	10	25		15	MOC NJ 1925-51
Norton, Oliver P.	Civil War	20	30	45		Civil War Gov. IN, U.S. Sen. IN
Norton-Taylor, Judy	Entertainment	10	15		20	Pin-Up SP $25
Norville, Deborah	TV News	8			15	TV News Anchor
Norvo, Red	Entertainment	15			40	Bandleader, Vibes, Xylophone
Norworth, Jack	Composer	100		225		"Take Me Out to the Ball Game"
Nouira, Hedi (Tunisia)	Head of State	7		15		
Nourse, Amos, Dr.	Senate/Congress	35	50			Senator ME 1/16-3/3/1857
Nourse, Joseph 1754-1841	Military	500	1250			DS/Content $2,000
Novak, Kim	Entertainment	6	8	15	15	Pin-Up SP $30
Novak, Michael	Clergy	15	20	35		
Novak, Vitezslav	Composer	40			150	Czech. Composer
Novarro, Ramon	Entertainment	35			95	Mexican Actor Murdered 1968
Novatna, Jarmila	Entertainment	15	45		35	Czech. Soprano
Novello, Ivor	Entertainment	25			75	Br.Actor, Composer, Film Star
Noyce, Phillip	Entertainment	10		25	20	Film Director
Noyes, Alfred	Author	15	40	55	30	Br. Poet, Poetic Plays, Stories
Noyes, Edward F.	Governor	10	20		15	Governor OH
Nugent, Elliott	Entertainment	6	10		15	
Nugent, Ted	Entertainment	15		35	35	
Nungesser, Charles	Aviation	135	225	290	300	
Nunn, Sam	Senate	10			25	Senator GA
Nureyev, Rudolf	Entertainment	100	125	225	275	Kirov Ballet
Nurmella, Kari	Entertainment	15			30	Opera
Nutter, Mayf	Country Music	10			20	
Nuyen, France	Entertainment	5	8	15	15	
Nye, Bill (Edgar Wilson)	Author	15		100		Humorist
Nye, Gerald P.	Senate	10	35		15	Senator ND
Nye, James W.	Senate	75	140	175		Gov. Nevada Terr. 1861. Sen.'64
Nyerere, Julius	Head of State	10	25	65	30	Tanzania

O

NAME	CATEGORY	SIG	LS/DS	ALS	SP	COMMENT
O'Boyle, Patrick A., Cardinal	Clergy	30	45	75	50	
O'Brian, Hugh	Entertainment	5	6	15	15	
O'Brien, Cubby	Entertainment	5			15	Mickey Mouse Club
O'Brien, Edmond	Entertainment	20	40		50	
O'Brien, George	Entertainment	20			40	
O'Brien, James	Business	5	10	15		
O'Brien, Lawrence F.	Cabinet	10	20	40	20	JFK Adviser-Strategist.P.M.Gen.
O'Brien, Margaret	Entertainment	10			20	
O'Brien, Pat	Entertainment	45	150		100	
O'Brien, Virginia	Entertainment	5			10	Singer-Comedienne
O'Callaghan, Mike	Governor	5	15		10	Governor NV
O'Casey, Sean	Author	100	275	375	315	Irish Playwright. Abbey Theatre
O'Connell, Arthur	Entertainment	30			65	
O'Connell, Charles	Business	10	15	30	15	
O'Connell, Daniel	Patriot	60	205	310		Irish Nationalist Leader
O'Connell, Helen	Entertainment	15			25	
O'Connell, William H., Cardinal	Clergy	50	65	75	65	
O'Conner, Flannery	Author	300	925			Am. Author. Died At Age 39
O'Connor, Basil	Celebrity	15	25		35	1st Pres.March Dimes Foundation
O'Connor, Bryan D.	Astronaut	5			15	
O'Connor, Carroll	Entertainment	6	8		20	
O'Connor, Donald	Entertainment	5			20	
O'Connor, Glynnis	Entertainment	5			15	
O'Connor, Sandra Day (SC)	Supreme Court	35	160	200	75	Bush Appointee
O'Connor, Una	Entertainment	40			85	
O'Connor,Thos.P.(Tay Pay)	Author	60	100			Irish Journalist
O'Conor, Charles 1804-84	Law-Politician	60	75			1st Catholic Presidential Cand.
O'Conor, Herbert R.	Governor	5	10			Gov. MD
O'Daniel, W. Lee 'Pappy'	Senate/Congress	15	50		45	Governor, Senator TX
O'Donald, Emmett	Aviation	15	30	50	35	
O'Driscoll, Martha	Entertainment	4			10	Pin-Up SP $20
O'Flaherty, Liam	Author	90	325			Ir. Novelist. "The Informer"
O'Hara, Geoffrey	Composer	20	45		25	AMusQS $65
O'Hara, John	Author	160	500	660		Am. Novelist, Short Stories
O'Hara, John F., Cardinal	Clergy	50	85	100	75	
O'Hara, Mary (Alsop)	Author	20	50	75		Am. Novelist."My Friend Flicka"
O'Hara, Maureen	Entertainment	12			20	
O'Herlihy, Dan	Entertainment	7			15	
O'Higgins, Bernardo	Head of State	750				Chile.Soldier,Statesmn,Dictator
O'Higgins, Harvey	Author	10	20	75	15	Am. Journalist, Novelist
O'Keefe, Dennis	Entertainment	5	6	15	15	
O'Keefe, Georgia	Artist	250	725	955	475	Austere Scenes S.W. Desert
O'Keeffe, Adrian	Business	5	15		10	CEO First National Stores

NAME	CATEGORY	SIG	LS/DS	ALS	SP	COMMENT
O'Laughlin, Gerald S.	Entertainment	10			20	
O'Leary, Brian	Astronaut	5			15	
O'Mahoney, Joseph	Senate	10	35			Senator WY
O'Malley, J. Pat	Entertainment	25			50	
O'Neal, Frederick	Entertainment	5			15	Afro-Am. Actor
O'Neal, Ralph A.	Military	22	40	85	70	
O'Neal, Ryan	Entertainment	10			35	
O'Neal, Tatum	Entertainment	15			40	
O'Neil, Barbara	Entertainment	175			355	
O'Neill, Charles	Military	10	20	45		Adm. USN
O'Neill, Charles	Senate/Congress	10		40		MOC PA 1863
O'Neill, Eugene	Author	195	525	1050	450	Playwright. Nobel & 3 Pulitzers
O'Neill, James	Entertainment	20	25	45	45	Vintage Actor
O'Neill, Jennifer	Entertainment	5	6	15	15	
O'Neill, Peggy	Entertainment	5	6	15	15	
O'Neill, Thomas 'Tip'	Senate/Congress	15	25		35	Speaker of the House
O'Sullivan, Gilbert	Entertainment	25	75			
O'Sullivan, Maureen	Entertainment	15		35	30	
O'Toole, Annette	Entertainment	10			30	
O'Toole, Peter	Entertainment	20			85	
Oak Ridge Boys, The (4)	Country Music	10			25	Gospel
Oakes, Randi	Entertainment	5			15	
Oakie, Jack	Entertainment	20	95		40	
Oakley, Annie	Markswoman	1350		3400	3225	Am. Markswoman/Buffalo Bill
Oakley, Violet	Artist	35	95			Her "The Tragic Muse" Famous
Oates, Joyce Carol	Author	10	30	60	25	Am.Novelist,Critic,Poet,Teacher
Oates, Warren	Entertainment	25			50	
Ober, W.O. 'Willy'	Aviation	25		55		
Oberhardt, William	Artist	30	65	135		Portraits.Eisenhower,Hoover....
Oberon, Merle	Entertainment	45			90	
Oberth, Hermann, Dr.	Science	40	250			
Oboler, Arch	Entertainment	12		35	25	Writer-Producer of Radio Dramas
Obratszova, Elena	Entertainment	10			35	Opera
Ocasek, Ric	Entertainment	25			50	Rock
Ochles, Wubbo	Astronaut	10	25		25	
Ochoa, Ellen	Astronaut	5			20	
Ochoa, Severo, Dr.	Science	22	35	85	30	Nobel Physiology & Medicine
Ochs, Adolph S.	Business	50	165		65	Publisher-Founder NY Times
Odell, Benjamin Baker, Jr.	Senate/Congress	10	30	40		MOC 1895, Governor NY 1900
Odell, George C.D.	Author	5	15	30		Educator, Theatre Arts
Odell, Moses F.	Senate/Congress	10	20	30		MOC NY 1861
Odets, Clifford	Author	35	90	210	135	Playwright."Golden Boy", etc.
Oersted, Hans Christian 1777-1851	Science	2500	4750	750		Discovered Electromagnatism
Oesau, Walter 'Gulle'	Aviation	130		415	275	
Offenbach, Jacques	Composers	145	240	375	275	ALS/Content 1,400
Offenhauser, Fred	Engineer	130	395			Automobile, Racing Engine Mfg.
Ogden, Aaron	Senator	35	110	225		Am. Rev. War Soldier, Gov. NJ
Ogden, Francis B.	Military	10	35	80		Inventor
Ogle, Samuel	Colonial Am.	65	185			Colonial Gov. MD
Ogle, William	Celebrity	5	10	15	8	
Oglesby, Richard James	Civil War	40	60	95	150	Union Gen., Gov. IL, US Sen. IL
Oh, Soon-Teck	Entertainment	5			15	
Ohms, Elizabeth	Entertainment	35			150	Opera
Ohrbach, Jerry	Entertainment	8			20	
Oi, Narimoto	Military	40	125	195		
Oland, Warner	Entertainment	150			275	

NAME	CATEGORY	SIG	LS/DS	ALS	SP	COMMENT
Olcott, Chauncey	Composer	65	90	150	75	"My Wild Irish Rose" etc.
Oldenburg, Claes Thure 1929-	Artist	15	35	95	35	Swe. Sculptor. Soft Scuptures
Older, Charles H.	Aviation	12	30	45	32	ACE, WW II, Flying Tigers
Older, Charles S.	Civil War-Gov.	25	40	55		CW Gov. NJ
Olds, Ransom E.	Business	200	950			REO & Oldsmobile Motor Cars
Olds, Robin	Aviation	15	30	45	32	ACE, WW II, Korea, Nam
Olin, John M.	Business	6	12	20	12	Olin Industries
Olin, Lena	Entertainment	20			50	
Oliphant, Laurence	Author	10	25	60		Br. Writer. Cape Town, S.A.
Oliver, Andrew	Revolutionary War	65	185	240		Am. Colonial Politician
Oliver, Edna May	Entertainment	45			120	
Oliver, Henry W., Jr.	Business	45	60			Oliver Tractor Co.
Oliver, Jane	Entertainment	6			15	
Oliver, Paul A.	Civil War	25	50	75		Credit For Inventing Dynamite
Oliver, Sy	Entertainment	30			75	Trumpet, Composer, Arranger
Olivero, Magda	Entertainment	20			70	Opera
Olivier, Laurence & Leigh, Vivien						SEE Leigh, Vivien
Olivier, Laurence, Sir	Entertainment	65	225		195	Special DS $2,000
Olmos, Edward James	Entertainment	5	6	15	15	
Olmstead, Frederick Law	Architect	80	175	340		Landscape Arch, NY Central Park
Olney, Richard	Cabinet	15	25	50	30	Att'y General
Olney, Thomas	Clergy	85	125	250		
Olsen & Johnson	Entertainment	35			75	"Hellzapoppin"
Olsen, Ole	Entertainment	25			50	
Olson, Merlin	Entertainment	9	10	20	25	
Olson, Nancy	Entertainment	6	8	15	15	
Onassis, Aristotle	Business	175	475		225	Gr.Millionaire Shipping Magnate
Onassis, Jacq. Kennedy	Celebrity	350	750	1250	1050	good content letter $10,000
Onizuka, Ellison S.	Astronaut	125			175	
Ono, Yoko	Entertainment	40		100	75	
Ontkean, Michael	Entertainment	5	6	15	15	
Opatoshu, David	Entertainment	6	8		20	
Opp, Julie	Entertainment	12			25	Opera
Oppenheimer, Robert, Dr.	Science	395	1050			Exec. Dir. Manhattan Project
Opper, Frederick Burr*	Cartoonist	25			275	Happy Hooligan
Orbison, Roy	Country Music	75			175	Blind Singer-Pianist
Orczy, Emmuska, Baroness	Author	35	55	105	145	Br. Novelist, Playwright
Ord, E.O.C.	Civil War	50	145	210	750	Union Gen-Indian Fighter
Orient, John H., Bishop	Clergy	5	10	15		
Orita, Zenji	Military	50	160	255	100	
Orlando, Vittorio E.	Head of State	55	135	275		It. Prime Minister, President
Ormandy, Eugene	Conductor	25	45	90	75	Hung.-Am. Conductor
Orpen, William, Sir	Artist	45	120	185	350	Portrait, Genre, War Painter
Ortega, Katherine D.	Gov't Official	3	8		10	
Ory, Edward "Kid"	Entertainment	100			200	Dixieland Bandleader
Osborne, Baby Marie	Entertainment	10			20	
Osborne, Henry Z.	Senate/Congress	10	20		15	MOC CA 1917
Osborne, John	Author	10	20	35	15	Br. Playwright, Screenwriter
Osborne, Ozzy	Entertainment	20			35	
Osborne, Sidney P.	Governor	10	15		10	Governor AZ
Osborne, Thomas A.	Governor	10	15		10	Governor KS
Oscar I, Joseph-Francois	Royalty	70	215	425		King Sweden & Norway
Oscar II	Royalty	25	70	145		King Sweden & Norway
Osgood, Charles	TV News	4			15	TV News, Host
Osgood, Samuel	Revolutionary War	125	385	535		Cont'l Congress,First P.M. Gen.
Osler, William, Dr.	Science	350	1050	1750		Can. Phys., Medical Historian

NAME	CATEGORY	SIG	LS/DS	ALS	SP	COMMENT
Oslin, K.T.	Entertainment	5			15	
Osmena, Sergio	Head of State	65	200			Pres. Philippines 1944-46
Osmond Brothers (3)	Entertainment	10			30	
Osmond, Donny	Entertainment	5	8	15	15	
Osmond, Marie	Entertainment	5	15	20	22	
Ostenso, Martha	Author	25	45	70		Am. Novelist, Poet
Osterhaus, Peter J.	Civil War	30	70	110		Union Gen.
Osterkamp, Theo	Aviation	35	60	130	70	
Osterman, Kathryn	Entertainment	20			50	Silent Films
Osvoth, Julia	Entertainment	20			45	Opera
Oswald, Lee Harvey	Assassin?	2250	7500			Murdered John F. Kennedy
Oswald, Marina (now Porter)	Celebrity	40	125	150	55	Mrs. Lee Harvey Oswald
Oswald, Mark	Entertainment	10			25	Opera
Oswald, Steve	Astronaut	5			15	
Otis, Elita Proctor	Entertainment	10	15	25	25	
Otis, Elwell S.	Civil War	25	40	65		Union Gen.
Otis, Harrison Gray	Civil War	50	175	295		Union Gen.,CW-Sp. Am. War
Otis, Harrison Gray 1765-1848	Senator/Congress	20	30	70		MOC 1797, Senator 1817 MA
Otis, James 1725-83	Revolutionary War	180	550	750		Statesman, Eloquent Lawyer
Otis, Johnny	Entertainment	20			40	R & R Producer, Director. HOF
Otto I (Othon I)	Royalty	105	365	560		Greece. King of the Hellenes
Otto I (The Great) 912-973	Royalty	2150				King of Germany, Holy Rom.Emp.
Oudinot,Charles N. Duc de	Napoleonic Wars	70	150			Marshal of Napoleon
Ouida (Louise de la Ramee)	Author	25	60	125		Br.Novelist."A Dog of Flanders"
Ouspenskaya, Maria	Entertainment	150			375	
Outcault, Richard*	Cartoonist	75			450	Yellow Kid, Buster Brown
Outlaw, Edward C.	Aviation	12	25	40	32	ACE, WW II, Ace in a Day
Overall, Park	Entertainment	5			20	
Overmyer, Robert	Astronaut	5			25	
Ovington, Earle	Aviation	45		245	175	Pilot 1st Air Mail Plane
Owen, David, Sir	Economist	10	25	40	15	Internat'l Planned Parenthood
Owen, John	Clergy	10	10	15	20	
Owen, Reginald	Entertainment	25			35	
Owen, Ruth Bryan (Rohde)	Diplomat	10	20		15	1st Woman Diplomat-MOC FL
Owens, Buck	Country Music	5			15	
Owens, Buck	Aviation	12	28	45	30	ACE, WW II, Marine
Owens, Tex	Country Music	10			20	
Oxenberg, Catherine	Entertainment	25			45	
Oxnam, G. Bromley, Bishop	Clergy	35	50	95	45	
Oz, Frank	Entertainment	5	6	15	15	Self Caricature S $50

P

NAME	CATEGORY	SIG	LS/DS	ALS	SP	COMMENT
PRESIDENTIAL OATH	President		5500			FIVE PRES.(Printed Transcript)
PRESIDENTS	President				3250	FOUR PRESIDENTS
Paar, Jack	Entertainment	6	8	25	20	

NAME	CATEGORY	SIG	LS/DS	ALS	SP	COMMENT
Pabst, Fred	Business	150	395		225	Pabst Brewing Co.
Paca, William	Revolutionary War	300	940	1500		Signer Decl. of Independ.
Pacca, Bartolomeo, Cardinal	Clergy	45	300			Sec'y of State to Pope Pius VII
Pacetti, Iva	Entertainment	25			65	Opera
Pache, Jean Nicholas	Fr. Revolution	20	65	145		
Pacino, Al	Entertainment	10			40	
Pack, Denis, Sir	Military	25	80	125		
Packard, David	Business	20	45	90	25	Co-Founder Hewlett-Packard Co.
Packard, Vance	Author	10	20	45	15	Am. Nonfiction Writer
Packwood, Bob	Senate/Congress	10	25		35	Senator OR
Pacula, Joanna	Entertainment	9	10		25	
Paderewski, Ignace J.	Composers	170	550	450	525	Pianist,Statesman AMusQS$550
Padgett, Lemuel P.	Senate/Congress	5	15		10	MOC TN 1901-22
Paduca, Duke of	Country Music	20			40	
Paer, Ferdinando	Composer	40	110	200		Italian Opera Buffo
Paganini, Nicolo	Composer	300	850	2100		Revolutionized Violin Technique
Page, Anita	Entertainment	10			15	
Page, Carroll S.	Senate/Congress	10	25		20	Governor 1890, Senator VT 1908
Page, Geraldine	Entertainment	30			60	
Page, Patti	Entetainment	4			12	
Page, Thomas Nelson	Author	10	20	40		Am. Novelist, Diplomat.
Page, William Tyler	Senate/Congress	20				
Paget, Debra	Entertainment	20			45	
Pagliughi, Lina	Entertainment	35			140	Opera
Pahlavi, Mohammed Reza	Head of State	135	200	375	375	Shah of Iran
Paige, Janis	Entertainment	10		15	15	
Paige, Mabel	Entertainment	10			25	Vintage Radio
Paine, John Knowles	Composer	15	40	50		Paine Hall at Harvard
Paine, Robert Treat 1731-1814	Revolutionary War	295	645	1245		Signer Decl. of Indepen.
Paine, Thomas	Revolutionary War	3200		13500		Am. Philosopher-Author
Pakula, Alan J.	Entertainment	5	10		15	Director
Pal, George	Entertainment	50			125	
Palacio, Ernesto	Entertainment	5			30	Opera
Palade, George E., Dr.	Science	20	35		25	Nobel Medicine 1974
Palance, Jack	Entertainment	15			60	
Palet, Jose	Entertainment	60			240	Opera
Paley, William S.	Business	15	30	65	25	Founded CBS in 1928
Palfrey, F.W.	Civil War	25		75		Union Gen.
Palfrey, John G.	Clergy	35	50	75		
Pallette, Eugene	Entertainment	60			85	
Palma, Tomas Estrada 1835-1908	Head of State	20	30	45		1st President Cuba
Palme, Olaf	Head of State	35	60	125	40	
Palmer, A. Mitchell	Cabinet	10	25	40	30	MOC PA. Att'y General
Palmer, Alice Freeman	Educator	15	35	50		Pres. Wellesley. Member HOF
Palmer, Betsy	Entertainment	4	4	9	9	
Palmer, Gregg	Entertainment	15			35	
Palmer, John McCauley	Civil War	80	140	225		Union General
Palmer, Lilli	Entertainment	15	15		70	
Palmer, Potter	Business	30	65	110		Palmer House Hotel, Chicago
Palmer, Robert	Entertainment	20			35	
Palmerston, Henry J.Temple, Lord	Head of State	30	95	145		Prime Minister
Paluzzi, Luciana	Entertainment	5			15	Pin-Up SP $25
Pan, Hermes	Entertainment	30			65	Choreographer
Panerai, Rolando	Entertainment	5			25	Opera
Pangborn, Clyde	Aviation	75	140	250	250	Aviation Pioneer
Pangborn, Franklin	Entertainment	30			50	

NAME	CATEGORY	SIG	LS/DS	ALS	SP	COMMENT
Pankhurst, Emmeline 1858-1928	Women's Rights	40	120	255	385	Br. Leader of Women's Suffrage
Pankhurst, Estelle Sylvia	Women's Rights	60	145	250	75	Br. Woman Suffrage Advocate
Pankhurst,Christabel,Dame	Women's Rights	25	65	160		Br. Woman Suffrage Advocate
Pannenberg, Wolfhart A.	Clergy	35	85	100	75	
Pantoliano, Joe	Entertainment	5			15	
Papen, Franz von	Military	40	185	230	150	Vice-Chancellor Under Hitler
Papp, Joseph	Entertainment	30	40		55	Major Producer, Theatre
Paris, Joel B., III	Aviation	10	22	40	35	ACE, WW II
Park, Charles E.	Clergy	15	20	25		
Park, Frank	Senate/Congress	5	15	25		MOC GA 1913
Park, Roy H.	Business	10	25	55	20	Duncan Hines.Broadcast Stations
Parke, John Grubb	Civil War	45	75	150		Union General
Parker, Alton B.	Jurist-Pres.Cand.	15	35	75	20	Judge, Pres. Candidate 1904
Parker, Amelia, Mrs.	Celebrity	5	15	30		Alton B. Parker Wife
Parker, Charlie	Entertainment	400			1300	Alto Sax Jazz Musician
Parker, David	Military	15	35	60		
Parker, Dorothy	Author	25	40	95	30	Critic, Poet, Humorist
Parker, Edward P.	Business	65	150			Parker Bros. Pen Co.
Parker, Eleanor	Entertainment	6	8	15	15	Pin-Up SP $20
Parker, Ely Samuel	Civil War	300	195			Seneca Indian Chief,Union Gen.
Parker, Fess	Entertainment	10	15	25	30	
Parker, Graham	Entertainment	20			35	
Parker, Isaac C. 1768-1830	Law	2500		3250		"Hanging Judge", MOC MA 1796
Parker, Jameson	Entertainment	5			20	
Parker, Jean	Entertainment	15		30	30	
Parker, Joel	Governor-CW	15	30	50		Civil War Gov. NJ
Parker, Robert A.	Astronaut	6			20	
Parker, Roy, Jr.	Entertainment	5	6	15	15	
Parker, Sarah Jessica	Entertainment	9	10	25	25	Pin-Up SP $75
Parker, Suzy	Entertainment	6	8	15	15	
Parker, Theodore	Clergy	50	90	175		Abolitionist, Social Reformer
Parker, Thomas	Revolutionary War	55	90	145		Off''r Cont. Army. General
Parker, Tom, Colonel	Entertainment	5			15	Elvis Pressley's Manager-Agent
Parkhurst, Charles H.	Clergy	25	30	60	30	Reformer. Anti Tammany Hall
Parkins, Barbara	Entertainment	6	8	15	20	Pin-Up SP $25
Parkinson, Dian	Playboy Cover	5			15	Pin-Up SP $25
Parkman, Francis	Author	25	70	150		Historian. "The Oregon Trail"
Parks, Bert	Entertainment	10			30	
Parks, Gordon	Author	10	35	70	35	
Parks, Larry	Entertainment	20			50	
Parks, Rosa L.	Activist	100			125	Civil Rights, Bus Boycott
Parnell, Charles Stewart	Statesman	45	130	295		Ir.Nationalist.Home Rule Confed
Parr, Ralph	Aviation	12	28	42	32	ACE, Korea, Double Ace
Parran, Thomas	Senate/Congress	5	8	10		MOC MD
Parrish, Anne 1760-1800	Philanthropist					NRPA
Parrish, Anne 1888-1957	Author	15	20	30		Am. Novelist
Parrish, Helen	Entertainment	8			20	
Parrish, Julie	Entertainment	4	4	9	10	
Parrish, Maxfield	Artist	175	625	800		Repro S $600. TLS/Cont.$950
Parry, Charles Hubert H., Sir	Composer	10	25	50		Historian, Dir.Royal Coll.Music
Parry, William E., Sir	Explorer	40	85	210		Adm. Arctic Explorer
Parsons, Albert Ross	Composer	5	10	15	5	
Parsons, Estelle	Entertainment	5	8		20	
Parsons, Louella O.	Entertainment	20	30	75	50	Hearst Entertainment Journalist
Parton, Dolly	Country Music	10			30	
Parton, Stella	Country Music	4			10	

NAME	CATEGORY	SIG	LS/DS	ALS	SP	COMMENT
Partridge, Wm. Ordway	Artist	10	20	50	30	Am.Sculptor. Portrait Busts
Parvis, Taurino	Entertainment	40			110	Opera
Pasch, Moritz	Science	60		95		Ger. Mathemat'n. Pasch's Axiom
Pasero, Tancredi	Entertainment	30			75	Opera
Paskalis, Kostas	Entertainment	15			45	Opera
Pasquarella, Gus	Photographer	55				Photo Hindenburg Burning $1500
Passman, Otto E.	Senate/Congress	5			10	MOC LA
Pasternak, Boris	Author	375	675	1325		Rus.Poet,Novelist."Dr. Zhivago"
Pasternak, Joe	Entertainment	30	65	100	70	Film Director
Pasteur, Louis	Science	500	900	2850	2000	Pasteurization, Vaccines
Pastor, Tony	Entertainment	10			20	
Pastore, John A.	Governor	5	10		15	Governor RI
Patat, Frederic	Astronaut	12	25		25	
Patch, Alexander M.	Military	85	225	395	205	Am. General WW II
Pate, MIchael	Entertainment	5			15	
Paterson, John 1744-1808	Revolutionary War	70	200	325		Berkshire Minute-Men. General
Paterson, William 1745-1806	Supreme Court					Continental Congress NRPA
Patey, Janet	Entertainment	25		80		
Patman, J. Wm. Wright	Senate/Congress	5			10	MOC TX 1929
Paton, Alan	Author		195	400		S.Afr.Author,Political Activist
Patrick, Butch	Entertainment	10		25		
Patrick, Dennis	Entertainment	4			10	
Patrick, Gail	Entertainment	9	10	20	15	
Patrick, John	Author	4	15			
Patrick, Marsena Rudolph	Civil War	35	50	205		Union General
Patten, Gilbert (Burt Standish)	Author	30	70	160	50	Fictional Hero "Frank Merriwell
Patten, Luana	Entertainment	15			25	
Patterson, Daniel Tod 1786-1839	Military	45	145	225		Navy Commandant vs Jean Lafitte
Patterson, John	Governor	12	25			Governor AL
Patterson, Paul L.	Governor	5	10		10	Governor OR
Patterson, Richard North	Author	5			10	Fiction
Patterson, Robert 1792-1881.	Civil War	25	55	80		Oldest Commissioned CW Maj.Gen.
Patterson, Robert P.	Cabinet	20	35	45	25	Sec'y War
Patterson, William Allan	Business	3	7	12	5	
Patti, Adelina (Niccolini)	Entertainment	85	180	385	425	Opera
Patti, Amalia	Entertainment	40		135	150	Opera
Pattison, Robert T.	Governor	10	25		15	Governor PA
Patton, Francis L.	Clergy	15	20	25	20	
Patton, George S., III	Military	10	20	45	15	Son Of WW II General
Patton, George S., Jr.	Military	1450	3850	6050	2550	Spec'l SIG $2,250
Paul I & Frederica	Royalty	250				Greece
Paul I, Pavel Petrovich	Royalty	230	750	1625		Emperor Russ.Son of Cath. Great
Paul II, Pope	Clergy		400			
Paul III, Pope	Clergy		1300			
Paul VI, Pope	Clergy		500			
Paul VI, Pope	Clergy	300	475	1100	600	Giovanni Battista Montini
Paul, Alexandra	Entertainment	4			15	Pin-Up SP $20
Paul, Arthur	Celebrity	3	7	12	15	
Paul, Les	Entertainment	25	35		75	And Manufacturer of Guitars
Paulding, Hiram	Civil War	25	45	70		Commanded Navy Yard NY
Paulding, James Kirke	Cabinet -Author	30	90	155		Van Buren Sec'y Navy
Pauley, Jane	TV News	4	10	15	15	
Paulham, Louis	Aviation	40	75	135	80	
Pauling, Linus	Science	60	240	340	90	Nobel in Chemistry, Nobel Peace
Paulsen, Valademar	Science	40	120			
Paulsson, Pat	Entertainment	5	6	15	15	

NAME	CATEGORY	SIG	LS/DS	ALS	SP	COMMENT
Paulter, Thomas C.	Celebrity	12	20			
Paulton, Harry	Entertainment	3	3	6	8	
Paulucci, Jeno F.	Business	15	25	35	20	
Pavarotti, Luciano	Entertainment	15	100	150	50	Opera, Concert
Pavie, Auguste-Jean-Marie	Diplomat	40	145	230		Fr. Explorer. Laos, Mekong
Pavlova, Anna	Entertainment	275		450	625	Russian Ballerina
Pawnee Bill (Lillie,G.A.)	Entertainment					SEE Lillie, G.A.
Paxinou, Katina	Entertainment	150		300	275	
Paxton, Elisha Franklin "Bull"	Civil War	750	1450			CSA Gen., Stonewall Brigade
Paycheck, Johnny	Country Music	8			25	
Payer, Julius von	Explorer-Artist	90	225		285	Austr-Hung. No.Polar Expedition
Payne, Cril	Celebrity	4	8	15	10	
Payne, Eugene B.	Civil War	25	45	65		Union General
Payne, Freda	Entertainment	4			10	
Payne, Henry C.	Cabinet	15	20	35		P.M. General 1902
Payne, John	Entertainment	20	30	55	50	Film Actor
Payne, John Barton	Cabinet	7		15		
Payne, John Howard	Composer	90	250	385		Actor, Author."Home Sweet Home"
Payne, T.H. (Act'g)	Cabinet	5	25			
Payton, Gary	Astronaut	8	20		15	
Peabody, A. P.	Clergy	15	20	35		
Peabody, Charles, Dr.	Science	10	20	25		
Peabody, Eddie	Entertainment	15	15	35	30	
Peabody, Endicott	Clergy	35	45	60		Founder Of The Groton School
Peabody, Francis	Celebrity	10	25	85		
Peabody, Francis G.	Clergy	10	10	10	15	
Peabody, George 1795-1869	Business	50	140			Merchant, Financier
Peabody, George F. 1852-1938	Banker	35	90	250	150	Merchant,Financier,Philanthropy
Peale, Chas. Willson 1741-1827	Artist-Rev. War	235	525	900		Officer. Portrait Painter, Engr
Peale, Norman Vincent	Clergy	20	60	125	60	
Peale, Rembrandt 1778-1860	Artist	175	475	1550		Am.Portrait & Historical Artist
Peale, Titian 1799-1885	Artist		225			ALS/Content $695
Pearce, James Alfred	Senate/Congress	10	30	35		MOC, Senator MD 1835
Pearce, Richard	Entertainment	10	15		20	Film Director
Pearl Jam	Entertainment	35			75	Rock
Pearl, Minnie	Country Music	5			12	
Pearson, Lester B.	Head of State	35	80	175	45	P.M. Canada, Nobel Peace Pr.
Peary, Harold	Entertainment	20			45	
Peary, Robert E.	Military	75	195	245	600	Adm. Arctic Explorer
Peck, Gregory	Entertainment	10		35	45	
Peck, Robert Newton	Author	10	15	25		Am. Novelist
Peckham, Rufus W. (SC)	Supreme Court	50	120	195	125	
Peckinpah, Sam	Entertainment	7	10		15	Director
Peddie, G.	Military	10	25			Gen. WW II
Pederson, Monte	Entertainment	10			30	Opera
Pederzini, Gianna	Entertainment	15			45	Opera
Pedro II	Royalty	80	240	305		Emperor Brazil
Peel, Robert, Sir	Head of State	60	115	150		Prime Minister
Peeples, Nia	Entertainment	15			25	
Peerce, Jan	Entertainment	30			75	
Pegler, Westbrook	Author	15	20	35	20	Am. Journalist, Columnist
Pegram, John	Civil War	185	300	445		CSA General
Pei, I.M.	Architect	35	75	140		Internationally Recognized
Peirce, Benjamin 1809-80	Science	20	30	75		Mathematician, Astronomer
Pelham, Henry 1696-1754	Head of State	45	150	265		Prime Minister
Pelham-Holles,Thomas	Head of State	50	105	170		Brother of Henry. Prime Min.

NAME	CATEGORY	SIG	LS/DS	ALS	SP	COMMENT
Pell, John	Historian	10	25			Museum Director
Pell, Stephen H.P.	Historian	10	25			Curator
Pellegrini, Margaret	Entertainment	15			35	
Pemberton, John C.	Civil War	80	350		400	CSA Gen.
Pena, Elizabeth	Entertainment	10			20	
Pender, William Dorsey	Civil War	410				CSA Gen. War Dte. ALS $3,250
Penderecki, Krzysztof	Composer	20		90		Pol. Opera, Religious Music
Pendergast, Thomas J.	Political	17	50	105	35	KS Democratic Political "Boss"
Pendleton, Alex 'Sandie'	Civil War	205	525	475		CSA Staff Officer-T.J. Jackson
Pendleton, Edmund	Revolutionary War	350	680	975		Continental Congress
Pendleton, George Hunt	Senate	20	35	75		Presidential Candidate. Sen. OH
Pendleton, Nat	Entertainment	30	45	60	45	
Pendleton, William Nelson	Civil War	320		485	935	CSA Gen., Pre War Clergyman
Penn & Teller	Entertainment	10			25	
Penn, Arthur	Entertainment	10			20	
Penn, John	Revolutionary War	1525	2000	3225		Signer Decl. of Indepen.
Penn, Sean	Entertainment	5	15	30	35	
Penn, William	Religious Reform	1500	3500	5850		AMsS $9,000
Penn, William 1644-1718	Colonialist	1500	4250	7500		Religious Reformer
Pennell, Joseph	Artist	55	160	320		Am. Artist, Printmaker
Penner, Joe	Entertainment	19	25	45	45	
Penney, J. C.	Business	60	150	245	175	Founder of J.C. Penney
Penney, Joe	Entertainment	8		25	20	
Pennington, Ann	Entertainment	25	30	70	70	Ziegfield Star
Pennoyer, Sylvester	Governor	10	15			Governor OR
Pennypacker, Galusha	Civil War	70	165	235		Union General
Pennypacker, Samuel W.	Governor	15	25		30	Jurist, Author, Gov. PA
Penrose, Boies	Senate/Congress	12	15			Senator PA. Pres. Pro Tempore
Penske, Thomas H.	Business	10	30		20	
Penzias, Arno, Dr.	Science	15	35	65	25	Nobel Physics
Peppard, George	Entertainment	6	8	15	19	
Pepper, Art	Entertainment	30			75	Bandleader
Pepper, Claude	Senate	15	25		20	Champion of the Elderly Sen.FL
Pepper, George Wharton	Senate/Congress	5	15			Senator PA 1922
Pepperell, William, Sir	Military	95	550	375		Merchant.Gen. in Fr-Indian War
Pepys, Samuel	Author-Diarist	570	1990			Br. Sec'y of the Navy
Pequet, Henri	Aviation	16		37		
Perceval, Spencer	Head of State	120	250			Only Br. P. M. Assassinated
Percival, John 'Mad Jack'	Military	30	95	145		Am.Navy. War 1812 Exploits
Percy, Charles	Senate/Congress	10	15		25	Senator IL
Percy, Walker	Author-Doctor	60		235		Am. Novelist
Pereira, William L.	Architect	10	35	75	20	Internationally Recognized Arch
Perelman, S.J.	Author	45		160		Humorist, Film Scripts
Peres, Shimon (Isr)	Head of State	25	100		30	Israeli Statseman
Perez, Mariano	Head of State	15	25	85	20	President Colombia
Perignon, D.C. Marquis de	Military	65	180	375		Marshal of Napoleon
Perkins, Anthony	Entertainment	25			75	
Perkins, Carl	Country Music	15			35	
Perkins, Frances	Cabinet	25	90	145	60	1st Woman Cabinet Member
Perkins, George C.	Senate/Congress	14	20			Governor, Senator CA 1893
Perkins, Marlin	Zoo Director	12			20	Animal Expert
Perkins, Millie	Entertainment	10			30	
Perkins, Osgood	Entertainment	35			75	
Perkins, Thomas H.	Business	20	45	90		
Perkins, Tony	Entertainment	25			45	
Perlman, Itzhak	Entertainment	20			35	Am. Violinist

NAME	CATEGORY	SIG	LS/DS	ALS	SP	COMMENT
Perlman, Rhea	Entertainment	5	6	15	15	"Cheers" SP $45
Perlman, Ron	Entertainment	8	12	40	30	
Peron, Eva (Evita)	Head of State	1500	1175			Argentina. Statesman
Peron, Juan & Peron, Eva	Heads of State		750			
Peron, Juan Domingo	Head of State	125	365	525	250	President Argentina
Perot, H. Ross	Business	30	80		100	Presidential Candidate
Perpich, Rudolph G.	Governor	10	15		15	Governor MN
Perrault, Charles 1628-1703	Author			2600		Fr. Poet. Fairy Tales. NRPA
Perrine, Valerie	Entertainment	5	6	15	10	Pin-Up SP $30
Perris, Adriana	Entertainment	5			30	Opera
Perry, Lucas	Entertainment	20			75	
Perry, Madison S.	Governor	15	45			Governor FL
Perry, Matthew C.	Military	275	775	1725		Opened Japan to Trade
Perry, Nora	Author	3	10	20		Novelist
Perry, Oliver H.	Military	750	1000	1250		
Perry, Ralph Barton	Author	10	20	35		Philosopher, Pulitzer Prize
Perryman, Lloyd	Country Music	10			20	
Pershing, John J.	Military	60	170	295	285	Comm.-in-Chief AEF WW I
Persichetti, Vincent	Composer	10	25	60	15	
Persoff, Nehemiah	Entertainment	5	6	15	15	
Persons, Wilton B.	Gov't Official	5	15	25	10	Gen. Chief Ass't to Pres. DDE
Pertile, Aureliano	Entertainment	40			125	Opera
Perulli, Franco	Entertainment	20			50	Opera
Perutz, Max	Science	20	40	75	25	Nobel Chemistry 1962
Pesci, Joe	Entertainment	15			50	
Petain, Henri-Phillippe.	Head of State	35	105	265	50	Hero WW I. Treason WW II
Peter & Gordon (Both)	Entertainment	75			125	
Peter I	Royalty	90	225	400		King of Serbs, Croats, Slovenes
Peter I, The Great	Royalty	910	4500			Czar of Russia
Peters, Absalom	Clergy	15	20	35		
Peters, Bernadette	Entertainment	5	6	20	25	Pin-Up SP $35
Peters, Brock	Entertainment	5	6	15	15	
Peters, Jean	Entertainment	10		30	25	
Peters, Mike*	Cartoonist	5			45	Mother Grimm
Peters, Richard Jr.	Revolutionary War	40	90	150		Soldier,Jurist,Continental Cong
Peters, Roberta	Entertainment	10			25	Opera, Concert
Peters, Susan	Entertainment	35		85	75	
Petersen, Paul	Entertainment	5			15	
Peterson, Bruce A.	Astronaut	5			15	
Peterson, Chesley	Aviation	15	30	55	40	ACE, WW II, Eagle Squadron
Peterson, Donald H.	Astronaut	5			15	
Peterson, Forrest (RADM)	Astronaut	5			15	
Peterson, Oscar	Entertainment	25			45	Jazz Pianist
Peterson, Roger Tory	Author	20	35		25	
Peterson, Rudolph A.	Business	4	6	15	10	
Petiet, Claude	Fr. Revolution	125	265			
Petion, Alexandre	Head of State	275				Haitian General, President
Petrella, Clara	Entertainment	20			50	Opera
Petrie, Wm. Matthew Flinders, Sir	Egyptologist	95	170			Pyramids At Giza
Petrillo, James C.	Labor	20	55			Czar of Musician's Union
Petroff, Paul	Entertainment	30			100	Am. Ballet Dancer-Teacher
Petrova, Olga	Entertainment	35			75	Silent Films
Pettet, Joanna	Entertainment	5	6	15	15	
Pettigrew, James J.	Civil War	130	305			CSA General
Pettit, Charles	Revolutionary War	70	185	315		Continental Congress
Pettus, Edmund W.	Civil War	85	170	360		CSA Gen.ALS War Dte $3500

NAME	CATEGORY	SIG	LS/DS	ALS	SP	COMMENT
Petty, Tom	Entertainment	35			95	
Peugeot, Eugene	Business	50	130	315		Fndr. Peugeot Automobile Co.
Pfeiffer, Michelle	Entertainment	30			85	Pin-Up SP $90
Pflug, Jo Ann	Entertainment	3	5	15	12	
Phelan, James D.	Senate	10	25	40		Senator CA 1915
Phelps, Austin	Clergy	20	30	40		
Phelps, John Smith	Civil War	25	65	100		Union General, Gov. MO
Phelps, John Wolcott	Military-CW	45	135	200		Raised 1st Negro Troops
Phelps, Noah 1740-1809	Military	50	165			Soldier, Patriot, Spy
Philbin, Mary	Entertainment	25			55	
Philbin, Regis	TV Host	5			10	TV Host
Philbrick, Herbert A.	Celebrity	15	30	60	25	"I Led Three Lives" Agent
Philip (Duke Edinburgh)	Royalty	110	175	325	350	Prince Consort Elizabeth II
Philip II (Sp)	Royalty	245	1370			Special DS $2,350
Philip III (Sp) Philip II (Port)	Royalty	250	750			
Philip IV (Sp),III (Port)	Royalty	150	550	1250		
Philip V (Sp)	Royalty	150	390			Founder Bourbon Dynasty
Phillip, Jack W.	Military	27	80			Captain USN
Phillips, Bill	Country Music	10			20	
Phillips, Chynna	Entertainment	30			75	Singer-Actress
Phillips, J.B.	Clergy	35	50	95	50	
Phillips, John	Entertainment	15			35	Founder "Mamas & the Papas"
Phillips, Julianne	Entertainment	30			65	Pin-Up SP $65
Phillips, Lou Diamond	Entertainment	10	15	45	30	
Phillips, Mackenzie	Entertainment	10			35	
Phillips, Michelle	Entertainment	10			35	
Phillips, Phil	Composer	15			35	Singer-Songwriter
Phillips, Robert	Astronaut	6			16	
Phillips, Wendell	Reformer	35	50	115	50	Abolitionist, Orator,Civ.Rights
Phillips, William	Revolutionary War	200	550	825		Br. Major General
Phillips, Wm.	Cabinet	4	15	20		
Phillpotts, Eden (Harrington Hext)	Author	10	35	55		Br.Novelist.Plays,Poems,Mystery
Phillpotts, Henry	Clergy	25	35	40		Under Sec'y
Phipps, Spencer	Colonial	55	175			Br. Colonial Gov. MA
Phoenix, River	Entertainment	35			75	
Piaf, Edith	Entertainment	150	385		200	Legendary Internat'l Chanteuse
Piatigorsky, Gregor	Entertainment	120	190	300	300	Rus./Am. Cellist
Picard, Emile	Science	70	215	475		Fr. Mathematician
Picasso, Pablo	Artist	1010	1125	2500	2300	Signed sketch of fish $4,000
Picasso, Paloma	Artist	25		95		Artist-Designer. Daughter
Piccaluga, Nino	Entertainment	30			80	Opera
Piccard, Auguste	Science	35	115	180	110	Sw. Physicist. Bathyscaphe
Piccard, Jacques	Science	15	40	75	20	
Piccard, Jean-Felix	Science	65	195		125	Chemist, Aeronautical Eng.
Piccaver, Alfred	Entertainment	75			225	Br. Tenor, Opera
Piccolomini, Marietta	Entertainment	100	275		275	It. Soprano
Pichegru, Charles	Fr. Revolution	35	115	195		Fr. Gen. Strangled In Prison
Pick, Lewis A.	Military	35	125		40	Gen. WW II
Pickens, F.W.	Civil War	35	80			Civil War Gov SC
Pickens, Jane	Entertainment	13			25	(Pickens Sisters)
Pickens, Slim	Entertainment	25	30		55	
Pickens, T. Boone	Business	20	55		45	Corporate Raider. Controversial
Pickering, John	Senate/Congress	50	250			Impeached & Convicted by Congr.
Pickering, Thomas	Diplomat	10			20	Ambassador to Russia
Pickering, Timothy	Cabinet-Military	200	550	1440		Soldier, Politician, Rev. War
Pickering, William, Dr.	Science	15	35	60	25	Astronomer.Lowell Observatory

NAME	CATEGORY	SIG	LS/DS	ALS	SP	COMMENT
Pickett, Cindy	Entertainment	3	3	6	6	
Pickett, George Edward	Civil War	515	1250	2765		CSA Gen. Sig Offered @ $2,500
Pickford, Jack	Entertainment	50			150	
Pickford, Mary	Entertainment	55	150		135	Co-Founder of United Artists
Picon, Molly	Entertainment	15	20		45	
Pidgeon, Walter	Entertainment	20			45	
Pied Pipers, The (3)	Entertainment	20			45	Big Band Singing Group
Pierce, Benjamin	Revolutionary War	60	135	200		Father of Pres., Gov. NH
Pierce, Franklin	President	320	1085	1700		
Pierce, James	Entertainment	25			65	
Pierce, Jan	Entertainment	20			50	Opera
Pierce, Jane M.	First Lady	215	500	1100		
Pierce, N. B.	Civil War	30	60	90		
Pierce, Walter M.	Senate/Congress	3	5	10		MOC OR
Pierce, Web	Country Music	4			10	
Pierne', H.C. Gabriel	Composer	15	50	125		Conductor. AMusQS $250
Pierrepont, Edwards	Cabinet	15	45	90		Att'y General 1875
Pierson, Roland	Aviation	10	25	35	30	
Pigni, Renzo	Entertainment	15			35	Opera
Pike, Albert	Civil War	130	225	315		CSA Gen.
Pike, Christopher	Author	4		15	10	Novelist
Pike, James A., Bishop	Clergy	85	185	320	125	
Pike, Zebulon 1751-1834	Revolutionary War	40	75	135		Officer Revolutionary Army
Pike, Zebulon M.1779-1813	Military	230	685	1250		General. Discovered Pike's Peak
Pilatre De Rozier, Jean Francois	Aeronaut	125		500		Pioneer Balloonist
Pillow, Gideon J.	Civil War	185	440	750		CSA General.ALS/Cont. $3,750
Pillsbury, John S.	Business	30	45	70	35	Governor MN, Pillsbury Flour
Pillsbury, Parker	Reformer	15	25	60		
Pilsudski, Joseph Klemens	Military	115	320	550	275	Pol. Gen., Statesman,Dictator
Pinay, Antoine (Fr)	Head of State	15	35	50		Fr.
Pinchback, Pinckney	Senate	125	350	495		Early Black Elected Official
Pinchot, Bronson	Entertainment	5			15	
Pinchot, Gifford	Governor	35	95	120		Governor PA, Forester
Pinckney, Charles (1757-1824)	Revolutionary War	375		1500		Continental Congress,MOC,Sen.SC
Pinckney, Charles C. (1746-1825)	Revolutionary War	175	525	725		General, Diplomat, "XYZ Affair"
Pinckney, Pauline	Author	5	10	20		
Pinckney, Thomas	Revolutionary War	200	475			Continental Army, Gov. SC
Pincus, Harry	Artist	10	30	60		
Pine, Phillip	Entertainment	3	3	6	8	
Pinero, Arthur Wing, Sir	Author	15	35	65	60	Br. Dramatist, Actor
Ping, Deng Xiao	Head of State	200		700		China. NRPA
Pingel, Rolf	Aviation	10	15	30	25	
Pingree, Hazen S.	Governor	10	15			Governor MI
Pink Floyd	Entertainment	75			140	
Pinkerton, Allan	Am. Detective	225	675	1365		Dir.Union Secret Service Bureau
Pinkerton, Robert A.	Business	35	105	220	75	CEO Pinkerton's Inc.Detectives
Pinkerton, William A.	Civil War	80	250			U.S. Army Secret Service 1861
Pinkney, William	Cabinet	90	185	245		MOC, Senator MD. Att'y Gen.1811
Pinochet, Augusto	Head of State	30	115	245	50	Chilean Mil. Leader
Pinza, Ezio	Entertainment	70			175	It. Basso, Opera, Films
Pioneers, Sons of the	Country Music	100			300	
Piper, William Thomasr.	Aviation	175	380			Founder Piper Aircraft Corp.
Pirandello, Luigi	Author	70	175	425		Nobel Lit. ALS/Content $2,400
Pirchoff, Nelly	Entertainment	10			30	Opera
Pire, Dominique George	Clergy	55		90	65	
Piscopo, Joe	Entertainment	10			35	

NAME	CATEGORY	SIG	LS/DS	ALS	SP	COMMENT
Pissarro, Camile	Artist	200	740	1465		Fr. Impressionist-Pointillist
Piston, Walter	Composer	75	225	470	95	Pulitzer Music 1947 & 1960
Pitkin, William 1694-1769	Colonial Am.		350			Soldier, Colonial Gov. CT
Pitney, Gene	Entertainment	5			25	
Pitńey, Mahlon (SC)	Supreme Court	25	50	145	30	MOC NJ 1895
Pitt, Brad	Entertainment	20			60	
Pitt, John, Sir 1756-1835	Military	45		95		Gen. Cmdr.Failed Walcheren Exp.
Pitt, William (Elder)	Head of State	110	225	365		"The Great Commoner"
Pitt, William (Younger) 1759-1815	Head of State	115	225	355		England's Youngest Prime Min.
Pitts, Zazu	Entertainment	40			100	
Pius IX, G.M. Mastori	Clergy	175	250	400		G. M. Mastori
Pius IX, Pope	Clergy	40	150	275		
Pius VII, Pope	Clergy		1500			
Pius X, Pope	Clergy		750			Giuseppe Sarto
Pius XI, Pope	Clergy	350	950	3200	950	A.D. Achille Ratti
Pius XII, Pope	Clergy		1500		770	Eugenio Pacelli
Plainsmen, The	Country Music	25			50	
Planck, Max	Science	80	225	440		Nobel Physics 1918
Plancon, Pol	Entertainment	125			400	Opera
Plant, Robert	Entertainment	35			100	
Plato, Dana	Entertainment	5			15	
Platt, Ed	Entertainment	75			160	
Platt, Marc	Entertainment	5			35	Dancer-Choreographer
Platt, Orville H.	Senate/Congress	5	15			Senator CT
Platt, Thomas C.	Senate/Congress	15		33	20	Senator NY
Playfair, Lyon, 1st Baron	Science	10	25	40		Br. Chem. Modern Sanitation
Pleasant,Mary E.('Mammy')	Celebrity	400				
Pleasanton, Alfred	Civil War	75	185			Union Gen.ALS War Dte $1,200
Pleasence, Donald	Entertainment	15			40	
Pleshette, Suzanne	Entertainment	6	8	15	15	
Plimpton, George	Author	7	20	25	15	
Plishka, Paul	Entertainment	5			25	Opera
Plitsetskaya, Maya	Entertainment	15			40	Ballet
Plowright, Joan	Entertainment	10			25	
Plummer, Christopher	Entertainment	6	8		25	
Plunkett, Edw. John,Lord Dunsany	Author	50		225		Soldier,Traveler,Big Game Huntr
Podmore, Thomas	Clergy	10	10	15	20	
Poe, Edgar Allan	Author	4500				AMsS $35,000
Pogany, Willy	Artist	70	190			Illustrator, Muralist,Designer
Poggi, Gianni	Entertainment	10			25	Opera
Pogue, William R.	Astronaut	6			20	
Poincare, Raymond	Head of State	25	60	140	110	Prime Minister France
Poindexter, John	Military	40			150	US Adm. Iran-Contra
Poindexter, Joseph B.	Governor	10	15			Governor Hawii, Federal Judge
Poindexter, Miles	Senate/Congress	5	15		10	MOC, Senator WA 1909
Poinsett, Joel R.	Cabinet	70	460	350		Sec'y War. Poinsettia
Pointer Sisters	Entertainment	30			60	
Poitier, Sidney	Entertainment	6	10		35	
Poland, Luke P.	Senate/Congress	10	15	30		MOC, Senator VT 1865
Polando, John	Aviation	30	60	110	75	
Polanski, Roman	Entertainment	20			125	Fugitive Director
Polaski, Deborah	Entertainment	5			25	Opera
Poli, Afro	Entertainment	10			45	Opera
Police, The	Entertainment	70			275	
Poling, Daniel A.	Clergy	20	30	60	35	
Polk, James K.	President	475	1640	3540		

NAME	CATEGORY	SIG	LS/DS	ALS	SP	COMMENT
Polk, Leonidas	Civil War	425	685	2050		CSA General
Polk, Sarah Childress	First Lady	300	600	1050	1200	
Pollack, Sydney	Entertainment	8	15	30	20	Director-Actor
Pollard, Snub	Entertainment	50			200	Keystone Cop
Pollen, Tracy	Entertainment	10			35	
Pollock, Channing	Author	30	55	145	45	Am. Playwright, Essayist
Pomeroy, Samuel Clarke	Senate/Congress	12	20			Senator KS 1861
Pometti, Vincenzo	Entertainment	5			15	
Pompadour, Mme J. A,Duchess.	Royalty	135	470	1130		Louis VI Mistress
Pompidou, Georges	Head of State	10	25		20	Premier, President France
Ponchielli, Amilcare	Composer	175		1200		It. Opera. La Gioconda.Ballets
Pond, Enoch	Clergy	15	25	30		
Pond, Julian	Science	50		325		
Ponder, James	Governor	12	20			Governor DE
Poniatowski, Jozef Antoni, Prince	Military	370	1175	2150		Rarest Napoleon Marsh'l
Pons, Juan	Entertainment	5			25	Opera
Pons, Lily	Entertainment	50			150	Coloratura Soprano Met. Star
Ponselle, Rosa	Entertainment	25		75	85	Opera
Ponti, Carlo	Entertainment	15	20		30	It. Film Producer
Ponting, Herbert George	Celebrity	25	60	165		
Ponty, Jean-Luc	Entertainment	6	8	15	15	
Pool, Tilaman E.	Aviation	10	22	38	28	ACE, WW II, Navy Ace
Poor, Enoch	Revolutionary War	175	550	875		General. Patriot, Hero
Pope Pius X	Clergy	500			1975	Giuseppe Melchiorre Sarto
Pope, Alexander	Artist	150	370	600		Am. Painter
Pope, Alexander	Author	600	1850	2845	3500	Br. Poet, Satirist, Critic
Pope, Generoso Jr.	Business	10	40	50	25	It.-Born Publ. "Il Progresso"
Pope, James Pinckney	Senator	10	15		20	Senator ID. Dir. TVA
Pope, John	Civil War	90	115	200	400	Union General
Popovic, Cojetko	Celebrity	40		270		
Popovich, Pavel	Astronaut	45			175	Rus. Cosmonaut
Popp, Lucia	Entertainment	15			50	Opera
Porizkova, Paulina	Entertainment	25			75	Model-Actress. Pin-Up SP $80
Porsche, Ferdinand, Dr.	Business	225	385		400	Inventor-Designer VW & Porsche
Portal, Charles	Aviation	20	40	80	50	
Porter, Cole	Composer	250	625	1135	1600	
Porter, David 1780-1843	Military	45	145	250		Am.Naval Off. Fought 3 Wars
Porter, David Dixon	Civil War	105	285	410		Union Adm., Mex. War,Civil War
Porter, Don	Entertainment	5	5	10	13	
Porter, Fitz-John	Civil War	40	100	155	750	Union General
Porter, Gene Stratton	Author	50	145	295	65	Am. Novelist. "Freckles"
Porter, George, Sir	Science	15	35	60	25	Nobel Chemistry 1967
Porter, Horace	Civil War	45	190	185		Union General-MOH
Porter, James D.	Governor	5	20	35		Governor TN
Porter, James M.	Cabinet	20	65	135		Sec'y War 1843
Porter, Jane 1776-1850	Author	100		300		Br. Romance Novelist
Porter, Katherine Anne	Author	70	175	385	150	Am."Ship of Fools", Pulitzer
Porter, Noah	Clergy	30	65	100		Editor
Porter, Quincy	Composer	17	45			Dean & Dir.New Eng.Conservatory
Porter, William Sidney (O.Henry)	Author	300	850	1325		Successful Short Story Writer
Portes-Gil, Emilio	Head of State	35		85		Pres. Mexico
Portland, 3rd Duke of	Head of State	45	200			W.H.C.Bentinck, Prime Min.
Portman, Eric	Entertainment	35			95	
Portsmouth, Duchess (Chas II)	Royalty	65	270	550		Louise-Renee' Keroualle
Poshetko, Joseph	Aviation	5	15	25	15	
Possart, Ernst	Entertainment	15		55	50	Classical Musician

NAME	CATEGORY	SIG	LS/DS	ALS	SP	COMMENT
Post, Augustus	Aviation	25	45	55	50	Pioneer Aviator, Balloonist
Post, Emily	Author	25	50	125	35	Leading US Etiquette Authority
Post, Marjorie Merriweather	Business	15	35	70	25	Philanthropist, Postum Cereal
Post, Markie	Entertainment	6	8		20	Pin-Up SP $35
Post, Wiley	Aviation	300	475	650	950	1st Solo Around the World
Poston, Tom	Entertainment	5			15	
Potter, Beatrix	Author	105	300	750	145	Illustr.Own Children's Books
Potter, Cora	Entertainment	10	15	30	25	
Potts, Annie	Entertainment	5			15	
Poulenc, Francis	Composer	130	375	650		Member of the Group of Six
Poulson, Norris	Mayor	4	30		10	Mayor L.A.
Pound, Ezra	Author	200	575	1050		Poet, Editor, Critic
Povey, Len	Aviation	5	10	25	20	
Povich, Maury	TV Host	10			20	TV Host
Powderly, Terence V.	Labor	45	95		50	Am. Labor Leader
Powell, Adam Clayton	Congress	30	40	55	35	MOC NY. Barred,Reelected
Powell, Colin L.	Military	20	100		75	Chmn. Joint Chiefs of Staff
Powell, Dick	Entertainment	25	30	60	60	
Powell, Eleanor	Entertainment	10	25		35	
Powell, Jane	Entertainment	9	10	20	25	Pin-up SP $30
Powell, John Wesley	Explorer	250				Geologist.Pioneer Expl. West US
Powell, Lewis F.,Jr. (SC)	Supreme Court	25	100			In Robes-SP $950
Powell, Maud	Entertainment	20			90	Violinist
Powell, Max	Country Music	10			20	
Powell, Ross E.	Military	10	15	30		
Powell, Talmage	Author	10	20	45	15	Am. Novelist Mysteries
Powell, William	Entertainment	30	50		95	
Power, Tyrone	Entertainment	75	90		250	
Powers, Bert	Celebrity	4	10	15	10	White House Aide
Powers, Francis Gary	Aviation	80			100	U2 Downed Pilot Over USSR
Powers, Hiram	Artist	45	160	425	150	19th Cent. Major Sculptor
Powers, John 'Shorty'	Astronaut	45	95		50	NASA Spokesman. "A-OK"
Powers, John Robert	Business	10	20	25	20	Fndr.One of 1st Modelling Agy.
Powers, Mala	Entertainment	5	7		15	
Powers, Preston	Artist	25	65	165		
Powers, Ridgely C.	Governor	10	15	30		Governor MS
Powers, Stephanie	Entertainment	9	10	20	25	Pin-Up SP $25
Pownall, Thomas	Colonial Am.	165	425	630		Lt. Gov. NJ, Gov. MA Bay, SC
Powter, Susan	Author	5			10	Non-Fiction
Powys, Llewelyn	Author	30	65	115	35	Essayist, Novelist
Poynter, Edward John, Sir	Artist	10	35	80		Pres. Royal Academy
Pozzo de Borgo, Chas. A.	Corsican Diplomat	50		200		Opponent of Napoleon
Pran, Dith	Celebrity	10	20	45	20	
Pratt, Thomas G.	Senate/Congress	5	20	25		Gov. 1845, Senator MD 1849
Preble, George H.	Civil War	20	60	85		Adm. USN.DS/Cont. $250
Precourt, Charlie	Astronaut	7			15	
Preddy. George E.	Aviation	10	30	45	30	
Preger, Kurt	Entertainment	5			20	Opera
Prelog, Vladimir	Science	20	30	45	25	Nobel Chemistry 1975
Preminger, Otto	Entertainment	25	35		55	Film Director
Prentice, John*	Cartoonist	10			40	Rip Kirby
Prentiss, Paula	Entertainment	6			15	Pin-Up SP $25
Prescott, Oliver	Revolutionary War	70	175	465		Suppression of Shay's Rebellion
Prescott, Wm. Hickling	Author	30	60			
Presley, Elvis	Entertainment	640	1360		1160	AN/Content $10,000-$13,000
Presley, Priscilla	Entertainment	10		40	35	Pin-Up SP $35

NAME	CATEGORY	SIG	LS/DS	ALS	SP	COMMENT
Presser, Jackie	Celebrity	10	25		15	
Preston the Magician	Entertainment	4	6		8	
Preston, Robert	Entertainment	10			45	
Preston, William Ballard	Cabinet	25	50	110		CSA Gov VA.Wardte SP $3,000
Pretenders	Entertainment	12			65	
Preuss, Georg	Military	20		40		
Previn, Andre	Conductor-Comp.	15		80	75	
Previn, Dorey	Composer	5	10	20	10	
Prey, Hermann	Entertainment	10			30	Opera
Price, James H.	Governor	5	15			Governor VA
Price, Leontyne	Entertainment	15		45	50	Am. Soprano, Opera
Price, Margaret	Entertainment	15			45	Opera
Price, Sterling	Civil War	165	350			CSA General
Price, Vincent	Entertainment	40			75	
Pride, Charley	Country Music	5			15	
Prien, Guenther	Military	300			750	
Priest, Ivy Baker	Cabinet	10	15	30	20	U.S. Treasurer
Priest, Royce W.	Aviation	10	22	35	30	ACE, WW II, USAAF Ace
Priestley, J. B.	Author	35	110	220	80	Playwright
Priestley, William O., Sir	Medical	50	120	200		Obstetric Physician
Priestly, Jason	Entertainment	20			50	
Priestly, Joseph 1783-1804	Science	350	1200	2200		Br. Clergyman, Chemist.
Prieur-Duvernois, Claude-A.,Count	Fr. Revolution	35	125			Fr. Revolutionist
Prigogine, Ilya	Science	20	30	45	25	Nobel Chemistry 1977
Prima, Louis	Entertainment	20			45	Big Band Leader-Trumpeter
Prince	Entertainment	110			200	
Prince, Harold 'Hal'	Entertainment	15	20	30	30	
Prince, Henry	Civil War	30	65	85		Union Gen.Pre War ALS $650
Prince, John Dyneley	Educator	10	25		15	Dean Graduate School NYU
Principal, Victoria	Entertainment	10	10		25	
Pringle, Aileen	Entertainment	15	15	35	30	
Prinz, Dianne	Astronaut	4			12	
Prinz, Rosemary	Entertainment	3	4		10	
Prinze, Freddie	Entertainment	45			85	
Pritchard, Jeter C.	Senate/Congress	10	15			Senator NC 1895
Procol Harum	Entertainment	35			65	
Proctor, Edna Dean 1838-	Author	35		80		Am. Poet, Magazine Writer
Proctor, Redfield	Cabinet	12	25	50	30	Gov, Senator VT, Sec'y War
Proctor, Richard Anthony	Science	5	15	25		Br. Astonomer, Science Writer
Profumo, John	Politician	40	65		100	Br.Traitor.Member of Parliament
Profumo, Valerie (Hobson)	Entertainment	10		25	25	Br. Film Star
Prokofieff, Serge	Composer	465	975	1750	550	AMusQS $2,900, $5,000
Prosky, Robert	Entertainment	5	6	15	15	
Protti, Aldo	Entertainment	5			20	Opera
Prouse, Juliet	Entertainment	6	8	15	20	Pin-Up SP $25
Proust, Marcel	Author	500	875	1865	6000	ALS/Content $3,300, $3,500
Prouty, Jed	Entertainment	30			45	
Provine, Dorothy	Entertainment	5	6		10	
Provost, Jon	Entertainment	25			55	
Prowse, Dave	Entertainment	10			25	"Darth Vadar"
Proxmire, William	Senate/Congress	5	10		15	Senator WI
Pryor, David	Governor	5	15			Governor AR
Pryor, Richard	Entertainment	9	10	35	25	
Pryor, Roger	Entertainment	15	20		45	
Pryor, Roger A.	Civil War	85	200	325		CSA Gen. US MOC 1859-61
Prévost, Eugene-Marcel	Author	10	25	55		Fr. Moralist, Feminist Fiction

NAME	CATEGORY	SIG	LS/DS	ALS	SP	COMMENT
Pucci, Emilio	Business	10	25	40	15	It. Fashion Designer
Puccini, Giacomo	Composer	450	850	1525	1375	AMusQS $1,900-$4,000
Puck, Wolfgang	Business	5	10		15	Owner of Spago
Puelo, Johnny	Entertainment	10			25	
Puett, Clay	Business	25	60		35	
Pulitzer, Joseph	Business	125	350	595		Pulitzer Pr. Editor-Publisher
Pulitzer, Joseph, Jr.	Business	15	25		20	Editor-Publisher
Pulitzer, Roxanne	Celebrity	5	15	35	20	Pin-Up SP $25
Pullman, George M.	Business-Inventor	225	510	500	225	Pullman RR Car.DS/Cont.$1,200
Pullman, Hattie Sanger	Philantropist	15	25	30		Mrs. George M. Pullman
Puma, Salvatore	Entertainment	5			20	Opera
Punshon, W. Morley	Clergy	25	40	50		
Pupin, Michael, Dr.	Science	90	305	300	225	Physicist-Inventor-Author
Purcell, Edward M., Dr.	Science	20	30	45	25	Nobel Physics 1952
Purcell, Lee	Entertainment	4	5	12	10	
Purcell, Sarah	Entertainment	5	6	15	10	
Purdy, James	Author	15	50			
Purl, Linda	Entertainment	6	8	15	15	
Purvis, Melvin	Lawman	25	125	165	100	
Purvis, Robert	Anti-Slavery	15	40	85		Underground Railroad
Pusey, Edward B.	Clergy	25	35	95	30	
Pusey, Nathan M.	Educator	15	45	100	30	President Harvard
Pusey, Pennock	Political	10	15			Government Official
Pushkin, Alexander	Author	825	3250	16200		Rus. Poet, Dramatist,Novelist
Pusser, Buford	Lawman	50	150			"Walking Tall"Tennessee Sheriff
Putnam, George Haven	Business	9	25	50		
Putnam, George Palmer	Business	15	40	75	30	Book Publisher, Author
Putnam, Israel 1718-90	Revolutionary War	195	455	910		"Don't Fire Till You See......"
Putnam, Rufus	Revolutionary War	175	405	825		General. Ohio Pioneer
Putney, Mahlon	Celebrity	20	55			
Puzo, Mario	Author	20	75	100	45	Am. Novelist. "The Godfather"
Py, Gilbert	Entertainment	5			25	Opera
Pyle, Denver	Entertainment	4	6	10	10	
Pyle, Ernie	Author	250	400	485	350	Correspondent WWII, Pulitzer
Pyle, Howard	Artist	170	375			Am.Art Nouveau Illustrator-Auth
Pynchon, John 1621-1703	Colonial America			3750		Statesman, Soldier. NRPA

Q

NAME	CATEGORY	SIG	LS/DS	ALS	SP	COMMENT
Qaddafi, Muammar el-(Alg)	Head of State	85	225	500	150	Chairman Libyan-Arab Republic
Quaid, Dennis	Entertainment	20			50	
Quaid, Randy	Entertainment	6	8		20	
Quale, Anthony	Entertainment	20	25	55	45	
Qualen, John	Entertainment	10			20	
Quang, Thich Tri	Head of State	20	45	125	30	NRPA
Quant, Mary	Business	5	10	20	10	Br. Fashion Designer.
Quantrill, Wm. C.	Military	900	3000	4150		CSA Army Guerilla Leader

NAME	CATEGORY	SIG	LS/DS	ALS	SP	COMMENT
Quarles, William A.	Civil War	70	225			CSA General
Quarry, Robert	Entertainment	10			25	
Quasimodo, Salvatore	Author	25	40	55	30	Nobel Literature 1959
Quay, Matthew Stanley	Senate/Congress	12	25			Senator PA 1887
Quayle, Dan (V)	Vice President	40	200		75	
Quayle, Marilyn	2nd Lady	20			55	
Queen, Ellery	Author					SEE DANNAY
Queensberry, Wm. Douglas	Celebrity	15	40	95		
Quesada, E.R. 'Pete'	Military	15	35	55	25	
Quesada, Elwood R.	Aviation	16	30	45	30	
Quie, Albert Harold	Senate/Congress	5			10	MOC MN
Quigg, Lemuel Ely	Senate/Congress	5	10			MOC NY 1894
Quillan, Eddie	Entertainment	20			45	
Quincy, Josiah 1772-1864	Senate/Congress	140	300			MOC MA. Pres. Harvard
Quinn, Anthony	Entertainment	10	20		75	
Quinn, Carmel	Entertainment	5			15	
Quinn, Martha	Entertainment	4			10	MTV
Quinn, Robert E.	Governor	10	15			Governor RI
Quinn, William F.	Governor	5	10		15	Governor HI
Quintard, Charles Todd	Clergy	75	95	160		Served Confed. Army as Phys.
Quirk, Michael J.	Aviation	12	25	40	30	ACE, WW II
Quiros, Jean B.	Head of State	45	70			
Quisling, Vidkun	Military	115	220	475	450	Nor. Collaborator

R

NAME	CATEGORY	SIG	LS/DS	ALS	SP	COMMENT
Raab, Julius	Head of State	5	15	35	15	Chancellor Austria
Raabe, Meinhardt	Entertainment	25			50	
Rabi, Isador I.	Science	35	55	80	40	Nobel Physics 1944
Rabin, Yitzhak	Head of State	210	540	775		Prime Minister, Nobel Peace
Raboy, Mac*	Cartoonist	10			95	Flash Gordon
Rachin, Alan	Entertainment	5			15	
Rachmaninoff, Sergei	Composer	300	1105	2000	550	AMusQS $2,000, $3950, $4500
Racine, Jean 1639-99	Author	4500				Fr. Dramatist. NRPA
Rackham, Arthur	Artist	55	175	425		Illustrator Children's Books
Radford, William	Senate/Congress	10	15	30		MOC NY
Radhakrishnan, Sarvepalli	Head of State	65	180	380	75	Pres. India, Philosopher
Radner, Gilda	Entertainment	25			95	
Rae, Charlotte	Entertainment	5			15	
Raeder. Erich	Military	65	195	290	125	Ger. Navy Cmdr., War Crimes
Raff, Joseph Joachim	Composer	25		150		Ger. Wide Variety Of Music
Rafferty, Frances	Entertainment	4			10	
Raffin, Deborah	Entertainment	6	8	15	15	
Rafko, Kaye Lani	Entertainment	12			17	Miss America 1988
Raft, George	Entertainment	40	105		125	11" x 14" Vintage SPI $200
Raglan, Fitzroy Somerset, Lord	Military	40	115	150		Crimean War. Raglan Sleeve

NAME	CATEGORY	SIG	LS/DS	ALS	SP	COMMENT
Ragsland, Rags	Entertainment	40			75	
Rahman, Abdul	Head of State	10	35	80	15	Malaysia. 1st Ambass. U.S.
Raimondi, Ruggero	Entertainment	20			50	Opera
Rain-in-the-Face	Indian Chief	13000				
Rainer, Luise	Entertainment	15	20	40	45	
Raines, Ella	Entertainment	10			25	
Rainey, Ford	Entertainment	3	5		15	
Rainey, Henry Thomas	Senate/Congress	5	15			MOC IL 1903-21, Speaker
Rainger, Ralph	Composer	20			40	AMusQS $55, $85
Rainier III, Prince	Royalty	70	95	205	125	Monaco
Rains, Claude	Entertainment	90			150	
Rainwater, Leo James	Science	20	30	45	25	Nobel Physics 1975
Rainwater, Marvin	Country Music	15			30	
Raisa, Rosa	Entertainment	25	45		60	Opera
Raitt, Bonnie	Entertainment	5			30	
Raitt, John	Entertainment	5	7	15	15	
Raleigh, Cecil	Entertainment	6	8		10	
Raleigh, Sara	Entertainment	6	8		10	
Rall, Guenther	Military-Aviation	30	75	150	90	#3 ACE, WW II, Ger./275 Kills.
Ralston, Esther	Entertainment	12	15	25	20	
Ralston, Jobyna	Entertainment	30	35	65	60	
Ralston, Vera Hruba	Entertainment	10	15		25	
Ralston, William	Business	55	90	150		Founder Bank of California
Rama VI	Royalty	135				King Siam (Thailand)
Rambeau, Marjorie	Entertainment	20	25	45	45	
Rambo, Dack	Entertainment	15	20		50	
Rambo, Dirk	Entertainment	20			40	
Ramey, Samuel	Entertainment	10			35	Opera
Rampling, Charlotte	Entertainment	5			20	Pin-up SP $35
Ramsay, William, Sir	Science	150	410	640		Nobel Chemistry 1904
Ramsey, Alexander	Cabinet	20	45	90		CW Gov. MN, Hayes Sec'y War
Ramsey, Michael, Archbishop	Clergy	35	45	50	45	
Ramsey, Norman F., Dr.	Science	15	25		20	Nobel Physics 1989
Rand, Ayn	Author	500	1175		750	Objectivist Novels
Rand, Sally	Entertainment	25			55	"Fan Dancer"Pin-Up SP $60
Randall, James R.	Writer-Composer	70				"Maryland, My....." MsS $1,900
Randall, Samuel J.	Senate/Congress	7	20			MOC PA 1863-90
Randall, Tony	Entertainment	5	5	15	15	
Randell, Mike	Business	3			5	TV Exec.
Randolph, Beverly	Revolutionary War	100	325			Early Gov. Virginia 1788
Randolph, Boots	Entertainment	5			15	Country Rockabilly Saxaphonist
Randolph, Charles D.	Showman	75	210	315		"Buckskin Bill" Assoc./Wm. Cody
Randolph, Edmund J.	Revolutionary War	200	665	575		Sec'y State, Statesman
Randolph, Geo. Wythe	Civil War	200	550	565		CSA General
Randolph, John (of Roanoke)	Revolutionary War	85	265	485		MOC, Senator VA
Randolph, Joyce	Entertainment	4			15	
Randolph, Lillian	Entertainment	100			250	
Randolph, Peyton	Am. Revolution	400	2100			1st Pres. Continental Congress
Randy & the Rainbows (3)	Entertainment	20			40	Rock
Rangel, Charles B.	Senate/Congress	5			10	Congressman NY
Rank, J. Arthur, 1st Baron	Entertainment	25		75	55	Br.Industrialist, Film Magnate
Rank, Otto	Science	200		425		Austrian Psychoanalyst
Rankin, Jeannette	Senate/Congress	80	200			Voted against both World Wars
Rankin, Nell	Entertainment	10	20		25	Am. Contralto
Rankin, Robert J.	Aviation	12	25	42	35	ACE, WW II, Ace in a Day
Ransier, Alonzo Jacob	Senate/Congress	75				MOC SC

NAME	CATEGORY	SIG	LS/DS	ALS	SP	COMMENT
Ransom, John Crowe	Author	35	85	200		Am. Poet, Critic, Professor
Ransom, Matt W.	Civil War	80	285			CSA Gen.
Rapaport, Lester	Artist	10	15	30	15	
Raphael	Artist	3500	9800	25000		
Raphael, Sally Jessy	TV Host	5			30	TV Talk Show Hostess
Rapper, Irving	Entertainment	15			35	40's Film Director
Rappold, Marie	Entertainment	30			95	Opera, Concert
Rashad, Phylicia	Entertainment	5			15	
Raskob, John J.	Business	10	20		15	CEO General Motors
Rasmussen, Knud J.V.	Explorer	200		325	150	Danish Arctic Explorer, Author
Rasputin, Gregori E.	Clergy	2000	4500	7500		Rus. Mystic. Assassinated
Rathbone, Basil	Entertainment	200	275	350	485	
Rathbone, Monroe J.	Business	4	8	15	10	Exxon.Important Oil Innovations
Ratner, Payne	Governor	5	15			Governor KS
Ratoff, Gregory	Entertainment	20	65		60	Film Director
Ratzenberger, John	Entertainment	5			15	"Cheers" SP $35
Raum, Green B.	Civil War	30	65			Union Gen., MOC
Ravel, Maurice	Composer	350	780	2005	850	AMusQS $1,675-$3,800
Rawdon-Hastings, Francis, Lord	Revolutionary War	25	60	110		Br. Off'r. Bunker Hill
Rawlings, Edward V.	Military	10	20			
Rawlings, Marjorie Kinnan	Author	45	150			Am. Pulitzer. "The Yearling"
Rawlins, John A.	Civil War	65	160	245		Union Gen., Sec'y War 1869
Rawlinson, Herbert	Entertainment	15	20	45	35	
Rawls, Lou	Entertainment	15	30		35	Singer
Rawson, Edward 1615-1693	Colonial America	125	350	685		Colonial Sec'y
Ray, Aldo	Entertainment	4	5		15	
Ray, Charles	Entertainment	25	35	65	60	
Ray, Dixie Lee	Governor	15			40	Governor WA
Ray, James Earl	Assassin	55	150	275		Shot Martin Luther King, Jr.
Ray, Leah	Entertainment	10			15	
Ray, Man (Rudnitsky)	Artist	150	575			Painter,Photographer,Surrealist
Ray, Robert D.	Governor	5			10	Governor IA
Ray, Susan	Country Music	5			10	
Rayburn, Sam	Senate/Congress	35	65		75	Speaker of the House, TX
Raye, Collin	Country Music	10			25	
Raye, Martha	Entertainment	20	75		35	Pin-Up SP $35
Raymond, Alex*	Cartoonists	60			55	Flash Gordon
Raymond, Alex*	Cartoonist	15			75	Rip Kirby, Secret Agent X-9
Raymond, Gene	Entertainment	10	15	25	25	
Raymond, Henry J.	Business	30	75	150		Fndr.New York Times, MOC NY
Raymond, Jim*	Cartoonist	15			75	Blondie
Raymond, Paula	Entertainment	5			15	
Razaf, Andy	Composer	45		225		Lyricist "Ain't Misbehavin' "
Re'jane, Gabrielle-Charlotte Re'ju	Entertainment	15	70	105		
Read, Albert Cushing	Aviation	40	85	180	115	Adm. Record Flight, WW I &II
Read, Dolly	Entertainment	5	6	15	15	Pin-Up SP $15
Read, George	Revolutionary War	175	425	750		Signer Decl. of Indepen.
Read, T. Buchanan	Artist	17	29	40		
Readdy, William F.	Astronaut	4			12	
Reade, Charles	Author	30	70	135		Br. Novelist, Dramatist
Reagan, John H.	Civil War	105	525	620		CSA Postmaster Gen.
Reagan, Maureen	Celebrity	5	15	30	15	Political Daughter of President
Reagan, Nancy	1st Lady		75	120	75	
Reagan, Ronald	President	175	595	2010	285	Personal Paternal ALS $18,000
Real, Pierre F., Count	Fr. Revolution	15	35	80		
Reale, Antenore	Entertainment	20			55	Opera

NAME	CATEGORY	SIG	LS/DS	ALS	SP	COMMENT
Ream, Vinnie				450		Am. Sculptor
Reason, Rex	Entertainment	10			20	
Reasoner, Harry	TV News	15			40	"60 Minutes"
Reaumur, Rene-Antoine de	Science	200		825		Fr. Physicist, Naturalist
Rector, George	Business	20			35	World Famous Chef-Rector's NY
Rector, Henry M.	CSA Governor	190	650			CSA Gov. Arkansas
Reddy, Helen	Entertainment	5		20	15	
Redenbacker, Orville	Business	4		10	15	Popcorn King
Redfield, Billy	Entertainment	4	7		15	
Redfield, William C.	Cabinet	10	20	45	15	Sec'y Commerce 1913
Redford, Robert	Entertainment	40	225		125	
Redgrave, Lynn	Entertainment	10			25	
Redgrave, Michael, Sir	Entertainment	32		55	45	
Redgrave, Vanessa	Entertainment	20	30		65	
Redman, Don	Entertainment	20			45	Jazz Musician
Redmond, John E. 1856-1918	Politician	5	15	40	15	Ir. Leader of Home Rule
Redon, Odilon	Artist	70		450		Also Lithographer & Engraver
Redouté, Pierre Joseph	Artist	210	900	1450		Fr. Painter, Lithographer
Reed, Alan	Entertainment	25			50	
Reed, Carol, Sir	Entertainment	45			150	Br. Film Director
Reed, David H.C.	Clergy	20	25	35	30	
Reed, Donna	Entertainment	40	50		125	Pin-Up SP $180
Reed, Erik	Entertainment	4			10	
Reed, Frances	Entertainment	10	12		20	
Reed, James Alexander	Senate/Congress	5	15		10	Senator MO 1910
Reed, James F.	Celebrity	1250				NRPA
Reed, Jerry	Entertainment	5			12	
Reed, John	Author	200	1200	1350	300	Radical Am.Journalist
Reed, Joseph	Revolutionary War	75	200	550		PA Statesman, Continental Cong.
Reed, Lou	Entertainment	20			50	
Reed, Oliver	Entertainment	10			30	
Reed, Phillip	Entertainment	15	20	35	30	
Reed, Rex	Entertainment	5	6	16	16	
Reed, Robert	Entertainment	20	45		55	
Reed, Roland	Entertainment	15			35	Vintage Actor
Reed, Stanley (SC)	Supreme Court	40	90	150		
Reed, Thomas Brackett	Senate/Congress	15	35	45		Speaker of the House. ME
Reed, Walter	Entertainment	10			25	
Reed, Walter	Science	400	1050	1400	675	Proved Mosquito=Yellow Fever
Reedy, George	Cabinet	3			5	
Rees, Roger	Entertainment	4			10	
Rees, Thomas	Business	10	25	45	25	
Reese, Della	Entertainment	5			15	
Reeve, Christopher	Entertainment	25			60	
Reeves, George	Entertainment	1200	1200	1800	4250	
Reeves, Keanu	Entertainment	10			50	
Reeves, Marth	Composer	5			20	Composer-Entertainer
Reeves, Ronna	Entertainment	5			10	Singer
Reeves, Steve	Entertainment	30			50	
Reeves-Smith, Olive	Entertainment	5	7	15	15	
Regan, Donald	Cabinet	10	15		30	Sec'y Treasury
Regan, Phil	Entertainment	10	75		25	
Reger, Max	Composer	75	250	550		Ger. Composer
Reginald, Lionel	Entertainment	10			20	
Regnaud de Saint-Jean etc	Fr. Revolution	30		105		
Rehan, Ada	Entertainment	20			40	Fine Vintage Shakespearean Actr

NAME	CATEGORY	SIG	LS/DS	ALS	SP	COMMENT
Rehm, Dan	Aviation	12	25	45	30	ACE, WW II
Rehnquist, William H.(SC)	Supreme Court	45	160	185	100	
Reich, Wilhelm	Science	120	325	650		Austr. Psychoanalyst. Author
Reichers, Lou	Aviation	30	45	60	65	
Reid, Tim	Entertainment	5	6	15	15	
Reid, Wallace	Entertainment	180			650	
Reid, Whitelaw	Journalist	30	75		50	Correspondent, Ambassador
Reifel, Benjamin	Senate/Congress	5			10	MOC SD
Reightler, Ken	Astronaut	5			16	
Reik, Theodor	Science	105	285	590		Austrian Psychoanalyst
Reilly, Charles Nelson	Entertainment	5			10	
Reinburg, J. Hunter	Aviation	15	35	50	40	ACE. WW II, Marine Ace
Reinecke, Karl	Composer	55	145	225	250	Ger.Pianist, Conductor, Teacher
Reiner, Carl	Entertainment	10		30	25	
Reiner, Fritz	Entertainment	50	150		225	Hung. Conductor
Reiner, Rob	Entertainment	10			25	Film Director
Reinhardt, Max	Entertainment	110		470	215	Austrian Innovative Theatre Dir
Reinking, Ann	Entertainment	5	10	20	15	
Reischauer, Edwin O.	Celebrity	3	5	10	5	
Reiser, Paul	Entertainment	10			25	
Reiserer, Russell	Aviation	15		40		ACE WW II
Reitsch, Hanna	Aviation	65	160	270	185	
Reitz, Francis W.	Head of State	50	135			South Africa
Rejane, Gabrielle-Charlotte	Entertainment	35		115	90	Vintage Fr. Stage Actress
Remarque, Erich Maria	Author	40	150	285	50	"All Quiet on the Western Front"
Rembrandt van Rijn	Artist	2800		3600		Dutch Painter-Etcher
Remick, Lee	Entertainment	25			55	Pin-Up SP $65
Remington, Frederic	Artist	550	910	2475	895	Sculptor,Writer,War Correspond.
Renaldo, Duncan	Entertainment	25			75	
Renaud, Maurice	Entertainment	35			125	Opera
Renaud, Paul	Head of State	50			100	Premier France
Renault, Louis	Jurist	35	95	125		Nobel Peace Prize 1907
Renner, Karl, Dr.	Head of State	25	50	105	40	Fndr.,Pres.Austrian Republic
Rennie, Michael	Entertainment	35			100	
Reno, Marcus A.	Military	950	2750			Battle of Little Big Horn
Renoir, Jean	Entertainment	120	340			Fr. Inovative Film Maker
Renoir, Pierre-Auguste	Artist	250	700	2620	3500	Repro Artwork S $3,000-$5,000
Renquist, William	Supreme Court	75			150	Chief Justice
Renwick, Edward Sabine	Inventor	20	45	75		Father Modern Poultry Industry
REO Speedwagon	Entertainment	35			65	Rock
Repplier, Agnes	Author	5	15	35		Am.Dean of Essayists,Biographer
Requesens, Luis de Zunig	Military	750				NRPA
Resnick, Mike	Author	10	20	40	10	Hugo award winner
Resnick, Regina	Entertainment	15			60	Opera
Resnik, Judith	Astronaut	100	275		225	
Respighi, Ottorino	Composer	70	200	450		It.Opera, Orchestral,Choral
Reston, John 'Scotty'	Author	10	20	35	15	Journalist, Synd. Columnist
Rethberg, Elisabeth	Entertainment	40			155	Opera
Rethy, Ester	Entertainment	10	15	35	30	Opera, Operetta
Rettig, Tommy	Entertainment	10			25	
Reuter, Edzard	Business	35	60	250	150	
Reuther, Walter P.	Labor	25	40	95	30	Pres. UAW-CIO
Revelle, Hamilton	Entertainment	4	5	10	10	
Revels, Hiram Rhoades	Clergy-Civil War	500				1st Black U.S. Senator, MS
Revere, Anne	Entertainment	15			40	
Revere, Paul	Revolutionary War	1700	5400	9400		Rev. War Dte ADS $29,000

NAME	CATEGORY	SIG	LS/DS	ALS	SP	COMMENT
Rexroth, Kenneth	Author	10	35	65	20	Am.Columnist, Poet, Avant-Garde
Rey, Alvino	Entertainment	10			25	Big Band Leader
Reybold, E.	Military	15	35	55		Gen. WW II. Engineer Corps.
Reymann, Hellmuth	Aviation	30		75		
Reynolds, A.W.	Civil War	65	145	190		CSA General
Reynolds, Burt	Entertainment	8			20	
Reynolds, Craig	Entertainment	10			25	
Reynolds, Debbie	Entertainment	6			20	Pin-Up SP $25
Reynolds, Donn	Country Music	10			20	
Reynolds, Gene	Entertainment	5	6	15	15	
Reynolds, John Fulton	Civil War	350	1445			Union Gen. KIA Gettysburg
Reynolds, Joseph Jones	Civil War	45	110	190		Union General, Indian Fighter
Reynolds, Joshua, Sir	Artist	200	390	780		Br. Portraitist, Pres. R.A.
Reynolds, Marjorie	Entertainment	5	8	15	15	Pin-Up SP $15
Reynolds, R.J.	Business	225	750			Founder Tobacco Empire
Reynolds, Richard Samuel	Business	45	110	240	55	Reynolds Metal Co., Aluminum
Rhea	Entertainment	10	15	30	25	
Rhee, Syngman	Head of State	175	375	955	250	1st Pres. So. Korea
Rhett, Alicia	Entertainment	300				SP N/A
Rhett, Robert Barnwell	Civil War	140	285	610		CSA Gen. ALS/Content $2,500
Rhett, Robert G., Mrs.	Celebrity	3		10		Blanche Rhett
Rhodes, Billie	Entertainment	15			35	
Rhodes, Cecil John	Head of State	135	230	395	600	S.Afr. Fndr.De Beers Mining
Rhodes, Erik	Entertainment	20			45	
Rhodes, John J.	Senate/Congress	5	15		10	MOH AZ 1953-83
Ribbentrop, Joachim von	Military	160	525	645	325	Hitler Foreign Affairs Advisor
Ribbentrop, Rudolf von	Military	65	95	150		
Ribicoff, Abraham	Cabinet	10	15	35	25	Gov., Senator CT. Sec'y HEW
Ricciarelli, Katia	Entertainment	5			25	Opera
Rice, Alexander H.	Senate/Congress	5	15	20		MOC MA 1859-67
Rice, Alice C.	Author	65		220		"Mrs. Wiggs of Cabbage Patch"
Rice, Anne	Author	15			30	Novelist
Rice, Donna	Model	15			30	Hart Stopper. Pin-Up SP $35
Rice, Elmer	Author	80	250		100	Pulitzer Prize. Playwright
Rice, Florence	Entertainment	5	9		15	
Rice, Henry M.	Senate/Congress	5		15		Senator MN 1858-63
Rice, Merton S.	Clergy	20	20	40		
Rice, Tim	Composer	10	30	65	30	
Rice-Davies, Mandy	Celebrity	5	10	25	20	Involved In Br. Scandal
Rich, Buddy	Entertainment	30			75	Big Bandleader-Drummer
Rich, Irene	Entertainment	6	8	15	15	
Richard, Cliff	Entertainment	20			45	Rock
Richards, Ann	Governor	7			20	Governor TX
Richards, Dickinson W.	Science	25	35	70	30	Nobel Medicine 1956
Richards, J.K. (Act'g)	Cabinet	3	15	25		
Richards, Keith	Entertainment	25			85	
Richards, Richard N.	Astronaut	10			35	
Richards, William	Senate/Congress	15		50		Rep. NY 1871
Richardson, Dorothy	Author	35	110	285		Br. Introduced New Technique
Richardson, Elliot	CabinetP	7	25	45	15	Att'y Gen. Watergate Period
Richardson, Ian	Entertainment	5	6		15	
Richardson, John P.	Governor	15	25			Governor SC 1840
Richardson, John, Sir	Science-Explorer	20	60	150		Surgeon-Naturalist Franklin Exp
Richardson, Miranda	Entertainment	20			75	Br. Actress
Richardson, Ralph, Sir	Entertainment	20	25	50	45	
Richardson, Robert Vinkler	Civil War	535	805			CSA General

NAME	CATEGORY	SIG	LS/DS	ALS	SP	COMMENT
Richardson, Tony	Entertainment	10			20	
Richardson, William A.	Cabinet	15	50	85		Sec'y Treas.1873, Jurist, Auth.
Richelieu,Armand E. du 1766-1822	Head of State	85	240	340		Military, Prime Minister France
Richelieu,Armand-Jean, Card'l	Head of State	245	890	2150		1585-1642.Special DS $3,450
Richey, Helen	Aviation	20	50		55	
Richey, Lawrence	Cabinet	3	10			
Richie, Lionel	Composer	10	20		40	Composer-Singer-Arranger
Richman, Charles	Entertainment	10	15	30	25	
Richman, Harry	Entertainment	15	20	35	35	
Richter, Burton, Dr.	Science	20	45	70	35	Nobel Physics 1976
Richter, Hans	Music	150		750		Ger. Conductor. AMusQS $350
Richters, Christine	Playboy Ctrfold	3			10	Pin-Up SP $15
Richthofen, Manfred von	Aviation	850	2750	5000	5200	ACE, WW I, The Red Baron
Rickard, George L. "Tex"	Business	200	475		275	Boxing Promoter DS $1,500
Rickenbacker, Edward V.	Aviation	75	310	585	275	ACE, WW I, CMH, Top US Ace
Rickles, Don	Entertainment	5	6	15	15	
Rickover, Hyman G.	Military	100	365	570	325	Adm. Atomic Sub.
Riddle, George	Country Music	10			20	
Ride, Sally K.	Astronaut	15	100		55	1st Woman in Space
Riders in the Sky (3)	Entertainment	5			10	
Ridgway, Matthew B.	Military	40	125	175	95	Supreme Allied Cmdr. WW II
Riefenstahl, Leni	Photographer	25	45	80	75	Hitler's Photographer
Rieger, Vince	Aviation	12	25	40	30	ACE, WW II, Navy Ace
Riegger, Wallingford	Composer	20	65	125	35	Am. Orchestral, Choral, 12 Tone
Rigal, Delia	Entertainment	15			45	Opera
Rigg, Diana	Entertainment	15	20	45	45	
Riggs, Tommy	Entertainment	5	8	15	15	
Righteous Brothers	Entertainment	45			110	
Riis, Jacob A.	Author-Reformer	15	45	90		Journalist. ALS/Cont. $350
Riley, James Whitcomb	Author	140	175	480	225	Prolific Poet
Riley, Jeannie C.	Country Music	5			15	
Riley, Larry	Entertainment	4			10	
Rilke, Rainer Maria	Author	140	345	1400		Ger. Lyric Poet
Rimsky-Korsakov, Nicolai	Composer	450	1750	2625	650	Rus. 16 Operas, 3 Symphonies
Rinehart, Mary Roberts	Author	20	80	125	25	Am. Novelist, Playwright
Ringgold, George H.	Civil War	15	35	55		Union Paymaster
Ringling, Albert C. 1852-1916	Business-Circus	115	405			Ringling Bros.& Barnum & Bailey
Ringling, Charles 1863-1926	Business-Circus	115	435			Ringling Bros.& Barnum & Bailey
Ringling, Henry	Business-Circus	100	500		125	Special DS $1,250
Ringling, John 1866-1936	Business-Circus	125	300	615	700	Ringling Bros.& Barnum & Bailey
Ringling, Otto 1858-1911	Business-Circus	210	700			Ringling Bros.& Barnum & Bailey
Ringling, William	Business-Circus	100	325		125	2nd Generation Owners
Ringo, John	Outlaw	2000	6500			Cowboy Gunslinger
Ringwald, Molly	Entertainment	20		45	50	
Ripley, Eleazar W.1782-1839	Military	65		250		General War 1812
Ripley, George	Social Reformer	140	350	875		Critic,Editor,Unitarian Clergy
Ripley, James Wolfe	Civil War	55	185	210		Union General
Ripley, Robert*	Cartoonist	100			350	Believe It Or Not
Ripley, Roswell	Civil War	165	220	410		CSA Gen. Nephew of Union Gen.
Risner, James R.	Military	10	25	35	20	
Ritchard, Cyril	Entertainment	20			60	
Ritchie, Adele	Entertainment	15		50	40	Vintage Musical Theater Star
Ritchie, Neil, Sir	Military	15	35	60	30	General
Ritchie, Steve	Aviation	12	35	45	40	ACE, Nam, Only AF Ace
Ritt, Martin	Entertainment	30			65	Film Director
Rittenhouse, David 1732-96	Science	850	965	4500		Am Astronomer,1st US Telescope

NAME	CATEGORY	SIG	LS/DS	ALS	SP	COMMENT
Ritter, John	Entertainment	5	6	15	15	
Ritter, Tex	Country Music	60	75	150	135	
Ritter, Thelma	Entertainment	40			150	
Ritterscheim, Karl	Entertainment	5			20	Opera
Ritz Brothers, The (3)	Entertainment	75			150	Jimmy, Al, Harry
Ritz, Jimmy	Entertainment	15			40	
Rivera, Diego	Artist	295	620	1050		Political-Social Muralist
Rivera, Geraldo	Entertainment	20	40		30	TV Host
Rivers, Joan	Entertainment	6	8	25	15	
Rivers, Larry	Artist	40	75	160		Forerunner Pop Art Movement
Rivington, James 1724-1802	Revolutionary War	100	225			Journalist-Publisher-Spy
Ro'Al, Zhang	Artist		700			
Roach, Hal, Jr.	Entertainment	5			15	
Roach, Hal, Sr.	Entertainment	100	190		125	Film Pioneer. "Our Gang" Comedy
Roarke, Hayden	Entertainment	25			45	
Robards, Jason	Entertainment	10	15		25	
Robbins, Frederick C., Dr.	Science	20	30	45	25	Nobel Medicine 1954
Robbins, Gale	Entertainment	15	15	35	30	
Robbins, Harold	Author	20	100	150	35	Am.Novelist."The Carpetbaggers"
Robbins, Jay T.	Aviation	10	25	40	35	ACE, WW II
Robbins, Jerome	Entertainment	30	75	125	50	Ballet Dancer, Choreographer
Robbins, Marty	Country Music	25			65	Country & Pop Singer
Robbins, Reg. L.	Aviation	25			60	Pioneer Aviator
Robbins, Tim	Entertainment	4			10	
Roberti, Margherita	Entertainment	15			30	Am. Soprano
Roberts, Barbara	Governor	7			20	Governor Or
Roberts, David	Artist	40	90	175		Scottish Painter
Roberts, Doris	Entertainment	6	8	15	15	
Roberts, Eric	Entertainment	10			25	
Roberts, Frederick Sleigh, Earl	Military	40	55	85	100	Field Marshal, Kandahar
Roberts, Jack	Country Music	10			20	
Roberts, Jonathan 1771-1854	Senate	60		350		Introduced Important Legislatio
Roberts, Julia	Entertainment	80			200	
Roberts, Kenneth	Author	20	80	150		Am. Historical Novels
Roberts, Lee S.	Composer	30	65	150		AMusQS $285
Roberts, Oral	Clergy	20	35	50	25	
Roberts, Owen J. (SC)	Supreme Court	50	150	220	100	
Roberts, Pernell	Entertainment	35			75	
Roberts, Ralph	Author	10	20	40	15	1st U.S. book computer viruses
Roberts, Robin	TV News	4			10	ESPN News
Roberts, Roy	Entertainment	15			35	
Roberts, Tanya	Entertainment	10			25	Pin-Up SP $35
Roberts, Tony	Entertainment	5	6	15	15	
Roberts, Xavier	Business	15	20	35	25	
Robertson, Alice Mary	Senate/Congress	5		20	25	MOC OK,Self-Taught Creek Indian
Robertson, Beverly H.	Civil War	55	140			CSA General
Robertson, Cliff	Entertainment	5	6		20	
Robertson, Dale	Entertainment	10			35	
Robertson, J. Forbes-, Sir	Entertainment	15			55	
Robertson, Morgan	Author	15		60		Sea Stories
Robertson, Pat, Rev.	Clergy	15	25	50	20	
Robeson, George M.	Cabinet	20	50	95		Sec'y Navy 1869
Robeson, Paul	Entertainment	105	210	280	265	Am. Singer, Actor, Athlete
Robespierre, Maximilien	Fr. Revolution	1150	3500	12500		Special DS $4,275
Robin, Mado	Entertainment	40			155	Opera
Robinson, Bill "Bojangles"	Entertainment	150	190	450	375	Black American Dancer

NAME	CATEGORY	SIG	LS/DS	ALS	SP	COMMENT
Robinson, C. Roosevelt	Celebrity	5	15	20	5	
Robinson, Dwight P.	Business	5	15	25	15	
Robinson, Edward A.	Author	55	125	275		Am. Poet, 3 Pulitzers
Robinson, Edward G.	Entertainment	25	45	100	125	
Robinson, John 1761-1828	Revolutionary War	60	175	340		Soldier, Merchant
Robinson, John C.	Civil War	60	180	215		Union Gen., CMH Gettysburg
Robinson, Lucius	Governor	10	20	40		Governor NY 1876
Robinson, Smokey	Country Music	30			65	
Robson, Flora, Dame	Entertainment	20	25	40	60	
Robson, May	Entertainment	30			75	
Robson, Stuart	Entertainment	20	25	45	45	Vintage Actor
Rochambeau, Jean B. de, Count	Revolutionary War	270	820	1080		Fr. Gen. in Am. Revolution
Roche, James M.	Business	5	15	30	15	Pres. Ford Motor Co.
Rochefort, Henri	Author	10	25	50		Fr.Journalist.Anti Napoleon III
Rock, Blossom	Entertainment	25			45	
Rock, John	Science	25	80			
Rockefeller, Abby A.	Business	14	30	65	20	Socialite.Wife of John D., Jr.
Rockefeller, David	Business	20	55	75	25	Banker
Rockefeller, Happy	Business	5	15	25	10	Wife of Nelson Rockefeller
Rockefeller, John D.	Business	300	1125	1550	700	Standard Oil. Philantropist
Rockefeller, John D., Jr.	Business	35	145	225	75	Rockefeller Ctr. Philanthropist
Rockefeller, Laurance	Business	5	15	25	10	Philanthropist
Rockefeller, Nelson A.	Vice President	30	125		110	Governor NY
Rockerfeller, John D., IV	Governor	5	15		10	Governor WV
Rockerfeller, Winthrop	Governor	10	20		15	Governor AR
Rockwell, George Lincoln	Activist	50	110	200	95	Am. Nazi Party TLS $450
Rockwell, Norman	Artist	100	255	575	250	Am. Illustrator-Artist
Rockwell, Robert	Entertainment	5	10		25	
Roddy, Philip Dale	Civil War	110	285	425		CSA Gen.ALS War Dte $3,000+-
Roden, George	Civil War	30	55	85		
Roderick, Milton David	Business	5			10	CEO U.S. Steel
Rodes, Robert Emmett	Civil War	340		1050		CSA General
Rodgers, Geo. Washington	Military	40	105	195		Naval Officer War !812
Rodgers, John	Aviation	55	125	240	135	
Rodgers, John 1812-82	Civil War	105	335	445		Un. Naval Commodore,-Explorer
Rodgers, Richard	Composer	150	340		170	Pulitzer. AMusQS $460
Rodgers, Richard & Hammerstein	Composers	250				Oscar Hammerstein III
Rodgers, Richard & Hart, Lorenz	Composers	375	1350			
Rodgers, Robert L.	Senate/Congress	3	7		10	MOC PA
Rodin, Auguste	Artist	150	300	675	975	SP of Sculpture $1,700
Rodman, Hugh	Military	35				Adm. USN
Rodman, Judy	Entertainment	5	6	15	15	
Rodney, Caesar	Rev. War-Cabinet	185	670	1250		Signer Decl. of Indepen.
Rodzinski, Artur	Conductor	30	75		75	Pol.-Am. Conductor
Roe, Edward Payson 1838-88	Author	15	25	35		Novelist, Clergy
Roe, Tommy	Entertainment	10	15		20	Singer
Roebling, John A.	Engineer	75	165	325		Designer of Brooklyn Bridge
Roebling, Washington A.	Science	100	225	450		Builder of Brooklyn Bridge
Roebuck, Alva Curtis	Business	65	215	320		Co-Fndr. Sears & Roebuck
Roederer, Pierre C., Count	Fr. Revolution	20	50	95		
Roehm, Ernest	Celebrity	200	540			
Roentgen, Wilhelm	Science	450	1300	1875		1st Nobel in Physics
Roethke, Theodore	Author	35	135	250	40	Am. Poet. Pulitzer
Rogers, Bernard W.	Military	10	25	50	40	
Rogers, Buddy	Entertainment	15	20	40	15	
Rogers, Carroll P.	Business	8	20	40	15	

NAME	CATEGORY	SIG	LS/DS	ALS	SP	COMMENT
Rogers, Fred	Entertainment	5	15		15	Mr. Rogers
Rogers, Ginger	Entertainment	40			190	
Rogers, Jean	Entertainment	25			65	
Rogers, Jimmy	Country Music	75			175	Vintage Entertainer
Rogers, John	Military		350	375		
Rogers, Joseph W.	Aviation	15	30	60	35	
Rogers, Kenny	Country Music	10			30	
Rogers, Marianne and Kenny	Country Music	10			35	
Rogers, Robert	Revolutionary War	335	1195	3300		Frontier Soldier
Rogers, Roy	Entertainment	25			55	
Rogers, Samuel 1763-1855	Author	10	25	55		Br. Poet.Patron Of The Arts
Rogers, Wayne	Entertainment	20			35	
Rogers, Will (Wm. Penn A.)	Entertainment	285	450	1030	850	America's Favorite Humorist
Rogers, Will Jr.	Senate/Congress	10			25	Congressman CA, Actor
Rogers, William F.	Civil War	15	25	35		Union General
Rogers, William Findlay	Senate/Congress	5		10		MOC NY, Soldier CW
Rogers, William P.	Cabinet	12	20	35	25	Sec'y State
Roget, Peter M., Dr.	Author	30	65	140		Br.Physician. Roget's Thesaurus
Rohmer, Eric	Entertainment	35	250			Fr. Director
Rohmer, Sax (A.S.Ward)	Author	75	240	465	100	Br. Mystery Novels. "Fu Manchu"
Roland de La Platiere,Jean	Fr. Revolution	30	95	185		Fr. Statesman. Suicide
Roland, Gilbert	Entertainment	9	10		25	
Roland, Ruth	Entertainment	25	35		45	
Roldan, Salv. C.	Head of State	10	20	50	10	Columbia
Rolfe, William James	Author	5	10	20	5	
Rolland, Romain	Author	30	85	125	40	Nobel Lit. 1915, AMsS $2,000
Rolle, Esther	Entertainment	5			20	
Rolling Stones (All)	Entertainment	600			12000	
Rollins, Edward Henry	Senate	15	25	35		NH Railroad & Bank Executive
Rollins, Sonny	Entertainment	30			55	Jazz Tenor Sax
Rolls, Charles S.	Business	175	300	550		Roll-Royce Motors
Rolph, James	Governor	10		35	20	Governor CA
Roman, Ruth	Entertainment	10			25	
Romanoff, Michael, 'Prince'	Business	40	65	145	55	Romanoff's.Hollywood Restaurant
Rombauer, Irma S.	Author	5	15	30	10	"The Joy of Cooking"
Romberg, Sigmund	Composer	150	250	385	225	AMusQS $650
Rome, Harold	Composer	15	50	105	30	AMusQS $125
Rome, Sydney	Entertainment	5	6	15	15	
Romero, Cesar	Entertainment	35			50	
Romjue, Milton Andrew	Senate/Congress	5	12		10	Rep. MO 1917
Rommel, Erwin	Military	750	2400	3650	1500	Ger. Field Marshal WW II
Romnes, Haakon I.	Business	4	10		9	CEO A T & T
Romney, George 1734-1802	Artist	150	475	600		Signed Original Sketch $1,500
Romney, George W.	Business-Governor	15	30	55	20	Pres. American Motors. Gov. MI
Romulo, Carlos P.	Head of State	20	70	95	50	Philippines. Pres.UN, Pulitzer
Ronstadt, Linda	Entertainment	10		40	30	
Rooney, Mickey	Entertainment	10			35	
Roosa, Stuart R.	Astronaut	10			25	
Roosevelt, Alice (Longworth)	Pres. Daughter	35		275		
Roosevelt, Edith Kermit	First Lady	50	240	275	400	
Roosevelt, Eleanor (Anna)	First Lady	95	290	480	225	S White House Cd.$90-$225
Roosevelt, Franklin D.	President	365	950	1905	745	
Roosevelt, Franklin D.(As Pres.)	President	400	1480			WH Card $450.ALS/Cont $19,000
Roosevelt, Franklin Jr.	Senate/Congress	10			20	Rep.NY.Bussinessman-Farmer
Roosevelt, James	Senate/Congress	8	25	45	15	Rep. CA. General Marine Corps
Roosevelt, Nicholas J.	Revolutionary War	25	60	135		Inventor

NAME	CATEGORY	SIG	LS/DS	ALS	SP	COMMENT
Roosevelt, Quentin	Business	5	15	25	10	
Roosevelt, Sarah D.	Presidential	25	70	85	50	FDR Mother
Roosevelt, Theodore	President	225	775	2935	1185	TLS/Content $1,250-$9,000
Roosevelt, Theodore (As President)	President	700	1065	2000	1490	TLS/Cont.$12,000, WH Cd. $450
Roosevelt, Theodore II	Celebrity	10	20	45	15	
Roosevelt, Theodore, Jr.	Military	20	50	110	40	WW I & II. Gov. Puerto Rico
Root, Elihu	Cabinet	65	140		140	Sec'y War, Sec'y State, Nobel
Root, George F. (G.Wurzel)	Composer	50	150	400		AMQS $1,195
Root, Jesse	Revolutionary War	25	60	125		Continental Congress
Roper, Daniel	Cabinet	10	30	50	15	Sec'y Commerce 1933
Rops, Felicien	Artist	55	165	350		Belg. Licentious Subjects
Rorem, Ned	Composer	15	45	110		Pulitzer, AMusQS $175
Rorke, Hayden	Entertainment	25			45	
Rosas, Juan M. de	Head of State	10	25	40		Argentina
Rose, Axl (Guns N' Roses)	Entertainment	20			40	Rock
Rose, Billy	Entertainment	25		35	55	Entrepreneur, Producer
Rose, David	Composer	10	20	35	20	
Rose, Fred	Country Music	30			60	
Rose, Juanita	Country Music	10			20	
Rosebery, Archibald P., 5th Earl	Head of State	30	70	165		Prime Minister
Rosecrans, William S.	Civil War	160	270	365		Union Gen.
Rosellini, Albert D.	Governor	5	15		10	Governor WA
Rosenberg, Alfred	Military	175	340		450	Nazi Head of Foreign Policy
Rosenbloom, "Slapsie" Maxie	Entertainment	55			120	Heavyweight Boxer-Actor
Rosendahl, Charles	Aviation	75	115	225	200	
Rosenman, Samuel I.	Jurist	5	20	55	10	Confidant-Advisor to FDR
Rosenquist, James	Artist	20	60	150		Am. Pop Art. Huge Canvases
Rosenthal, Joe	Artist	75	200	290	180	Photogr. Iwo Jima Flag Raising
Rosenthal, Laurence	Composer	3	10	20	10	
Rosenthal, Moriz	Entertainment	75				Pol. Pianist
Rosenwald, Julius	Business	150	750			Bought out Roebuck (of Sears..)
Rosing, Bodil	Entertainment	10			30	
Ross, Charles J.	Entertainment	5	6	15	15	
Ross, Charlotte	Entertainment	4	6		10	
Ross, Dianna	Entertainment	40	70	165	125	
Ross, G.	Military	10	35	55		
Ross, George	Revolutionary War	165	505	645		Signer Decl. of Independ.
Ross, Jerry L.	Astronaut	5			15	
Ross, Joe E.	Entertainment	100			250	
Ross, John [Coowescoowe]	Am. Indian Chief	275	1365	1800		Chief Cherokee Nation
Ross, John, Sir 1777-1856	Explorer	40	180	205		Arctic Expeditions
Ross, Katharine	Entertainment	20			40	
Ross, Lanny	Entertainment	5		25	20	Vintage Radio Tenor
Ross, Lawrence Sullivan	Civil War	165	600			CSA General, Texas Governor
Ross, Lewis W.	Senate/Congress	10	15	30		Rep. NY 1863
Ross, Marion	Entertainment	15			35	
Ross, Nellie Tayloe	Governor	35	75	145		1st Woman Governor in U.S., WY
Ross, Robert	Author	5	10	20	5	Mystery Writer. Poe Award
Ross, Sobieski	Senate/Congress	10	15	25		Rep. PA 1873
Rosselini, Isabella	Entertainment	10			40	
Rosser, Thomas L.	Civil War	125	255	305	375	CSA General
Rossetti, Christina	Author	45	125	245		Br. Poet. Sister of Dante
Rossetti, Dante Gabriel	Artist	180	220	475		Br. Poet & Painter
Rossi, Dick	Aviation	10	25	45	32	ACE, WW II, Flying Tigers
Rossini, Gioacchino	Composer	500	1150	1950	3875	AMusMsS $2,300
Rossman, Edmond	Aviation	10	30	45	25	

NAME	CATEGORY	SIG	LS/DS	ALS	SP	COMMENT
Rostand, Edmond E.-A.	Author	65	200	450		Fr. Playwright. "Cyrano de...."
Rostenkowski, Dan	Senate/Congress	5	10		20	Powerful Rep. IL
Rostropovich, Mstislav	Entertainment	25	55	100	85	Cello Virtuoso, Conductor
Roth, David Lee	Entertainment	30			75	
Roth, Lillian	Entertainment	35	40	80	75	Vintage Vocal Star
Roth, Philip	Author	16	35	70	25	Novels. "Portnoys' Complaint"
Rothafell, S. L. 'Roxy'	Entertainment	15	20	40	45	NY Entrepreneur,Theatre Owner
Rothenstein, William, Sir	Artist-Writer	20	45	75		Off'l Artist WW I & II
Rothschild, Alfred (b.1843)	Banker	35	90	150		Grandson of Nathan Mayer
Rothschild, Alix de	Banker	70	190	375		
Rothschild, Guy de	Banker	15	40	80	85	
Rothschild, Leopold (b.1845)	Banker	35	75	150		Grandson of Nathan Mayer
Rothschild, Lionel Nathan (b.1808)	Banker	25	75	125	45	Son of Nathan Mayer
Rothschild, Mayer Amschel (b.1743)	Banker	135	400	550		Founder House of Rothschild
Rothschild, Nathan (b.1840)	Banker	50	150			Eldest son of Lionel
Rothschild, Nathan Mayer (b.1777)	Banker	475	1085			Founder London Bank Branch
Rotia, Rocky	Business	5	15	30	25	
Roualt, Georges	Artist	175	475	1240		Landscapes,Religious,Clowns....
Rouget de Lisle, Claude-Joseph	Military,Composer	110	295	550		Composed "La Marseillaise"
Rountree, Richard	Entertainment	10			25	Opera, Concert
Rourke, Mickey	Entertainment	20			50	
Rous, F. Peyton, Dr,	Science	20	30	45	25	Nobel Medicine 1966
Roush, Clara	Author	10	15		15	
Rousseau, Jean-Jacques	Author	295	1050	2950		Fr. Philosopher, Political
Rousseau, Lovell Harrison	Civil War	50	165			Union General
Rousseau, Theodore	Artist	75	175	350		Fr. Leader of Barbizon School
Roux, Pierre Paul Emile	Science	20	45	90	40	Fr. Bacteriologist with Pasteur
Rovero, Ornella	Entertainment	15			45	Opera
Rowan, Andrew S.	Military	35	95	165	90	Delivered Message to Garcia
Rowan, Dan	Entertainment	15			35	
Rowan, John 1773-1853	Senate/Congress	90	250			Rep. 1807, Senator KY 1825
Rowan, Stephen C.	Civil War	25	60	85		Union Naval Commodore
Rowe, Leo S.	Cabinet	5	20	35	10	Ass't Sec'y
Rowe, Misty	Entertainment	6			20	Pin-Up SP $25
Rowland, David	Colonial America	40	150			Member Stamp Act Congress
Rowland, Gena	Entertainment	5	6	15	15	
Rowlandson, Thomas 1756-1827	Artist	250	625	900		Br. Caricaturist, Illustrator
Rowling, William E.	Head of State	10	15	20	20	New Zealand
Roxas, Manuel	Head of State	30	90	230	110	1st Pres. Philippines Republic
Roy, Maurice, Cardinal	Clergy	30	30	40	35	
Royce, Henry, Sir	Business	350	700			Rolls-Royce, Ltd.
Roylance, Pamela	Entertainment	3	3	6	6	
Roze, Marie	Entertainment	40			145	Opera
Rozema, David Lee	Clergy	10	15	25	15	
Rubattel, Rudolph	Head of State	30	55			Switzerland
Rubens, Alma	Entertainment	65	85	165	150	
Rubens, Peter Paul	Artist	2000	9250	21750		Flem.Baroque Landscapes, Portr.
Rubik, Erno	Science	35	65	85	45	Hung.Mathematician.Rubik's Cube
Rubin, Jerry	Celebrity	15		35	20	
Rubini, Jan	Entertainment	20			65	
Rubinoff	Entertainment	18			35	"Rubinoff & His Violin"
Rubinstein, Anton	Composer	75	220	365	445	AMusQS $625-$1250 AMsS $4,750
Rubinstein, Artur	Entertainment	40	125	250	175	Pol./Am. Pianist
Rubinstein, Helena	Business	50	145	225	350	Invented the Cosmetics Industry
Rubinstein, Ida	Entertainment	125			500	Rus. Ballerina/Nijinsky
Rubinstein, John	Entertainment	5	6	15	15	

NAME	CATEGORY	SIG	LS/DS	ALS	SP	COMMENT
Ruby, Harry	Composer	30	90	200	50	AMusQS $265
Ruby, Jack	Assassin	275	505	1200		Killed Lee Harvey Oswald
Rucker, Daniel H.	Civil War	25	65	80	120	Union Col., Bvt. General
Rudel, Hans-Ulrich	Aviation	85	295	395	345	Most Highly Decorated Ger. Ace
Rudman, Warren B.	Senator	10			20	Senator NY
Rudolf I [Hapsburg (Aus)]	Royalty			750		
Rudorffer, Erich	Aviation	35			85	Ger. World's 7th Highest Ace
Ruehl, Mercedes	Entertainment	25			60	
Ruff, Charles F.	Civil War	20	45	60		Union General
Ruffo, Titta	Entertainment	105			410	Opera
Ruge, Friedrich	Military	55			175	Ger. Vice Adm.
Ruger, Thomas H.	Civil War	30	50	75		Union General
Ruggles, Charles	Entertainment	25			75	
Ruggles, Daniel	Civil War	75	250	590		CSA General. LS Wardte $750
Ruggles, Wesley	Entertainment	20	25	45	45	Film Director
Ruick, Barbara	Entertainment	4	6	15	10	
Rukeyser, Louis	Business	4	15	25	15	"Wall Street Week"
Rulter, John (SC)	Supreme Court	0				No Entry
Rumpler, Edward	Aviation	20	40	75	50	
Rumsfeld, Donald	Cabinet	10	20	45	15	Sec'y Defense
Runcie, Robert A.K., Archbishop	Clergy	30	40	50	40	
Runco, Mario	Astronaut	8			16	
Rundstedt, Karl R. Gerd von	Military	225	415	370	275	Ger.Fld. Marshal.Pol.,Fr.,USSR
Runger, Gertrud	Entertainment	15			50	Opera
Runkel, Louis	Business	5	15		10	
Running Horse, Chief	Native American	5		30		
Running Water, Chief	Native American	75		275		Model For US Indian Head Nickel
Runyon, Damon	Author	150	375	650	195	Short Stories & Sports Writer
Ruppert, Jacob	Business	95	300	415	225	Founder Ruppert Brewing Co.
Rush, Barbara	Entertainment	5	6	15	15	Pin-Up SP $20
Rush, Benjamin	Revolutionary War	650		1600		Signer Decl. of Indepen.
Rush, Isadore	Entertainment	12			30	Stage
Rush, Richard	Cabinet	50	160	275		Att'y General 1814
Rusk, Dean	Cabinet	25	80		50	Sec'y State
Rusk, Jeremiah M.	Civil War-Cabinet	25	55	110		Union Gen.,Sec'y Agri. 1889
Rusk, Johnny	Country Music	4			12	
Rusk, Thos. Jefferson	Military	350	445	700		TX Provisional Gov., Sec'y War
Ruskin, John	Artist	50	130	230		Br. Painter, Critic, Author
Rusling, James F.	Civil War	15	30	40		Union Gen. Bvt.
Russell, Annie	Entertainment	10		25	20	Vintage Stage
Russell, Bertrand	Author	85	260	285	300	Philosopher, Mathematician
Russell, Bruce*	Cartoonist	25			50	Political Cartoonist, Pulitzer
Russell, Charles	Governor	5	15			Governor NV
Russell, Charles M.	Artist	250	750	1650		Known For Cowboy-West Art
Russell, David Abel	Senate/Congress	10	20	35		Rep. NY 1835
Russell, David Allen	Civil War					Union Gen.-Killed at Gettysburg
Russell, Donald J. M.	Business	5	10	20	10	
Russell, Harold	Entertainment	5	10	20	25	Military Hero, Academy Award
Russell, Jane	Entertainment	5	10	20	25	Pin-Up SP $35
Russell, John	Entertainment	20			45	
Russell, John, Lord, 1st Earl	Head of State	40	80	105		Br. Prime Minister, 1864-65
Russell, Johnny	Entertainment	5			13	Singer-Songwriter
Russell, Jonathan 1771-1832	Diplomat	390	800			Min. to Nor,Swe.Treaty of Ghent
Russell, Kurt	Entertainment	15			35	
Russell, Lillian	Entertainment	100	145	225	310	Vintage Musical, Operetta Star
Russell, Mark	Entertainment	4			10	

NAME	CATEGORY	SIG	LS/DS	ALS	SP	COMMENT
Russell, Richard B., Jr.	Senate/Congress	20	35		35	Gov., Senator GA
Russell, Richard M.	Senate/Congress	5	10			Rep. MA
Russell, Rosalind	Entertainment	35	45		100	
Russell, Sol Smith	Entertainment	15			35	Vintage Comedian
Russell, Theresa	Entertainment	10	15	30	25	
Russell. George W.	Author	40	145		55	Leader Ir. Literary Renaissance
Rust, Albert	Civil War	70	180	195		CSA General
Rustin, Bayard	Activist	15	35	70	25	Afro-Am Civil Rights Activist
Rutan, Dick	Aviation	15	70		30	
Rutan, Dick & Jeana Yeager	Aviation		75		125	
Rutgers, Henry 1745-1830	Revolutionary War	95	295	345		Benfactor Rutgers University
Rutherford, Ann	Entertainment	10	15		30	Pin-Up SP $35
Rutherford, Ernest	Science	155	490	925	225	Br. Physicist. Nobel Chem. 1908
Rutherford, Margaret, Dame	Entertainment	50		145	185	
Rutledge, Edward	Revolutionary War	220	500	1225		Signer Decl. of Independ.
Rutledge, John (SC)	Supreme Court	195	600	1775		Continental Congress
Rutledge, Wiley B. (SC)	Supreme Court	30	115	265	50	
Ruttan, Susan	Entertainment	5			15	
Ryan, Irene	Entertainment	75			250	
Ryan, Meg	Entertainment	25			65	
Ryan, Peggy	Entertainment	10	15	35	30	
Ryan, Robert	Entertainment	20	30		60	
Ryan, Sheila	Entertainment	5	6	15	15	
Ryan, T. Claude	Aviation	85	250		225	Ryan Aircraft Mfg.-Designer
Rydell, Bobby	Entertainment	10			15	Rock
Ryder, Albert P. 1847-1917	Artist	90	250	560		Am. Landscapes,Marine,Portraits
Ryder, Wynona	Entertainment	25			80	
Ryle, Martin, Sir	Science	35	110	190	45	Nobel Physics 1974

S

NAME	CATEGORY	SIG	LS/DS	ALS	SP	COMMENT
Saarinen, G. Eliel	Architect	20	65	150	40	Am. Foremost Arch. Of His Day
Sabatini, Rafael	Author	25	70	95		It. Historical Romance Novels
Sabin, Albert Bruce, Dr.	Science	25	90	150	120	Polio Vaccine
Sabin, Dwight May	Senate/Congress	5	10		10	Rep. MN 1883
Sablon, Jean	Entertainment	20	25	45	45	Vintage Fr. Romantic Singer
Sabu	Entertainment	50			150	
Sacco, Nicola	Political Radical			3700		With Vanzetti Convicted Murder
Sacher-Masoch, Leopold von	Author	130	275	420		Word "Masochism" Attributed
Sackler, Howard	Author	5	15	25	10	
Sacks, Oliver, Dr.	Science	15	45		30	"Awakenings". Neurologist
Sackville-West, Lionel, Sir	Diplomat	10	25	40		2nd Baron
Sackville-West, Victoria Mary	Author	100		415		Br. Poet and Novelist
Sadat, Anwar	Head of State	50	145	325	300	Assassinated Pres.of Egypt
Sade	Entertainment	15			30	
Sade, Marquis de	Author	240	725	1900		Sadist, Sadistic Attributed

NAME	CATEGORY	SIG	LS/DS	ALS	SP	COMMENT
Safer, Morley	TV News	5	10		15	"60 Minutes"
Sagan, Carl, Dr.	Science	10	30	55	25	Am. Astronomer, Author.Pulitzer
Sage, Russell	Business	70	185	360	135	Financier, Speculator/J.Gould
Sager, Carole Bayer	Composer	5	15	20	10	
Saget, Bob	TV Host	4			10	TV Host
Sahl, Mort	Entertainment	5	8	15	15	Political Humorist
Said, Nuri	Head of State	5	15	35	10	Pr. Minister Iraq
Saint Hilaire, L.V. Jos.	Fr. Revolution	30	75	155		
Saint James, Susan	Entertainment	20			55	
Saint Laurent, Yves	Business	20	35	75	45	Fashion Designer
Saint, Eva Marie	Entertainment	10	15		25	
Saint-Cyr, Gouvion	Military	50	175	190		Fr. Marshal, Minister of War
Saint-Exupery, Antoine de	Aviation	50	145	225	135	Fr. Aviator and Author
Saint-Gaudens, Augustus	Artist	100	335	675		Known For Monumental Projects
Saint-Just, Louis A.L. de	Fr. Revolution	375	1235			Guillotined Fr. Revolutionary
Saint-Saens, Camille	Composer	125	325	380	400	Opera, AMusQS $450-$650
Saito, Hiroshi	Celebrity	5	15	35	20	
Saito, Makoto, Baron	Head of State	85	190	350		Prime Minister Japan
Sakai, Saburo	Aviation	35			85	3rd Highest Japanese Ace
Sakall, S.Z. "Cuddles"	Entertainment	150			350	
Sakharov, Andrei & Elena Bonner	Science	425				Nobel Phys.,Political Activists
Salalm, Abdus	Science	20	30	55	25	Nobel Physics 1979
Salan, Raoul	Military	20	55	95	50	
Salazar, Jose, Cardinal	Clergy	30	30	35		
Sale, Chic	Entertainment	25	35	65	60	
Sales, Soupy	Entertainment	5	8		15	
Saleza, Albert	Entertainment	15			45	
Salinger, J[erome] D[avid]	Author	575	3050	2400		Novelist. "Catcher in the Rye"
Salinger, Pierre	Journalist	10	20	40	20	Press Sec'y Pres. JFK
Salisbury, 3rd Marquis, Robert C.	Head of State	25	45	80		Prime Minister
Salisbury, Harrison	Author	15			25	Pulitzer Journalist, Editor
Salk, Jonas, Dr.	Science	40	150	175	70	Polio Vaccine Booklet S $200
Salling, John	Civil War	15	25	50		Union General
Salmi, Albert	Entertainment	25			40	
Salminen, Sally	Author	15	40	75		
Salt, Jennifer	Entertainment	3			10	
Salt, Titus, Sir 1803-76	Business	5	20	40		Pioneer Wool Industry.Inventor
Salten, Felix 1870-1946	Author	35	100	235		Austrian Author of "Bambi"
Saltonstall, Leverett	Senate/Congress	12	20		15	Senator MA
Salvini, Tomaso	Entertainment	45			175	Tragedian with Booth
Sam the Sham (Domingo Samudio)	Entertainment	10			20	Tex-Mex Rock
Sambora, Richie	Entertainment	10			35	
Samms, Emma	Entertainment	6	8		20	Pin-Up SP $35
Sammt, Albert	Aviation	30			65	
Samples, Candy	Entertainment	25			60	
Sampson, Will	Entertainment	35	55	85	100	
Sampson, William T.	Military	30	80	135	75	Adm. Cmdr-in-Chief, Sp.-Am. War
Samuelson, Paul A., Dr.	Economics	25	40		35	Nobel Economics
San Giacomo, Laura	Entertainment	20			65	
San Juan, Olga	Entertainment	5			10	
San Martin, Jose de	Head of State	500	895	2650		Soldier Hero of Argentina
Sanborn, Franklin B.	Author	5	15	35	15	Journalist, Editor, Biographer
Sanborn, Katherine A.	Author	5	20	35		
Sand, George	Author	100	200	615		Fr. Novelist
Sandburg, Carl	Author	65	255	305	365	Orig. Pencil Portr. S $750
Sanders, George	Entertainment	45	80		150	

NAME	CATEGORY	SIG	LS/DS	ALS	SP	COMMENT
Sanders, Gregg	Entertainment	10	12	25	20	
Sanders, Harland	Business	25	75		90	KFC Colonel Sanders
Sanders, Horace T.	Civil War	20	35	60		Union General
Sanderson, Julia	Entertainment	10	20	30	30	Vintage Radio/Frank Crummit
Sandoz, Marie	Author	25	70	170	40	
Sands, Tommy	Entertainment	10			15	
Sandwich,4thEarl(Montagu)	Statesman	65	200	550		The Sandwich Attributed To Him
Sanford, Edw. Terry (SC)	Supreme Court	75	195			
Sanford, Isabel	Entertainment	5	7	15	15	
Sanger, Frederick	Science	20	35	60	25	Nobel Chemistry 1958
Sanger, Margaret	Reformer	65	210	350	105	Birth Control Reformer
Sangster, Margaret E.	Author	30	55	140		Journalist, Poet, Editor
Sangster, William E.	Clergy	25	40	55		
Sankey, Ira D.	Clergy	75	95	150	100	
Sankford, Henry	Clergy	35	50	60		
Sano, Roy L., Bishop	Clergy	20	25	35	25	
Sansom, Art	Cartoonist	5			20	The Born Loser
Santa Anna, Antonio L. de	Head of State	235	1285	1570	585	General,Revolutionist,Pres.Mex.
Santa Cruz, Andres 1792-1865	Head of State	95	245			General. Pres.Bolivia. Exiled
Santa Rosa, Annibale S.,Count	Military	25	70	150		It.Piedmontese Insurgent
Santana	Entertainment	10			30	Singer-Musician
Santayana, George	Author	65	175	350		Poet, Philosopher, Critic
Santos, Joe	Entertainment	5	6	15	15	
Santos-Dumont, A.	Aviation	300	390	580	720	Brazil. Aeronaut. PioneerAirman
Santunione, Orianna	Entertainment	5			20	Opera
Sarandon, Susan	Entertainment	9	15		35	Pin-Up SP $38
Sarasate, Pablo de	Composer	100		250		Violin Virtuoso, AMusQS $275
Sardi, Vincent	Business	4	15	25	10	Fndr. Sardi's Restaurant NYC
Sardou, Victorien	Playwright	20	45	100	150	Fr. Librettist, Bourgeois Drama
Sarett, Lew	Author	75	100			
Sarfatti, Margherita	Author	10	30	50		
Sargent, Dick	Entertainment	5			15	
Sargent, John G.	Cabinet	15	30	60	25	Att'y General 1925
Sargent, John Singer	Artist	95	245	400		Am. World Famous Portraitist
Sargent, Kenny	Entertainment	20			45	Big Band Singer
Sargent, Winthrop	Revolutionary War	30	100	240		Cont'l Army, 1st Gov. MS Terr.
Sarnoff, David	Business	60	110	145	70	Broadcasting Pioneer
Sarocco, Suzanne	Entertainment	10			25	Opera
Saroyan, William	Author	60	225	285	80	Pulitzer "The Time of Your Life
Sartain, John	Artist-Engraver	25	100	155		Sartain's Union Magazine
Sarton, May	Author	5	15	40		
Sartre, Jean-Paul	Author	100	325	500		Leader Existentialist Movement
Sassoon, Beverly	Entertainment	3	3	6	15	
Sassoon, Siegfried	Author	130	225	365		Br. Poet.Anti-War Verse
Sassoon, Vidal	Business	15	20	25	20	Hair Design & Products
Satie, Erik	Composer	210	825	1650		Eccentric, Avant Garde Music
Sato, Eisaku	Head of State	20	55	150	35	Premier Japan. Nobel Peace
Sauckel, Fritz	Military	50	200			Nazi War Criminal. Hanged
Sauer, Emil	Entertainment	15	15	35	30	
Sauguet, Henri	Composer	65		275		Fr. Opera, Ballet AMQS $250
Saulsbury, Grove	Governor	5	15	30		Governor DE
Saumarez, James, Sir, Baron de	Military	90	265	600		Br. Adm., Battle of the Nile
Saunders, Alvin	Senate/Congress	15	35	80		Sen.KY, CW Gov. Nebr.Territory
Saunders, Edward Watts	Senate/Congress	10	20			Rep. VA 1906
Saunders, Hugh W.	Aviation	5	10	20	15	
Saunders, Lori	Entertainment	4			15	

NAME	CATEGORY	SIG	LS/DS	ALS	SP	COMMENT
Saunders, Stuart J.	Business	3	7	15	10	
Saunders, Stuart T.	Business	5			10	CEO Penn-Central RR
Savage, Ann	Entertainment	12	15		35	
Savage, Fred	Entertainment	7			25	
Savage, M. J.	Clergy	15	30	45		
Saval, Dany	Entertainment	5		25	20	Pin-Up SP $25. Fr. Actress
Savalas, George	Entertainment	10			25	
Savalas, Telly	Entertainment	15			40	
Savles, Thomas F, Bishop	Clergy	30	40			
Savoia, Attilio	Artist	15	40	75		
Sawyer, Charles	Cabinet	5	25	30	10	Sec'y Commerce 1948
Sawyer, Diane	Journalist	5	20		25	TV Broadcast Journalist
Sawyer, Joe	Entertainment	75			200	
Sax, Adolphe	Science	55	135	230		Invented Saxophone & Others
Saxbe, William B.	Cabinet	8	12	20	15	Att'y General 1974
Saxe, John G.	Author	10	30	55	30	
Saxon, John	Entertainment	5			15	
Saxon, Rufus, Jr.	Civil War	25	55	70		Union General
Sayao, Bidu	Entertainment	15			90	Opera
Sayers, Dorothy	Author	110	495	575	125	Br. Mystery Novelist
Saylor, Anna, Mrs.	Socialite	5	10			
Scacchi, Greta	Entertainment	10			30	
Scaggs, Boz	Entertainment	15			35	
Scagliarini, Eleanora	Entertainment	10			40	Opera
Scalchi Lolly	Entertainment	35			75	
Scalia, Antonin (SC)	Supreme Court	30	90		55	
Scalia, Jack	Entertainment	10			25	
Scammell, Alexander 1746-81	Revolutionary War	350		1500		Officer. Wounded Died 1781
Scancarelli, Jim*	Cartoonist	10			45	Gasoline Alley
Scarborough, John	Clergy	10	15	20		
Scarlatti, Alessandro 1660-1725	Composer	725	4150	12000		115 Operas, Over 600 Cantatas
Scarwid, Diana	Entertainment	5		15	20	
Schaal, Richard	Entertainment	3	3	6	8	
Schaal, Wendy	Entertainment	3	3	6	6	
Schacht, Hjalmar	WW II	60	160	300		Nazi Minister WW II
Schafer, Natalie	Entertainment	20			35	
Schaff, Phillip	Clergy	40	55	75	50	
Schaffner, Franklin J.	Entertainment	30			75	
Schaffner, Hans	Head of State	10			20	Pres. Austria
Schall, Thomas D.	Senate/Congress	5	15			Rep., Senator MN 1915
Schallert, William	Entertainment	5	6	15	15	
Schally, Andrew V., Dr.	Science	22	30	45	30	Nobel Medicine 1977
Schanberg, Sydney, H.	Author	10	30	75	15	
Scharwenka, Franz Xavier	Composer	25		75	150	Pianist.Founder of Conservatory
Schary, Dore	Entertainment	15		25	30	Producer, Director, Writer
Schary, Emanuel	Artist	10	25	35		
Schawlow, Arthur L., Dr.	Science	22	30	35	25	Nobel Physics 1981
Scheer, Reinhard 1863-1928	Military	20	45	95	40	Ger. Adm. Battle of Jutland.
Scheff, Fritzi	Entertainment	15	15	30	25	Theatre & Silent Films
Scheidemann, Philippe	Head of State	10	20	50	40	1st Chancellor of Repub. 1919
Scheider, Roy	Entertainment	10			25	
Schell, Maria	Entertainment	5	7	20	15	
Schell, Maximillian	Entertainment	10	15	35	30	
Schenck, Robert C.	Civil War	35	45	70		Union Gen., Rep OH, Ambassador
Scherer, Paul	Clergy	20	25	40	30	
Schick, Bela, Dr.	Science	60	135	225	75	Schick Test for TB

NAME	CATEGORY	SIG	LS/DS	ALS	SP	COMMENT
Schiele, Egon	Artist		1400			Austrian Expressionist Painter
Schiff, Jacob H.	Business	15	40	65		
Schiffer, Claudia	Entertainment	20			45	Pin-Up SP $55
Schifrin, Lalo	Composer	5	15	25	15	AMusQS $40
Schildkraut, Joseph	Entertainment	60	110		150	
Schiller, Hans von	Aviation	20		45		
Schilling, David	Aviation	18	38	60	45	ACE, WW II
Schine, G. David	Business	20			40	Hotel Chain Owner
Schiotz, Fredrik A.	Clergy	20	25	35	30	
Schipa, Tito	Entertainment	45			180	Opera
Schirach, Baldur Von	Ger. Politician	125	515			Nat'l Dir.Hitler Youth Movement
Schirra, Walter M.	Astronaut	20	75		85	Mercury 7 Astro.
Schlafly, Phyllis	Political	10	20	35	25	Activist, Feminist
Schlesinger, Arthur Jr.	Author	10	30	50	15	
Schlesinger, James R.	Cabinet	5	10	25	15	Sec'y Defense 1973
Schlesinger, John	Entertainment	5			20	Film Director
Schley, Winfield Scott	Military	90	260	425	250	Arctic rescue of Greely
Schliemann, Heinrich	Archaeologist	245		1025		ALS re Mycenae $5,000
Schmalz, Wilhelm	Military	15	40	75	30	
Schmidt, Friedrich	Astronaut	30				
Schmidt, Helmut	Head of State	15	25	40	20	Ger. Political Leader, Chanc.
Schmidt, Maarten, Dr.	Science	10	25	30	20	
Schmidtmer, Christiane	Entertainment	4			15	Ger. Actress. Pin-Up SP $25
Schmitt, Harrison H.	Astronaut	15			50	Moonwalker Astro
Schmitt-Walter, Karl	Entertainment	10			35	Opera
Schnabel, Artur	Entertainment	25	135	190		Austrian Pianist
Schnaut, Gabriella	Entertainment	5			25	Opera
Schneider, John	Entertainment	4	10		15	Singer-Actor
Schneider, Romy	Entertainment	75			130	
Schneider,Wm. C.(SKYLAB)	Astronaut	6			20	
Schoenberg, Arnold	Composer	300	950		675	AMusQS $2,250
Schoene, Heinrich	Military	125	450		195	Ger. Gen. Storm Trooper
Schoenebeck, Karl August	Aviation	30	65		75	
Schoenert, Rudolf	Aviation	10	20	40	25	
Schoepfel, Gerhard	Aviation	5	15	25	15	
Schofield, John Arthur	Civil War	98		185		Union General
Schofield, John McAllister	Civil War	95	120	160		Union General, Sec'y War 1868
Schopenhauer, Arthur	Author	700	17500	5000		Ger. Philosopher
Schorner, Ferdinand	Military	40		120		
Schrader, Paul	Entertainment	5	15		20	Film Director
Schram, Emil	Business	3	10	20	5	
Schramm, Margit	Entertainment	5			15	Opera, Operetta
Schreiber, Avery	Entertainment	3	5	8	12	
Schricker, Henry F.	Governor	5	20		10	Governor IN
Schrieffer, John R.	Science	10	20	35	15	Nobel Physics 1972
Schriver, Edmund	Civil War	40	90	125		Union General
Schroder, Ricky	Entertainment	10			35	
Schroeder, Patricia	Senate/Congress	5	10		15	Rep. CO
Schroeder-Feinen, Ursula	Entertainment	5			30	Opera
Schubert, Franz	Composer	2200	5400	10000		
Schuk, Walter	Aviation	25	45		85	Ger. 12th Highest ACE
Schulberg, Budd	Author	5	10		10	Novelist, Screenwriter
Schuller, Robert	Clergy	15	20		25	
Schultz, Theodore William	Agri-Science	10	15	25		Nobel Economics
Schulz, Charles*	Cartoonist	100	145	680	700	Peanuts S Orig. Strip $1,500+-
Schuman, William	Composer	10	30	75	60	

NAME	CATEGORY	SIG	LS/DS	ALS	SP	COMMENT
Schumann, Clara	Pianist-Composer	60	165	350	175	ALS/Content $3,000
Schumann, Elizabeth	Entertainment	40			130	Opera
Schumann, Robert	Composer	815	1100	4850	5000	
Schumann-Heink, Ernestine	Entertainment	45		100	150	Opera, Concert
Schurz, Carl	Civil War	55	95	165		Union Gen., U.S.Sen. MO
Schuschnigg, Kurt von	Head of State	50	85	220	75	Deposed Austrian Chancellor
Schuyler, Philip J.	Revolutionary War	200	570	950		Soldier, Statesman
Schwab, Charles M.	Steel Business	20	65	105	100	Pres. Carnegie,US & Bethlehem
Schwantner, Joseph	Composer	10		55	40	Pulitzer, AMusQS $95
Schwarzenegger, Arnold	Entertainment	30	35	75	115	
Schwarzkopf, Norman	Military	30	125		90	Gen. Desert Storm
Schwatka, Frederick	Celebrity	10	20	55		
Schwedtman, Ferd. D.	Science	5	15		10	
Schweickart, Russell L.	Astronaut	7			25	
Schweiker, Richard S.	Senate/Congress	5	10		10	Rep., Senator PA 1961
Schweitzer, Albert, Dr.	Science-Music	175	315	675	1050	Nobel Peace Prize, Clergy
Schwellenback, Lewis B.	Cabinet	10	35	70	15	Sec'y Labor 1945
Schwinger, Julian, Dr.	Science	20	30	55	25	Nobel Physics 1965
Sciorra, Annabella	Entertainment	10			30	
Scobee, Dick	Astronaut		425		175	Challenger Victim
Scofield, Glenni W.	Senate/Congress	10	15	25		Rep. PA 1863
Scofield, Paul	Entertainment	10			35	
Scoggins, Tracy	Entertainment	5	8	25	20	Pin-Up SP $25
Scopes, John T.	Educator	200	1800			Defendant In "Monkey" Trial
Scorsese, Martin	Entertainment	10			40	Film Director
Scott, Robert L., Jr.	Aviation	15	30	60	35	
Scott, Charles	Revolutionary War	90	195	350		General, Indian Fighter,Gov.KY
Scott, Charles Wm. A.	Aviation	25	50	80	50	Br. Won Harmon Trophy
Scott, Cyril Meir	Composer	15	50	105	20	Br. Orchestral, Piano, Chamber
Scott, David C.	Business	5	10		10	CEO Allis-Chalmers
Scott, David R.	Astronaut	10			25	
Scott, Eric	Entertainment	4	6		10	
Scott, Fred	Entertainment	20			55	
Scott, George C.	Entertainment	20			80	
Scott, Gordon	Entertainment	15			35	
Scott, Gustavus	Revolutionary War	35	90	140		Lawyer, Patriot (MD)
Scott, Hazel	Entertainment	35	45		130	Piano-Organ
Scott, Hugh	Senate/Congress	5	15		25	Senator PA
Scott, Jack	Entertainment	10			25	Rock
Scott, Jerry*	Cartoonist	10			45	Nancy
Scott, John Morin	Revolutionary War	35	85	150		General, Patriot, Rep.NY
Scott, Lizabeth	Entertainment	8	10		20	Pin-Up SP $25
Scott, Martha	Entertainment	5			20	
Scott, Randolph	Entertainment	40	45		100	
Scott, Raymond	Composer	25			50	Big Band Leader, Arranger
Scott, Robert Falcon	Explorer	90	255	500	195	Br. Arctic Expeditions
Scott, Robert Kingston	Civil War	55				Union Gen.,Scoundrel Gov. SC
Scott, Robert Lee, Jr.	Aviation	15	35	55	38	ACE, WW II, God's Co-Pilot
Scott, Thomas	Clergy	40	50	75		
Scott, W. Kerr	Senate	5			25	Gov. NC 1949, Senator NC 1954
Scott, Walter, Sir	Author	135	540	700		Poet, Novelist, Historian
Scott, Willard	Entertainment	4	4		10	
Scott, William R.	Business	5	15			RR Exec.
Scott, Winfield	Civil War	125	330	430	450	Union Gen., Pres. Candidate
Scott, Zachary	Entertainment	25			50	
Scotti, Antonio	Entertainment	40			185	It. Baritone, Opera

NAME	CATEGORY	SIG	LS/DS	ALS	SP	COMMENT
Scotto, Renata	Entertainment	15			50	Opera
Scowcroft, Brent	Military	10	30		20	Gen., Statesman,Pres. Advisor
Scranton, Bill	Governor	5	15		15	Gov. PA. Pres. Candidate
Scriabin, Alexander	Composer	650	3500	5000		Rus. 3 Symphonies, etc.
Scribe, Eugene 1791-1861	Author	10	35	60		Fr. Librettist.Meyerbeer,Halevy
Scripps, William E.	Aviation	15	90		40	
Scudder, Horace E.	Author	10	25	50		Ed.Atlantic Mnthly, Biographer
Scuderi, Sara	Entertainment	34			85	Opera
Scully, Thomas	Artist	190	375	650		
Scully-Power, Paul	Astronaut	25				
Seaborg, Glenn	Science	40	95	150	125	Chm. AEC. Nobel Chemistry 1951
Seaforth, Susan	Entertainment	5			20	Pin-Up SP $30
Seals, Dan	Country Music	5			20	
Searle, Ronald	Artist	10	35	80		
Sears, Edmund	Clergy	20	25	35		
Seaton, George	Entertainment	35			70	Film Director
Seawell, Molly Elliot	Author	5	15	35	10	
Seawell, William T.	Business	3	10	15	15	
Seberg, Jean	Entertainment	65	75		155	Early Suicide
Sedaka, Neil	Composer	5			25	And Entertainer
Seddon, James A.	Civil War	100	450	250		CSA Sec'y War Dte. DS $1,000
Seddon, Margaret R.	Astronaut	6			20	
Sedgewick, John	Civil War	135	350			Union General ("Uncle John")
Sedgwick, Catherine M.1789-1867	Author	10	20	45		Am. Early Novelist. Moral Tales
See, Elliot M. Jr.	Astronaut	225			250	
Seeburg, Justus Percival	Business	40	120	195		
Seeger, Pete	Composer	40	50	95	50	Entertainer
Seeley, Blossom	Entertainment	5	6	15	15	
Seeley, Jeannie	Country Music	10			20	
Seelye, Julius Hawtry	Clergy	15	20	25		College Pres., Rep.MA
Segal, George	Entertainment	5	8	15	20	
Segal, George	Artist	25		35		
Segal, Steven	Entertainment	15			60	
Segar, Elzie C.*	Cartoonist	125			575	Popeye
Segar, Joseph E.	Senate/Congress	10	20			Rep. VA 1862
Seger, Bob	Entertainment	20			40	
Seger, C.B.	Business	15	45	85	40	
Segovia, Andres	Entertainment	120		365		Classical Guitar Virtuoso
Segre, Emilio, Dr.	Science	20	35	50	30	Nobel Physics 1959
Segura, Wiltz	Aviation	15	25	40	30	ACE, WW II, USAAF Ace
Segurola, Andres de	Entertainment	45			150	Sp. Bass
Seidelman, Susan	Entertainment	5	10		10	Film Director
Seignolle, Claude	Author	120	175	220		
Seinfeld (Cast)	Entertainment	150			385	Four Main Characters
Seinfeld, Jerry	Entertainment	15			40	
Seipel, Ignas Dr.	Head of State	10	30	80	40	Austrian Prelate & Chancellor
Seka	Entertainment	9	10	20	25	Pin-Up SP $35
Selassie, Haile	Head of State	160	380	740	700	Ethiopia
Selfridge, Harry G.	Business	10	40	110	35	Founder "Selfridge's", London
Selfridge, Thos. O.	Civil War	40	85	120		Union Naval Commander
Sellecca, Connie	Entertainment	10			30	
Selleck, Tom	Entertainment	10	15	25	20	
Sellers, David Foote	Military	20	55	95	50	
Sellers, Peter	Entertainment	80			150	
Sellers, Winfield S.	Military	15	40	75	40	
Selman, John	Celebrity		1500			

NAME	CATEGORY	SIG	LS/DS	ALS	SP	COMMENT
Selznick, David O.	Business	120	400		150	Film Producer
Selznick, Irene	Entertainment	10	15		20	Film Executive
Sembrich, Marcella	Entertainment	70		300	255	Opera, Concert. Polish Soprano
Semmelweis, Ignaz 1818-65	Science	500	1200	3200		Hung. Obstetrician.Antisepsis
Semmes, Paul	Civil War	255	975	900		CSA General
Semmes, Raphael	Civil War	285	750	1900	1500	CSA Admiral
Senechal, Michel	Entertainment	5			25	Opera
Senn, Nicholas	Civil War	35		140		Union Surgeon
Sennett, Mack	Entertainment	310	1275		550	Historic DS $4,500
Sergeant, John	Celebrity	10	20	35		
Sergeant, John 1779-1852	Senate/Congress	15	35	55		Rep.PA 1815.Missouri Compromise
Sergievsky, Boris	Aviation	75			150	
Serkin, Rudolf	Entertainment	45		155	150	Piano Virtuoso, AMusQS $175
Serling, Rod	Author-Entertain.	125	260	375	340	
Serpico, Frank	Law	10	20	45	20	Undercover Detective-Hero
Serurier, Jean M.P., Count	Fr. Revolution	50	145	215		Marshal of Napoleon
Service, Robert W.	Author	75		260	400	Canadian Poet, Author
Sessions, Roger	Composer	15	45	165		Pulitzer, AMusQS $225
Sessions, William L.	Government	25	75		30	Dir. FBI
Seton, Ernest Thompson	Author	55	95	230	60	Help Found Boy Scouts of Am.
Seuss, Dr. (Theodore S. Geisel)*	Author	75	125		535	Repro "Cat In The Hat" S $150
Severance, Joan	Entertainment	5			20	Pin-Up SP $25
Severeid, Eric	Journalist	10			20	TV-Radio Broadcast Journalist
Severeid, Susanne	Model	4			15	Pin-Up SP $20, Actress
Severinson, Doc	Entertainment	6	8	25	20	Trumpet, Big Band
Seversky, Alex. de	Aviation	50	95	175	120	ACE WW I. Seversky Aircraft
Sevier, John	Revolutionary War	615	1650	750		Historical DS $3,750
Sewall, David	Revolutionary War	20	50	110		Jurist, Patriot, Justice Peace
Sewall, Samuel 1652-1730	Colonial America	275	1250	1300		Salem Witchcraft Trials
Sewall, Samuel 1757-1814	Senate/Congress	25		60		Rep. MA 1796.MA Chief Justice
Seward, Frederick Wm.(son of W.H.)	Cabinet	30	55	80		Ass't Sec'y State
Seward, William H.	Cabinet	75	240	310	250	LS/Re Assassination $1,750
Sewell, William J.	Civil War	40	90	130		Union Gen., U.S. Sen. NJ
Sexton, Walton R.	Military	10	30	45	30	Adm. US Navy. WW II
Seymour, Anne	Entertainment	10			20	
Seymour, George F., Bishop	Clergy	25	25	40		
Seymour, Horatio	Governor	45	60	80		Civil War Gov. NY
Seymour, Jane	Entertainment	10			30	Pin-Up SP $30
Seymour, Stephanie	Entertainment	20			45	Model-Actress
Seymour, Truman	Civil War	75	110	205		Union General
Shackelford, Ted	Entertainment	5			15	
Shackleton, Ernest H., Sir	Explorer	90	265	645	450	Br. Antarctic Explorer
Shaffer, Paul	Entertainment	5			15	
Shaffer, Peter L.	Author	10	20	35	15	
Shafter, William H.	Military	15	40	75	35	
Shafter, William R.	Civil War	35	55	110	150	Union Gen.
Shaftesbury,7th (A.A. Cooper)	Reformer	25	75	160		Politician, M.P.
Shahn, Ben	Artist	55	150	240	145	Am.Painter-Graphic Artist
Shalamar	Entertainment	12	15	60	50	
Shaler, Alexander	Civil War	35	60	110		Union General
Shalikashvili, John	Military	10	25		20	Chm. Joint Chiefs of Staff
Shamir, Yitzhak	Head of State	20	30	55	30	Prime Minister Israel
Shannon, Del	Entertainment	35			80	Country Music
Shannon, Wilson	Governor	25	65	100		Kansas Peacmaker 1870
Shapiro, Harry	Artist	10	25	45		
Shapiro, Karl	Author	10	30	70	20	

NAME	CATEGORY	SIG	LS/DS	ALS	SP	COMMENT
Shapley, Alan	Military	10	35	50		
Shapley, Harlow	Science	35	275			Astronomer. Dir.Harvard Observ.
Shapp, Milton J.	Governor	10	20			Governor PA
Sharan, Shri Chakradhar	Head of State	15	35		75	Pres. India
Sharett, Moshe (Shertok)	Head of State	45		275		Israeli Prime Minister
Sharif, Omar	Entertainment	20	25	65	75	
Sharkey, Ray	Entertainment	5			20	
Sharnova, Sonia	Entertainment	10			25	Am. Contralto
Sharon, Ariel	Military	20	50	90	45	Israeli General, Politician
Sharon, William	Senate-Business	45	110	200		Senator NV, Banker & Financier
Sharp, U. S. Grant	Military	10	25	35	15	
Sharp, William	Artist	15	40	105		
Sharpe, George H.	Civil War	20	45			Union Gen., Diplomat
Sharpe, Karen	Entertainment	4	6		8	
Sharpe, William, Dr.	Economist	22	30		25	Nobel Enconomics 1990
Shatner, William	Entertainment	12	15		45	"Star Trek" SP $75
Shaunessy, Charles	Entertainment	5	6	15	15	
Shavelson, Melville	Entertainment	5	10		25	
Shaver, Helen	Entertainment	10			25	
Shaw, Anna Howard 1847-1919	Women's Rights	35	80	175		Physician, Suffragist, Clergy
Shaw, Artie	Entertainment	25			50	Big Band Leader-Clarinetist
Shaw, Bernard	Journalist	15			25	TV Broadcast Journalist
Shaw, Brewster H.	Astronaut	6			15	
Shaw, George Bernard	Author	175	1025	1640	1725	Ir. Playwright, Critic. Nobel
Shaw, Irwin	Author	25	70	170	40	Am.Novelist, Short Story Writer
Shaw, Lemuel	Revolutionary War	15	40	75		Chf.Justice MA Supreme Court
Shaw, Leslie M.	Cabinet	25	35	50		Sec'y Treasury 1902
Shaw, Robert	Entertainment	40			150	
Shawn, Dick	Entertainment	40			100	
Shawn, Ted	Entertainment	45			100	Am. Dancer-Choreographer
Shay, John	Entertainment	4	6		10	
Shayne, Robert	Entertainment	10			30	
Shea, George Beverly	Clergy	15	20	25	30	Singing Evangelist
Shea, William A.	Business	5	20	40	10	
Shear, Rhonda	Entertainment	10			20	
Shearer, Moira	Entertainment	20		50	45	Ballet. "Red Shoes"
Shearer, Norma	Entertainment	70	105		340	
Shearing, George	Entertainment	20			45	Jazz Pianist
Sheedy, Ally	Entertainment	10	15		30	
Sheen, Charlie	Entertainment	8	15		25	
Sheen, Fulton J., Archbishop	Clergy	50		90	50	
Sheen, Martin	Entertainment	9	45		25	
Sheffer, Chris	Entertainment	6	8	15	15	
Sheffield, Johnny	Entertainment	10			25	
Shehan, Lawrence J., Cardinal	Clergy	35	45	50	60	
Shelby, Isaac	Revolutionary War	110	350	625		Officer VA Militia. 1st Gov. KY
Shelby, Joseph O.	Civil War	225	950	1250		CSA General
Sheldon, Charles M.	Clergy	20	35	50	40	
Sheldon, Sidney	Author	5	15	25	15	Am. Novelist
Shelley, Mary Wollstonecraft	Author	475		1850		"Frankenstein"
Shelley, Percy Bysshe	Author	1060	2150	4000		ALS/Content $14,000
Shelton, Deborah	Entertainment	8	9		20	Pin-Up SP $30, Miss USA
Shepard, Alan B.	Astronaut	25			70	Mercury 7 Astro
Shepherd, Cybill	Entertainment	15	15		35	Pin-Up SP $40
Shepherd, William M.	Astronaut	5			15	
Sheppard, Dick	Clergy	25	35	50	30	

NAME	CATEGORY	SIG	LS/DS	ALS	SP	COMMENT
Sheppard, Morris	Senator/Congress	10	20		15	Rep.,Sen. TX.Author 18th Amend.
Shera, Mark	Entertainment	5			20	
Sheridan, Ann	Entertainment	45			120	
Sheridan, Nicollette	Entertainment	15			35	Pin-Up SP $60
Sheridan, Philip H.	Civil War	195	425	655	1765	Union Commanding Gen. Cavalry
Sheridan, Richard Brinsley	Author	65	120	325		Ir. Dramatist
Sherlock, Nancy	Astronaut	7			15	
Sherman, Forrest P.	Military	20	50	95	50	Adm.WW II.Ch. Naval Operationsl
Sherman, Frederick C.	Military	20	45	70	35	Adm. Cmdr Carrier Lexington
Sherman, George	Entertainment	10			25	
Sherman, James S. (V)	Vice President	75	225	325	230	
Sherman, John	Cabinet-Senate	70		150	85	Sherman Anti-Trust Act, OH
Sherman, Richard and Roger	Composer	40	60	100		AMusQS $150
Sherman, Roger	Revolutionary War	150	655	715		Signed All 4 Major Fed. Papers
Sherman, Thomas West	Civil War	30	55	85		Union General
Sherman, William T.	Civil War	375	550	1400	3800	Union Gen.War Dte ALS $4,500
Sherwood, (Mary) Martha 1775-1851	Author	10	15	35		Br. Author Juvenile Tales
Sherwood, Bobby	Entertainment	6	8	15	15	
Sherwood, Isaac R.	Senate/Congress	10	15		20	Rep. OH 1873
Sherwood, Percy	Composer	25			60	Ger. Pianist. AMusQS $75
Sherwood, Robert E.	Author-Cabinet	30	95	195	50	Am.Plays,Speeches FDR,Pulitzers
Sherwood, Samuel	Senate/Cogress	20	35	50		Rep. NY 1813
Shields, Arthur	Entertainment	10			25	Actor-Brother Barry Fitzgerald
Shields, Brooke	Entertainment	9	10	35	30	Pin-Up SP $36
Shields, James	Civil War	50	80	115		Union Gen., U.S Sen.IL,MN,MO
Shigeta, James	Entertainment	6	8	15	20	
Shimmerman, Armin	Entertainment	15			35	"Star Trek"
Shippen, Edward	Revolutionary War	45	95	165		Ch. Justice PA, Statesman
Shipstad, Henrik	Senate/Congress	5	20		25	Senator MN 1922
Shiras, George, Jr. (SC)	Supreme Court	75	250	375		
Shire, Talia	Entertainment	15			35	
Shirer, William L.	Author	15	40		20	News Commentator
Shirley, Anne	Entertainment	15	15	35	30	
Shirley, William 1693-1771	Colon'l Gov. MA	155	445	885		Cmdr.-in-Chief, Explorer, Author
Shivers, Allan	Governor	12			30	Governor TX
Shockley, William, Dr.	Science	30	125	150	100	Nobel Physics 1956
Shoemaker, Lazarus D.	Senate/Congress	10	20		15	Rep. PA 1871
Shoemaker, William L.	Author	5	8	15		
Shoen, Sam	Business	5	15	35	25	
Shoma, William	Aviation	15	32	50	40	ACE, WW II, CMH
Shoop, Pamela Susan	Entertainment	5	6	15	15	
Shor, Bernard "Toots"	Business	30	45	75	35	NY Restaurateur.Celebrity Host
Shore, Dinah	Entertainment	15			35	Singer-Actress-TV Host
Short, Martin	Entertainment	6			25	
Shortridge, Samuel	Senate	10	20			Senator CA 1920
Shostakovich, Dmitri	Composer	600	720	800	2000	ALS/Content $3,200
Shoumatoff, Elizabeth	Artist	25	45	60		FDR Portrait AT Time Of Death
Shoup, David M.	Military	15	40	75	35	
Shoup, George L.	Senator	12	20	35		1st Gov. ID, Senator ID 1890
Showalter, Max	Entertainment	4	4	9	15	
Shrimpton, Jean	Entertainment	5	6	15	10	
Shriner, Herb	Entertainment	4	5		15	
Shriver, Eunice Kennedy	Celebrity	15			35	Sister JFK,Wife Sargent Shriver
Shriver, Loren J.	Astronaut	5			15	
Shriver, Maria	Journalist	6			15	Broadcast Journalist
Shriver, Sargent	White House	4	10	25	20	Created Job Core

NAME	CATEGORY	SIG	LS/DS	ALS	SP	COMMENT
Shroyer, Sonny	Entertainment	3			7	
Shubert, John	Entertainment	5	9		15	
Shubert, Lee	Business	20	60	85	30	Theatrical Mgr.-Producer
Shugart, Alan	Inventor	10	20		20	Computer Disk Drive
Shulman, Ellen L.	Astronaut	6			20	
Shulman, Max	Writer	10			20	Creator "Dobie Gillis"
Shultz, George P.	Cabinet	10	25	55	30	Sec'y State 1982
Shuman, Charles B.	Celebrity	3	7	15	5	
Shuster, W. Morgan	Business	10	15	35	15	Chm.Appleton-Century-Crofts
Sibelius, Jan	Composer	440	950	2000	1200	Fin.Symphonies,Incidental Music
Sibley, Henry H.	Civil War	100	210	295		Pioneer, Indian Fighter. Gov MN
Sickles, Daniel E.	Civil War	110	225	290	175	Union General, CMH winner
Sickles, Noel*	Cartoonist	20			175	Scorchy
Siddons, F. Scott, Mrs.	Entertainment	25			50	Vintage Actress
Siddons, Sarah Kemble 1755-1831	Entertainment	215		860		Br. Tragedienne
Sidmouth, Viscount	Head of State	35	65	105		Henry Addington, Prime Minister
Sidney, George	Entertainment	15			35	Film Director
Sidney, Sylvia	Entertainment	10	15	25	25	
Siegbahn, Kai Manne	Science	30	55	100	90	Nobel Physics 1981
Siegbahn, Karl Manne G.	Science	35	65	130	100	Nobel Physics 1924
Siegel & Roy	Entertainment	10			20	Animal Trainers
Siegel & Shuster*	Cartoonist	150			900	Superman
Siegel, Don	Entertainment	20	65			Film Director
Siegel, Franz	Civil War	40	85	200		Union General
Siegel, Jerry	Entertainment	10	25		15	One of Creators "Superman"
Siegel, Joel	Journalist	4			10	TV Film Reviewer
Siegmeister, Elie	Composer	25	85	175	40	
Siems, Margarethe	Entertainment	45			110	Opera
Siepi, Cesare	Entertainment	10			25	Opera. Self-Taught Bass
Sierra, Gregory	Entertainment	4	4	9	9	
Sierra, Margarita	Entertainment	3	3	6	6	
Sigall, Joseph	Artist	100	190	385		Pres. Portraits & Eur. Royalty
Sigel, Franz	Civil War	45	115	200		Union General
Sighele, Mietta	Entertainment	10			30	Opera
Sigler, Kim	Governor	5	15		10	Governor MI
Signac, Paul	Artist	75	170	350		Watercolor Land & Seascapes
Signoret, Simone	Entertainment	35	40		125	
Sigsbee, Charles D.	Military	35	105	165	75	Capt. USN "The Maine"
Sihanouk, Prince	Head of State	30	95	140	75	Cambodia
Sikes, Cynthia	Entertainment	5			15	Pin-up SP $25
Sikking, James B.	Entertainment	6	8	15	15	
Sikorsky, Igor I.	Aviation	80	295	350	275	Designed & Built 1st Helicopter
Silja, Anja	Entertainment	15			40	Opera
Silliman, Benjamin 1816-85	Science	30	65	125		Am.Chemist. Editor. Professor
Sills, Beverly	Entertainment	15			30	Am. Soprano
Sills, Milton	Entertainment	30	40	75	65	
Silver, Abba Hillel	Zionist	15	50			Zionist Leader
Silver, Ron	Entertainment	15			40	Actor-Director
Silverheels, Jay	Entertainment	175			350	
Silverman, Fred	Business	3	9	20	10	Broadcasting Executive
Silverman, Jonathan	Entertainment	5			10	
Silvers, Phil	Entertainment	30	50		85	
Simenon, Georges	Author	40	125	275	125	Fr-Belg. Creator Insp. Maigret
Simeon, Charles	Clergy	45		75		
Simmons, E.H.H.	Business	25	40			Pres. NY Stock Exchange
Simmons, Gene (Kiss)	Entertainment	9			30	

NAME	CATEGORY	SIG	LS/DS	ALS	SP	COMMENT
Simmons, Jean	Entertainment	8	10	20	20	
Simmons, Richard	Entertainment	15			40	Actor
Simmons, Richard	Entertainment	5			15	Diet & Aerobics
Simms, William G.	Author	35	100	250		Lawyer, Pro-Slavery Editor
Simon and Garfunkel	Entertainment	40			125	
Simon, Carly	Entertainment	20			50	Singer-Composer
Simon, Claude	Author	150				Nobel Literature 1985
Simon, Herbert A.	Science	20	35	50	25	Nobel Economics
Simon, Neil	Author	45	75	150	75	Playwright, Screenwriter
Simon, Norton	Industrialist	15	35	65	25	Norton Simon, Inc.,Philanthropy
Simon, Paul	Composer	20			75	Entertainer
Simon, Paul Martin	Senate/Congress	5			10	Rep.,Senator IL
Simon, Simone	Entertainment	15			35	
Simon, William E.	Cabinet	5	15	25	20	Sec'y Treasury
Simpson, Alan	Senate/Congress	5	10		15	Senator WY
Simpson, James Y., Sir	Science	25	90	195		Scot.1st Obstetric Ether Use
Simpson, Russell	Entertainment	50			120	
Simpson, Wallis Warfield	Head of State	110		450		Duchess of Windsor
Simpson, William H.	Military	25	100		75	Gen. WW II
Sims, William S.	Military	30	55	115	50	Adm. USN WW I, Pulitzer Author
Sinatra, Frank	Entertainment	100	125		330	MGM DS $375
Sinatra, Nancy	Entertainment	5	10	20	20	Pin-Up SP $25
Sinclair, Harry F.	Business	140	175	350	200	"Teapot Dome"
Sinclair, Upton	Author	35	75	145	125	Am. Writer-Socialist Politician
Sinding, Christian A.	Composer	45	120	210		Symphonies, Concertos, Sonatas
Singer, Isaac Bashevis	Author	40		155	45	Nobel Literature 1978
Singer, Isaac M.	Inventor	575		2500		Singer Sewing Machine
Singer, Marc	Entertainment	10	12		30	
Singlaub, John K.	Military	10	20	35	20	General WW II
Singleton, Penny	Entertainment	10	10	15	25	
Sioli, Franco	Entertainment	5			15	Opera
Siple, Paul A.	Aviation	22	45			Explorer, Geographer
Sirica, John J.	Jurist	20	35		50	Watergate Judge
Sirk, Don	Entertainment	65				Film Director
Sisley, Alfred	Artist	150	400	850		Fr.Impressionist. Landscapes
Sissle, Noble	Entertainment	25			50	Big Band Leader-Arranger
Sitgreaves, John	Revolutionary War	30	75	145		Officer. Continental Congress
Sitting Bull (T. Iyotake)	Indian Leader	7700			15000	Sioux Indian Leader
Sitwell, Edith, Dame	Author	70	135	250		Br.Poet, Critic, Novelist
Sitwell, Osbert, Sir	Author	35	70	210		Playwright, Novelist
Sixty Minutes (all)	Entertainment	25			45	
Sizoo, Joseph R.	Clergy	20	25	35		
Skaggs, Ricky	Country Music	10			20	
Skala, Lilia	Entertainment	10	15	25	30	
Skelly, William Grove	Business	320				Founder Skelly Oil, Financier
Skelton, Red	Entertainment	15	20	40	40	
Skerrit, Tom	Entertainment	8	10	20	20	
Skinner, B. F.	Author	20	30	50	75	Behavioral Psychology-Theorist
Skinner, Cornelia Otis	Author	15	30	45	25	Actress, Monologuist
Skinner, Cortlandt 1728-99	Military	40	85	155		Born NJ. Loyalist General
Skinner, Otis	Entertainment	32	40	70	65	Vintage Stage Star
Skinner, Samuel K.	Cabinet	10	20			Sec'y Transportation
Skinner, Stella	Artist	25	40	75		
Skipworth, Alison	Entertainment	15	15	30	25	
Skorzeny, Otto	Military	165	275	540	500	
Skouras, Spyros	Business	15			85	Fndr-Pres-Chm 20th Century Fox

NAME	CATEGORY	SIG	LS/DS	ALS	SP	COMMENT
Skovhus, Boje	Entertainment	10			25	Opera
Slater, Christian	Entertainment	15			55	
Slater, Helen	Entertainment	8	15	30	55	
Slaughter, Frank G.	Author	8	15	35	10	
Slayton, Donald K. "Deke"	Astronaut	35	95		75	Mercury 7 Astro (Deceased)
Sledd, Patsy	Country Music	4			12	Pin-Up SP $15
Slezak, Leo	Entertainment	45	60		155	Great Austrian Tenor, Opera
Slezak, Walter	Entertainment	15			35	
Slick, Grace	Entertainment	25			40	
Slidell, John	Civil War	75	150	195		Statesman, CSA Diplomat
Slim, Wm. Joseph, Sir	Military	30	75	120	60	Br. General WW II
Sliwa, Lisa	Celebrity	6	15		10	NY Street Protection Group
Sliwinski, Josef	Entertainment	20		100	75	Pol Pianist
Sloan, Alfred P. Jr.	Business	30	45	90	50	Sloan-Kettering Inst. CEO GM
Sloan, John	Artist	85	275	550		Am.Painter,Etcher,Illustrator
Sloan, John 1779-1856	Cabinet	20	45	95		Fillmore Treasurer of U.S.
Sloane, Everett	Entertainment	30			55	
Sloat, John Drake	Civil War	45	95	130		Union Naval Officer
Slocum, Henry Warner	Civil War	50	75	150		Union General, Rep. NY
Small, John Humphrey	Senate/Congress	5		15		Rep. NC 1899
Smart, Jean	Entertainment	5			15	
Smathers, George A.	Senate/Congress	5		25	15	Rep., Senator FL 1947
Smedley, Richard	Entertainment	3	3	6	8	
Smetana, Bedrich	Composer	1500		9000		Czech. Operas, Symphonies etc.
Smiley, Delores	Country Music	10			20	
Smirnoff, Yakov	Entertainment	8			15	
Smith, Adam 1723-1790	Economist	3000				Architect of Br. Political Econ
Smith, Addison T.	Senate/Congress	5	10	15		Rep. ID 1913
Smith, Al*	Cartoonists	15			60	Mutt & Jeff
Smith, Alexis	Entertainment	15	45		30	Pin-Up SP $35
Smith, Alfred E.	Governor	50	110	400	125	Presidential Candidate, Gov NY
Smith, Armistead B.	Aviation	10	22	38	28	ACE, WW II, Navy Ace
Smith, Ashbel	Civil War	140		615		TX Historical Politician, CSA
Smith, Bernie	Entertainment	6	8	15	15	
Smith, Betty	Author	50	110		65	
Smith, Buffalo Bob	Entertainment	10	15		30	"Howdy Doody"
Smith, C. Aubrey	Entertainment	35			80	
Smith, C.R.	Military	25	75			Adm. Flagship Fleet
Smith, Caleb	Cabinet	40	150	365		Lincoln Attorney General
Smith, Carl	Country Music	5			12	
Smith, Charles E.	Cabinet	15		25	20	P.M. General 1898
Smith, Charles M.	Entertainment	10			25	
Smith, Charles M.	Governor	5	15			Governor VT
Smith, Connie	Country Music	5			12	
Smith, Edmund Kirby	Civil War	255		560		CSA General
Smith, Elinor	Aviation	45	100	160	130	
Smith, Elizabeth Oakes	Reformer	90	205	385		Early Supporter Woman Suffrage
Smith, Elmo	Governor	10	25			Governor OR
Smith, F. E.	Celebrity	36				
Smith, Francis Hopkinson 1838-	Artist	15	20	35		Am.Engineer-Artist-Illustrator
Smith, Francis M. "Borax"	Business	30	65	95		Founder U.S. Borax Co.
Smith, Frank, Bishop	Clergy	15	20	25	25	
Smith, Frederick W.	Business	15	30	55	20	Fndr., Chm. Federal Express
Smith, George Washington	Senate/Congress	5	15			Rep. IL 1889
Smith, Gerrit	Senate/Congress	45		325		Abolitionist, Reformer,Rep.NY
Smith, Gipsy	Clergy	25	45	75	35	

NAME	CATEGORY	SIG	LS/DS	ALS	SP	COMMENT
Smith, Green Clay	Civil War	50	65	140		Union Gen., Congress KY
Smith, Gustavus Woodson	Civil War	120	270	475		CSA General
Smith, H. Allen	Senate/Congress	5	10		10	Rep. CA 1957
Smith, Hamilton	Science	20	30	45	25	Nobel Medicine 1978
Smith, Harry	Journalist	4	10		5	Broadcast Journalist
Smith, Harsen	Business	3	10	25	10	
Smith, Hoke	Cabinet	10	35	70	30	Gov.,Sen. GA, Sec'y Int.1911
Smith, Holland M."Howlin Mad",Gen	Military					Iwo Jima Flag Raising FDC $550
Smith, Ian	Head of State	10	20	50	30	
Smith, Ida B. Wise	Reformer	30	55	95		Temperance Advocate, WCTU
Smith, J. Gregory	Governor	5	15		10	Governor VT
Smith, Jaclyn	Entertainment	6	8	20	20	Pin-Up SP $30
Smith, James	Revolutionary War	235	525			Signer Decl. of Indepen.
Smith, James Y.	Governor	35	55			Civil War Gov. RI
Smith, James, Jr.	Senate/Congress	10	15			Senator NJ 1911
Smith, Joe	Entertainment	15			45	
Smith, John	Colonial Am.	2200	11500	29000		NRPA
Smith, John Pye	Clergy	20	25	35		
Smith, Joseph	Religious Leader	700	1775			Founder Morman Church
Smith, Kate	Entertainment	40	195	175		
Smith, Keely	Entertainment	10			30	Band Vocalist
Smith, Kent	Entertainment	6			15	
Smith, L. C.	Business	50	135	240		L.C.Smith Typewriters, etc.
Smith, Maggie	Entertainment	15	15	30	30	
Smith, Margaret Chase	Senate/Congress	6	20		15	Columnist, Rep., Sen. ME
Smith, Martha	Entertainment	5			15	
Smith, Martin Luther	Civil War	50	135	240		CSA General
Smith, Matthew	Revolutionary War	25	75			
Smith, Melancton 1744-98	Revolutionary War	75	185			Continental Congress
Smith, Melancton 1810-93	Civil War	40	85	120		Un. Adm. Served Under Farragut
Smith, Michael J.	Astronaut	275			300	Died on Challenger
Smith, Nels H.	Governor	5	10		15	Governor WY
Smith, R.T.	Aviation	10	28	40	35	ACE, WW II, Flying Tigers
Smith, Richard	Revolutionary War	50	130	250		Continental Congress
Smith, Robert 1757-1842	Cabinet	55	170	290		Att'y Gen.,Sec'y Navy,Sec'y St.
Smith, Robert H. "Snuffy"	Aviation	15	30	50	35	ACE, WW II, Flying Tigers
Smith, Rodney "Gipsy"	Clergy	50	50	85	50	
Smith, Roger	Entertainment	5			20	
Smith, Roy L., Bishop	Clergy	20	30	45	30	
Smith, Samuel 1752-1839	Revolutionary War	55	165	225		General, Rep.,Senator MD
Smith, Samuel Francis	Clergy-Poet	100	275	390		AQS "America" $500-$2,000
Smith, Shelley	Entertainment	4			10	Pin-Up SP $20
Smith, Stanley	Entertainment	9			25	Stage
Smith, Susan M.	Playboy Ctrfold	3			10	Pin-Up SP $15
Smith, Sydney*	Cartoonist	30			150	The Gumps
Smith, Thomas A.	Military	95	240			Fort Smith Arkansas. General
Smith, Thomas Church Haskell	Civil War	29	55	80		Union General
Smith, Tom E.	Business	10	20	30	25	Pres. Food Lion Grocery Chain
Smith, Truman 1791-1884	Senate-Cabinet	10	25	40		Rep., Sen. CT, Sec'y Interior
Smith, W. Angie, Bishop	Clergy	20	25	35	25	
Smith, W. Wallace	Clergy	40	45	60		
Smith, Walter Bedell	Military	35	50	95	45	Gen. WW II,Ambass.,Dir. CIA
Smith, William 1797-1887	Civil War	85	215	330		CSA Gen., Congress, Gov. VA
Smith, William Farrar	Civil War	45		180		Union Gen.
Smith, William S.	Revolutionary War	35	95	185		Rev.Soldier.Pres.Soc.Cincinnati
Smith, William Sidney, Sir 1764-	Military	50		185		Br.Adm. Napoleonic War

NAME	CATEGORY	SIG	LS/DS	ALS	SP	COMMENT
Smith, Willy "The Lion"	Entertainment	75			125	Jazz Alto-Baritone Sax,Clarinet
Smithers, Jan	Entertainment	6	8		15	
Smoot, Reed	Senate/Congress	25	45			Senator UT
Smothers Bros. (both)	Entertainment	10			25	Tommy and Dick
Smucker, Paul	Business	10			25	"Smuckers" Jams & Jellies
Smuts, Jan Christian	Head of State	45	130	265		Fld. Marshal. Pres. Un. So. Afr
Smythe, Reg*	Cartoonist	10			40	Andy Capp
Snell, George D., Dr.	Science	15	30	45	45	Nobel Medicine 1980
Snipes, Wesley	Entertainment	15			40	
Snodgrass, W.D.	Author	25	75			
Snow, Charles Percy, Baron	Author	25	80	170	60	Br. Novelist, Physicist
Snow, Hank	Country Music	25			50	
Snyder, Simon	Governor	5	15	35		Governor PA
Soarez, Alana	Playboy Ctrfold	3	5	10	10	Pin-Up SP $15
Sockman, Ralph	Clergy	15	20	25		
Soddy, Frederick, Dr.	Science	60	160	275	125	Nobel Chemistry 1921
Soglow, Otto	Cartoonist	20			75	The Little King
Sokoloff, Vladimir	Entertainment	25			65	
Soles, P. J.	Entertainment	5			15	
Solow, Robert M., Dr.	Economics	22	30		25	Nobel Economics 1987
Solti, Georg, Sir	Entertainment	20			50	Conductor
Solzhenitsyn, Alex.	Author	100	250	495	185	Sov. Novelist. Nobel Lit. 1970
Somers, Suzanne	Entertainment	6			20	Pin-Up SP $25
Somerset, Lord Fitzroy	See Raglan					SEE RAGLAN
Somervell, Arthur, Sir	Composer	20	55	85		Br.Oratorios...AMusQS $150
Somervell, Brehon B.	Military	35	125			Gen. WW II
Sommer, Elke	Entertainment	9	10	20	25	Pin-Up SP $30
Sommers, Joanne	Entertainment	3	5		10	
Somoza, Anastasio	Head of State	20	95			Nicaragua
Sondergaard, Gale	Entertainment	40			75	
Sondheim, Stephen	Composer	25	80	135	125	AMusQS $275, $350
Sonny & Cher	Entertainment	30			100	
Sontag, Henrietta Rossi	Entertainment	70			375	Opera
Sontag, Susan	Author	10	25	45	20	
Soo, Jack	Entertainment	25			55	
Soong, T.V. (Tzu-wen)	Diplomat	35	50			Chinese Financier, Negotiator
Sooter, Rudy	Country Music	10			20	
Soper, Donald O.	Clergy	20	25	30	30	
Sopwith, Thos. O. M., Sir	Aviation	65	115	190	100	Br. Pioneer. ALS/Content $850
Sorenson, Ted	Author	6			15	JFK Aide
Sorkin, Arleen	Entertainment	4	5		10	Pin-Up SP $20
Sorrel, Gilbert Moxley	Civil War	165	370	550		CSA General
Sorrvia, Agnes	Entertainment	20			45	Opera
Sorvino, Paul	Entertainment	15			35	
Sothern, Ann	Entertainment	9	10	25	25	
Sothern, E. A.	Entertainment	30	85	120		19th Century Romantic Idol
Soto, Talisa	Entertainment	10			20	Pin-Up SP $25
Soul Asylum	Entertainment					Rock. No Price Available
Soul, David	Entertainment	5	10	20	15	
Soule, Pierre	Civil War	60	170			Sessessionist. US Sen. LA
Soult, Nicolas Jean de Dieu, Duke	Fr. Military	105	245			Nap.Marshal of Fr.,Minister War
Sousa, John Philip	Composer	145	400	475	960	AMusQs$650-$1250
Soustelle, Jacques	Head of State	5	15	40	15	
Souter, David H. (SC)	Supreme Court	40			55	
Southampton, 1st Earl of 1505-50	Royalty	75	215	450		Politician. Sec'y to Cromwell
Southcott, Joanna	Clergy	45	60	90		Br. Religious Fanatic

NAME	CATEGORY	SIG	LS/DS	ALS	SP	COMMENT
Southey, Robert	Author	95	280	500		Br. Poet Laureate 1813
Sovine, Red	Country Music	12			35	
Soyer, Raphael	Artist	20	50	125	100	Signed Repro. $200-$300
Soyinka, Wole (Akinwande O.)	Author	25	80			Nigerian. Nobel Literature 1986
Spaak, Paul-Henri	Head of State	15	30	50	25	Belg. Fndr. EEOC, NATO
Spaatz, Carl "Tooey"	Military-Aviation	55	85		75	Gen. WW II, AF Commander
Spacek, Sissy	Entertainment	10	15		40	
Spaight, Richard Dobbs 1758-1802	Revolutionary War	115	350			Continental Congress
Spain, Fay	Entertainment	10			30	
Spalding, Albert	Entertainment	35			75	Violinist, AMQS $85-$250
Spalding, J. Walter	Business	25	7	140	55	
Spallanzani, Lazzaro 1729-99	Science	120	400	700		It. Physiolog.Artificial Insem.
Sparkman, John	Senate/Congress	12			25	Senator AL
Sparks, Chuncey	Governor	5	20			Governor AL
Sparks, Jared	Author	15	35	50		US Historian, Editor,Publisher
Sparks, Ned	Entertainment	25	30	60	70	
Sparks, William E.	Military	15	30	50		
Sparv, Camilla	Entertainment	8	9	25	20	
Spaulding, Albert	Composer	25	65			
Spaulding, R.Z.	Business	15	40	55	25	
Speakes, Larry	Cabinet	4	10	16	10	
Speaks, Oley	Composer	50	90	175		"On The Road To Mandalay"
Spector, Phil	Entertainment	75			200	Rock
Speed, James	Cabinet	45	80	135		Lincoln's Att'y General
Speed, John Gilmer	Author	5	15	25		Journalist. Biographer
Speer, Albert	Military	55	115	275	175	Hitler's Architect
Speer, Robert Elliott	Clergy	15	20	25		
Speer, Robert Milton	Senate/Congress	5	10	20		Rep. PA 1871
Speidel, Hans	Military	35	90	165	75	Nazi Gen.,Rommel Chief-of Staff
Speight, J. J.	Senate/Congress	5	10			
Speir, Dona	Entertainment	5			15	Pin-Up SP $20. Playboy Ctrfold
Spelling, Aaron	Entertainment	6	10		20	Film Producer, Writer
Spelling, Tori	Entertainment	5			15	Pin-up SP $40
Spellman, Francis, Cardinal	Clergy	30	45	95	45	
Spencer, George Eliphaz	Civil War	35	80	145		Union General, Senator AL 1868
Spencer, Herbert, Sir	Author	50	200	270		Br. Philosopher
Spencer, John C.	Cabinet	15	60	70		Tyler Sec'y War
Spencer, John P. 5th Earl	Politician	10	15	35		Liberal Leader House of Lords
Spencer, Susan	TV News	4			10	CBS News
Spender, Stephen	Author	65	185	260	75	Br.Poet, Critic. Protest Poetry
Spenser, Tim	Country Music	15			25	Fndr. "Sons of the Pioneers"
Sperry, Elmer A.	Science	165	375	535	225	Inventor Gyroscope
Sperry, Roger W.	Science	22	30	35	25	Nobel Medicine 1981
Spielberg, David	Entertainment	5	6	15	200	
Spielberg, Steven	Entertainment	75			185	Producer-Director
Spillane, Mickey	Author	50	75	110	150	Am. Writer of Detective Fiction
Spiner, Brent	Entertainment	15			35	"Star Trek"
Spinner, Francis Elias	Cabinet	25	155	200		Treasurer for 4 Presidents
Spivak, Charlie	Entertainment	20			40	Big Band Leader-Trumpeter
Spock, Benjamin, Dr.	Science	25	75	115	50	Am. Pediatrician-Psychiatrist
Spofford, Harriet P. 1835-	Author	10	25	40		Am. Romantic Poet, Novelist
Spong, Hilda	Entertainment	20			45	
Spontini, Gaspare, Count de	Composer	95		385		It. Influenced Wagner Operas
Spooner, John C.	Senate/Congress	5	15		10	Senator WI 1885
Spooner, William A.	Clergy	25	35	45		Br. Creator Of The "Spoonerism"
Sprague, Charles A.	Governor	10	20		15	Governor OR

NAME	CATEGORY	SIG	LS/DS	ALS	SP	COMMENT
Sprague, Frank Julian	Science	55	100	165	115	Inventor Ass't To Thos. Edison
Sprague, William	Civil War	75	90	105		Union Gen., CW Gov. RI, Senate
Sprague, William Buell	Clergy	45	70	110		
Spreckels, Claus	Business	95	325		175	Am. Sugar Manufacturer
Spring, Gardiner	Clergy	25	35	45		
Spring, Samuel	Clergy	20	25	35		
Spring, Sherwood C.	Astronaut	6			15	
Springer, Robert C.	Astronaut	5			15	
Springfield, Rick	Entertainment	12			25	
Springsteen, Bruce	Entertainment	50	75	150	165	
Spruance, Presley	Senate/Congress	12	20	40		Senator DE 1847
Spruance, Raymond A.	Military	25	75	130	60	Am. Adm. Victor Midway WW II
Spurgeon, Charles H.	Clergy	65	90	165		
Squibb, Edward R.	Business	80	150	255		Pioneer Mfg. of Pharmaceuticals
Squier, Emma	Author	5	10	15		
St. Clair, Arthur	Military-Rev. War	135	315	560		Gen.,Pres. Continental Congr.
St. Cyr, Lili	Entertainment	10	15	30	25	Pin-Up SP $35
St. Denis, Ruth	Entertainment	50	140	250	150	Dancer, Choreographer
St. Jacques, Ramond	Entertainment	15			45	
St. John, Al "Fuzzy"	Entertainment	150			350	
St. John, Jill	Entertainment	8	9	20	20	Pin-Up SP $30
St. Johns, Adela Rogers	Author	10	25	45	15	Star Hearst Reporter. Novelist
St. Laurent, Louis	Head of State	10			50	P. M. Canada
St. Vincent, John Jervis, Earl	Military	35	65	135		Br. Adm. 1735-1823
Stabile, Dick	Entertainment	20			40	Big Band Leader
Stacey Q	Entertainment	5			10	Rock
Stacey, John	Aviation	8	20	30	20	
Stack, Robert	Entertainment	10			20	
Stack, Rose Marie Bowe	Entertainment	4	5		9	
Stacpoole, Henry de Vere	Author	15	45	80		Writer, Publicist
Stadlman, Anthony	Aviation	10	20	30	20	
Stael, Anne-Louise, Madame de	Author	65	185	380		Fr. Writer. Exiled By Napoleon
Stafford, Jo	Entertainment	5			15	40's-50's Top Vocalist
Stafford, Robert T.	Governor	8	15	20		Governor VT
Stafford, Thomas P.	Astronaut	15			65	
Stager, Anson	Civil War	20	60	110		Gen.Supt.Govt.Telegraphs
Stahl, Leslie	Journalist	5	15		10	TV. "60 Minutes"
Stalin, Joseph	Head of State	1290	3500	8600	2150	USSR
Stalin, Svetlana	Celebrity	35	105	250	45	Daughter of Stalin
Stallone, Sylvester	Entertainment	20	40	75	85	
Stamos, John	Entertainment	10			35	
Stamp, Terence	Entertainment	10			25	
Stanbery, Henry	Cabinet	10	20	45		Att'y General 1866
Stander, Lionel	Entertainment	10	15	25	25	
Standing, Guy, Sir	Entertainment	25			55	
Standish, Myles	Colonial America	1885	8800	26400		"Mayflower" Colonist. NRPA
Stanford, Leland	Senate	115	325	450	125	Railroad Pres., Philanthropist
Stanford, R. C.	Governor	6	15		10	Governor AZ
Stang, Arnold	Entertainment	5			15	
Stanhope, Edward	Military	10	20	30		
Stanhope, Hester, Lady 1776-1839	Non-Conformist	15	45	95		Adopted Eastern Ways.Prophetess
Stanhope, Phil. H., 5th Earl	Historian	10	20	25		Lord Mahon. M.P., Author
Stanhope, Phil.H., 7th Earl	Celebrity	7	20	45		
Stanhope, Philip D. 1694-1773	Author-Politician	125		625		4th Earl Chesterfield
Stanislavski, Konstantin	Entertainment	350			1750	Rus. Actor, Director, Producer
Stanislaw II Augustus Poniatowski	Royalty	95	375	730		Last King of Poland

NAME	CATEGORY	SIG	LS/DS	ALS	SP	COMMENT
Stanley, Arthur	Business	3	5		7	Pres. Stanley Works
Stanley, David Sloane	Civil War	25	65	90		Union Gen. Wardte ALS $750
Stanley, Freelan O.	Inventor	325		1400		Auto. Pioneer. Stanley Steamer
Stanley, Henry Morton, Sir	Br. Explorer-CW	125	230	520	565	Br. Author, Journalist, CSA
Stanley, Henry, Capt.	Military	10	25	40		
Stanley, Wendell M.	Science	20	45	90	30	Nobel Chemistry 1946
Stans, Maurice	Cabinet	15	35		40	Sec'y Commerce. Watergate
Stansbury, Howard 1806-63	Explorer	20	55	100		Surveyor, Military
Stanton, Benjamin	Senate/Congress	20	45	100		Rep. OH.ALS/Content $250
Stanton, Edwin M.	Cabinet	115	225	350	150	ALS War Dte $950, Sec'y War
Stanton, Elizabeth Cady	Women's Suffrage	105	225	335		1st Pres.Nat'l Women's Suffrage
Stanton, Frank L.	Author	5	15	25		Am. Journalist, Poet, Publ.
Stanton, Frank, Dr.	Business	15	45	80	30	Pres. CBS
Stanton, Harry Dean	Entertainment	6	8	1	20	
Stanwyck, Barbara	Entertainment	35	40		75	Pin-Up SP $85
Stapleton, Jean	Entertainment	5			20	
Stapleton, Maureen	Entertainment	8	10		25	
Stapp, John, Col.	Military	5	15	20	10	
Stapp, Olivia	Entertainment	10			35	Opera
Star Wars (Cast)	Entertainment				175	SP (7) $175
Stark, Harold R.	Military	15	40	75	40	Adm.,Cmdr.Eur.Waters WW II
Stark, John	Revolutionary War	410	625	1565		Often Quoted General
Starker, Janos	Entertainment	6	8	15	15	
Starkey, Thomas A., Bishop	Clergy	20	35	40		
Starr, Belle	Outlaw	2000	6500			Early West Bandit Queen
Starr, Blaze	Entertainment	15			50	Pin-Up SP $50. Stripper
Starr, Kay	Entertainment	20			35	Big Band Singer. Vocalist
Starr, Leonard*	Cartoonist	25			160	Little Orphan Annie
Starr, Ringo	Entertainment	95			200	Beatles' Drummer
Starrett, Charles	Entertainment	30	35		65	
Starry, Donald A.	Military	5	6	15	10	
Stassen, Harold	Governor	10	15	35	20	Governor MN
Statler, Ellsworth M.	Business	75	205	375	150	Statler Hotel Chain
Statlers, The	Country Music	25			50	
Stead, Wm. Thomas	Journalist	20	60	140	45	Died On Titanic
Stebbins, George C.	Clergy	45	70	95		
Steber, Eleanor	Entertainment	20			55	Opera, Concert
Stedman, Edmund C.	Author	20	35			Poet, NY Stock Broker, Publ.
Steel, Danielle	Author	10	20		25	Novelist
Steele, Barbara	Entertainment	20			35	
Steele, Bob	Entertainment	20	25	45	45	
Steele, Frederick	Civil War	45	95	185		Un.Gen. War Dte/Content $2500
Steele, Karen	Entertainment	4	5		10	
Steele, Richard, Sir 1672-1729	Author	200	600	1320		Essays, Drama. "The Tatler"
Steele, Tom	Entertainment	15		25	25	
Steely Dan	Entertainment	25			50	
Steenburgen, Mary	Entertainment	10			35	
Stefansson, Vilhjalmur	Explorer	60	155	250		Arctic Explorer, Ethnologist
Steffens, Lincoln	Author	20	100	175	25	Journalist. Leading Muckraker
Steger, Will	Celebrity	35	90			
Stegner, Wallace	Author	20		45		Am. Novelist. Pulitzer
Steichen, Edward J.	Artist	80	210	375		Pioneer Photgraphy as Art Form
Steig, William*	Cartoonist	20			100	New Yorker Cartoonist
Steiger, Rod	Entertainment	8			30	
Steimle, Edmund A.	Clergy	10	15	20		
Stein, Gertrude	Author	225	400	895	795	Expatriot Am. Writer

NAME	CATEGORY	SIG	LS/DS	ALS	SP	COMMENT
Stein, Jules	Humanitarian-Bus.	50	200			Founder MCA
Steinbeck, John	Author	300	875	3100	950	Pulitzer, Nobel Lit., DS $2,500
Steinem, Gloria	Feminist	15	25	45	25	Fndr.,Editor "Ms"Magazine
Steinhoff, J. 'Mickey'	Aviation	15	25	50	30	
Steinlen, Theophile	Artist	35	105	250		Fr. Known For Posters, Lithogr.
Steinmetz, Charles P.	Science	60	250	425		Ger.-born Electrical Engineer
Steinway, Henry Z.	Business	20	55	85	30	Steinway Piano
Steiwer, Frederick	Senate/Congress	5		15		Senator OR 1926
Stekel, Wilhelm	Science	60	275			Austrian Psychiatrist
Stella, Antonietta	Entertainment	25			65	Opera
Stemple, Robert	Business	25				Pres. General Motors
Sten, Anna	Entertainment	15	15	30	35	
Stendhal (Marie H. Beyle)	Author	350	1020	2315		19th Cent. Fr. Novelist
Stengle, Charles I.	Senate/Congress	5	15	25		Rep. NY 1923
Stennis, John C.	Senate/Congress	10	15			Sen. MS 1947. Pres. Pro Tem.
Stephanie, Princess	Royalty	10			25	Princess of Monaco
Stephen, Adam 1730-1791	Revolutionary War	60	165	320		General. Trenton, Brandywine
Stephenopolus, George	Government	10	20		25	White House Aide
Stephens, Alexander Hamilton	Civil War	165	340	550		US Congress GA, VP CSA
Stephens, William D.	Senate	10	30			Governor CA, Senator CA
Stephenson, George 1781-1825	Science	150	425	875		1st Practical Steam Locomotive
Stephenson, Henry	Entertainment	35			75	
Stephenson, Robert	Science	90	245	410		Br. Railroad Engineer-Designer
Stepp, Hans	Aviation	5	15	20	15	
Steppenwolf	Entertainment	75			150	
Sterling, Andrew B.	Composer	15	50	100		
Sterling, Robert	Entertainment	5			20	
Stern, Henry Aaron	Clergy	20	20	25		
Stern, Isaac	Entertainment	15	35	45	35	AMQS $80,ALS/Cont. $110
Sterne, Laurence 1713-68	Author	95	375			Br.Whimsical,Eccentric Humor
Sterrett, Cliff*	Cartoonist	35			300	Polly And Her Pals
Stettinius, Edward R.,Jr.	Cabinet	40	90	190	45	FDR, Truman, Sec'y State
Steuben, Friedrick von	Revolutionary War	1225	3425			ALS/Content $9,750
Stevens, Andrew	Entertainment	8	9	20	20	
Stevens, Brinke	Entertainment	5			15	Pin-Up SP $20
Stevens, Cat	Entertainment	20			35	
Stevens, Clement	Civil War	175				
Stevens, Connie	Entertainment	6	8	15	15	
Stevens, Craig	Entertainment	8	9	20	20	
Stevens, Ebenezer	Revolutionary War	65	195			Memb. Boston Tea Party
Stevens, George	Entertainment	30			60	Film Director
Stevens, Inger	Entertainment	75			150	
Stevens, John 1748-1838	Revolutionary War	20	45	90		Engineer Perfected Steam Engine
Stevens, John Paul, III (SC)	Supreme Court	40	90		150	
Stevens, K.T.	Entertainment	4	5		10	
Stevens, Onslow	Entertainment	30			65	
Stevens, Ray	Country Music	5			10	
Stevens, Rise	Entertainment	20			40	Opera, Concert, Films
Stevens, Robert T.	Cabinet	10	25		20	Sec'y Army
Stevens, Stella	Entertainment	6	8		20	Pin-Up SP $30
Stevens, Tabitha	Entertainment	10			25	
Stevens, Thaddeus	Senate/Congress	35	110	200		Rep. PA 1849-68, Abolitionist
Stevens, Wallace	Author	250	835		2000	Am. Poet, Pulitzer
Stevens, Walter Husted	Civil War	250				CSA Gen.
Stevens, Warren	Entertainment	4	4	15	15	
Stevenson, Adlai E.	Governor	40	65	145		Gov. IL, Pres. Candidate

NAME	CATEGORY	SIG	LS/DS	ALS	SP	COMMENT
Stevenson, Adlai E. 1835-1914	Vice President	55	200	305	160	Cleveland Vice Pres.
Stevenson, Adlai E., III	Governor	5	10		10	Gov. IL
Stevenson, Andrew	Senate/Congress	10	20	30		Rep. VA 1821
Stevenson, Carter L.	Civil War	95	205	500		CSA General
Stevenson, Coke	Governor	5	15			Governer TX
Stevenson, McLean	Entertainment	10	35		30	
Stevenson, R. H.	Civil War	10	20	30		
Stevenson, Robert Louis	Author	335	845	1785		Novelist, Poet, Essayist
Stewart, Alexander P.	Civil War	175	295			CSA Gen.
Stewart, Alexander T.	Business	10	25	40		Am. Merchant, Garden City, L.I.
Stewart, Catherine Mary	Entertainment	4			15	
Stewart, Charles	Military	95	275			Cmdr. USS Constitution
Stewart, Elaine	Entertainment	4			10	Pin-Up SP $15
Stewart, James (Jimmy)	Entertainment	35	125		60	S "Harvey" Original $300+
Stewart, James C.	Aviation	12	25	40	30	ACE, WW II
Stewart, James S.	Clergy	30	45	60	45	
Stewart, John A.	Business	3	10	25		
Stewart, Lisa	Entertainment	5			15	
Stewart, Paul	Entertainment	10			30	
Stewart, Peggy	Entertainment	4			10	
Stewart, Potter (SC)	Supreme Court	25	110		95	
Stewart, Rex	Entertainment	75	95		150	Cornet
Stewart, Robert L.	Astronaut	5			20	
Stewart, Rod	Entertainment	10	15		65	Rock
Stewart, William	Senate	34	45	70		Drafted US Mining Law-1872 (NV)
Stewart, Wynn	Country Music	10			20	
Stickney, Dorothy	Entertainment	5	7	20	25	
Stieglitz, Alfred	Artist	200	675	925		Revolutionized Camera Technique
Stiers, David Ogden	Entertainment	30			150	
Stigler, George J.	Economist	20	25	40	25	Nobel Economics 1982
Still, William Grant	Composer	120	265	385	250	1st Afro-Am. Symphony Conductor
Stills, Stephen	Entertainment	40			75	
Stilwell, Joseph W.	Military	125	250		450	Gen. WW II
Stimson, Henry L.	Cabinet	40	115	195	50	Sec'y State 1929
Sting	Entertainmebt	25			40	
Stirling, Linda	Entertainment	5			20	
Stirling, Wm. Alex., Lord 1726-83	Revolutionary War	385	950			General Continental Army
Stock, Frederick A.	Composer	20	55	100	45	Dir. Chicago Symphony Orch.
Stock, Harold	Business	10	35	50	20	
Stockdale, James B.	Military	22	30		25	Adm. WW II. Perot Running Mate
Stockton, Frank R.	Author	25	125		35	Juvenile Fiction. Novels.Editor
Stockton, Richard 1730-81	Revolutionary War	300	1150	3500		Signer Decl. of Indepen.
Stockton, Richard 1764-1828	Senate/Congress	20	35	50		Rep., Senator NJ 1796
Stockton, Robert Field 1795-1866	Military	125	375	490		Sen. NJ, Stockton, CA Named
Stockwell, Dean	Entertainment	10			30	
Stockwell, Guy	Entertainment	10			30	
Stockwell, Harry	Entertainment	50			150	
Stoddard, Richard H.	Author	20	30	45		Poet, Writer, Literary Critic
Stoddart, James H.	Entertainment	20			40	Vintage Actor
Stoddert, Benjamin	Revolutionary War	95	340	510		1st Sec'y Navy 1798
Stoker, Bram	Author	90	225	375		Ir. writer of "Dracula"
Stokes, Carl Burton	Celebrity	5	15	35	10	
Stokes, Louis	Senate/Congress	10	20		15	Afro-Am. Congressman OH
Stokes, William	Civil War	60				Union Gen., Rep. TN
Stokowski, Leopold	Entertainment	75	90	180	150	Conductor
Stolle, Bruno	Aviation	5	15	20	15	

NAME	CATEGORY	SIG	LS/DS	ALS	SP	COMMENT
Stoltz, Eric	Entertainment	9	10	20	25	
Stolz, Teresa	Entertainment	40	75			ALS/Content $400
Stone Temple Pilots	Entertainment	25			75	Rock
Stone, Cliffie	Country Music	10			20	Singer, Songwriter, Record Exec
Stone, Ezra	Entertainment	30			50	Vintage Radio's "Henry Aldrich"
Stone, Fred	Entertainment	18		30	30	
Stone, George E.	Entertainment	20			45	
Stone, Harlan Fiske (SC)	Supreme Court	70	135	175	225	Chief Justice
Stone, Harold J.	Entertainment	10			30	
Stone, Irving	Author	20	75	100	40	Historical Biographical Novels
Stone, John Samuel	Clergy	20		85		
Stone, Lewis S.	Entertainment	30	40	75	65	
Stone, Lucy (Blackwell)	Reformer	90	290	350		Suffragist, Women's Rights
Stone, Milburn	Entertainment	45	55	100	100	
Stone, Oliver	Entertainment	10			30	Film Director, Writer, Producer
Stone, Paula	Entertainment	4		10	20	
Stone, Sharon	Entertainment	15			55	Pin-Up SP $75
Stone, Thomas	Revolutionary War	285	930	1750		Signer Decl. of Indepen.
Stoneman, George	Civil War-Gov.	60	155	195		Union General, Gov. of CA
Stooges, The Three (3)	Entertainment	1500			3500	
Stoopnagle, Colonel Lemuel Q.	Entertainment	15	15	30	30	Vint.Radio (Fred. C. Taylor)
Stoppard, Tom	Author	30	80	155	35	Br. Plays of Verbal Brilliance
Storch, Larry	Entertainment	6	8	12	15	
Storm, Gale	Entertainment	10			20	Star of Early TV Series
Storm, Tempest	Entertainment	10	15	28	25	Pin-Up SP $35
Storms, Harrison A.	Business	9		25		
Storrs Richard Salter	Clergy	25	35	50		
Story, Joseph (SC)	Supreme Court	75	150	300		ALS/Content $2,500
Stott, John	Clergy	15	25	30		
Stoughton, William 1632-1701	Colonial America	450	1200			Gov. MA, Stoughton Hall,Harvard
Stout, Rex	Author	35	110	215	40	Created Detective Nero Wolfe
Stowe, Harriet Beecher	Author	185	320	535	2100	Anti-Slavery. AMsS $3,850
Stowe, Madeline	Entertainment	10			30	Pin-Up SP $30
Stracciari, Riccardo	Entertainment	50			180	Opera
Strachey, Lytton	Author	70	175	475		Br. Member of Bloomsbury Group
Stradlin, Izzy	Entertainment	15			40	"Guns N' Roses"
Straight, Beatrice	Entertainment	5	6	15	15	
Strait, Donald G.	Aviation	12	25	40	35	ACE, WW II
Strait, George	Country Music	10			30	
Strait, Horace Burton	Senate/Congress	10	15			Rep. MN 1873, Banker, Agri.
Stranahan, Robert A., Jr.	Business	5			10	CEO Champion Spark Plugs
Strange, Glenn	Entertainment	50			150	
Strasberg, Lee	Entertainment	30	35	55	75	Drama Coach. Hd. Actor's Studio
Strasberg. Susan	Entertainment	5	15	35	20	Pin-Up SP $30
Stratas, Teresa	Entertainment	25			50	Opera
Stratemeyer, George F.	Military	30	40		50	
Stratten, Dorothy	Entertainment	100			250	
Stratton, Chas. S.(Tom Thumb)	Entertainment	200		475	500	General Tom Thumb
Stratton, Samuel S.	Senate/Congress	5	10		10	Rep. NY. Navy Intelligence
Stratton, William G.	Gov-Congress	4	10			Rep., Gov. IL
Straub, Robert W.	Governor	5	15			Gov. OR
Straus, Jack I.	Business	4	10	25	10	3rd Generation R.H.Macy Dept...
Straus, Nathan 1848-1931	Business	45	70		55	Owner R.H. Macy Co. Dept Store
Straus, Oscar	Composer	150	240	525	200	Fr. "The Chocolate Soldier"
Strause, Charles	Composer	8	15	30	25	
Strauss, Adolf	Military	10	15	35	15	

NAME	CATEGORY	SIG	LS/DS	ALS	SP	COMMENT
Strauss, Franz Josef	Head of State	15	45	125	35	
Strauss, Johann 1804-49	Composer	250	445	1050		Aus. Waltzes. Cond. Own Orchest
Strauss, Johann, Jr. 1825-99	Composer	450	1225	900	1125	"The Waltz King"
Strauss, Levi	Business					1850 Establ'd Levi Strauss & Co
Strauss, Peter	Entertainment	15			45	
Strauss, Richard	Composer	200	545	1055	695	AMusQS $700-$1,500
Strauss, Robert	Cabinet	4	12	20	10	
Strauss, Robert	Entertainment	25			45	
Stravinsky, Igor	Composer	275	720	1350	875	AMusQS $975-$1,150-$1,750
Straw, Ezekiel A.	Governor	5	15			Governor NH
Strawbridge, James Dale	Senate/Congress	5	15			Rep. PA/. CW Brigade Surgeon
Stray Cats	Entertainment	35			100	Rock
Strayhorn, Billy	Entertainment					Jazz Musician-No Price Availabl
Streep, Meryl	Entertainment	20	30	45	45	
Street, Julian	Author	15			75	
Streett, St. Clair	Aviation	50	165			Alaskan Air Expedition
Streich, Rita	Entertainment	10			25	Opera
Streicher, Julius	Journalist	50	170			Nazi Anti-Semetic, Hanged
Streight, Abel	Civil War	50	165			Union Gen. Escaped Libby Prison
Streisand, Barbra	Entertainment	150			240	Pin-Up SP $275
Stribling, Thomas S.	Author	12	25	60		Am. Novlist. Pulitzer
Strindberg, August	Author	275		725		Swe.ALS's/Cont. $1,400-$2,200
Stringham, Silas Horton	Civil War	55	105			Union Adm.
Stritch, Samuel, Cardinal	Clergy	40	45	75	45	
Stroheim, Eric von	Entertainment	160			490	Classic Film Director
Stromberg, Hunt	Entertainment	10	15		30	Film Producer, Director
Strong, Caleb	Revolutionary War	60	200	475		1st U.S. Senator Mass.
Strong, Susan	Entertainment	12			20	Vintage Actress
Strong, William (SC)	Supreme Court	80	170	305		
Stroud Twins	Entertainment	18			40	
Stroud, Robert,Birdman of Alcatraz	Convict-Ornithologist					Remarkable 7 pp. ALS $15,000
Strouse, Charles	Composer	15			30	
Struthers, Sally	Entertainment	4		10	15	
Stryker (4)	Entertainment	10			20	Gospel Singers
Stuart, Alexander H. H.	Cabinet	25	60	95		Fillmore Sec'y Interior
Stuart, George R.	Clergy	10	15	20		
Stuart, Gilbert 1755-1828	Artist	200	500	850		Portraitist. Presidents-Royalty
Stuart, Gloria	Entertainment	5			15	
Stuart, J.E.B.	Civil War	1835	4950	7300		CSA Gen.,War Dte.ALS $19,000
Stuart, Marty	Country Music	10			25	
Studebaker, Clement	Business	200	500	765		Auto Pioneers.Studebaker Bros.
Studebaker, Jr., Clement	Business	40	105	195	75	Studebaker Bros. Mfg. Co.
Studer, Cheryl	Entertainment	10			35	Opera
Stultz, Wilmer	Aviation	50	135		150	Pioneer Aviator/A. Earhart
Stump, Felix B.	Military	25	80		50	Adm. Capt. Lexington WW II
Sturge, Joseph 1793-1859	Philanthropist	10	20	45		Pacifist,Reformer,Abolitionist
Sturgeon, Daniel	Senate-Cabinet	25	70	125		Sen. PA 1839, US Treasurer 1853
Sturges, John	Entertainment	5	6	15	15	
Sturges, Preston	Entertainment	20			50	Film Director, Producer, Writer
Sturgis, Samuel D.	Civil War	50	105			Union Gen.
Styne, Jule	Composers	25			60	AMusQS $180, $370
Styron, William	Author	15	35	80	75	"Sophie's Choice" MsS 1p $200
Styx	Entertainment	25			50	
Suchet, David	Entertainment	10			30	Br. Actor. "Poirot"
Suchet, Louis G.,Duc d'A	Napoleonic Wars	85	215	390		Marshal of Napoleon
Sucre, Antonio de	Military	295	1050			Liberator of Venezuela, General

NAME	CATEGORY	SIG	LS/DS	ALS	SP	COMMENT
Sudarmono, Pratiwi	Astronaut	12	25		25	
Suenens, Leo Joseph, Cardinal	Clergy	45	75	90	65	
Suharto, General	Head of State	15	30	75	35	Indonesia
Sul, Terra	Entertainment	4			10	
Sullavan, Margaret	Entertainment	40			150	
Sullivan, Anne (Annie)	Educator	100		425		TLS/Content $1,000
Sullivan, Arthur, Sir	Composer	175	400	775	1275	AMusQS $1,200
Sullivan, Barry	Entertainment	10	15		25	
Sullivan, Ed	Entertainment	25	35	60	70	Columnist, TV Host
Sullivan, Francis L.	Entertainment	10	20		25	
Sullivan, James	Revolutionary War	50	95	200		Continental Congress, Gov. MA
Sullivan, John	Revolutionary War	150	250	575		Continental Congress, General
Sullivan, Kathleen	Entertainment	10			20	TV Hostess
Sullivan, Kathryn D.	Aviation-Astro.	10	25	45	30	
Sullivan, Pat*	Cartoonist	50			400	Felix The Cat
Sullivan, Peter John	Civil War	55	105	160		Union General
Sullivan, Susan	Entertainment	5	6	20	15	
Sullivan, William 1774-1839	Author	20	40	95		Politician, Gen. Militia, Orato
Sully, Alfred	Civil War	35	80	110	150	Union General
Sully, Thomas 1783-1872	Artist	165	410	775		Leader Portrait Painter His Day
Sully-Prudhomme, René F.A	Author	40	135	225		Fr. Poet, 1st Nobel Literature
Sulzberger, Art Ochs, Jr.	Business	10	25	30	15	NY Times
Sulzer, William	Congress-Gov.	15	35		25	Rep.,Gov. NY, Impeached 1913
Summer, Donna	Entertainment	10	15		20	
Summerall, Charles Pelot	Military	10	20	35	25	Gen., Pres. Citadel 1931-53
Summerfield, Arthur E.	Cabinet	15	20	30	20	P.M. Genera, Modernized Systeml
Summersby, Kay	Military-WWII	95	325		125	D.D. Eisenhower's WW II Aide
Summerville, Slim	Entertainment	35			75	
Sumner, Charles	Civil War	85	160	195		Abolitionist. Founder Rep.Party
Sumner, Increase	Governor	65	190			Rev. War Jurist & Stateman
Sumter, Thomas	Revolutionary War	375	1200			Soldier, Rep.,Sen., SC 1789
Sun Yat-Sen	Head of State	500	925	1550		1st Pres. Chinese Republic
Sunday, William A. 'Billy'	Clergy	85	160	275	400	Evangelist
Sununu, John	Cabinet	12	15	25	15	Chief of Staff White House
Supertramp	Entertainment	35			75	
Suppe', Franz von	Composer	110	225	450	395	Aus. Opera, Operetta,Choral
Susann, Jacqueline	Author	20	35	45	40	"Valley of the Dolls" etc.
Sutherland, Donald	Entertainment	10	15	20	20	
Sutherland, George (SC)	Supreme Court	65	165	350	250	
Sutherland, Joan	Entertainment	15		35	40	Opera, Concert
Sutherland, Keifer	Entertainment	10			45	
Sutro, Adolph H. J.	Business-Engineer	35	80	185		Mining magnate. Sutro Tunnel
Sutter, John A.	CA Pioneer	700	3400	8875		Sutter's Fort.ALS/Cont. $15,000
Sutton, Grady	Entertainment	8	10		15	
Sutton, Willy	Criminal	45		290	75	Bank Robber. Prison Escapes
Svanholm, Set	Entertainment	15			45	Opera
Svenson, Bo	Entertainment	4	5	9	10	
Swaggart, Jimmy	Clergy	10	30	35	30	Evangelist
Swan, James	Revolutionary War	180	595	650		Finan'l Speculator.
Swann, Thomas	Senate/Congress	5	15			Senator,Gov, MD. Pres. B & O RR
Swanson, Claude A.	Cabinet	10	25	55	20	Sec'y Navy 1933
Swanson, Gloria	Entertainment	40	330		140	
Swanson, J.	Civil War	65	135	180		
Swart, Charles R.	Head of State	5		20		
Swarthout, Gladys	Entertainment	25			90	Opera and Film Star
Swasey, Ambrose	Business	40	90			

NAME	CATEGORY	SIG	LS/DS	ALS	SP	COMMENT
Swayne, Noah H. (SC)	Supreme Court	45	115	195		
Swayne, Wager	Civil War	25	45	105		Union General
Swayze, John Cameron	Entertainment	5			10	Radio, TV News & Commercials
Swayze, Patrick	Entertainment	25			60	
Swearingen, John	Business	10	25	40	15	CEO Continental Ill. Corp.
Sweat, Lorenzo DeMedici	Senate/Congress	10	15	25		Rep. ME 1863
Swedenborg, Emanuel 1688-1772	Science	3000				Swe.Science,Philosophy,Religion
Sweeney, Brian	Law Enforcement	4			10	Law Enforcement No. Ireland
Sweeney, Walter C.	Military	5	15	25	15	Gen. Tactical Air Cmd.
Sweet, Blanche	Entertainment	20		30	35	
Sweet, John H.	Business	5	15		10	CEO US News & World Report
Swenson, Ruth Ann	Entertainment	10			25	Opera
Swett, James E.	Aviation	15	30	50	42	ACE, WW II
Swift, Frederic W.	Civil War	55	135	195		Union General, MOH
Swift, George B.	Political	10	25			Mayor of Chicago
Swift, Harold Higgins	Business	20	50	95	35	Chm. Swift & Co., Meatpackers
Swift, John W. 1750-1819	Revolutionary War	65	180			Merchant. Soldier
Swift, Jonathan 1667-1745	Author	2500	7300	13230		Satirist,Poet,Clergy,Political
Swigert, John L. Jr.	Astronaut	40	75		125	
Swinburne, Algernon C.	Author	185	295	600		Br. 19th Cent. Lyric Poet
Swinnerton, Frank	Author	20	55	100		Br. Novelist, Critic
Swinnerton, James*	Cartoonist	35			180	Little Jimmy
Swinton, Ernest D.,Col.	Military	45	110	175		British Inventor of Tank
Swit, Loretta	Entertainment	15			30	
Switzer, Carl "Alfalfa"	Entertainment	200			525	
Swope, Gerard	Business	60				CEO General Electric
Swope, Herbert Bayard	Author	10	35	75	20	Journalist, War Corresp.,Pulitz
Swope, James S.	Aviation	10	22	40	30	ACE, WW II
Sykes, Jerome H.	Entertainment	15			30	Light Opera
Sylva, Carmen (Queen of Romania)	Author	50	75			Elizabeth, Queen of Romania
Sylva, Marguerite	Entertainment	15			40	Vintage
Sylvia	Entertainment	5	6	15	15	
Symington, Stuart	Cabinet	5	15	35	20	Sen. MO, Sec'y Air Force
Symmes, John Cleves	Revolutionary War	110	375	550		Patriot. Continental Congress
Szell, George	Entertainment	10			35	Hung. Conductor
Szent-Gyorgyi, Albert	Science	40	65	125	50	Nobel Medicine 1937
Szold, Henrietta	Zionist Leader	140	435	600		Founder, Pres. Hadassah
Szymanowski, Karol M.	Composer	125		560		AMusMsS $1250

T

NAME	CATEGORY	SIG	LS/DS	ALS	SP	COMMENT
T Hooft, Visser	Celebrity	3	5	10	10	
T, Mr.	Entertainment	10			20	
Tabb, John Banister	Civil War Clergy	40		200		Rom.Cath. clergyman, Poet
Taber, Robert	Entertainment	6	8	15	15	
Taft, Charles P.	Publisher	10	15	25	10	Owner-Ed. Cincinnati Times-Star
Taft, Helen Herron	First Lady	100	200	550		ALS White House $1,200
Taft, Helen Manning	First Lady	80	185	300	500	Daughter
Taft, Henry Wallace	Lawyer	3	7	15		Noted Brother Of Pres. Taft
Taft, Lorado	Artist	60	95	160		Influential Am. Sculptor-Author
Taft, Robert A. 1889-1953	Senate/Congress	20	50		25	SIGned caricature $75, OH
Taft, Robert, Jr. 1917-	Senate/Congress	7	15		10	Rep., Senator OH.
Taft, William Howard	President	185	556	900	445	
Taft, William Howard (As President	President	220	695		490	
Tagliabue, Carlo	Entertainment	45			175	Opera
Tagliavini, Ferruccio	Entertainment	35			160	Opera
Taglioni, Marie	Entertainment	300		935		It. Premier Ballerina
Tagore, Rabindranath, Sir	Author	105	265	490	350	Nobel Prize Lit., Indian Poet
Tait, A.C., Archbishop	Clergy	25	35	50		
Tait, Arthur Fitzwilliam	Artist	25	55	100		Landscape Artist
Taka, Miiko	Entertainment	15			25	Japanese Actress
Takei, George	Entertainment	15			35	
Talbert, Melvin, Bishop	Clergy	20	25	30	35	
Talbot, Gloria	Entertainment	10			20	
Talbot, Helen	Entertainment	10			25	
Talbot, Lyle	Entertainment	5	10	15	15	
Talbot, Nita	Entertainment	4	6		20	
Talbot, Wm. Henry Fox	Science	295		1250		Br.Inventor of Photogr. Process
Talbott, Harold D.	Cabinet	10	15			Sec'y AF
Talcott, Joseph 1669-1741	Colonial America	30	75	160		Colonial Governor CT
Talese, Gay	Author	10	25		15	Am. Novelist
Talking Heads	Entertainment	20			60	
Tallchief, Maria	Entertainment	15	20	35	30	Ballerina
Talley, Marion	Entertainment	15		45	50	Am. Soprano
Talleyrand, Charles Maurice de	Head of State	185	615	950		Grand Chancellor of Napoleon
Talmadge, Benjamin 1754-1835	Revolutionary War	220	465			Served Throughout War. Rep. NY
Talmadge, Constance	Entertainment	35			80	
Talmadge, Eugene	Governor	20	60	95		Governor GA
Talmadge, Herman	Senate/Congress	10	20		15	Gov., Senator GA
Talmadge, Norma	Entertainment	50			175	
Talmage, T. Dewitt	Clergy	50	70	95		America Divine, Editor
Talman, William	Entertainment	50	70	150	125	Regular on Original Perry Mason
Talvela, Marti	Entertainment	30			75	Opera
Tamblyn, Russ	Entertainment	6	8		20	
Tambor, Jeffrey	Entertainment	6	8	15	15	

NAME	CATEGORY	SIG	LS/DS	ALS	SP	COMMENT
Tamiroff, Akim	Entertainment	30	40	75	70	
Tandy, Jessica	Entertainment	20	35	45	50	
Taney, Roger B. (SC)	Supreme Court	60	275	560		Chief Justice., Dred Scott Case
Tanner, Henry Ossawa	Artist	35	85	185		Religious Subjects,Realistic
Tanner, John Riley	Governor	12	20			Governor IL
Tansman, Alexandre	Composer	40	125		280	
Tappan, Arthur 1786-1865	Abolitionist	25	65	120		Merchant, Philanthropist
Tappan, James C.	Civil War	35	70	110		CSA General
Tarbell, Ida M.	Author	20	45	95	25	Author of Expose's
Tarkington, Booth	Author	35	125	195	125	Playwright, Novelist. Pulitzer
Tarleton, Banastre, Sir	Revolutionary War	135	365	715		Barbaric Br.General. Am. Rev.
Tarnower, Herman Dr.	Medical	15	50	135	20	Diet Dr. Murdered
Tashman, Lilyan	Entertainment	30	40	75	70	
Tassigny, J.M.G. de	Military	35	90	140		
Tate, Allen	Author	10	30	45		Am. Poet, Critic, Biographer
Tate, Henry, Sir, 1st Baronet	Business	40	95	240		Br. Philanthropist,Tate Gallery
Tate, Jackson R.	Military	5		30	25	Adm. WW II.
Tate, Sharon	Entertainment	200	300	500	550	Murdered By Manson Gang
Tattersall, Richard 1724-95	Business	20	45	100		Rendevous For Sporting-Betting
Tatum, Edward L.	Science	45	70	125		Nobel Medicine 1958
Taube, Henry, Dr.	Science	22	35		25	Nobel Chemistry 1983
Tauber, Richard	Entertainment	40			125	Opera, Austrian Tenor
Taufflieb, Gen.	Military	45	120	215	100	
Taurog, Norman	Entertainment	50			150	Film Director
Taussig, Frank William 1859-1940	Economist	10	25			Author. Chm Tariff Bd.
Tawes, J. Millard	Governor	5	15			Governor MD
Tawney, James A.	Senate/Congress	5	15	25		Rep. MN 1893
Tayback, Vic	Entertainment	15			40	
Taylor, Bayard 1825-78	Author	20	70	135		Journalist, Traveller, Diplomat
Taylor, Charles H.	Congress	5	10		10	Congressman NC
Taylor, Deems	Composer	20	80	85	50	Musicologist, Critic, Author
Taylor, Don	Entertainment	5			20	
Taylor, Dub	Entertainment	10			40	
Taylor, Elizabeth	Entertainment	150		275	365	
Taylor, Estelle	Entertainment	10	25	45	45	
Taylor, George	Revolutionary War	1400	3575	7050		Signer Decl. of Indepen.
Taylor, Glen H.	Senate	10	25		25	Sen. ID, Actor, Singer
Taylor, Graham	Clergy	15	25	35		
Taylor, H. C.	Military	10	24	40		
Taylor, James	Composer	35	100	250	65	Singer-Guitarist
Taylor, James (Afro-Am.)	Entertainment	40			75	
Taylor, James Willis	Senate/Congress	4	10	20		Rep. TN 1919
Taylor, Joan	Entertainment	7			15	
Taylor, John	Celebrity	50	130			
Taylor, John W.	Senate/Congress	15		40		Early Rep. 1813, Speaker
Taylor, Kent	Entertainment	5			15	
Taylor, Laurette	Entertainment	15	20	40	35	
Taylor, Margaret	First Lady					Only 1 Known. No Price Avail.
Taylor, Mary	Country Music	10			20	
Taylor, Maxwell D.	Military	25	75	110	65	Gen. WW II
Taylor, Niki	Model	20			75	
Taylor, Richard	Civil War	225	525			CSA Gen. Son of Pres. Taylor
Taylor, Richard E., Dr.	Science	20	50			Nobel Physics 1990
Taylor, Robert	Entertainment	35	65	125	175	
Taylor, Robert L.	Senate	10	15		15	Gov., Rep. & Senator TN
Taylor, Rod	Entertainment	4	6		20	

NAME	CATEGORY	SIG	LS/DS	ALS	SP	COMMENT
Taylor, Thomas H.	Civil War	45	75	210		CSA General
Taylor, Vaughn	Entertainment	20			50	
Taylor, Walter H.	Civil War	40	90			CSA Col. Aide-de-camp R.E. Lee
Taylor, William, Bishop	Clergy		40	50	75	
Taylor, Wm. Levi (Buck)	Celebrity	175				NRPA
Taylor, Zachary	President	730	3450	6200		DS As Pres. $4,500-$7,800
Taylor-Young, Leigh	Entertainment	5	8	15	15	
Tazewell, Littleton	Senate/Congress	45	135	250		Rep. 1800, Sen. 1824,Gov. VA
Tchaikovsky, Piotr I.	Composer	2000	3450	4200	5000	Rus. Opera,Symphony,Ballet,Etc.
Tchernihovsky, Saul	Author	175		550		Rus-Hebrew Dr., Poet,Translator
Te Kanawa, Kiri, Dame	Entertainment	25	55		75	Opera, Concert
Teagarden, Charlie	Entertainment	10			25	Jazz Trumpet
Teagarden, Jack	Entertainment	60	100		125	Big Band Leader-Trombonist
Teal, Ray	Entertainment	50			150	
Tearle, Conway	Entertainment	20			50	Vintage Br. Actor
Teasdale, Veree	Entertainment	20	25	45	45	
Tebaldi, Renata	Entertainment	20			90	Opera
Tedrow, Irene	Entertainment	3	4		16	
Teitjens, Therese	Entertainment	50			190	Opera
Telfair, Edward	Revolutionary War	30	95	150		Continental Congress from GA
Teller, Edward, Dr.	Science	50	130	210	125	Fermi Award
Teller, Henry M.	Cabinet	15	25	50	20	Sec'y Interior 1882
Telva, Marion	Entertainment	15			45	
Temin, Howard M., Dr.	Science	20	35	55	25	Nobel Medicine 1975
Tempest, Marie	Entertainment	25	35	50	65	
Temple, Shirley (Black)	Entertainment	25	25	35	40	
Temple, Shirley (as a child)	Entertainment	150			475	
Temple, Wm.	Clergy	40	45	85	65	Archbishop Canterbury
Templeton, Ben	Cartoonist	5			20	Motley's Crew
Templeton, Faye	Entertainment	25	30	60	65	Musical Career For Over 50 Year
Temptations	Entertainment	40			125	
Ten Broeck, Abraham	Revolutionary War	100		245		Gen. Judge, Banker
Tennant, F.R.	Clergy	15	20	25		
Tennant, Victoria	Entertainment	5	8	25	20	
Tenniel, John, Sir	Artist	70	110	260		Illustr. "Alice in Wonderland"
Tennille, Toni	Entertainment	5			15	Singer
Tennyson, Alfred, Lord	Author	155	335	595	595	Br. Poet Laureate
Tennyson, Jean	Entertainment	10			20	Am. Soprano
Teresa, Mother	Clergy	125	225	350	250	Nobel Peace Prize
Tereshkova, Valentina	Cosmonaut	200	250		250	1st Woman in Outer Space
Terhune, Alfred Payson	Author	25	50	110	50	Famous Writer of Dog Stories
Terhune, Max	Entertainment	100			250	
Terkel, Studs	Author	10	15	25	15	Columnist, Biographer, TV
Terry, Alfred Howe	Civil War	55	70	155		Union Gen., Cmdr. Dakota Terr.
Terry, Clark	Entertainment	50				Trumpet, Fluegelhorn
Terry, Ellen, Dame	Entertainment	30	60	150	75	Actress Partner of Henry Irving
Terry, Fred	Entertainment	10	15	25	25	
Terry, Henry D.	Civil War	45	100	160		Union General
Terry, Luther, Dr.	Celebrity	3	5	10	5	
Terry, Paul*	Cartoonist	50			250	Animator-Mighty Mouse
Terry, Phillip	Entertainment	5	6	15	15	
Terry, William Richard	Civil War	75	175	245		CSA General
Tesla, Nikola, Dr.	Science	425	950			Physicist, Electrical Genius
Tetard, J.	Aviation	45	60	170	100	
Tetrazzini, Luisa	Entertainment	75	90	200	250	Opera
Teyte, Maggie	Entertainment	35			130	Opera

NAME	CATEGORY	SIG	LS/DS	ALS	SP	COMMENT
Thackeray, William Makepeace	Author	100	375	725		Br. Novelist
Thagard, Norman E.	Astronaut	10			25	
Thalberg, Irving	Entertainment	250	375	585	350	MGM's Boy Genius Producer
Thant, U	Head of State	75	130	295	200	UN Sec'y General
Tharp, Sister Rosetta	Entertainment	65				Jazz Vocalist-Guitar
Tharp, Twyla	Entertainment	20	25		40	Dancer-Choreographer
Thatcher, Henry Knox	Civil War	50	95	140		Union Naval Commander
Thatcher, Margaret, Dame	Head of State	45	140	225	150	Prime Minister
Thatcher, Peter	Clergy	75	100	150		
Thaves, Bob	Cartoonist	5			20	Frank & Ernest
Thaw, Harry K.	Business	40	95	195	75	"Playboy". Shot Sanford White
Thaxter, Celia	Entertainment	20	25	45	45	
Thaxter, Celia 1835-94	Author	20	45	95	150	Am. Poet
Thayer, Abbott	Artist	15	35	70		Am. Ideal Figures, Landscapes
Thayer, Celia	Author	5	10	15		Am. Novelist, Screenwriter
Thayer, John Milton	Civil War	45	85	180		Union Gen., Gov. WY Terr.
Thayer, Silvanus 1785-1872	Military	60	140	245		"Father of the Military Academy
Thebaw	Head of State	145				Burma
Thebom, Blanche	Entertainment	20	35		85	Am. Contralto, Opera, Concert
Theiss, Ursula	Entertainment	10	15	25	25	
Thelen, Bob	Aviation	10	25	40	35	ACE, WW II, Blue Angels
Thesiger, Ernest	Entertainment	225			650	
Thicke, Alan	Entertainment	5			15	
Thielicke, Helmut	Clergy	30	50	65	60	
Thiers, Louis-Adolphe	Fr. Revolution	30	65	155		1st Pres. 3rd Republic
Thieu, Nguyen Van	Head of State	20	60	150	35	So. Viet Nam
Thinnis, Roy	Entertainment	5	6	20	10	
Thirsk, Bob	Astronaut	5	15		15	
Thomas, B.J.	Entertainment	4			10	
Thomas, Betty	Entertainment	5	6	15	10	
Thomas, C.-L.-Ambroise	Composer	70	105	275		Fr. Operas,etc. AMusQS $525
Thomas, Charles 1840-78	Military		800			45 Yrs. Service. Union Gen.
Thomas, Clarence (SC)	Supreme Court	30			45	
Thomas, Danny	Entertainment	20			45	
Thomas, Dave	Business	10	20		25	Founder of "Wendy's"
Thomas, Dylan	Author	510		2050	1500	Welsh Poet
Thomas, E. Donnall, Dr.	Science	15	25		30	Nobel Medicine 1990
Thomas, George Henry	Civil War	100	195	435		Union Gen."Rock of Chickamauga"
Thomas, Heather	Entertainment	10	10	30	25	
Thomas, Isaiah	Colonial Printer	135	380	725		Publ. 1st Eng. Bible in America
Thomas, James, Bishop	Clergy	20	25	35	30	
Thomas, Jess	Entertainment	15			40	Opera
Thomas, John	Revolutionary War	350	855	1750		Am. Physician & Gen. Cont.Army
Thomas, John Charles	Entertainment	20	30	45	50	Multi Media Am. Baritone
Thomas, Kurt	Entertainment	5	6	15	15	
Thomas, Lorenzo	Civil War	90	140	270		Union General
Thomas, Lowell	Entertainment	15		35	40	World Traveller, Top Radio News
Thomas, Marlo	Entertainment	4	6		15	
Thomas, Michael Tilson	Entertainment	15			50	Am. Conductor
Thomas, Norman	Socialist Leader	25	115	215	55	6 Times Presidential Candidate
Thomas, Olive	Entertainment	65	70	150	150	Jack Pickford Wife.Suicide at36
Thomas, Philip Evan	Business	6	17	29		
Thomas, Richard	Entertainment	5	6	15	15	
Thomas, Robert Bailey	Author	20	45	105		Pulbl.,Editor "Farmer's Almanac
Thomas, Samuel	Civil War	45				Union General
Thomas, Seth E.	Business	125	250	475		Founder Seth Thomas Clock Co.

NAME	CATEGORY	SIG	LS/DS	ALS	SP	COMMENT
Thomas, Seth E.,Jr.1816-88	Business	65	175	350		Cont'd Seth Thomas Clock Co.
Thomas, Terry	Entertainment	50			150	
Thomas, Theodore	Entertainment	15			30	Conductor. NY & Chic. Symph.
Thomberg, Kerstin	Entertainment	15			35	
Thompson Twins	Entertainment	25			80	
Thompson, Benj. von Rumford	Revolutionary War	275	450			Br.Physicist, Inventor,Loyalist
Thompson, Benjamin 1798-1852	Senate/Congress	5	10	25		Rep. MA 1845
Thompson, Denman	Entertainment	15			30	Vintage Stage Actor
Thompson, Dorothy	Author	35	80	110	85	Journalist,Corresponent,Column.
Thompson, Emma	Entertainment	20			50	Pin-Up SP $75
Thompson, Ernest Seton	Author	40	100	195		Wild Life Stories, Naturalist
Thompson, Gordon	Entertainment	8	9		20	
Thompson, Hank	Country Music	6			15	
Thompson, J. Walter	Business	25	70	130	50	J. Walter Thompson Adv. Agency
Thompson, Jacob	Cabinet, CW	145	315	1380		Sec'y Interior, CSA Secret Agt.
Thompson, Jim	Governor	5	10		20	Governor IL
Thompson, John P.	Business	15	30	65	20	Pres. Southland Corp.
Thompson, Lea	Entertainment	5	10		10	
Thompson, Linda	Entertainment	4			10	Pin-Up SP $20
Thompson, M.E.	Governor	5	15			Governor GA
Thompson, Marshall	Entertainment	15		25	35	
Thompson, Merriwether Jefferson	Civil War	135	425	450		CSA General
Thompson, Orlo and Marvis	Country Music	20			40	
Thompson, Richard W.	CabinetP	20	45	65		Sec'y Navy 1809
Thompson, Robert E.	Clergy	10	10	15		
Thompson, Ruth Plumly	Author	450				
Thompson, Smith (SC)	Supreme Court	75	150	185		
Thompson, Sue	Country Music	10			25	
Thomson, Andrew	Clergy	35	65	75		
Thomson, Charles	Revolutionary War	450	1480			LS As Sec'y Cont'l Congr.$1,750
Thomson, Elihu 1853-1937	Science	525	1250			Electrical Engineer-Inventor
Thomson, Hugh	Br. Illustrator	25		100		
Thomson, James E.	Business	5	15	30	10	Pres. Merrill-Lynch.
Thomson, Virgil	Composer	45	85	150	125	& Music Critic, AMusQS $125
Thorborg, Kerstin	Entertainment	20			50	
Thorburn, Grant	Colonial Am.	40	95			Grocery, Seed Merchant. Hero
Thoreau, Henry David	Author	1540	3000	7200		Am.Schoolmaster, Naturalist
Thorndike, Sybil, Dame	Entertainment	30	45		75	
Thorne, Charles Robert	Entertainment	65	80		120	
Thornhill, F. D.	Military	15	25	40		
Thornton, Charles Tex	Business	5	15	25	15	
Thornton, Dan	Governor	5	15		10	Governor CO
Thornton, Dr. William E.	Astronaut	5			20	
Thornton, Kathryn	Astronaut	10			25	
Thornton, Matthew	Revolutionary War	455	1950	1925		Signer Decl. of Indepen.
Thornton, William	Astronaut	5			20	
Thornton, William	Revolutionary War	140	350			Am. Architect. Designed Capitol
Thorpe, Jeremy	Politician	10	20	45	15	Br. Parliamentarian
Thorpe, Rose Hartwick	Author	10	20	35		Am. "Curfew Must Not Ring....."
Thorson, Ralph'Papa'	Law	10	25	45	15	Bounty Hunter
Thorvaldsen, Bertel	Artist	105	325			Dan. Sculptor "Lion of Lucerne"
Three Sons, The	Entertainment	15			45	Jazz Musicians
Three Stooges, The	Entertainment	1000			2200	With Moe, Curly and Larry
Throop, Enos T.	Governor	25	55			Governor NY 1829
Thruston, Gates P.	Civil War	25	30	55		Union General
Thuot, Pierre	Astronaut	5			15	

NAME	CATEGORY	SIG	LS/DS	ALS	SP	COMMENT
Thurber, James	Author	105	250	505	110	Am. Humorist & Comic Artist
Thurber, James*	Cartoonist	105			500	New Yorker Illust. & Cartoonist
Thurman, Allen G.	Senate/Congress	10	30			Senator OH
Thurman, Howard	Clergy	35	40	50	50	
Thurman, Uma	Entertainment	15			35	Pin-Up SP $75
Thurmond, J. Strom	Senate/Congress	10	20		15	Senator, Governor SC
Thurston, Howard	Entertainment	60	250	250		Thurston "The Magician"
Thurston, John M.	Senate/Congress	15		30		Senator NE 1895
Tibbett, Lawrence	Entertainment	50	125		145	Opera, Concert, Films
Tibbetts, Paul W.	Aviation	35	120	175	75	Pilot of Enola Gay
Tidball, John C.	Civil War	60	135	175		Union General Bvt.
Tiegs, Cheryl	Entertainment	8	9		20	Model. Pin-Up SP $25
Tierney, Gene	Entertainment	20	25	50	45	Pin-Up SP $50
Tierney, Harry	Composer	40	95	195		AMusQS $350
Tietjens, Therese	Entertainment	60			135	Ger. Soprano . Opera
Tiffany, Charles Lewis	Business	175	500		1500	Founder Tiffany and Co.
Tiffany, Louis Comfort	Artist-Business	175	500			Stained glass artist. Painter
Tiffin, Pamela	Entertainment	5	8	15	15	
Tilden, Samuel J.	Governor	75	160	250		Gov. NY, Presidential Cand.
Tilghman, James	Revolutionary War	25	70	165		Lawyer, Politician
Tilghman, Lloyd	Civil War	140	290	415		CSA General. NRPA
Tilghman, Matthew	Revolutionary War	200		950		Cont. Congress.ALS/Cont. $2,750
Tilghman, William M.	Law	200	850	1450		Early Western Sheriff
Tilkin-Servais, Ernest	Entertainment	25			85	Opera
Tillich, Paul	Clergy	70	95	125	100	
Tillinghast, Charles C. Jr.	Business	8	20	40	15	CEO TWA. Merrill-Lynch
Tillis, Mel	Country Music	5			15	
Tillman, Floyd	Country Music	10			20	
Tillman, Pitchfork Ben	Senate/Congress	25	40	55		Senator SC 1894
Tillotson, Johnny	Country Music	6			20	
Tillstrom, Burr	Entertainment	25			50	
Tilly, Jennifer	Entertainment	4		10	15	Pin-Up SP $35
Tilly, Meg	Entertainment	4	6	20	15	Pin-Up SP $35
Tilton, Charlene	Entertainment	25			40	
Tilton, Wm. Stowell	Civil War	45	100			
Timken, William Robert	Business	35	95	155	60	Fndr. Timken Roller Bearings
Ting, Samuel C. C., Dr.	Science	20	35	50	30	Nobel Physics 1976
Tingey, Thomas	Military	60	165	225		Continental Navy
Tingley, Clyde	Governor	12	20		15	Governor NM 1935
Tinker, Grant C.	Entertainment	8	9		15	TV Film Producer
Tiny Tim	Entertainment	19	35		25	
Tiny, Texas	Country Music	10			20	
Tiompkin, Dimitri	Composer	35		175	95	AMusQS $225
Tippett, Michael Sir	Composer	40			150	
Tisserant, Eugene, Cardinal	Clergy	35	45	50	40	
Tissot, James	Artist	75	170	230		Fr. Painter, Engraver, Enameler
Titchener, Paul	Business	10	35	45	20	
Titian (Vecelli, Tiziano)	Artist					It. NRPA
Tito, Marshal (Josip Broz)	Head of State	85	205	280	250	Yugoslav Statesman. Communist
Titov, Gherman	Astronaut	40			135	
Tobey, Charles W.	Senate/Congress	5	15		10	Governor, Rep., Senator NH
Tobey, Ken	Entertainment	10			25	
Tobias, George	Entertainment	50			150	
Tobin, Genevieve	Entertainment	15		30	35	
Tobin, James, Dr.	Economist	22	30		25	Nobel Economics 1981
Tobin, Maurice	Cabinet	10	20	30	15	Sec'y Labor 1948, Gov. MA

NAME	CATEGORY	SIG	LS/DS	ALS	SP	COMMENT
Tocqueville, Alexis de	Author	45	140	350		Fr.Politician,Statesman,Writer
Tod, David	Governor	10	26			Governor OH
Today Show (Early)	Entertainment	35			75	
Todd, Alexander Robertus, Sir	Science	30	85		40	Nobel Chemistry 1957
Todd, Ann	Entertainment	20			40	
Todd, Charles Scott	Celebrity	5	15	40		
Todd, Richard	Entertainment	7			20	
Todd, Robert	Aviation	15	30	45	25	
Todd, Thelma	Entertainment	150	195	350	500	
Tognini, Michel	Astronaut	15	25		25	
Togo, Heihachiro	Military	95	315	495	185	Jap. Adm. Sino-Jap. War
Togo, Shigenori	Diplomat	250			400	Jap. Foreign Minister-Statesman
Tojo, Hideki	Military	250	700	1500	475	
Toklas, Alice B.	Author	30	95	200		Companion of Gertrude Stein
Tokody, Ilona	Entertainment	5			25	Opera
Tokyo Rose (Iva I. Toguri)	Military	225	330		250	WW II Radio Propagandist
Toledo, Francisco, Cardinal	Clergy	15000				
Toler, Sidney	Entertainment	150			425	Charlie Chan
Tolkien, John Ronald R.	Author	350	1250	1575		ALS/Content $2,000
Tolstoy, Leo, Count	Author	1200		2965	1750	Rus. Novelist
Tombaugh, Clyde W.	Science	40	180	265	100	Am. Astronomer, Proved Pluto
Tomei, Marissa	Entertainment	25			80	
Tomlin, Lily	Entertainment	5		15	25	
Tompkins, Angel	Entertainment	10	15	20	25	Pin-Up SP $35
Tompkins, Daniel (V)	Vice Pres.	85	320	475		Monroe VP, Governor NY
Tompson, Alexander K.	Clergy	15	25	35		
Tone, Franchot	Entertainment	20		35	45	
Toombs, Robert Augustus	Civil War	135	250	350		CSA General & Sec'y State
Toomey, Regis	Entertainment	15	20		45	
Toones, Fred "Snowflake"	Entertainment	150			300	
Toorop, Jan (Dutch)	Artist	20	100	210	125	Posters, Tiles, Stained Glass
Topal	Entertainment	10			30	
Topp, Erich	Military	35		175	95	Ger. U Boat Cmdr. WW II
Topping, Dan	Business	10	15	30	15	Millionaire Owner NY Yankees
Torisu, Kennosuke	Military	60		175	75	
Tork, Peter	Entertainment	10	35		20	Singer-Actor "The Monkees"
Torme, Mel	Entertainment	15			25	Vocalist, Composer
Torn, Rip	Entertainment	10			20	
Torrence, Ridgely	Author	10	25	40	15	Am. Poet, Editor, Dramatist
Torres, Raquel	Entertainment	20			45	
Torrey, R.A.	Clergy	20	35	50		
Tors, Ivan	Entertainment	15			35	Producer-Director
Toscanini, Arturo	Entertainment	300	500	1150	795	AMusQS $750, AMusMs $3,750
Tosti, Paolo	Composer	25	60	155		It.
Toto	Entertainment	65			295	
Totten, Jos. G.	Civil War	15	35	70		Union Gen. Wardte DS $400
Totter, Audrey	Entertainment	5	15		15	Pin-Up SP $20
Toucey, Isaac 1792-1869	Cabinet	25	80	130		Att'y Gen. 1848, Sec'y Navy '57
Toulouse-Lautrec, Henri	Artist	1050	3200	5900		Fr. Parisian Nightlife. Lithogr
Toumanova, Tamara	Entertainment	30			95	Rus-Am Ballerina
Tourel, Jennie	Entertainment	20			50	Opera
Tourgee, Albion W.	Author	15	20	35		Lawyer, Judge, Diplomat
Tower, John	Senate/Congress	5	15		25	Senator TX
Tower, Zealous B.	Civil War	20	35	55		Union General
Towers, Constance	Entertainment	5	6	10	10	
Towl, E. Clinton	Business	20		55		

NAME	CATEGORY	SIG	LS/DS	ALS	SP	COMMENT
Townes, Charles Hanson	Science	25	40	65		Inventor
Townley, James	Clergy	35	50	75		
Townsand, Colleen (Evans)	Entertainment	5	9	20	15	
Townsend, Edward Davis	Civil War	30	55	60		Union General
Townsend, Francis Everett	Science	40			150	Social Reformer & Physician
Townsend, Frederick	Civil War	15	30	45		Union General
Townsend, George A. (Gath)	Author	15		40		War Correspondent
Townsend, Lynn	Business	10	20	35	15	CEO-Pres. Chrysler Corp.
Townsend, M. Clifford	Governor	10	15			Governor IN
Townsend, Pete	Entertainment	30			70	Lead Singer "The Who"
Townsend, Peter	Military	10	35	50	25	
Townsend, Robert	Entertainment	10	15		20	Film Director
Townsend, Washington	Senate/Congress	10	20			Rep. PA 1969
Toynbee, Arnold 1852-83	Author	25	105	190	75	Br. Historian, Sociologist
Toynbee, Arnold Joseph	Author	20	45	120	30	Br.Historian, Prof.,Peace Conf.
Tracy, Arthur	Entertainment	20			45	"The Street Singer"
Tracy, Benjamin F.	Cabinet	20	45	70		Sec'y Navy 1889
Tracy, Edward Dorr	Civil War	190	500	725		CSA Gen., War Dte.DS $800
Tracy, Lee	Entertainment	10			25	
Tracy, Spencer	Entertainment	175	300	375	425	
Train, Arthur	Author	10	15	35		
Trapier, James Heyward	Civil War	140	290	420		CSA General
Trask, Diana	Country Music	10			20	
Traubel, Helen	Entertainment	45			100	Opera. Am. Soprano
Travalena, Fred	Entertainment	5	8	15	15	
Travanti, Daniel J.	Entertainment	6	8	15	20	
Traven, Berwick (Torsvan)	Author	265	800	1765		Ger. Novelist, Actor, Pacifist
Travers, Henry	Entertainment	100			250	
Travers, Patricia	Entertainment	5		10	15	
Traverso, Giuseppe	Entertainment	15			45	Opera
Travis, Merle	Country Music	20			40	
Travis, Randy	Country Music	15			30	
Travis, William Barret	Military		5000			Co-Cmdr. Alamo.Texas Frontier
Travolta, John	Entertainment	9	10	20	25	
Treacher, Arthur	Entertainment	25		40	45	Perrenial Br. Butler
Treadway, Allen Towner	Senate/Congress	4	15			Rep. MA 1913
Treadwell, John	Revolutionary War	25	60	95		Del. CT. Elected to Cont.Congr.
Treas, Terri	Entertainment	3	3	6	6	
Trebek, Alex	Entertainment	9	10	20	25	
Tree, Herbert Beerbohm, Sir	Entertainment	30	85	135	75	Br.Actor-Mgr.Fndr.Royal Academy
Treen, Mary	Entertainment	10	15	30	25	
Treilhard, Jean-Baptiste	Fr.Revolution	10	25	50		Fr. Politician
Tremayne, Les	Entertainment	5			20	
Trench, Richard C., Archbishop	Clergy	45	60	95	65	
Trenholm, George A.	Civil War	70	145	250		CSA Sec'y Treasury
Trent, William	Celebrity		600			
Trettner, Henrich 'Heniz	Aviation	20	45		50	
Trevelyan, George Otto, Sir	Author	15	35	65		Br.Historian,Sec'y To Admiralty
Treves, Frederick, Dr.	Science	200		440		Dr. To "Elephant Man"
Trevor, Claire	Entertainment	15			30	
Trilling, Lionel	Author	10	25	55		Am. Lit. Critic. Professor
Trimble, Isaac Ridgeway	Civil War	200	900			CSA General
Trinh, Eugene	Astronaut	8			20	
Tripler, Charles E.	Science	75	185			Inventor Liquid Air
Tripplehorn, Jeanne	Entertainment	25			80	
Trist, Nicholas P.	Diplomat	75	225			Am.Negotiated Treaty Guadaloupe

NAME	CATEGORY	SIG	LS/DS	ALS	SP	COMMENT
Tritt, Travis	Country Music	15			40	
Tritton, William Ashbee, Sir	Science	25	70	125	40	Developed Military Tank
Trollope, Anthony	Author	95	225	350		Br. Novelist. 50 Novels
Trollope, Frances	Author	30	115	225		Br. Novelist. Mother of Anthony
Trotsky, Leon	Head of State	950	1950	3200	1050	Communist leader-Assassinated
Trotter, Mark C.	Clergy	15		35		
Troubridge, Thomas, Sir	Military	75		250		Br. Admiral, Battle of the Nile
Troup, Bobby	Entertainment	10			20	Pianist, Composer, Vocalist
Trower, Robin	Entertainment	15			30	
Troyanos, Tatiana	Entertainment	15			35	Opera
Truax. Ernest	Entertainment	10	15		30	
Trudeau, Gary*	Cartoonist	30			175	Doonesbury
Trudeau, Pierre	Head of State	25	65	90	80	Prime Minister Canada
Trueblood, D. Elton	Clergy	15	30	45	35	
Truett, George W.	Clergy	15	35	50	35	
Truffaut, Francois	Entertainment	55	160			Dir. & Critic, ALS/Content $800
Trujillo, Rafael	Head of State	35	80		45	Dominican Republic.Assassinated
Truly, Richard H.	Astronaut	20	75		40	
Truman, Bess W.	First Lady	55	140	235	175	
Truman, Harry S.	President	275	585	4000	740	ALS/Content $14,000
Truman, Margaret (Daniel)	First Family	25	35	80	30	Daughter Of Harry S. Truman
Truman,Harry (Mt.St.Helens)	Celebrity	5		25	25	Resident Volcano Eruption
Trumbo, Dalton	Author	50	200		75	Blacklisted Oscar Winner.
Trumbull, John 1750-1831	Author-Lawyer	75	230			CT Poet & Lawyer
Trumbull, John 1756-1843	Artist	90	275	425		ALS Content $8,000
Trumbull, Jonathan 1710-85	Revolutionary War	295	365	900		Supplied Cont. Army,"Bro. John"
Trumbull, Jonathan 1740-09	Military-Senate	125	300	565		Sec'y Washington's Staff
Trumbull, Lyman	Senate	25	80	140	95	U.S. Senate IL 1855-1873
Trump, Donald J.	Business	10	60	75	50	Millionaire Entrepreneur
Trump, Ivana	Celebrity	10			40	Ex Mrs. Donald Trump
Trump, Marla Maples	Celebrity	15			40	Current Mrs. Donalt Trump
Truscott, L.K., Jr.	Military	15	40			
Truth, Sojourner	Abolitionist					RARE in any form. 3 Known
Truxton, Thomas	Revolutionary War	110	320	675		Cmdr. USS Constellation
Truxton, William Talbot	Civil War	20	45	75		Union Naval Officer. Adm. 1882
Tryggvason, Bjarni	Astronaut	5			16	
Tryon, Tom	Entertainment	10	20	25	20	Author-Actor
Tryon, William	Revolutionary War	145	375	770		Colon'l Gov. NC, NY
Tshombe, Moise	Head of State	40	75	145	90	Katanga Pr.,Zaire(Congo Rep.)
Tsongas, Paul E.	Senator	15		25	20	Senator MA, Pres. Hopeful
Tubb, Ernest	Country Music	15			35	
Tubb, Justin	Country Music	5			10	
Tuchman, Barbara W.	Author	35		155	45	2 Time Pulitzer Pr., Historian
Tucker, Forest	Entertainment	25	30	40	45	
Tucker, Orrin	Entertainment	15			25	Big Band Leader
Tucker, Richard	Entertainment	20	25		105	Opera
Tucker, Samuel	Revolutionary War	125	325	675		Am. Naval Hero. Commodore
Tucker, Sophie	Entertainment	20			55	
Tucker, Tanya	Entertainment	6	8		25	
Tucker, Thomas	Revolutionary War	45	115	225		Soldier, Statesman, Treasurer
Tucker, Tilghman M.	Senate/Congress	15	30	55		Senator 1838, Governor MS 1841
Tudor, Anthony	Entertainment	35			125	
Tuell, Jack M., Bishop	Clergy	20	25	35	30	
Tufts, Cotton	Revolutionary War	75	175			Highly Esteemed Physician
Tufts, Sonny	Entertainment	20	25		35	
Tulford, Nellie Hughes	Astronaut	5			16	

NAME	CATEGORY	SIG	LS/DS	ALS	SP	COMMENT
Tully, Alice	Celebrity	16	30		20	Lincoln Ctre. Tully Hall
Tully, Grace G.	White House	10	25	50	20	Sec'y to FDR
Tully, Tom	Entertainment	25			45	
Tully, Tom	Cabinet	5	15	35	15	
Tumulty, Joseph P.	White House	15	35	75	40	Aide to President Wilson
Tune, Tommy	Entertainment	6	8	15	20	Dancer, Choreographer
Tunnell, James M.	Senate/Congress	10	30		25	Senator DE 1940
Tunney, John V.	Senate/Congress	5	10		10	Rep., Senator CA
Turgenev, Ivan 1818-33	Author	205	525	1150		Russ. Novelist, Dramatist
Turkel, Ann	Entertainment	4	6		15	Pin-Up SP $20
Turkel, Studs	Author	10	20	35	20	Columnist. TV Commentator
Turner, J. M. W.	Artist	225	605	1500		Br. Landscape Painter
Turner, Janine	Entertainment	20			80	
Turner, John Wesley	Civil War	100	125	300		Union General
Turner, Kathleen	Entertainment	10			40	Pin-Up SP $45
Turner, Lana	Entertainment	20			45	Pin-Up SP $50
Turner, Morrie	Cartoonist	5			20	Wee Pals
Turner, Philip	Revolutionary War	55	135	275		Unrivalled Sugeon During War
Turner, Roscoe, Col.	Aviation	75			200	Pioneer Aviator
Turner, Ted	Business	10	75		30	
Turner, Tina	Entertainment	15	20	40	45	
Turpie, David	Senator/Congress	15	25	35		Senator IN 1863
Turpin, Ben	Entertainment	150			450	
Turreau De Garambouville	Fr. Revolution	20		85		
Turtles	Entertainment	35			75	
Tuttle, Lurene	Entertainment	5	6	15	15	Radio Dramatic Star
Tuttle, Wes & Marilyn	Country Music	15			30	
Tutu, Desmond, Bishop	Clergy	65	100	225	145	Nobel Peace Prize
Tutwiler, Margaret D.	Cabinet	10	15		15	Ass'y Sec'y State
Tuve, Merle Antony 1901-82	Science	35	80	155	50	Neutron, Ionosphere, Radar
Twain, Mark (see Clemens)	Author	750		2500		
Tweed, Shannon	Entertainment	6	10	20	25	Pin-Up SP $30
Tweed, William Marcy 'Boss'	Political Giant	120	230	385	350	Corrupt Tammany Hall Politician
Twiggs, David Emanuel	Civil War & 1812	200	375	715		CSA General
Twiggy	Entertainment	10		15	20	
Twining, Nathan F.	Aviation	45	135	185	65	Gen. WW II
Twiss, Peter	Aviation	7	15	30	20	
Twitty, Conway	Country Music	40			70	
Two Gun White Calf	Blackfoot Chief	225			940	Chief posed for Buffalo Nickel
Tydings, Millard E.	Senate/Congress	20	50		25	Rep., Senator MD, Author
Tyler, Beverly	Entertainment	5			20	
Tyler, Bonnie	Entertainment	15			30	
Tyler, Edward Burnett, Sir	Science	15	30	50		!st Prof. Anthropology Oxford
Tyler, Gerald E.	Aviation	10	25	40	30	ACE, WW II
Tyler, John	President	400	1575	1250		As VP. ALS/Content $7,500
Tyler, Julia Gardiner	First Lady	195	545		650	Special DS $1,100
Tyler, Moses Coit	Author	5	15	25		Historian. Am. Historical Assoc
Tyler, Robert C.	Civil War	220	580	850		CSA General
Tyler, Royall	Revolutionary War	20	50	120		Jurist, Author, Playwright
Tyler, T. Texas	Country Music	15			30	
Tyler, Tom	Entertainment	60			150	
Tyndale, Hector	Civil War	30	55	85	150	Union General
Tyndall, John	Science	45	85	175		Irish Physicist, Philosopher
Tyner, James N.	Cabinet	10	40	75		P. M. General 1876
Tyner, McCoy	Entertainment	10	20		30	Jazz Pianist-Composer
Tyson, Cicely	Entertainment	5	10	20	15	

U

NAME	CATEGORY	SIG	LS/DS	ALS	SP	COMMENT
U-2 (All)	Entertainment	185			300	Irish Rock Group
Ubico Casteneda, Jorge	Head of State	25	75			
Udall, Morris K.	Senate/Congress	4			10	Rep. AZ
Udet, Ernst	Aviation	225	375	700	475	ACE, WW I, German Ace
Ueberroth, Peter	Business	10	25	40	10	
Uecker, Bob	Entertainment	5	8	15	15	
Ufford, Edward S.	Clergy	40	50	70		
Uggams, Leslie	Entertainment	5	10	15	20	
Ullman, Liv	Entertainment	6	8	20	30	
Ullman, Tracey	Entertainment	20			50	
Ulmanis, Karlis	Head of State	90				1st Pres. Latvia. Fate Unknown
Ulmar, Geraldine	Entertainment	6	8	15	15	
Umberto I (It)	Royalty	50	150	375		King Italy
Umeki, Miyoshi	Entertainment	245			450	
Umstead, William B.	Governor	5	15	20		Governor NC
Underwood, Oscar W.	Senate/Congress	4	10		10	Rep., Senator AL
Unger, Jim	Cartoonist	15	20		25	Henry
Unreal, Minerva	Entertainment	25			60	
Unruh, Howard B.	Celebrity	80				
Untermeyer, Louis	Author	20	55	90	25	Am. Poet,Critic,Satirist,Biogr.
Updike, John	Author	25	75	150	40	Am. Novelist,Poet,Short Story
Upjohn, E. Gifford, Dr.	Business	125	450			Founder Upjohn Pharmaceuticals
Upshaw, Dawn	Entertainment	10			25	Opera
Upshaw, William D.	Senate/Congress	5	15		10	Rep. GA 1919, Evangelist
Upshur, Abel Parker	Cabinet	25	65	80		Tyler Sec'y Navy
Upton, Emory	Civil War	25	55	85		Union Gen. Wardte DS $465
Urbanowicz, Witold A.	Aviation	30	70	125	60	Pol. ACE, WW II
Ure, Mary	Entertainment	5	10	20	20	
Urey, Harold Clayton	Science	90	295	550		Nobel in Chemistry 1934
Urich, Robert	Entertainment	10	15	25	30	
Uris, Leon	Author	20	75	125	65	Am. Novelist
Urso, Camilla	Entertainment	25			40	Fr. Violinist
Urvanowicz, Witold A.	Aviation	20	45	75	50	ACE, WW II, Polish Ace
Usher, John P.	Cabinet	40	110	195		Sec'y Interior 1863-65
Ustinov, Peter	Entertainment	25	45	60	75	And Playwright, Author
Utrillo, Maurice	Artist	155	395	650	200	Fr. Montmartre, Paris Scenes

V

NAME	CATEGORY	SIG	LS/DS	ALS	SP	COMMENT
Vaccaro, Brenda	Entertainment	4	6	15	10	
Vaccaro, Tracy	Entertainment	5			15	Pin-Up SP $30
Vacio, Natividad	Entertainment	3	3	6	6	
Vadim, Roger	Entertainment	20			50	
Vai, Steve	Entertainment	15			35	Rock
Valdengo, Giuseppe	Entertainment	15			40	Opera
Valens, Richie	Entertainment	500	600		1000	
Valenti, Jack	Entertainment	5	10		15	Pres. Moving Picture Assoc.
Valentine, Karen	Entertainment	4	6	10	15	
Valentine, Lewis	Law	35	105		50	Legend'y NY Police Commissioner
Valentino, Rudolph	Entertainment	1000		1550	2200	
Valery, Paul A. 1871-1945	Author	45	105	170		Fr. Noted Poet, Philosopher
Valette, A.J.M.	Fr. Revolution	15		75		
Valetti, Cesare	Entertainment	20			50	Opera
Vallandigham, Clement L.	Civil War	115		325		Civil War "Copperhead"
Vallee, Rudy	Entertainment	15	35	45	35	
Vallejo, Mariano Guadalupe	Military	140	450			Early CA Off'l & Military Leadr
Valli, Frankie	Entertainment	15			45	Singer
Vallone, Raf	Entertainment	5	6	15	15	
Van Allan, Richard	Entertainment	5			25	Opera
Van Allen, James	Science	40	135	260	100	Nobel Physics
Van Ark, Joan	Entertainment	5	8	15	15	
Van Buren, Abigail	Journalist	5	15	30	10	Am. Syndicated Columnist
Van Buren, Angelica	First Lady					NRPA
Van Buren, Hannah	First Lady					No Known Examples
Van Buren, James D.	Gov't Official	5	15			Son of Pres. Van Buren
Van Buren, Martin	President	335	990	725		DS As Pres. $975- $2,500
Van Buren, Raeburn*	Cartoonist	10			50	Abbie & Slats
Van Cleef, Lee	Entertainment	25			45	
Van Dam, Rip 1662-1736+	Colonial America	60	175	360		Merchant,Politics,Col. Gov. NY
Van Damme, Jean-Claude	Entertainment	15			55	
Van Den Berg, Lodewik, Dr.	Astronaut	5			16	
Van Devanter, Willis (SC)	Supreme Court	40	125	200	75	
Van Dine, S.S. (W.H.Wright)	Author	45	100	200	225	Created Philo Vance
Van Dongen, Kees	Artist	30	45	120		Fauvist Painter, Portraitist
Van Doren, Carl	Author	15	45	95	20	Pulitzer in Biography
Van Doren, Mamie	Entertainment	10	15	25	25	Pin-Up SP $35
Van Doren, Mark	Author	10	30	50	25	Critic, Editor, Pulitzer Poetry
Van Dorn, Earl	Civil War	250		685		CSA General
Van Dresser, Marcia	Entertainment	15			40	Vintage Actress
Van Druten, John W.	Author	10	20	35	15	Playwright, Novelist
Van Dusen, Henry P.	Clergy	15	15	25	20	
Van Dyck, M. Ernest	Entertainment	15	25		40	Tenor

NAME	CATEGORY	SIG	LS/DS	ALS	SP	COMMENT
Van Dyke, Dick	Entertainment	5	8	15	20	
Van Dyke, Henry	Clergy-Author	35	50	105		Minister To Netherlands-Luxem.
Van Dyke, Jerry	Entertainment	5			20	
Van Dyke, Nicholas 1738-89	Revolutionary War	110	305	625		Statesman, Continental Congress
Van Fleet, James, Gen.	Military	20	75	95	40	Gen. WW II
Van Fleet, Jo	Entertainment	10	20	45	40	
Van Halen (All)	Entertainment	40			100	Rock
Van Halen (all-original)	Entertainment	80			170	Rock
Van Halen, Alex	Entertainment	20			50	
Van Halen, Eddie	Entertainment	25	30		50	Rock
Van Heusen, James (Jimmy)	Composer	60	90	175	75	AMusQS $250
Van Hoften, James D.	Astronaut	5			20	
Van Horn, Burt	Senate/Congress	10	20			Rep. NY 1861, Manufacturer
Van Horne, David	Revolutionary War	10		75		
Van Kirk, Theodore	Aviation	50	130		95	
Van Loon, Hendrik Willem	Author	15	30	65	40	Historian, Journalist, Lecturer
Van Loon, William	Journalist	10		50		Lecturer
Van Ness, Cornelius P.	Governor	15	35	60		Jurist, Gov. VT, Minister Sp.
Van Nuys, Frederick	Senate/Congress	10			25	Senator IN 1932
Van Patten, Dick	Entertainment	5	6	15	15	
Van Patten, Joyce	Entertainment	4	4	10	15	
Van Rensselaer, Henry	Civil War	225				Rep. NY 1841, Union General
Van Sloon, Edward	Entertainment	125			250	
Van Stade, Frederica	Entertainment	15			45	Opera
Van Sweringen, Otis P.	Business	15	40	90	35	RR Exec-Developer Shaker Height
Van Valkenburgh, Debbie	Entertainment	6	8	15	15	
Van Vechten, Carl	Author	40	80	220	45	Am. Novelist, Staff NY Times
Van Vleck, John H., Dr.	Science	30	45	75		Nobel Physics 1977
Van Vliet, Stewart	Civil War	45		100		Union Gen.
Van Vooren, Monique	Entertainment	4	6	10	15	Pin-Up SP $25
Van Wagoner, Murray D.	Governor	5	20		15	Governor MI
Van Wyck, Charles Henry	Civil War	40	70	90		Union General, Senator NE
Van Zandt, Philip	Entertainment	50			150	
Van Zant, Ronnie	Entertainment	25			100	
Van Zealand, Paul, Viscount	Head of State	15			35	Premier Belgium, Foreign Min.
Van, Bobby	Entertainment	5			20	Dancer
Van, Gloria	Entertainment	5	6	15	15	
Van, Isabelle	Entertainment	5			10	Dancer
Van, Jackie	Entertainment	5			15	Dancer
Vance, Cyrus	Cabinet	10	20	35	25	Sec'y State, Sec'y Army
Vance, Louis Joseph	Author	15	35	90		Am. Novelist
Vance, Robert Brank	Civil War	60	145	225		CSA Gen., Rep. NC 1873
Vance, Vivian	Entertainment	125	150		250	
Vance, Zebulon Baird	Civil War	175		650		CSA Gov. NC, Opposed J.Davis
Vandamme, Dominique Rene	Napoleonic Wars	50	150	210		Battle of Waterloo
Vandenberg, Arthur H.	Senate/Congress	20	60		25	Senator MI, Pres. Pro Tem.
Vandenberg, Hoyt S.	Military-Aviation	25	150		100	
Vander Pyl, Jean	Entertainment	10			20	Voice Wilma-Pebbles Flintstone
Vanderbilt, Alfred Gwynn	Business	15	35	65	25	
Vanderbilt, Amy	Author	10	25	40	35	Columnist, Authority on Manners
Vanderbilt, Cornelius 1794-1877	Business	370	890	1100		"Commodore". Financier
Vanderbilt, Cornelius, Jr.	Business	20	75	105	35	RR Exec.,Head of Family 1885
Vanderbilt, George Washington	Business	50	145	270	100	"Biltmore House"
Vanderbilt, Gloria	Business	25	45	80	30	Fashion Designer
Vanderbilt, William H. 1821-85	Business	50	175	475	150	RR Exec., Philanthropist
Vanderbilt, William H., Jr.	Business	20	45	90	35	Governor RI

NAME	CATEGORY	SIG	LS/DS	ALS	SP	COMMENT
Vanderbilt, William K. 1849-1920	Business	55	220		125	RR Exec.,Financier-Yachtsman
Vandergrift, Alexander A.	Military	35	100	160	50	Marine Corps Gen. WW II
Vanderlyn, John 1775-1852	Artist	250		750		Am. Pres. Portraits, Capitol
Vane, John R., Dr.	Science	20	30	50	25	Nobel Medicine 1982
Vaness, Carol	Entertainment	10			35	Opera
Vanili, Milli	Entertainment	10			50	
Vanilla Ice	Entertainment	20			40	Rock
Vanity	Entertainment	4	7		15	Pin-Up SP $25
Vanzetti, Bartolomeo	Political Radical	600	1800	5650		Convicted Murderer,Electrocuted
Varese, Edgard	Composer	185	400	675		Fr.-Am. Music Pioneer
Varga, Francis	Celebrity	30				
Vargas, Alberto	Artist	135	350	575		Repro "Varga Girl" S $325-$450
Vargas, Getuilio	Head of State	50	150		75	Revolutionist Pres. Brazil.
Varick, Richard	Revolutionary War	75	200	290		Soldier, Washington's Sec'y
Varmus, Harold E., Dr.	Science	25	60		35	Nobel Medicine 1989
Varney, Astrid	Entertainment	5			25	Opera
Varney, Jim	Entertainment	10			25	
Vasquez, Roberta	Playboy Ctrfold	4			10	Pin-Up SP $20. Actress
Vassar, Matthew	Business	45	105	210		Founder Vassar College
Vassarely, Victor	Artist	55	130			Op Art Repro S $150
Vaubois, J.F.G.	Fr. Revolution	5	15	40		
Vaughan, Robert	Clergy	10	10	10		
Vaughn, George A.	Aviation	35	55	95	65	ACE, WW II
Vaughn, Herbert, Cardinal	Clergy	30	50	90	75	
Vaughn, John C.	Civil War	90				CSA Gen. Wardte. DS $2,500
Vaughn, Robert	Entertainment	5	8	15	15	
Vaughn, Sarah	Entertainment	35			100	Jazz Vocalist-Pianist
Vaughn, William S.	Business	4	10		10	Pres. Eastman Kodak
Vaughn-Williams, Ralph	Composer	105	320	425	150	Br. Symphonies To Theatrical
Vaux, Roberts	Philanthropist	110		450		Prison Reform, Houses of Refuge
Veach, Charles L.	Astronaut	5			15	
Vedder, Elihu	Artist	50	135	225		Drew From Dreams & Fantasy
Vedral, Joyce L.	Author	5			10	Non-Fiction
Vedrines, Jules	Aviation	200	395	650	265	
Vee, Bobby	Entertainment	5			15	
Veidt, Conrad	Entertainment	85	90	130	250	
Veit, Stan	Author	5	10	20	20	Computer Shopper, PC historian
Velez, Lupe	Entertainment	85	95	175	200	
Veloz & Yolanda	Entertainment	6	8	15	15	30-40's Ballroom Dance Team
Venable, Evelyn	Entertainment	15	20	40	35	
Venable, William Webb	Senate/Congress	5	15		10	Rep. MS 1916, Judge
Vendela	Entertainment	20			45	Model-Actress
Vendome, L.J., Duke de 1654-1712	Fr. Military	150	450			Marshal of France
Vera Ellen	Entertainment	20			45	Dancer, Films. Pin-Up SP $50
Verdi, Giuseppe	Composer	1000	1750	2275	5250	AMusQS $5,000, $5,700, $7,500
Verdon, Gwen	Entertainment	5	6	15	15	
Verdy, Violette	Entertainment	10			30	Opera
Vereen, Ben	Entertainment	5			20	
Vergennes, Chas. G.,Le Comte de	Statesman	175	375			Fr. Ambass. Supported Am. Rev.
Verlaine, Paul	Author	175	490	750		Fr. Symbolist Poet
Vermehren, Werner	Aviation	14	35	55	30	
Verne, Jules	Authors	185	655	1150		Fr. Sci-Fi Novelist
Vernier, Theodore, Count	Fr. Revolution	30	100			
Vessey, John W.	Military	10			30	
Vetch, Samuel 1668-1732	Colonial America	80	225	450		Colonial Governor
Vetri, Victoria	Entertainment	4			10	Pin-Up SP $20

NAME	CATEGORY	SIG	LS/DS	ALS	SP	COMMENT
Veverka, Jaroslav	Entertainment	20			45	Opera
Viardot, Pauline	Entertainment	30			100	
Vickers, Jon	Entertainment	15			45	Opera
Vickers, Martha	Entertainment	3	3	6	6	
Victor Emmanuel II (It)	Royalty	70	250	475	100	
Victor Emmanuel III & B.Mussolini	Royalty, Hd of St					Fine DS by both $850-$1050
Victor, Claude Perrin	Military	30	75	140		
Victoria, Empress (Fred. III, Ger)	Royalty	30		125		Eldest Daughter Queen Victoria
Victoria, Mary Louisa	Royalty	40	110	175		Mother of Q. Victoria
Victoria, Queen	Royalty	145	550	925	1385	
Victors, Henry	Entertainment	65			200	
Vidal, Gore	Author	10	20	30	15	Am. Novelist,Playwright,Critic
Vidor, Florence	Entertainment	30	35	65	60	
Vidor, King	Entertainment	25			55	Film Director. LS/Cont. $250
Vieira, Meredith	TV News	4			15	Commentator
Viele, Egbert L.	Civil War	25	40	55	85	Union General, Engineer
Vigneaud, Vincent du	Science	10	25	45	15	
Vigran, Herb	Entertainment	10	15		20	
Vila, George R.	Business	7	20	40	15	CEO Uniroyal Tire
Vilas, Jack	Aviation	6	16			
Vilas, William F.	Cabinet	15	30	45	35	P.M. Gen., Sec'y Interior 1888
Viljoen, Benjamin	Celebrity	5	15	40	10	
Viljoenk, B.J.	Military	35		145		
Villa, Francesco (Pancho)	Military	550	1975	3050	1125	Guerilla Leader, Revolutionary
Villa-Lobos, Hector	Composers	100	225	525	125	AMusQS $500
Villalpando, Catalina Vasquez	Cabinet	15			30	US Treasurer
Villechaize, Herve	Entertainment	15	25		35	
Villiers, Frederic	Artist	10	20	50	25	
Vincent, Jan-Michael	Entertainment	10		15	20	
Vincent, Romo	Entertainment	5	10	20	15	
Vincent, Stenio J.i	Head of State	125				Pres. Haiti. Lawyer, Diplomat
Vincent, Thomas M.	Civil War	30	55	100		Union General, Bvt.
Vinci, Leonardo da	Artist	5100	13000	34000		NRPA
Vinson, Carl	Senate/Congress	5	20		10	Rep. GA 1914
Vinson, Frederick M. (SC)	Supreme Court	95	235	425	200	Chief Justice, Cabinet, Rep. KY
Vinson, Helen	Entertainment	15	20	40	35	
Vinton, Bobby	Composer	5			15	AMusQS $40
Vinton, David	Civil War	125	325			Union Gen., 1st P.O.W.
Vinton, Will	Celebrity	12	25			
Virchow, Rudolf 1821-1902	Science	175		850		Founder Cellular Pathology
Virtanen, A. I.	Science	30	85	140	50	Nobel Chemistry 1945
Vishinsky, Andrei	Head of State	70	230	580	120	Rus.1st Deputy Foreign Minister
Visitor, Nana	Entertainment	15			35	"Star Trek"
Vittor, Frank	Artist	40		165		
Vivian, Richard H. Sir	Revolutionary War	45	125	255		
Vlaminck, Maurice de	Artist	105	235	650	325	Fr. Fauvist Painter
Voelker, John D.	Author	5	10	15	15	
Voight, Deborah	Entertainment	5			25	Opera
Voight, Jon	Entertainment	5		20	25	
Voisin, Gabriel	Aviation	65	135	225	125	Fr. Airplane Mfg. Pioneer
Vokes, Christopher	Military	15	30	40	25	
Vokes, Rosina	Entertainment	6	8	15	15	
Volcker, Paul A.	Cabinet	5		10	10	Chm. Federal Reserve
Volkov, Vladislav	Cosmonaut	75			160	
Voll, John J.	Aviation	18	40	65	45	ACE, WW II
Volstead, Andrew J.	Senate/Congress	70	210	250		Rep. MN 1903. Volstead Act

NAME	CATEGORY	SIG	LS/DS	ALS	SP	COMMENT
Volta, Alessandro	Science	400	2500	2500		Volt, Electrical Unit, For Him
Voltaire, Francoise Marie	Author	400	1885	2760		Fr. Writer-Philosopher
Volz, Nedra	Entertainment	4			10	
Von Behr, Henrich, Baron	Military	10			30	
Von Braun, Wernher	Science	75	540	740	295	Ger-Am Rocket Pioneer
Von Bulow, Claus	Celebrity	15	25		20	Danish Count. Accused Murderer
Von Debizka, Hedwig	Entertainment	40			150	Opera
Von Däniken, Erich	Author	10	30	75	20	Sci-Fi
Von Edelsheim, Macmilian	Military	20			45	Panzer General
Von Gazen, Waldemar	Military	20			50	Panzer General
Von Gronau, Wolfgang	Aviation	40			175	
Von Gronau, Wolfgang	Aviation	165			500	Ger. ACE, WW I
Von Hesse-Nassau, Adolph	Royalty	100	300			1st Duke of Luxembourg
Von Kleist, Paul	Military	50	85		100	Ger. WW II Tank Commander
Von Kretchmer, Otto	Military	35	90			Top Ger. U Boat Cmdr. WW II
Von Oy, Jenna	Entertainment	5			15	"Blossom"
Von Papen, Franz	Military	95	200	395	175	Ger.Acquitted Major War Crimes
Von Paulus, Friedrich	Military	165	600			Ger. WW II Field Marshal
Von Sauken, Dietrich	Military	25			75	Panzer General
Von Sternberg, Joseph	Entertainment	30	100		45	Film Director
Von Stroheim, Erich	Entertainment	150			300	Vintage Film Director
Von Sydow, Max	Entertainment	10		15	20	
Von Tilzer, Albert	Composer	30	110	200	45	Founder ASCAP
Von Trapp, Maria, Baroness	Celebrity	35	90	175	45	"Sound of Music" Fame
Von Zell, Harry	Entertainment	10	15	25	25	Radio Announcer-Comedian
Von der Chevaerie, Kurt	Military	10			40	
Vonnegut, Kurt	Author	20	90	105	50	Am. Black-Humor Novels.
Voorhees, Daniel W.	Senate/Congress	15	40			Rep., Senator IN 1861
Vorster, Balthazar J	Head of State	25	70	165	50	Prime Minister South Afr.
Voss, James	Astronaut	5			14	
Voss, Janet	Astronaut	5			10	
Vosseller, Aurelius B.	Military	35	95			
Voysey, Charles	Clergy	35	50	75		
Vraciu, Alex	Aviation	15	25	50	35	ACE, WW II
Vuillard, Edouard	Artist	140	290	700		Fr.Painter,Printmaker, Illustr.

W

NAME	CATEGORY	SIG	LS/DS	ALS	SP	COMMENT
Wade, Benjamin Franklin	Senate/Congress	40	95	160		Senator OH 1851-69
Wade, Leigh	Aviation	30	55	100	45	
Wadopian, Eliot	Entertainment	10			25	Bassist. Paul Winter Consort
Wadsworth, James S.	Civil War	50	95	185		Union Gen.
Wadsworth, James W., Jr.	Senate/Congress	12	30			Senator NY
Wadsworth, Jeremiah 1743-1804	Revolutionary War	145	490	585		Army Officer. Rep. CT. Merchant
Wadsworth, Peleg	Revolutionary War	105	315			General, Aide Artemas Ward
Waesche, R.R.	Military	20	50			US Coast Guard Commandant

NAME	CATEGORY	SIG	LS/DS	ALS	SP	COMMENT
Waggin, Patti	Entertainment	3	3	6	6	
Wagner, Jane	Author	10	15		20	Playwright. Emmy & Peabody
Wagner, Lindsay	Entertainment	6	8	15	20	
Wagner, Richard	Composer	1000	1865	3250	2750	ALS/Content $5,000, $5,500
Wagner, Robert	Entertainment	15	15	25	30	
Wagner, Robert F.	Senate/Congress	25	120	225	40	Senate NY 1926, Wagner Act
Wagoner, Porter	Country Music	5			15	
Waigel, Theo, Dr.	Ger. Government	4	10		12	Ger. Government Official
Wainwright, Jonathan	Military	125	270	315	225	Gen. WW II
Waite, H. Roy	Aviation	15	25	40		
Waite, Morrison R. (SC)	Supreme Court	40	95	170	60	Chief Justice Supreme Court
Waite, Ralph	Entertainment	5	6	15	15	
Waite, Terry	Hostage	30		40	35	Also Hostage Negotiator
Wakely, Jimmy	Country Music	30			100	
Wakeman, Rick	Entertainment	15			30	
Waksman, Selman A., Dr.	Science	40	75	95	60	Nobel Medicine 1952
Walburn, Raymond	Entertainment	10	15	45	35	
Walcott, Fred C.	Senate/Congress	10	30			Senator CT 1929. Mfg., Banker
Walcutt, Charles C.	Civil War	30	65	85		Union General
Wald, George	Science	15	30	50	25	Nobel Medicine 1967
Wald, Lillian D. 1867-1940	Reformer	30	90	175	50	1st City School Nurse Service
Waldheim, Kurt	Head of State	25	65	150	45	Prime Minister Austria
Waldo, Anna Lee	Author	15			20	
Waldron, Hicks B.	Business	5			10	CEO Heublein Inc.
Walesa, Lech	Head of State	25	65		110	Nobel Peace Pr., Pres. Poland
Walgreen, Charles Rudolph	Business	35	60	145		Pharmacist Fndr. Walgreen Drugs
Walken, Christopher	Entertainment	20		45	35	
Walker, Benjamin	Revolutionary War	105	315			Rev. Army Officer. Rep. NY
Walker, Bree	TV News	5			10	TV News
Walker, Charles	Astronaut	5			14	
Walker, Clint	Entertainment	35	50	100	125	
Walker, David M.	Astronaut	5			30	
Walker, Francis Amasa	Civil War	45	105	145		Union Gen. Rose From Private
Walker, Frank C.	Cabinet	5	15		10	P.M. General 1940
Walker, Fred L.	Military	10	35	50		
Walker, Gilbert C.	Governor	12	20	25		Gov. VA 1869, Rep. VA 1875
Walker, James	Clergy	15	20	45		
Walker, James J.	Politician	25	70	155	40	Mayor NYC. Corruption Charges
Walker, Jerry Jeff	Entertainment	10	15	30	35	
Walker, Jimmy	Entertainment	5			15	
Walker, John Brisben	Journalist	10	30			Editor Cosmopolitan Magazine
Walker, John George	Civil War	75	170	255		CSA General
Walker, Leroy Pope	Civil War		1100			CSA Gen.-1st CS Sec'y of War
Walker, Mary E.	Civil War	215		575		Union Nurse & Surgeon, CMH
Walker, Mort*	Cartoonist	15			75	Beetle Bailey
Walker, Nancy	Entertainment	20			40	
Walker, Robert J.	Cabinet	25	75	175		Polk Sec'y Treasury
Walker, Robert Jarvis C.	Senate/Congress	12	20			Rep. PA. 1881.
Walker, Robert, Sr.	Entertainment	50		150	155	
Walker, T. Bone	Entertainment	30			85	Jazz Guitar-Vocalist
Walker, Walton H.	Military	30	55	95	50	General. Killed in Korea 1950
Walker, William	Military					
Walker, Wm Henry Talbot	Civil War	130	270	520		CSA General
Wallace, Alfred R.	Science	75	160	300		Developed Theory of Evolution
Wallace, Dee	Entertainment	5	6	15	15	
Wallace, Dillon	Author	5	15	30	10	

NAME	CATEGORY	SIG	LS/DS	ALS	SP	COMMENT
Wallace, Edgar 1875-1932	Author	85	270	345	450	Popular Thriller Writer
Wallace, George C.	Governor	10			20	Governor AL
Wallace, Hal	Entertainment	15			40	
Wallace, Henry A. (VP)	Vice President	45	135	275	130	
Wallace, Henry C.	Cabinet	10	25	50	20	Sec'y Agriculture 1921
Wallace, Irving	Author	20	125	200	75	Am. Novelist
Wallace, Jean	Entertainment	10	15	20	25	
Wallace, John	Civil War	100	300			Black Leader 1860's
Wallace, Lewis "Lew"	Civil War, Author	85	300	500		Union Gen.-Statesman-Author
Wallace, Lila Acheson	Business	10	25	35	20	
Wallace, Lurleen B.	Governor	20	75		25	Governor AL
Wallace, Mike	Journalist	5	10	15	15	News Journalist." 60 Minutes"
Wallace, William H.	Civil War	85	258			CSA (Prices Courtesy Seagrave)
Wallach, Eli	Entertainment	5	6	15	15	
Wallburg, Donnie	Entertainment	10			45	
Wallenberg, Knut	Financier	60	155			Swe. Enskilda Bank, Statesman
Wallenstein, Alfred, Dr.	Conductor	20			75	Am. Cellist/Conductor
Waller, Littleton	Military	100				Marine General 1880-1920
Waller, Robert James	Author	5			10	Novelist
Waller, Thomas "Fats"	Composer	150	425	775	450	Jazz Pianist. AMusQS $900
Waller, Thomas M.	Governor	15	25	40		Governor CT 1883
Walley, Deborah	Entertainment	5	6	15	15	
Wallis, Barnes, Sir	Aviation	30	75			Br. Aircraft Designer. Inventor
Wallis, Ruth	Entertainment	10			25	
Wallis, Shani	Entertainment	4	5	8	6	
Wallmann, Jeff	Author	5	10	15	5	
Walpole, Horace	Author	150	450	1000		Br.Wit, Letter Writer, Novelist
Walpole, Hugh Seymour, Sir	Author	30	105	120		Novelist, Playwright,Biographer
Walpole, Robert, Sir, Earl Orford	Head of State	85	270	575		Prime Minister
Walpole, Spencer H.	Celebrity	5	15	25		
Walsh, Blanche	Entertainment	15			35	Vintage Actress
Walsh, David I.	Senate/Congress	10	15			Governor MA 1914, Senator 1919
Walsh, John	Entertainment	4	5		10	Fox TV Host
Walsh, Kenneth	Aviation	15	25	50	35	ACE, WW II, CMH
Walsh, M. Emmet	Entertainment	5	6	15	15	
Walsh, Raoul	Entertainment	35			75	Film Director
Walsh, Thomas J.	SenateCongress	15	40		20	Senator MT 1912
Walston, Ray	Entertainment	8	9	15	20	
Walter, Bruno	Entertainment	60			200	Ger. Conductor
Walter, Jessica	Entertainment	6	8	15	15	
Walters, Barbara	Entertainment	5	10	20	15	TV Anchor, Specials Hostess
Walters, Julie	Entertainment	5	6	15	15	
Walters, Vernon A.	Military	5		10		
Walthall, Edward C.	Civil War	85		305		CSA Gen.
Walthall, Henry B.	Entertainment	25		55	65	
Walton, Ernest T.S.,Dr.	Science	75				Nobel Physics 1951
Walton, George	Revolutionary War	170	525	995		Signer. ADS/Content $2,500
Walton, Gladys	Entertainment	5	6	15	15	
Walton, Jayne	Entertainment	5	6	15	10	
Walton, Sam M.	Business	70	145		80	Founder Walmark
Walton, William	Composer	35	90	195	150	AMusQS $375
Wambaugh, Joseph	Author	10	20	35	15	Am. Novelist re Law Enforcement
Wanamaker, John	Business-Cabinet	40	55	125	100	Dept. Store Pioneer, P.M. Gen.
Wang, Cheng-T'ing	Diplomat	20	60	90		Chin. Political Leader, Ambass.
Wang, Taylor	Astronaut	7			20	
Wapner, Jos. A., Judge	Jurist	4			12	TV Judge

NAME	CATEGORY	SIG	LS/DS	ALS	SP	COMMENT
War	Entertainment	15			35	Rock
Warburton, Irvine "Cotton"	Entertainment	30		45		Oscar Film Editor,Football Star
Ward, Aaron	Senate/Congress	15	35	50		General, War 1812, Rep. NY 1825
Ward, Artemas	Revolutionary War	350	1300			Revolutionary War Commander
Ward, Artemas (pseud of C.Browne)	Author	15	35	65	20	Humorist
Ward, Burt	Entertainment	20			50	"Bat Man"
Ward, David	Entertainment	10			35	Opera
Ward, Genevieve	Entertainment	3	5		8	
Ward, Henry 1732-97	Revolutionary War	150	430	870		Colon'l Cong.Pro Independence
Ward, J.H. Hobart	Civil War	35	60	75		Union General
Ward, John Quincy Adams	Sculptor	25	80	100	40	Am. Sculptor
Ward, Joseph, Sir	Head of State	15	25	60		PM New Zealand
Ward, Marcus L.	Senate/Congress	15	25			Rep. NJ 1873
Ward, Mary A. (Mrs. Humphrey)	Author	10	30	60		Br. Moral, Reforming Novels
Ward, Rachel	Entertainment	9	10	20	25	Pin-Up SP $30
Ward, Sela	Entertainment	15			30	
Warden, Jack	Entertainment	6	8	15	15	
Wardlaw, Ralph W.	Clergy	30	35	45		
Ware, Henry	Clergy	15	25	35	30	
Ware, Linda	Entertainment	3	5		15	40's Teen Singing Star in Films
Warfield, David	Entertainment	30	40	75	75	
Warfield, Marsha	Entertainment	5			20	
Warfield, William	Entertainment	6	8	20	25	
Warhol, Andy	Artist	150	320	575	240	Repro M.Monro S $2,000
Waring, Fred	Entertainment	15	45	50	35	Inventor of Waring Blender
Warner, A.P.(Borg-Warner)	Business	45	145		75	Fndr.Stewart-Warner.Speedometer
Warner, Adoniram J.	Civil War	25		115		Union Gen., Rep. OH 1879
Warner, Charles Dudley	Author	20	65	110		Am. Man of Letters, Essays
Warner, H.B.	Entertainment	25			65	
Warner, Harry M.	Business	95	285	395	150	Fndr. Warner Bros.(One oF Four)
Warner, Jack L.	Business	80	175	300	150	Fndr. Warner Bros.(One of Four)
Warner, James	Aviation	25		40		
Warner, John W.	Senate-Cabinet	10	15		10	Sec'y Navy 1972,Senator VA
Warner, Malcolm Jamal	Entertainment	10	30		25	
Warner, Seth 1743-84	Revolutionary War	200		1200		Officer.Leader With Ethan Allen
Warnow, Mark	Entertainment	10			25	Big Band Leader
Warrant	Entertainment	25			50	Rock
Warren Commission	Kennedy Assass.				975	Photograph of Entire Comm.
Warren, Chas. Marquis	Author	5	15	25	10	
Warren, Earl (SC)	Supreme Court	75	125	215	250	Chief Justice, Governor CA
Warren, Francis	Senate/Congress	15	25	40		CW CMH, Gov.,Senator WY
Warren, Gouverneur K.	Civil War	65	190	250		Union Gen., ALS/Cont. $1,250
Warren, Harry	Composer	30	100		40	AMusQS $450
Warren, James	Revolutionary War	110	375	540		Continental Army Paym'r
Warren, Jennifer	Entertainment	4		10	15	
Warren, Joseph 1741-1775	Revolutionary War	6875				Physician, Patriot. NRPA
Warren, Joseph, Sr.	Colonial America	45	135	175		
Warren, Lavinia	Entertainment	45			295	Mrs.Tom Thumb, Charles Stratton
Warren, Leonard	Entertainment	75			350	Opera
Warren, Leslie Ann	Entertainment	5	6	15	20	
Warren, Michael	Entertainment	3	3	10	15	
Warren, Robert Penn	Author	30	100	125	75	Am. Poet, Novelist. Pulitzers
Warrick, Ruth	Entertainment	9	10	20	25	
Warsitz, Erich	Aviation	15	35	65	40	
Warwick, Countess Evelyn F.	Celebrity	35	125			Mistress of Edward VII
Washburn, Bryant	Entertainment	5	9	20	20	

NAME	CATEGORY	SIG	LS/DS	ALS	SP	COMMENT
Washburn, Cadwallader C.	Civil War	45	75		85	Union Gen., Gov. WI 1855
Washburn, Israel, Jr.	Governor	30	80	135		Civil War Gov. ME
Washburn, W. D.	Senate/Congress	4	15			Rep. MN 1879, Senator 1889
Washburne, Elihu B.	Cabinet	20	40	70		Sec'y State 1869, Minister Fr.
Washington, Booker T.	Author	185	385	745	1000	Afro-Am. Educator-Author
Washington, Bushrod (SC)	Supreme Court	115	340	795		
Washington, Denzel	Entertainment	15	20		50	
Washington, Dinah	Entertainment	125			200	Vocalist
Washington, George	President	4285	13800	24000		
Washington, George C.	Senate/Congress	15	35	55		Rep. MD 1827
Washington, Harold	Senate/Congress	4	15	35	15	Rep. IL 1981,Mayor Chicago 1983
Washington, John A.	Civil War	125		590		CSA Lt.Col.,Gen. R.E.
Washington, Ned	Composer	45			100	
Washington, William 1752-1810	Military	65	165	315		Patriot. General
Wassel, Corydon M., Dr.	Military	45	85	150	50	Med.Missionary China.WW II Hero
Wasserman, Dale	Composer	15		35	30	"Man of LaMancha"
Watanabe, Gedde	Entertainment	9	10	20	25	
Waterhouse, Benjamin 1754-1846	Science	255	765	1500		Pioneer in Vaccination
Waterhouse, J. W.	Artist	10		50		
Waterhouse, Richard	Civil War	150	320	550		CSA General
Waterloo, Stanley	Author	10	20	35		
Waterman, F.D.	Business	75	195			Waterman Pen
Waterman, W.	Aviation	15		25		
Waters, Ethel	Entertainment	55	135		100	Actress-Singer
Waters, Muddy	Entertainment	20	100		50	Jazz Musician
Waterston, Robert Classie	Clergy	10	15	30		
Waterston, Sam	Entertainment	6	8	15	20	
Watkins, Henry George "Gino"	Explorer	125		450		Youngest Arctic Expl.Died at 25
Watkinson, William L.	Clergy	15	20	35		
Watson, Harold F.	Aviation	10	30	45	25	
Watson, J. Crittenden	Civil War	25	60	105		Union Commodore
Watson, James D., Dr.	Science	28	35	55	30	Nobel Medicine 1962
Watson, Minor	Entertainment	5	6		15	
Watson, R.J. "Doc"	Aviation	10	22	38	28	ACE, WW II, USAAF Ace
Watson, Thomas Augustus	Science	65	155	315		Ass't To A.Bell.Teleph. Pioneer
Watson, Thomas J., Jr.	Business	10	20	50	75	Chmn. IBM in Productive Years
Watson, Thomas J., Sr.	Business	110	145		125	Founder IBM
Watt, James	Cabinet	4	10	20	15	Sec'y Interior 1981
Watt, James 1736-1819	Science	400	895	1850		Inventor. Steam Engine
Watt, James, Jr. (1769-1848)	Science	40	85	185		Marine Engineer.Son of Inventor
Watterson, Bill*	Cartoonists	25			180	Calvin & Hobbes
Watterson, Henry	Journalist	15	40	75		CSA Army. Editor, Pulitzer
Watts, George Frederick	Artist	75	225	350		Painter & Sculptor
Waugh, Evelyn	Author	45	195	325	50	"Brideshead Revisited"
Wavell, Archibald, Sir	Military	35	85	150	60	Br. Field Marshal,Viceroy India
Wayne, Anthony	Rev. War Military	625	1750	3000		Rev. War Gen. "Mad Anthony ..."
Wayne, Carol	Entertainment		55	130	150	
Wayne, David	Entertainment	5	6	15	15	
Wayne, Henry C.	Civil War	95	200	325	250	CSA General
Wayne, James M. (SC)	Supreme Court	75	200	350		
Wayne, John	Entertainment	400	550	750	925	DS Wayne & John Ford $1,500
Wayne, Pat	Entertainment	10			20	
Weatherhead, Leslie D.	Clergy	30	35	60	40	
Weathers, Carl	Entertainment	6	8	15	20	
Weaver, Dennis	Entertainment	6	8	15	20	
Weaver, Doodles	Entertainment	20			30	

NAME	CATEGORY	SIG	LS/DS	ALS	SP	COMMENT
Weaver, James B.	Civil War	30		140		Union Gen., Pres. Candidate
Weaver, Robert C.	Cabinet	25	45		30	1st Afro-Am. Cabinet. Sec'y HUD
Weaver, Sigourney	Entertainment	10			40	Pin-Up SP $45
Webb, Alexander S.	Civil War	20	45	55		Union General
Webb, Charles Henry	Author	5	15	30		
Webb, Clifton	Entertainment	35			65	
Webb, Del	Business	5	15	20	30	Desert Inn Casino
Webb, Jack	Entertainment	40	45	110	125	
Webb, James E.	Astronaut	10			25	Admiral
Webb, Jimmy	Composer	20			65	
Webb, Richard	Entertainment	15			35	"Capt. Midnight"
Webb, Samuel B.	Revolutionary War	105	325	615		Fndr. Soc. of Cincinnati
Webb, U.S.	Political	6		25		California Official
Webb, W.R. "Spider"	Aviation	15	30	45	35	ACE, WW II, Ace in a Day
Webber, Andrew LLoyd	Composer	100	250		300	Br. Musical Theatre
Webber, Robert	Entertainment	15	20		35	
Weber and Fields	Entertainment	95			150	Vintage Comedians
Weber, Joe	Entertainment	20	25	45	45	Vintage Comedian
Weber, Karl Maria von	Composer	375	1035	1320		
Webster, Ben	Entertainment	125				Tenor Sax-Arranger
Webster, Daniel	Cabinet-Senate	110	295	430	375	Statesman, Orator
Webster, H.T.*	Cartoonist	20	30		125	The Timid Soul
Webster, Jean	Author	15	45	135		Am. Novelist."Daddy-Long-Legs"
Webster, Noah	Author	295	795	1485		Am.Lexicographer,Editor etc.
Webster, Paul Francis	Composer	20	50	70	45	
Wedell, Jimmie	Aviation	10	30	40	35	
Wedemeyer, A.C.	Military	25	75		35	Gen. WW II
Wedgwood, John H., Sir	Business	10	20	35	15	
Weed, Marian	Entertainment	15			50	Opera
Weed, Thurlow	Politician	15	30	50		Political Leader NY, Journalist
Weede, Robert	Entertainment	10			35	Opera, Concert, Operetta
Weeks, John W.	Cabinet	15	35	70		Sec'y War 1921
Weeks, Sinclair	Cabinet	5	15	35	15	Sec'y Commerce 1953
Weems, Ted	Entertainment	10	20		40	Big Band Leader-Trombone
Weicker, Lowell Jr.	Senate/Congress	5	10		15	Rep.CT 1969, Senator 1971
Weidler, Virginia	Entertainment	7	9	20	15	
Weidman, Jerome	Author	5	10	20	5	
Weikl, Bernd	Entertainment	5			20	Opera
Weill, Kurt	Composer	250	805	1200	375	Opera, Ballet, Musical Comedy
Weinberg, Steven, Dr.	Science	25	35		30	Nobel Physics 1979
Weinberger, Casper	Cabinet	5	10	25	15	Sec'y HEW, Sec'y Defense
Weingartner, Felix von	Composer	100		250	150	Austrian Conductor
Weir, Benjamin M.	Celebrity	12	15	25	15	
Weir, Julian Alden	Artist	40	135	250		Early Am. Impressionist
Weir, Robert Walter	Artist	50	140	265		Prof. Drawing. Taught R.E. Lee
Weiser, Jan Conrad	Fr. Revolution	290	950	1600		
Weiss, John	Clergy	10	15	20		
Weissmuller, Johnny	Entertainment	115			225	
Weitz, Paul J.	Astronaut	8			25	
Weitzel, Godfrey	Civil War	30	45	60		Union Gen.
Weizman, Vera	First Lady	25	80		35	Widow of 1st Pres. Israel
Weizmann, Chaim	Head of State	460	1075	2335	875	Chemist, Zionist Leader
Weizmann, Ezer	Head of State	25	65			Israeli AF Gen. Pres. of Israel
Welch Herbert, Bishop	Clergy	15	25	30	35	
Welch, Raquel	Entertainment	10	15	20	25	Pin-Up SP $30
Welch, Robert A.	Business	25	40	90	30	Batchelor Oil Multi-Millionaire

NAME	CATEGORY	SIG	LS/DS	ALS	SP	COMMENT
Weld, Tuesday	Entertainment	10	15	30	25	
Welden, Ben	Entertainment	10			25	
Weldon, Felix de	Artist	60				Iwo Jima Memorial Statue
Welensky, Roy, Sir	Head of State	15	55	115		
Welk, Lawrence	Entertainment	20		35	25	
Weller, Peter	Entertainment	10	15	25	25	
Weller, Thomas H., Dr.	Science	25	35	50	30	Nobel Medicine 1954
Welles, Gideon	Cabinet-CW	95	175	300	675	Sec'y of Navy, LS Wardte $775
Welles, Orson	Entertainment	95	350		275	Special DS $650
Welles, Sumner	Diplomat	25	65	150	55	State Dept.,Ambassador
Wellington, 1st Duke of	Head of State	140	250	385		Arthur Wellesley,Prime Minister
Wellington, George Louis	Senate/Congress	12	20			Rep. 1895, Senator MD
Wellman, Walter	Aviation	60	145	230	75	Aviator-Explorer-Writer
Wells, Carolyn	Author	10	25	40	15	Sketches, Parodies,Detective
Wells, Carveth	Author	20	45	110	25	Explorer, Author, Lecturer
Wells, Dawn	Entertainment	5	6	15	15	
Wells, H.G. (Herbert George)	Author	150	275	440	200	Br. Sci-Fi Novelist, Historian
Wells, Henry	Business	200	750	1500		Wells-Fargo, American Express
Wells, Henry & Fargo, James	Business	850	1375			Wells-Fargo, American Express
Wells, Henry & Fargo, William G.	Business		3375			Wells-Fargo, American Express
Wells, James M.	Governor	15	40			Governor LA 1865
Wells, Junior	Entertainment	4			10	
Wells, Kitty	Country Music	5			15	
Welty, Eudora	Author	35	120	225	100	Am.Short Stories, Novelist
Wenck, Walter	Military	25	60	120	55	
Wendelin, Rudolph*	Cartoonist	20			125	Smokey the Bear
Wendorf, E.G. "Wendy"	Aviation	10	25	40	30	ACE, WW II, Navy Ace
Wendt, George	Entertainment	5			30	
Wenrich, Percy	Composer	55	125			AMusQS $175, $350
Wentworth, Benning 1696-1770	Colonial America	95	270	550		Col. Gov. NH. "Bennington", VT
Wentworth, John 1737-1820	Revolutionary War	80	250	340		
Wermuth, Arthur W.	Military	15	35	50	25	WW II Hero
Werner, Oskar	Entertainment	20		45	50	
Wert, Richard L.	Military	5	15	25	15	
Wesley, Charles	Clergy	150				
Wesley, John	Clergy	375	650	1500		Methodist Fndr, ALS/Cont.$3000
Wessell, Vivian	Entertainment	10		40	35	
Wesselowsky, Alessandro	Entertainment	40			160	Opera
West, Adam	Entertainment	10	25		25	"Batman"
West, Benjamin	Artist	150	825	1400		Am. Historical Painter
West, Dottie	Country Music	10			40	
West, F.H.	Civil War	40	110			Union Gen. War Dte LS $250
West, Jessamyn	Author	12	30	35	15	Popular Novelist
West, Mae	Entertainment	65	135		225	
West, Morris L.	Author	15	45	80	30	"Shoes Of The Fisherman"
West, Rebecca, Dame	Author	15	45	125		Br. Novelist & Critic
West, Richard L.	Aviation	10			30	ACE WW II
West, Roy O.	Cabinet	25	40			Sec'y Interior 1928
Westall, William	Artist	15	40	95		
Westheimer, Ruth, Dr.	Medical	4	15	25	15	Sex Therapist
Westinghouse, George	Business	125	720	835	350	Inventor. Fndr. Westinghouse Co
Westman, Nidia	Entertainment	15	15	35	30	
Westminster, 2nd Earl	Royalty	15	50			Robert Grosvenor
Westmore, Wally	Entertainment	15			50	Hollywood Makeup Director
Westmoreland, Wm. C.	Military	20	50	75	40	Gen. Korea, Viet Nam
Weston, Agnes, Dame	Celebrity	6	20	40	25	

NAME	CATEGORY	SIG	LS/DS	ALS	SP	COMMENT
Weston, Edward 1850-1936	Business	40	125	315	70	Weston Electrical Instruments
Weston, Edward 1886-1958	Artist	35		600		Am. Western Photographer
Westover, Russ*	Cartoonist	15			75	Tillie The Toiler
Wetherbee, James D.	Astronaut	5			15	
Weyer, Kurt	Military	15			60	
Weygand, Maxime	Military	40	75	150	125	Fr. Gen.,Foch's Chief of Staff
Weyman, Stanley J.	Author	15	35	75		Brit. Novelist
Whalen, Grover	NYC Official	10	30		15	Merchant-NYC Official Greeter
Whalen, Michael	Entertainment	15	15	35	30	
Wharton, Edith N.	Author	190	475	1225		Pulitzer, Age of Innocence
Wharton, John A.	Civil War	150	450			CSA Gen. ALS Wardte $1,950
Wharton, Thomas 1735-1778	Revolutionary War	115	300	565		Gov. PA, Patriot. Pres. PA 1777
Wheatley, Melvin E., Bishop	Clergy	20	25	35	30	
Wheaton, Will	Entertainment	15			35	"Star "Trek"
Wheatstone, Charles, Sir	Science	100	320	565		Br. Physicist, Inventor
Wheeler, Bert	Entertainment	25			75	Comedy Team "Wheeler & Woolsey"
Wheeler, Burton K.	Senate	25	70		35	Senator MT 1922
Wheeler, Earle G.	Military	10			50	
Wheeler, Ellie	Entertainment	10	15	25	25	
Wheeler, Joseph	Civil War	80	225	475	950	CSA Gen. LS Wardte $1,650+
Wheeler, William A. (V)	Vice President	75	225			Hayes VP
Whelan, Arleen	Entertainment	10		25	20	
Whelchel, Lisa	Entertainment	5			10	
Whipple, Abraham 1733-1819	Revolutionary War	250	750			Fired 1st Gun of Rev. on Water
Whipple, Amiel Weeks 1818-1863	Civil War	115	235	350		Astronomer, Surveyor, Union Gen
Whipple, Fred L. 1906-	Author-Science	10	25		15	Astronomer. Rocket Research
Whipple, George H.	Science	45	75	150		Nobel Medicine !934
Whipple, Henry B.	Clergy	50	100	200		
Whipple, William	Revolutionary War	315	900	1335		Signer Decl. of Ind.
Whipple, William D.	Civil War	25	40	50		Union General
Whisner, William T.	Aviation	20	45	75	50	ACE, WW II
Whistler, James McNeill	Artist	300	575	1030		Am.Painter,Etcher. Lived Abroad
Whitaker, Johnnie	Entertainment	10			25	
White, Alice	Entertainment	25			75	Vintage Actress
White, Andrew Dickson 1832-1918	Educator-Diplomat	20	45	70	50	Co-Fndr. Cornell University
White, Anthony Walton 1750-1803	Revolutionary War	55	165	250		Washington Aide de Camp. Genera
White, Betty	Entertainment	9	10	20	25	
White, Byron R. (SC)	Supreme Court	55	125	170	55	
White, E.B.	Author	30	110			"Charlotte's Web"
White, Edward D. (SC)	Supreme Court	50	190	225	135	
White, Edward H. II	Astronaut	200	325		325	1st Am. To Walk In Space
White, George	Entertainment	60	70	120	100	Theatrical producer
White, George Stuart	Military	20		70		Br.Fld.Marshal. Ladysmith Seige
White, Hugh	Governor	5	20		15	Governor MS 1936
White, I.D.	Military	10			25	
White, Jesse	Entertainment	10			20	
White, Jim	Explorer	40		175		Discover Carlsbad Caverns
White, Josh	Entertainment	55			225	Am. Folk Singer
White, Julius	Civil War	25	55	120		Union General
White, Paul Dudley, Dr.	Science	45	125		80	Heart Specialist
White, Pearl	Entertainment	150		320	300	Queen of the Silent Serials
White, Sanford	Architect	100	305	790	150	TLS/Content $1,600-5,500
White, Stewart E.	Author	10	20	40	15	Am. Western Adventure Stories
White, Theodore	Author	8	15	25	10	Detailed Presidential Campaigns
White, Vanna	Entertainment	5			15	Pin-Up SP $25
White, Vanna & Pat Sajak	Entertainment	10			25	

NAME	CATEGORY	SIG	LS/DS	ALS	SP	COMMENT
White, Wallace H., Jr.	SenateCongress	10	15			Rep. ME 1917, Senator 1930
White, William 1748-1836	Clergy	130	265	250		1st P.E. Bishop
White, William Allen	Author	15	40	85	25	Journalist "Sage of Emporia"
White, Windsor T.	Business	110		550		Pioneer Auto-Truck Mfg.
Whitelaw, Billie	Entertainment	15			30	
Whiteman, Paul	Entertainment	55	140	170	145	"King of Jazz".Intro Gershwin
Whiting, Jack	Entertainment	6	8	15	15	
Whiting, Margaret	Entertainment	15			30	Vocalist
Whiting, Richard	Composer	50		135	100	AMusQS $150
Whiting, William Henry	Civil War	200				CSA General
Whitlam, Gough	Head of State	10			25	Prime Minister Australia
Whitley, Ray	Country Music	10			35	
Whitman, Charles S.	Governor	10	30		15	Governor NY 1915
Whitman, Slim	Country Music	5			15	
Whitman, Walt	Author	1265	1250	2935	2780	Controversial Am. Poet
Whitmore, James	Entertainment	5		10	15	
Whitney, C.V.	Business	15	35	70	25	
Whitney, Casper	Publisher	10	25	35		Publisher
Whitney, Courtney	Military	15	40	75	35	General WW II. MacArthur Aide
Whitney, Eli	Science	650	1800	3875		Am. Inventor Cotton Gin
Whitney, Grace Lee	Entertainment	15			35	"Star Trek"
Whitney, Richard	Business	35	50			Pres. NY Stock Exchange
Whitney, William Collins	Cabinet	20	35	65	25	Financier, Cleveland Sec'y Navy
Whittaker, Charles E.(SC)	Supreme Court	50	75	165	85	
Whitten-Brown, Arthur, Sir	Aviation	250	375			Pioneer Aviator/John Alcock
Whittier, John Greenleaf	Author	60	350	450		"Quaker Poet"
Whittle, Frank, Sir	Aviation	15	50		45	
Whittle, Josephine	Entertainment	5	6	15	15	
Whitty, Dame May	Entertainment	35	45	85	75	
Who, The (All 4)	Entertainment	450	2050		750	Rock
Wickard, Claude	Cabinet	15	25			Sec'y Agriculture 1940
Wicke, Lloyd C., Bishop	Clergy	15	25	35	30	
Wicker, Irene	Entertainment	10			25	Vintage Radio's "Singing Lady"
Wickersham, George W.	Cabinet	15	35	60		Att'y Gen. 1909
Wickes, Mary	Entertainment	4	4	15	15	
Wickliffe, Charles A.	Cabinet	30	65	95		P.M. Gen. 1841
Widmark, Richard	Entertainment	9	10	20	25	
Wieck, Dorothea	Entertainment	15	15	35	30	
Wieghorst, Olaf	Artist	60	225	350	180	"Dean of Western Art"
Wiemann, Ernst	Entertainment	5			20	Opera
Wien, Noel	Aviation	25	55	105	65	
Wiere Brothers	Entertainment	15			25	
Wiesel, Elie	Author	20	45	55	25	Nobel Peace Prize 1986
Wiesel, Torsten S., Dr.	Science	22	30	45	25	Nobel Medicine 1981
Wiesenthal, Simon	Activist	20	45	90	35	Famed Nazi Hunter
Wiest, Diane	Entertainment	10			55	
Wigfall, Lewis T.	Civil War	150	290			CSA Gen. CSA Senator
Wiggin, Kate Douglas	Author	125		190	95	
Wigglesworth, Richard B	Senate/Congress	5	10			Rep. MA 1928, Diplomat
Wigner, Eugene P. Dr.	Science	15	25	40	20	Nobel Physics 1963
Wihan, Hanus	Entertainment	30		120		Czech Viol-Cellist.AMusQs $85
Wilberforce, Samuel, Bishop	Clergy	30	45	60		
Wilberforce, William	Abolitionist	45	145	305		Br. Anti-Slavery Polititian
Wilbur, Curtis D.	Cabinet	10	25	35	15	Sec'y Navy 1924
Wilbur, Ray Lyman	Cabinet	10	25	55	20	Sec'y Interior 1929
Wilbur, Richard	Author	5	15	35	10	Novelist

NAME	CATEGORY	SIG	LS/DS	ALS	SP	COMMENT
Wilbur, W.H.	Military	5	15	25	10	
Wilcott, Terry	Astronaut	5			10	
Wilcox, Ella Wheeler, Mrs.	Author	20	35	100		Journalist, Poet, Essayist
Wilcoxon, Henry	Entertainment	20		35	45	
Wild Choir	Entertainment	5			10	Rock
Wild, Edward A.	Civil War	70	150	210		Union General
Wilde, Cornel	Entertainment	20	25	40	45	
Wilde, Oscar	Author	550	1550	3250	575	Ir. Poet, Playwright, Wit
Wilde, Percival	Author	20	55	120		Playwright, Novelist
Wilder, Billy	Entertainment	10			30	Film Director
Wilder, Gene	Entertainment	10	25		25	
Wilder, Marshall P.	Entertainment	12	20	30	15	Reciter, Imitator
Wilder, Thornton	Author	55	110	230	200	Pulitzer, ALS/Content $675
Wilding, Michael	Entertainment	30			55	
Wilentz, David T.	Celebrity	25				
Wiley, Alexander	Senate/Congress	15	40			Senator WI 1938
Wiley, Harvey W., Dr.	Science	80	195			Created FDA
Wilhelm I (Ger)	Royalty	75	215	435		King of Prussia, Emperor Ger.
Wilhelm II (Kaiser)(Ger)	Royalty	170	415	525	295	
Wilhelm, August	Military	120			500	Ger. Gen. Storm Trooper
Wilhelmj, August	Entertainment	25			75	Ger. Violinist
Wilke, Robert J.	Entertainment	10			25	
Wilkerson, Guy	Entertainment	25			65	
Wilkes, Charles	Civil War	50	105	200		Union Adm., Explorer
Wilkes, Earle	Military	10			50	
Wilkie, David, Sir	Artist	35	80	160		Genre Paintings, Portraits
Wilkins, George Hubert, Sir	Explorer	30	50	115	55	Led Arctic & Antarctic Exped.
Wilkins, Hans	Aviation	10	25	45	30	
Wilkins, Roy	Activist	15	35	85	20	Sr. Statesman of Civil Rights
Wilkins, T. H.	Science	15	25	40	20	
Wilkinson, Geoffrey	Science	15	25	40	20	Nobel Chemistry 1985
Wilkinson, James	Revolutionary War	120	390	485		General
Wilkinson, June	Entertainment	6	8	15	25	Pin-Up SP $30
Wilks, Matthew	Clergy	15		25	50	
Willard, Charles	Aviation	15			35	
Willard, Edward S.	Entertainment	15		35	30	Vintage
Willard, Frances E.	Temperance	40	70	160		Pres. W.C.T.U.
Willard, Frank*	Cartoonist	35			190	Moon Mullins
Willard, Fred	Entertainment	4	6	10	15	
Willcox, Orlando B.	Civil War	40	85	155		Union Gen.
Willebrands, John, Cardinal	Clergy	30	45	65	40	
Willett, Marinus 1740-1830	Revolutionary War	75	150	250		Officer Cont. Army.Mayor NYC
William III (Eng)	Royalty	560	1685	2500		
William IV (Eng)	Royalty	85	240	370		"The Sailor King", DS $575
William, 4th Duke of Devonshire	Head of State	75	185	355		Prime Minister 1756
William, Warren	Entertainment	10	15	40	45	
Williams, Andy	Entertainment	20			45	
Williams, Barry	Entertainment	4	6	10	15	
Williams, Bart	Entertainment	5			20	
Williams, Ben Ames	Author	15	25	40	20	Am. Novelist
Williams, Bill	Entertainment	10	15		25	
Williams, Billy Dee	Entertainment	10	15		25	
Williams, Cindy	Entertainment	4	6	15	15	
Williams, Clifton C.	Astronaut	6			25	
Williams, Donald E.	Astronaut	5			15	
Williams, Edward B.	Law	5	15	40	10	Top Criminal Lawyer

NAME	CATEGORY	SIG	LS/DS	ALS	SP	COMMENT
Williams, Edward M.	Business	35	90	155		
Williams, Edy	Entertainment	5			20	Pin-Up SP $30
Williams, Eleazer 1787-1858	Clergy	45	115	270		Missionary.Louis XVII ???
Williams, Esther	Entertainment	8	10	20	25	Pin-Up SP $20
Williams, Geoffrey	Science	10	20	35	20	
Williams, George H.	Cabinet	10	25	40		Att'y Gen. 1872, Senator OR 186
Williams, Gluyas*	Cartoonist	10			75	New Yorker Cartoonist
Williams, Grant	Entertainment	40			100	
Williams, Guinn "Big Boy"	Entertainment	75			150	
Williams, Gus	Entertainment	12			25	Showman
Williams, Guy	Entertainment	100	125		150	
Williams, Hal	Entertainment	4			12	Afro-Am Actor
Williams, Hank	Country Music	600	1200		1250	
Williams, Hank Jr.	Country Music	30			45	
Williams, Harrison A., Jr.	Senate	15	35		20	Rep. 1953, Senator NJ
Williams, J.R.*	Cartoonist	20	25		100	Way Out West
Williams, JoBeth	Entertainment	10			30	
Williams, Joe	Entertainment	15			40	Jazz Vocalist
Williams, John	Composer	20	65	150	75	AMusQS $225
Williams, John Sharp	Senate/Congress	10	20		20	Rep. MS 1893, Senator 1910
Williams, Jonathan	Author	5	15	25		
Williams, Jr., Alford J.	Aviation	30	45	95	125	
Williams, Mary Alice	Journalist	10			20	TV News Journalist
Williams, Mason	Composer	10			20	Guitar Soloist
Williams, Otho 1749-1800	Revolutionary War	140	400	735		Officer. Fought/Gates & Greene
Williams, Paul	Composer	5	7	15	15	
Williams, Robin	Entertainment	5	15	30	30	
Williams, Roger	Entertainment	4		10	15	Pianist-Arranger
Williams, Seth	Civil War	30	65	85		Union General
Williams, Tennessee (Thomas L.)	Author	150	340	650	395	Pulitzer, Cat on a Hot Tin Roof
Williams, Tex	Country Music	10			20	Big Band
Williams, Treat	Entertainment	5	15	25	20	
Williams, Van	Entertainment	25			75	
Williams, Vanessa	Entertainment	25			50	Miss America, Pin-Up SP $ 55
Williams, William	Revolutionary War	175	475	790		Signer Decl. of Indepen.
Williams, William Carlos	Author	275	375		300	Am. Poet, Novelist, Physician
Williamson, Fred	Entertainment	10			20	Afro-Am. Actor
Williamson, Hugh	Revolutionary War					Continental Congress
Williamson, Marianne	Author	5			10	Non-Fiction
Willing, Foy	Country Music	10			20	(Riders of the Purple Sage)
Willing, Thomas	Revolutionary War	75	250			Banker,Continental Congress
Willis, Bruce	Entertainment	20			50	
Willis, Nathaniel P. 1806-67	Author	20	35	75		Major Editor Poetry Mags.
Willis, Richard S.	Clergy	20	25	35		
Willkie, Wendell	Politician-Gov.	25	150		100	Pres. Candidate, Governor IN
Wills, Bob	Country Music	75			200	
Wills, Chill	Entertainment	40			75	
Willson, Meredith	Composer	25	60	155	80	"The Music Man"
Willys, John North	Business	60	110	245	90	Auto Pioneer, Diplomat
Wilmer, Richard Hooker, Bishop	Clergy	8	25	40		
Wilmot, David	Senator/Congress	85	230			Rep.,Senator PA. Wilmot Proviso
Wilson, August	Author	10	30	45	20	Dramatist, Dir., Pulitzer,Tony
Wilson, Brian	Entertainment	325			550	"Beach Boys"
Wilson, Charles E.	Business-Cabinet	20	35	70	30	Pres. GM., Sec'y Defense 1953
Wilson, Charles Edward	Business	20	75			Pres. General Electric
Wilson, Demond	Entertainment	10			25	

NAME	CATEGORY	SIG	LS/DS	ALS	SP	COMMENT
Wilson, Dennis	Entertainment	95			190	
Wilson, Dooley	Entertainment	350			900	Supporting Player "Casablanca"
Wilson, E. Willis	Governor	12	25			Governor WV 1885
Wilson, Earl	Journalist	10	15	30	15	Powerful Synd. Columnist
Wilson, Edith Bolling	First Lady	70	225	430	200	ALS as 1st Lady $500
Wilson, Edmund	Author	25	90	165		Am. Critic.ALS/Content $650
Wilson, Edmund Beecher	Author-Science	350	450			Am. Biologist
Wilson, Ellen Louise	First Lady	100	365	600		1st Wife - Pres. Wilson
Wilson, Flip	Entertainment	10			25	
Wilson, Francis	Entertainment	12		15	25	Vintage Actor
Wilson, Gahan*	Cartoonist	10		75	50	Mag. Cartoonist
Wilson, George W. Lt.	Celebrity	15	35	120		
Wilson, Harold, Sir	Head of State	40	105	130	45	Prime Minister
Wilson, Henry (VP)	Vice President	80	150	275		Grant VP
Wilson, Jackie	Entertainment	15			40	
Wilson, James (SC) 1742-98	Supreme Court	350	625	1600		Signer. ALS/Content $4,000
Wilson, James 1835-1920	Cabinet	15	50	95		Sec'y Agriculture 1897
Wilson, James H.	Civil War	85	180	245		Union Gen. Cavalry
Wilson, John L.	Senate/Congress	15	30	40		Rep. 1889, Senator WA 1895
Wilson, Joseph R.	Celebrity	40		175		Father of Woodrow Wilson
Wilson, Julie	Entertainment	10			35	
Wilson, Kemmons	Business	15	35	80	50	Founder Holiday Inn
Wilson, Lois	Entertainment	15	15	35	40	
Wilson, Marie	Entertainment	25	35	65	60	"My Friend Irma" Early TV
Wilson, Pete	Governor	10			20	Governor CA
Wilson, Robert, Dr.	Science	15	25	35	20	Nobel Physics 1978
Wilson, Sloan	Author	15	35	75	20	"Man in the Grey Flannel Suit"
Wilson, Teddy	Entertainment	25		75	90	Pianist-Arranger
Wilson, Tom*	Cartoonist	10			30	Ziggy
Wilson, W. and Roosevelt, F.D.	Presidents		1500			DS
Wilson, William B.	Cabinet	10	25	50	15	Sec'y Labor 1913
Wilson, Woodrow	President	205	710	2115	760	
Winans, Ross	Inventor	85	250			Railroad Equipment
Winchell, Paul	Entertainment	10	20	35	30	
Winchell, Walter	Author	25	35	45	35	Radio-Newspaper Columnist
Winchester, Oliver F.	Industrialist	250	700	1100		Winchester Repeating Arms, Inc.
Winchester, Wm.P.Sir,1st Marguis	Elizabethan					Lord Treasurer Eng. 1485-1572
Winder, John Henry	Civil War	110	435	450		CSA Gen.,Wardte. DS $1,275
Windgassen, Wolfgang	Entertainment	15			45	Opera
Windom, William	Entertainment	4	6	10	15	
Windom, William	Cabinet	25	35	70	40	Sec'y Treasury 1881
Windsor, Claire	Entertainment	10	15		25	
Windsor, Marie	Entertainment	5	8	15	15	Pin-Up SP $20
Windsor,Duchess of (W.Simpson)	Royalty	130	265	560	175	Content ALS $775
Winfield, Paul	Entertainment	5	6	15	15	
Winfrey, Oprah	Entertainment	25			50	
Wing, Toby	Entertainment	10	15	25	25	
Wingate, Francis R., Sir	Military	30	75	155	75	Gen. Succeeded Kitchener
Winger, Debra	Entertainment	10	15	30	35	Pin-Up SP $40
Winkler, Betty	Entertainment	5	6	15	15	
Winkler, Henry	Entertainment	5	8	15	20	
Winkler, K.C.	Entertainment	4			10	Pin-Up SP $20
Winner, Septimus	Composer	85	205	350		AMusQS $495-$1,000
Winninger, Charles	Entertainment	25		50	60	
Winslow, Edward 1699-1753	Colonial America	225	675			Silversmith.Government Official
Winslow, Edward 1714-84	Revolutionary War	20	50	90		Loyalist.Port Plym'th Collector

NAME	CATEGORY	SIG	LS/DS	ALS	SP	COMMENT
Winslow, John 1753-1819	Revolutionary War	20	55	95		Soldier, Hero, Patriot, General
Winslow, John Ancrum	Military	95	275	385		Union Naval Officer
Winslow, John F.	Civil War	55	150	225		Builder of the "Monitor"
Winsor, Kathleen	Author	15	35	90	25	Novelist "Forever Amber"
Winter Consort, Paul	Entertainment	50			125	Enviromental Music, Grammy
Winters, Jonathan	Entertainment	9	10	20	25	
Winters, Roland	Entertainment	30	45	85	75	
Winters, Shelley	Entertainment	6	8	20	25	Pin-Up SP $30
Winthrop, John 1714-1779	Revolutionary War	200	685			Physicist-Astron.Science Leader
Winthrop, John, The Younger	Colonial America	800	1900	4750		Col. Gov. CT. NRPA
Winthrop, Robert C.	Senate/Congress	15	30	40		Rep. 1840, Senator MA
Winthrop, Thomas L. 1760-1841	Revolutionary War	25	50	95		Merchant. Widely Esteemed
Winwood, Estelle	Entertainment	25	35		45	
Wire, Calvin C.	Aviation	8	15	28	20	ACE, WW II
Wirt, William	Cabinet	35	100	170		Att'y General 1817
Wirtz, Willard	Cabinet	5	10	20	10	Sec'y Labor 1962
Wirz, Henry Hartmann	Civil War	450	3850	4950		CSA Gen., Comd. Andersonville
Wisch, Theodor	Military	110		65		NRPA
Wise, Henry A.	Civil War	110	195	285		CSA General. Gov.,Senator VA
Wise, Robert	Entertainment	10	40		25	Film Director
Wise, Stephen	Clergy	20	50	110	35	
Wiseman, L.H.	Clergy	10	15	25	15	
Wiseman, Nicholas, Cardinal	Clergy	30	45	90		
Wister, Owen	Author	50	140	215	75	Am. Novelist, "The Virginian"
Withers, Jane	Entertainment	8	10	20	20	
Withers, Robert E.	Civil War	25	40	75		CSA Colonel, US Sen. VA
Witherspoon, Jimmy	Entertainment	10			35	Musician
Witherspoon, John 1723-94	Revolutionary War	675	2235	3000		Signer Decl. of Indepen.
Wittber, Bill	Aviation	20	50	75	80	
Witte, Serge (1st Prem Rus)	Head of State	20	50	95		1st Constitutional Russian Prem
Wittig, Georg F.K.	Science	25	50		40	Nobel Chemistry 1979
Wixell, Ingvar	Entertainment	20			45	Opera
Wodehouse, P. G.	Author	160	525	765	350	Br. Novelist Creator of "Jeeves
Woggon, Elmer	Cartoonist	5			20	Big Chief Wahoo
Woidick, Franz	Aviation	15	25	45	30	
Wolcott, Derek	Author	15	20		25	Poet. Nobel Literature
Wolcott, Edward O.	Senate/Congress	15	25			Senator CO 1889
Wolcott, Oliver	Revolutionary War	140	480	1075		Signer Decl. of Ind.
Wolcott, Oliver, Jr.	Cabinet	55	175	355		Washington Sec'y Treasury
Wolf, Gary	Entertainment	5			15	Voice of Roger Rabbitt
Wolf, George (Wolfe)	Governor	35	90	175		Gov. PA 1829, Statesman
Wolfe, Ian	Entertainment	10			25	
Wolfe, James 1727-59	Military	1550		8250		Br. Gen. French & Indian War
Wolfe, Thomas	Author	425	1800	2800		Early Death For Gifted Writer
Wolfe, Tom	Author	15	40	75	30	Am. Novelist
Wolfe-Barry, John, Sir 1836-1918	Civil Engineer	10	25	45		London Electr.RR, Docks,Bridges
Wolff, Amalie	Entertainment	15	15	30	25	
Wolff, Joseph	Clergy	35	40	50		
Wolff, Karl	Military	175	550			Ger. Gen. SS
Woll, Matthew	Labor	10	30	80		Lux.-Am. Labor Leader
Wolper, David	Entertainment	5	6	15	15	
Wolseley, Garnet J.,Viscount	Military	25	65	135	35	Field Marshal; C-in-C Army
Wolsey, Thomas 1475?-1530	Statesman		7800			Influential Cardinal, Statesman
Wonder, George*	Cartoonist	10			75	Terry & The Pirates
Wonder, Stevie	Entertainment	5	6		15	
Wong, Anna May	Entertainment	85		160	200	

NAME	CATEGORY	SIG	LS/DS	ALS	SP	COMMENT
Wood, F. Derwent	Artist	10	25	60		
Wood, Fernando	Civil War	20	55	90		Civil War Mayor NYC
Wood, Garfield 'Gar'	Science	60		80	75	Boat Designer, Builder, Racer
Wood, Grant	Artist	150	350	575		"American Gothic"
Wood, Haydn	Composer	20	55	85	30	AMusQS $150
Wood, James 1750-1813	Revolutionary War	50		120		House of Burgesses; Gov. VA
Wood, Lana	Entertainment	4	6	10	15	Pin-Up SP $30
Wood, Leonard, Dr.	Military	25	45	70	250	T. Roosevelt's"Rough Riders"
Wood, Natalie	Entertainment	100			200	
Wood, Nigel	Astronaut	7			24	
Wood, Peggy	Entertainment	15			35	
Wood, Robert	Astronaut	5			16	
Wood, Robert E.	Military	20	75			Business (Sears), Gen. WW II
Wood, Robert W.	Science	10	25		15	Physicist. Manhattan Project
Wood, Sam	Entertainment	40			90	Film Director-Producer Westerns
Wood, Sterling Alexander M.	Civil War	95	280	305		CSA General
Wood, Thomas J.	Civil War	45	105			Union Gen.
Wood, Thomas Waterman 1823	Artist	10	20	55		Pres. Am. Water-Color Society
Woodbury, Levi (SC)	Supreme Court	55	190	225		Gov., Sen., Sec'y Navy & Treas.
Woodcock, Amos Walter, Gen.	Military	10	20		20	War Crimes Prosecution Staff
Woodfill, Samuel	Military	10	30	50	25	Major WW I CMH Winner
Woodford, Stuart L.	Civil War	30	100	225		Union Gen., Gov. NY
Woodhull, Victoria C.	Reformer	115	240	510		1870's Feminist
Woodring, Henry H.	Cabinet	15	45	65	30	Sec'y War 1936
Woodruff, Wilford	Religion	25	65	130		Am. Morman Religious Leader
Woods, Charles Robert	Civil War	30	55	85		Union General
Woods, Donald	Entertainment	15	20	35	35	
Woods, James	Entertainment	10	15	25	20	
Woods, Phil	Entertainment	15			45	Jazz Alto Sax-Clarinet
Woods, Rose Mary	White House	15		30		Nixon Sec'y. Watergate
Woods, William B. (SC)	Supreme Court	40	85	190	125	
Woodward, Bob	Author	10	20	35	25	Uncovered Watergate/C.Bernstein
Woodward, Edward	Entertainment	10	15	25	20	
Woodward, Joanne	Entertainment	15	65		30	
Woodward, Marjorie	Entertainment	4	6	10	15	
Woodward, Robert Burns	Science	20	40	85	25	Nobel Chemistry 1965
Woodworth, Samuel	Author	45	140	350		Wrote "The Old Oaken Bucket"
Wool, John E.	Civil War	85	210	375		Union General & Vet. of 1812
Wooley, Mary E.	Celebrity	30	90	215		
Wooley, Monty	Entertainment	25	35		45	
Wooley, Sheb	Country Music	5			15	
Woolf, Virginia	Author	330	685	1705	4500	Br. Novelist, Essayist
Woolrich, Cornell	Author	150	550			Am. Writer of Detective Fiction
Woolworth, Charles S.	Business	40	110	205		F.W. Woolworth Co.
Woolworth, Frank W.	Business	295	890	1550		Fndr. F.W. Woolworth Co.
Woorinen, Charles	Composer	10	25	40		Pulitzer, AMusQS $100
Wooster, David	Revolutionary War	235	700			General; Continental Army
Wopat, Tom	Entertainment	6	8	15	15	
Worden, Al M.	Astronaut	15			30	
Worden, Hank	Entertainment	15			35	
Worden, John L.	Civil War	125	185	385		Union Navy, Comdr. Monitor
Wordsworth, Christopher	Clergy	20	30	35	35	
Wordsworth, William	Author	225	910	1685		Br. Romantic Poet Laureate
Work, Hubert	Cabinet	20	45	110	30	Sec'y Interior 1923
Worth, Irene	Entertainment	10			25	
Worth, William J. 1794-1849	Military	30	75	125		General; Mexican War

NAME	CATEGORY	SIG	LS/DS	ALS	SP	COMMENT
Wouk, Herman	Author	30	100	175	125	Am. Novelist; "Caine Mutiny"
Wray, Fay	Entertainment	25			100	
Wren, Christopher	Architect-Science	1550	5600	4500		St. Paul's Cathedral, London
Wright, Bobby	Country Music	7			15	
Wright, C.S.	Celebrity	15	35			
Wright, Cobina Sr. & Jr.	Entertainment	5			10	Socialite-Actresses of the 40's
Wright, Frank Lloyd	Architect	840	2215	4950	1175	ALS/Content $4,000, $4,750
Wright, Harold Bell	Author	10	20	35	15	Am. Novelist.
Wright, Henry C. 1797-1870	Reformer	10	20	35		Anti-Slavery Reformer-Lecturer
Wright, Horatio G.	Civil War	40	75	200		Union General
Wright, Jerauld	Military	10	35		20	
Wright, Jim (James Claude)	Senate/Congress	10	30		15	Rep. TX 1955, Speaker
Wright, John J., Cardinal	Clergy	40	75	95	70	
Wright, Luke E.	Cabinet	15	45	90	35	Sec'y War 1908, Ambass. Japan
Wright, Marcus Joseph	Civil War	125	160	200		CSA General
Wright, Orville	Aviation	500	990	1750	2450	TLS/Historical Content $15,000
Wright, Orville & Wright, Wilbur	Aviation				12500	First Flight Pioneers
Wright, Richard	Author	70	225		375	Afro-Am. Suffering, Prejudice
Wright, Silas, Jr. 1795-1847	Senate/Congress	20		75		Gen'l,Statesman, Gov. & Sen. NY
Wright, Theresa	Entertainment	25		40	45	
Wright, Turbutt 1741-1783	Revolutionary War	25	60	95		Continental Congress
Wright, Wilbur	Aviation	875	2595	4500	4500	Historic SP $12,500,TLS $15,000
Wrigley, Philip K.	Business	50	145	200	75	Wrigley Gum; Chicago Cubs
Wrigley, William, Jr.	Business	90	200	285	100	Founder Wrigley Gum Mfg.
Wunderlich, Fritz	Entertainment	75			500	Opera
Wyant, Alexander Helwig	Artist	85		350		ALS/Cont.$750
Wyatt, Jane	Entertainment	5			15	
Wyatt, Wendell	Senate/Congress	5	10		10	Rep. OR 1964
Wyeth, Andrew	Artist	225	450	1025	1025	Eminent Am. Painter
Wyeth, Henriette	Artist	75	225			
Wyeth, Jamie	Artist	125	540	400	325	Orig. Ink Sketch Pig $550-$950
Wyeth, John A.	Medical Author	65		250		Noted Surgeon
Wyeth, N. C.	Artist	140	375	600		Am. Illustrator & Painter
Wyler, Gretchen	Entertainment	5	6	15	15	
Wyler, William	Entertainment	30			75	3 "Best Picture" Acad. Awards
Wylie, Elinor	Author	60		285		Am. Poet, Novelist
Wylie, Philip	Author	15	30	65	20	Iconoclastic Author.
Wylie, Robert 1839-1877	Artist	45	150			
Wyman, Jane	Entertainment	15		125	40	
Wyman, Willard G.	Military	15	25	40	25	4 Star General WW II
Wymore, Patrice	Entertainment	8	9	15	15	
Wyndham, Charles, Sir	Entertainment	15	35		45	
Wyndham, Mary, Lady	Entertainment	4	6	10	10	
Wynette, Tammy	Country Music	5			15	
Wynn, Ed	Entertainment	60	65	100	150	Special DS $350
Wynn, Keenan	Entertainment	25	30		45	
Wynter, Dana	Entertainment	6			15	
Wynyard, Dianna	Entertainment	5	6	15	25	
Wysong, Forrest R.	Aviation	10	15	30	20	
Wyszynski, Stefan, Cardinal	Clergy	50	65	95	75	
Wythe, George	Revolutionary War	350	1100	2450		Signer. ALS/Cont.Wardte. $7,500

X

NAME	CATEGORY	SIG	LS/DS	ALS	SP	COMMENT
Xenia Alexandrova	Head of State	65		300		Russia

Y

NAME	CATEGORY	SIG	LS/DS	ALS	SP	COMMENT
Yalow, Rosalyn S.	Science	15	25	40	20	Nobel Medicine 1972
Yamaer, George	Celebrity	10	20	80	15	
Yamamoto, Isoroku, Adm.	Military	150	295	625	475	Pearl Harbor Attack, 12/7/1941
Yamanashi, Hanzo	Military	95	265			
Yamasaki, Minoru	Celebrity	10	25	60	20	
Yamashiro, Katsumari	Military	100			300	
Yamashita, Tomoyuki	Military	115	275	500	275	Jap. General. Hanged
Yang, Chen N.	Science	15	20	35	20	Nobel Physics 1957
Yang, Y. C.	Diplomat	10			20	Ambassador to Republic of Korea
Yankovic, Frank	Entertainment	4	4	9	10	
Yarnell, Harry E.	Military	15	35		20	Adm. Fleet Commander
Yarnell, Lorine	Entertainment	3	3	6	6	Shields & Yarnell
Yarrow, Ernest A.	Clergy	15	20	25		
Yates, Peter W.	Revolutionary War	30	120	165		Continental Congress
Yates, Richard	Civil War	40	110			Civil War Governor IL 1861
Yaw, Ellen Beach	Entertainment	30			200	Am. Soprano
Yeager, Chuck	Aviation	20	45	85	60	ACE, WW II, Pioneer Ace
Yeager, Jeana	Aviation	15	65		35	
Yeager, Jeana & Dick Rutan	Aviaton	75	75		125	Voyager
Yearwood, Trisha	Country Music	10			25	Singer
Yeates, Jasper 1745-1817	Revolutionary War	15	35	60		Jurist
Yeats, Jack Butler	Artist	25	60	150		Brother of Wm. Butler Yeats
Yeats, Wm. Butler	Author	190	405	1085		Poet, Dramatist;Abbey Theatre
Yeltsin, Boris	Head of State	750	1350			Russia
Yen, C.K.	Head of State	50	175			Pres. Republic China
Yerby, Frank G.	Author	35	80	165	40	Afro-Am. Novelist
Yerkes, Charles T.	Business	35	100			Capitalist. TLS/Content $450
Yes	Entertainment	40			80	
Yo Yo Ma	Entertainment	20			125	Concert Cellist
Yogananda, Paramhansa	Religious (Yoga)			495		

NAME	CATEGORY	SIG	LS/DS	ALS	SP	COMMENT
Yokum, Dwight	Country Music	10			25	
Yorgesson, Yogi	Country Music	10			20	
York, Alvin, Sgt.	Military	200	340	700	425	CMH WW I
York, Dick	Entertainment	25			50	
York, Michael	Entertainment	8	10	20	20	
York, Susanna	Entertainment	6	8	15	20	
Yorty, Sam	Political	5	10		10	Rep. CA, Mayor L.A.
Youmans, Vincent	Composer	55	165	255	150	"Tea for Two". MusMsS $800
Young, Alan	Entertainment	6	8	15	15	
Young, Andrew	Political	10	20	35	25	Afro-Am. Mayor Atlanta
Young, Art*	Cartoonist	20			125	Political Cartoonist
Young, Brigham	Clergy	590	1775	4450	1875	Am. Morman Leader, Gov. UT
Young, Burt	Entertainment	6			20	
Young, Charles Augustus	Science	35	140	225		Am. Astronomer, Author
Young, Chic*	Cartoonist	35			200	Blondie
Young, Clara Kimball	Entertainment	40			75	Vintage Stage Actress
Young, Coleman	Political	5	15		20	Afro-Am. Mayor of Detroit
Young, David H.	Aviation	10	25		30	
Young, Dean	Cartoonist					Dagwood. Orig. Strip $275
Young, Faron	Country Music	5			15	
Young, Gig	Entertainment	30	50	70	50	
Young, Henry E.	Civil War	25	45	70		CSA Major, Judge Advocate
Young, John	Astronaut	30			145	Moonwalker Astro
Young, John	Senate/Congress	15	25	45		Rep. NY 1836
Young, Lester	Entertainment	70	75	145	150	Jazz, Tenor Saxophone
Young, Loretta	Entertainment	9	15	25	25	
Young, Lyman*	Cartoonist	10			50	Tim Tyler's Luck
Young, Neil	Entertainment	15			40	
Young, Owen D.	Business	15	25	50	20	CEO Gen. Electr.,Financier, Law
Young, Robert	Entertainment	15	25	45	45	
Young, Roland	Entertainment	20			50	
Young, Samuel B.M.	Civil War	30	55	80		Union General Bvt.
Young, Sean	Entertainment	15			35	Pin-Up SP $40
Young, Trummy	Entertainment	15			45	Jazz Musician
Young, Whitney	Activist	5	20	45	15	Am. Civil Rights Leader. Author
Youngdahl, Luther	Governor	5	15		10	Governor MN 1947
Younger, Bob	Outlaw	2500				Fought/Quantrill.Died in Prison
Younger, Cole (Thomas Coleman)	Civil War	2000	2950	4200		Served/Quantrill; Bank Robber
Youngman, Henny	Entertainment	6	8	15	15	
Ysaye, Eugene	Composer	30			225	Belg. Violin Virtuoso,Conductor
Yudenich, Nikolay N.	Military	95			175	Rus. Gen. Russo-Jap.& WW I
Yukawa, Hideki	Science	35	45	70		Nobel Physics 1949
Yulee, David Levy	Civil War	45		140		CSA Congress
Yung, Carl Gustav	Science	375	1710			Swiss Founder Analytical Psych.
Yung, Victor Sen	Entertainment	35			65	
Yurka, Blanche	Entertainment	20			45	
Yutang, Lin (Lin Yutang)	Author	50	165			Chin. Novels,Philosophy,Plays

Z

NAME	CATEGORY	SIG	LS/DS	ALS	SP	COMMENT
Zabach, Florian	Entertainment	5			20	
Zablocki, Clement John	Senate/Congress	5			20	Rep. WI 1949
Zabriskie, Andrew C.	Business	35		140		Capitalist, Financier
Zadora, Pia	Entertainment	5			15	Pin-Up SP $20
Zahn, Timothy	Author	10			35	"Star Wars Trilogy"
Zais, Melvin	Military	10	20	35	15	
Zajic, Dolora	Entertainment	5			25	Opera
Zancanaro, Giorgio	Entertainment	10			30	Opera
Zangwill, Israel	Author	35	110	170	55	Br. Playwright, Novelist, Poet
Zanuck, Darryl F.	Entertainment	50	300		75	Producer. Exec.20th Century Fox
Zanuck, Richard Darryl	Entertainment	6	8	15	15	Film Producer, Exec.
Zapata, Emiliano	Revolutionist	500	1350	1625		Mex. Guerilla Leader
Zappa, Frank	Entertainment	25			50	
Zapruder, Abraham	Celebrity	40				Filmed JFK Assassination
Zavodszky, Zoltan	Entertainment	30			85	Opera
Zeani, Virginia	Entertainment	15			45	Opera
Zefferelli, Franco	Entertainment	10			25	Film Director
Zellerbach, James D	Business	15	40	85	35	US Ambassador, Industrialist
Zeman, Jacklyn	Author-Actress	5	8	15	10	Pin-Up $20
Zemke, Hubert "Hub"	Aviation	15	35	65	40	ACE, WW II, Triple Ace
Zemlinsky, Alexander	Composer	90	285			Aus. Conductor
Zenatello, Giovanni	Entertainment	45			125	Opera
Zeppelin, Ferdinand von, Graf	Aviation	275	875	1200	650	Inventor Dirigible Air Ship
Zerbe, Anthony	Entertainment	10		25	25	
Zetland, 2nd Earl, Thos. Lawrence	Freemason					Master of the Freemasons NRPA
Zetterling, Mai	Entertainment	15			35	
Zhukov, Georgi K.	Military	80	200	500	325	Rus. Marshal. Soviet Hero WW II
Ziegfeld, Florenz	Entertainment	245	390	575	525	ALS/Content $950
Ziegler, George M.	Civil War	40	55	75		Union General, Bvt.
Ziegler, Karl	Science	45	85	170	55	Nobel Chemistry 1969
Ziegler, Ronald L.	White House	5	10	25	15	White House Aide
Ziegler, Vincent C.	Business	5			10	CEO Gillette Safety Razor Co.
Zimbalist, Efrem, Jr.	Entertainment	5	8		20	
Zimbalist, Efrem, Sr.	Entertainment	45			275	Violinist, Composer
Zimbalist, Stephanie	Entertainment	6	8	15	20	Pin-Up SP $30
Zimmer, Norma	Entertainment	3	5		15	
Zindel, Paul	Author	10	20		30	Playwright
Zinnemann, Fred	Entertainment	20		35	35	Film Director
Ziolkowski, Korczak	Artist	20	35	65	40	
Zmed, Adrian	Entertainment	5	6	15	15	
Zog I	Royalty	40			85	King Albania
Zola, Emile	Author	165	350	725		Fr. Novelist & Social Reformer
Zollicoffer, Felix K.	Civil War	175	350	540		CSA General

NAME	CATEGORY	SIG	LS/DS	ALS	SP	COMMENT
Zorina, Vera	Entertainment	10			25	Ballerina, Films
Zuazo, Hernan Siles	Head of State	10	15	25	15	
Zucco, George	Entertainment	100			250	
Zukoffsky, Louis	Author	25		80	50	Am. Poet
Zukor, Adolph	Business	75	145	200	120	Founder Paramount Pictures
Zuloaga, Ignacio	Artist	25	75			Sp. Painter
Zumwalt, Elmo	Military	15	75	125	45	Adm. WW II
Zweig, Arnold	Author	25	65		50	Ger. Novelist, Playwright
Zweig, Stefan	Author	30	90	195	45	Aus. Psychoanalytical Biogr.
Zweigert, Eugen, Lt.	Aviation	100			300	Ger. ACE WW II
Zwicky, Fritz	Science	20	35		45	Am. Astronomer. Jet Propulsion
Zworykin, Vladimir	Science	55	120	230	75	Am. Inventor TV System
ZZ Top	Entertainment	35			70	

George Sanders, Ted Koppel, and Vice President of ABC (News) Tom O'Brien at the 1968 Republican Convention. As a working journalist back in those days, George happily garnered lots of good autographs.

PHOTOGRAPHS

A few more bonus photographs of our friends–just so you can see what a few of the folks you may be dealing with look like!

Christophe Stickel and George Sanders. This California dealer is one of the top sellers of the Sanders books.

George with Ann Krafthofer.

Dealer Roger Epperson with George at an autograph show in Florida.

Gerry Stodolski, George, and Catherine Barnes attending a UACC show in Florida.

George with R&R's Bob Eaton.

Jim Hayes, noted expert on The War Between the States, and George.

In the Dallas, Texas offices of Shirley and Eugene Muchin.

The 1994 SANDERS PRICE GUIDE to AUTOGRAPHS

Section III: FACSIMILES

NUMBER 3

FACSIMILES

Facsimiles are copies–Xerox, photograph, etc.–of actual, *authentic* signatures. Facsimiles play a very important role in the collecting of autographs.

Some people, alas, are less than honest. Anyone can sign John Wayne's name, and often do. A document or photograph signed by anyone other than the actual celebrity is worthless. If a move star's secretary or a politician's autopen (a device that automatically signs an approximation of a real person's signature) sign instead of the real person, that autograph is worth less than the paper it's on.

So, naturally, any serious collector wants to make sure the autographs he or she receives are authentic. This is done by comparing known *good* signatures with the one in question. Reputable dealers have usually already done this for you and guarantee the autograph's authenticity. Autographs you buy at a flea market or receive through any other source need checking!

Following is 42 pages of known authentic facsimile signatures. There are also numerous facsimiles in the first section of this book, such as all of the First Ladies in Chapter 3. You will want to also find other sources of facsimiles. One very good one is to get and save as many dealer catalogs as possible (see the last section in this book for dealer addresses, and tell them you read about them in **The 1994 Sanders Price Guide to Autographs**).

Enjoy our wonderful hobby, but don't take any wooden autographs!

ARTISTS AND PHOTOGRAPHERS

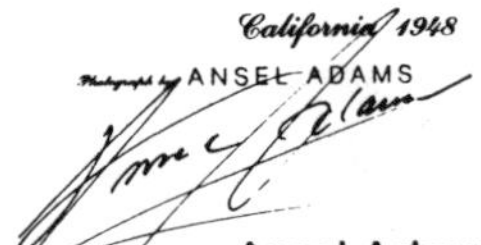

Ansel Adams

Jean Baptiste Camille Corot

George Eastman

Charles Dana Gibson

Winslow Homer

Edouard Manet

Henri Matisse

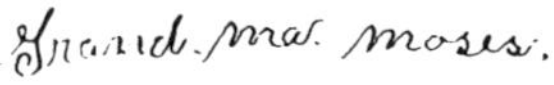

Grandma Moses

Joan Miro

Georgia O'Keeffe

Pierre Auguste Renoir

August Rodin

Norman Rockwell

James McNeil Whistler

Andrew Wyeth

ASTRONAUTS

Guion Bluford, Jr.

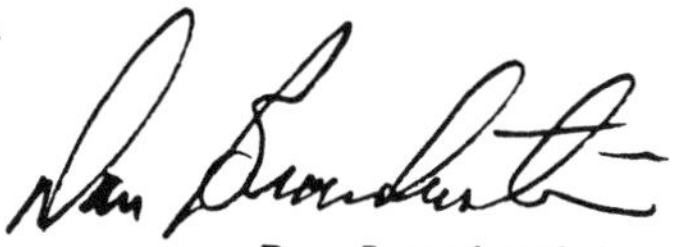

Dan Brandenstein

Apollo 15 Astronaut

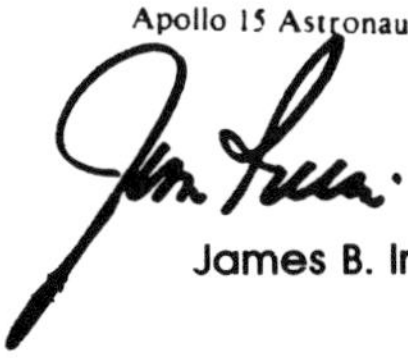

James B. Irwin

Frank Borman

Scott Carpenter—Second U.S. Astronaut to Orbit Earth

Pilot: Fitz Fulton

Fitz Fulton

"Gus" Grissom

John A. Glenn, Jr.

Gurraycha—First Mongolian Cosmonaut

Hank Hartsfield

Ivanov—Cosmonaut

Sigmund Jahn—East German Cosmonaut

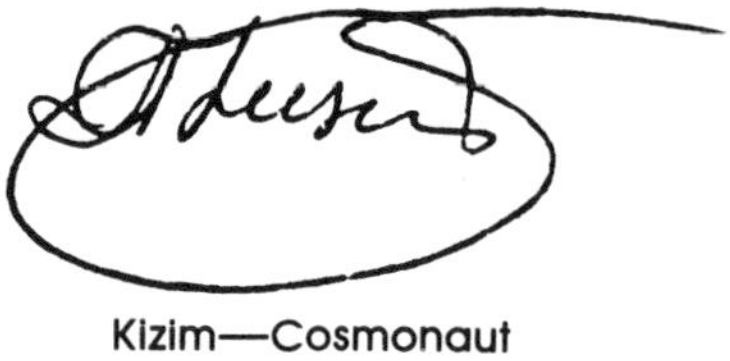

Kizim—Cosmonaut

Christopher Kraft—Houston Mission Control

Sir Bernard Lovell

Maguari—First Hungarian Cosmonaut

FACSIMILE SECTION

FACSIMILE SECTION

ASTRONAUTS

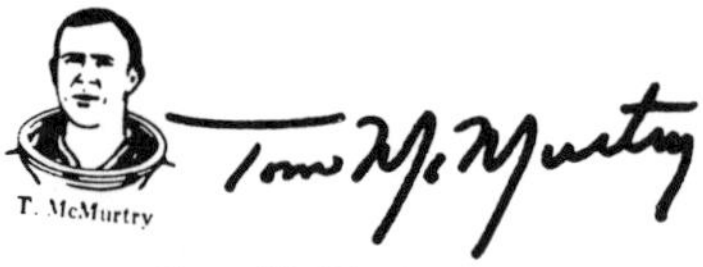

Tom McMurtry

Eugene Kranz—Apollo Flight Director

Ed Mitchell

Story Musgrove

R. Nebel

Andryen Grigoryevich Nikolayev

Ellison Onizuka—*Challenger* Crew Member

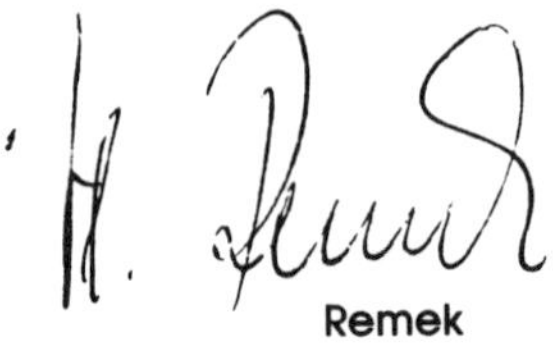
Remek

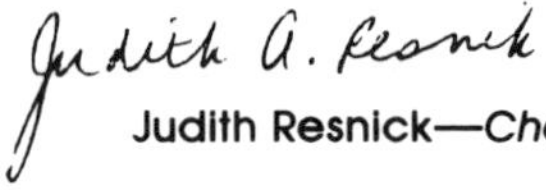
Judith Resnick—*Challenger* Crew Member

David Scott

Dick Scobee—*Challenger* Crew Member

Stu Roosa

Alan B. Shepard, Jr.—*Apollo 15*

Valentina Vladimirovna Tereskova—First Woman in Space

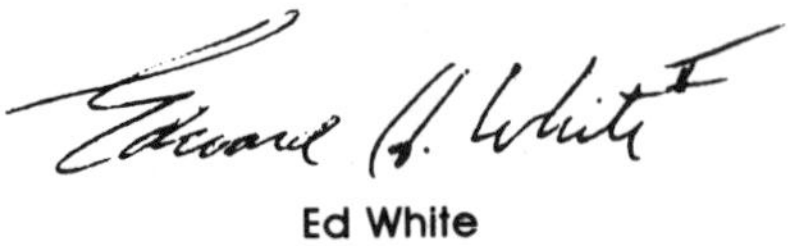
Ed White

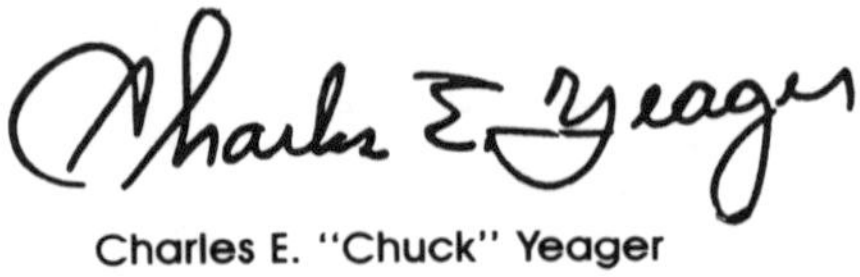
Charles E. "Chuck" Yeager

AUTHORS

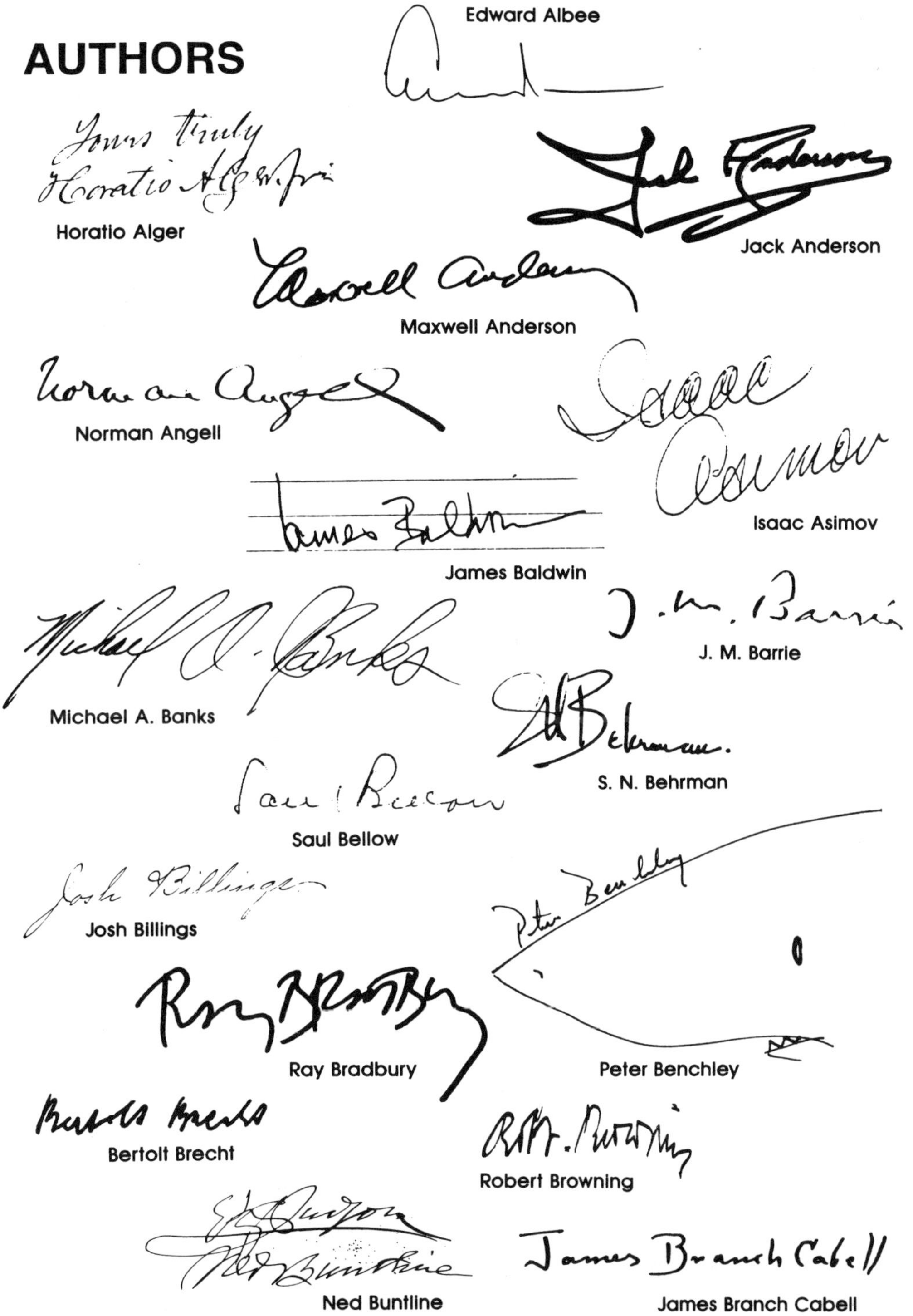
Edward Albee
Horatio Alger
Jack Anderson
Maxwell Anderson
Norman Angell
Isaac Asimov
James Baldwin
J. M. Barrie
Michael A. Banks
S. N. Behrman
Saul Bellow
Josh Billings
Ray Bradbury
Peter Benchley
Bertolt Brecht
Robert Browning
Ned Buntline
James Branch Cabell

FACSIMILE SECTION

AUTHORS

Albert Camus

Truman Capote

Dale Carnegie

Bruce Catton

G. K. Chesterton

Irvin S. Cobb

Michael Crichton

Dr. A. J. Cronin

E. E. Cummings

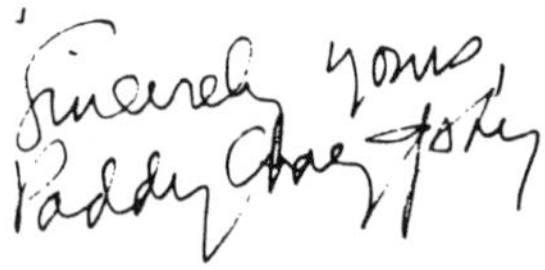
Paddy Chayefsky

John Dos Passos

Lloyd C. Douglas

Arthur Conan Doyle

Ralph Waldo Emerson

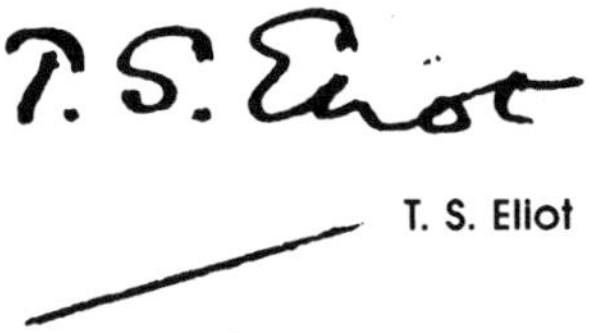
T. S. Eliot

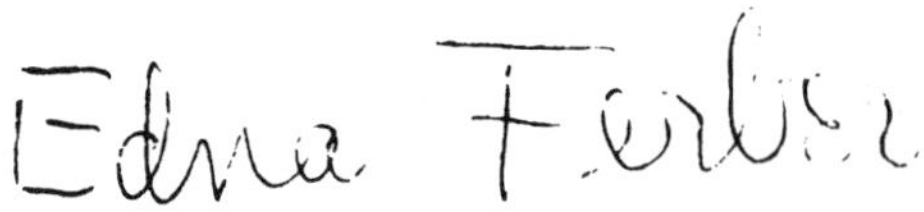
Edna Ferber

Eugene Field

E. M. Forster

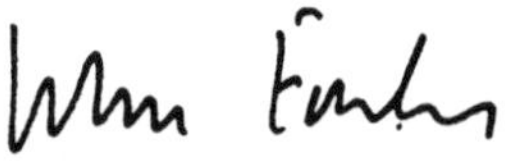
John Fowles

John Galsworthy

Erle Stanley Gardner

AUTHORS

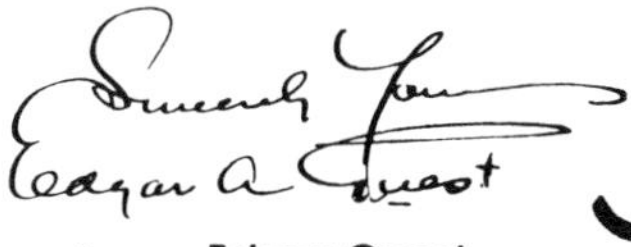
Edgar Guest

Zane Grey

Thomas Hardy

H. Rider Haggard

Joel Chandler Harris

Paul Harvey

Joseph Heller

Lillian Hellman

Frank Herbert

Victor Herbert

John Hersey

Oliver Wendell Holmes

Julia Ward Howe

Victor Hugo

Henrik Ibsen

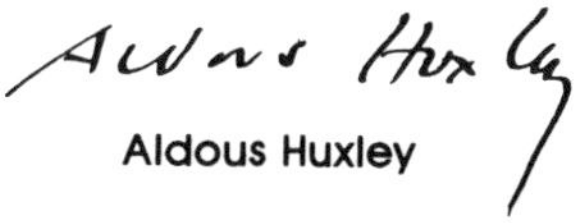
Aldous Huxley

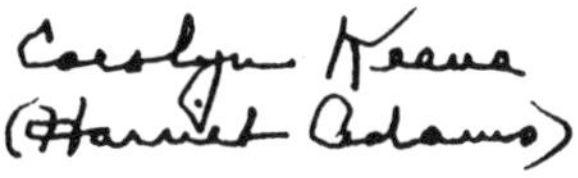
Carolyn Keene

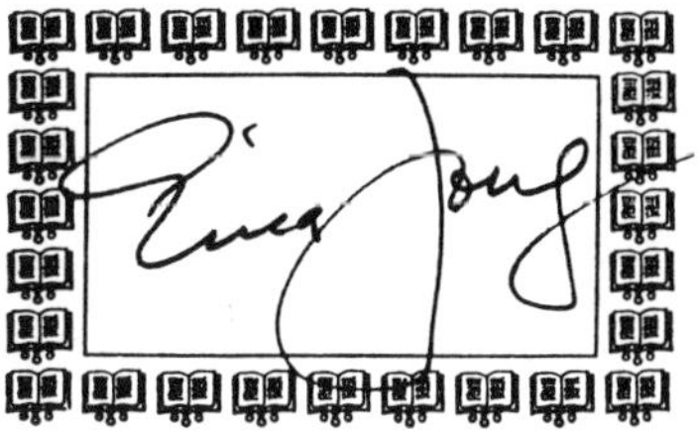
Erica Jong

Ring Lardner

John LeCarré

James Russell Lowell

Clare Boothe Luce

FACSIMILE SECTION

FACSIMILE SECTION

AUTHORS

Emily Post

Mario Puzo

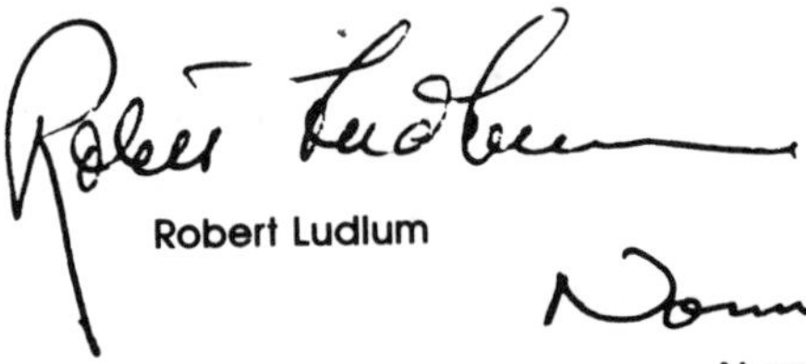
Robert Ludlum

Archibald MacLeish

Norman Mailer

Bernard Malamud

Thomas Mann

W. Somerset Maugham

E. L. Masters

Arthur Miller

Christopher Morley

John Lothrop Motley

Henry Miller

Ogden Nash

Alfred Noyes

Clifford Odets

Eugene O'Neill

Baroness Emmuska Orczy

George Plimpton

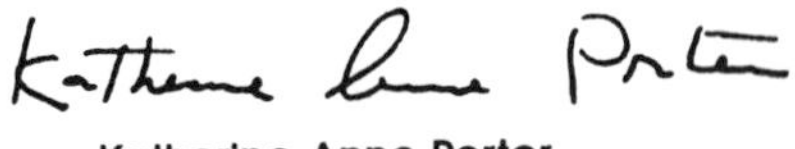
Katherine Anne Porter

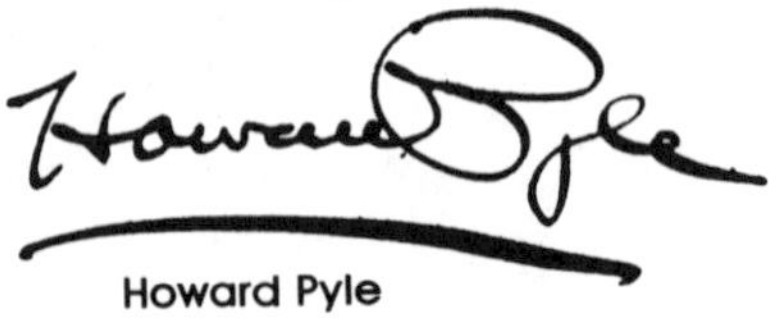
Howard Pyle

Eugene M. Prevost

AUTHORS

Robert Reud

James Whitcomb Riley

Kenneth Roberts

Sigmund Romberg

Bertrand Russell

Damon Runyon

Rafael Sabatini

George Sand

Carl Sandburg

Arthur Schlesinger, Jr.

Sir Walter Scott

Dr. Seuss

George Bernard Shaw

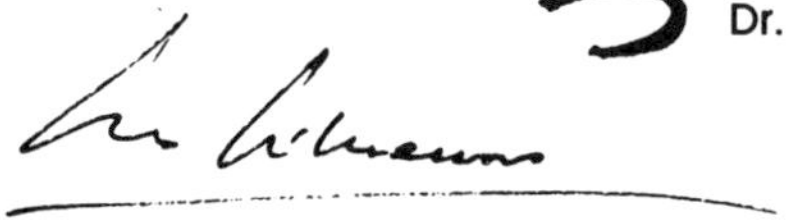
Georges Simenon

Neil Simon

Upton Sinclair

Isaac Bashevis Singer

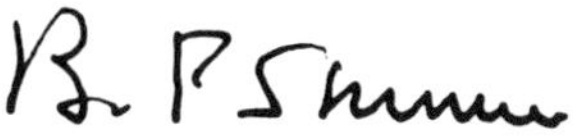
B. T. Skinner

Mickey Spillane

Rex Stout

FACSIMILE SECTION

FACSIMILE SECTION

AUTHORS

Frank Yerby

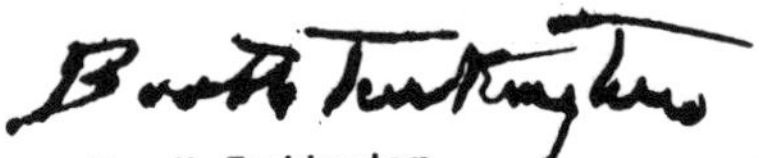

Booth Tarkington

Studs Terkel

Leon Uris

S. S. Van Dine

Carl Van Doren

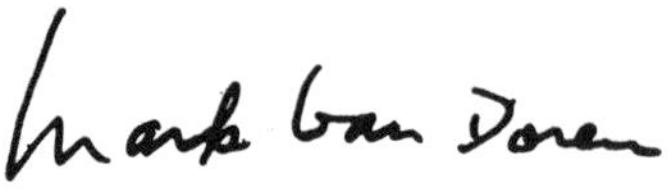

Mark Van Doren

Jules Verne

Erich Von Däniken

Irving Wallace

Jessamyn West

Robert Penn Warren

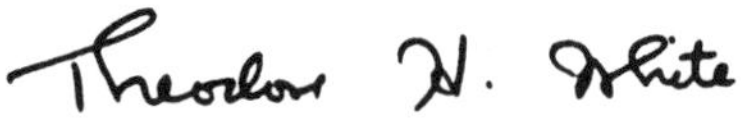

Theodore H. White

Walt Whitman

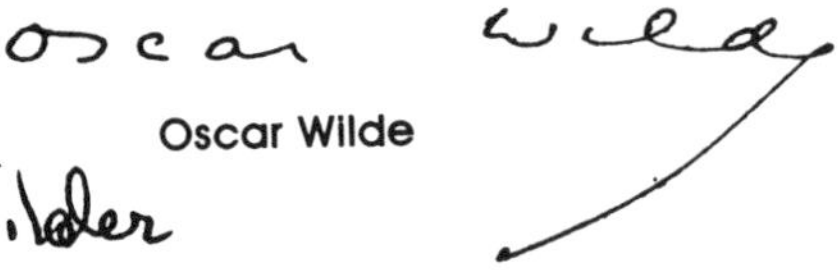

Oscar Wilde

Thornton Wilder

Ben Ames Williams

Tennessee Williams

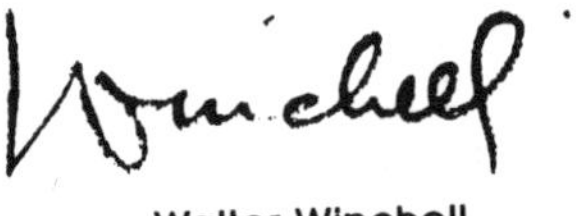

Walter Winchell

Owen Wister

Grant Wood

Thomas Wolfe

AVIATORS

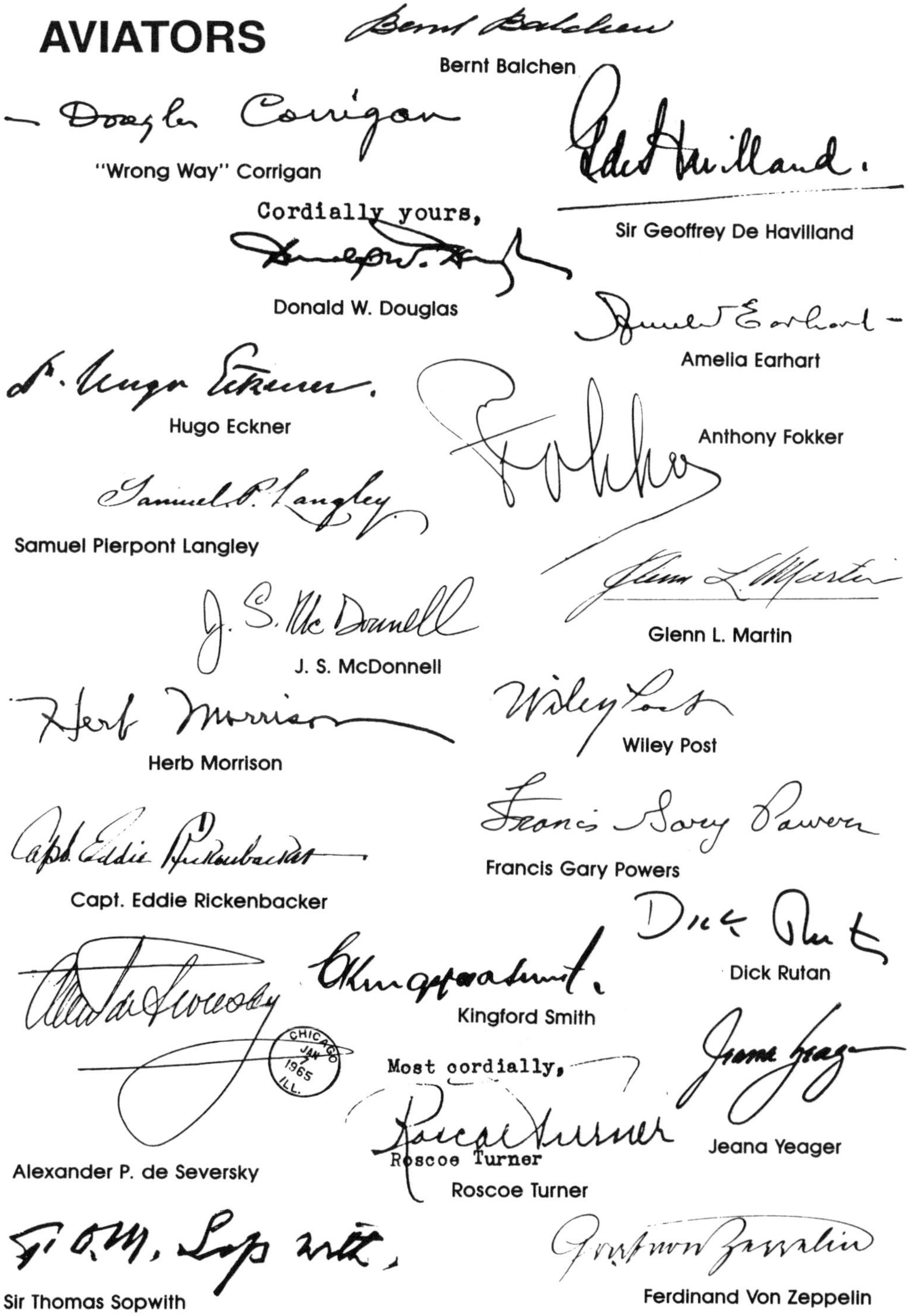

Bernt Balchen

"Wrong Way" Corrigan

Sir Geoffrey De Havilland

Donald W. Douglas

Amelia Earhart

Hugo Eckner

Anthony Fokker

Samuel Pierpont Langley

Glenn L. Martin

J. S. McDonnell

Herb Morrison

Wiley Post

Francis Gary Powers

Capt. Eddie Rickenbacker

Dick Rutan

Kingford Smith

Jeana Yeager

Alexander P. de Seversky

Roscoe Turner

Sir Thomas Sopwith

Ferdinand Von Zeppelin

FACSIMILE SECTION

FACSIMILE SECTION

BUSINESS LEADERS AND FINANCIERS

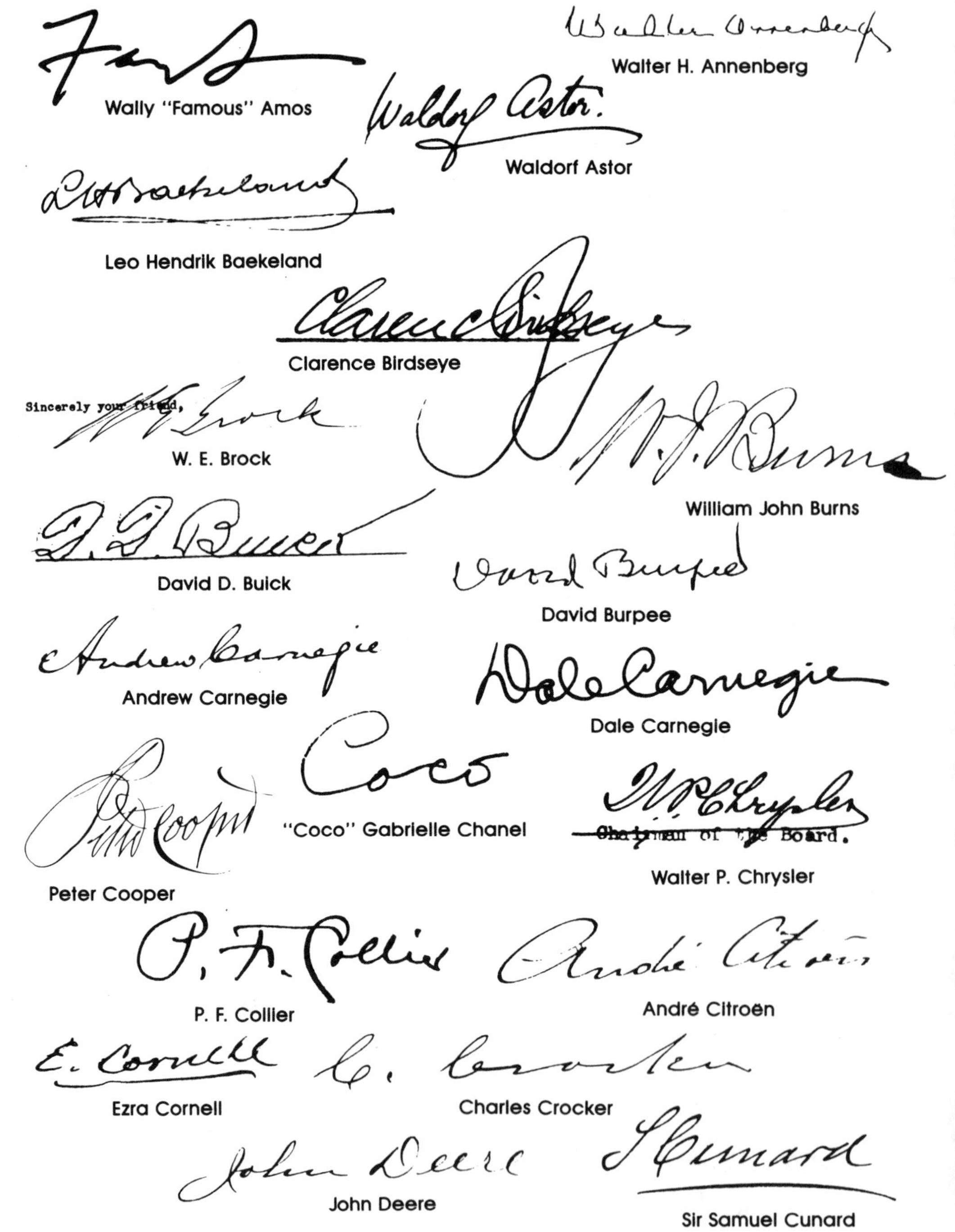

Wally "Famous" Amos

Walter H. Annenberg

Waldorf Astor

Leo Hendrik Baekeland

Clarence Birdseye

W. E. Brock

William John Burns

David D. Buick

David Burpee

Andrew Carnegie

Dale Carnegie

Peter Cooper

"Coco" Gabrielle Chanel

Walter P. Chrysler

P. F. Collier

André Citroën

Ezra Cornell

Charles Crocker

John Deere

Sir Samuel Cunard

BUSINESS LEADERS AND FINANCIERS

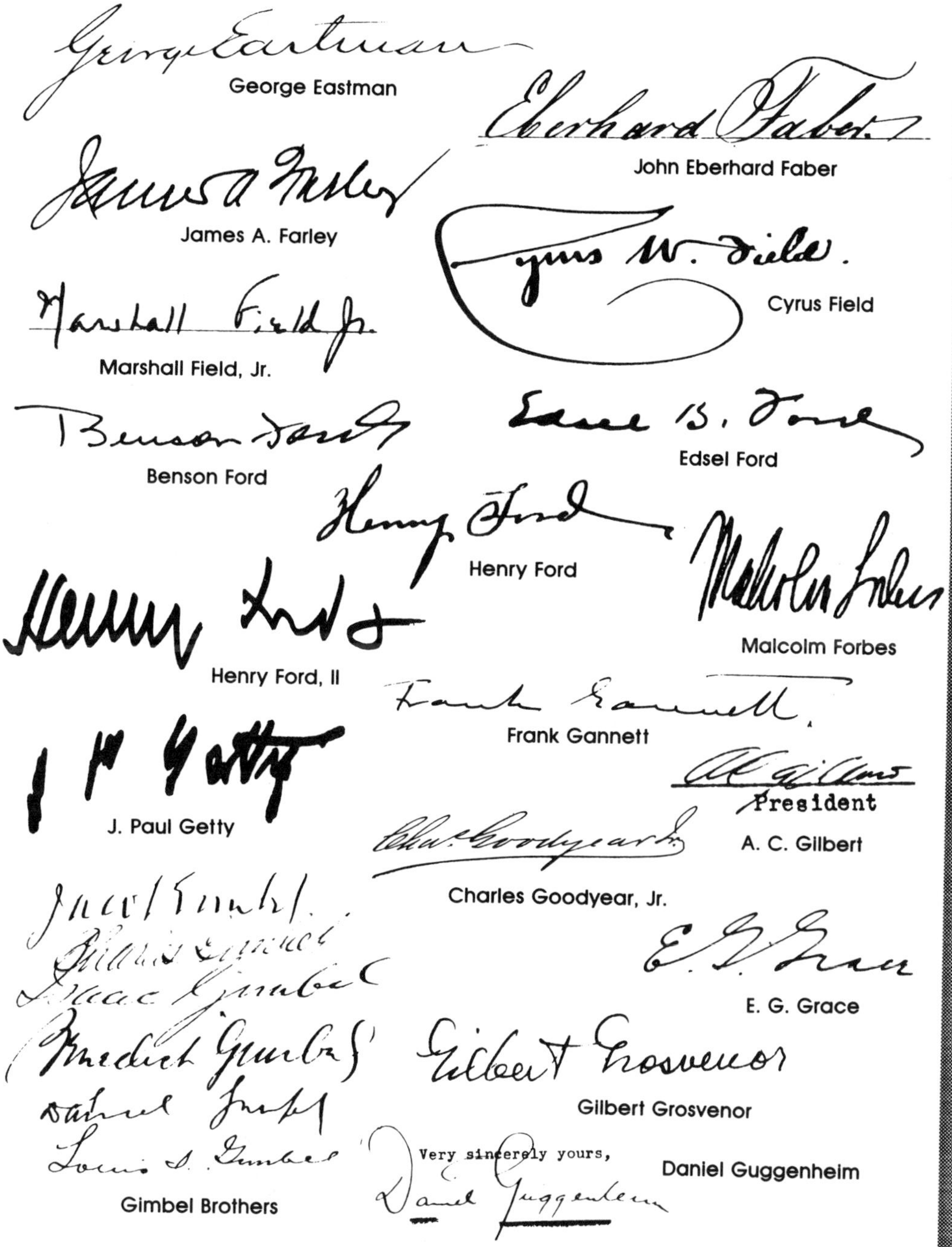

George Eastman
John Eberhard Faber
James A. Farley
Cyrus Field
Marshall Field, Jr.
Benson Ford
Edsel Ford
Henry Ford
Malcolm Forbes
Henry Ford, II
Frank Gannett
J. Paul Getty
A. C. Gilbert
Charles Goodyear, Jr.
E. G. Grace
Gilbert Grosvenor
Gimbel Brothers
Daniel Guggenheim

BUSINESS LEADERS AND FINANCIERS

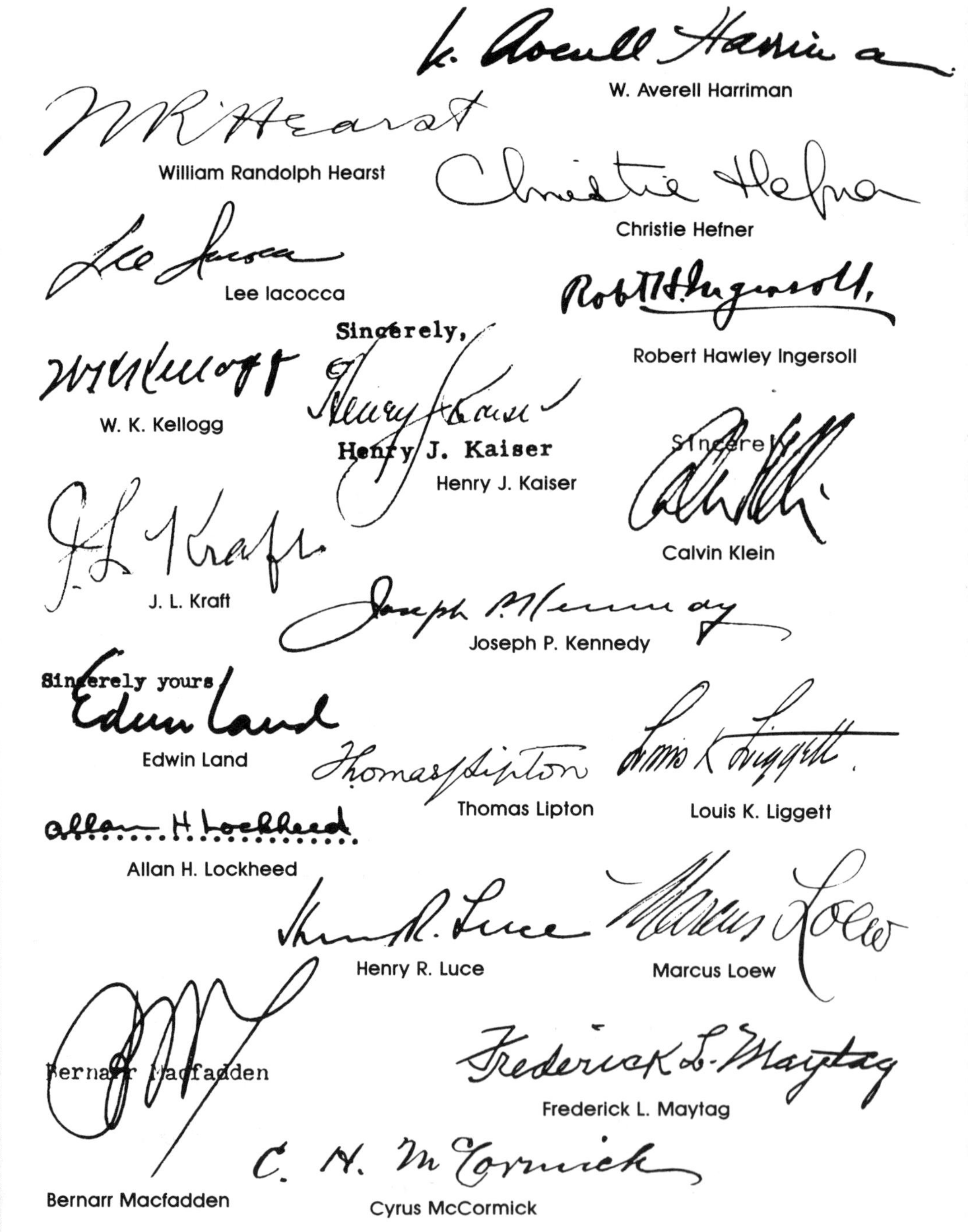

FACSIMILE SECTION

BUSINESS LEADERS AND FINANCIERS

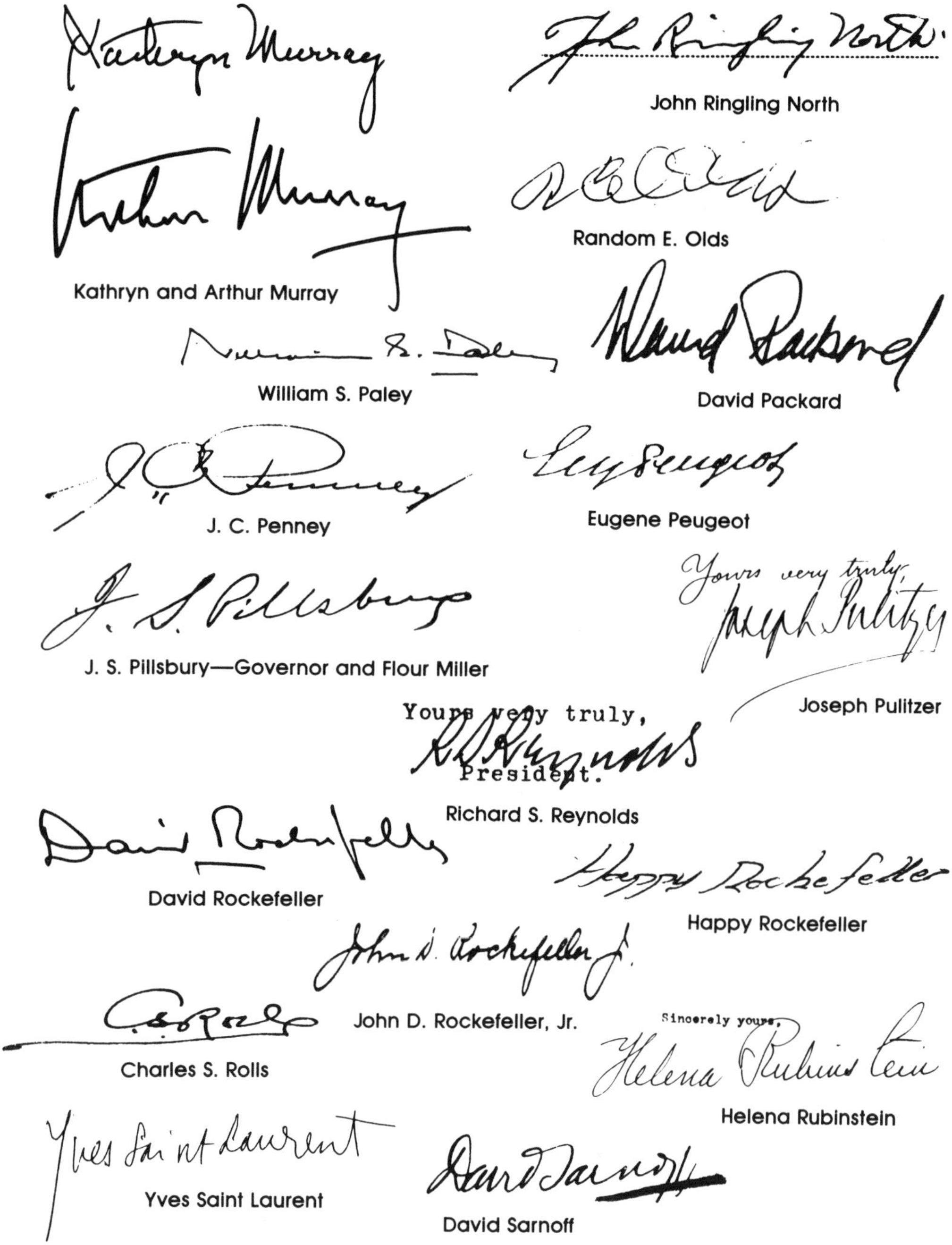

John Ringling North

Random E. Olds

Kathryn and Arthur Murray

William S. Paley

David Packard

J. C. Penney

Eugene Peugeot

J. S. Pillsbury—Governor and Flour Miller

Joseph Pulitzer

Richard S. Reynolds

David Rockefeller

Happy Rockefeller

John D. Rockefeller, Jr.

Charles S. Rolls

Helena Rubinstein

Yves Saint Laurent

David Sarnoff

FACSIMILE SECTION

BUSINESS LEADERS AND FINANCIERS

Dr. Armand Hammer

Rupert Murdock

Charles M. Schwab

Vidal Sassoon

Harry F. Sinclair

Alfred P. Sloan, Jr.

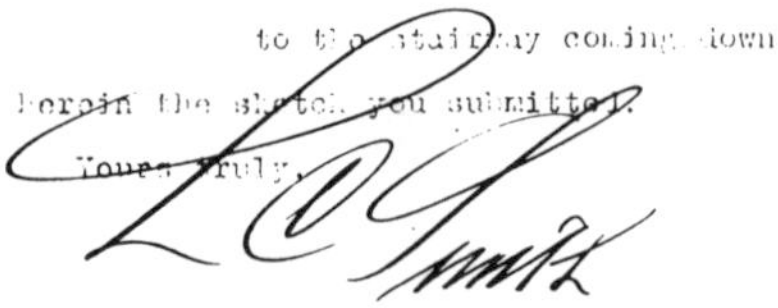
L. C. Smith

Edward Robinson Squibb

Frank Stanton

Harold H. Swift

Donald J. Trump

Ted Turner

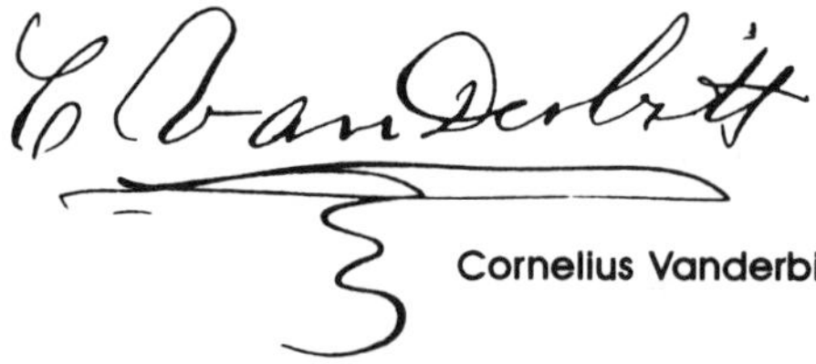
Cornelius Vanderbilt

George W. Vanderbilt

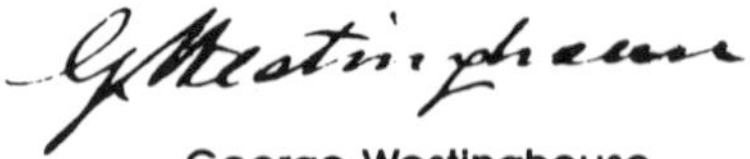
George Westinghouse

Thomas J. Watson

Eli Whitney

CABINET MEMBERS AND U.S. VPs

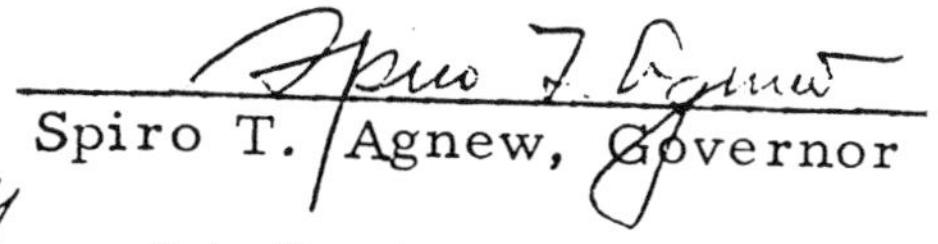

Spiro Theodore Agnew (Richard Nixon's V.P.)

Alben William Barkley (Harry Truman's V.P.)

John Cabell Breckinridge (James Buchanan's V.P.)

Aaron Burr (Thomas Jefferson's V.P.)

John Caldwell Calhoun (John Quincy Adams' V.P.)

George Clinton (V.P. for Thomas Jefferson and James Madison)

Schuyler Colfax (U. S. Grant's V.P.)

Calvin Coolidge (Warren G. Harding's V.P.)

Charles Curtis (Herbert Hoover's V.P.)

George Mifflin Dallas (James K. Polk's V.P.)

Charles G. Dawes (Calvin Coolidge's V.P.)

FACSIMILE SECTION

FACSIMILE SECTION

CABINET MEMBERS AND U.S. VPs

Charles W. Fairbanks (Theodore Roosevelt's V.P.)

John Nance Garner (Franklin D. Roosevelt's first V.P.)

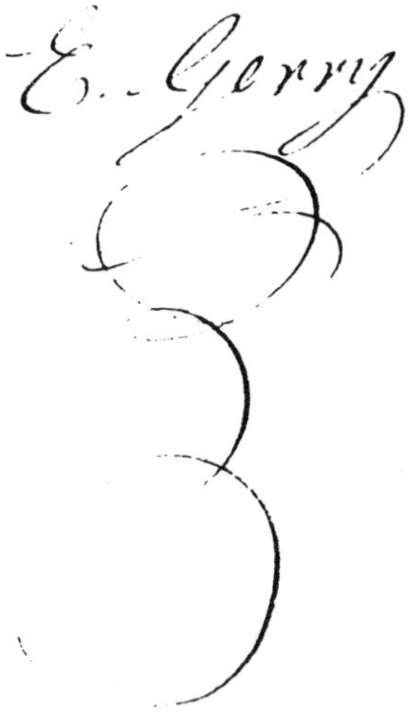

Elbridge Gerry (James Madison's V.P.)

Hannibal Hamlin (Abraham Lincoln's V.P.)

Thomas Andrews Hendricks (Grover Cleveland's V.P.)

Garret Augustus Hobart (William McKinley's first V.P.)

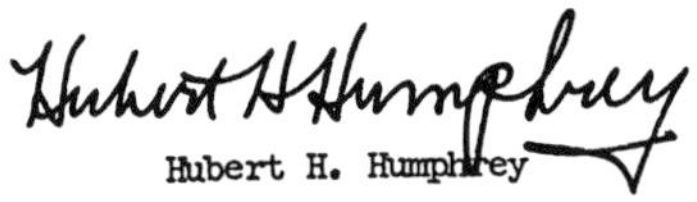

Hubert Horatio Humphrey (Lyndon Johnson's V.P.)

Thomas Riley Marshall (Woodrow Wilson's V.P.)

Lyndon Baines Johnson (John F. Kennedy's V.P.)

Richard Mentor Johnson (Martin Van Buren's V.P.)

William Rufus DeVane King (Franklin Pierce's V.P.)

CABINET MEMBERS AND U.S. VPs

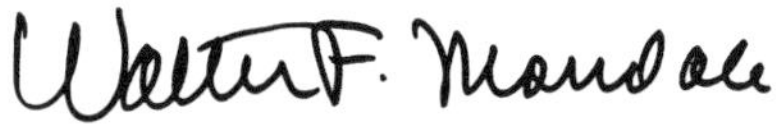

Walter Frederick Mondale (Jimmy Carter's V.P.)

Levi Parsons Morton (Benjamin Harrison's V.P.)

Dan Quayle (George Bush's V.P.)

Nelson Aldrich Rockefeller (Gerald Ford's V.P.)

James Schoolcraft Sherman (William Howard Taft's V.P.)

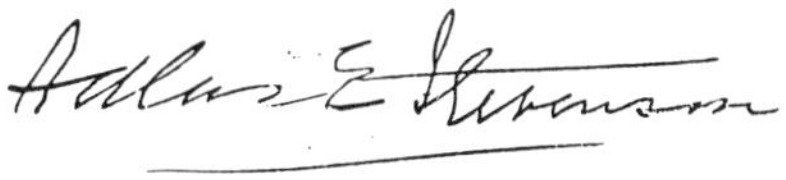

Adlai E. Stevenson (Grover Cleveland's V.P.)

Daniel D. Tompkins (James Monroe's V.P.)

Henry Agard Wallace (Franklin D. Roosevelt's second V.P.)

Henry Wilson (U. S. Grant's V.P.)

FACSIMILE SECTION

CARTOONISTS AND ILLUSTRATORS

Herb Block—"Herblock"

Dik Browne

Milton Caniff

Al Capp

Ed Dodd

Jim Davis

Fred Fredericks

Dave Graue

Chester Gould

Johnny Hart

Walter Lantz

Bil Keane

Hank Ketcham

George McManus

Russell Myers

Dick Moores

Gary Trudeau

Charles Schulz

Robert Ripley

CELEBRITIES

Cesar Chavez

Red Adair

Joseph Alsop

Lady Astor

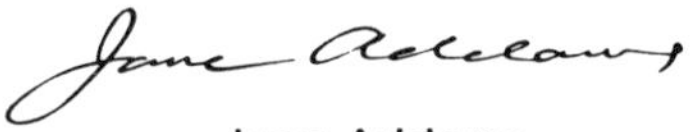

Jane Addams

F. Lee Bailey

P. T. Barnum

Roald Ammundsen

Clara Barton

Bernard M. Baruch

Ezra Taft Benson

Dan Berrigan

Hugo Black

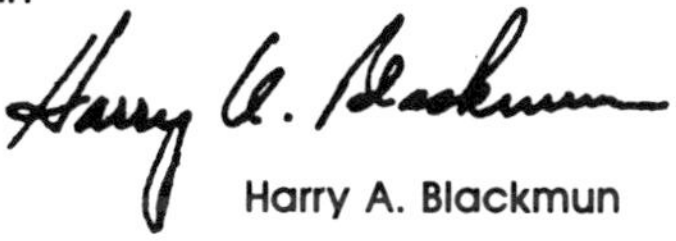

Harry A. Blackmun

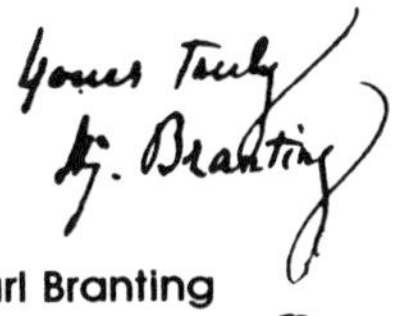

Karl Branting

Julian Bond

Evangeline Booth

Louis D. Brandeis

Justice William J. Brennan, Jr.

Ralph Bunche

Kellye Cash

Warren E. Burger

Whittaker Chambers

FACSIMILE SECTION

FACSIMILE SECTION

CELEBRITIES

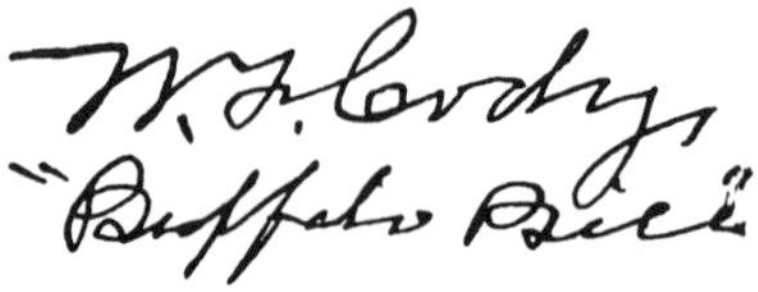

William F. "Buffalo Bill" Cody

Roy Cohn

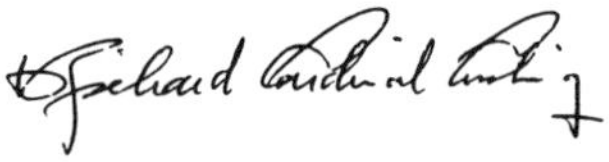

Richard Cardinal Cushing

Richard J. Daley

Richard Harding Davis

Thomas Dewey

William O. Douglas

William Du Bois

Abba Eban

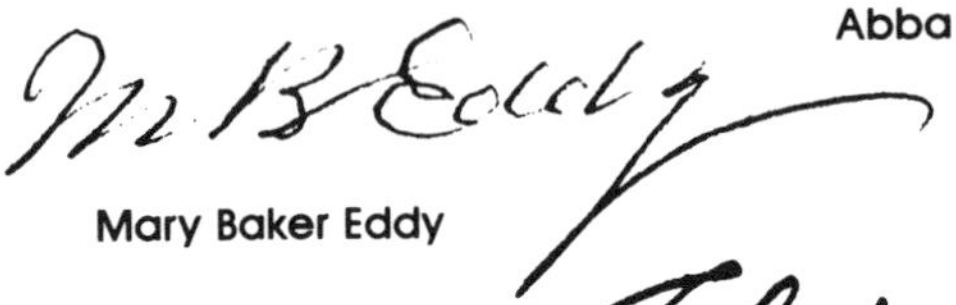

Mary Baker Eddy

Julie Nixon Eisenhower

Charles Evers

James A. Farley

Mayor Diane Feinstein

Bobby Fischer

Father Edward Flanagan

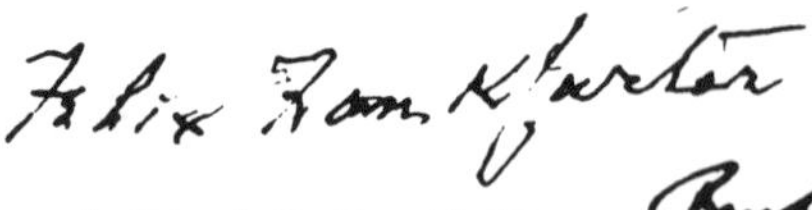

Justice Felix Frankfurter

R. Buckminster Fuller

Milton Friedman

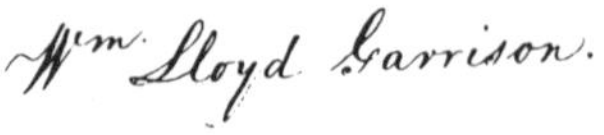

William Lloyd Garrison

CELEBRITIES

Horace Greeley

Oliver Wendell Holmes

Sir Edmund Hillary

Thor Heyerdahl

Samuel Gompers

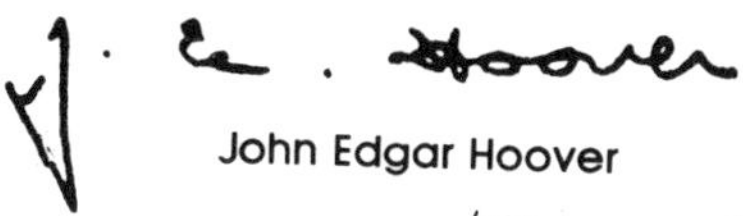
John Edgar Hoover

Charles E. Hughes

Aimee McPherson Hutton

Jesse Jackson

Leon Jouhau

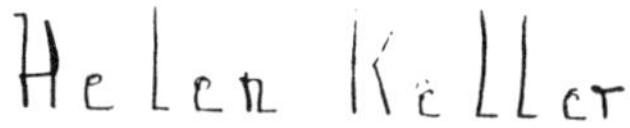
Helen Keller

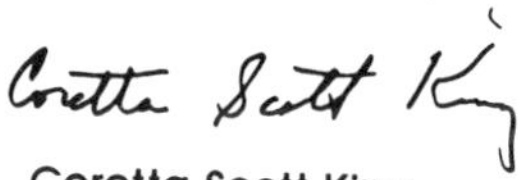
Coretta Scott King

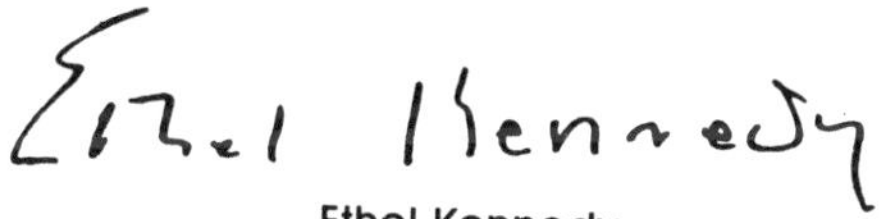
Ethel Kennedy

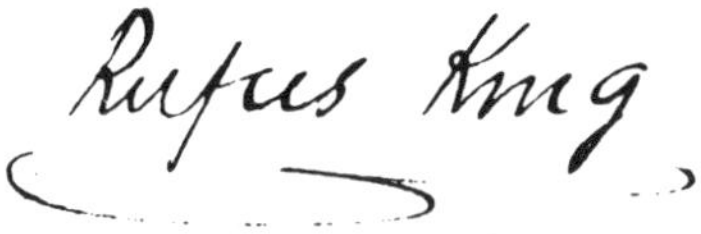
Rufus King

Lane Kirkland

Edward I. Koch

Evel Knievel

Fiorello LaGuardia

Simon Lake

Bert Lance

Ann Landers

Alf Landon

CELEBRITIES

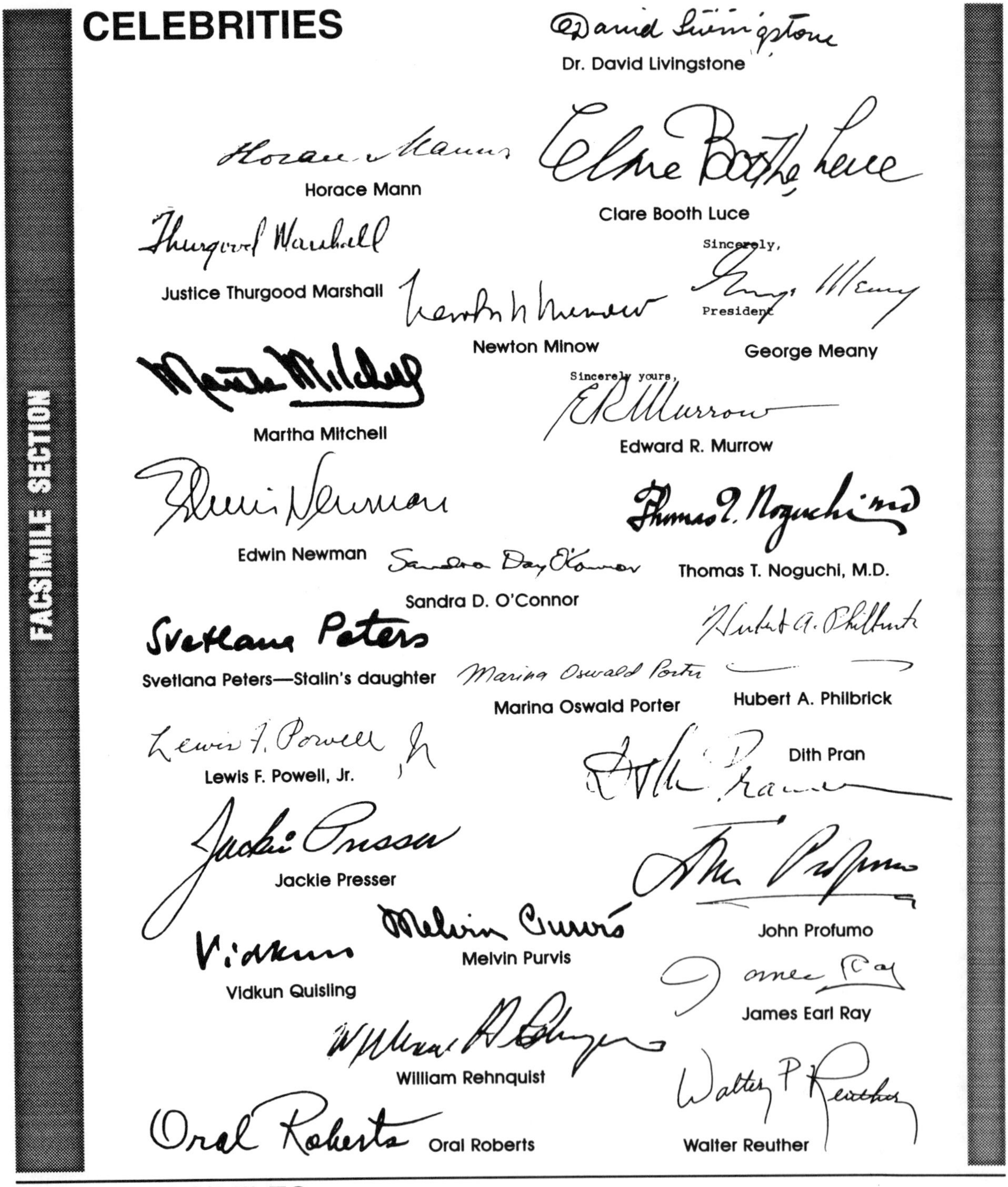

CELEBRITIES

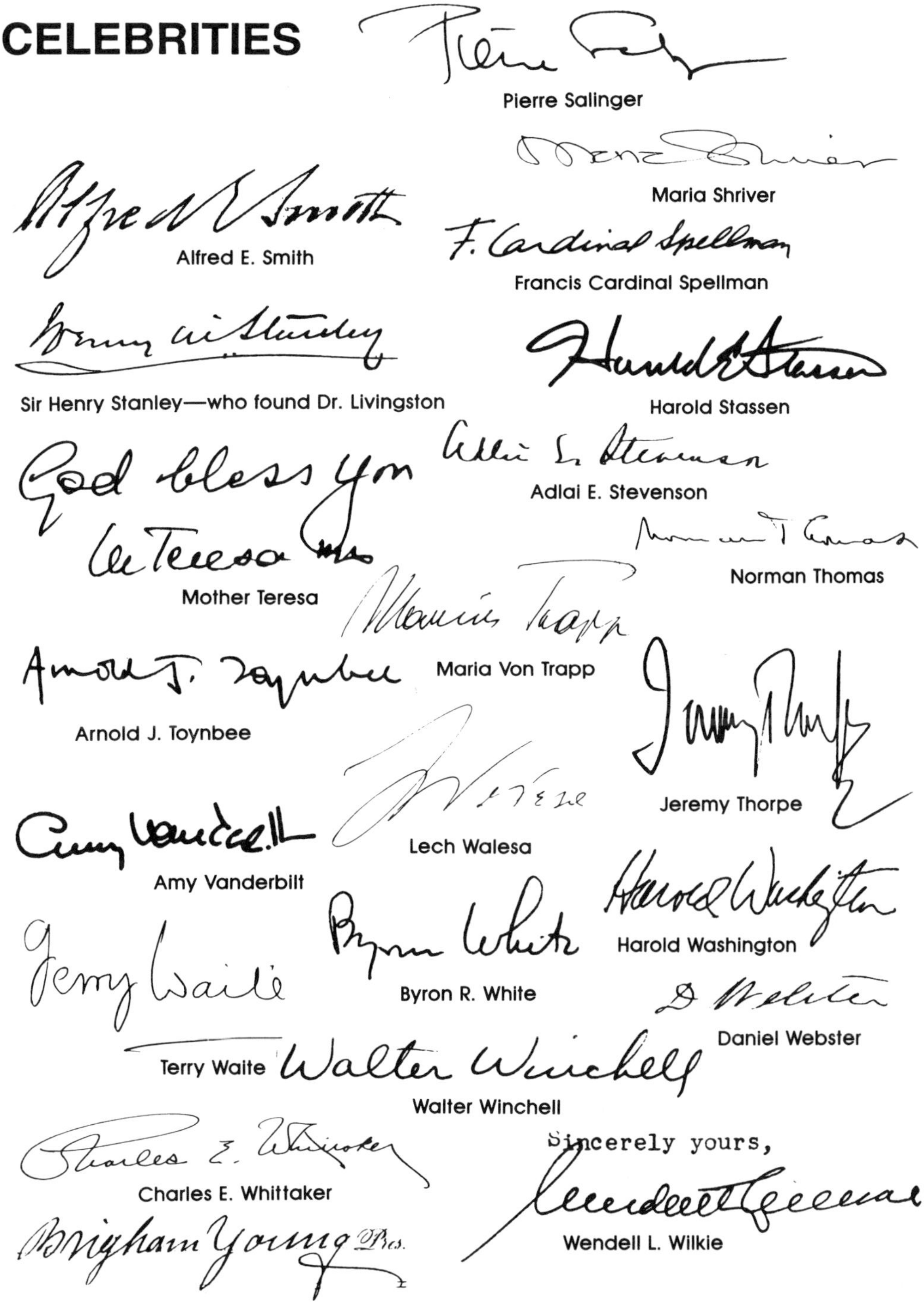

Pierre Salinger

Maria Shriver

Alfred E. Smith

Francis Cardinal Spellman

Sir Henry Stanley—who found Dr. Livingston

Harold Stassen

Adlai E. Stevenson

Norman Thomas

Mother Teresa

Maria Von Trapp

Arnold J. Toynbee

Jeremy Thorpe

Lech Walesa

Amy Vanderbilt

Harold Washington

Byron R. White

Daniel Webster

Terry Waite

Walter Winchell

Charles E. Whittaker

Wendell L. Wilkie

Brigham Young

FACSIMILE SECTION

FACSIMILE SECTION

CIVIL WAR LEADERS

Gen. D. C. Buell

Maj. Gen. Benjamin F. Butler

Ambrose E. Burnside

Maj. Gen. Howell Cobb, C.S.A.

General Samuel Cooper—Highest-Ranking Confederate Officer

Jefferson Davis

Maj. Gen. Abner Doubleday

Lt. Gen. Jubal Early, C.S.A.

John Charles Fremont

Maj. Gen. John White Geary, U.S.A.

Brig. Gen. Joseph Hawley, U.S.A.

Maj. Gen. Oliver Otis Howard, U.S.A.

Robert Edward Lee

General George McClellan

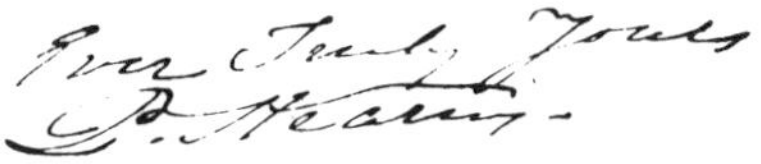

Maj. Gen. Philip Kearny

Maj. Gen. George Meade, U.S.A

Nelson Appleton Miles

Maj. John S. Mosby, C.S.A.—"The Gray Ghost"

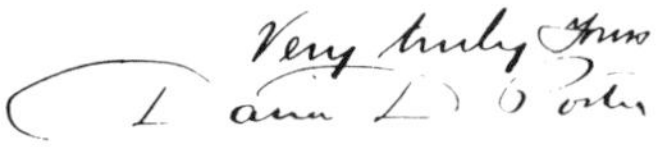

Adm. David D. Porter

Gen. William S. Rosecrans

Gen. Philip Sheridan

Winfield Scott

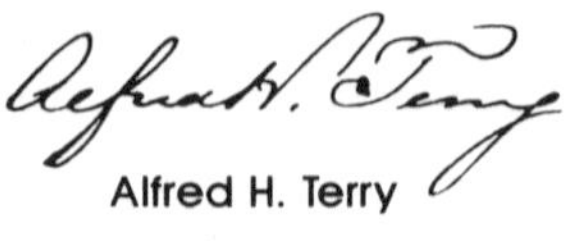

Alfred H. Terry

COMPOSERS

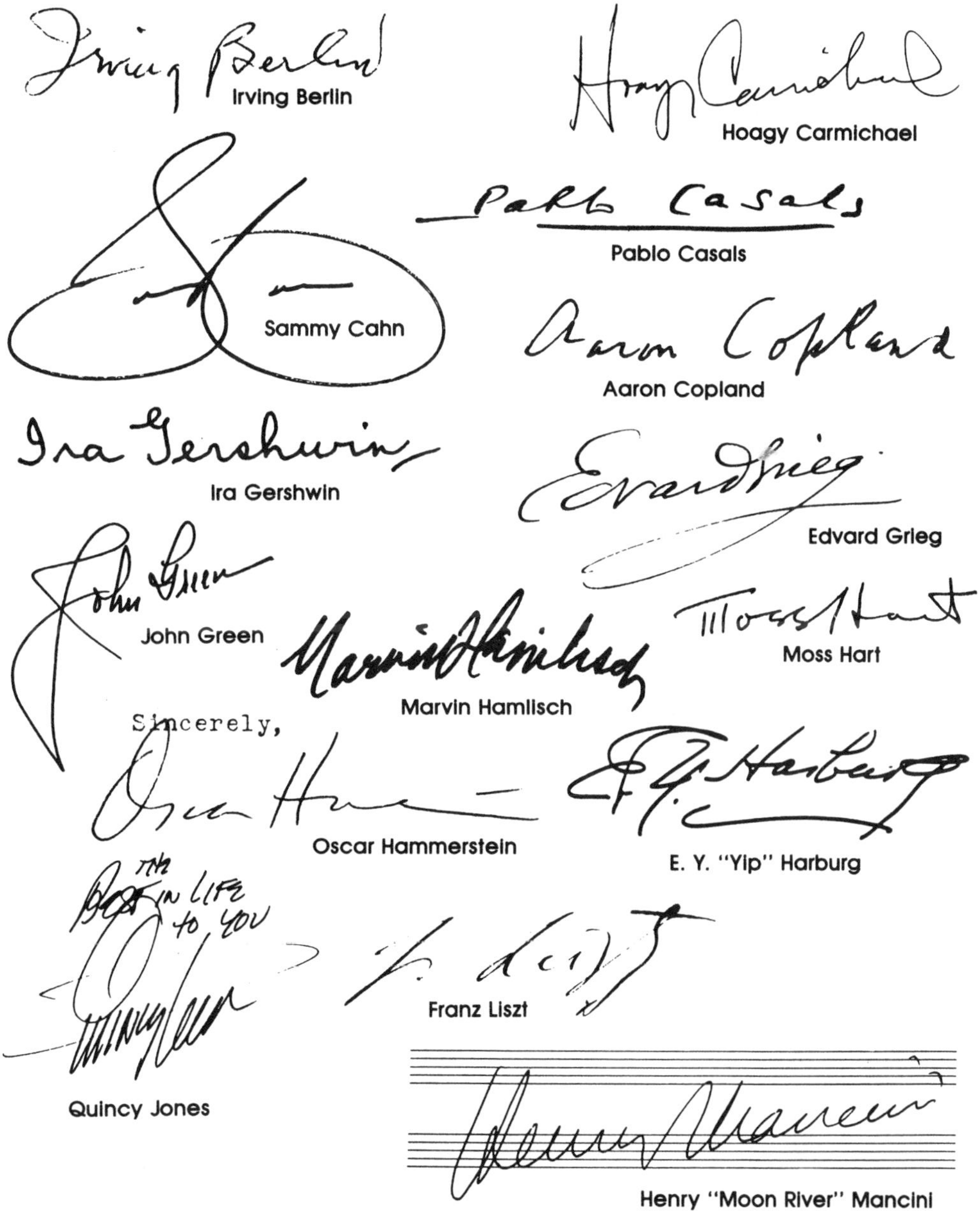

Irving Berlin

Hoagy Carmichael

Sammy Cahn

Pablo Casals

Aaron Copland

Ira Gershwin

Edvard Grieg

John Green

Marvin Hamlisch

Moss Hart

Oscar Hammerstein

E. Y. "Yip" Harburg

Quincy Jones

Franz Liszt

Henry "Moon River" Mancini

FACSIMILE SECTION

COMPOSERS

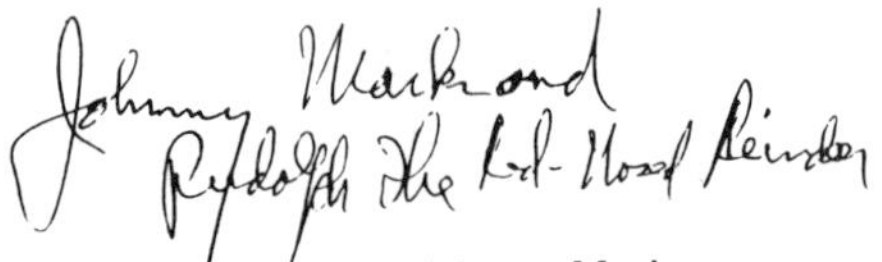

Johnny Marks

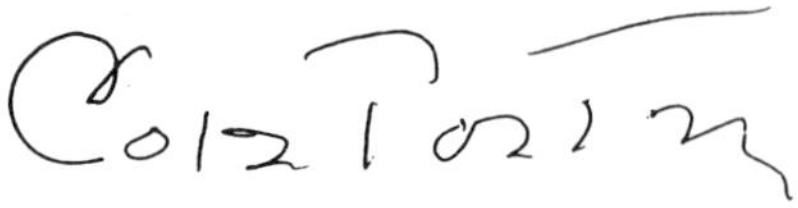

Cole Porter

André Previn

Richard Rodgers

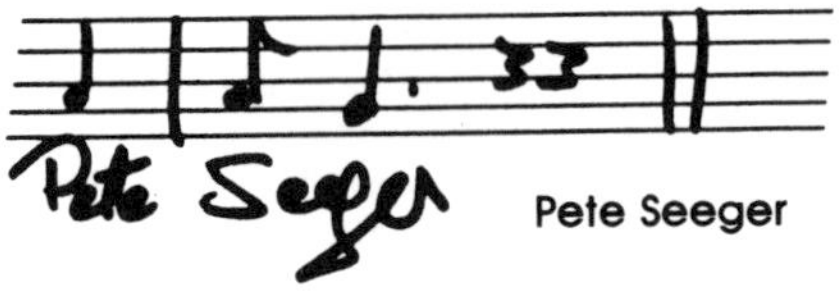

Pete Seeger

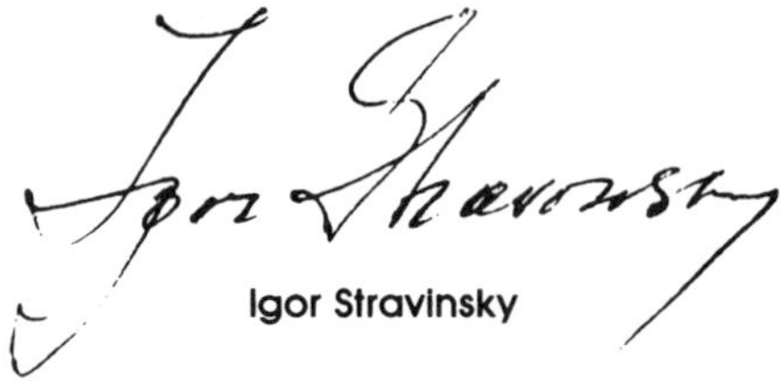

Igor Stravinsky

Sir Arthur Sullivan (of Gilbert and Sullivan)

Mason Williams

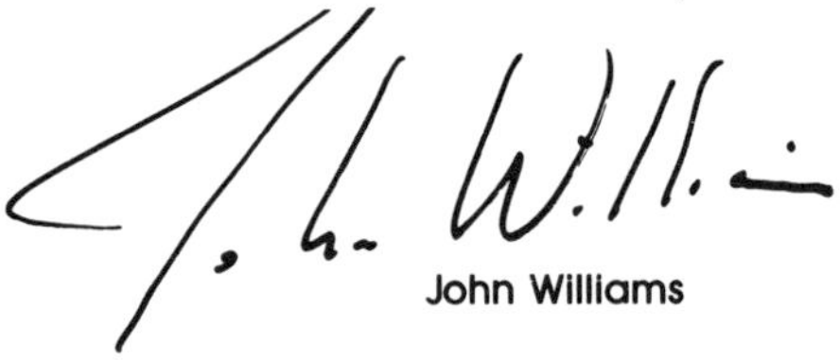

John Williams

Paul Williams

Meredith Willson

ENTERTAINERS

ENTERTAINERS

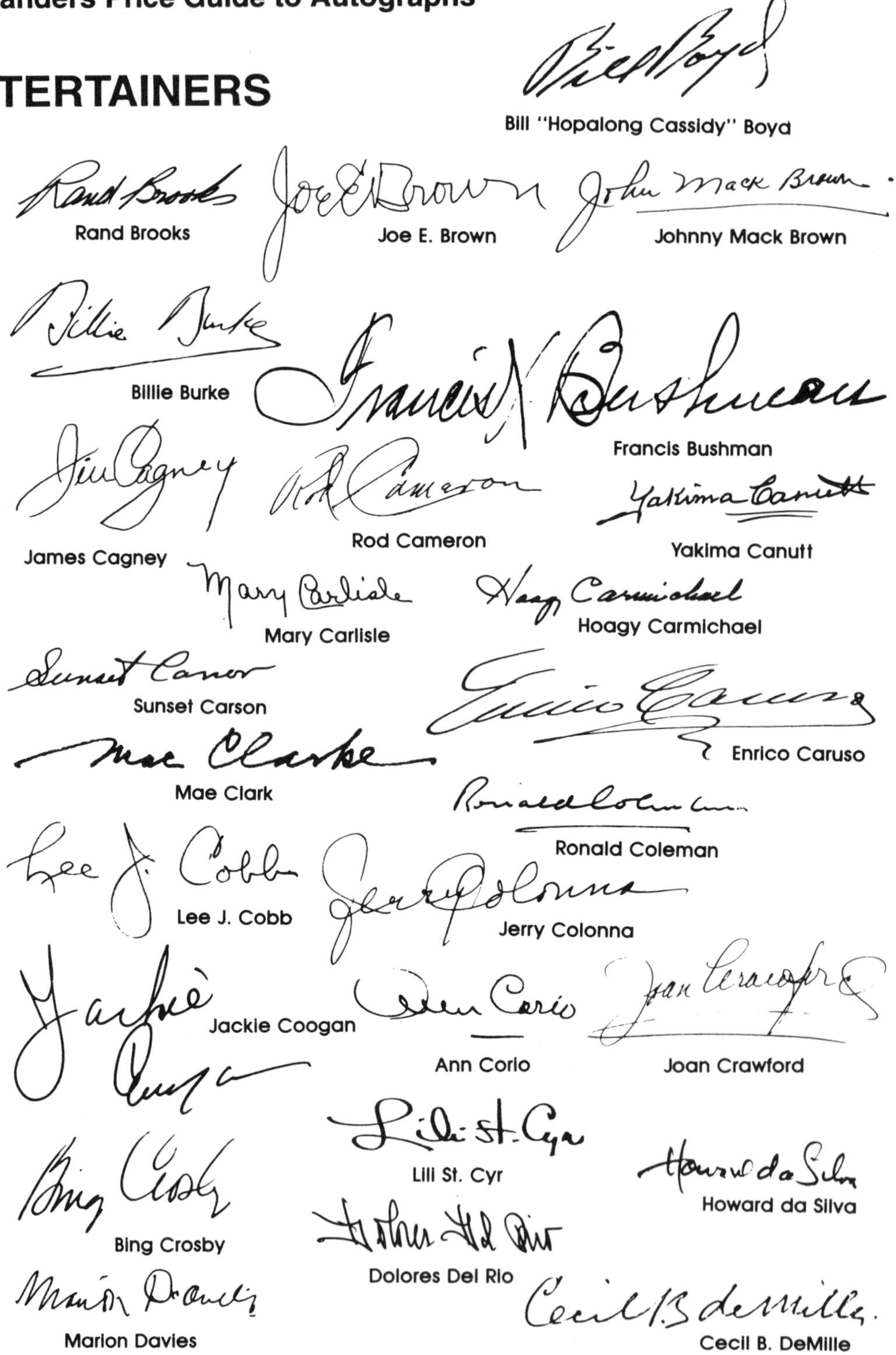

Bill "Hopalong Cassidy" Boyd

Rand Brooks

Joe E. Brown

Johnny Mack Brown

Billie Burke

Francis Bushman

James Cagney

Rod Cameron

Yakima Canutt

Mary Carlisle

Hoagy Carmichael

Sunset Carson

Enrico Caruso

Mae Clark

Ronald Coleman

Lee J. Cobb

Jerry Colonna

Jackie Coogan

Ann Corio

Joan Crawford

Lili St. Cyr

Howard da Silva

Bing Crosby

Dolores Del Rio

Marion Davies

Cecil B. DeMille

ENTERTAINERS

Joan Fontaine

Arthur Fiedler

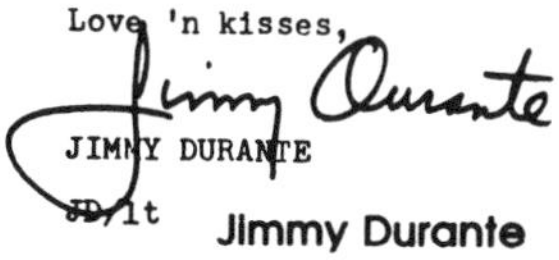

Jimmy Durante

Errol Flynn

David Frost

Cary Grant

Greta Garbo

Ava Gardner

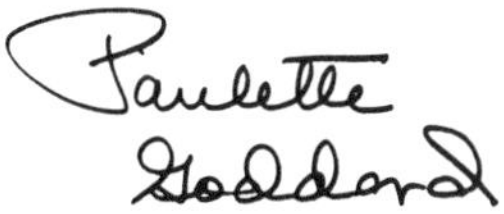
Paulette Goddard

Lillian Gish

Arthur Godfrey

Samuel Goldwyn

Benny Goodman

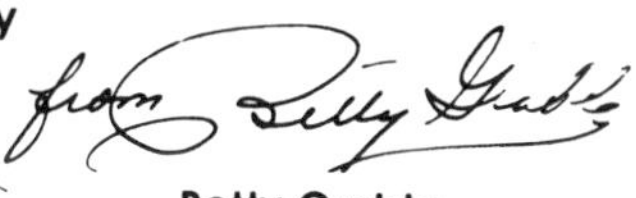
Betty Grable

D. W. Griffith

Josephine Hall

Ann Harding

Oliver Hardy

June Haver

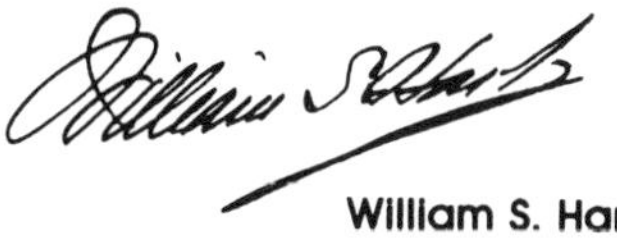
William S. Hart

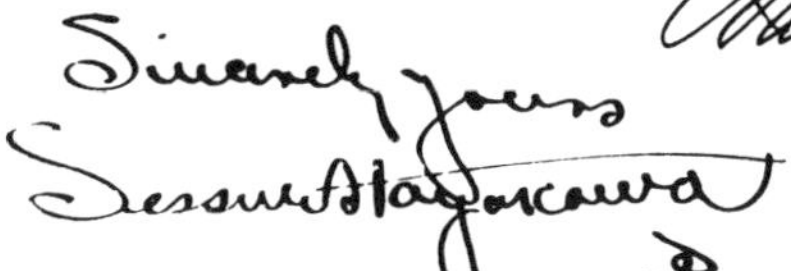
Sessue Hayakawa

Susan Hayward

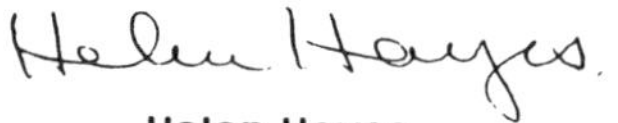
Helen Hayes

Jascha Heifetz

Katharine Hepburn

FACSIMILE SECTION

FACSIMILE SECTION

ENTERTAINERS

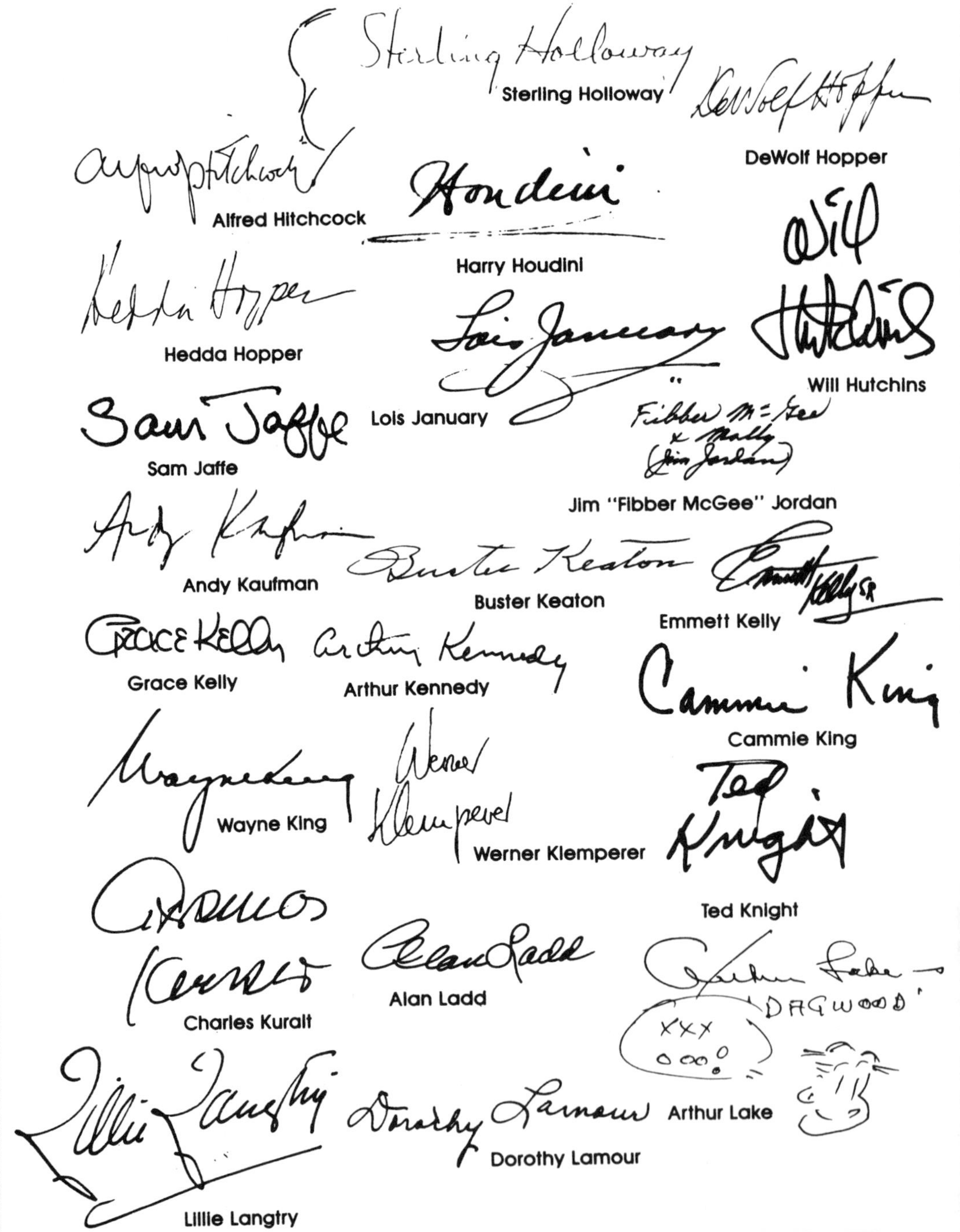

Sterling Holloway

DeWolf Hopper

Alfred Hitchcock

Harry Houdini

Hedda Hopper

Lois January

Will Hutchins

Sam Jaffe

Jim "Fibber McGee" Jordan

Andy Kaufman

Buster Keaton

Emmett Kelly

Grace Kelly

Arthur Kennedy

Cammie King

Wayne King

Werner Klemperer

Ted Knight

Charles Kuralt

Alan Ladd

Arthur Lake

Lillie Langtry

Dorothy Lamour

ENTERTAINERS

Lash LaRue
Stan Laurel
Gertrude Lawrence
David Lean
Norman Lear
Anna Lee
Gypsy Rose Lee
Lila Lee
Beatrice Lillie
Liberace
Jenny Lind
Harold Lloyd
Gina Lollobrigida
Marion Mack
Jeanette MacDonald
Mantovani
Ted Mack
Sheila MacRae
Groucho Marx
Zeppo Marx
Harpo Marx
Raymond Massey
Marlee Matlin

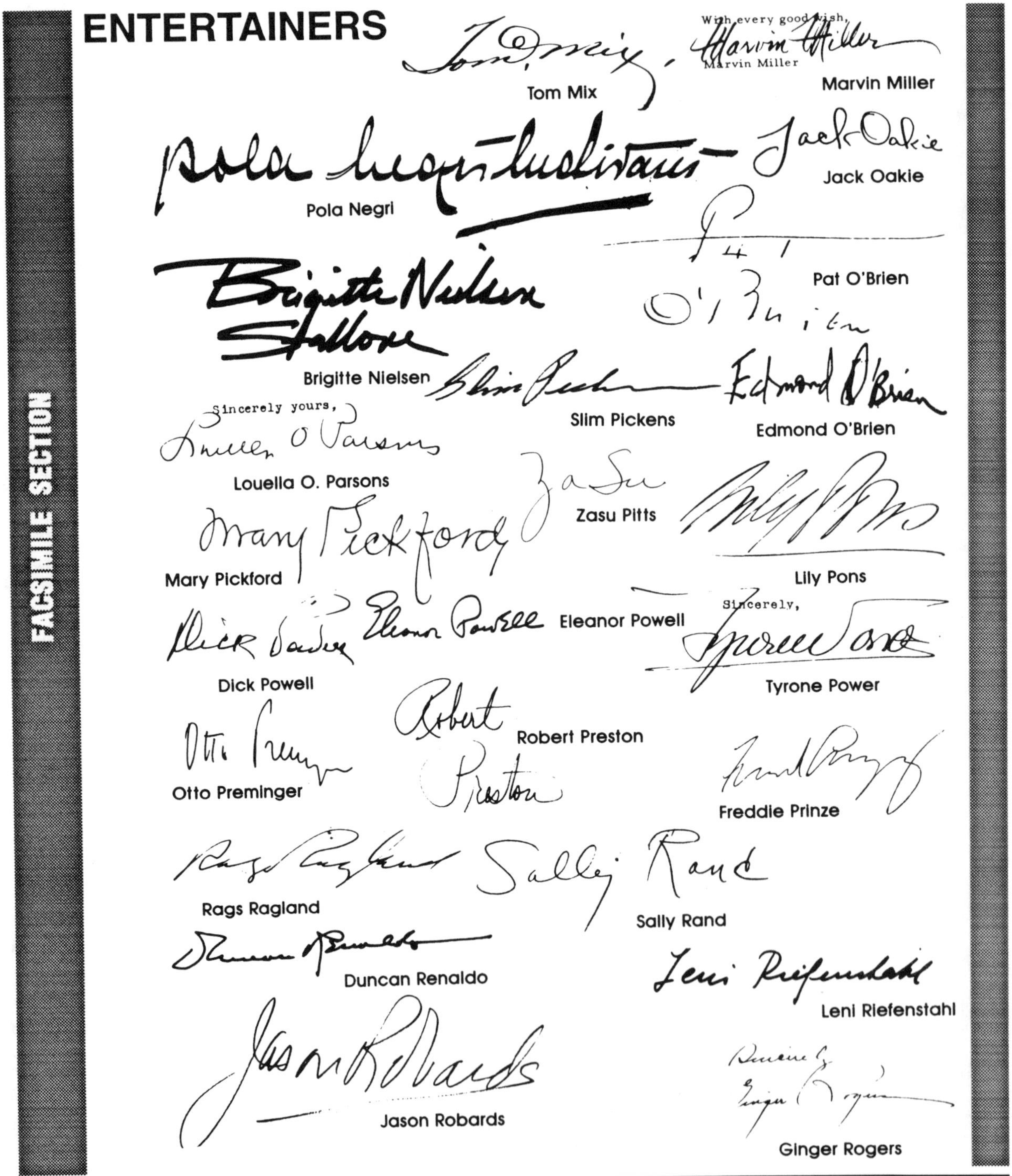
ENTERTAINERS
FACSIMILE SECTION
Tom Mix
With every good wish,
Marvin Miller
Marvin Miller
Pola Negri
Jack Oakie
Pat O'Brien
Brigitte Nielsen
Slim Pickens
Edmond O'Brien
Sincerely yours,
Louella O. Parsons
Zasu Pitts
Lily Pons
Mary Pickford
Eleanor Powell
Sincerely,
Dick Powell
Tyrone Power
Robert Preston
Otto Preminger
Freddie Prinze
Rags Ragland
Sally Rand
Duncan Renaldo
Leni Riefenstahl
Jason Robards
Ginger Rogers

ENTERTAINERS

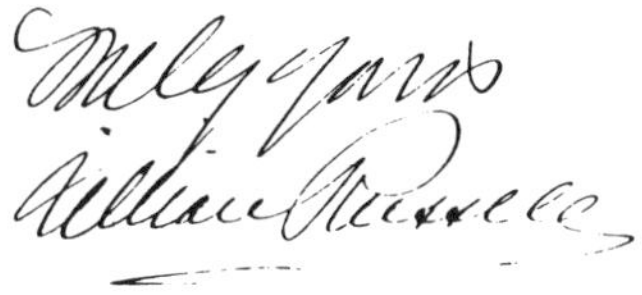
Lillian Russell

Ann Rutherford

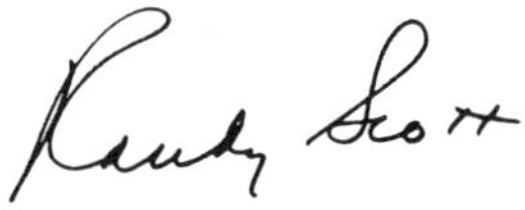
Randolph Scott

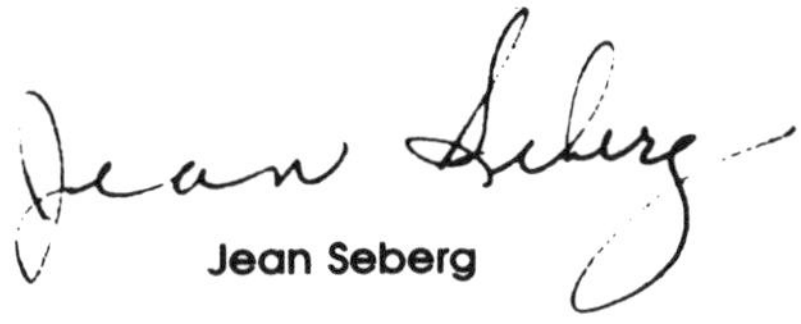
Jean Seberg

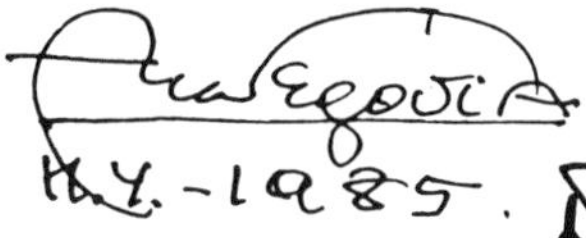
Andres Segovia

David O. Selznick

Mack Sennett

Norma Shearer

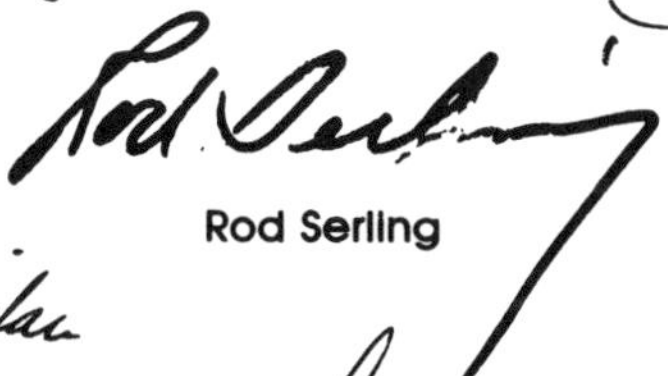
Rod Serling

Ann Sheridan

Frank Sinatra

Phil Silvers

Jimmy Stewart

Ann Sothern

Tempest Storm

Howard Thurston

Forrest Tucker

Barbara Walters

John Wayne

Charlie Weaver (Cliff Arquette)

Esther Williams

FACSIMILE SECTION

FACSIMILE SECTION

HEADS OF STATE

Clement R. Attlee

Louis Napoléon Bonaparte

Menachem Begin

Willy Brandt

King Juan Carlos, Spain

Joe Clark, Canadian Prime Minister

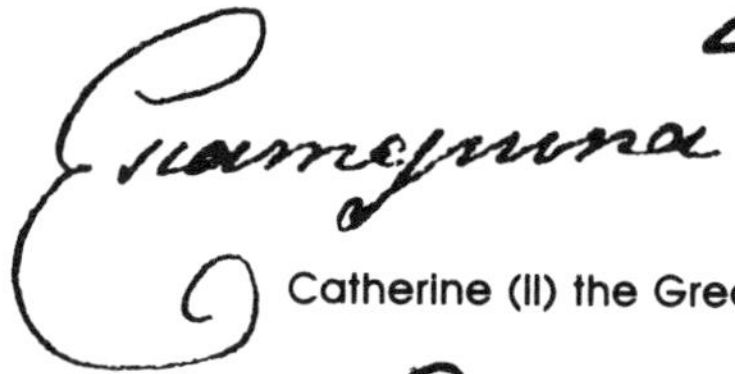

Catherine (II) the Great

Idi Amin Dada

Benjamin Disraeli

Francis Duvalier, Haiti

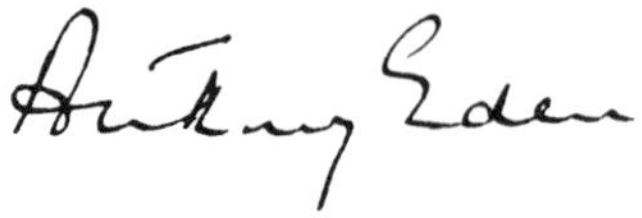

Sir Anthony Eden

Queen Elizabeth II, England

Frederick the Great, Prussia

Indira Gandhi

Mahatma Gandhi

Guiseppe Garibaldi

Charles de Gaulle

King George I, England

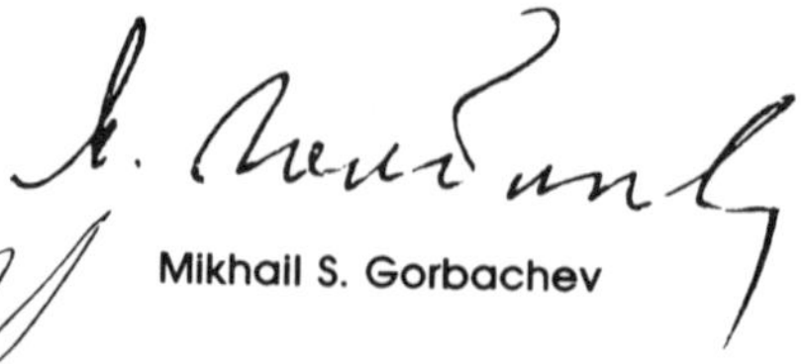

Mikhail S. Gorbachev

Salvador Allende Gossens

HEADS OF STATE

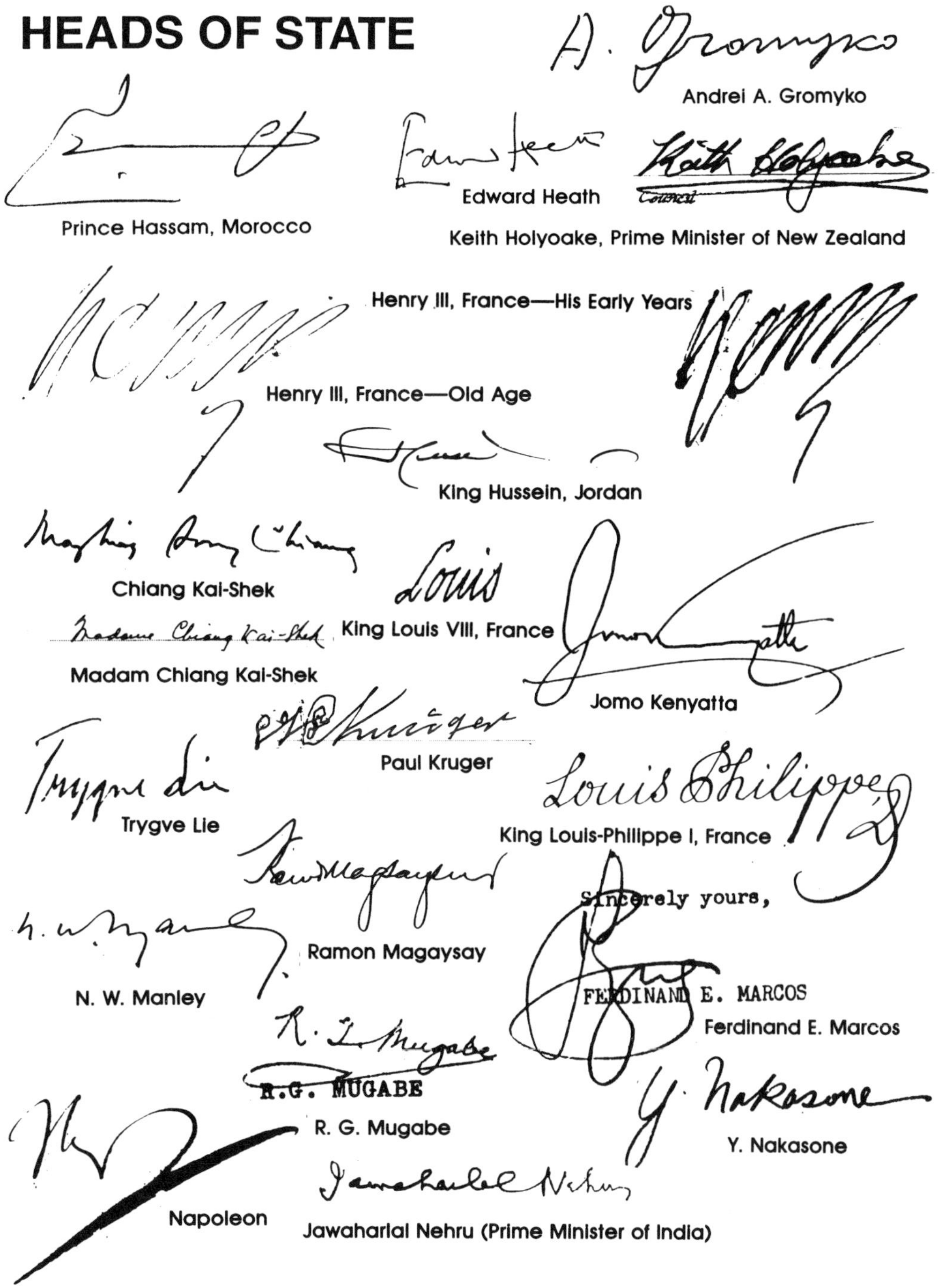

Andrei A. Gromyko

Prince Hassam, Morocco

Edward Heath

Keith Holyoake, Prime Minister of New Zealand

Henry III, France—His Early Years

Henry III, France—Old Age

King Hussein, Jordan

Chiang Kai-Shek

King Louis VIII, France

Madam Chiang Kai-Shek

Jomo Kenyatta

Paul Kruger

Trygve Lie

King Louis-Philippe I, France

Ramon Magaysay

N. W. Manley

Ferdinand E. Marcos

R. G. Mugabe

Y. Nakasone

Napoleon

Jawaharlal Nehru (Prime Minister of India)

FACSIMILE SECTION

HEADS OF STATE

Olaf Palme

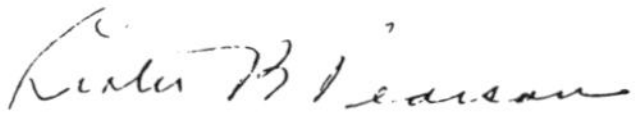

Lester B. Pearson

Sir Robert Peel

Lord North

Col. Muammar Al-Qaddafi, Libya

Prince Rainier, Monaco

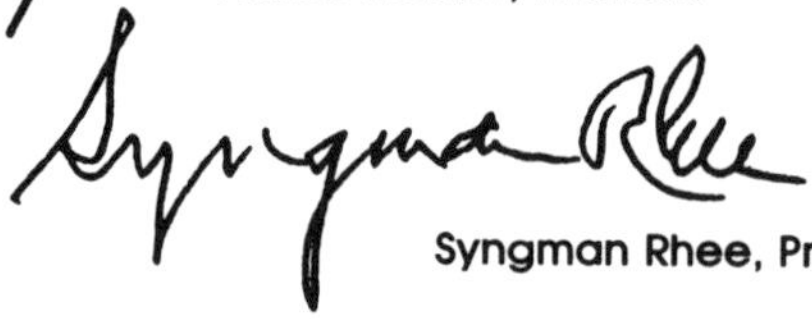

Syngman Rhee, President of Korea

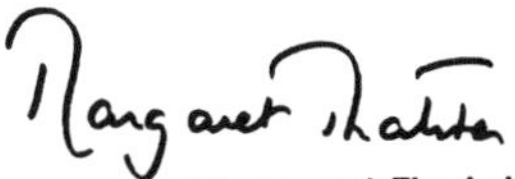

Margaret Thatcher

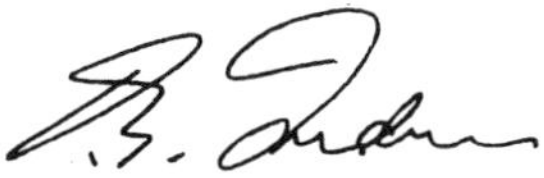

Pierre Trudeau, Canadian Prime Minister

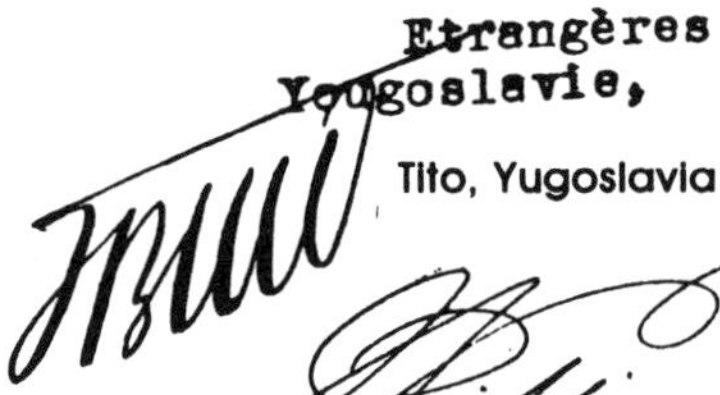

Tito, Yugoslavia

Kurt Waldheim

Queen Victoria

William IV, England

MILITARY LEADERS

Robert Anderson

Theodorus Bailey

G. T. Beauregard

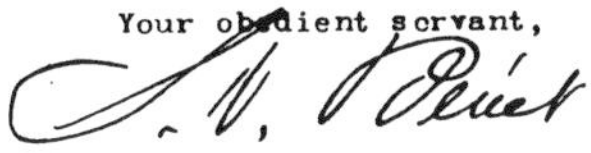

Steven Vincent Benet

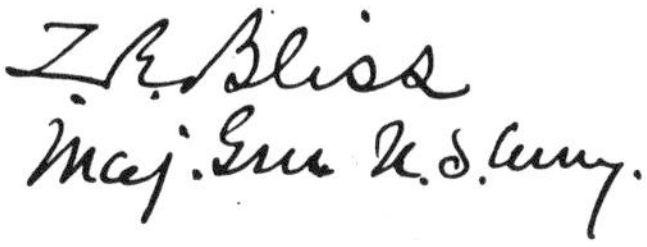

Maj. Gen. Zenas Bliss

D. C. Buell

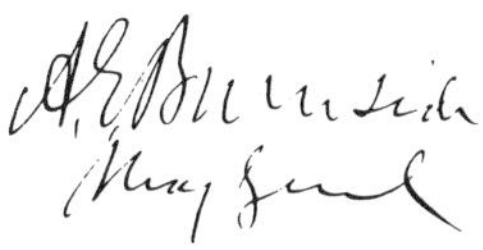

Gen. Ambrose Burnside

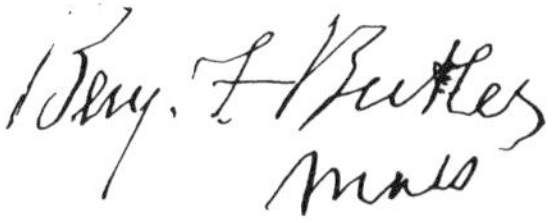

Benjamin F. Butler

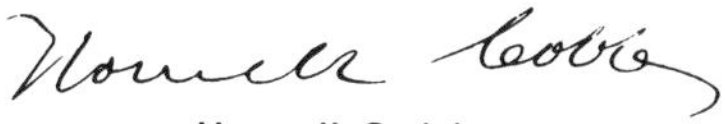

Howell Cobb

Samuel Cooper

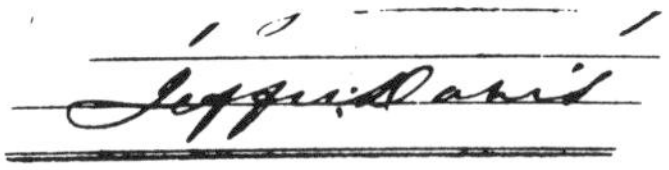

Jefferson Davis

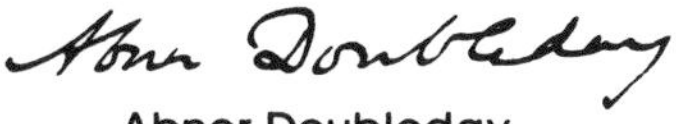

Abner Doubleday

Jubal Early

John Charles Fremont

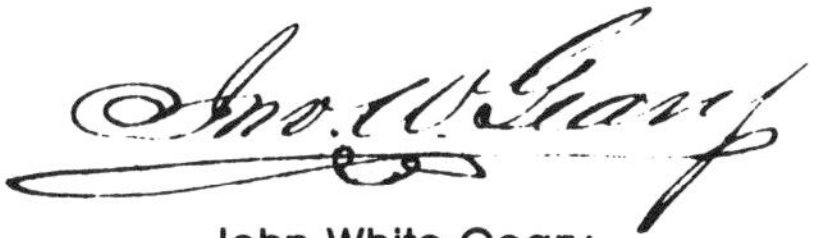

John White Geary

Joseph R. Hawley

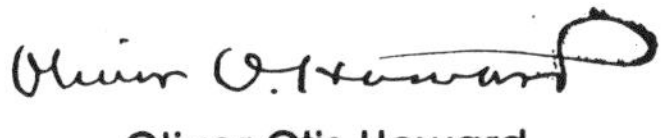

Oliver Otis Howard

FACSIMILE SECTION

FACSIMILE SECTION

MILITARY LEADERS

Philip Kearny

Robert E. Lee

George McClellan

George Meade

Nelson Appleton Miles

John S. Mosby

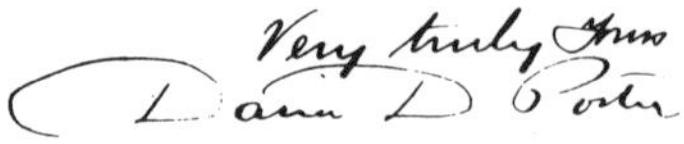

David D. Porter

W. S. Rosecrans

Winfield Scott

Philip Sheridan

W. J. Sherman

Alfred Terry

George A. Trenholm

SCIENTISTS AND TECHNOLOGISTS

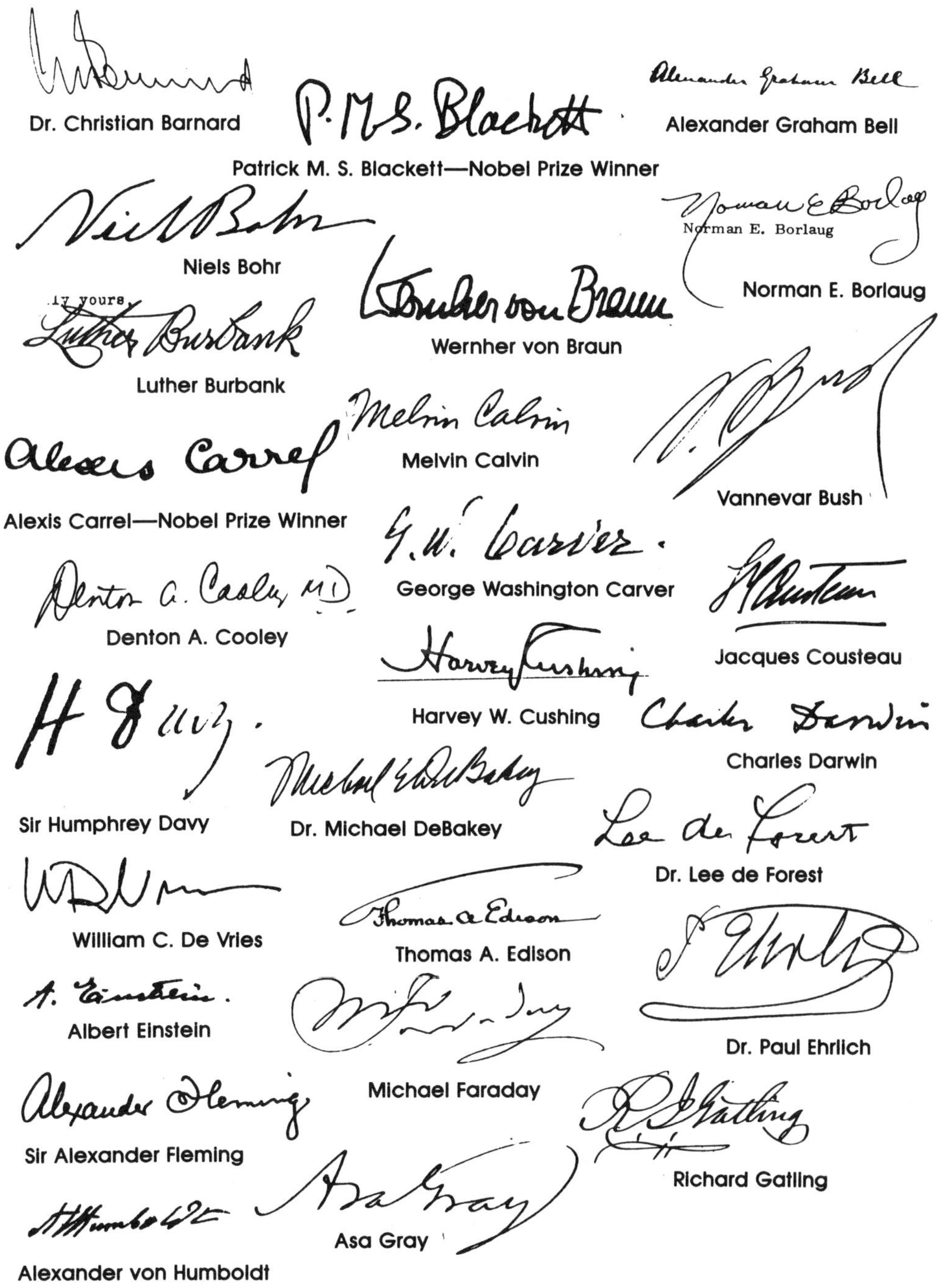

Dr. Christian Barnard

Patrick M. S. Blackett—Nobel Prize Winner

Alexander Graham Bell

Niels Bohr

Norman E. Borlaug

Wernher von Braun

Luther Burbank

Melvin Calvin

Vannevar Bush

Alexis Carrel—Nobel Prize Winner

George Washington Carver

Denton A. Cooley

Jacques Cousteau

Harvey W. Cushing

Charles Darwin

Sir Humphrey Davy

Dr. Michael DeBakey

Dr. Lee de Forest

William C. De Vries

Thomas A. Edison

Albert Einstein

Dr. Paul Ehrlich

Michael Faraday

Sir Alexander Fleming

Richard Gatling

Asa Gray

Alexander von Humboldt

FACSIMILE SECTION

SCIENTISTS AND TECHNOLOGISTS

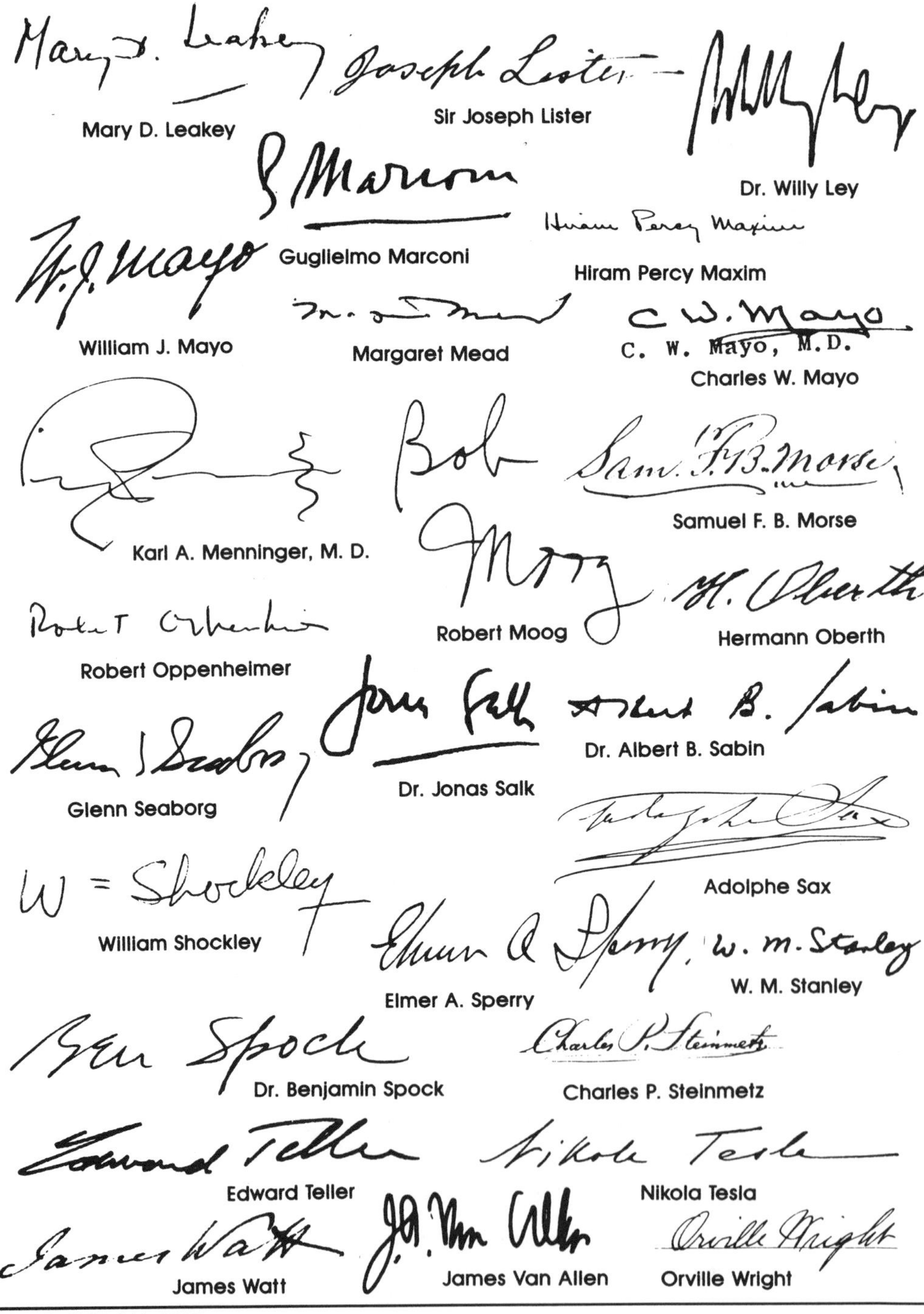

U.S. PRESIDENTS

John Adams

John Quincy Adams

Chester A. Arthur

David R. Atchison—
President of the U.S. for One Day

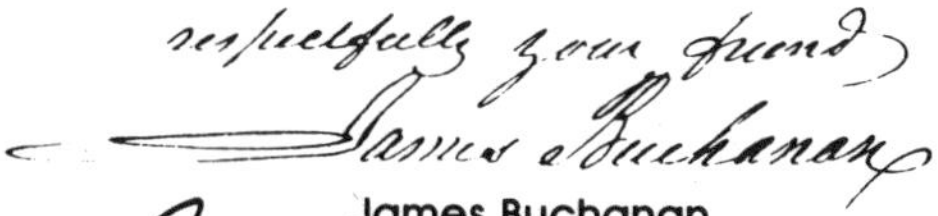

James Buchanan

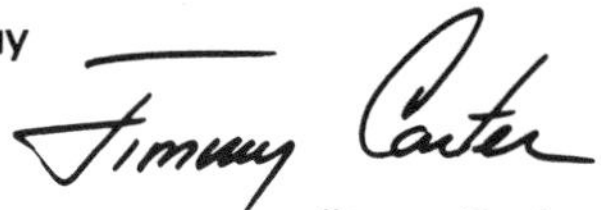

Jimmy Carter

Grover Cleveland

Dwight D. Eisenhower

Calvin Coolidge

Millard Fillmore

Gerald R. Ford

James A. Garfield

Charles Guiteau—Assassin of President Garfield

U. S. Grant

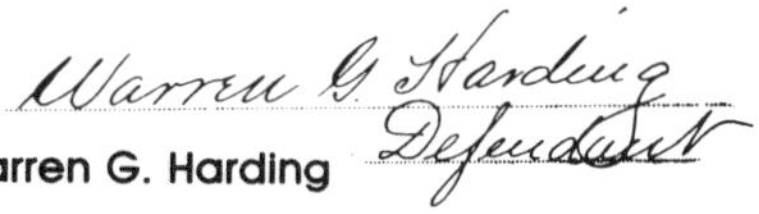

Warren G. Harding

Benjamin Harrison

William Henry Harrison

Herbert Hoover

Rutherford B. Hayes

Andrew Johnson

Andrew Jackson

Lyndon Johnson

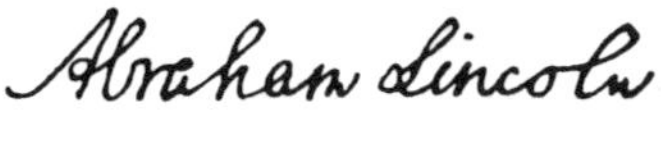

Abraham Lincoln

U.S. PRESIDENTS

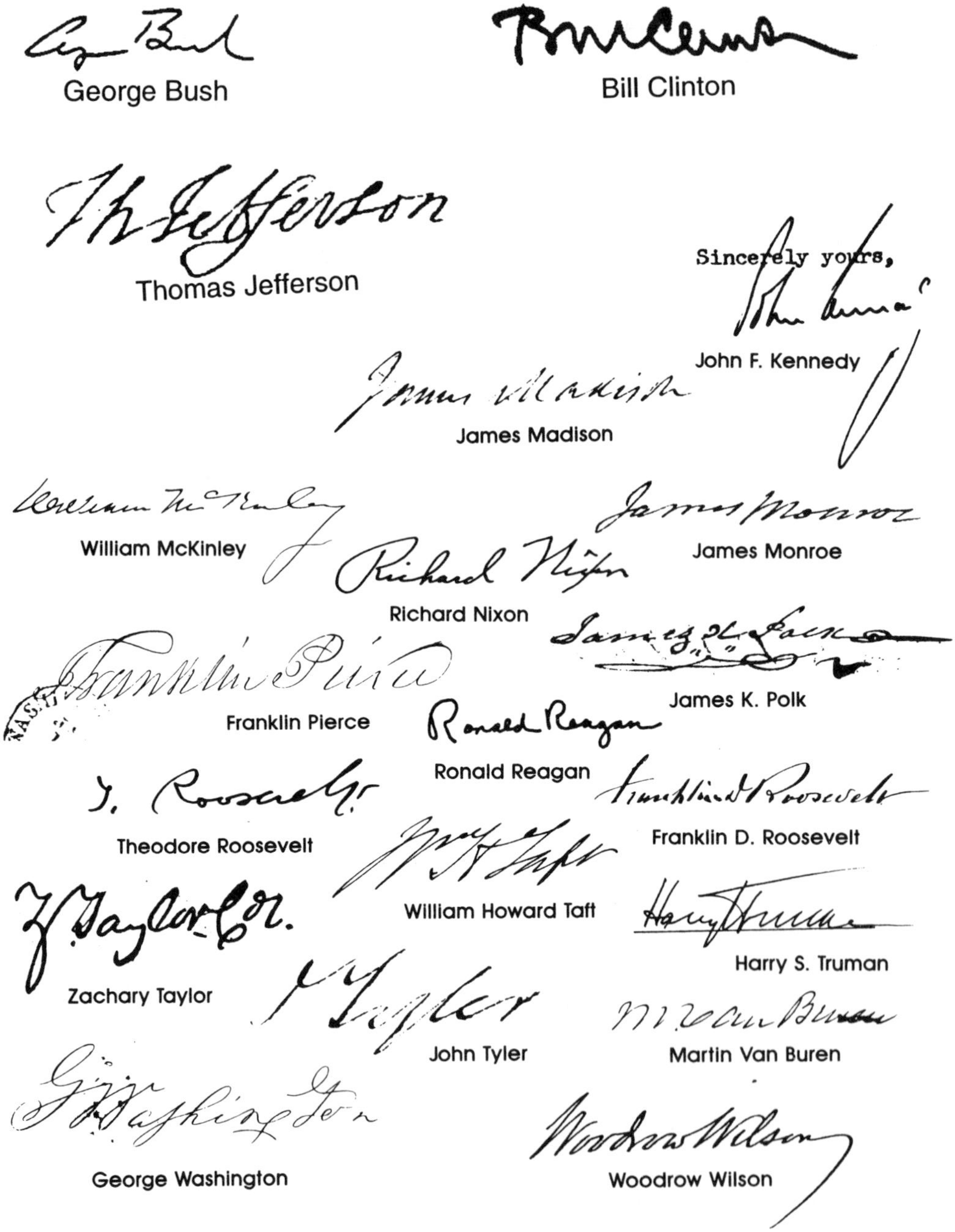

George Bush

Bill Clinton

Thomas Jefferson

John F. Kennedy

James Madison

William McKinley

James Monroe

Richard Nixon

James K. Polk

Franklin Pierce

Ronald Reagan

Theodore Roosevelt

Franklin D. Roosevelt

William Howard Taft

Zachary Taylor

Harry S. Truman

John Tyler

Martin Van Buren

George Washington

Woodrow Wilson

FACSIMILE SECTION

The 1994 SANDERS PRICE GUIDE to AUTOGRAPHS

Section IV: DEALERS

NUMBER 3

SEARLE'S AUTOGRAPHS

An excellent selection of autographs in the middle price ranges.

Monthly catalogs issued in all fields of collecting since 1973, with emphasis on TV, movies, and theatre. Contact us for a free list. We are looking for items to purchase in all fields and are very competitve with our prices. Consignment items accepted.

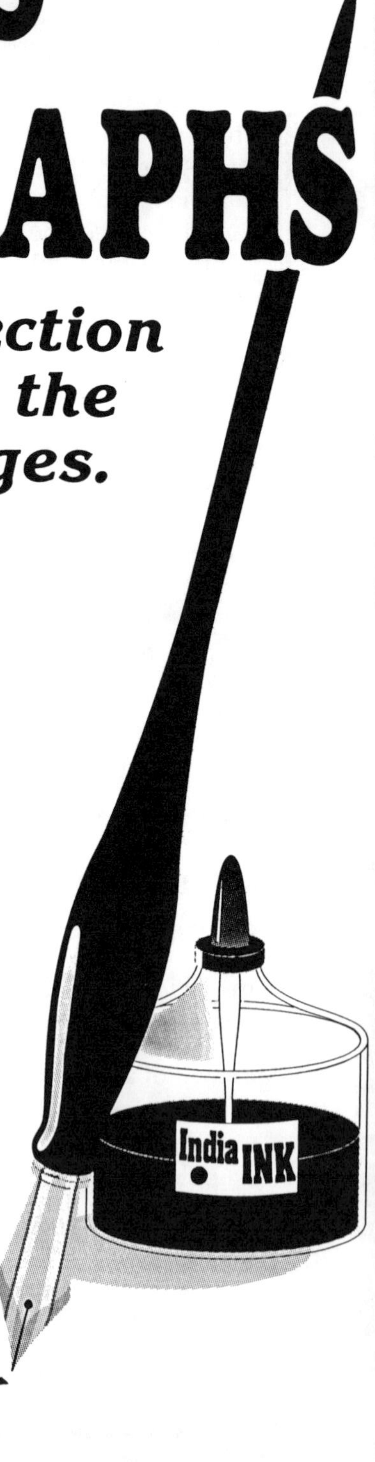

P.O. Box 18509
Asheville, NC 28814
(704) 258-8096
(704) 252-4584 fax

Entered according to Act of Congress, in the year 1866, by VANNERSON & JONES, in the Clerk's Office of the District Court for the District of Columbia.

WAR BETWEEN THE STATES

"The Congressional Record of March 2, 1928, reports Senate joint resolution No. 41 wherein Congress recognized the title "War between the States as proper."

A war was waged from 1861 to 1865 between two organized governments: the United States of America, and the Confederate States of America. These were the official titles of the contending parties. It was not a "Civil War," as it was not fought between two parties within the same government. It was not a "War of Secession," for the Southern States seceded without a thought of war. The right of a State to secede had never been questioned. It was not a "War of Rebellion" for sovereign, independent States co-equal, cannot rebel against each other. It was a War between the States, because twenty-two non-seceding States made war upon eleven seceding States to force them back into the Union of States. It was not until after the surrender of 1865 that secession was decided to be unconstitutional.

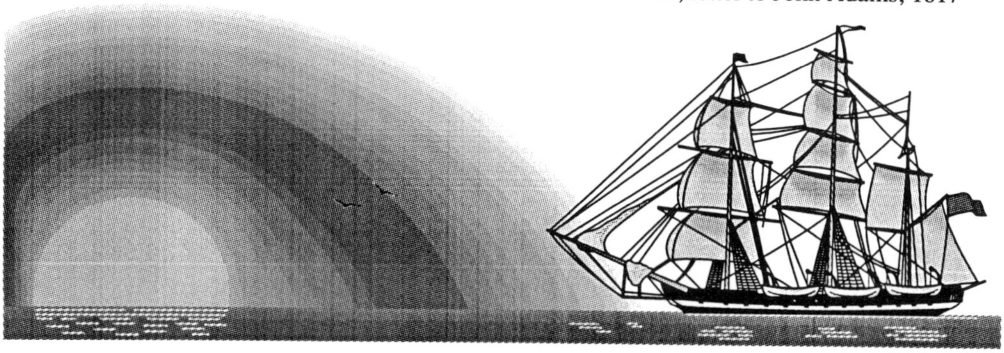

AUTOGRAPH HOUSE

Helen & George Sanders

We Buy and Sell
All Authentic Autographs
Up to and Including the Very Rarest

Autographed copies of our books always available:

Authors of:
The Price Guide to Autographs
The Collector's Guide to Autographs
The Sanders Price Guide to Sports Autographs
The Sanders Price Guide to Autographs

P.O. Box 658, Enka NC 28728, (704) 667-9835